Down and DIRTY

Down and DIRTY

THE PLOT TO STEAL THE PRESIDENCY

JAKE TAPPER

LITTLE, BROWN AND COMPANY
Boston New York London

To Dad

Contents

Preface

Usually when Americans go to Florida for a spell, they come back looking better — tan, refreshed, relaxed, a few piña coladas under their belt.

It didn't quite work out that way for America as a whole.

America is the greatest country in the history of the world, and the fact that we had a peaceful transfer of power even after everything that went down from November 7 through December 13, 2000, is a testament to that fact. But what happened in Florida brought out the ugliest side of every party in American politics, as if the state became a fun-house mirror with harsh lighting, magnifying the nation's blemishes and cellulite.

Democrats were capricious, whiny, wimpy, and astoundingly incompetent. Republicans were cruel, presumptuous, indifferent, and disingenuous. Both were hypocritical — appallingly so, at times. Both sides lied. Over and over and over. Far too many members of the media were sloppy, lazy, and out of touch. Hired-gun lawyers pursued their task of victory, not justice. The American electoral system was revealed to be full of giant holes.

The people themselves were split into three groups: Those who cared so much about their candidate winning they lost all sense of reason, consistency, or civility. Those who were so apathetic they couldn't care one way or another, they just wanted it to be over. And people like you, gentle reader, who fell somewhere in between.

In many ways, Florida was the perfect setting for the freak show. Long before Vice President Al Gore and Gov. George W. Bush began battling over Florida — pouring millions of dollars and days and days in campaign stops in pursuit of its 25 electoral votes — the area currently known as the Sunshine State was ground zero for the eighteenth-century struggle for domination over the New World. With Britain, France, and Spain tripping over one another in the northern end of the state — Britain in Georgia, France in Louisiana, and Spain in Florida — the three superpowers constantly squared off against one another.

Gore isn't even the first to refuse to concede Florida in the face of crushing evidence to the contrary. When Seminole chief Billy Bowlegs surrendered after the Third Seminole War, going west in 1858 with about one hundred of his fellow Native Americans, more than three times that number remained in the Everglades. The Seminole tribe never officially conceded, remaining to this day in a declared state of war with the United States. Even Gore didn't prove that tenacious.

What happened in Florida was the perfect ending to campaign 2000. Gore was an uninspiring technocrat politician — cold and ruthless — who constantly sold out his friends, staffers, and values in his pursuit of power. So anemic were his campaign and communication skills, so apparent and easily exploitable were his vulnerabilities (especially his tendency for puffery), he couldn't manage that last final step to the crown that he had been groomed from the crib to assume. His three debate performances were so different in tempo and temperature, it was as if he hadn't spent his entire adult life in the public eye. More important, the multiple personality disorder seemed to symbolize the larger problem of a man who didn't really know who he was.

The Republicans caricatured him as one who would do anything to get elected, but Gore happily handed them the Magic Markers. And while Gore's lack of an inner core — behind closed doors as vice president, he reportedly argued with other Clinton advisers against affirmative action, while he tried to slam Bush for opposing it during presidential debates — may have created no more than an uneasiness among middle-of-the-road undecided voters, it had disastrous consequences in his party's white left wing. After the campaign-finance abuses of the Clinton-Gore 1996 reelection campaign and his administration's actions on trade agreements like NAFTA and GATT, Gore's protestations to be a fighter for the little guy rang so hollow that 2,878,000 lefty and disillusioned Americans voted for Ralph Nader — including almost 100,000 Floridians.

Bush, conversely, was a brilliant schmoozer and deft liar, but he had the intellectual inquisitiveness of your average fern. Not only did the Yale grad actually utter the word "subliminable" — not once but twice — but in the closing months of the presidential race he was still expressing ignorance about federal institutions, like the Food and Drug Administration, laws, like the Employment Non-Discrimination Act, and long-passed bills, like the Violence Against Women Act, through which $50 million had been given to his state's budget during his tenure. He do-si-do'ed his way to the White House with little to recommend him but a fratty charm that wore thin quick. It was barely enough to recommend him for president of DKE, much less commander of the known universe. More darkly, during his South Carolina primary campaign against Arizona senator John McCain, Bush seemed more than willing to cozy up to the eviler forces in his party. His first stop in the Palmetto State: fundamentalist Bob Jones University, where anti-Catholic dogma is the norm, and interracial dating was banned until 2000. McCain and his family were attacked ruthlessly, disingenuously, by Bush and his forces and their allies. Once, after I wrote a story criticizing Bush for "the race-, gay-, and Jew-baiting campaign that he and his allies waged in South Carolina," a senior Bush staffer called me to angrily complain. "Where was the Jew-baiting?!"* he asked, not even remotely understanding the pathetic hilarity underlying his selective defensiveness.

Both candidates were wanting. After the first presidential debate, I wrote that "Gore's still unlikable, Bush still seems dumb. Feels like a tie." And that pretty much summed up the whole shebang. Neither man deserved it. Neither man captured the hopes of the nation as had, say, Ronald Reagan in 1980.

So it was only fitting that both Gore and Bush were forced to continue their respectively unconvincing pitches for the White House for more than a month after the race was supposed to have ended. Neither of them had proved worthy of the job to begin with, and neither deserved to win as desired a prize as others had. They needed to fight for it even more, and more desperately, and whoever ended up winning it needed the position deflated.

When it became clear in 1961 that New York Yankee Roger Maris might well break the revered Babe Ruth's sixty-home-run record, commissioner of baseball Ford Frick made a ruling that would forever sully Maris's achievement. Frick ruled that since the Babe's record was set in 1927, when seasons lasted 154 games, Maris would have to break the record in the exact same number of games. Maris broke the record, hitting sixty-one homers,

---

*After he learned that a Democrat in Columbia, South Carolina, named Sam Tanenbaum was supporting McCain, Bush mentioned Tanenbaum's name with suspicious frequency. Additionally, Christian activist Pat Robertson placed thousands of prerecorded phone calls to likely supporters, letting them know that McCain's New Hampshire campaign had been co-chaired by "an anti-Christian bigot" — former New Hampshire Republican senator Warren Rudman, a Jew. (Rudman himself, not exactly a Gore supporter, feels that this was Jew-baiting.) Rudman's religion was mentioned, and his name was mispronounced in other pro-Bush Christian conservative–channeled phone calls to sound more ethnic, "ROOD-mahn."

but, because the baseball season in 1961 consisted of 162 games, an asterisk stained his appearance in the record books until 1992, when Frick's ruling was scrapped. Of course, by then Maris had been dead for seven years.

Far more so than in the case of Maris, between Gore and Bush it wasn't tough to argue that whoever ended up winning the presidency needed to have, forever more, an asterisk next to his name.

And one big mother of an asterisk President Bush did get. We will never know who would have won Florida had all the ballots been hand-counted by their respective canvassing boards. Adding to the confusion were thousands of trashed or miscast ballots — including Palm Beach County's infamous "butterfly ballot." We will never know who, therefore, truly was the choice of the most Floridians and who, therefore, really earned the state's critical electoral votes and therefore the presidency. That Gore ended up winning more than a half million popular votes over Bush complicated matters. Of course, had Gore been the one who successfully engineered a victory, there would have been innumerable reasons why he, too, was undeserving. Perhaps reasons even greater than Bush's.

How the figurative asterisk came to pop up next to Bush's name is a fascinating tale, both for lofty, academic reasons — for what it says about our republic — as well as for the sheer insanity of it all. I spent two years, 1999 and 2000, following Bush and Gore around, and most of the thirty-six days following the November 7 Election Day in Florida, watching in horror and amusement — mostly amusement — the circus. I spent the following months tracking down the players who briefly appeared on our TV screens and catching up on what the rest of us who weren't in their shoes missed. The following is what I saw and what I learned from the players after it was all over.

★   ★   ★

About the research methods for the book.

Quotes are taken directly from transcripts, reconstructed by one or more of the players in the conversation, or — where noted — from specific media stories. Thoughts attributed to an individual come from an interview with that individual.

So as not to disrupt the narrative flow of the book, news scoops contained within are seldom attributed to an individual. Two examples: Bill Daley chewing out Bob Butterworth, and Katherine Harris wanting to certify the election results on November 14 despite Judge Lewis's order but being advised not to by her lawyers. Except where noted, such stories always came from one or more individuals present at the time of the incident and have been checked against the recollections of other participants in the event and either confirmed or at the very least not contradicted.

I owe a debt to the following individuals for taking their time to talk with me about what happened in this whole mess, while it was going on and afterward.

Deborah Allen, Jill Alper, Jennifer Altman, Eli Attie, Jenny Backus, Rep. Kevin Bailey, Nick Baldick, Brenda Barnett, Mickey Barnett, Fred Bartlit, Jeremy Bash, Katie Baur, Phil Beck, Mitchell Berger, Achim Bergmann, Harold Blue, David Boies, Kathy Bowler, Daryl Bristow, Rep. Corinne Brown, George and Ethel Brownstein, Judge Charles Burton, Carretta King Butler, Kerey Carpenter, Michael Carvin, Warren Christopher, Judge Nikki Ann Clark, Rep. Garnet Coleman, Barbara Comstock, Jack Corrigan, Denise Cote, Jim Cunningham, Bill Daley, Anita Davis, William Davis, Miguel De Grandy, Rep. Peter Deutsch, Russell Doster, Dexter Douglass, Herman Echavarria, Tony Enos, Randy Enwright, Tucker Eskew, Mark Fabiani, Mike Feldman, Rep. Harold Ford, Jr., Donnie Fowler, Rep. Lois Frankel, Sean Gallagher, Joe Geller, Bert Gluck, John Giesser, Ben Ginsberg, Sandra Goard, Sen. Bob Graham, Murray Greenberg, Peter Greenberger, Jan Crawford Greenburger, Commissioner Suzanne Gunzburger, Armando Gutierrez, Douglas Hattaway, Nicolas Hengartner, Mark Herron, Ed Hollander, Karen Hughes, Harry Jacobs, Rev. Jesse Jackson, Gov. Bill Janklow, Frank Jimenez, David Johnson, Ed Kast, Deborah Kearney, Gov. Frank Keating, Sen. Bob Kerrey, Ron Klain, Joe Klock, Justice Gerald Kogan, Ben Kuehne, David Lane, Henry Latimer, Michael Lavelle, Michael Leach, David Leahy, Judge Robert Lee, Chris Lehane, Theresa LePore, Judge Terry Lewis, Nan Markowitz, Roberto Martinez, Scott McClellan, Jim McConnell, Judge Michael McDermott, Mayor Patrick McManus, Terrell McSweeney, Ken Mehlman, George Meros, Dennis Newman, John Newton, Tom Nides, Mayor Alex Penelas, Dean Ray, Barry Richard, Gerald Richman, Commissioner Carol Roberts, Bruce Rogow, Don Rubottom, Ion Sancho, Joe Sandler, Cindy Sauls, Chris Sautter, Ned Siegel, Judge William Slaughter, Dorrance Smith, Doug Smith, Mark Steinberg, Mark Steitz, Graham Streett, Ray Sullivan, Irv Terrell, George Terwilliger, David Treece, Larry Tribe, Mindy Tucker, Steve Uhlfelder, Jason Unger, Mayco Villafana, Mark Wallace, Craig Waters, Willie Whiting, Michael Whouley, Jim Wilkinson, Quiounia Williams, Jackie Winchester, Anne Womack, Jack Young, Steve Zack.

I would also like to thank those brave souls who agreed to help me get to the bottom of it all but for understandable reasons preferred to keep their names out of it.

Special notes of thanks to:

My editors at Salon.com, Kerry Lauerman, Joan Walsh, and David Talbot, and publisher Michael O'Donnell for all their support.

Daryl Kessler, Dan Karp, John Scully, Chris Haber, David Dimlich, Dan Weiss, and, especially, Nancy Ives for their love and friendship.

The inspired Geoff Shandler and the wonderful Pamela Marshall at Little, Brown and Company and my gorgeous, brilliant agent, Christy Fletcher, for making this book a reality.

Mom, Aaron, Stone, Shelly, Lisi, Becky, and Debby, for being so wonderful. And of course my father, to whom this book is dedicated.

Jake Tapper
Motel 6
Apalachee Parkway
Tallahassee
January 2001

Down and
DIRTY

BUSH
COUNTIES

GORE
COUNTIES

Pensacola

Escambia

Santa Rosa

Okaloosa

Walton

Holmes

Washington

Bay

Jackson

Calhoun

Gulf

Liberty

Franklin

Wakulla

Gadsden

Tallahassee

Leon

Jefferson

Madison

Taylor

Hamilton

Columbia

Suwannee

Lafayette

Dixie

Bradford

Baker

Union

Alachua

Gilchrist

Levy

Nassau

③ Duval

Clay

St. Johns

Putnam

Flagler

De Land

Volusia

Seminole

Marion

⑤

Sumter

Citrus

Hernando

Pasco

Lake

Orlando

Orange

Osceola

Brevard

Indian River

St. Lucie

Martin

Palm Beach

West Palm Beach

Fort Lauderdale

Plantation

Broward

Miami
Beach

Miami

① Miami-
Dade

Monroe

Collier

Hendry

Glades

⑥ Lee

Charlotte

Desoto

Highlands

Okeechobee

Hardee

Polk

Sarasota

Manatee

② Hillsborough

④ Tampa

Pinellas

1

"Do you get the feeling that Florida might be important in this election?"

At 5:55 A.M. in Tampa, Florida, on Election Day 2000, Vice President Al Gore makes a run for the Florida Bakery.

It's his third stop of the day — he's already headlined a South Beach, Miami, midnight rally alongside Robert DeNiro and Stevie Wonder, as well as made a visit to a Tampa hospital. At the bakery, Gore meets up with his running mate, Sen. Joe Lieberman, D-Conn.

The Sunshine State is so critical to his victory, Gore earlier in the year had thought about picking Florida's Democratic senator, Bob Graham, as his running mate. Instead he went with Lieberman, who has demographic pluses as well: an Orthodox Jew is a big hit in southern Florida.

The two are offered small Cuban coffees in teeny plastic sample cups.

"*L'chaim*," Gore says to Lieberman.

"That's good. That feels like eight hours of sleep," Gore says, downing his coffee. He's been going for more than thirty hours now.

"What do you recommend instead of doughnuts?" He asks the woman behind the counter what a nice Cuban pastry would be.

Too little too late. Ever since April, when the Clinton administration sent Immigration and Naturalization Service officers to seize Elián González at gunpoint from the bungalow of his Miami relatives in Little Havana, Gore's been struggling for Cuban-Americans to give him a chance. And in this tight, tight race in Florida he needs their support. Any way he can get it.

The woman behind the counter recommends guava and cream cheese.

"We'll get some of those instead of doughnuts," Gore says. Gore gives her a $20 bill for the $14.45 check. "Keep that as a tip," he says. "*Gracias.*"

At 6:10 A.M., Gore's motorcade arrives at the local Democratic HQ, in a small cement building in a Cuban section of Tampa. Lieberman — with his hound-dog mug and subtle, bubbly glee — jumps onstage.

"Do you get the feeling that Florida might be important in this election?" Lieberman jokes. "The dawn is rising on Election Day, right here in Tampa Bay."

"This is the last official stop of Campaign 2000," Gore adds. "It's not an accident that it's here in Tampa. It's not an accident that it's in west-central Florida, because Florida may very well be *the* state that decides the outcome of this election."

He tells the crowd about his South Beach rally. "Just before I went out to make the speech, somebody had one of the cable television networks on, and it was reporting news at the top of the hour, and it was a roundup of the campaign activities. And it said, 'At this hour, George W. Bush is asleep, and Al Gore is preparing to speak to twenty-five thousand people in Florida.'" The crowd goes wild.

A napping Dubya was not exceptional, especially after a campaign day as busy as was Monday, spent flipping the political bird to Gore and President Clinton, swooping in on his campaign plane to stump in their respective home states of Tennessee and Arkansas. Bush finished up his campaigning Monday night with an airport rally in Austin, and then it would be bedtime. Bush likes sleep. He hits the sack by 9:30 P.M. He carried a down pillow — nicknamed "pilly" — with him on the campaign trail.

"Well, it's almost 5:30 A.M. Texas time, and George W. Bush is STILL asleep and I'm still speaking to people HERE IN FLORIDA!!" Gore says. The crowd again goes wild.

Soon enough, Gore and Lieberman leave the Tampa rally, head to the airport, and fly to Tennessee to watch the returns. Now it's in the hands of the people.

People like Theresa LePore.

★   ★   ★

LePore, elections supervisor for Palm Beach County, has been awake for three full hours. At 2:30 A.M. she eased herself out of bed. She was at work by 3:45 A.M. Voters start calling her to make sure they know the proper place to vote at around 4:30 A.M. or so. LePore feels like crap; she has a sinus infection; she didn't get home the previous night until around 10 P.M.; she hasn't really slept. But she's jazzed.

LePore loves elections. Lives for them. Says elections are in her blood. At the age of eight, she helped her Republican dad lick envelopes for his favorite candidates. In the summer of 1971, at the age of sixteen — when most girls in her school had their sights set on less lofty pursuits — LePore walked into the Palm Beach County elections office and took a job as a part-time typist, making $1.75 an hour, under good ol' boy elections supervisor Horace Beasley, aka Mr. B. She wasn't even old enough to vote.

LePore's now worked at the elections office for twenty-eight years. Originally she had registered to vote as a Republican, like her dad, a disabled Korean War veteran who never told her just how he injured his left arm. But he never really was about partisan politics, and in 1979 LePore re-registered as an independent. When a third-party formally registered as "Independent," she changed her registration to "no party."

LePore earned her associate degree from Palm Beach Junior College and even attended Florida Atlantic University for a spell. But she never got her bachelor's. She really wasn't all that interested in pursuing an education; she's not even a political junkie. She'd found what she wanted to do. And she'd found a mentor in Jackie Winchester, the Palm Beach County supervisor of elections, appointed to the position after Mr. B died in office in 1973. Winchester was first elected to the post in 1974, and not long afterward, Winchester handpicked LePore to be her chief deputy.

When Winchester announced her retirement in January 1996, it was only natural that LePore would take her place. Soon after Winchester told her of her plans, in the fall of 1995, LePore registered as a Democrat and ran. LePore won by 25,000 votes, and in 2000 she has the best kind of reelection match: she's running unopposed. So she's not even on the ballot.

But LePore's job this time was a little tougher than it had been in the past. Historically, Florida had been a tough place for third-party candidates. To get on a ballot, third-party candidates had to secure the signatures of 3 percent of all voters in the district on a petition. Democratic and Republican candidates had a much easier time, enjoying the option of either securing the signatures of 3 percent of just local members of their party or paying a qualifying fee. But in 1998, Libertarians launched a campaign to level the playing field, proposing Amendment 11 to the state constitution, "grant(ing) equal ballot access for independent and minor parties" by allowing members of those parties to pay the ballot-access fee instead of getting signatures. On that Election Day — the same day that Jesse "The Body" Ventura was elected governor of Minnesota as a Reform

Party candidate — Amendment 11 passed overwhelmingly, with 64 percent of the vote. As a result, instead of the most restrictive ballot-access requirements in the country, Florida now had one of the loosest. LePore had no fewer than ten presidential candidates, and ten vice presidential candidates, to put on her ballot.

In September, LePore went to voting systems manager Tony Enos, thirty-six, and asked for help. Enos was, like her, an experienced elections board employee — he'd been there for eighteen years, since he was eighteen. He soon gave her three ballot options.

One of them was a one-pager, as they'd always done in the past. But the twenty names meant that the type was really small. This troubled LePore. She remembered the 1988 Senate race, when Republican Connie Mack defeated Democratic representative Buddy MacKay by just 33,000 votes. During the recount, Democrats complained that 54,000 ballots didn't register a vote for Senate — a full 17 percent. A closer inspection of these undervotes, as they were called, brought blame on the ballot design. Since the Senate race had been on the same page as the presidential race — a lot of names on one page — the race, written in small letters at the bottom of the first page of the ballot, had apparently escaped some voters' notice. Winchester and her equals in Hillsborough, Broward, and Miami-Dade Counties came under some heavy criticism for the 170,000 total undervotes in their four counties.

That experience, combined with her work for a federal task force dedicated to making it easier for the blind, disabled, and sight-impaired to vote, made LePore sensitive to the needs of voters who didn't have the best vision. There had been numerous complaints from older voters after all the referenda and initiatives appeared on the 1998 ballot in 10-point type. This time, the names, she decided, would be better spread out over two pages. Like a butterfly. They called it a "facing-page ballot."

Enos had two designs with that option. One listed five candidate tickets on the left page, all huddled near the top of the page, with the other five pairs on the right page, near the bottom. But LePore didn't like this design. She wanted the list of candidates in essentially the same location on each page, with the holes to punch staggered between pages.

So it came down to Enos's third option. Bush and Cheney listed first on the left page, with their hole first in the middle; Reform ticket Pat Buchanan and Ezola Foster first on the right page, their hole second in the middle; Gore and Lieberman listed second on the left page, with their hole third in the middle, and so on.

★ ★ ★

In Miami-Dade County, the voting machines are being set up at two of the most Democratic precincts in the county, two places where Gore's gonna win big.

Precinct 255, Lillie C. Evans Elementary School, is located at 1895 NW 75th Street. Its voters are 89.8 percent Democratic, 95 percent African-American.

Precinct 535, Dunbar Elementary School, is at 505 NW 20th Street. Its registered voters are 88.48 percent Democratic, 93.25 percent black.

Before the voting machines leave the elections warehouse, they're tested to make sure that they're functioning properly. The ten machines at Dunbar and the ten at Evans had both been deemed to be working fine. But at Evans Elementary on Tuesday morning, poll worker Larry Williams does a test ballot, and a punch he attempts for Gore doesn't register at all. Seven of the ten machines at Evans miss punches when tested. No one ever tells precinct clerk Donna Rogers. When Rogers is asked about the problems her precinct experiences today, she'll say that no voter complained to her, no poll worker told her about anything wrong, how was she to know. She'll say that the *Miami Herald* and I are the only ones — including the elections commission — to tell her that there were undervotes in her precinct, so as far as she's concerned, it's all hearsay.

But it's true. By the end of the day, 113 out of the 868 ballots cast at Evans Elementary School will not register a vote for president. This is a precinct that Gore will win with 98.81 percent to Bush's .66 percent — of the votes that register.

Six of the ten machines at Dunbar miss punches as well in their morning tests. At Dunbar Elementary, 105 out of the 820 ballots won't register a vote for president. This is a precinct that Gore will win with 98.74 percent of the vote to Bush's 1.12 percent.

These rates of discarded ballots — roughly 13 percent for both precincts — will be the highest rate of unread ballots in the county.

★ ★ ★

Liz Hyman, thirty-four, sits outside the Delray Beach Gore HQ. She's a lawyer at Akin Gump in Washington, D.C., but she's also worked for the Justice Department, Gore's office, and for the U.S. trade representative for the Clinton administration, and she's taken some vacation time to help volunteer with the Gore campaign. A friend has a house in Palm Beach, so that just happened to be where she chose to do her volunteering.

Since 7 A.M., Hyman's been sitting at a table outside the building where she's trying to snag volunteers for various "Get Out the Vote" activities. She keeps hearing something weird about the ballot. Volunteers who have voted already complain that it's difficult to understand; many are upset. Word gets out: it's a problem elsewhere in the county, too. Conspiracy theories start cropping up: it makes it look like you're voting for Buchanan; maybe someone tampered with it!

At around 8 A.M., Hyman busts out her cell phone and calls her dad, Lester Hyman, another D.C. attorney. "You're not going to believe what's going on down here," she says. It's something that maybe people at Gore HQ in Nashville should know about. At the Justice Department, Hyman was once deputy to Ron Klain, a hotshot Democratic attorney and Gore guy. Maybe call him?

Klain's on his way to work that morning when he gets the call. Lester Hyman doesn't really understand the problem — something about people accidentally voting for Buchanan? — but says Liz is upset.

Klain knows that Liz does not upset easily. When he arrives, he goes into the "boiler room," where Gore's main on-the-ground political adviser, Michael Whouley, is working away. Klain gives Whouley Liz's name and number, vouches for her credibility.

Seconds later, Liz Hyman's cell phone rings. It's Joe Sandler, general counsel of the Democratic National Committee.

"I hear there's a problem with the ballot?" he asks.

★　★　★

There is a problem with Palm Beach County's butterfly ballot. People are confused. Many are angry. At a Greenacres condominium clubhouse John Lazet, sixty-six, votes the right way after a proctor gives him a second ballot. But he decides to take matters into his own hands.

He calls the supervisor's office but finds the man who answers the phone less than sympathetic. So he and two buddies drive to LePore's office. There they find her outside in the middle of a TV interview. Lazet starts verbally coming at her, but that quickly ends when LePore says that she doesn't have time to talk to him. She thinks it's just a few cranky old men. Nothing to worry about.

★　★　★

Assistant poll clerk Ethel Brownstein, seventy-one, arrives at the Lucerne Point Club from her home in Lake Worth at around 5:45 A.M. By seven, there's already a long line of voters, mostly seniors. She starts directing traffic: "You go here, you go here, you go here."

At around 8 A.M., a woman comes to Brownstein and tells her she's having a problem.

"I put this thing in, but it doesn't go in," she says.

Brownstein enters the voting booth to see what she's talking about. The rectangular ballot has gone in straight, in the slot underneath the ballot, but for some reason the stylus to punch the hole isn't going through.

"I want to vote for Mr. Gore," she says.

Brownstein looks at the ballot. "This is confusing," she thinks. Gore is listed second, but his is the third hole. And for a lot of these voters, who are elderly, who don't see so well, who are used to having the second hole correspond to the second name, well, they might not really understand how to vote correctly, Brownstein realizes.

"The first hole is Bush, the second is Buchanan, and the third is Gore," Brownstein says. Worried about crossing the line between assistance and instruction, Brownstein quickly hustles out of the booth. But she thinks, "You know, something's wrong here. People don't know how to punch these things." She starts saying to voters, "Please be careful. The first hole is Bush, the second is Buchanan, the third is Gore." Repeatedly she warns people, "Be careful."

Not everyone hears her or even with her advice can figure it out. Others just shrug off her warnings altogether; they've been voting since Truman, they don't need directions. The complaints start flooding in from the crowd: that the stylus didn't work properly, that they voted for the wrong person, that since there were two holes next to Gore and Lieberman's box they punched both holes. A couple women come to her in tears, afraid that they voted for Buchanan, knowing that it's too late since their ballots have been put into the box.

Brownstein's husband, George, seventy-six, is going through a similar ordeal at the Masonic Temple, precinct 121-D, where he's serving as a poll clerk. People are having problems, but when he tries to phone the elections office, he can't get through.

"This is unreal," he thinks.

At precinct 154-G in Bethesda Health City, assistant clerk Bert Gluck, seventy-six, is also seeing the meltdown. From inside the polling stations, voters are oohing and aahing, confused, punching more than one hole, griping that on some of the ballots the arrows don't line up with any holes. He cautions voters, don't turn in your ballot if you've punched more than one hole! Forty-nine voters take him up on the offer, turning in to him their double-punched ballots, which otherwise would have been voided.

At 10:30 A.M. in Nashville, Gore spokesman Douglas Hattaway and Democratic National Committee spokeswoman Jenny Backus have already heard about the butterfly ballot problems. In their first briefing of the day, Hattaway and Backus tell reporters to caution Palm Beach County voters to look carefully at their ballot. At 11:24 A.M., Bobby Brochin, counsel for the DNC in Florida, faxes LePore a letter from his Miami office. The Democrats aren't entirely sure what the problem is, just that there is one. "Apparently certain presidential ballots being utilized in several precincts in Palm Beach County are quite confusing," Brochin writes. "They contain two pages listing all of the presidential candidates, which may cause electors to vote twice in the presidential race. You should immediately instruct all deputy supervisors and other officials at these precincts that they should advise all electors (and post a written advisory) that the ballot for the presidential race is two pages long, and that electors should only vote for one presidential candidate."

LePore doesn't respond to Brochin's fax.

★   ★   ★

In Tallahassee, Anita Davis, past president of the local branch of the NAACP, is running around, going precinct to precinct. She returns from District 1 polling centers, jubilant. Turnout is way high.

After Gov. Jeb Bush formally introduced his "One Florida" initiative in March — which would effectively end affirmative action in the state — local NAACP activists were rejuvenated, launching their "We'll remember in November" voter registration/revenge drive. Today, November 7, black voters do indeed seem to be remembering. Davis's first trip out was at around 9 A.M., to one precinct where hundreds had already voted.

The overall numbers bear out her enthusiasm. Just under sixty thousand African-Americans registered to vote between February and October, a 7 percent increase. White registration grew by about half that. And while black voters constitute 934,261 of the Florida electorate, compared to 6,564,813 whites and Latinos, today, state black turnout is so high — the highest ever — that black voters will constitute 16 percent of the total turnout. In 1996, that number was just 10 percent.

Today in the Sunshine State, 93 percent of black voters will go for the vice president.* Little of this seems attributable to Gore, whose consultants reportedly kept blacks out of photographs with the veep during the

---

*This anti-Bush African-American zeitgeist will be outdone, remarkably, in Bush's home state of Texas, where a full 95 percent of black voters will pull levers against the self-described compassionate conservative.

campaign, so as to keep him from seeming too liberal. (In September, Gore was pulled from directly addressing the National Baptist Convention for fear of scaring away the soccer moms and blue-collar dads and other white swing voters the campaign lusted after so unattractively.[1]) No, but blacks are turning out in record numbers today, in Leon and Duval and Gadsden and Miami-Dade and elsewhere, not so much for Gore, but against Bush.

And not just Bush — and his Bob Jones University–visiting, Confederate flag–waving, itchy-death-row-trigger-finger-wiggling, South Carolina racist–pandering cracker Texas ass. But also his brother Jeb — whom many NAACP officials call "Jeb Crow" — as well as Poppy Bush, whose aides bragged in 1988 that they would make black murderer Willie Horton seem like Gov. Mike Dukakis's running mate when it was all said and done.

Which is not to say that the African-American community doesn't have issues with Dubya. In the second presidential debate, Bush defended his opposition to a hate crimes bill, saying that it wasn't needed, since all of the killers of his fellow Texan James Byrd, Jr., had been sentenced to death. But not all three had been put to death. One had been given a life sentence. And while the mainstream press ignored that fact, giving Bush a bye on this as they did on so much else, black radio hosts sure as hell noticed. So did the NAACP, which ran a TV ad against Bush, featuring Byrd's niece, Renee Mullins, saying that when Bush refused to support the hate crimes bill that bore her uncle's name, it felt like he'd been killed all over again. Incendiary stuff, stuff that whites decried as over the line, but it had an impact in the right neighborhoods.

And it goes beyond the descendants of the late Connecticut senator Prescott Bush. Despite its reputation in the Northeast as a somewhat anomalous Southern state, Florida has a fairly ugly racial history.

This isn't just *ancient* history, the 1889 Florida poll tax, the 1920 Ococee County murders and arson and other retaliations against blacks who had dared to try to vote, the 1951 Christmas Day murder of the NAACP's Harry T. Moore, who launched a Brevard County registration drive. No, it's more recent than that in the minds of much of Florida's black community. For Godsakes, post-Reconstruction, no black Floridian had been elected to the U.S. House until *1992*.[2]

When Davis, sixty-four, moved down to Tallahassee from Buffalo in 1979 — her son had been recruited to play football for FSU, and she was eager to get away from Buffalo's winters — Leon County didn't have one countywide black elected official. Not one. Post-Reconstruction, after all, the first black ever elected to the Tallahassee city commission was James Ford, and that hadn't been until 1971. Writing before the primary that year, the *Tallahassee Democrat* had described Ford, the Leon High School vice principal, as a "mature Negro. . . . We are impressed that he may be the best-qualified Negro ever to offer for public office in Tallahassee. We would expect him to serve, if elected, as a proper representative of his racial minority without antagonistic attitudes toward the majority that might result in more frustration and discord than genuine advancement."

The name "Tallahassee" comes from a Creek word for "old town," and for African-Americans that was true, and it wasn't good.

But Davis and others like her had worked hard, and things had changed. The U.S. Justice Department sued the city of Tallahassee in 1974 for engaging "in a pattern or practice of discrimination based on race in hiring." In 1975, the District Court for the Northern District of Florida ordered Tallahassee to "hire, assign, promote, transfer, and dismiss employees without regard to race or color."[3] Davis herself served for ten years as NAACP branch president, worked on the 1980s lawsuits that ended the at-large election system that kept blacks without a representative on the county commission or the school board. The first African-American county commissioner was finally elected in 1986, and not long after that came the first black member of the school board.

So when whites fretted that blacks in Tallahassee, or Florida, wanted "special rights," when they acted as if society was so far beyond institutional racism there was no longer any need for institutional remedies, Davis wondered just what planet they lived on. It was just 1990 that a black school board member had been first elected in a regular election. 1990!

At 11:30 A.M., Davis starts getting phone calls from friends right here in District 1. There's a Florida Highway Patrol road stop right near a black voting district, she's told, a checkpoint on Woodville Highway and Oak Ridge Road, a black area of town, just one mile from Woodville First Baptist Church, a polling place where a third of the voters are black.

Davis calls the FHP.

Yes, they have people doing some spot-checking, she's told. Nothing odd. Nothing illegal. Just normal procedure. Turns out that in September, the FHP was $1 million in the hole in its gasoline budget, so in October it started conducting checkpoints, which don't require cops to be driving around and burning fuel so much. They've done thirty-one of these so far, asking motorists to show their licenses and insurance information.

But this seems strange. "It's odd for them to be out there on Election Day," Davis thinks. "It just doesn't smell right." And why in a black neighborhood? Davis has seen too much to come to any other conclusion: "It's a method to keep people from the polls," she thinks.*

And that's not all. In the early afternoon, Davis's grandson, Jamarr Lyles, twenty, a student at Florida A&M, is getting ready to go to his job at Subway. Lyles worked hard to register his friends at the polls, and he's disappointed, he tells his grandmother. A bunch of them have called him, having been turned away at the polls, told that their names aren't there. He's bummed. All that hard work, and for what? Something is going wrong — or, depending on what you want, right — in Leon County.

★   ★   ★

At the Orange Bowl in Miami, Cuban-American activist Armando Gutierrez, who served as the spokesman for Elián González's Miami relatives, is getting his revenge.

Just as Davis has been activated to seek vengeance against Jeb by defeating his brother in the presidential election, Gutierrez has been motivated to seek vengeance against Al Gore because of the actions of his president, Bill Clinton, and Attorney General Janet Reno for what they did to little Elián. Gutierrez usually makes his money working on campaigns for local judges and smaller ballot issues — like one today on off-street parking. But the main cause today for both him and his poll workers is the defeat of Al Gore.

Though Gore attempted to distance himself from the Clinton administration's position that Elián should be returned to his father, who still lives in Cuba, Gutierrez didn't buy it for one minute. The day before Election Day, Gutierrez even held a press conference at Elián's Little Havana home with the boy's two great-uncles, telling the Cuban-American community to come and vote for Bush. "It's important to remind people that this is how you get even — at the polls," Gutierrez would say.

Today he has two precincts to watch, both at the Orange Bowl. Voters keep coming up to him, saying, "We're here because of Elián," or even "I voted for Elián," meaning Bush. Things are going well, Gutierrez thinks.

★   ★   ★

*In the coming days, assistant state attorney general Paul Hancock will say that the FHP checkpoint "was not done in accordance with normal procedure." By not getting the location approved, or announcing the checkpoint ahead of time to the media, the checkpoint violated standard FHP protocol.

Some voting snafus are garden-variety bureaucratic incompetence. Others are perhaps rooted in something else.

In November 1997, incumbent Miami mayor Joe Carollo was narrowly beaten by Xavier Suarez, mayor from '86 until '93. After losing that runoff, Carollo sued for fraud. A handwriting expert Carollo hired cast doubt over the legitimacy of about a fifth of the five thousand absentee ballots cast in the election. In March 1998, the Third District Court of Appeals threw out all five thousand of the absentee ballots, ruling that the "absentee ballot is a privilege," not a right. Carollo was installed as mayor.

In the wake of the embarrassing election, in 1998, the Florida legislature passed a state voter-fraud law, creating an ineligible-voter list as part of the central voter file, and requiring all sixty-seven counties to purge their voter registries of ineligible voters, including felons. In 1998, the state became the only one in the nation to hire a private firm to complete the task of accumulating the names of ineligible voters, signing a $4 million contract with DBT Online, since merged into ChoicePoint.

Early in the year, ChoicePoint sent its latest list of eight thousand ex-felons to the state. Linda Howell, the elections supervisor of Madison County, on the Georgia line, knew immediately that something was wrong with the list. Her name was on it. Linda Howell might be plenty of things, but a felon wasn't one of them. The husband of Duval County elections supervisor John Stafford's press officer was on the list, too. He also was not a felon. That was enough: neither Madison nor Duval County used Choice-Point's information.

As the ChoicePoint lists were examined, it became clear that this wasn't a case of a name or two accidentally being included. It turned out that only thirty-four voters actually belonged on Leon County's felon list. But Choice-Point had provided elections supervisor Ion Sancho with more than seven hundred names. Over the summer, ChoicePoint admitted its error, blaming the mistake on erroneous data that listed thousands who had been convicted of misdemeanors as felons. But by then, confusion had set in.

Sancho repeatedly complained to state division of elections director Clay Roberts, a Jeb Bush appointee who endorsed Jeb's brother for president. But Roberts didn't seem to care. "It's not that bad," Sancho remembers Roberts telling him. "Improvements have been made. It keeps getting better. We're working to solve the problems." By Election Day 2000, Sancho has been complaining about this list for two years, but Secretary of State Katherine Harris and Roberts have paid his and his colleagues' concerns little attention.

ChoicePoint, those looking for conspiracies in the coming days will point out, bought one of its bum lists from a company in Texas, and its founder was a major GOP donor. That Harris, Roberts, and Jeb Bush did little from November 1998 to November 2000 to allay the fears of elections supervisors who were concerned about ChoicePoint's shoddy lists — with a roughly 85 percent accuracy rate — will fuel anger as well. And today, ChoicePoint's incompetence will have a double-edged impact. Because its information is so frequently wrong, some counties ignored the list altogether, and hundreds of felons are able to vote. But because its information is so frequently wrong, some counties disenfranchised legitimate voters. In Hillsborough County, for instance, 54 percent of the voters on the Choice-Point list were African-American, despite the fact that blacks are only 11 percent of the county's voting population.[4] Now, a cynic might argue that if it were individual voters named Hilton Mayberry IV being confused with a felon of the same name — as opposed to Miguel Dominguez or Ronnie Jefferson — then maybe Clay Roberts and Katherine Harris would have been quicker to respond to the problem. A cynic might argue that Florida is a state that has pockets of poverty and despair that recall nothing so much as Civil War documentaries. And such a cynic might further point out that Jeb Bush's biggest and boldest race-related initiative has been to end affirmative action, and thus it would be almost silly to expect him to care about this.

At around 6 P.M. in Tallahassee, Willie Whiting, Jr., fifty, a pastor in the House of Prayer Church, goes with his wife, son, and daughter to St. John's United Methodist Church to vote. But Whiting's name isn't on the voter rolls.

"You have been purged from our system," he's told by one of the white poll workers.

What? That can't be true, he says. Double-check. The poll worker calls the Leon County elections office. The database has Whiting listed as a convicted felon.

This shocks Whiting. But unlike most who get caught in a similar situation, Whiting isn't going to walk away, scratching his head. "Do I need to call my lawyer?" he asks. Eventually the mistake is cleared up, and Whiting is allowed to vote.

In January of 2000, protesting Jeb's executive order repealing affirmative-action programs for state contracts and university admissions, African-American protesters, led by Sen. Kendrick Meek, D-Miami, and Rep. Tony Hill, D-Jacksonville, staged a twenty-five-hour sit-in in the office of Lt.

Gov. Frank Brogan. Jeb instructed aides to "kick their asses out." (Jeb later claimed that he had been talking about reporters.)

Pastor Whiting cannot escape the feeling that somehow, in some way, Jeb and others are today just trying to kick his ass out — of the voting rolls.

★   ★   ★

Other problems voters have today are less conspiratorial in nature. But they do, for whatever reason, seem to impact black voters more so than whites.

Quiounia Williams is eighteen. It's her first election, and she's excited. She enters the voting booth at First Timothy Baptist Church, on Biscayne Road in Jacksonville, and puts the card inside the slot. But she's never done this before, and no one's shown her how to do it, and for some reason the card won't go down. It doesn't sit still. Every time she punches a hole, the card moves.

She leaves the booth.

"I couldn't put the card all the way down," she tells a poll worker.

"Well," says the worker, "what actually happened?"

"When I pushed down, every time I got ready to punch a hole, it would move again."

"Don't worry about it, baby," the poll worker, an African-American woman, says, handing her an "I voted!" sticker, telling her to put the card in the box.

The elections office in Duval County, surrounding Jacksonville, is suffering its own distinct chaos. Despite having decided not to use Choice-Point's scrub list, Duval County is having some serious problems, particularly in its predominantly African-American precincts. Just last weekend, Stafford made sure that 170,000 copies of a sample ballot were inserted into the Sunday editions of the *Florida Times-Union*. "Step 4 Vote all pages," it read. But on the Duval ballot, the ten presidential candidates are spread over two pages. Stafford realized that the sample ballot's instructions were incorrect and could result in overvotes disqualifying the ballot. So today the official ballot has different instructions. "Step 4 Vote appropriate pages," it reads.

Ernest Lewis, for one, is confused. It's his first time voting. Whether it's because he remembers the instructions from the sample ballot, or whether it's because he's new at this and he just figured you vote on every page, Lewis votes on both presidential pages and voids his ballot in the process. More than twenty thousand voters in Duval County will do this today.

Some Florida counties have systems in place that notify voters immediately if their ballot is invalid, but only 26 percent of black voters live in these counties as opposed to 34 percent of white voters. That means by sheer numbers white voters have an advantage.[5]

In the cotton belt's Gadsden County on the Georgia line, union officials hustled all June to register two thousand African-American voters, many of them seniors who had never voted before. But today in Gadsden polling booths, many seem to be making up for lost opportunities by picking more than one candidate for president. Some are voting for all ten presidential candidates, then penning Gore's name on the write-in line. The ballot directions don't exactly help. "Vote for ONE," it says above the race for Senate. "Vote for Group," it says above the presidential contest.

From the Ochlockonee River to the Apalachicola, more than 2,000 of the 16,812 ballots cast in Gadsden today — two-thirds of which are going to Gore — will be thrown out. It's a full 12.33 percent of all ballots cast, the highest percentage in the state.[6] It's just another uncomfortable superlative for Gadsden — the state's third-poorest, and only majority-black, county, the only county in Florida that went for Walter Mondale over President Ronald Reagan in 1984. Here 94 percent of the students at Chattahoochee High School read below the minimum standard, the county's schools rank last in the state in reading for fourth, eighth, and tenth grades, and the school district's graduation rate — 46 percent — is the lowest in Florida.

The pattern is not unique to Gadsden, however. In Miami-Dade County, predominantly black precincts will register an undervote rate of 10 percent, while areas with few blacks have an undervote rate of 3 percent.[7] Some black neighborhoods in largely black Liberty City and Overtown will register overvote rates of 10 percent, while the countywide rate will be just 2.7 percent.[8] Undervotes and overvotes will result in 23 percent of the ballots cast — that's almost one out of every four ballots — by voters in largely black Palm Beach County areas like Belle Glade, Pahokee, and South Bay being chucked.[9]

★   ★   ★

By noon in Palm Beach County, WPEC-TV is reporting the story of the butterfly ballot, explaining the problem a hell of a lot better than the Democrats are. Joan Joseph, a Gore coordinator for the north end of the county, instructs her phone-bank supervisor to urge voters not only to hit the polls but to be wary of the ballot's confusing design.

They're getting other weird reports, too. In precinct 162-G, the almost entirely Jewish retirement community called Lakes of Delray, Pat Buchanan — who has defended accused Nazis, called Hitler "a great man," argued that the

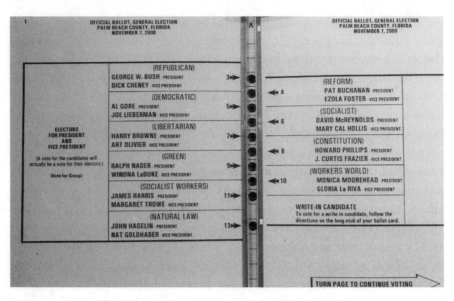

Palm Beach County's infamous butterfly ballot

United States fought the wrong side in World War II, and accused Holocaust survivors of having delusions of martyrdom — is racking up surprising support.

Sylvia Robb, wife of Lakes of Delray community president Arthur Robb, is just one of forty-seven voters who punches hole no. 2, thinking it's for Gore. By the end of the day, no precinct in Palm Beach County will show more votes for Buchanan than this one.

At 2:57 P.M., Brochin faxes his letter to LePore again, since he never heard from her the first time.

By 3 P.M. in Nashville, Whouley decides to switch the phone-script on the paid phone bank calls. Their telemarketing company, TeleQuest, is called in Texas. The Dems want them to make seventy-four thousand calls in Palm Beach. TeleQuest says they can't get anywhere near that number, but the company does make a change. "Some voters have encountered a problem today with punch-card ballots in Palm Beach County," the new TeleQuest script reads. "These voters have said that they believe that they accidentally punched the wrong hole for the incorrect candidate." To voters who had yet to vote, instructions were given: "punch number 5 for Gore-Lieberman," and "do not punch any other number, as you might end up voting for someone else by mistake.

"If you have already voted and think you may have punched the wrong hole for the incorrect candidate, you should return to the polls and request that the election officials write down your name so that this problem can be fixed."

Around that time in Palm Beach, the butterfly-ballot cacophony gets cranked up when outspoken Gore-backing talk-radio host Randi Rhodes tells listeners to WJNO-radio — 1290 on your A.M. dial — that she had the same problem.

"I got scared I voted for Pat Buchanan," she says on the air. "I almost said, 'I think I voted for a Nazi.' When you vote for something as important as leader of the free world, I think there should be spaces between the names. We have a lot of people with my problem, who are going to vote today and didn't bring their little magnifiers from the Walgreens. They're not going to be able to decide that there's Al Gore on this side and Pat Buchanan on the other side. . . . I had to check three times to make sure I didn't vote for a Fascist."

In retirement condos from Jupiter to Boca Raton, Rhodes's fans start wondering if they voted correctly.

Many of these seniors are deeply upset. Harold Blue, eighty-seven, enlisted in the cavalry right after Pearl Harbor, landing in Normandy at D day plus two, remaining in Europe long enough to carry out the cease-fire orders at the end of war, establishing contact with the Russians. Blue and his wife are legally blind, so at the polling station in a Greenacres public school, he requests help.

"Number one is Republican, number two is Democrat," the poll worker advises him. Later, Blue will realize that he punched the wrong hole. He fought for democratic principles in France, he thinks. But this sure as hell wasn't a democratic election.

At the elections office, Democratic officeholders like state representative Lois Frankel, state senator Ron Klein, and U.S. representative Robert Wexler come in and start complaining about the "widespread problem" of the butterfly ballot.

LePore has a real sick feeling in her stomach. "Oh, shit," she finally thinks.

Calls are coming in from people complaining because they had a problem voting. Poll workers and voters are calling and complaining that the phones have been busy, because of all the other calls. Harangued by the Democratic officials, LePore finally agrees to write an advisory about the ballot, though she tells the Democrats that she doesn't have the support staff to get it to every precinct, that they'll have to distribute it. They print out 531 copies:

ATTENTION ALL POLL WORKERS. PLEASE REMIND ALL VOT-
ERS COMING IN THAT THEY ARE TO VOTE ONLY FOR ONE (1)
PRESIDENTIAL CANDIDATE AND THAT THEY ARE TO PUNCH
THE HOLE NEXT TO THE ARROW NEXT TO THE NUMBER
NEXT TO THE CANDIDATE THAT THEY WISH TO VOTE FOR.

At around 4 P.M., Judge Charles Burton — chairman of the Palm Beach County canvassing board — sits in the conference room with LePore and the third member of the board, Democratic county commissioner Carol Roberts.

An elections office employee brings Burton over a ballot.

"Vote for Gore," she instructs him. Burton had voted the week before, via absentee ballot.

Burton looks at the ballot, sees the clear arrow from the Gore-Lieberman ticket to the third hole, punches the hole, *bang.*

"What's the problem?" he asks.

"Well, people are getting confused," she says.

"I don't really see it," says Burton, a low-key guy. "But, well, OK."

Roberts, a strong partisan Democrat, says, "You know they're starting to say this ballot was illegal. You may need to get your own lawyer," she advises LePore.

The phone lines are all jammed. LePore learns that Democratic voters are being hepped up, told by a phone bank to call her to complain if they think they may have screwed up the ballot. The lines are being blocked from voters at the polls right now, she thinks.

LePore asks Burton what he thinks. Was the ballot illegal? He gets a book of election law, reads the statute. It's clearly OK. The section of law the Democrats are referring to — 101.151 (3) (a) — applies only to paper ballots, not ones for punch-card voting.

"I don't really think it's illegal," he tells LePore. "But whatever."

It's not "whatever" for LePore. She feels like her world is crashing down around her.

★　★　★

At 5:30 P.M., Lieberman calls Rhodes in a previously arranged "Get Out the Vote" interview.

"You've got a very confusing ballot in Florida, have you heard?" Rhodes asks Lieberman.

"I just heard as I was listening and waiting to come on," Lieberman says, "and that's the first I heard about it."

"We have a serious problem," Rhodes says. "And in fact, for those who found the ballot confusing, we have an attorney at one of our big law firms" asking us to "please file an affidavit." The Democrats have already set up a phone number and retained an attorney to hear voters' complaints. "I'm not sure if I voted for you and Al Gore, or Pat Buchanan and Ezola Foster," Rhodes adds.

"Wow!" Lieberman responds. "Now, there's a big difference. You've got to be careful. The affidavit idea is very important. Because if the election is close, there's going to be contests all over America."

★   ★   ★

At that moment, Mitchell Berger is preparing for such an event.

Berger has known Al Gore since the early 1980s, when he was helping his dad's flailing mall development/management business in Chattanooga and Gore was a young congressman. Berger was interested in environmental issues, new economy issues, things that few politicians were discussing except for young Congressman Gore. They further bonded after Berger moved to Florida — where he built a successful law practice with offices in Miami, Fort Lauderdale, and Tallahassee — and Gore ran for president in 1988 with few other contacts in the Sunshine State.

Berger's respect for Gore knows no bounds. If you give Berger a minute, he'll spend five telling you how Gore's 1988 presidential run paved the way for Clinton's successful bid four years later. How New Democrat Gore was distancing himself from Jesse Jackson during the 1988 New York primary, thus allowing Clinton to do the same to rapper Sister Souljah four years later. He thinks that one of the most unreported stories about Al Gore is how Gore essentially ran the country while Clinton was stuck in the impeachment quagmire but had to keep such a fact quiet for the country's sake. And Berger has disdain for the reporters who covered the Clinton administration so aggressively, necessitating his giving Gore advice during some of the veep's own fund-raising scandals.

In frequent contact with Brochin and Palm Beach County Democratic chieftain Monte Friedkin, Berger's alarmed. He tells Brochin and lawyers in his firm, mainly Leonard Samuels, to get ready to litigate. He doesn't know who's going to litigate, he doesn't know how, but he wants to be prepared.

At 7 P.M., Berger's at the Miami airport, on the phone with Gore attorneys Joe Sandler and Lynn Utrecht and Gore's chief of staff, Charles Burson. He's getting ready to hop onto a 7:15 Southwest Airlines flight to Nashville, hopefully for the Gore celebration, but he's not so sure that he should go.

"Should I stay in Florida?" he asks the Gore attorneys. "'Cause there's a lot of bad things that went on here today." Some in Nashville were under the impression that Berger was ready to file a lawsuit against the butterfly ballot at that very moment.

Come to Nashville, Sandler says. There's nothing you can do. The polls are about to close. And hopefully everything will be the way it's supposed to be.

So Berger gets on the plane.

2

"You don't have to be snippy about it."

He's fucked!" Mark Fabiani, Gore's communications director, cackles.

I just told Fabiani that Bush is huddling back at the mansion instead of at the Four Seasons, where he was originally scheduled to watch the election returns.

"He's in retreat!" Fabiani says. "He's running home!"

It's Tuesday, November 7, 2000, around 9 P.M. And at this particular point in the evening, it doesn't look good for Bush. I do, in fact, picture Bush clutching his pilly, curled up in the fetal position, holding on to his daddy's leg. The exit polls have been coming in all day, and they've been bad. Bush, not surprisingly, is glum. His chief strategist, Karl Rove, had been telling him that it was going to be a Reaganesque landslide. Not quite.

Florida, a state Bush wanted to win, needed to win — little brother, Jeb, is the governor there, after all — is called for Gore at 7:48 P.M. EST. And with that, Bush's odds of becoming president have plummeted.

Jeb — an acronym for his full name, John Ellis Bush — calls his first cousin John Ellis in New York City. As luck and the fabled "vast right-wing conspiracy" would have it, Ellis helms Fox News Channel's election decision team, which means he's in charge of calling states.* Ellis has already spoken to George W. twice earlier in the day, reassuring the candidate not to "worry about your early numbers," since "your dad had bad early numbers in 'eighty-eight, and he wound up winning by seven. So who knows?"[1]

But now the news he has for Jeb is far more pessimistic.

"Are you sure?"[2] Jeb asks Ellis, after Fox News calls Florida for Gore, at 7:52 P.M., after three other networks have done so.

"We're looking at a screen full of Gore," Ellis replies.

"But the polls haven't closed in the Panhandle," Jeb says.

"It's not going to help," Ellis says. "I'm sorry."

So in a sudden turnabout, the normally cocky Bush abandons plans to watch the returns from a suite at the Austin Four Seasons and instead opts to run for the cover of the governor's mansion.

An election that his advisers had been predicting he'd win by 7 percentage points and 50 electoral votes is actually turning out to be too close to call.

★   ★   ★

At the Grand Hyatt in Manhattan, President Clinton is like a voracious animal, and what he wants is information about the election. In her quest for the U.S. Senate seat from New York, Hillary cruised to an easy victory, so the president's mind is focused on his no. 2. In his suite, each time a state pops up on the TV in front of him (ABC News) or to his right (MSNBC), he commands one of the aides around him to get more information. More, more, he's still not satisfied!

Earlier, when Florida was still in play, he had his former senior aide, Jonathan Prince, call Nick Baldick, Gore's man on the ground in Tallahassee. When Gore is trailing in Arkansas, Clinton called up his fellow Arkansan Secretary of Transportation Rodney Slater to see what he knew.

Gore's not down by so much, he tells Slater. "We've seen that turn around before."

Nevada comes on the screen.

---

*In a July 3, 1999, op-ed for the *Boston Globe* entitled "Why I Won't Write Any More About the 2000 Campaign," then-columnist Ellis wrote, "I am loyal to my cousin, Governor George Bush of Texas. I put that loyalty ahead of my loyalty to anyone else outside my immediate family. That being the case, it is not possible for me to continue writing columns about the 2000 presidential campaign. A columnist's allegiance must be to the reader. This is an annoying and pretentious thing that journalists say, but it is, in fact, true. Columns depend upon trust. . . . There is no way for you to know if I am telling you the truth about George W. Bush's presidential campaign because in my case, my loyalty goes to him and not to you."

"Where's Brian Greenspun?" Clinton asks, referring to the publisher of the *Las Vegas Sun* and a former classmate from Georgetown. "Get Brian Greenspun on the phone!" Clinton tells his aide, Doug Band.

"He's down the hall" at one of the First Lady's many receptions, Band says.

"Go get him!" Clinton says.

West Virginia comes on the screen. A state that has gone for Republican presidential candidates only three times in eighty years — all three times when the Republican in question was the incumbent president — is a solid Bush win.

"That's my fault," Clinton says, turning to chief of staff John Podesta. The environmentally friendly strip-mining policies Clinton pushed fostered resentment for Gore among the coal-mining community. "That policy screwed him," Clinton says.

It's a small crowd in the room, which consists primarily of Clinton, Podesta, Prince, Band, pollster Mark Penn, deputy chief of staff Steve Richetti, and Joel Johnson, senior adviser to the president for policy and communications. But even with such a small group, there's a hell of a lot of frustration and disdain toward Gore's consultants — Carter Eskew, Bob Shrum, and Tad Devine. The consensus seems to be that they ran a shitty campaign for Gore, that they never really cared about him the way James Carville cared about Clinton in '92, or Dick Morris did in '96. Devine's the guy who — when Clinton's speech at the Democratic convention in 1988 went more than a little long — supposedly turned the lights down on him, and Clinton's never forgiven him for that. Eskew and Shrum are seen as just part-of-the-problem Washington guys who could envision losing, guys for whom Gore was just another client.

Then there's the campaign they waged, the running away from Clinton, from the unprecedented peace and prosperity. They barely used the president, since their poll numbers showed that post-Lewinsky he hurt them with swing voters. But to not even get him to Arkansas until that last week?! Even worse, Shrum and pollster Stan Greenberg concocted this pose for Gore that was a total diversion from the New Democrat thing he and Clinton had sold so well to the public.

Clinton has a term for it tonight. He calls it "consultant populist bullshit."

★   ★   ★

In Miami, Democratic senator Bob Graham has just completed an interview with Tom Brokaw when a producer asks him if he'll be willing to remain miked-up and in front of the camera to talk to MSNBC anchor Brian Williams. Graham says yes and is flabbergasted when only a few minutes later NBC calls Florida for Gore.

There are a few congressional districts not even completed with their voting, Graham thinks, those west of the Apalachicola River. And as the senior Democrat in the state, Graham knows just how razor-thin the race is, how anyone can win it.

"They're really stretching it," Graham thinks.

★   ★   ★

In Fort Lauderdale, the three members of the Broward County canvassing board are in the supervisor of elections' warehouse, watching TV with mouths agape. They and the election workers haven't even counted one Broward County ballot before the state is awarded to Gore. They typically don't watch TV while they count the ballots, but this is the closest election in recent memory, and no one can resist.

"Oh, that's very kind of Mr. Brokaw to just give this away," says longtime supervisor of elections Jane Carroll, seventy, one of the few Republican officeholders in the overwhelmingly Democratic stronghold.

The chairman of the canvassing board, Judge Robert Lee, a Democrat, is incredulous at Brokaw's pronouncement. Not one precinct has come in! And Florida's in two time zones — the polls aren't even closed in the western part of the Panhandle!

As the night goes on and the ballots start pouring in — accompanied by sheriff's deputies — Lee, Carroll, and Democratic county commissioner Suzanne Gunzburger occasionally poke their heads into the back room, where every fifteen minutes they transmit the county results via a computer.

On the secretary of state's special Web site — for which they need a special password — Lee sees that Gore is hardly running away with the state. "Why are they calling Florida for Gore when it's so close?" he wonders.

Soon a few local Republican muckety-mucks — Shari McCartney and Ed Pozzuoli — storm into the warehouse. Where are the ballots from Weston? they ask.

Weston is one of the few GOP areas in the county, as far west as you can get without standing in the Everglades. It's a place of wealth and power, where several members of the Miami Dolphins live. Interstate 595 was built for Weston.

McCartney and Pozzuoli think something's amiss. Where are the Weston ballots?! Have they been stolen? Are they going to be counted?!

Have they even arrived yet?! Carroll explains that it's no big mystery, Weston is forty-five to sixty minutes away, and it's not as if there are two deputies assigned for each of the county's 609 precincts. Each team is assigned several precincts where they're to pick up and escort the ballots back to the warehouse. The ballots will get there.

★   ★   ★

At a party in Washington, D.C., Supreme Court justice Sandra Day O'Connor watches Dan Rather give Gore Florida.

"This is terrible," she says.

She rises to get a plate of food. Her husband explains that his wife, a Reagan appointee and former Republican leader of the Arizona state senate, wants to retire, but feels that she can do so only if a Republican is in the White House to name her successor.[3] But what can she do? She's had her one vote.

★   ★   ★

The press "pool" — the dozen or so members of the press whose turn it is to experience smaller events firsthand, after which we have to report back to the larger, more unwieldy, press corps — is bused to the governor's mansion.

"He preferred to be at home," says an aide, Gordon Johndroe, to the pool. "He found his house was more relaxing than the hotel, where there was a lot of activity."

As the pool waits for the call from Bush to allow us to walk in to see him, big news comes in via cell phone. One of the networks is about to call Pennsylvania for Gore, filling the last third of the Florida, Michigan, and Pennsylvania trifecta that is essential to a Gore victory.

Minutes later, as I walk into the upstairs living room of the governor's mansion, Bush doesn't look so panicky. He's sitting with his wife and parents, and though a handful of reporters swarms in — and a cameraman knocks over a vase, spilling water and flowers all over the place — Bush stays cool.

Appearances mean so much in the Bush campaign plan. His easygoing demeanor, as with his campaign's bold victory predictions, is all about conveying an air of inevitability. And that's kind of the story of W. Grandson of one senator, son of a president, W. has had a life that's been largely about coasting, failing upward, from Andover to Yale to Harvard Business School. His daddy's connections got him a cushy spot in the Texas Air National Guard during Vietnam; he started an oil business and ran it into the ground, but no matter, because one of his daddy's friends bailed him out of that, too. His daddy's rich friends helped him raise the dough to be the public face of the partners that bought and ran the Texas Rangers. And suddenly he was governor, and then he was the ordained candidate for president, and then he was here, in this room.

"We're not conceding anything until we see the actual vote," Bush says on the phone to Pennsylvania governor Tom Ridge. "Tom, I appreciate your calling."

He hangs up.

"I think Americans oughta wait until all the votes are counted," Bush says to us. "I don't believe the projections," he says, about both the Keystone State and Florida. "In states like Florida, I'm gonna wait for them to call all the votes," he says.

Jeb, who earlier in the night was saddened and apologetic when the networks handed his state to his brother's nemesis, has had a shift in mood. His political people back home have the race too close to call — at the very worst.

Jeb shares the news with his brother's chief strategist, Karl Rove, who is pleased to hear it. He directs his staffers to call up the networks and yell at them for their premature projections. Rove thinks that the nets have a double standard — other states that Bush will end up winning far more handily, like Ohio and Alabama, are still "too close to call." Giving Gore Florida is insanity, Rove thinks. Not to mention that six counties at the western Panhandle of the state are under the central time zone, so the polling locales for those voters in those largely Republican areas were still open when the nets told them, essentially, to go on home, Gore won. Rove and other Republicans will later argue that the early call cost Bush maybe 10,000 votes.

★   ★   ★

In Nashville, Gore's field strategist, Michael Whouley, is sitting in the "boiler room" he's set up, watching Rove dispute the networks' gift of Florida to Gore.

He's confused. Is Rove trying to send a message to the western states that things are still in play enough, that Bush can still win without Florida, as it is his obligation to do? Or does he actually believe that Bush is gonna win Florida? Rove had been talkin' smack all week, saying Bush was gonna win by 6 or 7 points, a Reaganesque sweep.

Whouley isn't sure which one it is.

★   ★   ★

Bush has his jacket off and is sitting between his wife, Laura, and mother, Barbara. His father, former president George H. W. Bush, is leaning back on the sofa, gripping his hands, legs crossed.

"I'm pretty darn upbeat about things," W. says. "I don't believe some of these states they've called."

His father is asked if this is anything like the mood in 1992, when he lost to Bill Clinton.

"Helluva lot worse," Bush Sr. says.

"Ditto," Barbara Bush says.

"I'm pleased to carry Tennessee," Bush says. "That's an interesting development."

Indeed, news of that had been a real psychic blow to Gore, who always held out hopes that, despite daunting poll numbers, he'd pull out a state victory.

Born to Tennessee senator Albert Gore, Sr., Gore Jr. was always child of both Carthage, Tennessee, where his family still owns land, and Washington, D.C. As a congressman, Gore was far more conservative on issues like abortion and guns than his later political incarnations, as he proceeded up the political food chain to senator (elected in 1984) and vice president (1992). Unlike Bush, who seemed to stumble into all this, Gore has been running for president from the time he was a zygote, and he was constantly trying to figure out what others wanted him to be — his positions on issues, his circle of advisers were always changing, changing, changing. His public manner was stilted, often condescending; his inner turmoil peeked out and reared its head from time to time, and it wasn't pretty.

Clinton-Gore carried Tennessee's 11 electoral votes in 1996, but only barely, and only after sinking unconscionable amounts of cash into the state in the last weeks of the campaign. (Whouley called 'em "the most expensive electoral votes in history.") Tonight it is official: Gore can now officially consider D.C. his home, because Tennessee has rejected him. Bush is pleased.

We're escorted out of *maison Bush*. In minutes, the networks pull Florida from Gore's column and put it back under "too close to call."

★   ★   ★

All the networks are taking their lead from the election-projections folks over at Voter News Service, or VNS, which was formed in 1990 as a cost-cutting measure. (Each network used to have its own projections staffs.) But it's more than just costs that VNS has cut — it's reliability, and quality, and accuracy.

At this moment, the rocket scientists at VNS are projecting that Gore will beat Bush in Florida by 7.3 percentage points. Almost half of this — 2.8 percentage points — comes from bad sampling at the polls, picking the wrong people at the wrong places. VNS's exit poll in Tampa is off by a full 16 points, inflating Gore's lead like hot air in a balloon.

Its Miami numbers are totally crazy. They overestimate the black turnout and underestimate the Cuban-American turnout. Not surprisingly, these sample groups in Miami are much smaller than the ones the networks and AP used before VNS was created.

Another 3.2 points in Gore's 7.3-point "lead" come from VNS decision makers having picked a bad exit-poll model. More than 1.3 points from this figure come from an underestimation of absentee ballots. VNS thinks absentee votes will account for 7.2 percent of the turnout, when the real figure is 12 percent. They're also underestimating how many of these absentee ballots will end up coming in for Bush — they guess that absentee voters will be Bush backers 22.4 percent more than regular voters, when the actual number is 23.7 percent.

Why do they think this? Because, unlike in other states, VNS didn't conduct any telephone polling in the Sunshine State to get a sense of what their parameters should be. It would cost too much, they decided.[4]

And then there's the question of voters who went to the polls to cast a vote for a candidate, and for some reason that vote didn't count — or counted for the wrong candidate, like, say, Pat Buchanan. To the VNS exit pollers outside, there's no way to check if a voter who tells them they voted for Gore may have actually, officially done so.

Moreover, VNS is beset with simple incompetence, the kind of mediocrity we settle for in normal life — think 411 or the Department of Motor Vehicles — that has disastrous consequences at moments of great importance, like Space Shuttle launchings and Election Night projections. Shortly after 9 P.M., one VNS operator, adding a number to Gore's vote total in Republican Duval County, gets a little frisky with the keys. Instead of 4,301 votes, the operator adds 43,023. Whoa, boy! Lake County totals for Gore will be inaccurately added — twice — giving vote totals that exceeded the number of voters. But even after these figures are fixed, another vote total shortchanges Gore 4,000 votes in Brevard County, 93,318 votes instead of the actual figure 97,318. This last mistake isn't fixed until 3:51 A.M.[5]

★   ★   ★

Within a half hour, Bush is up even further, 217 electoral votes to Gore's 167, now that Florida's 25 electors have been stripped from the vice president. Bush wins key second-tier swing states like Missouri, West Virginia, and New Hampshire. He's only 53 electoral votes away from the big enchilada. But then Gore picks up California, and the race narrows even further. Soon it becomes clear: whoever wins Florida wins it all.

Though Florida had gone for a Democratic presidential candidate only three times in forty years, demographic shifts in the state had made it far more up for grabs. Bush's team could never conjure a strategy for an electoral victory that didn't include the state; when Gore's poll numbers started going soft and then south in states like West Virginia, Arkansas, and Tennessee, his team, too, began to realize how important a Florida victory would be.

Gore's selection of Lieberman as his running mate helped him shore up disproportionately Jewish and Democratic southeastern Florida. Bush had Jeb, of course, and Jeb's organization, and the Panhandle and western side of the peninsula. So the battle was fought in the middle stretch of the state, between Tampa and Orlando — the fabled Interstate 4 corridor — which was full of younger voters, high-tech workers, and transplants from other swing states, like Michigan.

Gore and the Democrats would end up spending around $8 million in the state; Bush and the Republicans $14 million. After the Democratic convention — where aides had arranged it so Florida's delegates would be the ones to put Gore over the top, giving him the nomination — Gore spent fourteen days in the state, including high-profile days of debate preparation in Longboat Key. Bush spent nine days in the state, sending his parents and Ret. Gen. "Stormin'" Norman Schwarzkopf to stump for him. He spent his last Sunday before the election flying to four Florida cities.

Now Bush wants to know: was this all for naught?

At midnight, he directs Jeb: "Get me figures, little brother."[6]

Jeb punches keys at a computer, entering figures for each precinct.

"I can't believe this is happening," Bush says. "This is like running for a city council seat."

Bush leads Gore in the state, but as the last 10 percent of the precincts are counted, Bush's lead narrows.

In Nashville, Gore knows this. He's been watching the returns come in with his family, on the ninth floor of the Loews Vanderbilt Plaza Hotel. But at around 1 A.M. eastern, he comes down to the seventh floor to watch with his staff.

It looks promising. Bush's lead narrows from 80,000 to 60,000 to 30,000.

20,000.

10,000.

Gore and his team are well aware that a number of the last counties to report their tallies are largely Democratic ones in the southeast corner of the state — Palm Beach, Broward, Miami-Dade.

It looks as though Gore is going to pull into the lead again.

Suddenly Bush's lead pops up to an unsurmountable 50,000.

Gore staffers curse under their breaths. There must have been Republican-leaning counties holding their returns to the end, they think.

It's quiet on the seventh floor. Nobody is talking. Gore puts his hands on the shoulders of his staffers, to buck them up.

★   ★   ★

In New York City, Ellis calls his cousins in Austin.

"Our projection shows that it is statistically impossible for Gore to win Florida," he says to his cousins' delight.

At 2:17 A.M. EST, Ellis calls Florida for his cousin, thus giving him the presidency, Bush with 271 electoral votes (270 are needed to win), Gore 249.

"It's just Fox," Rove says at Austin HQ.

The guys in the office cheer, nonetheless. The women are a little more circumspect. But then NBC calls Florida for Bush, and the women cheer, too. Within thirty seconds, every other network follows Fox News Channel's lead.

Bush brother Marvin takes a moment to tease the Florida governor. "Jebby!" he jokes. "You can come in from the ledge now!"[7]

★   ★   ★

Now, of course, the VNS brain surgeons are fucking it up the other way.

At 2:10 A.M., 97 percent of the state's precincts have reported in. VNS wizards guess that 179,713 votes are still outstanding. It ends up being about 360,000. In Palm Beach County — decidedly Gore country — VNS guesses that there are only about 41,000 votes left to come in. It ends up being 129,000.

In Tallahassee, Gore's main man on the ground in Florida, Nick Baldick — who helped Clinton win the state in '96 — has been disappointed with the numbers coming in. But he's not ready to concede just yet. Yeah, some of the news is pretty grim: Gore's getting killed pretty bad in the north, Baldick thinks. Much worse than he'd thought. Clinton is hurting them, he thinks. We didn't go on TV in time, didn't let them know Gore was a vet and Bush was a National Guard draft dodger. Jews in the south are turning out huge (thank God for Lieberman!), but old people in the I-4 aren't going for Gore in the numbers they need them to. Yikes.

Studying the returns, suddenly Baldick realizes something's a bit off.

"What the fuck's going on in Volusia County?" Baldick thinks.

The Gore team had anticipated winning Volusia County, around Daytona Beach on the northeast coast, by 10,000 or so votes — but on the Volusia County Web site Gore has only won by 942 votes. Baldick dispatches a ground staffer, Deborah Tannenbaum, to the board of elections there, in DeLand.

When she calls him, she has good news. The Web site's all screwed, she says. Gore actually won Volusia by 15,000 votes, she says.

Baldick looks at the precincts that have yet to come in. Twelve in Broward, where they should be strong, a couple in Palm, ditto. One in Dade. Half of Sumter County and a little bit more than half in Union. Hmm.

VNS clearly doesn't know this — and in fact, based on Volusia's computer screw-up, VNS thinks that Bush is ahead by 20,000 nonexistent votes. VNS's fact checking is so sloppy, no one even realized the ridiculousness of an early report that 95 percent of largely Republican Duval County had voted for Gore.

Baldick wonders if Katherine Harris has the new Volusia numbers or the old Volusia numbers. He wonders if Whouley knows about this. He has a line open with Whouley and Charlie Baker, another Gore field guy, in Nashville. He tells them not to put too much faith in the networks. We're either gonna win by 50 or lose by 100, he says. But this thing's still too close.

"I can't see why the networks are even thinking of calling it," Baldick thinks.

★ ★ ★

In Nashville, Gore goes back upstairs to talk to his family. On his way, he runs into his chief speechwriter, Eli Attie, a thirty-three-year-old mop-topped New Yorker. Gore and Attie had spent some time earlier in the day working on his victory speech.

"Do you have an alternative statement?" Gore asks him.

Attie nods.

"Why don't you bring it to my room," Gore says.

In fact, Attie has a bunch of speeches on hand. One for victory. One for an electoral victory, but a popular-vote defeat. One for a victory but a loss in Tennessee. One for a result where it's all too close to call, and the winner won't be known 'til Wednesday; Tad Devine had told him that it might come down to the absentee ballots in one state. And finally, Attie has a concession speech, one he wrote on Sunday in Philadelphia, while sitting in the back of a van. Gore goes upstairs; campaign chair Bill Daley and chief media strategist Carter Eskew go with him. Daley is focused on what Gore's going to do; he thinks he should concede. Eskew is focused on what Gore's going to say. Campaign manager Donna Brazile, long since edged out of the immediate circle, sends Gore a page: "Never surrender. It's not over yet," it reads.

Gore takes Daley aside, asks him what he thinks.

"I think you oughta call them," Daley says, meaning the Bushies, meaning concession.

Lieberman, who has a tight race in his political history, tries to talk him out of it. But Gore isn't buying it. "I just want to thank everybody for everything they did," Gore says. He doesn't want a prolonged, protracted, divisive fight. Gore's kids start to cry.

Daley hands him a slip of paper.

"Is this the number?" Gore asks. Daley says yes.

At around 2:40 A.M., Gore calls Bush to concede. Bush tells Gore that he's a "good man." He sends his best to Gore's wife, Tipper. "I know this is hard for you," Bush says.

Soon after, Eskew and Daley come back down to the seventh floor. We're going to the War Memorial to concede, they say.

★   ★   ★

In Austin, word of the concession reaches the networks, and the world waits for Gore to appear on the steps of the War Memorial to announce that it's all over. Journalists scamper from the press tent into the party area in front of the capital, which has erupted in joyful cheers.

I run into Mark McKinnon, Bush's media adviser, one of the only decent guys in the higher echelons of the governor's staff. He's smiling, a little drunk, a few tequila shots under his belt. He's wearing a black Kangol backward.

"A little drama for you," he says to me, smiling, as he makes his way into the celebration held on the now-rain-soaked Congress Street. "A little drama."

McKinnon doesn't know the half of it.

Just as, a week and a half ago, Gore had no idea how prescient he was being, in an aside he makes to me between two local Charleston, West Virginia, TV interviews. Gore joked, "If it's going to be a close race, it might as well be a historic one."

★   ★   ★

It's almost 3 A.M., and Gore is in his motorcade, making its way from the Loews Hotel to Nashville's War Memorial Plaza.

Bearing Baldick's words in mind, Whouley frantically tries to reach the team upstairs. He watches the last few numbers from Florida as they come in. Suddenly that last-minute 50,000-vote bubble has popped. The lead is down to 6,000 — way too close to concede.

Whouley wants to confirm these numbers. Baldick says again that it's too close to call. Within a thousand votes either way.

"Are you shu-ah?" he asks Baldick, in his thick Boston accent.

Baldick's shuah.

Whouley checks the Florida secretary of state's Web site. He asks his numbers guy, Ken Strasma, what he thinks. Strasma says the numbers he's been getting from Florida show that Gore could still win, and that at the very least it is too close.

"Are you shu-ah?" Whouley asks.

DNC spokeswoman Jenny Backus starts calling the networks to alert them that Florida is still too close to call. Meanwhile, Whouley calls Monica Dixon, one of the "war room" rapid-response staffers. Her voice mail's on; she's already left. In a zone, intensely concentrating on clearing it all up, Whouley and the rest in the boiler room haven't talked to Gore and his senior staff. They had assumed that Gore, Daley, et al. would call down before making any decisions. But that doesn't seem to be the case.

Whouley's assistant, a young Harvard grad named Jeff Yarborough, has been working so closely with Whouley that he — like Radar from *M*A*S*H* — often takes actions on his boss's behalf just minutes before his boss thinks of them himself.

Yarborough frantically pages Gore's traveling chief of staff, Mike Feldman.

"CALL SWITCHBOARD. CALL HOLDING WITH MIKE WHOULEY. ASAP," reads the page.

"Wheah the fuck ahh these people?!" Whouley asks.

"I'm getting Feldman on through White House signal," Yarborough says, referring to the White House paging system.

Feldman doesn't know what to think. Whouley had been at campaign HQ on the speaker phone with the seventh floor, but after the networks called the race for Bush, everyone kind of forgot about him. Feldman wonders if Whouley even knows that Gore conceded. Feldman punches up the switchboard on his cell phone and is immediately connected to Whouley.

"Wheah ahh you guys?!" Whouley asks.

"About two blocks away from the memorial," Feldman says.

"WHY?!" asks Whouley.

"Because Gore's going to give a speech," Feldman says.

"Fuh WHAT?!" Whouley asks. "It's an automatic recount! This thing is only six thousand votes! Ahh you with Daley?"

"I better get him on the line right now," Feldman says.

Daley's in a different car, so Feldman conferences him in on the cell phone.

Whouley explains that this thing is still too close to call. Another Gore staffer, Charlie Koch, has called Florida attorney general Bob Butterworth, the Gore campaign's state chair, to find out the relevant law as it pertains to the Florida recount. If the margin of victory is within one-half of 1 percent, there's an automatic machine recount, Butterworth explains. Whouley shares this with Daley.

"It's too close to call," Whouley says, giving Daley the details. "We still may win this thing. At a minimum, Billy, it's an automatic recount. We got TV cameras going to Bob Butterworth's house right now! It's an automatic recount!"

"Oh fuck," Daley says. "Let's go to hold when we get there. We'll sort it out there. And we'll call you back from a land line."

Attie's sitting with Daley and Eskew. He wonders why Daley's head is down; he's not exactly the kind of guy to get weepy. Then he realizes Daley's on the phone. He gets off the phone and turns to Eskew.

"With-ninety-nine-point-seven-percent-of-the-vote-counted-in-Florida-we're-only-six-hundred-votes-behind, whadda-we-do?!!" Daley asks.

Feldman calls David Morehouse, a Gore aide, and tells him to take Gore straight to the holding room when they arrive. Do not let Gore hit the stage, Feldman says. They are only a block or so away from the War Memorial.

Daley phones Gore.

"Whatever you do, do not go out on the stage!" Daley bellows.

"What the fuck are they doing?" Whouley thinks. "You don't leave to concede without checking with the boiler room first! We're busy workin' to get Bush's face off the TV, and they're taking the networks' word for it?! We're hustling, and they're conceding?! What a fuck-up."

A block later, Gore is down by maybe only 1,300 votes.

The motorcade stops. Someone tells Attie to get to the holding room in the Memorial, so he begins clawing his way there. When he gets there, he sees Gore.

"With ninety-nine point seven percent of the vote counted, we're only six hundred votes behind," Attie tells him. "We need to change the language in the speech, and Carter and Daley need to talk to you."

Gore looks at him, taken aback. Hmm!

About ten minutes later, another aide, Greg Simon, says: "It's down to five hundred votes in Florida."

Lieberman tells Gore not to concede.

At 3:15 A.M., Daley calls his counterpart in Bush's camp, Don Evans, to tell him about their concerns. "You need to give us a little more time," Daley says to Evans. "You need to let us work this out."

★   ★   ★

Bush is not happy. Ellis has told him that Florida is, again, too close to call.

"You gotta be kidding me," Bush says.

After calling back to Tallahassee, Jeb says the same thing. "I'm not seeing the same thing they're seeing in the numbers," Jeb says.

When Gore calls him a few minutes later, Bush doesn't let on that he knows that Florida is still in play. From this moment on, Bush and his team will propagate a myth, repeating it over and over to the American people: he won, definitively, at the moment that his cousin called the election for him for Fox News Channel.

"Circumstances have changed dramatically since I first called you," Gore says to Bush. "The state of Florida is too close to call."

"Are you saying what I think you're saying?" Bush asks pointedly. "Let me make sure that I understand. You're calling back to retract that concession?"

"You don't have to be snippy about it," Gore responds.

Gore tries to explain: Florida is too close to call. If Bush wins it, Gore will concede again. But the reality is different than the networks have reported it.

Bush tells Gore that the networks are right. Jeb's right here, he says.

"Your *little brother* doesn't get to make that call," Gore says.

"Well, Mr. Vice President, you do what you have to do," Bush says. *"Thanks for calling."*

"You're welcome!" Gore says.

★   ★   ★

Inside the holding room at the War Memorial, Gore hangs up.

His staff cheers.

Except for Bill Daley, that is, his campaign chairman. He's holding his bald head in his hands.

In the holding room, Daley took Gore aside and apologized for not having served him well, for having taken the TV networks' word for it. Gore brushed it off, don't worry about it, he said. But now Daley's fretting again that Gore may have done the wrong thing in retracting his concession. "What if we find out within the next few hours that what had caused us to hesitate was some mistake, some problem with the secretary of state's office?" he worries. "Then all of a sudden it's Wednesday morning, and we should have pretty obviously conceded the night before." He's trying to get a handle on the chaos; he doesn't want Gore to look like a jerk.

★   ★   ★

In Austin, Bush calls John Ellis. "Gore unconceded," he tells him.

"You've got to be kidding me," Ellis says.

In Austin, the rain is unrelenting.

★   ★   ★

In Tallahassee, Jeb Bush's acting chief counsel, Frank Jimenez, is watching CNN at Lt. Gov. Frank Brogan's home. At 3:50 A.M., Ed Kast, the assistant director for the state division of elections, does a phone interview with CNN anchors Judy Woodruff and Bernard Shaw and analysts Jeff Greenfield and Bill Schneider.

"OK, Mr. Kast," Greenfield says, "I just want to review the bidding because we may be talking about the outcome of the presidential election here. Right now, Governor Bush is leading Vice President Gore by we think — it's thirteen hundred ten votes if Judy's math is right. You've got, roughly based on the past, a couple of thousand overseas absentee ballots, . . . I'm not trying to put words in your mouth, but is it a fair statement that we do not yet know who has won the state of Florida?"

"We've got George Bush ahead," Kast says. "But it's not — those are preliminary and unofficial figures. They're not by any means official."

Jimenez places a call to Kast's boss, Clay Roberts.

"How long would it take to conduct a recount, Mr. Kast?" Woodruff asks.

"If we're thrown into a recount, or if there is a recount, they'll start that just as soon as we notify them, which will probably be first thing tomorrow morning," Kast says.

The anchors ask Kast how long that would take. But while they're talking, Clay Roberts tells Kast to get off the phone.

"Wouldn't there still be a ten-day separation?" Shaw asks.

Pause.

"Did we lose Ed Kast?" Shaw asks.

"We may have," Woodruff says.

"He certainly was a lot of information," Shaw says.

Exactly the problem. Jimenez and Roberts do not want an elections officer going on TV and saying that Bush is actually not yet the official winner
of Florida.

★   ★   ★

Bush attorney Ben Ginsberg, former counsel for the Republican National
Committee, is in the streets to rejoice. With the rest of the crowd, the bald,
bespectacled, neon-orange-bearded attorney waits and waits for Gore to
concede and Bush to take the stage.

He waits. And waits.

It doesn't seem quite right, he thinks. Something's off. On the jumbo-
tron TVs set up for the crowds, CNN's Candy Crowley reports that Gore
has retracted his concession.

Ginsberg's cell phone goes off. It's Rove's assistant.

"You better get back here," she tells him.

Back at HQ, Ginsberg's sitting at a desk when Don Evans, Bush's oil-slick
good-ol'-boy campaign chair saunters by.

"Think it's a recount?" he asks Ginsberg.

"Yep," Ginsberg says.

"Better start gettin' people to fly," Evans says.

Others are already on it. Ken Mehlman, thirty-four, the national field
director for the Bush campaign, was standing — waiting — on Congress
Street when he soon enough realized something was up. He hightailed it
back to HQ and, working with Tony Feather, figured out who needed to get
to Florida ASAP. They decided on Brian Noyes, the regional political director whose territory included the Sunshine State; Coddy Johnson, a regional
political director who had the central states; policy guy Joel Kaplan; Kristin
Silverberg, and attorneys Kevin Murphy and Kevin Martin. All are notified:
go back to your apartments and get maybe two days' worth of clothes. They
have a 6 A.M. charter flight to Miami.

★   ★   ★

In Nashville, Daley calls an executive at CBS, tells him to take back the premature call that Bush won. Feldman calls the political director at ABC, tells
him the same thing. NBC soon declares Florida "too close to call." On
CNN, the check mark remains by Bush's name. But not for long. At 4:05
A.M., CNN removes the check mark from Bush's name. The electoral count
becomes: Gore 249, Bush 246.

Within the hour, Daley and Evans make their respective announcements to their respective perplexed crowds.

Daley says that he's "been in politics for a very long time, but I've never seen a night like this." The networks called the election, Daley said, but "it now appears that their call was premature. . . . Until the result is official, our campaign continues," he says to cheers in Nashville. Daley says that Gore and Lieberman are ready to concede — but only after the Florida tally is official.

In Austin, Evans addresses the sopping-wet crowd. "We hope and we believe we have elected the next president of the United States," Evans says. "They're still counting, and I'm confident when it's all said and done, we will prevail." He leaves the podium and returns to the shelter of the campaign HQ.

"Ladies and gentlemen," a voice says from the loudspeaker. "Thank you for coming. That concludes the program."

If only.

3

"Do you remember us hitting anything?"

In the wee hours of the morning, as Tuesday morphs into Wednesday, the Election Night that will never end gains power. Outside Florida, political and legal soldiers are being recruited for the tumultuous thirty-six days that will follow, while within the Sunshine State itself, chaos, confusion, and conspiracy take hold.

Strange things are afoot in Volusia County, for instance.

In one precinct, Socialist Workers presidential candidate James Harris racks up 9,888 votes. The fact that Harris has only received 19,507 nationwide, and that the precinct only has around 350 voters, seems to cast doubt about his new 10,000-vote stronghold in one tiny Volusia County precinct.

More significant, in the city of DeLand, Volusia County elections workers have realized a big glitch in the computer programming that transmits results via modem from precinct 216 to the elections supervisor's office. Gore had 16,000 votes that just vanished in the night. The problem has since been discovered and ironed out, but Democrats are all fired up. What else, they wonder, could have gone wrong?

At around 3:45 A.M., an elections worker named Deborah Allen, forty-seven, and her younger brother Mark Bornmann walk out of the elections supervisor's office to go home. Bornmann, forty-three, a volunteer who has spent the last three hours in the elections office napping, is carrying his sister's bags: a briefcase and a small bag containing casual clothing she'd been wearing at her day job, as well as some toiletries.

After Allen and Bornmann leave, operatives from both the Democratic and Republican parties freak out, wondering if she's heisting some ballots, telling the deputy sheriff on the scene to apprehend her. Supervisor of Elections Deanie Lowe is sure that everything's kosher but feels compelled to make sure nonetheless.

Other sheriff's deputies are notified. A "bolo" (be on the lookout) is put out on the two. On International Speedway Boulevard, a cop recognizes Allen's brown Wagoneer as she and her brother make their way back home to Ormond Beach.

They're stopped and told they have to come back to DeLand. They won't tell her where she's going or why she's being asked to turn around and drive back to DeLand escorted by two sheriff's cars.

"Do you remember us hitting anything?" Allen worriedly asks her brother. She's in a panic. She's afraid that in the elections office parking lot maybe she collided with someone, maybe someone's dead.

At around 4:20 A.M., Allen and Bornmann arrive under police escort back at the elections supervisor's office. The contents of the bags are poured out onto the pavement near the parking lot and photographed.

No ballots.

In the wake of this mess, the Volusia County office of elections is sealed, surrounded by yellow police tape and armed deputies.

★   ★   ★

In Nashville, meanwhile, Gore asks Daley to phone up former secretary of state Warren Christopher, to recruit him for the recount effort. In addition to being an attorney with O'Melveny & Myers, a diplomat, and a respected Democrat party elder, Christopher is in many ways responsible for helping Gore segue from senator to vice president, having helmed then-governor Clinton's 1992 search for a running mate. In 2000, Gore called upon Christopher to help find him a Gore of his own, a process that ended up in the selection of Lieberman.

At 3:30 A.M. Pacific time, Christopher's wife is shaken from her sleep when the phone rings.

"It's Bill Daley," she says.

Christopher takes the call. It's brief.

"The election's so close in Florida there's going to be an automatic recount," Daley says. Gore wants Christopher and him to run it.

The seventy-five-year-old springs out of bed. A 6 A.M. Pacific time flight to Nashville is arranged. He shaves, showers, and packs. On the morning shows, the Gore campaign is able to announce the selection of their éminence grise to project that the recount will be a dignified and orderly event.

In Gore-Lieberman HQ in Nashville, things are not so dignified or orderly. It's downright scrappy.

Most of the crew has spent the night waiting outside the Nashville War Memorial in the rain on an emotional roller coaster: overjoyed when Gore was awarded Florida, then despondent when it was taken from him, then mortified — almost in mourning — when it was given to Bush. After the networks took Florida away from the GOP governor, they were overjoyed again, chanting the Gore mantra "Stay and fight!"

Soaking wet and totally confused, the young Democrats gather in HQ after Daley has bid them adieu for the night. Gore strategist Tad Devine gathers the crew around and gives them a pep talk. They said Al Gore was dead in the water in New Hampshire, Devine says, referring to pre-primary polls that showed former New Jersey senator Bill Bradley with a sizable lead in the state Gore eventually won. "But we stayed and fought!" Devine says, and Gore won New Hampshire. They said Al Gore was going to get demolished by George Bush, Devine says. But we stayed and fought, and it looks like Al Gore's going to win the popular vote.

"I don't know what the outcome of this election will be," Devine says. "But I feel an obligation to go down there and figure it out, and stay and fight!" The exasperated Democratic masses cheer. There's an automatic recount in Florida, Devine says, and Gore needs guys on the ground to make sure it all goes right.

Donnie Fowler, deputy field director, jumps on a desk and starts shouting out names like he's in the army. "Backus, Jenny!" he says. "Bash, Jeremy!" He runs through several dozen. "You got an hour. Go home and pack. Bring about three days' clothing." A charter plane is shipping them all down to Florida at 6 A.M.

Someone chips in that he did the Virginia recount in 1998, and it took three weeks.

Everybody groans. Three weeks! That's forever!

Lieberman's campaign plane — nicknamed "El Al Gore" or "Air Force Jew" by Nashville staffers — is snagged. By 5:30 A.M., sixty to seventy staffers have been shuttled to the airport and loaded up onto the plane, which Gore campaign lawyer Jack Young has dubbed "Recount One."

Jill Alper briefs the young campaign staffers on what's going on, tells them to take off their campaign paraphernalia. As they all drink coffee and

OJ, Young and Joe Sandler, general counsel of the DNC since 1993, brief them on the recount process.

Weeks before the election, Whouley asked Sandler and Young to prepare an immense notebook containing the recount procedures of twenty states. Some states were dropped as they got closer to Election Day and poll numbers went outside the margin of error, but it's a pretty comprehensive volume, and it looks like a stroke of genius now. They thought they'd need it for Missouri. Earlier in the night, when Iowa looked too close to call, they pulled the book out. They looked to the binder again for information about Oregon, Washington, New Mexico. And, finally, Florida.

In August 1994, Young and two Democratic attorney colleagues — Chris Sautter and Tim Downs — self-published *The Recount Primer,* a forty-three-page booklet that deals with almost every issue the team will encounter — and the country will learn about — in the next thirty-six days. In the primer, they laid out the purpose of a recount for "partisan representatives": "a) preserving a margin of victory, b) identifying election night mistakes which will turn a narrow loss into a win, or c) creating doubt as to the outcome sufficient to require a new election." They will contrast these goals with those of election officials, who "are concerned with accuracy, not outcome."

In the front of the plane sits Ron Klain, the guy who's going to run the legal effort. He's snoozing.

Klain was Gore's chubby, assertive chief of staff at the White House before Gore's second campaign manager, Machiavellian former House Democratic whip Tony Coehlo, froze him out of Gore's inner circle in May 1999. Coehlo had decided to run the operation out of Nashville and didn't want Klain throwing in his two cents from the Old Executive Office Building in D.C., nor did Coehlo want Klain leaving the OEOB to play a role in the campaign, frankly. Klain thought he was unnecessarily cruel. By August 1999, Klain had announced that he was leaving. To spend time with his family, of course.

Despite years of loyal service to Gore, that was it, no postcards, no letters; he could barely even get through to Gore anymore. Gore looked away, as if Klain had never existed.

It was a very painful year. He'd tried to keep a sense of humor about it. His new office at the D.C. office of O'Melveny & Myers featured cue cards from a monologue from the *Tonight* show with Jay Leno, autographed by the host himself:

AND ANOTHER BIG SHAKE-UP IN THE AL GORE CAM-
PAIGN.... IT SEEMS HIS LONG TIME CHIEF OF STAFF HAS
QUIT....

THEY SAID TODAY ON THE NEWS THIS IS THE BIGGEST
SETBACK FOR THE GORE CAMPAIGN ... WELL ... SINCE AL
GORE.

It had seemed like a big fall for wunderkind Klain. The Hoosier had
come to D.C. in '79 to go to Georgetown, and he immediately began
interning for Indiana Democratic senator Birch Bayh. After Harvard Law,
Klain clerked for U.S. Supreme Court justice Byron White, served as chief
counsel to the Senate Judiciary Committee, domestic policy adviser to
Clinton in '92, associate counsel to the president, chief of staff to Attorney
General Janet Reno, and, as of November 1995, top aide to Gore.

Superconnected. On March 19, 1993, Justice White called him at the
White House and asked him to hand-deliver his resignation letter to Clinton. Clinton asked him to lead the team to pick a replacement. One of
Klain's first calls was to the Senate Judiciary chairman, Delaware Democratic senator Joe Biden. He knew them all.

He was moving, always moving, working his ass off, downing Cokes and
M&M's while his wife raised their three kids. In 1994, *Time* magazine had
named him one of America's fifty "most promising leaders" under age
forty. Now what?

To Gore, people are expendable. Klain was just one of several dissed in
the Coehlo era — Jack Quinn and dying media man Bob Squier were two
notable others. And as Gore tore through campaign managers like the rest
of us go through a box of Kleenex, Coehlo was soon shoved aside as well. It
helped that he had been sick, a better excuse than that "spend time with my
family" bullshit, and in June 2000, when Commerce Secretary Daley was
brought in to get the campaign functioning better, Klain was no longer persona non grata. He was, again, persona grata — though slightly demoted.
That summer and fall, Klain ran the campaign's war-room effort, getting
out instant response to Bush attacks against Gore's policies and character.

Now, however, Klain has an opportunity to be in charge again, to run
things for Gore, to get him elected president.

At around 8:30 A.M., Klain, Sandler, Young, DNC spokeswoman Jenny
Backus, and a few others get off the plane in Tallahassee; it will also stop in

Tampa and Fort Lauderdale. As Backus is interviewed by a local TV station — in a town like Tallahassee, it's kind of hard to miss a plane with "Gore-Lieberman" painted on its side — another plane lands. It belongs to Gov. Jeb Bush. He talks to the camera after Backus concludes.

★ ★ ★

At dawn, a plane leaves Austin packed with lawyers and political operatives, flying due east. There's Ben Ginsberg, of course, as well as other Bush-Cheney campaign lawyers, like Joel Kaplan and Ted Cruz.

Ginsberg's the expert; he's been through tons of recounts before. In fact, Ginsberg's life has been changed by recounts. It's something he'll tell junior lawyers repeatedly over the next thirty-six days: "Recounts change lives. I can't tell you how this one will change your life, but it will."

Ginsberg's career trajectory had always been shaped by serendipity. He was raised by liberal Jewish Democrats on Philadelphia's Main Line, but his politics were shaped as a sophomore at the University of Pennsylvania, where Ginsberg saw what he felt was the great fallacy of Great Society–style paternal liberalism in the Comprehensive Employment and Training Act, or CETA, which tried to help gang members by giving them jobs. It didn't accomplish anything, Ginsberg thought. It just threw money at the problem.

As editor of the *Daily Pennsylvanian,* he became a reporter — at the *Philadelphia Bulletin,* the *Boston Globe,* the *Berkshire Eagle* in Western Massachusetts, the *Riverside* (California) *Press-Enterprise.* Whenever he could, he'd ask to cover CETA, because he knew there would be good stories there.

In Riverside in the late '70s, in what was then the fastest-growing metropolitan area in the country, Ginsberg covered the housing-and-development boom and was shocked to discover how much he didn't know. So he applied to Georgetown Law and started in '79. In the meantime, flaky Jerry Brown was elected governor of California in '78, which convinced Ginsberg for the first time to register as a Republican.

In 1982, thirty-one-year-old Ben Ginsberg was just a "grunt associate" at the D.C. law firm Baker & Hostetler when the Republicans on the House Administration Committee hired the firm to find precedents on recounts. No one had bothered to look into it at all, and the committee wanted to have the information ready, if needed. Ginsberg did the work.

Just two years later came "the bloody eighth." In November 1984, in Indiana's 8th congressional district, one-term Democratic congressman Frank McCloskey was unseated by Republican Rick McIntyre by 34 votes out of 233,500 cast. McCloskey lost the recount as well. But the U.S. House was in Democratic hands, 252 to 182, and led by Speaker Tip O'Neill, D-Mass., the House conducted its own recount — which had Democrat McCloskey winning by four votes, 116,645 to 116,641. Though just a kid of thirty-three, Ginsberg had been flown to Indiana for the recount, and the whole experience radicalized him. It was a stolen election, he thought, it was not an honest process.

Ginsberg was hired as counsel for the National Republican Congressional Committee in June of '85, and as such was flown into Minnesota in '86 to supervise another recount. There he met up with aides to Republican Minnesota senator Rudy Boschwitz, head of the National Republican Senatorial Committee, who brought him in as counsel to that shop in '87. Through that office, Ginsberg observed another Florida recount, that between Republican businessman Connie Mack and Democratic representative Buddy MacKay — the race Theresa LePore had in mind when designing the butterfly ballot.

After talking with Bush campaign chair Don Evans, plans are made to phone up George Terwilliger at White & Case, as well as other high-profile GOP barristers — most notably Ted Olson and Michael Carvin. From time served in Indiana and Minnesota, Ginsberg knows that the team needs red-meat local boys. So he calls Jeb's counsel, Frank Jimenez.

"We need Florida lawyers," Ginsberg tells him. "We need a statewide firm. We need litigators."

Jimenez has one recommendation: Barry Richard, from the Tallahassee branch of Greenberg Traurig.

Richard's a Democrat — a former state rep from Miami Beach, whose dad was mayor there back in the 1950s — but he's nonpartisan in his legal work. He represented Jeb Bush in his '98 gubernatorial bid, as well as in a case this year brought by Democrats who objected to an absentee-ballot mailing — "From the Desk of Gov. Jeb Bush" — sent out to Republicans and using, improperly, the Dems alleged, a symbol that resembled the state seal. The mailing was eventually canceled, though the suit was thrown out of court before Election Day by circuit court judge Terry Lewis. But Richard has represented Democrats, having served as campaign counsel just the past year for Insurance Commissioner Barry Nelson, a Democrat, in his successful Senate race.

I'm interested, Richard says when Jimenez calls, but I'm flying off to Miami to visit my eighty-eight-year-old dad, who's ill. I'll be back in Tallahassee Thursday, Richard says. I'll meet up with you guys then.

★   ★   ★

In a downtown Miami office building, Murray Greenberg — a twenty-eight-year veteran of the Miami-Dade County attorney's office — calls Supervisor of Elections David Leahy. He can't contain himself.

"This is the best election we've ever had!" Greenberg, a short, sweet, longtime Miamian, gushes to Leahy, a twenty-year county vet himself. The county had close to 90 percent voter turnout, there were no close races in the county mandating a recount, no problems getting returns in, no allegations of lost ballot boxes. Since Bush's statewide margin of victory had been so slim, they had to conduct a mandatory machine recount like every other county, of course. But that day's machine recount results in less than a 100-vote difference from their original score, well within the norm.

"It just went off without a hitch!" Greenberg gleefully concludes.

★   ★   ★

In Fort Lauderdale, about half a dozen Democrats exit "Recount One," including Gore deputy field director Donnie Fowler and Jeremy Bash, who worked on military and foreign affairs issues for Klain in the Nashville war room.

Field operatives meet them and hand them keys to their own cruising vessels, courtesy of Alamo Rent-a-Car. Bash and Fowler shoot north on I-95 to meet with the Palm Beach Democratic chairman, Monte Friedkin.

Friedkin seems obnoxious and rude, a brash New Yorker who's under the impression that he's quite impressive. Bash and Fowler ask about the butterfly ballot, and Friedkin immediately starts tearing into Theresa LePore. "She's a fool!" he says. LePore's perfectly nice, Friedkin allows, "but an idiot!"

Bash, Friedkin, and Fowler head to Delray Beach, where the machine recount has commenced for some of the county's ballots. Democrat and Republican observers are shooting the shit good-naturedly. The floor is covered in the punched-out bits of cardboard from the ballot, called chad.* Bash and Fowler, under instructions from Gore lawyers Young and Sandler, are there just to observe. Not to argue, not to talk, just to check out what's being done, gathering information.

They soon hit the Delray Beach Democratic Party headquarters, at a strip mall, where half a dozen or so lawyers are taking affidavits from maybe thirty Palm Beach voters who are complaining about problems with the butterfly ballot. There are three or four notary publics certifying the statements. Inside, the phones are ringing incessantly, voters wanting to tell

*As with "fish" or "sheep," the correct plural of "chad" is actually "chad."

their tales of woe. The Democratic operatives take a hard line: I'm sorry, miss, there's nothing I can do for you unless you come down to headquarters and fill out an affidavit.

Lina Petty, an operative in charge of the affidavit database, keeps her ears perked for attractive stories to tell. Republicans and young people are in demand. At that point the Democrats don't want a parade of old Yiddish Bubbies running around on TV complaining. Democrats want to show that this wasn't just old lefty Democrats who had a problem with the butterfly ballot.

Elsewhere, phone calls are going out. Democrats are recording — and in some cases hepping up — complaints. "I understand you were called yesterday by the Florida Democratic Party," reads one phone-bank script. "I am following up on that call on behalf of the Gore-Lieberman campaign. Would you be willing to answer a few questions?" There's a line for name, address, phone number, county, age, race, voting precinct, polling place, time arrived at polling place, weather conditions. Then: "Did you intend to vote for Gore/Lieberman but think you voted for someone else?

"If so, describe why you think you voted for someone other than Gore/Lieberman.

"Did you (check all that apply):
____ punch the wrong hole
____ punch more than one hole
____ other (describe)

"Was the ballot difficult to understand or confusing? Did you think to bring the confusion to the attention of a poll worker? If so, who and with what results? Was the ballot difficult to punch or mark?"

And on and on.

★　★　★

Back in Austin, Bush, Cheney, and crew are discussing whom else they should send to Florida. Ginsberg will be great for legal, but they need someone to run the whole shop, someone to be their version of Christopher — whom the morning shows are saying is on his way to Florida on Gore's behalf. Cheney suggests a man with whom he'd been sitting watching the election returns come in the night before, former secretary of state James Addison Baker III. He's a natural — skilled at PR, the law, and politics.

Get Baker, they agree.

Baker, seventy, has just landed in Houston, is making his way from Hobby Airport to his Rice University office, where the bidnessman is scheduled to meet with a Mexican official. He's tired, having been up late with Cheney. His cell phone rings. He expects that it's someone bringing news that the Florida mess has been sorted out; he has a European hunting trip scheduled with Bush Sr.

It's Evans.

We need you, he says. We need you to get down to Florida to supervise the recount.

Baker agrees. He's used to it. He's gotten calls like this before.

In fact, he's constantly brought in to save the day — most recently after the Republican convention in 1992, when he was dragged kicking and screaming from the State Department to run Bush Sr.'s faltering presidential campaign. The Princeton grad — from a long line of wealthy Houston lawyers, one of whom started monster law firm Baker Botts — first befriended Bush Sr. in the early '50s, when he and his new wife, Mary, would play George and Barbara in mixed-doubles tennis at the Houston Country Club. After Mary died of breast cancer in February 1970 — leaving Baker with four boys to raise on his own — Bush asked him to help run the Houston arm of his Senate campaign.

Bush Sr. lost, but Baker got the political bug pretty quick. True, his one try for office — a 1978 race for attorney general — ended up with him getting stomped like a rattlesnake in a cattle herd, but that was partly due to the fact that he didn't really like "the people." Didn't have much need for them. No, he knew better uses of his time than shaking hands with strangers at the mall; like his buddy Cheney, Baker soon became pretty damn good at selling himself as a ruthless CEO-type to the powers that be, though not one entirely without his own agenda.

In 1976, as an undersecretary of commerce, Baker was tapped by then-president Gerald Ford to help stave off a convention challenge from Ronald Reagan. At the convention that summer, his code name was "Miracle Man."

Baker was less successful leading the charge against Reagan four years later, when he managed Bush Sr.'s ill-fated 1980 presidential run, but somehow even this worked out well for Baker, and after Reagan earned the GOP nomination, he named Baker senior adviser to his campaign. Like Bush, Baker seemed to leave no fingerprints; though he was in charge of prepping Reagan for his debates against then-president Jimmy Carter, Baker was never even remotely blamed for "Briefingate," in which Carter's briefing papers ended up in the Reagan campaign's possession.

He's always been shrewd, always manipulated his prey — whether press or politicians — with a deft arrogance. Reagan brought him in as chief of staff, and Baker was quickly dubbed "the velvet hammer." By his cousin.

Still, he worked his ass off for Reagan, negotiating with Capitol Hill law-makers on much of Reagan's legislative agenda — shoring up business support for his tax-cut package, for instance, crafting the right message on Social Security reform. He elbowed out others grappling for power — Secretary of State Al Haig and Defense Secretary Caspar Weinberger. He and Bush always had a close, if oddly competitive, relationship — Baker would privately yuk about Bush's selection of then-senator Dan Quayle as his veep in '88. But they would be forever partners in politics, and Baker was appointed secretary of state when Bush became president in '88.

He was reluctant to leave the Department of State in '92, however, and only came on board to run the reelection campaign reluctantly, and late, and some thought he didn't give it his all. Barbara and W. blamed Baker for Bush Sr.'s election loss in 1992. Some speculated that Baker was sick of being the handler, the fixer, thought he could do a better job than Bush Sr. anyway. And with that, Baker took off, falling into a life of big bucks and oil-rights negotiating in former Soviet republics.

But being the grown-up was his fate. And here it was again, only now it was the son whose hide he was being called upon to pull from the fire.

Sigh.

★ ★ ★

Don Rubottom, the administrative overseer of the five committees in the GOP-controlled Florida state house, wonders if the legislature might have a role to play in any future developments.

I mean, who knows what will happen? Bush is ahead by less than 2,000 votes — and it's certainly possible that a few thousand illegally cast votes might show up. What if Florida's electoral votes are invalidated? He starts researching the matter, and learns that four times — in 1788, 1864, 1868, and 1872 — states failed to award electors to any candidate. Were that to happen here, Rubottom realizes, then Gore would become president! After all, with Florida's 25 out of the picture, Gore has more electoral votes than Bush!

Wednesday morning, Rubottom approaches his boss, house speaker Tom Feeney, Jeb's running mate from his unsuccessful 1994 gubernatorial run. Rubottom points to Article II, Section 1 of the Constitution. "Each state shall appoint, in such manner as the Legislature thereof may direct, a number of electors," it says. The Legislature chooses the method of picking electors.

Feeney is intrigued. It might be the legislature's responsibility to step in. Rubottom asks Feeney if he has permission to sell the idea to Jeb's people.

"Go for it," Feeney says.

Feeney signs off on it. So Rubottom looks for four-term congressman Charles Canady, forty-five, Jeb's new counsel. A conservative who didn't run for reelection because of his belief in term limits, Canady is set to become Frank Jimenez's boss in a few days. Rubottom finds him in the conference room in Jeb's office.

Canady "was appreciative and will consider it as a possible route later," Rubottom e-mails to Feeney later that afternoon. Rubottom also calls Ginsberg, but Ginsberg seems a bit cagey about getting involved with the legislature. At least right now.

★ ★ ★

"I'm feeling some pressure," says Theresa LePore to a small pack of reporters. Outside the Governmental Center in West Palm Beach are reporters, and protesters, and voters — many of whom are upset, crying, angry. It's Wednesday, 10:30 A.M.

LePore is asked if 3,407 votes for Buchanan in liberal Palm Beach — with its high numbers of Jews and blacks — seems reasonable.

"There are types of people who would tend to be Buchanan supporters," she says. "That there are small amounts of votes for Buchanan in Democratic areas indicates a lot of those people did vote properly," she says.

Rep. Mark Foley, R-Fla., shows up and backs LePore. "In fairness to the Democratic supervisor of elections, there's fifty folks in Century Village who like that brand of politics," Foley says about Buchanan.

Yeah, but 3,407? A full 20 percent of his state total right here in Palm Beach? Broward's about 50 percent bigger than Palm Beach, and Buchanan only got 789 votes there. Miami-Dade's *twice* as big as Palm Beach, and Buchanan only garnered 561 votes there. Moreover, it seems odd that 19,120 ballots indicate more than one choice for president — an overvote. This is more than 4 percent of the 462,000 ballots cast in Palm Beach County. Were these voters confused by the butterfly ballot? In the U.S. Senate race, which didn't have the same ballot configuration, there were only 3,783 overvotes.

LePore hears that Haitian-American groups are complaining that ballots weren't written in Creole in areas where a significant percentage of voters needed them. This pisses her off; in the summer she'd told all three major local Haitian-American groups that she would provide such ballots if they did the translating for her, but not one of them bothered to take her up on the offer. Not one even called her! She'd tried! She would go into black churches in Belle Glade where they'd tell her she was the only official to ever visit them in person! She's not insensitive to black Americans, for Godsakes!

She hears that a lawsuit is coming her way. She talks to Bob Montgomery, an attorney arranged through county attorney Leon St. John. He tells her to avoid the press.

One reporter manages to catch her eye, asks if she's having an OK day.

"Trying to," she says.

★　★　★

From this moment on, the Bushies have decided on one message: Bush won, and everything that happens from this point on is crazy, illegitimate Gore-propelled nonsense.

With Cheney by his side, Bush strides to the governor's mansion patio. Not far from a pond and a small fountain sits a lectern, which he approaches. Bush seems tired. "This morning brings news from Florida that the final vote count there shows that Secretary Cheney and I have carried the state of Florida," Bush reads from a prepared statement. "And if that result is confirmed in an automatic recount, as we expect it will be, then we have won the election."

Bush takes one question, and then he and Cheney walk off, ignoring others as reporters shout them out. He and Cheney make a beeline for the mansion, stopping briefly to pose for photographers; Cheney waves, Bush gives a thumbs-up.

Another photo op is arranged in the dining room. With place settings, grilled cheese sandwiches, fruit, and cold squash soup before them, Bush sits at the end of the table, Laura to his left, Lynne Cheney to his right, Dick Cheney across the table.

"I'm upbeat," Bush says when asked how he feels.

"My soup is getting cold," Bush says after a few questions, trying to get the reporters away.

The soup, of course, is supposed to be cold. It's cold squash soup.

★　★　★

Warren Christopher walks into the Gore-Lieberman suite at the Loews Hotel. Lieberman looks at him with a twinkle in his eye.

"Look what you've gotten me into now," Lieberman says.

They go around the room, talking about what to do next. "I think we should be aggressive in asserting our position," Christopher says. "But we've got to temper what we do with the realization that the nation is focused on us and is expecting us to act responsibly."

There are a few communications issues going on. Daley doesn't want Chris Lehane, Gore's sharp-tongued campaign spokesman, to be representing the cause. He doesn't like his style — doesn't really like *him* — preferring communications director Mark Fabiani. Gore, too, wants Fabiani. But even before the election, anticipating a whole different post-election legal dispute, Fabiani wrote Gore a memo arguing that any post-campaign battle should not have campaign faces. In that memo — written in case Gore won the electoral vote but lost the popular vote — Fabiani argued that neither he nor Lehane would be appropriate for such a situation.

A first draft of Fabiani's memo read:

POST-ELECTION STRATEGY

Operational Issues

Successful management of the post-election period will require immediate and substantial enhancements to the current Gore team. It is important that we all recognize that the Gore team, as currently constituted, will not be well equipped to successfully manage this post-election period. This is true because the post-election period will require a different mix of skills than currently exists on the Gore team and because current members of the Gore campaign team will either be completely unavailable or physically and mentally exhausted after November 7th.

Scenarios

Post-election planning should focus on the following scenarios:

A clear popular vote and Electoral College victory for Gore.

A clear popular vote and Electoral College loss for Gore.

A clear Electoral College victory and popular vote loss for Gore.

A disputed Electoral College victory and popular vote loss for Gore.

The Basic Proposition

If Gore wins, he will not benefit from any traditional honeymoon period.

If Gore wins only a narrow popular vote plurality and an Electoral College majority, Gore will immediately come under heavy scrutiny by both the media and the political opposition. How Gore deals with this scrutiny could determine the course of his presidency.

If Gore wins the Electoral College but loses the popular vote, the period after the election will determine whether his presidency is seen as legitimate.

If Gore's Electoral College victory is disputed, the post-election period will determine whether Gore's young presidency even survives until Inauguration Day.

There are other factors, too. Fabiani doesn't think the recount effort can afford to have him traveling and out of pocket for so long. Plus, frankly, he's longing for his family and La Jolla, where he thought he'd be heading by now. The last place he wants to go right now is Tallahassee. But he has an idea. Fabiani's deputy, Douglas Hattaway, is very low-key and calm. Given that this is going to be a battle against the public's patience, Hattaway — a Tallahassee boy — might be a good idea.

Soon, Fabiani calls Hattaway into his office.

"Want to go to Florida?" Fabiani asks, almost like an afterthought.

There's a pause.

"Sure," Hattaway says.

"OK," Fabiani says, relieved. "You're going to go down with Christopher and Daley. It's leaving at four."

That's in an hour.

The small team actually leaves Tennessee closer to 5 P.M. central, shuttled on a Lear Jet and armed with a few documents. There's one about the disproportionate number of votes Buchanan got in Palm Beach County, a three- to four-page memo on butterfly ballots, a one-pager on Florida recount law, and something about the Florida Secretary of State, Katherine Harris — who was apparently one of Bush's campaign co-chairs and now holds a tremendous amount of power.

Daley and Christopher sit in the back, talking quietly, reviewing documents. Up front sit Hattaway, Daley aide Graham Streett, and Hattaway's assistant, Terrell McSweeney.

"Daley isn't into all these 'irregularity' things," Streett says, referring to the arguments many in the Gore camp want to make about the reports — all merely anecdotal, at this point — they've heard about, say, blacks being stopped at polls, harassed, and intimidated by cops. "He thinks we should be cautious talking about the irregularities."

Streett's right. Daley's been around politics since birth, so he knows a few hard and fast facts about this kind of thing, and it's made him pessimistic about it all. First off, Daley thinks, it's very, very rare that an election is turned over unless it's because of some bizarre accident or mistake, some number that was recorded incorrectly, some ballots that an angry elections judge took home. That kind of thing is usually sorted out within twenty-four hours. But barring some legitimate explanation like that, the longer it goes — whether it's a race for state rep or mosquito abatement district, it is very tough to turn an election over. The system is set up that way. Then there's the matter of all these rumors. Not that Daley is flip about it, but every election has allegations of roadblocks and people being arrested and yada yada yada. This stuff won't play in Peoria.

That isn't surprising, of course, Hattaway thinks. Daley frequently weighs the PR implications of every decision. Some of the Gore folks back in Nashville seemed a bit breathless in their allegations about various conspiracies, particularly ones that the Gore team doesn't plan on addressing.

Christopher wants to know about the butterfly ballot.

"What do we know about this?" he asks. "It's very interesting."

Christopher notices figures transposed on the butterfly ballot chart and points it out to Hattaway, who is immediately impressed with the sharpness and studiousness of the old bird.

The plane starts to bounce around in turbulence, and soon thunder and lightning surround the plane. Streett, Hattaway, and McSweeney roll their eyes at one another, concerned but almost slightly amused at the chaos into which they've been thrust.

★ ★ ★

At the Loews Hotel Wednesday night, Whouley's eating dinner with John Giesser, his deputy at the DNC, when Al Gore's son-in-law, Drew Schiff, walks in and asks him to come upstairs, to be with the old man, the man who calls Whouley his "brain."

Whouley gets up and follows Schiff to the elevator.

Whouley's old school, the kind of guy who speaks about his underlings with both an earthiness and a passion for their skill. He would describe an employee of his political-consulting firm, Dewey Square, as "a disheveled, schlumpy, fucking guy, but a great election law lawyer." Whouley's not a big man, but he talks tough, and he means it.

The Dorchester boy started in politics while still at Boston College, running a ward in a race against the incumbent mayor Kevin White. Whouley did a good job: his guy lost by only 50 votes in his ward, enough to recommend Whouley to a young lieutenant governor candidate named John Kerry in 1982.

He did Kerry's Senate race in 1984, slowly working his way up in Massachusetts politics: a mayor's race (W), a congressional seat (L), a state auditor's race (W). The latter put him in charge of a great patronage job, director of human resource management. In 1987, he was twenty-nine, earning $54,000 a year, with his own parking space on Beacon Hill and a bunch of his old pals from the neighborhood under him.

A year later, the governor, Mike Dukakis, was the Democratic nominee for president, and Whouley slated Illinois for him, worked for him in Iowa in the last month before the caucus. He met a couple guys named Clinton and Gore when he ran Louisiana for the Duke a bit later, and the two Southern Democrats came in to work on the Massachusetts governor's hapless campaign.

Clinton didn't remember him when Whouley introduced the Arkansas governor at the Florida straw poll in October 1991, but Whouley made Clinton the front-runner with the skills he'd picked up along the way.

After Clinton's poll numbers went down the shitter in the wake of the Arkansan's draft-avoidance-letter revelation and the bottle-blond cabaret-singer scandal, Whouley came up with the idea to drop off a seven-minute videotape of Clinton talking to voters at the homes of 20,000 likely voters. Clinton came in second — at that point exceeding expectations — and Whouley moved to Little Rock to serve as Clinton's national field director.

In 1996, he managed Gore's slice of the reelection campaign. This time, Gore asked Whouley to serve as campaign manager soon after, but neither Whouley nor his wife was in any mood for another move, this one to Nashville, so he declined. Three times. Gore really wanted him there. Whouley remained in D.C., serving as one of Gore's senior strategists. He played a leading role in picking the states Gore needed to win, working with strategist Tad Devine on how much money would be channeled to Democratic efforts in each one, planning the Democrats' "Get Out the Vote" activities.

In the end, Whouley's end of the campaign was the one thing that worked well. So it was no wonder that Gore called on him today.

"How do you think it's going down there?" Gore asks.

"I think they're doing a great job," he replies, praising Baldick and Alper in particular.

"When are you heading down?" Gore asks, smiling.

"I think I should be in Nashville tomorrah, and I'll be down theah on Friday," Whouley says, recognizing a nudge for what it was.

"Excellent," Gore says.

★ ★ ★

To get to the Gore campaign's last best place of hope, you head down Apalachee Parkway (U.S. 27 South), turn left on Crosscreek Road near the Sonny's Barbecue, and there's a mall there, a nondescript strip mall that houses a couple veterinarians and a CPA.

Gore attorneys Klain, Sandler, and Young are here.

The place is a dump. Dingy, with wires all over. Klain says he's going to pick up Daley and Christopher.

They meet Mark Herron. Herron's a local lawyer, an elections and campaign law expert who was working to get former governor Lawton Chiles off the hook for some free hunting trips he'd taken, when Chiles died. An FSU, FSU Law guy, Herron starts briefing them on Florida law and what they can do now.

Just last session, the legislature rewrote a lot of the statutes about challenging an election. The real meat of the coconut happened in the revisions to the protest/contest/recount statutes. A candidate can request a hand recount of the ballots, but if Gore wants to do it, a decision has to be made within twenty-four hours, Herron says. The statute gives seventy-two hours, but Friday is a holiday, and you can't count on government offices being open.

We need big swings, Young thinks. We're 1,700 votes down. We should go after those four counties where we know there were problems yesterday — Broward, Miami-Dade, Palm Beach, Volusia. We probably won statewide; by hitting those counties we can maybe pick up the difference.

When Klain returns, around 8:30, Sandler's embarrassed. Here's the dapper Christopher, former diplomat, in his famous tailored, elegant suit, and here's Sandler, sitting in this dump, wearing stained khakis, not having showered in forty hours. "This is not how you want to meet Warren Christopher with the presidency at stake," Sandler thinks.

As the counties' machine recounts continue, Bush's lead has shrunk from 1,784 to less than 400 votes by sunset, according to press accounts.

★ ★ ★

On *Larry King Live* that night, LePore sees Democrat Wexler and Republican Foley square off against one another. Ironically, even though a former Foley staffer ran against her in 1996, Foley's the one defending her today.

"If there was confusion, . . . the Democrats should have objected before this sample ballot was printed and published and distributed," Foley says.

"Good point," King says. "Congressman Wexler, you signed off on it."

"Well, that's not exactly so, Larry," Wexler says. "Many people did complain to the supervisor of elections when they saw the sample ballot."

That's not true! LePore thinks. In October, LePore mailed out 655,000 sample ballots. Even before the sample ballots had gone out, she'd sent them to all 150-some candidates, faxed and mailed them to Friedkin and Friedkin's counterpart at the Republican Executive Committee of Palm Beach County. The *Palm Beach Post* and the *Sun-Sentinel* printed copies in their papers. And not one complaint. Not one! Not a peep! What the hell was Wexler talking about?!

". . . the Palm Beach County supervisor herself, Larry, yesterday, sent out an urgent message to poll workers late in the afternoon, which I've never seen done, which said, 'Advise the people how to vote, because there's mass confusion,'" Wexler goes on.

"Ah, OK," says King.

"Ah, OK"?! LePore thinks. *Wexler* was the one to request that "urgent message"! And now he's citing it as evidence that there was something wrong with the ballot?! Acting like he had nothing to do with it, this whole "which I've never seen done" thing?! What a liar!

Maybe I was naive to call him a friend, she thinks.

☆　☆　☆

Whouley's deputy on the Gore campaign, Donnie Fowler, has been amassing information all day. He's jazzed as he steers his rental car to a Palm Beach Denny's shortly after midnight as Wednesday becomes Thursday. Over a Grand Slam breakfast at 12:20 A.M., Fowler writes a memo to Young, Sandler, Whouley, senior political adviser Monica Dixon, and Klain, which he faxes to them in his chicken scratch.

Summary —

- 19,000 ballots rejected by county because voters "double-voted" due to confusing and illegal ballot (voters punched Buchanan & Gore)
- rejected ballots equal 4% of total votes cast for president, but only 0.8% of ballots rejected in U.S. Senate race
- possible Voting Rights Act violation: although an average of *4% of ballots were rejected* for double-voting (or "overvoting") county-wide, up to *15–16% of ballots rejected in African-American precincts;* Cong. Robert Wexler highlights in press conference with 12 TV cameras
- Gore picks up net 650 votes in Palm Beach recount; certification expected Thursday by 5:00 P.M.

- Judge Charles Burton in recount press conference *admits that punch card system is faulty* because little dots punched out can interfere with actual counting by machine
- Judge Burton also admits precinct 29-E originally registered 0 votes because of human error; actual count was 368 Gore to 23 Bush
- Reports of voters in line at poll closing (7:00 P.M.) turned away by election judges
- Local activist & attorney both criticize antiquated ballot-counting machinery
- Evidence that Republican county commissioner coerced Democratic election commissioner into holding recount test less than 24 hours after polls closed
- 500 absentee ballots left at post office — un-picked up and undelivered on election day
- 3,000 complaints on file at county headquarters
- unable to get through to county election commission on election day via phone

In the wee hours, Fowler calls his ex-girlfriend on his cell phone, leaves a message on her voice mail: "We got something here," he says confidently. "This is where it's going to happen, Palm Beach. This is where I think we're gonna win the White House."

4

"Palm Beach County is a Pat Buchanan stronghold."

One thing becomes crystal clear very early on in the whole damn mess: Florida election law — especially as it pertains to recounts — is chaos.

Statutes collide. Provisions are vague. Unlike in other states, those supervising the process are often the harshest of partisans. And, most insanely, the standard by which ballots are assessed is vague, requiring that one assess the "intent of the voter," a gauge that can be interpreted differently in different counties. Especially if the counties use punch-card ballots.

When the Votomatic punch-card ballot machine was invented in 1962, elections officials were delighted. This was The Future! This was based on the computers of IBM! But little by little, glitches in the system were revealed, especially since the machines were created for speed, not accuracy. Over the years, wealthier counties began purchasing higher-technology voting machines. And over the years, at times of close elections, the weaknesses of the Votomatic were apparent. In a 1977 Miami Beach city council race, Robert "Big Daddy" Napp lost by 244 votes. But there were 710 overvotes unread by the machine, Napp said, though no court would listen to him. After losing a 1991 Oakland Park city council race by 3 votes, Al Hogan, too, lost in court when he tried to get a hand recount of the faulty punch-card ballots. In times of close elections, punch-card ballots provided little assurance that the Election Night tally was correct.

The Recount Primer had suggestions for what to do in times like this:

Punch Cards

Some argue that punch card computerized voting is inherently unreliable (see Duggers, "The Analysis of Democracy," *The New Yorker*, November 7, 1988). The Duggers thesis may be a bit overstated; however, it is true that recount totals in punch card jurisdictions will inherently vary from election night totals: at least one relevant chad (the little bits of card that are punched out when the voter punches the stylus through the card to record the vote) will randomly be removed as a result of the handling of the cards. Punch cards also raise the issue of what determines a valid vote: a machine or the judgment of an election official. Some of the most common problems experienced in punch card voting include:

- Putting the card in the frame backward so everything is out of alignment.
- Failing to fully punch out the perforated circle of paper (the chad), thus permitting the chad to slip back into place; when the computer reads the card, it detects no hole and records no vote).
- Mistakenly voting for two candidates for the same office.

The posture a campaign takes with regard to punch card problems will depend on whether the candidate is ahead or behind. If behind, a candidate should consider a request for a partial or complete hand count of punch cards to allow election officials to determine voter intent on questionable ballots. Punch card and paper ballot voting provide the greatest chance of change in voter totals.

— The Recount Primer, p. 33

At a November 9 meeting, Christopher and Daley — referred to as "The Flag" by their underlings since as former cabinet secretaries they had flags in their offices — discuss their options with Democratic D.C. lawyers Klain, Young, Sandler, Chris Sautter, and two Miami attorneys, Ben Kuehne and Kendall Coffey.

Coffey is considered something of a ringer. He's a former U.S. attorney, and someone who's known to be able to negotiate the tricky politics of Miami, which at least one Gore lawyer calls a "snake pit." Coffey — and his best friend, Kuehne — know election law in Florida. And looking at Tuesday night's election, they already see things they don't like, things they think are illegal: votes, ballots, and procedures that Coffey intends to challenge. And Coffey's no stranger to desperate situations and lost causes in Florida, having represented Elián González's Miami relatives.

More important, Coffey and Kuehne worked on the 1997 Miami mayoral election scandal, representing Joe Carollo. They were the guys who sued on Carollo's behalf, and it all ended up with Carollo in City Hall.

Of course, Coffey also brings to the recount table his share of controversy. As an attorney for Elián's Little Havana relatives, he was a major critic of President Clinton and Attorney General Janet Reno. And as a former U.S. attorney for South Florida, Coffey received high marks for his performance as a successful, high-profile prosecutor of major drug lords — until he had to resign after biting a stripper.

Ahem.

Let me back up.

★   ★   ★

A longtime Miami attorney involved with the Democratic Party, Coffey lost an election for the state Senate in 1992, scoring only 43 percent of the vote against Republican Al Gutman.

To Coffey's good fortune, however, Clinton was elected the same day. And after Clinton's problems with attorney general nominees were settled, Senator Graham recommended to Reno that Coffey become South Florida's U.S. attorney, prosecuting federal civil and criminal cases from Fort Pierce to Key West, replacing Republican appointee Roberto Martinez. Coffey was confirmed by the U.S. Senate in November 1993.

In February 1996, Coffey was prosecuting Augusto "Willie" Falcon and Salvatore "Sal" Magluta — known as "Los Muchachos" — who were charged with smuggling $2.1 billion worth of cocaine into the United States. Surprisingly, Los Muchachos were acquitted. It would later come out that a juror, Miguel Moya, received a bribe of $500,000 to throw the case. Eventually, Moya would be sentenced to seventeen and a half years in jail as a result.

But Coffey obviously didn't know about the Moya bribe at the time. Despondent on the night of February 22, at around midnight Coffey headed to Lipstik, a Miami strip joint. At some point he got very drunk, and he struck up a conversation with "Tiffany," a thin, blond former bank teller, then twenty-eight, whose real name is Tamara Gutierrez.

Coffey bought $200 in "Lipstik money," used to pay the dancers for private sessions and lap dances in the fabled "champagne room." With that destination on his itinerary, Coffey also purchased a $900 magnum of Dom Perignon.

In the champagne room, Coffey and Tiffany sat on one of the room's two expansive couches. He told her he'd lost a big case. He drank his Dom Perignon. He gave her little affectionate love bites. They had a moment.

Things got a little hairy, however, when Coffey tried to kiss Tiffany on the lips. She didn't want him to, and when she tried to wriggle away, he bit her left arm, only not so affectionately this time. He broke the skin and drew blood.

Tiffany screamed.

A bouncer and the night manager loaded Coffey headfirst into a cab.

Rumors immediately began to race through the area like a hurricane. In mid-March, Coffey told the *Sun-Sentinel* that the rumors were untrue. Had he been at Lipstik that night? asked a reporter. "No," Coffey said. He added that he'd "never" been to the club. "It absolutely never happened," Wilfredo Fernandez, a spokesman for the U.S. attorney's office, told the *Miami Herald*. On March 27, the incident was reported to the inspector general's office. On March 28, investigators were sent to South Florida to check out the charges.

It turned out that Coffey, by the way, had purchased his Dom Perignon, and his $200 in Lipstik money, with his American Express card.

In May, the *Miami Herald* reported that Coffey was under internal investigation for the incident. This was just two days before GOP presidential candidate Bob Dole — who had been making a campaign issue out of Clinton's federal appointments — was to arrive in Florida. Coffey was summoned to D.C. to talk to Reno.

A day later, Coffey resigned.

The husband of the bitten one said that he was "shocked" that Coffey quit. "I want to see him reinstated," he said to the *Sun-Sentinel*. "He bit her, but not like a crazy man."

F. Scott Fitzgerald was dead wrong: There are plenty of second acts — third acts, fourth acts — in American public life.

Here's Coffey's next act.

★　★　★

Daley and Christopher ask the accumulated Democratic lawyers for a brief discussion of Florida election law. They get one.

Florida has sixty-seven counties, but four ways of voting. Forty counties have high-tech "optical-scanning" cards, where you fill in circles with a no. 2 pencil, as you do the SATs. Martin County uses old-school mechanical-lever machines, Union County uses paper ballots, and twenty-five counties use punch cards.

There are some problems. Machines don't always read the card. You have to make sure that the bits of chad are completely punched out of the ballot, which the seldom-read instructions clearly state, or the machine won't be able to read any selection, and your ballot will be an undervote. And, of course, you can vote for only one candidate, lest your ballot be an overvote.

Given the way these things work, you could blame many of the problems on voter error. You could additionally blame it on the fact that punch-card ballots just suck. In 1988, the National Bureau of Standards studied the issue and recommended that punch-card ballots be scrubbed themselves because of "inaccuracy or fraud in computerized vote-tallying." (The report cited a 1984 election in Palm Beach County, where a candidate for property appraiser sued the county for a number of ballot problems, including "hanging chad." He had lost by 242 votes. He lost his court case, too.) There's pretty clear evidence that counties that use punch-card ballots disenfranchise their voters in the process. Brevard County, for instance, used punch cards in its 1996 presidential race tally, and 26 out of every 1,000 ballots were undervotes, not registering a vote for president. Brevard switched to "Opti-scan" ballots, and in the 2000 race that proportion fell to less than 2 in 1,000. An almost identical change happened in Volusia County.

Whoever you blame, in this year's presidential race, Palm Beach County is discarding 29,502 of its 461,988 ballots cast, because of both undervotes and overvotes. This is a high rate of ballot rejection, 6.39 percent, but by no means the highest in Florida. In Duval County, 9.23 percent of its ballots have been discarded — a full 26,909. Miami-Dade's discard rate was only 4.37, but since it's the most populous county in the state with 653,963 voters, that still means 28,601 ballots in the trash.

In 1992, 2.3 percent of Florida ballots weren't counted for president; in 1996 that was 2.5 percent. This year, the percentage is 2.85 percent. That's not exactly an improvement. A full 173,992 ballots will be thrown away statewide this year, from Key West to Pensacola. About 105,000 are overvotes, about 60,500 are undervotes. Many undervotes are voters rejecting all of the presidential candidates — but many aren't. In Gadsden County, twelve out of every hundred voters didn't vote right. Were they confused because the presidential ballot was two pages long? Because at the top of the second page it said "Constitution Party" and they thought that was a separate office?

There are two phases to the process, the lawyers explain. In the "protest" phase, parties can request a hand recount of ballots, which would unquestionably find votes in the 175,000 unread ballots. The process begins by looking at a 1 percent sample of the ballots in a county, and if a hand count of that 1 percent shows that there were enough votes missed that it could change the outcome of the election, a countywide hand recount is ordered.

Should they ask for a statewide hand count of these ballots? The Flag asks. Sautter says yes. Young and Sandler nod in agreement. After all:

> If a candidate is ahead, the scope of the recount should be as narrow as possible, and the rules and procedures for the recount should be the same as those used election night. . . . If a candidate is behind, the scope should be as broad as possible, and the rules for the recount should be different from those used election night. A recount should be an audit of the election to insure the accuracy and honesty of the results.
>
> — *The Recount Primer,* p. 5

But there's concern about the probability that the 1 percent statutory test wouldn't be met in a majority of the sixty-seven counties. Most of these counties don't use punch-card ballots, don't have such high numbers of undervotes and overvotes as are in the southeastern counties Broward, Miami-Dade, and Palm Beach. And anyway, the Democrats don't have the resources to send lawyers and observers to every county.

Then The Flag raises the political considerations. Though the Florida popular vote is split down the middle, most Florida counties are Republican (Gore won sixteen counties; Bush fifty-one), and the Democratic lawyers have their doubts about the cooperativeness of the elections supervisors in these counties. And, of course, they assume that undervotes in GOP counties will largely be for Bush. Moreover, there is no statutory provision for a statewide recount. It would have to be county by county, it would have to be either signed off by Jeb Bush, so they don't have to fight sixty-seven separate battles, or ordered by a higher court.

OK, they agree, we'll ask for a hand recount in some counties. Fine. Now The Flag wants to know: Who evaluates the ballots? What's the likelihood that they'd be able to get the recounts? What would be the fallout of being denied recounts?

The Florida lawyers answer, with Sandler and Young also jumping in.

The ballots will be looked at by county workers supervised by county canvassing boards made up of a judge, a local election official, and the elections supervisor. It's likely that they will be able to get recounts. But if they were to try to get a recount in a county where they have no case, that could undercut the legitimacy of their other claims. They have to be careful.

What about contesting the election? What about the butterfly ballot? Christopher wants to hear more about this.

"Ultimately, the test is 'Was the will of the electorate suppressed?'" Coffey says. "But Palm Beach County is the battleground. There are big numbers of overvotes, confusion over Buchanan."

"If we were to file, where would we do so?" asks Christopher.

"Probably Tallahassee," Coffey says.

"What about other non–Palm Beach claims?" Klain asks.

"We don't know," Coffey says. "We're still looking for hard facts."

"What about that state seal issue?" Klain asks, referring to Jeb Bush's absentee-ballot mailing to Republicans, which used, perhaps improperly, the state seal.

"That's not enough on its own," Coffey says. Underlying much of this discussion is the question of whether or not elections officials were purposely helping the Republican Party, which would open up a claim of fraud. There are stories of people being turned away at polling places, being denied replacement ballots, being told how to vote. These are just complaints and anecdotes at this point, however.

Christopher wonders if there's a federal question here, if federal courts have jurisdiction.

"We haven't ruled that out," Coffey says. "But the eleventh circuit is tough on finding jurisdiction in election irregularity cases."

"What's the Florida standard for invalidating election results?" Christopher asks.

Coffey says that the Florida Supreme Court will set aside an election "if there's a reasonable doubt that the election did not determine the true will of the people."

"Was the form of the ballot illegal?" Christopher asks.

"Probably," replies Coffey. "But it's a close call."

They talk about staffing, about getting people on board, getting them trained, what sort of resources they'll need. The Florida lawyers say that they have a whole network of attorneys and pols ready. Kuehne and Coffey say that they know Dave Leahy, the supervisor of elections in Miami-Dade. They know that Broward's supervisor, Jane Carroll, is retiring but aren't sure what that might mean. Everyone agrees that they need to get much more information about the members of the canvassing boards.

Klain brings up the hand count. Sautter maintains that the Gore campaign push for all counties to be counted. But he's shot down.

Klain sees a need to limit the recount to the fewest possible counties, so they aren't opening up random cans of worms. It'll be just Palm Beach and Volusia, where they have the clearest right to demand recounts in those counties. Daley agrees; to do any more would look like they're just shotgunning, like they're trying to slow things down and they really don't care about the system. We have to be a little more judicious.

"We must stake our requests on principled reasons for wanting a hand count," Christopher says.

Coffey agrees. "We have good cause in Palm Beach and Volusia." Not so in the whole state, he argues. They go with those two.*

★   ★   ★

After the meeting, however, Nick Baldick comes over to the Governor's Inn and grabs Klain.

"We have to count Dade and Broward," Baldick says.

Klain says tough luck. "Look, these guys have decided we're not going to expand this thing, we're going to pinpoint targeted —"

"We *have* to *count* Dade and Broward," Baldick repeats.

There are 10,750 undervotes in Miami-Dade — a county that went for Gore 328,808 to Bush's 289,533 — and more than 6,000 in Broward, which went for Gore 387,703 to Bush's 177,902. These are counties that went for Gore — overwhelmingly, in Broward's case. And the Gore political team suspects that undervotes come from Democrats. There are votes to be gleaned there. Uncounted Gore votes.

Klain walks to Daley's room, where Christopher is hanging out.

Look, the political people have come back and given us these reasons to push for hand recounts in Broward and Dade, Klain explains.

After some discussion, The Flag agrees.

Soon enough, Democratic lawyers are fanned out to Fort Lauderdale, Miami, West Palm Beach, and DeLand, with one marching order: Get the votes hand-recounted, ASAP.

---

*In an interview on January 16, 2001, Ron Klain will say, "What's so interesting and ironic about this, as this process unfolded, the decision by us that's been the most second-guessed was, 'Why not the whole state?' At the time, the pressure we felt was the exact opposite pressure.... It's painfully ironic; the pressure we felt was to count as little as possible, to keep the thing limited and confined."

Daley, meanwhile, thinks about the Miami lawyers, bright guys, smart guys. But this whole revote in Palm Beach? It's madness! "Well, they did that in Miami!" the lawyers would say. Gimme a break! Daley thinks. "Mayor of Miami?!" That's like a separate *island* out there right now. And it's not exactly viewed as the prototype of good government and good politics. Then this idea that some of Buchanan's votes could be allocated to Gore?! C'mon! It just doesn't happen!

★　★　★

Throughout the campaign, Daley tried to be nonchalant about the fact that he saw the media as being soft on Bush and way too hard on Gore. Bush would go before the world and claim to have worked with Democrats on a patients' bill of rights, when the truth was he'd vetoed such a bill in '95 and then, presented with a veto-proof majority in '97, let it pass without his signature. Almost no one wrote about it. Meanwhile, Gore couldn't fib a little about how much his dog's arthritis medication cost without it turning into Watergate. It would piss Daley off, but he'd been raised on politics, and he knew that sometimes one guy got the breaks. In '92, that guy was Clinton. In 2000, he thought, that guy was Bush.

And now, Daley thinks, Bush has been given the greatest gift of all: the networks had declared him the winner when, in fact, the actual winner of Florida had yet to be established by elections officials. If Bush's first cousin, fucking John Ellis,* hadn't declared him the winner on Fox, who knows what would have happened? The whole dynamic would have been different. The headline woulda been "Too Close to Call." Then everyone, led by the media, would be driven by the quest to find out what *really* happened, what *really* is going on. As opposed to Us trying to take it from Them, Daley thinks.

That puts Daley in a tough spot. He's always tried to be temperate in his comments. But now there's this impression out there that Gore is trying to *take* from Bush. Plus, there are rumors that Colin Powell will be named secretary of state tomorrow.

"We have to stop this inevitability shit, or else we're gonna get rolled," he thinks. "We have to lay a marker down, we gotta say, 'Lookit, this is serious, we ain't going away, don't try to just roll over us.'"

---

*When I ask Daley what would have been the reaction had a first cousin of Gore been the one to call the election for Gore for one of the networks, he laughs. "They would *indict* him!" He guffaws. "[Congressman Dan] Burton [R-Ind.] would haul him before his subcommittee!"

★ ★ ★

In these first few days in Tallahassee, we journalists just sit in the hearing room in the state senate and wait for the news to come to us.

Early afternoon on Thursday, November 9, Daley walks in, solid, stolid, and bald — but thinner than you'd expect. He looks like he's ready to tackle anyone at a moment's notice. Then there's the gaunt Christopher, who looks like he's melting into his expensive gray pinstripe suit. When he speaks, he's barely audible.

"Secretary Christopher and I have been in Florida now for over twenty hours," Daley says. "We're here to report that what we have learned has left us deeply troubled."

Daley specifically cites the reports of the voters in Palm Beach County. "More than twenty thousand voters in Palm Beach County who thought they were voting for Al Gore had their votes counted for Pat Buchanan or not counted at all," Daley says. "These logical conclusions are reinforced by the phone calls, faxes, and other reports from over one thousand residents of Palm Beach County that have poured into us, saying that they believe they were victims of this ballot confusion," he adds. He neglects to mention that the Democrats have used staffers and paid telemarketers to call Democratic voters to alert these residents to the problem. Out of thin air, Daley plucks a number of Buchanan votes that he would allocate to Gore. "Based on the totals from other counties, there seems every reason to believe that well over two thousand of these votes were votes for Vice President Al Gore, more than enough to make him the winner here in Florida," Daley says.

"Those numbers cry out for justice," adds Coffey.

"Here in Florida it also seems very likely that more voters went to the polls believing that they were voting for Al Gore than for George Bush," Daley says. "If the will of the people is to prevail, Al Gore should be awarded the victory of Florida and be our next president."

Of course, electoral victories are not built upon "the will of the people." They are built upon 270 electoral votes garnered from enough states where a plurality of voters cast their ballot — competently — for a particular candidate. In 1996, more than fourteen thousand Palm Beach County residents also had their ballots thrown out. The Flag doesn't point it out, but Palm Beach County has had problems before the butterfly ballot.

Finally he announces what Team Gore is up to. "Here's what we intend to do about this," he says. "Today, the appropriate Florida Democratic officials will be requesting a hand count of ballots in Palm Beach County as well as three other counties: Volusia, Dade, and Broward. In addition, today I'm announcing that we will be working with voters from Florida in support of legal actions to demand some redress for the disenfranchisement of more than twenty thousand voters in Palm Beach County.

"In addition, we are still collecting accounts of other irregularities, voter intimidation and other oddities in other parts of the state. And if substantiated and appropriate, they, too, will become part of legal actions."

Whoa! Litigation-a-go-go!

"That ballot is completely illegal," Coffey says of the poor little butterfly. "It confused voters. It led an unprecedented number of voters — many of whom are elderly, who waited for hours — to have their votes disqualified, because it was very hard looking at it to figure out exactly what to do.

"The law requires a simple linear listing so that the boxes are punched in the same order and you don't have this massive confusion," Coffey says. "Florida election law is very clear."

Actually it's not so clear at all, but the Gorebies point to a section of Florida law that discusses placing "a cross (X) mark in the blank space at the right of the name of the candidate for whom you desire to vote." Since half the candidates on the butterfly ballot require punching a hole to the candidate's left, this would be a violation.

But whether they're lying or incompetent or just innocently mistaken, it turns out that the Gorebies are grabbing an irrelevant section of law. The relevant section, which applies to counties that use voting machines, says that, "Voting squares may be placed in front of or in back of the names of candidates." Nevertheless, Daley alludes to other possible legal challenges.

Asked about Baker, Christopher feebly says, "We'll see if there's some way we can cooperate with them. I must say, the cooperation cannot extend to the point of our giving up justified legal challenges that are absolutely necessary to ensure the fairness of the process."

Daley adds that the Bush campaign has "blithely dismissed the disenfranchisement of thousands of Floridians as being the usual Florida mistakes made in elections."

True enough. The Bushies want this done. In Thursday newspapers, the Bush campaign has leaked the names of cabinet appointments — most notably Powell.

They want this thing to be over.

Now.

"They're trying to presumptively crown themselves the victors. To try to put in place a transition runs the risk of dividing the American people and creating a sense of confusion," Daley says. "Let the legal system run its course. Let the true and accurate will of the people prevail.

"And if, at the end of the process, George Bush is the victor, we will honor and obviously respect the results."

With that, Daley, Christopher, and Coffey walk out of the room. After they become aware of Coffey's involvement on the Gore team, the Miami relatives of Elián González cancel a celebration that night in honor of their attorneys.

★   ★   ★

Anita Davis, Tallahassee NAACP president, has been called to Gadsden County. More than 12 percent of the 16,812 ballots cast on Election Day weren't read by the machine, so, in addition to conducting their machine recount, members of the canvassing board there are going to review the 2,000-plus scrapped Opti-scan ballots. Republicans are there objecting to the whole process, of course.

As the board reviews the ballots, Davis deflates. Some of these voters have filled in every circle *except* for Gore's. Some had filled in Gore's circle and put an X through Nader's. Some are discernible, however, and the board ends up finding 187 votes — 170 for Gore and 17 for Bush.

Ken Sukhia, of the Tallahassee Republican law firm of Fowler, White, Gillen, Boggs, Villareal, and Banker, is objecting. This is not what the secretary of state ordered the canvassing board to do, he says. County GOP chair Russell Doster understands Sukhia's suspicion — this is the most Democratic county in the state, so he could see how at first blush this looks bad — but he knows the members of the canvassing board, he respects them, and he has faith in their ethics. Moreover, Doster has seen these newly approved 187 votes, and he agrees with their assessments. He assures Sukhia that everything's on the up-and-up.

But Davis has a larger concern. "We've fallen short," she thinks. "We're registering people to vote but failing to educate them on the use of the ballot. And we've been doing it this way for twenty years!"

★   ★   ★

Soon Baker walks in. And with the appearance of this former world leader, who carries with him a far greater sense of command than Daley and Christopher combined, the room falls silent. "I'll take a few questions, but I can't be here too long," he says.

He's asked about the butterfly ballot. "The ballot in Palm Beach County that has been alleged to be confusing is a ballot that has been used before in Florida elections; it is a ballot that was approved by an elected Democratic official; it is a ballot that was published in newspapers in that county and provided to the candidates, to the respective political parties, in advance of the election in order that complaints, if any, could be registered. And, hey, guess what? There were no complaints until after the election." He accepts a few more questions, and then he takes off.

It's a difficult task to figure out what really is going on.

The idea of a "revote" seems ridiculous on its face — the Constitution requires that the presidential election be held on the first Tuesday following the first Monday in November; it makes no allowances for re-doing it for any reason. Even if all 425,000 Palm Beach voters joined hands and yelled "do-over" at the top of their lungs.

And Daley, Christopher, and Coffey seem more than a little desperate in their "support" for voter lawsuits, in their insistence that the butterfly ballot was "illegal." Confusing, sure. But illegal?

The Bushies, however, have decided that they're not even going to acknowledge that anyone was confused. This despite the fact that that morning, Buchanan — in a rare moment of statesmanship — tells Charlie Gibson of ABC's *Good Morning America* that, "Yes, I did get thirty-four hundred votes. But I also agree that many of those very probably and almost certainly were intended for Al Gore.

"The ballot is confusing to those who move through it very rapidly," Buchanan agrees. "There's Bush and Gore as the first and second names on the left, but if you vote for the second dot, you vote for me, and my name's on the right. I can understand how people have made that mistake, and people coming out were very anguished in chagrin, and I don't think they're acting. I think they probably voted for me mistakenly."

"So what to do, Pat?" Gibson asks. "What's the remedy, do you think, in fairness for this?"

"There is none, Charlie," Buchanan says, before calling for Gore to concede. "That ballot was agreed upon. That ballot's been used before. And they used it again. There is no remedy for that. It happened. It was done."

That afternoon, Bush spokesman Ari Fleischer — who is known by reporters to have an on-again, off-again relationship with the truth — tries to explain why Buchanan did so well in the heavily Jewish community of Palm Beach.

"New information has come to our attention that puts in perspective the results of the vote in Palm Beach County," Fleischer says. "Palm Beach County is a Pat Buchanan stronghold, and that's why Pat Buchanan received 3,407 votes there."

I call up Buchanan's Florida coordinator, Jim McConnell, and read him Fleischer's comment.

"That's nonsense," McConnell says.

McConnell says that he and Jim Cunningham, chairman of the executive committee of Palm Beach County's Reform Party, estimate the number of Buchanan activists in the county to be between three hundred and five hundred — nowhere near the 3,407 who voted for him. "Do I believe that these people inadvertently cast their votes for Pat Buchanan? Yes, I do," says McConnell. "We have to believe that based on the vote totals elsewhere." Says Cunningham of Buchanan's actual number of supporters in Palm Beach County: "It's in the hundreds; it's not a significant amount."

Asked if the county is "a Buchanan stronghold," as the Bush campaign has asserted, Cunningham said: "I don't think so. Not from where I'm sitting and what I'm looking at. They can say that because they would like to believe that. Because the votes we received they would like to believe were not mistaken votes." Heck, the Buchanan campaign decided not to even advertise in the area, nor in most of southeast Florida, Cunningham says, adding that "the percentage of people down there who would be receptive to our message is much smaller than in other parts of the state."

Asked how many votes he would guess Buchanan legitimately received in Palm Beach County, Cunningham says, "I think a thousand would be generous."

In any other business, liars are called liars. There are penalties for perjury in the law, fines for inaccurate claims in advertising, libel laws against journalists and publishers. But many political spokespeople take to lies like mutts to kibble, knowing that their bosses are rarely held accountable for such lies. Politics, of course, by necessity utilizes spin, obfuscation, and a degree of hyperbole. But lines can still be crossed — when speakers say things for political purposes that are just plain false, whether aware that the matters were not true or simply indifferent to what the truth is. And the media rarely calls them on it. Democrats and Republicans both know this and exploit it in desperate circumstances. Perhaps because Gore already had a reputation for misleading voters and overstating his record, the Bush people got away with it much more. So by November 9, they're emboldened to say whatever the hell they want to.

After Fleischer's widely distributed nonsense, Bush strategist Karl Rove appears before the cameras in Austin to bolster the untruth, which he calls in great Orwellian fashion, "set(ting) the record straight."

"There are 16,695 voters in Palm Beach County who registered as a member of the Independent Party, the Reform Party, or the American Reform Party, which were the labels borne this year by the reform effort in Florida," Rove says. "This in an increase of 110 percent over the registration totals for the same party in 1996."

About the ballot itself, Rove says that "the Gore campaign has been handing out a somewhat hazy and fuzzy copy of it, so we are making available to you, and can do so electronically as well, a relatively clean and clear copy of the butterfly ballot, which indicates that this is not as susceptible to confusion as Chairman Daley indicated."

"The Bush campaign is inflating the numbers of Reform Party members to the limits of gullibility," McConnell says after hearing Rove's comments. "They're including everybody that can in any way be assumed to be members of the Reform Party." Members of the American Reform Party and the Independent Party "are absolutely not Buchanan supporters." The American Reform Party "is largely made up of people who supported [former Colorado governor] Dick Lamm against Ross Perot for the 1996 nomination," McConnell says. He doesn't even know what the Independent Party is.

Cunningham says that the Independent Party didn't *have* a presidential candidate on the Palm Beach County ballot and endorsed Buchanan's Reform Party rival, John Hagelin. And the American Reform Party split with Reform, and this year endorsed Ralph Nader for president.

★   ★   ★

In Nashville, Fabiani is shaking his head. Daley was too hot at the press conference, way too hot. He'd wanted Daley to say that the butterfly ballot story in that day's *New York Times* — one that the Gorebies had been working on with its author, Don Van Natta — was astonishing and proved beyond any doubt that Bush, had all the votes been counted accurately, had lost Florida. It was time for Bush to stand up and explain to people how he could claim the throne when he'd seemingly won because people were confused about the butterfly ballot.

Keep saying it was the media making the allegations — that was Fabiani's plan. But instead, Daley had gone out there and read a statement Klain had written for him, this one about the lawsuits and all. The press conference had moved the issue away from people talking about who really won and who really lost to whether or not Gore was a spoiler trying to win the presidency by suing.

★   ★   ★

"Speaking of automatic recounts," Bush campaign chair Don Evans says, before the press throngs in Austin, "I want to alert you that there are at least three other states in which automatic recounts are likely." Wisconsin, Iowa, and New Mexico — all of which went for Gore — may have recounts as well.

Rove is asked if the Bushies are going to ask for recounts in those three states.

"We are waiting to see the results of the canvass Tuesday night in Wisconsin, and to be guided by Governor [Tommy] Thompson," he says.

Rove adds that any comments by the Gorebies about their man's popular-vote win are premature. Just as he claimed before the election that Bush would win by 6 or 7 percentage points, Rove again offers a prognostication that in hindsight couldn't end up being further from the truth. Rove says that a vote count in Colorado, as well as the continued tallying of absentee ballots in Arizona, California, Oregon, and Washington, has made his team "confident that this will carry with it the likelihood of an increasing amount of popular votes for Governor Bush and a diminishing margin between the two candidates."

Bush communications director Karen Hughes is asked about Gore's rising 200,000-vote lead in the popular tally. "I would point out that Governor Bush, in this election, has received more popular votes than President Clinton did in either of his two elections, in either 1996 or in 1992," she says. For that matter, Bush also garnered more popular votes than George Washington, Abraham Lincoln, and Franklin D. Roosevelt.

Just not more than Al Gore.

★   ★   ★

The Gorebies are disappointed. Some top members of the blue-chip law firm Holland & Knight agreed on Wednesday to take the Gore case: Martha Barnett, a senior partner at the firm and president of the American Bar Association, and Chesterfield Smith, the H&K partner who's the dean of Florida lawyers. But by Thursday they tell the Gore lawyers that there's a potential conflict, which they're working on resolving. We'll get back to you, they tell the Gorebies.

But Team Gore never hears from them again. Bye-bye, Holland & Knight.

The Democrats are disappointed but not surprised. This is Jeb Bush's terrain. All the major law firms in the state have offices in Tallahassee, so all are beholden to an extent to Jeb and the GOP-controlled state house and state senate.

Imagine the Everglades in the mid 1930s. Gladesmen hunted gators and otters, poling their skiffs through mangroves for weeks at a time, sleeping on small piles of peat at makeshift campsites with names like Break-A-Leg and Buzzard and Camp Nasty.[1] They fended off predators and irritants ranging from gator fleas to moonshiners to God-knows-who and God-knows-what. Now picture dropping Harvard boy Albert Gore, Jr., smack-dab in the middle of it all. The Gladesman — who know their way around the marshes, the swamps, the jungles — are not inclined to help the foreign preppie.

One such Gladesman is Frank Jimenez — a slight, intense guy whom I run into one night at Tallahassee hot spot Café Cabernet. Jimenez sits with Katie Baur, Jeb's communications director. Jimenez is angry. He says chad are on the floor. He says Daley's a thug. When I point out that Daley was twelve when his dad helped JFK, Jimenez calls me naive. He's motivated by anger, and, having taken an unpaid leave as Jeb's assistant general counsel, his charge is whatever it takes to help his boss's brother. Three other members of Jeb's legal staff take time off to help as well, as does Baur.

Another Gladesman is J. M. "Mac" Stipanovich, a former Marine who helmed the gubernatorial campaigns of Bob Martinez in '86 and Jeb in '94, and who spent '98 helping both Jeb and Katherine Harris win. Stipanovich used to be much higher profile, always quick with a quote for reporters. But from '98 on, the lawyer/lobbyist at Fowler White learned to keep his trap shut while he sat in the money-laden nexus of Tallahassee politics, raising money for Republican candidates, then turning around and lobbying them on behalf of clients like Big Tobacco. Stipanovich, who has likened politics to the Vietnam War, was drafted into duty by a senior Bush adviser the Thursday after the election, and he has been closely advising Harris ever since. All the while, he's been talking to Bushies. And Stipanovich's call is not the call of law or justice. It is the call of victory.

Reporters will try to establish direct ties between Harris and W. It's not as if they need to — Harris is on the program from the get-go. But the fact that Stipanovich is by her side during most of the next month — while Ken Sukhia, Stipanovich's law partner at Fowler White, simultaneously represents George W. Bush — is one connection never made.

And Harris, chief elections officer of the state, is the Gladeswoman the Gorebies are most wary of. Harris, first elected in 1988, was Bush's Florida co-chair as far back as October 1999. "I am thrilled and honored to announce my support of George W. Bush for the Presidency," she said in a "Bush for President" press release. Harris said that working with Bush's younger brother, "has provided a constant reminder of the power of values-based leadership — the same leadership George has shown in Texas. I also share George's commitment to education, and I look forward to sharing his vision with Floridians." She would later serve as a Bush delegate during the Republican National Convention.

This is the woman whom the state is relying upon for fair and impartial service.

Democrats shake their heads as they read the opposition research brief their staffers have prepared. Harris's activities on behalf of Bush went far beyond the normal activities of a state chair. She was a presence on the Bush campaign back in January, traveling with Jeb and 138 other Floridians as they flew from Miami and Tallahassee to New Hampshire on a leased Boeing 727 to campaign for the Texas governor in his primary campaign against McCain. Harris's presence on the tour — called "Freezin' for a Reason" — brought lovely photo ops of her and her fellow Floridians handing out bags of Florida oranges and Plant City strawberries. It has also brought serious questions in light of her authority in the Florida controversy.

This isn't the first time that Harris's involvement with the Bush campaign has had her critics questioning her impartiality. An October story in the *Tampa Tribune* about the $100,000 of state funds that Harris had spent on trips to New York City, Washington, D.C., and abroad, reported that, "Speculation has Harris seeking an ambassadorship if Texas Gov. George W. Bush is elected president."

Additionally, it was Harris who reportedly personally enlisted Ret. Gen. H. Norman Schwarzkopf in a Florida public service TV announcement urging Floridians to go to the polls. Schwarzkopf, a well-known supporter of Bush, not only vouched for Bush during the Republican National Convention, but appeared with the Texas governor at numerous campaign stops throughout the Sunshine State. Democrats and others criticized Harris for selecting someone so clearly aligned with the GOP candidate.

The Democrats gripe. They want a Harris of their own. Instead they have Bob Butterworth, the state's Democratic attorney general.

Many leading members of the Gore team don't think too highly of Butterworth, not his smarts or his loyalty. They've heard that he wants to run against Jeb for governor in 2002, that his eyes are on that election, not this one.

The Dems get word that Jeb has announced that he's recusing himself from the three-person state elections board, on which he serves with Harris and Jeb Bush–appointed supervisor of elections Clay Roberts, also a Bush backer. Harris soon announces that Jeb will be replaced by Agriculture commissioner Bob Crawford, a Democrat. Crawford also happens to be a Democrat who endorsed Jeb Bush for governor in 1998, and George W. Bush for president in 2000.

Even those individuals not loyal to Jeb who are skiffing through the murky political swamps of Florida politics right now are more inclined not to help Gore. His brother stands an excellent chance of being sworn in as the next leader of the free world on January 20. This is his state; he's the governor; he appoints judges, promotes others, names individuals to boards, freezes people out, or plucks them from obscurity. This is the Jeberglades.

For a guy like Al Gore, it's pretty dangerous terrain.

★   ★   ★

On Thursday, Butterworth's office places a call to circuit judge Robert Rouse, chief judge of the Seventh Judicial Circuit, who picked Volusia's canvassing board's chairman, Judge Michael McDermott, a Republican. The three — McDermott, Rouse, and Butterworth — get a conference call to discuss Volusia's recount.

Butterworth wants to make sure that whoever's in charge of the Volusia recount knows that it's supposed to be a full recount. Some of the counties are just comparing the final count with the numbers from the machine tallies instead of rerunning the cards through the machine. Butterworth also wants to make sure that McDermott knows what he's supposed to be doing.

"Mr. Butterworth, with all due respect, I believe you should disqualify yourself from any involvement in this matter," McDermott says. Butterworth was, after all, Gore's state campaign chair until just the other day.

Butterworth seems to get a bit huffy. "Well, I guess I'll leave the room, then," he says.

Butterworth leaves his own office, slamming the door behind him.

★   ★   ★

In Palm Beach County, Theresa LePore is worried.

On Thursday, she, Judge Burton, and Democratic county commissioner Carol Roberts grant both the Democrats' and Republicans' requests — a hand recount for the D's, another machine recount for the R's.

Even though their votes were unanimous, LePore feels very much alone. Neither of her colleagues — Burton, forty-one, a Democratic former prosecutor appointed to the bench by Gov. Jeb in May, and Roberts, sixty-four, a very partisan Democrat and former West Palm Beach mayor first elected in '86 — is suffering the same slings and arrows as is she.

Thursday morning, county attorney Leon St. John phones up local legal hotshot Bruce Rogow, who represented the raunchy rappers from 2 Live Crew in their obscenity and copyright infringement cases and who sued to get ex-Klansman David Duke on the presidential ballot. Rogow, sixty, has been before the U.S. Supreme Court eleven times, more than any other Florida lawyer.

"It looks like Theresa's going to need a lawyer," St. John says.

It's unclear just what she'll need one for, but she'll assuredly need one, St. John says. The rhetoric in the air — that accusation that she lost the election for Gore, that the butterfly ballot was illegal — is scaring her, he says. More immediately, St. John says, LePore's the target of a federal lawsuit filed yesterday by an attorney named Lawrence Navarro on behalf of a voter named Milton Miller, and it's set for a hearing today before U.S. District judge Kenneth Ryskamp, a hard-ass Republican.

In the coming days, Miller will be joined in his anti–butterfly ballot, anti-LePore charge by seventeen other Palm Beach County plaintiffs, in several other lawsuits. Thursday alone brings four circuit court suits and one federal court suit demanding a revote. Some of the plaintiffs are surely sympathetic. Like Sylvia Szymoniak, eighty-four, of Palm Springs, a Democrat who hasn't missed an election since she began voting in the 1930s, who says that she was rushed out of the voting booth. Or Florence Zoltowsky, seventy, a Boynton Beach Holocaust survivor whose possible vote for Nazi-defender Buchanan literally makes her ill. Or Lillian Gaines, sixty-seven, of the Coalition for Black Student Achievement, the Urban League, and the Sickle Cell Foundation of Palm Beach County.

Then, of course, there's Andre Fladell. Fladell, fifty-three, a chiropractor and Democratic operative from Delray Beach — he and LePore once served together as judges in a hot dog–eating contest — who has more than once been referred to as the "unofficial prince of Palm Beach County," not always as a compliment. If there was ever a guy to stick himself into the middle of a mess, Fladell was him.

On Wednesday, looking out upon the sea of potential lawsuits, Rogow called an old friend of his, Environmental Protection Agency chieftain Carol Browner, whom he'd known since she was twelve. He left a message for her: You need to tell Gore to get somebody on the ground here. It's chaos in Palm Beach. It's insanity. Someone needs to squash these suits. But now his first order of business is not to make helpful suggestions to Gore, for whom he voted, but to represent LePore against Miller's suit. Miller went to the 1st Korean Christian Reform Church on Election Day, where voting at precinct 214 was taking place, and was immediately confused by the ballot. "The names were zigzagged so that the punch holes were not in the correct order," the complaint says. Miller told "agents" of LePore and Harris that he was having problems understanding the ballot "but took no action to rectify the situation."

Miller "will suffer irreparable harm due to the Defendants' actions in the event a preliminary and permanent injunction" — against the certification of Palm Beach County's tally — "is not granted. Defendants' actions have caused Plaintiff to suffer emotional distress for which he cannot adequately calculate money damages." Miller is asking for LePore and Harris "to order a new election in Palm Beach County."

It's nonsense, Rogow thinks.

Soon, as Rogow drives on I-95 to represent LePore before Ryskamp, Democratic attorney Mitch Berger calls him on his cell. "We want to get this case dismissed," Berger says.

"So do I," Rogow says. "But what do you want me to do?"

"We'd like to have the lawyers who are involved call us," Berger says. "So when you get there, see what you can do."

Rogow agrees, figuring that Berger and the Gore team — which apparently Berger's on — would rather be in state court than federal, since the former is generally more sympathetic to Democrats, the latter to Republicans. He also figures that the Dems are probably afraid of this chaotic litigation. Additionally, others in the legal community observe, Ryskamp is probably not the most sympathetic ear for Jews and African-Americans complaining about ballot woes. Nominated to the Eleventh U.S. Circuit Court of Appeals by then-president Bush in 1990, Ryskamp had his nomination rejected by the Senate Judiciary Committee in 1991. It wasn't just that Ryskamp belonged to a Coral Gables country club that didn't have any Jewish or African-American members, though that rubbed some people the wrong way. It was more the substantive complaints about his alleged hostility to plaintiffs with age, gender, and race discrimination complaints, whom he ruled against almost nine out of ten times, often exhibiting — as the St. Petersburg Times wrote — "an insensitivity sometimes bordering on the Neanderthal."

Berger, meanwhile, tells an attorney, Dawn Myers, to go to federal court and squash the suit. He has an idea for how the butterfly ballot case can be won, but these guys are putting the cart before the horse, asking for a remedy — a revote — before the ballot's even been proved to have been illegal. That's more appropriate litigation for the "contest" phase of an election challenge, not the "protest" phase. Berger and his team want to do everything they can to get the uncounted votes included in the tally before Gore breaks any new ground by contesting an official election result.

Berger thinks that he could possibly argue for some sort of remedy — an allocation of ill-cast votes isn't entirely unprecedented. He can sure meet one of the two criteria, showing that there was significant confusion. And in a Palm Beach County court case, after witness after witness after witness, perhaps the momentum would be with him. Then he could jump the second hurdle in proving the illegality of a ballot, convincing the judge to see the conflicting measures of ballot law the way he would present them.

But Navarro won't back off until he has a private phone conversation with Daley himself. So Daley calls him. Afterward, Navarro explains to reporters why his client brought, and is now withdrawing, his suit.

"Al Gore's going to step up and fight this battle."

★   ★   ★

As the masses of election protesters accumulate outside the Palm Beach elections office, the Rev. Thomas Masters, pastor at the New Macedonia Missionary Baptist Church, looks out contentedly at his handiwork.

Masters, the brother-in-law of former former D.C. mayor Marion Barry, is the local go-to man for civil rights causes, especially when televised. Not all of Masters's causes have necessarily been embraced by the community as a whole — not his March and April tirades against the Domino's, Pizza Hut, and Papa John's deliverymen who didn't bring their pies to black neighborhoods, for instance, though eventually the chains capitulated. And certainly not his June demonstration outside the state attorney's office after prosecutors decided to try as an adult a thirteen-year-old who killed his teacher. Didn't matter. What Masters saw as an injustice, he spoke out against. Considering the charge, he barely even blinked after a jury ruled in favor of a seventeen-year-old retarded kid who'd accused *Masters* of rape, awarding his family $2.45 million in damages from Masters and his church — which a judge was nice enough to reduce to just $1.3 million only from Masters.

As with Barry, Masters knew the Rev. Jesse Jackson a bit, had enlisted Jackson in a 1996 demonstration against a local supermarket where a thirty-three-year-old — suspected of shoplifting a toothbrush and toothpaste — died of asphyxiation after eight employees pinned him down. Yesterday, after hearing about the voter problems, he worked with a few others — including Representative Wexler, who specifically focused on getting Jews to participate — to organize this march. He told them he'd get Jackson there.

And sure enough, at around 1:30 P.M., the Rev. Jesse Jackson arrives in West Palm Beach. "In Selma, it was about the right to vote," Jackson says. "Today, it's about making votes count.

"While there is — over and over again — a call for a recount, in West Palm there must be a first count," Jackson says. "We find around the state various irregularities that undercut the credibility of a great election, a great campaign by two worthy opponents. In democracy, everybody counts. Every vote must count.

"This ballot" — Jackson says, awkwardly holding up the butterfly ballot — "is fuzzy," alluding to Bush's campaign slam that Gore used "fuzzy math."

★ ★ ★

Fabiani cringes. Jackson is not helping.

Their challenge is to create for the public the impression that this can all be resolved quickly and fairly and it's not going to be dragged down to a destabilizing situation. Anything that strays from that message will hurt — and Jackson leading rallies and calling for a revote certainly falls into that category. It's not that Gore doesn't care that people didn't get to vote because polling places were moved at the last minute, or about other problems, but a revote is never going to happen.

Donna Brazile is asked to talk to Jackson, to tell him what the campaign's thinking and how he can help, and how he can be unhelpful if he so chooses. Whether Brazile ever truly conveys that is another question.

★ ★ ★

Warren Christopher is pissed at Jim Baker. On Wednesday, Baker told reporters that he'd tried to call his fellow former secretary of state but had not heard back from him. Truth is, Christopher had been traveling all day, and he had tried to get back to Baker, but he was hard to reach, too. But Baker had made it sound like Christopher wasn't returning his phone calls, and that angered him. In any case, Christopher and Baker finally do connect, and they decide to all meet Thursday afternoon.

It's pretty friendly, considering. Baker comes to the Governor's Inn, where Daley and Chris — the name Christopher's close friends call him by — are staying, and he brings with him Bush campaign manager Joe Allbaugh and Baker's protégé Bob Zoellick. No agreements or anything are reached of course — they quickly realize that they're going to disagree, but they concur that this should be done in a respectful way. They bullshit a little — *How ya doin'? Isn't this crazy?* — and then they say their farewells. The whole thing takes maybe six minutes.

★ ★ ★

That evening, Barry Richard returns from visiting his pop in Miami and, in jeans, heads straight to the Bush Building, where he meets Baker and Ginsberg. Wiry and intense, Richard fields their questions, about Florida election law, the Florida courts, about strategy.

What do you think about the butterfly ballot case? he's asked.

Not much, Richard says. Not knowing anything more about it than what he'd seen on TV and in the newspapers, Richard doesn't think the case has a great deal of substance. It can be won, he says.

Baker listens a lot, Richard notices, supervising but not really running anything. Baker's Bush's eyes and ears here, Richard thinks, while Ginsberg's the one actually in charge of the legal team. It's like Baker's the general manager, Ginsberg the coach.

In that metaphor, Richard can be seen as the quintessential yeoman player, hopping team to team with each trade. His father, Melvin Richard, served for twenty-two years on the city council and one term as the mayor of Miami Beach, bringing Jackie Gleason's TV show to town. After getting his J.D. from the University of Miami Law School, Richard served for the navy's judge advocate general during the Vietnam War, stationed at a Northern California naval hospital.

There he was thrust into a position of being indispensable to everyone, including those at the local army and air force hospitals, which didn't have attorneys. He advised the admiral on discipline and court-martials, taught doctors about medical law that he himself had to learn, answered questions from patients and staffers about problems with their mortgages and marriages, having to rapidly determine the law in each of their hometowns. "It was like getting thrown overboard," he would later say. "You need to learn to swim pretty quickly."

Then it was back to Coral Gables, where he practiced law with his dad and then served as a clerk in the Dade County attorney's office. He moved up the ladder pretty damn quick: there he was, a young man in his thirties, assistant attorney general for Miami arguing a search-and-seizure case before the U.S. Supreme Court, then moving to Tallahassee to serve as deputy attorney general from '72 to '74.

After that he ran and won as state representative. In '78 he ran for attorney general but lost to Jim Smith in the primary. Soon he started a small law firm that grew and grew and eventually merged with Greenberg Traurig in '91. He's known for his silver tongue and his silver bouffant and a pretty decent command of the law.

The butterfly ballot confusion was a shame, Richard thinks, but it wasn't much more than that: a shame.

By Thursday, Bushies have set up their basic shop, which is almost entirely headquartered in the Tallahassee Bush Building.

Baker is in charge, assisted as he always is by Margaret Tutweiler, who has served him throughout his career in a variety of positions, perhaps most notably as State Department spokeswoman. Zoellick is on board as well, as is Bush domestic policy adviser Josh Bolten.

If Baker's the CEO, Bush campaign manager Joe Allbaugh is chief operating officer, running the day-to-day, ensuring that there are no gaps in communication, making sure the trains run on time. Ginsberg heads up legal, helped by George H. W. Bush administration deputy attorney general George Terwilliger, now a senior partner at White & Case, Kirk Van Tine from the D.C. office of Baker Botts, an elite firm formed by an ancestor of Jim Baker. Eventually, the Bush legal effort will draw from a cast of hundreds from the best firms in the nation. Terwilliger, called and drafted by Evans in the midst of an interview on Fox News Channel, is picked up at the Tallahassee airport by his fellow White & Case-ians Tim Flanigan and Bob Bittman — the latter of whom had been a key aide to Ken Starr in his pursuit of President Clinton.

Ken Mehlman and Randy Enwright — a Florida political operative who served as political director of the Florida GOP from 1995 through 1999 — run the ground team. Tucker Eskew and Mindy Tucker — with advice from Tutweiler — work on communications, always in conjunction with other Bush spinners in Austin, like Karen Hughes, Dan Bartlett, Ari Fleischer.

The whole team is concerned. The powers that be worry that the floor is slipping out from under them.

After Palm Beach County's machine recount, there's been a 643-vote shift for Gore, one that the elections supervisor there, LePore, cannot immediately explain. In Pinellas County, Gore gains 404 votes, and Bush loses 61. But then the elections officials retract those numbers, too. Gore picked up 153 net votes in heavily Democratic Gadsden County — just *what the hell is going on?!*

More bad news; Gore's popular-vote lead now exceeds 300,000 votes.

And Broward, Volusia, and Palm Beach Counties are going ahead with the first steps toward a hand recount; the Miami-Dade canvassing board has announced that it will hear arguments about the matter on Tuesday. And after the state-mandated machine recount concludes Thursday evening, Bush's lead has been cut from 1,784 votes to 327. Baker, Ginsberg, and the other Bush recount team leaders worry that at some point the lower fourth of the MSNBC TV screen will post a headline with Gore's vote lead over Bush.

They all sit in the Bush Building, in the room they call the "bull pit." Baker, Ginsberg, Olson. This is untenable, they think. Many think that the election is being stolen from them.

Word comes from Austin that the team needs to prepare, to think about how to argue from a PR standpoint when and if the numbers turn. Bush won, they say. Everything the Democrats are trying to do is a violation of preexisting Florida election law. Hand recounts are for when there's a problem, a malfunction, with the machines — not for when a candidate simply doesn't like the result.

GOP pols in the field report back to Tallahassee: "If they keep counting, we'll be behind," they say.

Additional worries come when Frank Jimenez hears that the Democrats on the ground are already making noise about the standards by which ballots will be judged in any hand recount. They want the most generous standard available — even mere impressions in ballots, so-called dents or dimples.

If this all keeps going on, Gore could win.

Baker won't have it.

What about their own hand recount? The deadline's Friday. They can cherry-pick a few of their own counties, glean some votes that way.

But Baker wants to draw a line in the sand. No recounts. No nothin'.

When Terwilliger flies down from D.C. Thursday night, he takes notes on the plane. Note number one: "Federal Court — On What Basis?" He's skeptical that there was a role at all. But when he arrives, Ginsberg tells him to figure out how to get the matter into federal court. Terwilliger and other lawyers talk about it, and the conventional wisdom is that this is a state issue.

"Not good enough," Terwilliger says.

Florida courts are considered rather liberal, rather Democratic, especially the state supreme court. In 1996, Terwilliger had represented John Walsh from TV's *America's Most Wanted,* in an open-documents, or "sunshine law," case involving the police files surrounding the homicide of Walsh's son. Walsh didn't want the file disclosed, because police and prosecutors were closing in on a suspect, and there were some details in the file that might jeopardize the case, Walsh thought. The courts were liberal, more inclined to side with newspapers than cops, Terwilliger learned. That experience, combined with the observations of Florida Republicans about the Florida courts, convinced Terwilliger that this has to end up in federal court, where they have friends, especially at the U.S. Supreme Court.

★   ★   ★

Around this time, Berger receives a phone call from a colleague, Harry Jacobs, a personal injury lawyer from Longwood who's given Gore and the Democrats more than $50,000.

"We have a problem in Seminole County, too, Mitchell," Jacobs says. "What do we do?"

Berger finds out the basic story. The state Republican Party screwed up the absentee ballot applications it had sent out, forgetting to include a line on the form for the voter ID number. In Seminole County, Republican elections supervisor Sandra Goard allowed Republican operatives to camp out in the elections office for ten days filling in these numbers on the voters' behalf. Berger is outraged.

"You file a protest, Harry," Berger tells him, walking him through the process.

Jacobs will eventually lie about this conversation. When asked by MSNBC's *Hardball* host, Chris Matthews, on November 29, "Have you had any contact with Ron Klain or any of the attorneys for the Gore campaign?" Jacobs will say, "No, sir."

"None at all?" Matthews asks. "No contact with the Gore people at all in Washington or in Florida?"

"Well, I can tell you that I've talked to a lot of Democrats; I've also spoken to a lot of Republicans. Whether or not they have some official capacity, that's something unknown to me. I'm pursuing this case on my own."

"Right," Matthews says. "You've got no signal urging you on, for example; no cheering section from anybody connected to Gore?"

"Not that I'm aware of," Jacobs will say.*

---

*In January 2001, Jacobs will tell me that he was not lying, that he "did not know the breadth or the depth of the involvement" of Berger on the Gore team. He'll say that he simply assumed that Berger — as well as Democratic National Committee counsel Joe Sandler, with whom he had also spoken by the time of the *Hardball* interview — were just outraged Democratic volunteer lawyers, much like him. That may have been true at the time of the talk, but it strains credibility that by November 29 Jacobs was *still* unaware of Berger's involvement.

★ ★ ★

Though we've heard all sorts of news reports here and there about results of the first machine recount, the world still has no official number. At 6 P.M. that evening in the state senate building, the three Florida officials in charge of the election certification who are now supervising the state's recount effort — Harris, Roberts, and Crawford, Bush supporters to a man — come before the cameras to tell us that they don't know, either.

"We will all remember these times as some of the most critical and defining moments in our nation's history," says Harris. "A time when we as Americans are working to ensure the meaning and vitality of our democratic system." Only fifty-three of the state's sixty-seven counties have provided her office with their official recount results, she says. Though Harris requested all the re-tallies by Thursday, the fourteen remaining counties legally have until Tuesday, November 14, to provide her with their results.

The unofficial results are as follows, she says: Her candidate, Bush, scores 2,909,661 votes; Gore gets 1,784 votes less than that, 2,907,877. But these numbers mean nothing. They reflect a mishmash, a casserole, the new numbers from the fifty-three counties that have recounted and certified their results* plus the old numbers from the fourteen counties that have yet to turn their re-tallies in. And some of these fourteen counties outstanding are unbelievably important for Gore's hopes. Miami-Dade and Palm Beach Counties, for instance. Also unreported is Pinellas County, which includes St. Petersburg and is near Tampa, and Orange County, which includes Orlando — major population centers of the fabled Interstate 4 corridor. Old tallies have Gore beating Bush in both these spots, but not by all that much; about 20,000 total. A small increase in any one of these places could completely flip the election results.

Harris says that some news organizations are calling the counties on their own and counting those as recount results. The official standards, she says, are a bit more stringent. "Until we have the physical certification in our hands, they are not officially certified," she says. Absentee ballots from overseas, Harris reminds us, must be both received in Tallahassee and counted by November 17.

---

*And it will turn out that, as Butterworth tried to explain to judges Rouse and McDermott, many of these fifty-three counties didn't even conduct a recount — some just double-checked their computer numbers with the total, some didn't even do anything at all.

Crawford seems to speak for all three when he says that his endorsement of Bush won't affect his duties. "Anybody who's going to serve on this commission had to vote for somebody," Crawford says, though he neglects to point out that Harris and Roberts voted the same way. It does seem a bit much, all three of them being Bushies.

"Nobody ever said that democracy is simple or efficient," Crawford says. "But this is democracy in action. If you want simplicity, just go about seventy miles south of Florida, and you got Cuba, and they're very simple, they have no elections."

They leave the building, and none of us is any closer to knowing really much of anything at all.

5

"That limp-dicked motherfucker."

In Fort Lauderdale on Friday, November 10, Judge Robert W. Lee, forty, is trying to keep things orderly.

Lee, appointed to the bench in 1997 by then-governor Lawton Chiles, had hated having to do the automatic machine recount two days before. Having gone to bed at 5 A.M., he awoke Wednesday at 6:30 to run 588,000 Broward County ballots through the ten tabulation machines again.

Things got a little odder on Thursday, when Democratic lawyers petitioned the canvassing board, asking them to do a hand recount of 1 percent of the county — roughly three precincts. Why? Lee wondered. The machines seemed to be functioning perfectly well. What would be the justification for a hand recount? And now it's Friday, and the canvassing board is voting on whether or not to begin the 1 percent hand recount, to see if it's needed countywide.

Supervisor of Elections Jane Carroll isn't even there. Carroll, the Republican who's retiring on January 3 after thirty-two years as elections supervisor, is in Beech Mountain, North Carolina. She participates in the canvassing-board meeting by phone.

All eyes are on Lee here. Everyone knows Carroll is opposed to the very notion of hand recounts. Commissioner Suzanne Gunzburger, meanwhile, has voted for hand recounts as far back as March 1995, when a campaign for the Lauderdale Lakes city council was lost by 2 votes, and another for Miramar commissioner was lost by 9. "I felt strongly then as I do now that we should bend over backwards to protect this democracy," says Gunzburger, a partisan Democrat elected city commissioner in 1982, county commissioner ten years later. "Whatever we need to do to allow voters to

90

have their voice counted, it is our responsibility as a canvassing board to do so."

There isn't a whole lot of law in this area, Lee thinks. The statute for a recount — signed in 1989 by then-governor Martinez, a Republican — is kind of vague, he thinks. Is the law for when there's a problem with the vote counting? With the vote tabulation? Lee turns to the county attorney. "This statute is extremely vague as to what it means. When do we have to do this manual recount?"

Leonard Samuels, a Gore lawyer, suggests that the board count just the county's 6,686 undervotes. Carroll says that separating the undervotes from the other 582,000 ballots won't be easy; it will mean manually removing them all. Gunzburger makes the motion that they do the 1 percent plus the undervotes.

Lee and Carroll refuse to second it. Not going to happen. They'll stick with the three-precinct rule. If anything.

The law allows the petitioner to select the 1 percent he wants counted. Not surprisingly, Samuels presents three districts that are almost laughably pro-Gore, the VP having won 91 percent of their 3,892 votes. Precinct 6-C, Sanders Park Elementary School in the Pompano Beach neighborhood of Liberty Park, is so overwhelmingly African-American that only a dozen whites are even on the voting roll. Democrats outnumber Republicans 1,755 to 78. On Election Night, there were 1,071 Gore votes, 19 Bush votes, and 59 undervotes. The other two precincts are in the largely Jewish retirement condo community of Wynmoor Village in Coconut Creek, where registered Democrats outnumber registered Republicans by a 10-to-1 margin. In precinct 1-F in the Wynmoor Village Entertainment Center, Gore racked up 1,308 votes, with, as was the case in precinct 6-C, more undervotes than Bush votes, 80 to 62. Precinct 6-F in Wynmoor Village was similar: 1,175 Gore votes, 52 Bush votes, and 43 undervotes.

Ed Pozzuoli, chairman of the Broward County Republican Party, is hardly delighted with Samuels's picks. "It is not about fairness," he says. "They're looking for more Democratic votes."

Lee agrees that the precincts they picked are skewed, but that's the law.

"I think we're setting a bad precedent," Carroll says. The canvassing board, she says, has no business deciding "whether a voter really intended to vote it. . . . That's the reason that I've not been in favor of this sort of thing before."

In fact, Broward County hasn't conducted a hand recount since March of '96, for the Lauderdale-by-the-Sea mayoral race, where Anna Mae

French lost to Thomas D. McKane III by 1 vote. And that hand recount just confirmed that French had, indeed, lost by 1 vote.

Not that Carroll likes punch cards. She's been trying to get the county commission to pony up for better machines for some time now. In 1993, she wrote a memo criticizing the commission's wait-and-see attitude on voter technology. "If the theory of waiting to see what will come along in the future had been employed, we would still be on a manual registration system and hand-counting paper ballots brought in by horse-drawn carriages," she wrote. Still, Carroll's mind is made up against a hand count. So is Gunzburger's, in the opposite direction. "We always say one vote makes a difference," she says. "Well, we're looking at the next leader of our democracy, the forty-third president."

Both Lee and Gunzburger support the 1 percent hand recount; Carroll opposes.

Carroll agrees to return by Monday early afternoon. The hand recount of the three precincts will commence then.

★ ★ ★

It's weird that they keep bumping into other players in this drama, Daley thinks. Small town. Last night, he, Chris, and Klain went out to dinner at a local restaurant, Cypress, where who should come over to say hi but Katherine Harris. She was perfectly nice, perfectly lovely. Her cousin is chef and co-owner. Still, it was weird.

Now Friday morning, at the Doubletree, Daley and Chris run into Baker and his gang — Allbaugh, Zoellick, Tutweiler. They'd had a nice meeting yesterday afternoon, Daley thinks, why not go over there and say hello?

"Hey, Jim, I got a proposition for ya," Daley jokes. "How about we give you Oregon and Iowa in exchange for Florida?"

Baker doesn't seem to find this funny. Daley's greeted by four stone faces; you can almost hear the distant sound of crickets. Something's changed, Daley thinks. These guys are in a different mode than they were yesterday. They're in full battle gear, he thinks. Daley awkwardly exits.

"I think he's really pissed off," Daley says to Christopher.

★ ★ ★

The fact that Bill Daley is the son of former Chicago mayor Richard Daley, who helped steal Illinois for JFK in 1960, is not the reason why Fabiani thinks he shouldn't be so out in front on all of this. Though it doesn't help. Daley's gene pool is an irony not lost on us in the media, and it becomes a major talking point of the GOP. Which is too bad, because Daley — who was twelve in November 1960 — has worked hard his entire life to embody the positive aspects of his father's politics and to shun the corruption.

A Pulitzer Prize–winning *Chicago Tribune* investigation into the Daley machine in 1972 detailed the myriad ways Daley's machine ensured victory: dead people voted; other mystery voters had official addresses that didn't exist. The names of bums were copied from guest registers in skid row motels, and somehow they voted, too. Many Republican judges were kept from supervising, while others worked with their Democratic counterparts for Daley. Poll workers walked into the voting booths to "help" senior citizens pull the straight Democratic lever.[1]

And it worked. In 1960, Kennedy beat Nixon nationally with a hair-thin margin, 49.7 percent of the popular vote to Nixon's 49.6. Kennedy won Illinois by 8,858 votes — out of a total 4,657,394 cast. And while it's true that there were credible allegations of vote fraud in downstate Republican areas of the Land of Lincoln, it was Mayor Daley's Chicago where Kennedy won 89.3 percent of the vote — 456,312 votes — which carried him over the top. And though Kennedy's electoral-vote margin of victory was large enough that he could have lost Illinois and still won, it was not large enough that he could have lost Illinois and Texas — another state where there were rampant allegations of vote fraud — and still won.

Already Republicans like Baker are pressuring Gore to concede, regurgitating the historical falsehood that Nixon conceded Election Night for the good of the country. In fact, Nixon didn't even formally concede until November 11, three days after the election, and he did so, by his own admission, with thoughts that a recount would take up to half a year, and with consideration of his future political viability paramount in his mind. And even after the concession announcement — made by his press secretary, not the candidate himself — the Republican Party began investigating allegations about Daley's machine. RNC chairman Sen. Thurston Morton of Kentucky flew to Chicago and announced the formation of the National Recount and Fair Elections Committee. Recounts and recanvasses were ordered. One precinct's recount tally went from Kennedy having 323 votes to Nixon's 78 to a much closer count: 237 to 162.[2]

Investigations were launched in Texas, too. In fact, that month in Chicago a first-year Kirkland & Ellis associate attorney named Fred Bartlit — who forty years later would emerge as a Bush lawyer in this dispute — was hired by the Republican Party to investigate vote fraud in Texas. Only six or so weeks on the job, Bartlit concluded that there was plenty of evidence of electoral shenanigans in Starr and Duval Counties in

South Texas, where the votes were still controlled by the same team — led by George Parr, "the Duke of Duval County" — who stole a Senate election for LBJ in 1948.* Some historical accounts have GOP chieftains concluding that they just didn't have enough hard evidence to mount the challenge. For whatever reasons, the Republican Party decided not to contest the results. But little, if any, of it was rooted in Nixon's magnanimity.

That said, before Bill Daley, the mayor's youngest son of four, turned thirty, he had seen his dad both disgraced during the 1968 Democratic convention and buried in 1976. He and his older brother Richie Daley had to struggle to be taken seriously, to be seen as anything other than anachronisms, relics from a corrupt and ugly era. Legendary *Tribune* columnist Mike Royko once famously described the two as "too dumb to tie their shoes."

The oldest of the Daley sons, Richie, won his dad's state senate seat in 1973 to little aplomb and even lower expectations. But working with his brother Bill, the two fashioned together a coalition of liberal Democrats, minorities, and — yes — good-government types, which elected Richie mayor in 1989 and has kept him there ever since. Their father's machine is dead, and they are clean.†

Bill Daley, in fact, had built such a stellar reputation, and been such an asset to Bill Clinton in his clean victory in Illinois in 1992, he was close to being named transportation secretary in early 1993. That is, until Clinton's self-imposed "cabinet that looks like America" quota led him to abandon Daley at the last minute in favor of Federico Peña.

Ever the loyal soldier, however, Daley agreed to come on board the Clinton administration during one of its hardest times — the August 1993 budget fight — to take on an even harder-seeming task: heading up the administration's then-floundering effort to get the controversial North

---

*The days following the nail-biter August 1948 runoff between LBJ and Gov. Coke Stevenson had plenty of vote buying and malfeasance on both sides. After a few days of this, however, LBJ was still behind by 157 votes. Until, six days after the election, in the town of Alice, 202 additional votes were found for LBJ in the fabled "Precinct Box 13." All of these votes, except for 2, went for LBJ, who thus won the election by 87 votes. These 202 voters had supposedly come to Precinct 13 and signed in using a different color ink than the previous 840 or so voters — and in alphabetical order. In a subsequent investigation, not one of the 202 voters claimed to have voted that day, and some even were, of course, not alive at the time of the election.

†When I interviewed them in December 2000, both Bartlit and his law partner Philip Beck — Illinois residents who worked on Bush's legal team — expressed deep admiration for both Richie and Bill Daley. Both used the word "cheap" to describe Republican potshots against Daley because of the sins of his father.

American Free Trade Agreement passed. Three months after he took the job, it was hard to imagine that it had ever been so questionable; thanks to Daley, NAFTA passed. Three years later, Clinton made him commerce secretary, where he earned marks for running a clean, effective, and bipartisan shop. He helped Republicans when they called, eliminated dozens of political appointee positions, cleaned up the trade mission shit and all that.

In June, Gore called Daley late one night to ask him to be his campaign chair — a job he'd turned down three times already. The controversial former chairman, Tony Coehlo, had made the tough decisions to chuck the deadwood, but Coehlo was sick and had to take leave. And, of course, Coehlo was doing a pretty crappy job. Daley got to work, to mixed reviews. Some thought that Coehlo fostered better communication among the staff, but Daley was a better face for the campaign than Coehlo — who was then under a criminal investigation run jointly by both the State Department inspector general and the Justice Department's public integrity section for financial dealings he'd made at the Expo '98 world's fair in Portugal.

Today it's tough to imagine Daley being brought on board the Gore campaign because of his stellar reputation. Rush Limbaugh calls him "Bugsy Daley," but it's not just talk radio that targets the man as dirty. On ABC's *Good Morning America* that morning, Daley appears — his comments far more serene than yesterday's — and is followed by former senator Bob Dole, the Kansas Republican whose own presidential run, in 1996, was the lamest GOP effort since Barry Goldwater.

"It's always good to hear from Bill Daley from Chicago, where even the dead vote on a regular basis for Democrats, and where Gore carried Chicago nine-to-one," Dole says. "Maybe we ought to take a look at Chicago, where the same ballots were used, to see if people understood that."

The ABC producer offers Daley the opportunity to return on air, to rebut the charge, but Daley demurs.

Still, he's not happy. "That motherfucker," Daley says. "That motherfucker. Talking about my father." His dad's been dead and buried for twenty-four years, for Chrissakes.

Daley hasn't slept in days, and he gets the game, he understands that his Thursday statement was hot, as he was told to make it, and he understands that he's going to take a hit for it. But going after his father is below the belt, he thinks.

"If they want to point to something in my background that they want to criticize and say, this is bad, and this guy's bad, and yada yada yada, fine," Daley thinks. "But all these people out there talking about Chicago and my dad and all that shit — it's some pretty chickenshit stuff." His mom's ninety-three years old, and she's sitting in Chicago watching this stuff on TV. "Don't let it bother you!" Momma Daley admonishes her son, reminding him of all the good things his father did. Still, Daley thinks, why does she have to deal with this thing?! Why does *she* need to hear this shit?

Oklahoma GOP governor Frank Keating* comes on Fox News Channel, railing against "the twenty-seven-inch-neck crowd . . . from Chicago . . . Boss Daley's boys" that he claims are intimidating canvassing boards. What the hell's Keating talking about?! "Twenty-seven-inch-neck crowd?!" What does that even mean?!

The problem is, Daley thinks, he can't respond without ratcheting it up. He's not about to call people who have flowed in from Oklahoma to help Bush, a bunch of Okies from a state that has nothing going on. And these are the same people who talk about how the tone of politics has gotten really horrible, and we gotta change that! Unbelievable!

And what's more, these guys are totally chickenshit, Daley thinks. Take Rep. Curt Weldon of Pennsylvania, the loud-mouthed former fire chief of Marcus Hook, who tells the *Washington Post,* "I will use every ounce of energy I have to deny the electors being seated if I believe the political will of the people was thwarted by the son of Mayor Daley of Chicago." After Daley sees this comment, he has an assistant call Weldon. All he wants to say is, "Hey, lookit, I hope twenty-six years from now, if you're dead and your kids are in this business, that somebody's not talking about you, and something you did or didn't do." He would be more than pleased to talk about the 1960 election, about the fact that the Democratic Party of Cook County offered to pay for a statewide recount and the Republicans said, "No way." He's prepared to tell Weldon that his dad was investigated for twenty-two years by every federal prosecutor that Republicans could sic on him — and Clinton thinks *he's* been investigated a lot?! — and no one could ever find anything on him.

Yeah, that's what Daley wants to tell Weldon. But Weldon doesn't return the call. So the next day, Daley has another call placed to Weldon's office. Still no return call. Then another. Then another. For eleven days in a row, Daley will call Weldon, and the bombastic Weldon will never take the call, nor will he even return it. "Chickenshit," Daley thinks.

*When it's all over, Keating will be denied a position in the Bush cabinet at least partially because of questions about *his* ethics, namely his acceptance of personal gifts of approximately a quarter of a million dollars from a financier.

The heft of Daley's ire will be reserved for Dole, however.

On Sunday, November 12, Sam Donaldson asks Dole, "If people's votes weren't counted fairly, you certainly wouldn't argue that they shouldn't be counted."

"Oh, I don't — I don't argue that, but where does it stop?" Dole says. "Are they going to — why don't they do all fifty states then? Why don't they go to Chicago, where they invented irregularities. You know, Bill Daley's an expert on irregularities."

As Daley watches this, one of his colleagues sneers and calls the World War II combat veteran and Viagra pitchman a "one-armed, limp-dicked motherfucker."

"You shouldn't attack somebody's war wound," Daley says.

"How about 'limp-dicked motherfucker'?" the colleague asks.

"That's different," Daley says. He himself refers to Dole as a "limp-dicked motherfucker" from then on. "We all knew he was dysfunctional from the waist down," Daley says, "now we know he's dysfunctional from the shoulders up, too."

But at least one of Daley's colleagues at the helm of the Gore recount effort notices something odd about Daley's reaction. After Daley's fury subsides, he gets more passive. He seems gun-shy. The Bush hardball tactics arouse in him a flash of anger, but then he retreats. Instead of fighting back even harder, he thinks, Daley pulls back. "It's like they threw a couple hard fast pitches at the head of our team captain, and he got less aggressive," the Gore chieftain will later say. In other words, according to this colleague and admirer of Daley, the GOP tactics worked.

Another close associate of Daley's will dispute this, saying that irrespective of his hot November 9 comments, Daley just tried to keep a cool head about both the ups and downs in the next month's battle. However, this associate adds, "Those people who went after his dad — he knows who every single one of them is."

★ ★ ★

Tucker Eskew arrives in Miami Friday, to work with Mindy Tucker in the Bush communications department, along with Scott McClellan and Ken Lisaius.

Eskew's presence is more telling than the others', however. He's kept relatively low-profile since he helmed the communications for Bush's nasty South Carolina primary campaign. And because when he flies in from Austin, he joins the three other chief Southern strategists who helped Bush score his ugly South Carolina primary win against McCain.

They are Bush's South Carolina clan: chief strategist Warren Tompkins, strategist Neal Rhoades, state director Heath Thompson, and Eskew — three of whom were thanked personally by Bush in his South Carolina victory speech. Each is a veteran of the hardscrabble ways of Southern politics, raised at the knee of legendary scumbag Lee Atwater. Which is a nice way of saying that there's little that they wouldn't do to get a candidate elected, especially when it comes to — at the very least — turning a blind eye to allied political mercenaries in the hinterlands who race-bait, slander, and dance around election law. After all, in the weeks leading up to the South Carolina primary on February 19, McCain suffered one of the dirtiest personal smear campaigns in modern American political history.

"We play it different down here," Tompkins once told reporters. "We're not dainty, if you get my drift. We're used to playin' rough."

Indeed. Push polls attacked McCain's personal life, exaggerated his role in the Keating savings-and-loan scandal, and disputed his war heroism. Leaflets slammed his wife, Cindy, for her past addiction to painkillers; Bush allies told South Carolinians that she had V.D., thanks to her husband. An e-mail from a Bob Jones University professor accused McCain of fathering children out of wedlock. A mysterious public action committee in favor of the Confederate flag — called "Keep It Flying" — sprang up overnight and slammed McCain in 250,000 leaflets. Phone calls and radio talk shows repeated that McCain had a black baby, had been driven insane while in a Vietnamese POW camp, was a lying, cheating whore.

Were there layers of people separating Bush from this scum? Of course; there always are. But Bush never ordered it stopped — why would he? It was working. Bush engaged in his own delightful activities, appearing at Bob Jones and telling a Christian radio station, "An openly known homosexual is somebody who probably wouldn't share my philosophy." He literally embraced a fringe Vietnam veteran activist who erroneously slammed McCain for doing nothing for veterans. He sank lower in the mud than any major presidential candidate in more than a generation.

"When the going gets tough for Governor Bush, he turns to the darker side of our party," a senior McCain adviser tells me, after I phone up and report that the four Palmetto State pols are now in Florida. "We saw that in South Carolina, and we see that today."

The McCain strategist sees where Tompkins, Eskew, Thompson, and Rhoades might be pushed into service. In Florida, as in South Carolina, Bush stalwarts have an interest in devaluing traditional Democratic voters.

Jews and blacks in Palm Beach and Broward Counties, for instance, who have complained about various ballot and voting irregularities, are dismissed by Bush surrogates and Baker every chance they get. Voters who misunderstood the butterfly ballot are called "confused," "stupid," or worse. "I'm sure that those Dixiecrats in South Carolina can rest assured that [Bush's South Carolina team] care deeply about the Holocaust survivors who accidentally voted for Pat Buchanan, or the black voters who were turned away at the polls," the McCain adviser says. "They can rest assured that they're being represented well."

★ ★ ★

In consultation with Bush, Ginsberg, Terwilliger, and the rest of the legal team, Baker gives the go-ahead to file a federal suit against the Broward, Miami-Dade, Palm Beach, and Volusia County canvassing boards for going ahead with hand recounts. After consulting with Ginsberg, Bush staffer Ted Cruz calls a former colleague, Michael Carvin, a Reagan administration Justice Department official, and tells him to get down here ASAP.

They're going to "go federal" — sue the canvassing boards in federal court. Screw the PR risks, they decide, characteristically. They want the *federalis* to step into the pending chaos and nip it all in the bud.

It's suggested that for jurisdictional reasons it makes more sense to have Florida voters suing the canvassing boards than just the Bush campaign. In Broward County, they enlist a Jeb ally, Fort Lauderdale attorney Georgette Sosa Douglas, who led that area's "Get Out the Vote" push. In Palm Beach, they get Ned Siegel, a big donor and multimillionaire real-estate developer. In Miami-Dade they snag Gonzalo Dorta, a Coral Gables lawyer who sits on the county judicial nominating commission, thus whispering the names of his favorite judge candidates to Jeb. They call Jim S. Higgins, chairman of the Martin County Republican Executive Committee. Hard to imagine Gore being able to network like this.

The other Floridians on the lawsuit constitute a somewhat motley crew. There's Carretta King Butler from Daytona Beach, a thrift-shop owner perhaps best known in the area for endorsing a city commissioner candidate who once was accused of trying to run over her daughter. Butler, one of the few African-American delegates at the Republican convention, speaks often about "the Holy Spirit" and maintains that she has a close relationship with the state party chairman, Al Cardenas, despite the fact that she refers to him as "Al Cardison."

There's also Dalton Bray, a former aide to Republican congressman Cliff Stearns and a Clay County sheriff who lost his reelection bid in 1992. And there's Roger Coverly from Seminole County, about whom the GOP lawyers know basically nothing. It doesn't matter.

★   ★   ★

Ted Olson, the man putting the federal case together, is a beloved member of the Washington GOP establishment. Known for his blond mane, his $1,500 Wilkes Bashford suits, and his pundit/author wife, Barbara, Olson plays an active role "at the heart" of "the vast right-wing conspiracy" — as he once joked at a meeting of the Federalist Society, a conservative legal organization.

One of former independent counsel Ken Starr's best friends, Olson helped ABC News negotiate an interview with Monica Lewinsky, and ran the Arkansas Project — a multimillion-dollar investigation into the life of President Clinton funded by right-wing billionaire Richard Mellon Scaife. Olson defended controversial Arkansas witness David Hale during the Senate hearings on Whitewater. He has also taken on some landmark conservative causes, defending the Virginia Military Institute in its failed attempt to remain all male and successfully representing four white students who sued the University of Texas Law School, claiming its affirmative-action policy denied them their rightful acceptance.

I call around, and while Olson is no less beloved for taking on Bush's fight, there are conservative lawyers in Washington who think the premise of Olson's fight — that the federal government should intrude on a local election — goes against conservative legal opinion. So why would he even take this on? Isn't it intellectually inconsistent? Does that even matter?

Olson's close friend Daniel Troy, a former clerk for Judge Robert Bork, a constitutional lawyer and an associate scholar at the American Enterprise Institute, explains it all. First, Olson is "sort of a lawyer of the right, clearly a Republican," not to mention one of the three co-chairmen of Lawyers for Bush-Cheney. Also, Troy says, Olson has "a very profound sense of fair play ... Ted is not as predictable as you might think. The left would caricature him as some true-blue conservative, but in his personal style he's more iconoclastic." An example, Troy says, is Olson's taking up the cause of fighting federal sentencing guidelines in the case of Los Angeles police officer Stacey Koon, one of the cops convicted of violating Rodney King's civil rights by beating him in March 1991, an argument Olson won before the U.S. Supreme Court in June 1997. On one level, defending a cop is almost always a conservative cause, and defending one of the guys who beat King isn't exactly left-wing. But federal sentencing guidelines have been a Republican charge for quite some time. So for Olson to have argued that a federal judge was appropriate in deviating from federal sentencing guidelines could be seen as unusual, especially for a lawyer considered by his peers to be a "Borkian originalist," Troy says. Or it could be seen as defending a bullying white cop who almost beat a black man to death. Depends.

Even more controversial — in GOP circles, at any rate — was Olson's defense of *New York Newsday* reporter Tim Phelps against a special prosecutor hired by the Senate to investigate leaks during the confirmation hearings for then–Supreme Court nominee Clarence Thomas. Phelps broke the story that Thomas had been accused of sexual harassment by law professor Anita Hill.

Not that defending Phelps cost Olson any friends. Olson's conservative bona fides are long established; he and Barbara, who wrote an anti–Hillary Clinton screed called *Hell to Pay,* are the Beautiful People among the Washington Right.

"He is good friends with just about everybody," Troy says, describing a scene this summer when Olson was at a reception for the Reagan Library in Philadelphia during the Republican National Convention. "Nancy Reagan was whispering things in his ear; Ted was chatting with Pete Wilson here, hugging Rudy Giuliani there," Troy says. "Everybody likes him, and that's saying a lot for someone as high profile and successful as he is."

Well, not everybody, of course. Olson's involvement in so many anti-Clinton activities (he even helped Paula Jones's attorneys practice for their case before the U.S. Supreme Court) raises the thought — in the minds of some Democrats, at least — that his presence on the Bush legal team really is evidence of a vast right-wing conspiracy.

"He's very competent, but he's very right-wing extreme," a Democratic strategist tells me. "It appears that the Republicans are employing the same extreme strategies that they've tried in the past six years. This kind of partisanship over pragmatism and strong policy has failed them in the past, and we feel it will fail them again in this case."

I dunno. Olson's pretty good. Call him a right-wing whacko at your own risk, I say.

★   ★   ★

At noon, Baker walks into the Florida senate hearing room. Somewhere in his journey from the Bush Building to here, "the velvet hammer" lost the velvet. Far from being the voice of caution and respect for the process that is his billing, Baker has overnight morphed into one of those irritating Type A Major League Baseball coaches whose machismo fades into girlish histrionics whenever his team starts losing. His latest urgent, impatient cause: to call this election for Bush even before all of the ballots are in.

As questionable and desperate as the Gorebies' complaints about unfair voting practices and their threats of lawsuits may seem, the Bush campaign meets the Gore camp's desperation and raises it: the final recount is not over, but they're telling everyone that it is. The overseas absentee ballots have until November 17 to be received and counted. But the Bushies are now starting to panic. They've decided on a strategy: discredit anything that happens from now on.

"Let me begin by saying that the American people voted on November seventh, and Governor George W. Bush won thirty-one states with a total of two hundred seventy electoral votes," Baker says. "The vote here in Florida was very close, and when it was counted, Governor Bush was the winner. Now, three days later, the vote in Florida has been recounted."

At this point, both assertions are essentially untrue. The first count, from Election Night, was official but uncertified, so Bush was never the official winner, since the state's automatic recount effort kicked in. As for the vote in Florida having been recounted, that's just not true.

"Now the Gore campaign is calling for yet another recount in selective and predominantly Democratic counties where there were *large unexplained* vote swings *in their favor* in the recount," Baker says.* He asserts that further recounts, especially by hand, will introduce further errors. "This frustrates the very reason why we have moved from hand-counting to machine-counting."

As for Palm Beach County, Baker says that there is "a rule of law" to be followed. The apparently confusing butterfly ballot was legal, set up by a Democrat and met with no objections before Election Day. He pooh-poohs the fact that some voters were apparently so flummoxed by the butterfly ballot that they voted twice.

---

*Actually, the "large unexplained shifts" have perfectly legit explanations: incompetence. In Palm Beach, it turns out that on Election Night, the card-reader computer operator inadvertently hit "cancel" instead of "accept" when reading the cards for West Palm Beach precinct 29-E. The mistake was corrected. In Pinellas County on Election Night, according to Republican elections supervisor Deborah Clark, one election worker counted 937 absentee ballots twice, and another completely missed counting 1,435 absentee ballots. So Gore was awarded an additional 417 votes from the Election Night count, and Bush lost 61. Nothing conspiratorial about either occurrence, however much making such a charge served Baker's duplications ends. Baker will never correct himself.

It's weird to have Baker here talking about the butterfly ballot and the elderly Jewish voters who mistakenly punched the chad for Buchanan. As ironic as is the presence of Daley, so is the presence of Baker, chief antagonist of the American Jewish community in the administration of President George H. W. Bush. Amid complaints from American Jews who found the Bush administration needlessly hostile to Israel, Baker is alleged to have said about Jews in 1992: "Fuck 'em. They didn't vote for us." In April of the same year, the executive director of the American-Israel Public Affairs Committee told attendees at the annual AIPAC conference that "we are most angry about the recent series of Washington leaks, accusations, alleged vulgarities, and the whole patronizing approach this administration's top officials have displayed toward Israel." He was talking about Baker.

One wonders how his presence is being received by the confused elderly Jews of Palm Beach.

Baker paints the whole dispute as sour grapes by Gore. "I understand personally . . . that it is frustrating to lose an election by a narrow margin," he says. "But it happens." He cites the case of Nixon in '60 and Gerald Ford's 1976 loss to Jimmy Carter. Both "accepted the vote for the good of the country," Baker says, though it is also true that neither Nixon nor Ford had his election come down to one state's disputed and 300-some-vote margin of victory.

It is at this moment that I realize I've got to stop counting on the truth coming out of any of these guys' mouths. These guys — Daley and Coffey and Christopher, too — are now starting to piss me off, and I wonder what the rest of the country thinks. How can you say these things with a straight face? Baker, in particular, is grating. How can he state that Bush won the machine recount? Nothing's official yet. So I raise my hand.

"Are you basing your assertion that Bush won the recount on the Associated Press's completely unofficial tally?" I ask.

"I'm making the assertion that Governor Bush won the recount. You all know what the numbers are," he says.

"But that's not the official —"

"Wait a minute," Baker says. "Just a minute. Do you want an answer, or do you want to make a speech?"

No, I don't want to make a speech, I think. But I would like somebody, please, to give me a straight answer. At this point, I've been in Tallahassee for only a day and a half, but it's already crystal clear that both Bush and Gore are behaving in the exact same respective charmless ways that made me hate covering their nakedly ambitious, morally ambiguous, and essentially empty campaigns this past year. No wonder the country couldn't make up its fucking mind.

"Let me say this," Baker goes on. "We know why the certifications have been delayed from these very same counties where we have these large unexplained shifts toward the other campaign. If the purpose here is to delay and endless wrangling, and recount after recount after recount, that game can be played.

"It is important, ladies and gentlemen, that there be some finality to the election process. What if we insisted on recounts in other states?" Like Wisconsin or Iowa. But when we ask about those states a minute later, he says that the Bush campaign hasn't eliminated challenges in those states from the realm of possibility. A recount is already taking place in New Mexico, which Gore slimly won.

Black is white. White is black. 2 + 2 = 5.

★   ★   ★

Whouley's deputy at the DNC, John Giesser, thirty-six, arrived at his Palm Beach hotel at around 2 A.M. Predictably, Giesser's from Boston — he met Whouley while working for Dukakis in '88. In Delray, Giesser meets with Jack Corrigan, another member of the Boston crew. Corrigan knows this shit firsthand. He was an assistant district attorney working under Norfolk County district attorney William Delahunt. In 1996, Delahunt ran for congress and lost in the primary by 266 votes to a rich environmentalist named Philip Johnston. A recount brought Johnston's margin of victory down to 175 votes. Then Delahunt's team — led by P. J. O'Sullivan, now also in Palm Beach for Gore — noticed that 1,540 people who cast Democratic ballots in areas where one would think Delahunt would have a strong showing didn't vote in the congressional race. Those undervotes were, at the time, called "blanks." A month later, a superior court ruled that Commonwealth law requiring elections officials to gauge the "intent of the voter" meant that 946 "dimpled" ballots were actual votes. Delahunt was awarded the primary win and went on to win that November.

Corrigan's not the only guy on the ground here who knows punch-card ballots and dimples. Boston attorney Dennis Newman, who represented Delahunt's opponent in the 1996 dispute, is also down here at Whouley's request. Then, of course, there's Chris Sautter, who, with Jack Young, worked on a 1989 gubernatorial recount in Virginia, when Lieutenant Governor Doug Wilder's victory over Attorney General J. Marshall Coleman wasn't official until forty-three days after Election Night. Last year Virginia was for Recount Lovers, as Young and Sautter worked on recounts for state senator (37-vote victory Election Night, 39-vote victory post-recount), Fairfax school board seat (77 votes Election Night, 79 post-recount), and Broad Run district supervisor (9 votes Election Night, 12 votes post-recount).

It's easier to be ahead, of course.

Florida law has the same standard as Massachusetts — "intent of the voter" — but it leaves it up to the canvassing boards to make such judgments. So, for these guys, the plan is to have the four canvassing boards use the most liberal interpretations possible, so that as many as possible of the predominantly Democratic counties' undervotes break in the same proportion as the vote in each county.

The Boston Boys, and other lawyers on the Gore team, will cite the *Delahunt* standard and the Supreme Court of Massachusetts *Delahunt* precedent — which will be, at the very least, an imperfect comparison, if not a completely disingenuous one, because Delahunt-Johnston was the *only* race on that particular ballot. So, in *Delahunt*, the idea that voters went to the polls and didn't cast a vote for anyone at all was, of course, less believable than the notion that Florida voters would go to the polls and not cast a vote for either Bush or Gore. Counting those Massachusetts dimples as votes was far more logical than counting every nick and scratch on Florida ballots.

But no matter. Applying the *Delahunt* standard will bring Gore more than enough votes to win, the Boston Boys conclude. And if they get the hand recounts going, and with the standard they want, and they do so quickly, Gore's name will be at the bottom of the MSNBC screen next to the number of votes by which *he* leads Bush. "To get there the fastest and get the mostest votes, to paraphrase General Forrest," Young will later say.

This is what they've been sent here to do.

★ ★ ★

In Austin, Bush sets up a White House-esque photo op, sitting in the governor's mansion with some of his advisers. "I'm here with Secretary Cheney; Larry Lindsey, my chief economic adviser; Condi Rice, my national security adviser; Andy Card, who you know; and Clay Johnson," he says. "There was a count on Election Night, and there's been a recount in Florida," he continues. "And I understand there are still votes to be counted. But I'm in the process of planning, in a responsible way, a potential administration.

There's been a series of ongoing meetings that the secretary and I have had on a variety of subjects, so that should the verdict that has been announced thus far be confirmed, we'll be ready.

"Larry in particular is going to talk about the markets, and Condi is going to bring us up-to-date on a lot of matters. There's issues in Israel right now that I'm looking forward to hearing about."

Bush refers all questions about Florida to Baker. Reporters don't ask him any tough ones, and the cameras go CLICK-CLICK-CLICK.

★   ★   ★

Shortly after 1 P.M., the Democratic big guns walk into the Florida Senate hearing room to assert a few points of their own. As the Bushies have had their volume turned up to a shrill decibel level, the Gorebies by necessity continue low-tempo, low-key. They've gone through further legal discussions and are off the butterfly ballot deal, at least for now, though Berger is still working with Whouley and Fowler in Palm Beach to secure as many voter affidavits as his team is able for possible future use, maybe in a contest. They're trying to separate the wheat from the chaff; the thousands of complaints Gore staffers have recorded from phone interviews range from the serious to whiny to the just plain silly:

"Confused by 2 holes," reads the complaint of Fedora Horowitz of Boynton Beach. "Thought 1 for Gore and 1 for Lieberman, so accidentally voted for Buchanan. No one would help her because there were too many people in line."

"Not enough staff. Small print. Many, many people were very upset. Lines were very long, seniors on walkers, etc., were waiting in long lines," reads the phone complaint of John and Shirley Birk of Coconut Creek.

"Rumored that Bush would win w/absentee ballots," reports Maldine Bush of Miami. "Overheard 2 men talking outside a bank a few days prior to election."

"Marine in Vietnam, PSYCHO!! Hates Cubans, ANSCESTORS on *Mayflower*. If we don't follow on Cuban Corruption, he will 'have to get [his] automatic weapons and take care of us!! . . .'" writes another Democratic phone interviewer.

Bob Bauer, a D.C. election lawyer, has been brought in to check it out. A Bradley supporter (he even played the role of Gore in Bradley debate prep) who is married to Bradley's former communications director, Anita Dunn, Bauer quickly comes to the conclusion that the butterfly ballot case lacks legal merit. It will be kept on the table until Thanksgiving, but by Wednesday, November 15, Klain will consider that flying insect to have been swatted.

Now they have new talking points, off the litigation-a-go-go from yesterday. One, they say, this isn't about them, it's about the people of Florida. Two, they say serenely, everything's fine, everything's good, this is a perfectly normal situation, no big deal. Three, they say, it's the other side that's behaving like crazed banshees. And four, they say that they want to get this over with as soon as possible, too — even though their actions speak otherwise.

At the press conference they're led by Daley, who today kind of reminds me of The Thing from Marvel Comics' Fantastic Four. Behind him strolls a lovely-double-breasted-suit-wearing Warren Christopher.

The recount has shown, so far, "a considerable narrowing of the margin between Vice President Gore and Governor Bush," Daley says. "When one considers the number of ballots yet to arrive from Americans overseas, and presumably mostly men and women in the military, then it seems very clear that the outcome here in Florida remains in doubt, as it will for several more days."

Daley says that in the last day, three of Florida's sixty-seven counties have agreed to hand-count their ballots, as opposed to machine-counting them, "at least on a sample basis." The hand-count request was made "because of oddities in the computer vote totals. I hope all Americans agree that the will of the people, not a computer glitch, should select our next president."

Daley puts on a happy face, acknowledging that this whole mess — particularly its wait — is "frustrating" not only to the world, but "to all of us in both campaigns." He says he hopes "that our friends in the Bush campaign would join us in our efforts to get the fairest and most accurate vote count here in Florida."

But Daley also slams these "friends." "Calls for a declaration of a victor before all the votes are accurately tabulated are inappropriate," he says. "Waiting is unpleasant for all of us. But suggesting that the outcome of a vote is known before all the votes are properly tabulated" — as the Bush campaign repeatedly has done, most notably just minutes before in the same exact place by Baker — "is inappropriate." He says that everyone should "carefully measure all of our words, recognizing the high stakes involved in these deliberations."

But it's doubtful that the words will stay measured, especially since Daley makes it clear that the Gore campaign's take on "all the votes" being "accurately tabulated" would include the tens of thousands of nullified or mistakenly cast ballots in Palm Beach County. "Our legal team has concluded that the ballot in Palm Beach County was unlawful, it was complained about on Election Day, a complaint that was implicitly acknowledged by the elections supervisor who put out a flier on Election Day warning about the problems."

AAARGH! LePore put out this flier only because the Democrats asked for it.

When will this all be over?

"As soon as the proper procedures would allow it," Daley says, elliptically. "All of us want this as quick as possible to be over, there's no question about that."

Sure there is. There are *plenty* of questions about that.

For the Gorebies, "as quick as possible" means as soon as every Democratic Floridian has gotten the chance to vote, and vote accurately, even if he screwed up his vote because of a confusing ballot. But for the Bushies, "as soon as possible" means yesterday. Final recount, final shmecount.

As the briefing winds on, Christopher calls the Bush campaign's bluff that they might challenge Iowa or Wisconsin or New Mexico. Bring it on, the old man says. "The team of Governor Bush has every right to consider challenges in other states if they think they have an obligation to do so, and perhaps they have an obligation to do so if they regard the count as inaccurate," offers the former secretary of state.

"What we are seeing here is democracy in action," Daley says.

Is it? Yuck.

6

"You fucking sandbagged me."

All right," says Judge Charles Burton. "Good morning, everyone. If we could have quiet in here, we can get through this meeting as quickly as possible and get to the matter at hand. Today is November 11th, 2000."

With LePore and Democratic commissioner Carol Roberts, Burton is supervising both a second machine recount of the county's 462,657 ballots upon request of the Bush team, and a 1 percent hand recount upon request of the Democrats. Not surprisingly, the Democrats — or, more specifically, Nick Baldick — picked three patches of land that couldn't be more Democratic if they were located in Hyannis Port — precincts 193 and 193-E in Boca Raton and 162-E of Delray Beach.

As stacked with Gore votes as the three precincts are, they still don't add up to 1 percent of the county; vote-wise, they're still 300 or so votes shy of 4,620. So the canvassing board itself picks the first county with a vote total — 349 — roughly the size of the debt, precinct 6-B in suburban Palm Beach Gardens.

The word goes forth, and the ballots are ordered in. Teams of three counters apiece, with two observers — one D, one R — per table, set up. Some of the observers want to be able to handle the ballots.

"There's no one at any time who is going to touch the ballots," Burton says, all business. "There's going to be law enforcement in here, and they are going to be instructed as to that. We've got the hand slappers here."

Burton's already seen enough from the Democrat and Republican attorneys to know that this is not a courtroom where he is the king. This is something far more bizarre and chaotic, something from the messy world of politics. For that reason he wants the observers to keep their traps shut.

"Their job is to observe, period. If they participate in the process, we will be here until God knows when.

"We are not going to be here until three weeks from Sunday to decide," he says in words that will prove awfully prophetic. Yes, the counters won't be here three weeks from Sunday. Instead, the counters will actually be here *two* weeks from Sunday. But of course, nobody knows that right now. Right now they think it might all be over soon.

★   ★   ★

So fearful are the Bushies of what a hand recount might bring, they actually seek a temporary restraining order against the four Florida canvassing boards, as if Bush were an abused ex-girlfriend and the canvassing boards drunk and deranged stalkers.

In a brief put together by Olson, Michael Carvin, and the Bush crew, the Florida "voters" — real-estate tycoon Ned Siegel, et al. — on Saturday, November 11, ask Judge Donald Middlebrooks of the District Court for the Southern District of Florida to stop the hand recounts. The brief gets relatively little notice from the media, since even conservative legal scholars wonder where there could possibly be a federal issue in all of this. But in terms of what will eventually happen in the whole grim saga, it's as if the brief were written by Nostradamus, with a possible assist from Machiavelli.

Olson argues that the federal government needs to stop the hand recount because of violations to the 1st and 14th Amendments to the U.S. Constitution. Any such hand recount, without a showing of fraud, corruption, or coercion, would "impermissibly impede the plaintiffs' constitutional right to have their votes certified in a uniform and even-handed manner.

"The votes of citizens across the State of Florida will be unconstitutionally diluted if the Defendants conduct a manual recount of only selected ballots in portions of four heavily Democratic counties," the brief goes on. "Under Florida's scheme for discretionary manual recounts, the question whether a vote is subject to a recount and how it is counted is left to the unfettered discretion of the county canvassing boards and will vary throughout the state.

"Simply stated," Olson's brief continues, "under Florida's scheme, *identical* ballots in two different counties will be treated differently. For example, where there is a partial punch for one candidate, a ballot may be counted where the county board has decided to conduct a manual recount and, pursuant to wholly subjective perceptions, has determined that the voter 'intended' to vote for the candidate. An identical ballot in another county will not be counted for that candidate in a county that has refused to engage in the manual recount."

This, Olson argues, violates the equal protection clause of the Constitution since Florida's county-by-county recount laws — which vary due to "the arbitrary and unfettered discretion of government officials" — violate the right of voters to be treated equally.

Olson includes other arguments that will not fare so well with the test of time. Having government officials implementing recount procedures that are "pervasively arbitrary" violates due process, he says. Even giving the government officials such discretion is a violation of the 1st Amendment, he goes on.

Carvin himself, who hoisted much of the 3 U.S.C. 5 argument* into the brief late last night with Columbia Law School professor John Manning, thinks Olson's equal protection argument is something of a reach. Not until there's a final count can this charge be credibly made, Carvin thinks.

But the brief — signed by Olson, Terwilliger, Marcos Jimenez (Frank's older brother), Barry Richard, and Ben Ginsberg (with his name spelled "Ginsburg") — will end up proving to be a document that the Democrats perhaps should pay more attention to. Not the courtroom lawyers so much as Whouley's Boston ground troops. At this point, though, since not one of the four counties has even begun its hand recount, the GOP complaints seem like, well, baseless whining.

★   ★   ★

Hours after the motion for a restraining order is filed before Middlebrooks, Klain phones up the Cambridge, Massachusetts, home of Harvard Law School professor Lawrence Tribe, like Olson one of the highest-regarded Supreme Court attorneys in the country. Klain is a friend and former student of Tribe's, and he and Tribe's wife, Carolyn, were once co-chairs of the unsuccessful Senate campaign of Rep. Ed Markey, D-Mass. Tribe recommended Klain to Justice White for his clerkship.

---

*United States Code, Title 3, Section 5 states that if "any State shall have provided, by laws enacted prior to" Election Day a way to settle any "controversy or contest" of the election "by judicial or other methods or procedures" and the shit's all come down and been decided by six days before the electors are to meet, December 18, that law "shall be conclusive." The argument can be made, of course, that what's going on is just "judicial or other methods or procedures," but the Bushies will show an interesting propensity to omitting that clause from their briefs.

Klain asks Tribe if he has any ideas on how to deal with the federal attack. Before Tribe knows it, there are fifteen or so people listening to him via speaker phone, as he finds fallacies in the Bush team's federal case.

The substantive complaint hammers the whole idea of manual recounts, Tribe observes. But this is a weak argument, he says. These counts take place under the watchful eyes of observers from both parties, and even sometimes the media. In some ways, they're much more accurate, not less. He goes on, poking holes in the due process argument, the equal protection argument, the whole idea of whether there is a federal issue at stake. The call soon ends.

Soon enough, Klain calls back.

"The Vice President would really like it if you could get on a plane immediately to argue this for us," he says. "We'll find a charter plane for you if you want."

Tribe says that he'll need a minute to confer with Carolyn, his chief adviser. She usually discourages him from taking on new projects, since he's so overextended. But this time she's on board. "This could determine who becomes the next president," she says. "The issue of making sure that all the votes get counted is awfully close to what you've spent your life struggling for, in terms of constitutional rights. I mean, if you don't do this, I don't know what you would do."

Tribe arrives in Palm Beach that evening. He flies commercial; the charter flight would have gotten him down to Florida later. Upon arriving, he hears that arguments have been scheduled for Monday.

★   ★   ★

The Volusia canvassing board changed its mind yesterday, and as soon as it finishes tabulating its 400 or so write-in votes today, it will commence with a full recount of its 184,019 ballots.

Broward's 1 percent sample hand recount will commence on Monday, and on Tuesday the members of the Miami-Dade canvassing board will vote to see if they'll go ahead with their test 1-percent hand recount.

The only action in South Florida today, therefore, is at the Governmental Center in West Palm Beach, where Team Gore's crucial Step One — a hand recount of 1 percent of a county's ballots — has begun.

LePore is numb, with butterfly ballots in her stomach. Ever since Tuesday, she's been unable to sleep — she dozes in and out. Her eyes are bloodshot. She has no appetite, and when she does try to eat, she can't hold it down, one way or another.

The other two members of the canvassing board are Carol Roberts and Judge Burton. Both the Republican and Democratic lawyers on-site have been sizing them both up.

Roberts is an unrepentant partisan Democrat, from the proclamations emanating from her frequently flapping mouth down to the Gore-Lieberman bumper sticker on the front of her Lexus SUV. She's always been ambitious; she smokes MOREs, and she's always wanted more, too, from the day she got engaged to a twenty-nine-year-old doctor at the age of sixteen (unbeknownst to him), to the impulsive beginning of her political career.

That began when the mother of six learned that the two West Palm Beach city commissioners were running unopposed. This bothered her. She drove down to City Hall and decided to run against the one she'd never heard of before. And she beat him. Other seeds of ambition were planted. She was elected to the county commission in 1986.

Blond and pink-lipsticked, Roberts is known as a fairly effective commissioner, with smarts that belie her lack of a college degree — if also with an ego that sometimes outmatches her talents. Her office is decorated with photographs of her with Bill, her with Hillary, her with Burt Reynolds. Her home is the same way — with Gregory Peck, Geraldine Ferraro, Ted Kennedy, Don Shula. When she was elected president of the Florida Association of Counties, she was thrown a big party. By Carol Roberts.

"I'm accustomed to being vocal," she would later say. "I don't mind having an argument if I think I'm right. It's part of my personality, it's what I taught my kids: stand up for what you believe in." The fact that two of her six kids are Republicans is proof that they took her advice to heart, she would argue.

So the Republican lawyers, led by local rich boy Miami attorney Mark Wallace, thirty-two, feel they know right off the bat where Roberts is coming from.

Burton's a different breed of cat.

They know he's a Democrat. But, on the other hand, he was appointed to the bench in May by Jeb. So, in Florida terms, he's complicated.

Gray-haired with icy blue eyes and a wattle of neck chub that practically swallows his chin, Burton's a Newton, Massachusetts, boy who moved down to Florida to follow in his older brother's footsteps and attend law school. He was with the state's attorney's office from the time he received his J.D. on, save for five years after he and his bro set out a shingle of their own in 1990.

Burton liked prosecuting, he liked nailing murderers, liked running the crimes-against-children unit, liked taking loser cases, because he found them challenging. His highest-profile case had been the 1987 trial against fast-living ex–National Hockey Leaguer Brian Spencer, who had been accused of kidnapping and murdering the son of a Palm Beach realtor who was a client of Spencer's hooker girlfriend. Burton lost the case in October 1987; Spencer was shot to death the next June.

Burton was picked to be on the canvassing board almost the same way he heard that Jeb had picked him to be a judge: a short, surprising, and very brief phone call came in and changed his life forever. In May, after being passed over twice for an appointment to the bench, Jeb phoned up.

"Mr. Burton, Jeb Bush, how you doing?"

"Um, fine," Burton said, not sure if it was really Jeb, pretty sure that it was a friend playing a prank.

"So you want to be a judge?" Jeb asked. Burton said yes. "All right, well, I just wanted to let you know that I'm appointing you to county court." Burton thanked him. His first day was May 8.

Three months and change later, at the end of August, Burton got a call from the secretary to the county's chief judge, Walter N. Colbath, Jr. The judge who normally sat on the canvassing board was on the ballot this year, so he had to recuse himself, and Colbath wanted Burton to take his place.

"That's fine," Burton said. "What do I do?" Burton didn't even know what the canvassing board was.

"You deal with elections stuff," the secretary said. It's no big deal, she said. "Go talk to Theresa LePore, and she'll give you a little background on what you'll need to do."

"That's fine," the easygoing Burton replied.

By today, Saturday, Burton has already had to do much more than he'd ever anticipated. There was the first machine count, which resulted in a net of 643 more Gore votes. There was the matter of speaking to the press, which he'd been used to in much smaller numbers — maybe a reporter or two from the local paper during a murder trial or something — though nothing like the ravenous wolf packs now camped outside the Governmental Center. But someone had to do it, and he was sent out to do so by county officials who were afraid of what Roberts might say and sympathetic to the shell-shocked LePore.

At 2:03 P.M., a bunch of bureaucrats carry in three silver metal suitcases containing the 4,627 ballots.

The sorting begins, as does the kibbitzing.

"You are going to have to leave if you tell anybody anything," Roberts says to an observer who's caught speaking to a sorter.

"Here is the deal," Burton adds. "'Observer' means you observe. That means the sense of your eyes. If you have a problem, write it down." Hands go up. A cell phone rings.

"Who has a phone?!" Roberts asks. "OUT!"

In interpreting just what permutation of incompletely punched-out piece of chad constitutes a vote, LePore had informed Roberts and Burton about a guideline that the board — under Jackie Winchester — had adopted in 1990, which ruled that ballots with partially punched chad could be counted as votes.

There's the "hanging chad," she explains, in which the chad is hanging on to the ballot with one corner; the "swinging door chad," in which the chad is connected by two corners; and the "tri-chad," in which the chad is connected in three corners, with one corner punched out. All of these are votes according to the 1990 standard. A "dimpled chad," however, in which all four corners are attached but there's a puffed indentation in the middle of the chad, does not count as a vote.

Nevertheless, when the board members start to examine the undervote and disputed ballots that afternoon, they seem to abandon the 1990 precedent. They begin holding ballots up to the light to see if any light can be seen through the chad — what they call the "sunlight" or "sunshine" standard. This meets the aggressive objection of Mark Wallace, the lead Republican attorney at their table.

Wallace has been on the Bush program since 5 A.M. or so Wednesday morning, when Jillian Inmon, executive director of the Bush-Cheney state effort, roused him from slumber in his Coconut Grove penthouse and convinced him to hop in his black BMW and get to Palm Beach to supervise the machine recount. After graduating from the University of Miami ('89) and University of Miami Law School ('92), Wallace worked at his venture-capitalist daddy's law firm for a bit before he took a leave to serve as an aide on the gubernatorial race of this cool guy Jeb he knew from Hurricanes games.

To Wallace, a couple things seem clear right from the get-go. One: Carol Roberts is on the other side. Two: the canvassing board has no idea what it's doing, or how to do it. And of course he's not exactly about to keep his opinions secret.

On the early afternoon of Wednesday, Coddy Johnson and Kevin Murphy — fresh from Austin — had met him in the Governmental Center parking lot. "Guys," he said upon their arrival, "it's a little crazy in there." It was a line they would repeat to each other frequently throughout the Palm Beach hand recount; and it was chaos they would use to their advantage throughout the Palm Beach ordeal.

Not surprisingly, Roberts and Burton take a fairly immediate dislike to him. They think that he's there to tie things up, to delay, to gum up the works. Wallace himself will refer to "the four-corner offense" — a reference to a strategy by various college basketball teams to run out the clock by leisurely throwing the ball around, eating up valuable seconds — though he will do so by way of denying that he's doing it.

And not only is Wallace slowing things down, but he can't even figure out a subtle way to do his damage. Wallace sits so close to Burton his knee lightly hits the back of Burton's chair. At another point, Wallace's chin makes contact with the back of Burton's left shoulder. Mouth agape, objecting to myriad ballots on which he says he doesn't see votes, Wallace very early gets on Burton's nerves.

"I'm going to voice my objection," Wallace says, when Roberts holds a ballot up to the light.

Again and again. Over and over. If Burton got a dollar for every time Wallace objected, before the day was done he could've afforded one of those fancy suits that Warren Christopher and Ted Olson favor. Though the bespoke pinstripe isn't quite South Florida style.

Fort Lauderdale attorney Ben Kuehne, Wallace's Democratic counterpart, also chimes in. He clearly wants the board to use the most liberal interpretation of the sunlight rule as they can. Kuehne's backed by three of Whouley's Boston Boys, Dennis Newman, Jack Corrigan, and David Sullivan. "Turn the card over," Kuehne says at one point — since light can sometimes be seen if the ballot is held at a different angle.

Wallace gets mad. The board, made up of three Democrats, is listening to Kuehne more than to him, he says.

Roberts insists that she was already holding the card at different angles, that Kuehne's advice was redundant.

"You're injecting a partisan flavor to the process," Wallace says. "It's not right."

At around 3:45, a ballot is held up that has light shining through the no. 3 chad — a Bush vote.

"There is light through there," Wallace says.

"I see light," Roberts agrees.

"Thank you, Carol," Wallace responds.

Roberts shows Burton a dimpled chad, sans light. "Somebody attempted to push something," she says.

"Even though you see someone attempted to do something, you see no light," he says.

Wallace tells them to be careful handling the ballots. Bending them could cause chad to improperly fall from the ballot, he cautions.

Burton sighs heavily.

"Yes on a number three right here," Burton says, pointing to a Bush vote.

"Woohoo!" Wallace cheers.

The canvassing board realizes that it's now being more lenient with the sunlight standard than it was at the beginning of the precinct's count. The board agrees to look at some of the earlier ballots with the newer, more lenient standard.

"That is completely not fair," Wallace says. "It's another recount."

"It's a changing standard, I suppose," Burton allows.

"Light is light," Wallace says.

"We're here to make sure everyone gets a fair chance," Roberts says.

But to Wallace, even if the board applies the same new standard — what he refers to when he objects that "the sunshine rule doesn't apply to a micron of light!" — it's pretty clear what's going on. Palm Beach County went for Gore over Bush 67 percent to 33 percent. Even if the pinhole votes are fairly distributed, that's still a 2-to-1 Gore advantage.

His objections reach a fever pitch. Sometimes. Burton shows him a ballot that appears to be unpunched. "The only argument would be right here," he says to Wallace, pointing to the Bush no. 3 slot. "That's no argument, that's light," a suddenly agreeable Wallace says.

Funny how that works.

At 4:25 P.M., Burton lets out an enormous bearlike yawn.

"We all feel the same way," an elections worker jokes.

★   ★   ★

In Austin, Bush spokeswoman Mindy Tucker is watching the count on TV.

"How ridiculous," she thinks. "I can't sit here and watch this. This is the most ridiculous thing! Everyone keeps saying: no one wants to see sausage made. This is proof of that."

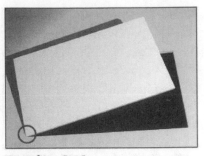

Chad are the perforated rectangles that are punched out of the ballots

Ballot card

Actual chad size ■

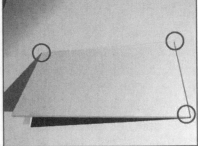

Hanging chad are attached to the ballot by one corner.

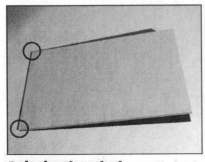

Swinging door chad are attached to the ballot by two corners.

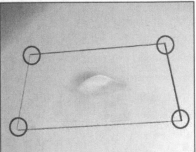

Tri-chad are attached to the ballot by three corners.

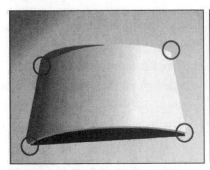

Pregnant chad bulge, but all four corners are still attached.

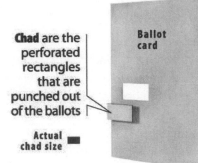

Dimpled chad are indented, but all four corners are still attached.

And that's the trick, she realizes. "If America sees this, everything we said about hand counts is being illustrated on national TV," she thinks. "This is playing right into our hands."

★   ★   ★

You know this meeting at the vice president's residence at the Naval Observatory, or "NavObs," is important, because Joe Lieberman's being asked to attend it on the Shabbos. His chief aide, Tom Nides, is sent to fetch him at a friend's house, where he's eating lunch after attending synagogue. During the campaign, Lieberman had said he would work on the Sabbath only if it were a matter of national importance, never if it was just a matter of politics. Clearly, Lieberman has no question in his mind as to which category this meeting falls into.

When Lieberman and Nides arrive, the meeting begins in Gore's dining room. Gore's there with Tipper, Daley, Christopher, Bob Shrum, Carter Eskew, with Klain and some of the Florida lawyers on the phone from Tallahassee, Fabiani from Nashville.

Daley's happy. The Bushies didn't file any recount requests within the seventy-two-hour period. It's a victory! Their attitude is clearly, "We ain't playing, period," but maybe that will be a mistake by them.

Gore suggests that he go on TV that night to give a simple message. Even though lots of people have clearly been disenfranchised by some irregularities at the polls, he will willingly back off any challenges about them — butterfly ballots, African-Americans kept from voting this way or the other — if Bush goes along with a statewide hand recount. It can be over in a matter of days, and it will be winner take all, and the matter will be settled.

Fabiani thinks that it's a good idea, but he wants to hold off on it until Sunday late afternoon. This is maybe the ultimate speech of your political career, Fabiani says. Doing it Saturday night, when few people are watching, and when it's too late to get into the Sunday newspapers, doesn't make sense. The speech still has to be written, there's no forum in which to give the speech yet, for such a major speech let's do it right. Let's do it after the football games Sunday afternoon.

Gore agrees.

But Klain, Lieberman, and others begin talking him out of the idea. You can't do this, they say. It's so early in the process; we don't know what would happen in a butterfly ballot lawsuit. We don't know if something terribly egregious happened on Tuesday with black voters that we have yet to hear about. You can't give these things up without knowing what the details are.

"I've been a lawyer, I was attorney general of Connecticut," Lieberman says. "One thing you learn when you're in those positions is you don't take anything off the table until you know all the facts. And we don't know all the facts."

Daley's a big basher of the butterfly ballot suit. It sucks, sure, but there's no remedy. "People get screwed every day," he says. He and Christopher are in favor of the four-county hand recounts.

But as the hours pass, Gore's idea to call for a statewide recount will be pretty much scrapped. Fabiani will spend the rest of his life kicking himself for not letting Gore give the speech, for not arguing more vociferously against the lawyers' demand that nothing be ruled out.

★　★　★

Kerey Carpenter, thirty-nine, an attractive strawberry-blond, is a litigator and assistant general counsel for Secretary of State Katherine Harris. On Friday, she was sent to Palm Beach because of all the butterfly ballot litigation that names Harris as a co-defendant along with LePore. Before she left, Carpenter was given a silver "Division of Elections" badge by division of elections director Clay Roberts, one she clips inside her wallet. She flashes it around, gets in everywhere she wants.

Kuehne wonders just who the hell she is. Initially he thinks she's the county attorney, Denise Dytrych, since Carpenter walked out with the canvassing board from the elections office into the counting room. And Carpenter almost immediately arouses Kuehne's suspicions when she offers advice about something innocuous, with an air of precision, that Kuehne doesn't think is right. Kuehne asks the Boston boys just who she is. They don't know. Newman, too, has been wondering who the "mystery woman" is. She's obviously important, because she has access to everyone.

Kuehne sidles up to Leon St. John, an assistant county attorney.

"Who is that?" he asks.

"She's one of the elections lawyers," St. John says.

"Oh, she's with the county?" Kuehne asks.

"No, she's with the state," St. John replies.

It hits Kuehne: this woman is with Harris's office.

From then on he views every word from her mouth from this perspective: Carpenter is from the Jeb Bush administration sent to help Jeb's big brother. She's a political hack who has little knowledge of election law, he thinks. She's giving political advice, not legal advice, he thinks. He's shocked to see the preeminent role she plays. She goes back with the canvassing board members when they go to their offices during breaks, as if she's the canvassing board's outside counsel. This, Kuehne realizes, is not good.

At about 5:00 P.M., the board decides to break. Roberts needs her MOREs, and Burton needs his Marlboro Lights.

In the small outdoor dining area adjacent to the Governmental Center, Wallace approaches Burton and implores him to stop adhering to the more lenient standard. He thinks the Democrats are stealing the election by finding votes where no votes are to be found. It's inappropriate, he thinks. He hadn't had a problem when they started with the sunshine rule, because he'd assumed it was going to be applied as it had been applied in the past in other counties. But it was ridiculous now, the things they were calling votes.

I don't think you can do this, Wallace says to Burton. You're a judge, you're a reasonable man. "Please," he says to Burton. "Think about it. Your actions are going to be judged for a long time."

Burton doesn't say anything. Wallace walks away.

Carpenter also approaches Burton, taking a drag on one of her Benson & Hedges DeLuxe Ultra Lights and talks to Burton about her office's position on when a full hand recount is allowable under the statute. It's supposed to be only when there's machine error, she says. Not voter error, which is how her office regards undervotes.

During this break, Burton tracks down county attorney Leon St. John. "I'm a little uncomfortable about this," he tells St. John, about the standards they were using before the break. Some of the chad they were counting as votes weren't even dimpled, they merely had a little pinprick of visible light. Burton thinks it's absurd, ridiculous. He doesn't think they're following the 1990 standard. "Bring it up," St. John says.

In the counting room, no one knows where Burton is. Time passes. Soon enough, he returns with something to share: the 1990 standard.

"The instructions in the voting machine are as follows:

TO VOTE, HOLD THE PUNCH STRAIGHT UP AND PUNCH DOWN *THROUGH* THE CARD NEXT TO THE PREFERRED CANDIDATE'S NAME OR ISSUE POSITION. (Emphasis added.)

"The guidelines assume that these directions have been understood and followed. Therefore, a chad that is hanging or partially punched *may* be counted as a vote, since it is possible to punch through the card and still not totally dislodge the chad. But a chad that is fully attached, bearing only an indentation, should not be counted as a vote. An indentation may result from a voter placing the stylus in the position, but not punching through. Thus, an indentation is not evidence of intent to cast a valid vote."

ADOPTED BY THE NOVEMBER 6, 1990, CANVASSING BOARD:

Robert Gross, County Court Judge

Jackie Winchester, Supervisor of Elections

Carol Elmquist, County Commissioner

Halfway through counting the precinct, Burton, LePore, and Roberts decide to adhere to the 1990 standard. If there is no detachment, it will not be counted. Kuehne protests, predictably, but the board disagrees. "My motion is that we stick by the November 6, 1990, guidelines," Burton says. "I want to do it, and I want to do it right." LePore and Roberts agree. All three members now restart. Burton takes a card, turns it around, and stays silent. His first card with the 1990 standard and already there's a change. "This is an example where there is light, but it's fully attached," Burton says. "The sun shines through it, but the four corners are attached. It's no." Kuehne tries to talk Burton out of the new standard, but he's shut down. "The board is no longer listening to comments from the spectators," he says. "Thank you."

The Boston Boys are not pleased. "We're in trouble," Newman whispers to Corrigan. "I think they screwed us." Newman and the Boston Boys had counted 30 new Gore votes and 19 new Bush votes. Those are now scrapped. After the canvassing board makes it halfway through precinct 193-E again, Gore has 19 new votes, Bush 9. The vote-pickup difference goes from +11 for Gore to +10. One vote here, one vote there, and Gore may not be able to catch up. And why was Burton gone for forty minutes during that break? they say to each other. Who was he talking to? How did his presentation and knowledge about this all get so polished and developed?

Now it's Kuehne's turn to be Mr. Objection.

Like the talent scout who discovered Shirley Temple, Kuehne sees dimples, and he likes them.

"Objection," he says when a ballot that would have been OK an hour ago is now not considered a vote.

Burton spends twenty or so seconds studying a ballot when finally: "I think we have to say no," he says.

"Objection on that one, too," says Kuehne. "I object again to the re-counting of something again using a different standard. This is contrary to what the public was informed of during the open part of the meeting."

"Objection noted," Burton responds.

"For clarification, members of the board, the corner rule applies?" Kuehne asks.

"The rule was stated in the memo," says Wallace.

"I was speaking to the board, thank you," Kuehne says dryly.

All these wasted votes! Roberts thinks. "How much is a new system?" she asks LePore.

"A lot of millions," LePore says. "And if you go to a new system, it has its own inherent set of problems."

Another ballot, another chad not counted, another objection from Kuehne.

"What party are you representing, Ben?" Wallace asks. "The Free The Chad Party?"

"The people of Florida," Kuehne says.

They are getting snippy about it.

★ ★ ★

Outside, Bush spokesman Eskew is bad-mouthing the hand-recount process.

"It's known that manual counting of ballots is prone to human error," the South Carolinian says. "It's prone to the kind of potential mischief, and it's prone to other influences that don't serve to create confidence in this process."

What Eskew doesn't mention is what the Gore folks have just learned, and are starting to share with selected Democrats and members of the media: George W. Bush himself signed a hand-recount provision into law in 1997. When Texas elections are recounted, the law states, "a manual recount shall be conducted in preference to an electronic recount."

Is it hypocrisy of the first order? Yes in a major way and no in a minor way. No because Texas has one standard for the whole state, while Florida varies county by county. But yes because Eskew and other Bushies will spend the next month mocking the very concept of hand, or manual, recounts, even while their main man happily signed a law stating that hand recounts are preferable. And yes because the standard Bush signed into law is one of the broadest in the nation. Texas Election Code — section 127.130 — says that a hand-counted punch-card ballot may not be counted unless:

(1) at least two corners of the chad are detached;

(2) light is visible through the hole;

(3) an indentation on the chad from the stylus or other object is present and indicates a clearly ascertainable intent of the voter to vote; or

(4) the chad reflects by other means a clearly ascertainable intent of the voter to vote.

And yes because as governor, Bush would joke with Texas state representative Rick Green, Republican of Dripping Springs, about his slim 1998 victory over the incumbent Democrat. Green lost on Election Night by 20 votes, but in his call for a hand recount — which went ahead because of the law Bush signed in 1997 — he ended up winning by 36. Bush got quite a kick out of that, calling him "Landslide" Green. And yes because New Mexico Republican National Committee chair Mickey Barnett is setting the stage for a possible recount in his state, where Gore's margin of victory was rather slim. And yes because Bush and his team had no problem with the hand recounts that went on in some Republican-leaning Florida counties the day after the election, where he picked up votes. And yes because the Bushies are contemplating hand recounts in Oregon and Wisconsin and Iowa and New Mexico. And yes yes yes yes yes yes yes. But Bush and his team don't care; they almost never do. Quite unlike the Gorebies, who shiver at the slightest negative clause in a *New York Times* op-ed.

I'm not quite sure which attribute is worse. But I'm pretty sure I know which is the one employed by the winners in political warfare.

★ ★ ★

Bush invites a bunch of reporters out to his ranch today, to show how calm, cool, and collected he is as he greets Cheney and Andy Card, his chosen chief of staff should he take the White House. The Connecticut-born, Andover- and Yale-educated scion is wearing his cute little cowboy suit today, minus the boots: big, LBJ-style 30-gallon hat, western coat with "Gov. Bush" on its breast, dungarees.

"I think it's responsible that Dick and I and others contemplate a potential administration," Bush says. "And so they've come, and we're going to spend the day here today. First Lady Bush will be arriving here soon. It's nice to be out here in the country. Last night it was such a wonderful feeling when we arrived at Crawford, at about nine-fifty —"

ARF! ARF! ARF!

Spot, his dog, seems to be channeling his anxiety.

"Hey, hey, hey, please," Bush says to Spot. "It's not your turn! Sorry, the dog wanted to have a few comments. What she says was, 'Let's finish the recount.'" Some of the more sycophantic reporters laugh. "Anyway, arrived —"

ARF! ARF! ARF! ARF!

"Hey, Spotty. Spotty!" Bush turns to his aide, Gordon Johndroe. "Gordon."

"Yes, sir?"

"Somebody needs to take care of the dog," Bush says. "Thank you, Gordon. Just go ahead and throw the ball. Heh, heh, heh." He's got a Band-Aid on the side of his head; a lanced boil. He takes a few questions. The lifeless Cheney says a few words. Then one last question is allowed.

"Given that this election is so close —"

ARF! ARF! ARF! ARF!

"Spotty, please," Bush pleads.

"— would you consider appointing Democrats to your cabinet?"

Bush dodges the question.

"Governor, how is your infection?" he's asked.

"My infection?" Bush says. "Well, I'm sure glad you asked. Heh, heh. What infection? Oh, that one. I was hoping nobody would notice this Band-Aid here." He hides the Band-Aid with his hand. "It's fine. It got pretty severely infected, and I had a doc look at it. And I'm taking antibiotics and putting on hot compresses, and it's beginning to retreat, thankfully."

★ ★ ★

Back outside the Palm Beach Governmental Center, Carpenter and Burton are taking another smoke break. Burton has come to like Carpenter. She's eminently likable.

Born in Jacksonville, Carpenter was raised in Michigan, where she dropped out of high school after tenth grade to give birth to her first daughter at seventeen. But she took night classes, even through her second delivery at age nineteen. She moved to Lake Park, Georgia, dumped her husband, and worked, worked, worked, earning a college degree in three and a half years from Valdosta State College and a J.D. from FSU shortly thereafter. A year or so ago, her friend Debbie Kearney — whom she met when she worked in Governor Lawton Chiles's legal office — brought her on board in Harris's office.

Carpenter is wary of Carol Roberts. She's told Roberts that the 1 percent sample hand recount can justify a full county recount only if it "could affect the outcome of the election." Roberts doesn't seem to care, Carpenter thinks. She wants a full county recount no matter what.

Burton asks Carpenter if the division of elections has an advisory opinion on the books about hand recounts, on what the standard is for one to be called. The statute says that one should be ordered only if there's "an error in vote tabulation," but what does this mean? An error in the machine? An error in the cards? Error by the voter? How soon could the division of elections get an advisory opinion to the canvassing board?

Carpenter says that she'll check and get back to him.

Carpenter places a call to Clay Roberts, director of the division of elections. Is there an advisory opinion on the books? Roberts says no. But he can have one for them on Monday. Carpenter, Clay Roberts, and Paul Craft — a division of elections mechanics expert who's also in Palm Beach — discuss the issue at length.

Carpenter walks back inside and tells the group that an opinion can come as soon as Monday if they want one. But they have to make a request in writing if they want it, she says.

Carpenter does not mention that if they make such a request, whatever response the division of elections gives them will be legally binding.

Whatever conversations Carpenter and Burton have do not go unnoticed by paranoid Democrats. One after another Democratic attorney sidles up to Kuehne to note how friendly Carpenter is being to Judge Burton. She looks like she's trying to get his attention, one says. She's sure hanging around him a lot, says another.

Wallace feels differently. Finally, some relative fairness, he thinks. He looks at the three-person board, Democrats every one. He feels outnumbered. But at least they're no longer finding sunshine in every glimmer of hope, he thinks.

★   ★   ★

At 7:10 P.M., a Socialist vote is noted.

"I think Fidel would be interested in knowing that," says Kuehne.

Another ballot is noted, one with something of a tri-chad, one corner being almost kinda sorta punched out. The board rules against it, though clearly they would have ruled for it earlier in the day.

"Changing the rules halfway through is not fair to the public," Kuehne says.

LePore says that they weren't quite halfway through the count of 193-E when they scrapped the sunshine rule.

"Changing a quarter of the way through is not fair to the public," Kuehne clarifies.

Sitting up front is Bob Montgomery, a wealthy local personal-injury lawyer who is taking the lead with Rogow in representing LePore. Three years ago, he was an attorney for no less than the entire state of Florida in its lawsuit against big tobacco, which resulted in a $13 billion settlement — $3.4 billion of which went to Montgomery and his team, though for various reasons they have yet to see dime one.

Montgomery's also a big Democrat, having given thousands of dollars to Democratic candidates over the years. Just in the past couple years he's given $1,000 to Sen. John Edwards of North Carolina; $500 to losing congressional candidate Elaine Bloom; a grand apiece to Florida's new senator, Bill Nelson, Sen. Max Cleland of Georgia, California representative Tom Lantos, Bill Bradley, a soft-money PAC for Hillary Clinton, the Democratic Leader's Victory Fund 2000, the Democratic Senatorial Campaign Committee; Sen. Ted Kennedy; Rep. Alcee Hastings; $10,000 to the Democratic Congressional Campaign Committee, and on and on. And though he originally backed Bradley, there were no hard feelings from Gore, especially after Gore himself came to Montgomery's Palm Beach home after the primaries for a $10,000-a-plate fiesta.

Roberts holds up a card.

"Be careful not to flex the card!" says Wallace.

"I'm not flexing it," says Roberts.

The count of precinct 193-E finally ends at 7:38 P.M. Burton needs a smoke. With him, Roberts, and Carpenter, the front of the room now smells like an ashtray.

They begin precinct 193 — about 70 percent of the voters from which are registered Democratic.

Sigh.

It's all over at 11:14 P.M. Gore picks up 33 votes, Bush 14, Hagelin 2, Constitution Party candidate Howard Phillips 6, Socialist Party candidate David McReynolds 1. More relevantly, it's a net gain of 19 for Gore. Roberts extrapolates this to mean 1,900 possible uncounted Gore votes in the remaining 99 percent of the county. Burton says that's faulty math. You can't take the 19 new net Gore votes from three of the most Democratic precincts in the world and apply their voting standards to the rest of the county. But Roberts doesn't care. She points out that the whole county is Democratic, if not necessarily *that* Democratic, and she wants a hand recount, and that's that.

In Tallahassee, Gore spokesman Doug Hattaway is also using appalling dishonest math. "When you multiply it out, one hundred percent of the vote would lead to a gain of nineteen hundred votes for Al Gore, an amount that could well change the result of the election," Hattaway has the nerve to say with a straight face. In Palm Beach, Democratic consultant Mark Steitz turns to Whouley. "That's fine that they're saying that," he says, "but let's not believe our own spin." Steitz figures the number to be closer to 300 votes or so. Still, the Gore people can't help but feel things are moving in the right direction, though clearly they feel the need to lie to nudge them along.

At 1:45 A.M., in front of the cameras and the crowds and everyone, the board announces the results.

"I move that this board conduct a manual recount of all the ballots for the presidential election!" Roberts says, to much cheering. But Burton is hesitant. "I believe we have the authority to request of the secretary of state or department of elections an advisory opinion, and it would be my intent as chair to do that," he says.

Roberts disagrees. "I'm asking for a vote," she says. "I don't believe we need an opinion on what we should do, because we are here in Palm Beach County. I represent the people of Palm Beach County. I move that this board conduct a manual recount of all the ballots for the presidential election for the year 2000!"

The crowd goes wild.

Burton is pissed. She never told him she was going to do this! And the crowd is cheering like they're in the middle of a Gore-Lieberman pep rally! Burton would prefer that Gore win as much as the next Palm Beach Jewish Democrat, but that's not what their job is!

"All right," Burton says. "We have to take the remainder of our meeting inside if we can't conduct our meeting out here in full public view."

The crowd quiets down a tad, but Burton still feels uncomfortable. They're not supposed to be politicians; they're not supposed to be partisan. He's just a county court judge in the criminal division; he has no idea what the election law is. And while Roberts is a county commissioner and has been on the canvassing board before, Burton doesn't think that she really knows either. And LePore's never had a recount like this before her!

"Quite honestly, this is a situation that I think is new to everyone," Burton says. He thinks about what Kerey Carpenter has been telling him all day. "I believe we have the authority to request of the secretary of state, or the department of elections, an advisory opinion."

"I don't believe this is, and I'm not giving an opinion, I'm asking for a vote," Roberts says. "I don't believe we need an opinion on what we should do, because we are here in Palm Beach County. I represent the people of Palm Beach County, and I believe the people of Palm Beach County deserve — I represent all the people in Palm Beach County, and I believe all the people in Palm Beach County deserve to have — as well as the people in the United States deserve to have — an answer, and this is the way I see best fit to get that answer."

The crowd cheers.

Burton's mood darkens further.

"I'd like to call for a vote!" Roberts says.

Burton asks Roberts — who clearly has more familiarity with Robert's Rules of Order (or at least Carol Roberts's Rules of Order) — what he can do if he wants to make a motion. Does he make a modified motion? She tells him he can make a substitute motion.

He does so. That before they vote on a full hand recount they "request an advisory opinion from the secretary of state."

LePore pauses. She's still in a state of shock from the Attack of the Butterfly Ballots. Then she says softly: "I'll second the motion."

Montgomery approaches her, whispers in her ear. No no no. LePore looks down on the ground.

"An advisory opinion on what, Mr. Chair?" Roberts asks Burton. She thinks the law is pretty clear. "What are we asking for advice on?"

Montgomery asks Roberts what she's doing.

"I believe that his motion was seconded," Roberts says. She turns to LePore: "Did you second the chair's —"

"No no no," Montgomery says to Roberts. "*Your* motion was seconded." Montgomery is acting as if LePore's not even there.

Roberts is confused. "Well I thought . . . ? Let's clear it up." She turns to LePore. "Did you second the motion of the chair also?"

"I seconded your motion for discussion," LePore says to Roberts. "And," she says, turning to Burton, "I second *your* motion —"

"No no no, you don't want to second his motion!" Montgomery says to LePore, cutting her off, telling her what to do, instructing her what to think.

"No," LePore says to no one in particular.

"You did not second his motion," Montgomery instructs her in a loud whisper. "Say, 'Excuse me, I misunderstood you, I misspoke.' So no, you withdraw your motion, you withdraw your second."

Wallace, Burton, and others watch the spectacle, appalled.

"I withdraw my second," LePore repeats. In the coming days, LePore will drop Montgomery. She'll start to think that he has his own agenda. But she's shell-shocked right now, and she trusts him.

"All right," Burton says. "I'd feel better making an informed opinion rather than a rash opinion."

"I don't think we need an opinion!" Roberts says. "Can I call for a vote now?"

GOP lawyer Jim Higgins "entreat[s] the board to seek an opinion."

Burton calls on Carpenter to speak. She says that they simply can't do a countywide hand recount, since those are only permissible if there's something wrong with the machines.

"What we found today was not an error of that type, but instead was voter error, and that caused the machine to not properly read the ballot," she says. At least wait until Harris gives them an opinion, she says.

"When can we receive an opinion?" Burton inquires.

"You can receive it tomorrow," Carpenter says. Once again, Carpenter neglects to tell Burton that such an opinion would be binding.

"I would like to call the vote!" Roberts says. "I would like to call the vote!"

All in favor?

Roberts votes aye.

"These people don't have a clue what is involved in going through half a million ballot cards," LePore thinks to herself. She doesn't know what to do. The presidency is involved here. But she still wonders about what the law says, whether the recount is allowed unless something has been proven to be malfunctioning with the machines. Then again, she feels horrible about the butterfly ballot.

She votes aye.

All opposed?

Burton votes aye.

And it's 2 to 1, LePore and Roberts for the hand recount, Burton against. The crowd cheers. Except for Democratic chair Friedkin. He's yelling. At Burton. "You'll never get elected in this county again!!" is what he cries.

When the three of them walk inside to the counting room, Burton lets loose. "I can't believe you fucking sandbagged me!" he yells. Roberts tries to explain about Florida's sunshine law mandating that all government business be done in the open air, in front of everyone. "Bullshit 'sunshine rule'!" he spits. She, Burton argues, should have let them know she was going to do that!

When he gets to his West Boca home that night, he vents to his wife. "This is unbelievable!" he tells her. "This is bullshit!" Then, thinking about the task he has before him and the partisan politics that entered the arena so annoyingly today, he says, "This is gonna be a nightmare."

Once again, Judge Charles Burton would prove to be a prophet.

7

"etc., etc."

Ken Mehlman, Bush's field director, was in his room at the Marriott Dadeland in Miami when he saw Carol Roberts's little power play on TV, and he couldn't believe it. First Palm Beach has this 600-vote surge for Gore during the machine recount — which Wallace, Johnson, and Murphy told him the canvassing board couldn't fully explain — and now this, Roberts pushing through a countywide hand recount. This process was totally becoming political, he thought.

So Sunday morning Mehlman gets up and he runs.

Normally he runs twenty-five to thirty miles a week, but with the election and all, he hasn't done so, and now he needs to. But there's no place to run around here, certainly nothing like his two favorite running trails — the Tow Path in Georgetown and the Reservoir in Central Park. There's not even anything like the trail he would tear through when he lived in Austin.

So Mehlman runs twenty-seven laps around a mall parking lot. Which in a sense is a lot like what all of Florida will be doing for the next few weeks.

After he's done, Mehlman screams up I-95 in his rental car, on his way to Palm Beach. He's been overseeing all the different people in all the different counties — Wallace, Johnson, and Murphy in Palm Beach; Bill Scherer and Ed Pozzuoli in Broward; Bobby Martinez, Miguel De Grandy, Kevin Martin, and all the rest in Miami-Dade. Broward's not doing anything 'til tomorrow; Miami-Dade has its hearing on Tuesday; Palm Beach looks like trouble. But there's hope. Wallace, Johnson, and Murphy have been calling Mehlman, telling him about the weirdness, the chad falling on the floor, the Democrats trying to get standards loosened up. The good news, Mehlman thinks, is that Florida has this sunshine law, requiring that all official government activities take place in public. And that, Mehlman has realized, is his secret weapon. If these Democratic canvassing boards were allowed to quietly count without the public knowing that they're counting dimples and such as votes, that would have been trouble. So Mehlman's going to make sure the shades are up and his guys are there to watch. He's going to set up a system where Republican volunteers are trained to observe. There are things they need to pay attention to — any irregularity, any ballot counted that shouldn't have been. Attorneys will be set up to interview observers to keep track of any weirdness. The system Mehlman sets up will then be able to be transferred to Broward, Miami-Dade, and anywhere else they need it.

Mehlman's feeling so much better.

★ ★ ★

Democratic attorney Jack Young is happy. In DeLand, the Volusia County canvassing board changed its mind on Friday and decided to go ahead with a full hand recount. Judge Michael McDermott and the two county council members — Republican Ann McFall and Democrat Patricia Northey — ruled on Friday that too much was at stake not to do a full hand recount, especially considering all the Election Night problems they had. Since the county uses Opti-scan ballots, the task will be much easier than it will be at the other three counties, which use punch-card ballots.

Which isn't to say that they're taking the task lightly. No siree. Especially not after the brouhaha surrounding the "heist" of ballots by Deborah Allen and her younger brother Mark Bornmann. So what if all they had were toiletries — McDermott has ordered the ballots moved across the street from the elections board office to the Thomas C. Kelly Administration Center, where the counting will take place. McDermott, who's retiring at the end of the year after twenty-four years on the bench, doesn't screw around.

And frankly, the Republican judge hasn't much liked the attitude of the Republican observers. They've been blowing smoke, dragging their feet. And McDermott's not going to put up with it. As chairman of the canvassing board, he has broad discretion to crack the whip. On November 9, he told David Brown, the finance chairman for the central Florida Bush-Cheney campaign that he was out of order.

"*You're* out of order!" Brown replied.

McDermott turned to the sheriff's deputy behind his shoulder.

"Remove him," McDermott said. "*Now.*" Brown was escorted out.

McDermott thinks the behavior of these guys is an embarrassment. He's embarrassed for himself as a fellow Republican. McDermott's secretary tells him of a phone message he received. "Judge McDermott's a Republican, but he's not acting like a Republican," it said. Exactly right, McDermott thinks. I'm acting like a judge.

McDermott has a much more pleasant experience with Young, with whom he chats during breaks about the *Canterbury Tales* and other works of English literature.

For his part, when he wasn't schmoozing McDermott, Young spent Saturday carefully observing the write-ins and other ballots the canvassing board is inspecting. That night, Young developed twenty-two rules of how to count a ballot, what he calls "certain principled approaches to getting votes." Young's whole plan is to get the yield rate up. When do you hit more home runs, he asks, if you're pitched two hundred balls or twenty thousand? We'll give Bush some votes, setting certain standards, so as to get more ballots allowed — which will then mean greater votes for Gore. So today, having carefully studied the ballots, Young has some ideas about how the 448 undervotes should be assessed. There are 184,019 ballots to review, and Young wants to get this right.

What if someone fills in a bubble for Bush but writes in McCain? Is that not an overvote, two candidates selected? No, Young says, that should count. McCain is not a qualified candidate for president, there are no electors slated for him.

Any mark circling the name — instead of shading in the bubble, as instructed? A vote. If someone wrote an X close to a name but not in the bubble? A vote. Random marks on the side of the ballot should be disregarded. These rules should count regardless of which candidate they benefit.

Sunday, Young and two other Democratic observers — Kathy Bowler, executive director of the California Democratic Party, and Floridian Sharon Liggett — give the Democratic observers a long list of instructions far exceeding what Volusia's Republican observers are being told to do.

Young and his team are ready — really ready. You can tell by their green felt-tip pens. Green because at the start of the day it had been announced that observers weren't permitted to take notes with pencils or blue or black pens, since such writing implements could be used to fill in Volusia's Optiscan ballots, creating new fraudulent votes.

The Republican observers have to scramble to get multicolored pens. Since stores are closed, sheriff's deputies open a supply closet and give them three boxes of red pens. Score it a draw, barely.

But Young and his team had more than the right colored ink. They have special forms for each precinct, on which they diligently record how many votes for each candidate there are, what ballots might be controversial, and why. They have pictograms for any ballot that they or the GOP observers challenge. On each pictogram, which is basically a Xerox of a ballot, the Democratic observers record why the ballot is considered controversial. After each precinct form is completed, the form is run to a local law office down the street, where a computer spreadsheet is being constructed. Young wants to keep close tabs on all the challenges so that when disputed ballots come up for discussion at the canvassing board, he knows what the disputed ballots are, and he knows what to say.

When the hand recount starts today, Young very early professes to the canvassing board his desire to have certain controversial Bush votes be counted. In the end he knows allowing those ballots will mean more Gore votes than Bush votes. Plus, he establishes some credibility by appearing fair-minded.

He's done this before. He wants the board to have confidence in him. He wants them to partner with him so the correct — and most generous — standard is applied. People forget, Young thinks, these are little administrative agencies. Be deferential but helpful. Treat them right, give them information so they look smart. Develop principled decision making so your guy gets more votes.

Twenty-two tables of counters and observers. The canvassing board in the corner, checking out the disputed ballots. Young on hand to share his thoughts. Go.

★   ★   ★

Burton drives from West Boca to his West Palm Beach judicial office to do some more research on when a countywide hand recount is legally allowed. He's still mad at Roberts, still upset about the partisan tone from last night.

"We need to at least talk about how to do this," he thinks. "Somebody oughta have a plan. If you're gonna start a business you don't know anything about, you don't just start it. You go work at a restaurant before you open one up."

A judge friend comes into the office to help him do research.

There are clearly conflicting statutes in the law. One provision allows for manual recounts. The other says that the election has to be certified by Tuesday. The secretary of state has discretion to postpone the certification if she so chooses, and it doesn't say anything about how that will only be at times of emergency — like during hurricanes — as Kerey Carpenter has been telling him. Hmm.

On his own, Burton faxes a letter to division of elections director Clay Roberts, asking if they can extend the certification deadline. If they do the hand recount and sent them the tally after Tuesday at 5 P.M., will their hard work — and any new votes they find — be ignored? Will they just be screwed? Are the voters whose ballots weren't recorded by the machine just shit out of luck?

He gets back a fax from Roberts. It says: Yes.

★   ★   ★

Clay Roberts also receives a phone call from Frank Jimenez today. Jimenez wants to know why Roberts hasn't yet issued forth an opinion on why counties can't conduct hand recounts. No one's yet requested one, Roberts says. Sunday night, state GOP chair, Al Cardenas, asks Roberts for the opinion. Roberts gladly issues it, and it is distributed to the world. Like turn-of-the-century Chicago Cubs infield double players Tinkers to Evers to Chance, the Jimenez to Cardenas to Roberts maneuver is but one example of how the Gorebies are at a distinct away-game disadvantage.

★   ★   ★

David Leahy, the Miami-Dade supervisor of elections, would never understand why the Palm Beach County canvassing board is going through such angst. Of course they have the discretion to do whatever they want, he thinks, and though he interprets the statute to mean an error in the vote-tabulation machines, and nothing else, he doesn't think there's any big rush to finish by Tuesday at 7 P.M.

Certainly that's part of the reason why the board decided to put off their hearing until Tuesday. Leahy is sure that if the board wants to amend its returns after November 7, it can. If it votes to complete a full countywide hand recount, it has some time. December 12 is the "safe harbor" date, by which the Legislature can step in if no electors have yet been assigned to a candidate; Leahy figures they have until December 1 to complete the count, if they want. Plenty of time.

★   ★   ★

Outside the Palm Beach County Governmental Center, protesters for both sides are takin' it to the streets.

"THEY! HAVE! NO CLASS!" cheers a Floridian woman with a face like Karl Malden whose rather generous dimensions have been impressively wedged into a tight floral pantsuit.

She's offended by a Gore backer who's carrying around an effigy of "King George II." It consists of a George W. Bush Halloween mask covered in Band-Aids wrapped around the head of an inflatable doll and dressed in an ensemble of K Mart's finest polyester. The whole rig hangs from a six-foot-long two-by-four.

"THEY! HAVE! NO CLASS!" the woman continues.

It's one of the few chants that doesn't catch on here, on the corner of North Olive and Fourth Streets, on a lovely Sunday afternoon.

The crowd that's gathered isn't one whose members, Bush backers or Gore backers, care much about class. This is a good guys/bad guys deal. There aren't many thoughtful debates about the nature of democracy or the hair-trigger media projections. No one's discussing why Bush signed his 1997 hand recount law for Texas but filed for a federal injunction yesterday to stop the same from happening here. No one's discussing the litigious nature of America, or why Gore ran such a piss-poor campaign — losing his home state even! — that it's even come down to dimples and such. No one's quoting historian David McCullough.

"No hand jobs," says one Bush backer's T-shirt, hastily scrawled in pen on Fruit of the Loom cotton. Yes, definitely not David McCullough.

"No More Lynching in America!" reads the sign of Jennifer Lowery-Bell, fifty-three, who drove down from Washington to join the call for a revote. She's drawn an African-American hanging from a noose.

How is this lynching? I ask.

"Anytime you have a violation and the people cannot do anything to help themselves, they go to extremes," she says. She cites the Palm Beachers confused by the butterfly ballot, the African-American voters who were supposedly intimidated from voting throughout the state. "What is that except lynching? It's just a different phrase for doing it," she says.

But Lowery-Bell is in the distinct minority today; the Bush forces are out and energetic. When they cheer "Bush won twice!" — as they do, quite often — she is relegated to standing on the curb and yelling "No!" after each line. She soon changes this to a long "Oooohhhh nooooo!" during the Bushies' cheer, which is at least competitive in its annoyance factor.

Maybe Lowery-Bell just chose the wrong day. A local merchant hawking "Re-Vote" T-shirts says he's sold four hundred since Friday, at $10 a pop. If he keeps it up, Bush's tax-cut plan may start looking more attractive.

Between the Bush backers and bashers, cops, journalists, and bystanders, there are only two hundred or so of us here today. But on TV it must look like many more, since anytime MSNBC's Suzanne Malveaux goes live, she immediately becomes the most popular kid in the playground. The crowd mobs her. As soon as the camera light goes off, the protesters quickly dissipate.

Otherwise, they don't seem to know what to do. A few times, the Bush crowd marches halfway up the one block of Fourth Street that has been cordoned off. Then they march back.

You get the feeling that they're all kind of new at this. One guy is so eager to join the fun that he marches while still in the midst of making his sign. He holds his posterboard awkwardly in front of him while he colors the block letters in the words "NO CONTROLLING LEGAL AUTHORITY/ BUSH WINS" with a thick green Magic Marker.

"GORE = MILOSEVIC" reads a completed sign by Wade Whitaker, twenty-two, of Las Vegas. "It's the same parallels," Whitaker says when I ask him about his sign. "When Milosevic was voted out of power, he wouldn't leave, either." Whitaker is here because, hepped up about the presidential controversy, he jumped on a red-eye that arrived in Orlando at 5:00 Saturday morning. He doesn't know anyone in town and isn't even sure where he's staying tonight.

Make no mistake: These protests are not to be confused with those seen at recent anti-globalization protests in Seattle or, to a lesser extent, in Washington. The local cops here in Palm Beach look bemused more than anything else. One tells me they aren't worried at all. "I don't think we're going to have any trouble," says a member of the Sheriff's Department. "Look at the ages of the people here. Two fifty-year-olds tend not to get in fistfights."

A local in an SUV keeps speeding by and riling up the crowd, yelling, "Bush is an alcoholic! No junkies in the White House!"

"Wexler's people cannot read directions," reads another sign, belonging to Carole Parsons, a fifty-five-year-old Palm Beach housewife whose sign refers to Florida representative Bob Wexler.

Who are "Wexler's people"? I ask, suspiciously.

"The people who elected him, who voted him into office," she says.

And who would those "people" be?

She pauses for a moment.

"Liberal Democrats," she finally says.

She later holds up a sign that says, "Wexler needs his Beano."

Both groups are pretty entrenched — both the side decrying "Jeb Crow" and the others who are constantly cheering "Jesse Go Home," a reference to Jesse Jackson, who has yet another rally scheduled for tomorrow.

A dozen or so religious leaders walk in, dressed in their Sunday best. "We're here to pray for peace," says Marc Murray, a local youth minister with Trinity Church International. They stand in a circle and are noticed only for the space they take up.

Heated arguments pop up here and there. Four older pro-Bush Cuban-Americans pretend to cry, mocking a young pro-Gore white girl. "Ayayay!" says one of the Cubanos, an older woman.

"You are not compassionate!" the young girl lectures. "Compassionate conservatives don't make fun of people!"

"Go home and cry!" responds an older man.

Another sign: "If arrows confuse you, you shouldn't be driving. Re-voke Palm Beach Dems driver's licenses."

Yet another: "Incompetents can't vote."

A few signs mention Elián González. Others mention Rush Limbaugh.

Soon the crowd decides that its new mission is to score supportive honks from passing cars. They stand at the police barricade and screech wildly every time a Grand Am toots. A woman powders her nose while a local idiot tries to hit on her. A guy with a sign saying "God Made Bush President" appears. Another, hyping the Web site Newsmax.com, starts shouting out that "Peter Jennings and Tom Brokaw have bald spots."

This guy has a bald spot, too.

Two middle-aged white men start challenging the bona fides of an effeminate, fortyish Gore supporter. "Let's see some ID!" yells one of the Bushies. "You're not from around here!" His chum joins in: "He's an out-of-town rabble-rouser! Just like Jesse Jackson!"

The Gore guy says he isn't about to show the two his driver's license. "Are you a cop?" he asks. "No? Then fuck you!" He crosses his arms defiantly. As the crowd converges on itself, a local teenager — Alex Baker, fourteen — jumps into the circle.

"Who wants water?" he asks at the top of his lungs. "We're selling water here! Who wants some?"

The crowd laughs and dissolves.

Baker and his buddy, Tyler Virgadamo, thirteen, are selling water for $1.50 and soda for $1.

"All the yelling that they do, their throats are going to start hurting," says Virgadamo of the crazy grown-ups all around them.

They've made $150 today, Baker says.

★   ★   ★

The world will never fully know what role Jeb Bush plays in all of this. He largely stays hidden from view, though his operatives — Jimenez, Harris,

Speaker of the State House Tom Feeney, who was his running mate in
'94 — play leading roles. Because of the sunshine law, reporters will be able
to obtain records of phone calls made and received, but we will never know
the content of those calls.

E-mail is different. Jeb is a wicked e-mailer, with at least three addresses.

The day after the election, Jeb spokeswoman Katie Baur sent an e-mail
to Frank Jimenez, who took official leave that day to help Jeb's big brother.
Jeb's chief of staff, Sally Bradshaw, had asked her to send him a message.

"SALLY WANTED ME TO REMIND YOU TO TALK TO BEN GINS-
BURG [sic] PRIOR TO PRE-BRIEF," she wrote. "SORRY FOR CAPS . . .
DRAMATIC TIMES."

Today, Monday, December 13, Jeb gets involved, too.

One woman writes Jeb: "Is there any way this can be stopped?" She keeps
getting phone calls, she complains, telling her, "Your vote along with nineteen
thousand others was thrown out."

Jeb forwards the note to Baur and Bradshaw, with a note: "This is a con-
certed effort to divide and destroy our state."

"Ve have our vays also," Baur — ever-sensitive to those Holocaust survivors of Palm Beach County — writes back. "I'm working on this."

Bradshaw writes: "This is obscene. I hope we are getting this to the press.
Shouldn't we give them a list of all the scare tactics the Gore campaign is
using?"

Three minutes later comes the note from Baur, whose boss has supposedly recused himself from it all: "That is what I am gathering."

★   ★   ★

In Miami, the Rev. Jesse Jackson — the man who once referred to New
York City as "Hymietown," who once said that "Zionism is a kind of poi-
sonous weed that is choking Judaism," who griped that he was "sick and
tired of hearing about the Holocaust" — is standing in front of the congre-
gation of Temple Israel of Greater Miami.

"It seems that in West Palm Beach, the African-Americans and the Jewish senior citizens were targeted," Jackson says. "Something systematic was
at work here. . . . It was large and systematic. Once again, sons and daugh-
ters of slavery and Holocaust survivors are bound together with a shared
agenda, bound by their hopes and their fears about national public policy."
He's trying to re-forge the brotherhood between Jews and blacks that was
so important to the civil rights movement, a connection that Jackson bears
more than a small share of the blame in having helped fracture. News stories in the coming days will report that Jews and blacks are working

together again, but these news stories are largely nonsense. Beyond a few rallies here and there, nothing really changes.*

Jackson's pet rabbi, Stephen Jacobs, whom he had to bring with him from Los Angeles, steps up. "Now, we blacks and Jews find ourselves fighting old battles we thought we had won," he says. "We must stand together, or we will perish alone."

The synagogue's leader, Rabbi Jeffrey Kahn, agrees. "Some people say what is happening here in Florida is hysterical. It's not hysterical, it's historical. And it's especially historical for us Jews and blacks as we come back together."

★   ★   ★

Time passes in Volusia.

What's this?

In Volusia County, Young has discovered 320 votes not included in the count on Election Night.

Apparently, in precinct 305 in DeBary at 9 P.M. Election Night, one machine stopped accepting ballots for some reason. After the elections tech-nerd didn't show, the clerk tried to fix it herself, turning the machine off and then on again. The machine flashed: "Prepare for election" which told her that it was starting over again, so she secured the ballots and wrote a note to "check these."

When he checks, Young notices that there are more ballots counted than were recorded in this precinct. Young wants this to be a lock-down indisputable recount, unchallengeable. So even though he knows that DeBary leans Republican and that these 320 votes mean a net gain of 58 votes for Bush, Young's not worried. Someone was going to discover this sooner or later, and he doesn't want a 58-vote difference to be the grounds for any GOP gripes about this being an inaccurate count. Young already knows that he'll be able to make up the 58 votes.

But the 320-vote discovery feeds into a larger concern everyone in the room has: will they have enough time to finish? After all, Harris has made it clear that all results have to be at her office by 5 P.M. Tuesday. "Every county must have official certifications of the voting returns from last Tuesday delivered to the Florida Department of State by 5 P.M . . . or those returns

---

* After it's all over, I'll go to hear a talk by Broward County commissioner Suzanne Gunzburger at a breakfast meeting of the Hollywood Hills Democratic Club at Orangebrook Country Club. There many members of the largely Jewish group — including several who think Bush stole the election — will roll their eyes and throw out a disgusted "Feh!" when I mention Jackson's name.

will not be included in the statewide canvass," she says in a statement. "No county canvassing board has ever disenfranchised all the voters of its county by failing to do their legal duty to certify returns by the date specified in the law. I am confident that no county canvassing board will do so in this election."*

Additionally, since no one wrote to Harris asking her opinion of hand recounts — despite Kerey Carpenter's lobbying in Palm Beach — Harris wrote a letter to state GOP chair Cardenas, saying that, indeed, she thinks hand recounts are only for times of extreme emergency, like a hurricane. The letter was then leaked to the media and everyone else.

Ten hours into the Volusia County hand recount, more than half the ballots have been checked out and 58 precincts out of 172. As the counting ends for the night, Bush is up a net 33 votes, much of this due to precinct 305.

Reporters and Democrats start questioning Young's methods. He hears thirdhand that some of the Big Gun Democrats in Tallahassee want him removed, they think he's not aggressive enough, they've heard he's being serene and not in-your-face with the board. But Young's not worried. He knows those votes will be picked up. He tells reporters that it's a "fluid process." On a cell phone, he tells one of the Gorebies in Tallahassee to "go to hell." Then he throws the cell phone across the parking lot.

* The thoroughly soporific items of law Harris depends upon are:
"101.111 (1) Immediately after certification of any election by the county canvassing board, the results shall be forwarded to the Department of State concerning the election of any federal or state officer. The Governor, the Secretary of State, and the Director of the Division of Elections shall be the Elections Canvassing Commission. The Elections Canvassing Commission shall, as soon as the official results are compiled from all counties, certify the returns of the election and determine and declare who has been elected for each office. In the event that any member of the Elections Canvassing Commission is unavailable to certify the returns of any election, such member shall be replaced by a substitute member of the cabinet as determined by the Director of the Division of Elections. If the county returns are not received by the Department of State by 5 P.M. of the seventh day following an election, all missing counties shall be ignored, and the results shown by the returns on file shall be certified."

and

"102.112 (1) The county canvassing board or a majority thereof shall file the county returns for the election of a federal or state officer with the Department of State immediately after certification of the election results. Returns must be filed by 5 P.M. on the seventh day following the first primary and general election and by 3 P.M. on the third day following the second primary. If the returns are not received by the department by the time specified, such returns may be ignored and the results on file at that time may be certified by the department."

★   ★   ★

As Sunday becomes Monday, the canvassing board in Polk County in Central Florida conducts a partial hand recount of its Opti-scan ballots that you won't hear one Bushie object to. That's because the board — consisting of two Democrats, Supervisor of Elections Helen Gienau, and county court judge Anne Kaylor, and Republican county commission chairman Bruce Parker — scraps about 108 net Gore votes. Most of this change comes from the 90 Gore votes from precinct 131 — the West Lakeland Church of God — that, upon second glance, seem to have been counted twice. A similar deal happened in Seminole County last week during a partial hand recount there; Bush picked up 98 votes in that one.

Of course, both Seminole and Polk Counties use Opti-scan ballots, which may be easier to decipher since counters are looking at the handiwork of voters with pens on paper, not styluses on punch cards. Still, there is the same subjectivity employed, and humans — with, presumably, the same frailties and partisan temptations — are doing the counting.

Incidentally, Seminole and Polk Counties both went for Bush over Gore by about 15,000 votes apiece.

★   ★   ★

The Bush lawyers do not anticipate that they will have a friend in Judge Donald Middlebrooks, into whose courtroom they stroll Monday morning at around 9 A.M. — Olson, Ginsberg, Marcos Jimenez, and a couple others. Middlebrooks is a Clinton appointee, the Bush legal team points out, downplaying its expectations.

And Middlebrooks sure does sound like a liberal — he worked for former Democratic governor Reubin Askew, even drafting the state's first sunshine law. In 1975, he got Askew to pardon two innocent African-American men wrongly convicted of two 1963 murders. He worked for powerhouse Steel Hector & Davis, but served as director of the Florida Bar Children's Fund and headed the Volunteer Lawyer Resource Center for inmates on death row. And while on the bench, Middlebrooks exacted a draconian financial penalty against Royal Caribbean Cruises for dumping hazardous waste into the sea and then lying about it.

What bad luck for the Republicans to draw such a judge!

But they're entering their case — entered their case, actually, since most of the documents have already been filed and responded to over the weekend — so as to get it to the more conservative Eleventh Circuit Court of Appeals in Atlanta and, if need be, the U.S. Supreme Court.

"I'm not under any illusion that I am the final word on any of this," Middlebrooks begins by saying, as he stares out on the sea of lawyers before him. "In fact, I take great, great comfort from that fact."

Rogow, representing LePore, points out that Olson hasn't sent him a statement of facts.

"We apologize," Olson says. "We attempted to fax copies of this material and data at an early hour in the morning to everybody connected with it, and I apologize to everyone who did not receive it."

"Well, the fax machines broke, all kinds of things happened," says Middlebrooks. "Last night around eleven o'clock our computer system crashed, so a lot of what we were working on disappeared."

You see what happens when you trust the infallibility of machines?

Olson begins. "It is particularly crucial that votes in presidential elections be counted according to consistent uniform and objective standards," he says. "Voters must know that their ballots will be treated fairly and equally, not distorted in a partisan standardless vote-counting process."

After Olson bashes the Dems for selectively plucking four Democratic-leaning counties for their hand recounts, Middlebrooks asks about media reports of a hand recount that took place in Seminole County. Wasn't that because of a Bush campaign request? No, says Olson. And even though it was a hand recount in a fairly partisan county, it wasn't done according to "the Florida statutes that we are attacking here, or that we are challenging here."

(More to the point: it's not true. Though just yesterday NBC's Tim Russert said "there was a hand recount in Seminole County," what actually happened was that some ballots had to be hand-fed into two of the counting machines, which is of course totally different.)

Olson says that the statute allowing canvassing boards to call hand recounts is wildly permissive. "The constraints are unlimited and unfettered," he says. "And there's no guidance for the exercise of the discretion with respect to initiating a recount." But Middlebrooks points out that the county-by-county nature of it all "seems to be a result of Florida's decentralized system." He wants to know what Olson suggests should be done about the fact that there is no statewide standard when it comes to assessing ballots.

"There should be a standard," Olson says.

How can Olson complain about counties making different decisions about recounts when there are at least four different ways that various counties vote? "But even the equipment is different, isn't it?" Middlebrooks asks.

"Pardon me?"

"The equipment looks like it's different," says the judge. "I thought all counties used that stylus punch system, but in something I saw, apparently there's a wide disparity in terms of even how counties vote. So it seems like the idea of 'the right standard' or 'more precise standard' might be difficult."

Olson says that some counties are doing things differently now from how they were done in the past. He says that Theresa LePore has said that in past Palm Beach recounts, observers weren't allowed to object, while they are this year. This is something that the Republicans don't seem to have a problem with in the counting rooms, since they're the ones doing most of the objecting, but here Olson trots it out as an example of the horror. Olson also complains about Palm Beach changing its counting rules in the middle of Saturday's count. But again, this was something done to the pleasure of the Republican attorneys — like Wallace, Johnson, and Murphy — who wanted the standard tightened up.

Middlebrooks wants to know: "Is y'all arguing there should be only a machine count and no manual count after that? Or that if you are going to have a manual count, you need more precise standards?"

"I think more closely the latter," Olson says.

On this issue, in many ways, the presidency doth hinge.

Of course, as exemplified by Brevard County — which switched from punch card to Opti-scan and saw its undervote rate plummet — it can also be observed that different voting systems provide different counties' voters with different odds as to whether their votes will be counted. This, too, would seem to be a violation of equal protection, and one doesn't have to be a history professor at Dartmouth to guess what sorts of Florida residents are more likely to have been stuck with antiquated and less accurate voting technology. But this argument is not one that Olson is concerned with today.

Olson now paints anyone looking at a ballot as if they're under suspicion of a crime. He ominously states that "Saturday in Palm Beach, according to one report, certain ballots were twisted and turned." He does not cite the one report. "There were pieces of chads found on the floor," he adds.

Olson further argues that due process will be violated, because there does not exist enough time to properly adjudicate the matter, because "the electors have to be selected and cast their ballots on November eighteenth."*

"Unless there are standards," Olson warns, "the votes of the plaintiffs may be evaluated differently by individuals who don't have any constraints on their exercise of that discretion and may have some reason to wish it to come out a certain way." Again, there is no mention of any Bush desire to have the hand-counted Seminole County ballots reconsidered. "The process, to sum it up, is selective, standardless, subjective, unreliable, and inevitably biased because people who have interests in the outcome of the election are making subjective judgments."

Now it's Tribe and Rogow's turn.

Tribe has spent the weekend submerging himself in it all, talking to friends and former students, faxing and reading and thinking. And then, Sunday night, a walk around the hotel swimming pool with his wife, off whom he bounces ideas.

"Mr. Olson has spent a lot of time on the merits of his argument, but what he forgets is that he's here on the question of whether or not a preliminary injunction should be issued," Tribe says. "All of this discussion about chads and how the system operates is interesting, but the truth is, he's put the chad before the horse.

"What counts is, does he have a case that says that a canvassing board using the Florida statutes is violating the Constitution?"

Middlebrooks interrupts. Having watched Palm Beach County's hand recount the day before, "it does seem like the rules in terms of what was penetration were changing some. Sometimes it was if you see a square through the light, and sometimes three corners. . . . It doesn't seem like a very clear process. Can you tell me something about that?"

Rogow brandishes a ballot. "I don't have one of those punchers with me, but if the court simply takes a paperclip and unwinds it and punches out a corner, you will be able to see that sometimes one would punch one corner, the other three corners would be connected. But when you punch out that one corner, you have penetrated the card, and therefore you have voted. And that is all that that process seeks to do, to make that determination.

"There is not an issue here of people fooling with these cards or making determinations with these cards that are partisan in any way. . . . Not only

---

* The actual date for this, of course, is *December* 18.

do you have observers from each party and you have people from the supervisor of elections' office, but the press is there." At least in part thanks to Middlebrooks, one might observe.

"How can there be irreparable injury in the public knowing what the outcome of the recount is?" Rogow asks. "They make the argument — and this I thought was quite startling — that somehow or other the public knowing . . . the result of the election may not have been for Governor Bush, but may have been for Vice President Gore, that somehow or other if that result is known, that will harm the nation's psyche.

"Is it messy?" Rogow asks. "Does it go on and on in some fashion? Yes, it does, but that's what democracy is about."

Rogow cites the Beckstrom Florida Supreme Court case, which holds that if a circuit court finds that an election has been held, and the result is such that there's reasonable doubt as to whether the will of the voters has been expressed, the court can call for a new election if it wants.*

"All right," Middlebrooks says. "Tell me two things. First, articulate the standard Palm Beach County is using to check these ballots."

"The standard is — and they use these words, I don't like them, but they are the words they use — if it's a hanging chad, if it's a swinging chad, if it's a tri . . . then that is counted as a vote. Pregnancy does not count in Palm Beach County; only penetration counts in Palm Beach County."

The courtroom laughs.

"All right," Middlebrooks says. "I had a second question, but I think you caused me to forget it."

★   ★   ★

So this is what hell looks like.

In Palm Beach County circuit courtroom 4-C, before Judge Stephen Rapp, the lawyers are stacked in the jury box and wedged ass-to-ass in the first three rows of the gallery, five thick, ten deep, as crowded and nearly as unruly as the mosh pit at a Nine Inch Nails concert.

---

* "Beckstrom" is a case that will be bandied about quite a bit. It stems from a November 1996 sheriff's election in Volusia County, in which fraud was alleged against the winner by Gus Beckstrom, the loser. In March 1998, the Florida Supreme Court upheld a circuit court judge's ruling that Beckstrom still was the loser — but it disagreed with one sentence in the trial court judge's decision: "I do not have jurisdiction to set aside this election." "The trial court clearly had jurisdiction" to do so if it wanted, the Florida Supreme Court wrote. "Thus, the correct statement is that the trial court found no factual basis for requiring that the election be set aside."

Al Gore may have put the butterfly ballot revote deal on hold for the time being, but eighteen plaintiffs and their lawyers haven't. Chief Judge Walter Colbath of the fifteenth circuit in Florida has consolidated the suits. In a way, it's not fair to lump them all together. Some of the plaintiffs are simply political plants. But others have genuinely moving stories, like those of Florence and Alex Zoltowsky, seventy and seventy-five, both of whom are Holocaust survivors. Florence spent two years in an underground cave hiding from the Nazis, while Alex survived a Polish concentration camp. The right to vote is paramount to them, they say. And the very idea that they cast their votes for Buchanan horrifying.

Then there are others, less compelling, attorney Henry Handler first and foremost among them. Handler, the County Democratic Executive Committee chairman from 1984 to 1986, filed the very first lawsuit, on behalf of that chronic man-in-the-middle Andre Fladell, Delray Beach commissioner Alberta McCarthy, and African-American community activist Lillian Gaines. Handler did this even though Gore attorney Mitch Berger repeatedly called him and beseeched him not to, arguing that he would end up hurting Gore's recount campaign and even a possible butterfly ballot legal challenge down the road. That didn't matter to Handler.

Bush lawyer Barry Richard is sitting at his desk in Tallahassee, participating by speakerphone. He says that the judge doesn't have the authority to grant a revote, that the venue should be moved to Tallahassee. Even if both of those requests are denied, Richard says, the court needs to allow a little more time before it all begins, so he can review evidence and depose witnesses and otherwise do this thing right.

But before Judge Rapp — a Republican appointed by former governor Martinez, nicknamed "Maximum Rapp" for his proclivity for tough sentences — can even commence, Handler steps forward with two affidavits. He wants Rapp to recuse himself.

According to the affidavits, attorney Joseph Thillman says that on Election Day he overheard Rapp in a courthouse elevator dissing Hillary Rodham Clinton and saying that he voted to "make sure the Democrats are run out of the White House." Another lawyer, Harry Winderman, claims that at 8:20 A.M. on November 8, he heard Rapp say from the bench that any voter who was confused by the butterfly ballot was "stupid" and did not deserve the right to vote.

Rapp takes a forty-minute break to consider Handler's motion. When he returns, he denies the claims but recuses himself. The case is going to be reassigned to circuit judge Catherine Brunson, he says.

But Brunson will recuse herself because one of the attorneys in the courtroom recently worked for her husband. Judge Edward Fine will recuse himself because last week one of the attorneys asked his advice in seeking a judge's recusal. Judge Thomas Barkdull III will recuse himself because his dad represents Butterworth. Judge Peter Blanc will recuse himself because two of the lawyers served as treasurers on his reelection campaign. And Chief Judge Colbath will recuse himself — claiming he was given the case accidentally. Judge Jorge LaBarga will be given the case. But he's away at lunch.

As he sits at his desk in Tallahassee doing some other work, Richard is somewhat amused as one after another judge recuses himself. In the coming days, he'll start to doubt that all those judges had personal involvements that in any other circumstance would require recusal. Richard will think that their revolving-door recusals may have been motivated by the simple fact that the butterfly ballot's a highly charged issue, one that they don't want to get involved with. A Democrat more partisan than Richard might add that finding a judge who'd risk displeasing Jeb would be pretty unusual.

★   ★   ★

The case before Middlebrooks continues.

Tribe offers a lengthy discourse. Providing Florida's first touch of shameless O.J.-ness, Harvard professor Alan Dershowitz makes a cameo on behalf of some voter or something. The canvassing boards' lawyers stand and briefly speak.

"We heard references to the manual recount in Texas," Olson says. "The Texas provision, which has been mentioned for obvious reasons, has a list of very specific standards. The ballot may not — and this is in the statute to control the discretion of the official — the ballot may not be counted unless at least two corners of the chad are detached; light is visible through the hole; an indentation on the chad in the stylus; etc., etc., I'm not going to go through all of the details with respect to it. But that is an example of an effort by the state to articulate clearly standards by which individual judgment can be exercised in very specific limited situations."

"Boy, that's disingenuous," Rogow thinks, surprised, as he hears Olson's "etc., etc." He leans over to Tribe and makes a comment about it. That kind of footwork might be common in politics, but it's not supposed to be that way in law.

Rogow's right; it's one of the more dishonest bits of lawyering in a scandal with more than its share coming full tilt from every side. The provisions Olson's leaving out are the full sentence of (3) which is "an indentation on the chad from the stylus or other object is present and indicates a clearly ascertainable intent of the voter to vote." And, most notably, the big one Olson is just too busy to mention is Texas's fourth possible way to assess that an incompletely punched ballot is a vote, that "(4) the chad reflects by other means a clearly ascertainable intent of the voter to vote."

In other words, essentially the same subjective standard that Florida has as well. But Ted Olson isn't going to let anyone know this. And the Democrats don't have a rebuttal, so nobody can correct him.

★   ★   ★

Warren Christopher is perpetually dour. But when he emerges from Katherine Harris's office Monday morning, he looks like he's been sucking on an extra-strength lemon. He reports that Harris plans on certifying the election, as mandated that she "may" do if she so chooses, tomorrow, Tuesday, at 5 P.M. He's one big tsk-tsk.

Isn't she just following the law? he is asked.

"We believe not," says Christopher. "We think it is arbitrary and unreasonable. She has discretion under the statute, and she's declined to exercise the circumstance, even though it can be exercised, according to her, if there's a hurricane. Isn't it a strange situation where she would exercise discretion in other situations, but not where the presidency of the United States is at stake?"

Asked to characterize the meeting, Christopher says that "she said that the local boards have to certify by five o'clock tomorrow. So whatever they certify is what she will count and nothing thereafter."

This is one pissed-off old man.

★   ★   ★

Middlebrooks doesn't take long to slap down Olson and the Bushies.

"The state election scheme is reasonable and nondiscriminatory on its face," he rules. He says that there's nothing wrong with hand recount, that "the manual recount provision is intended to safeguard the integrity and reliability of the electoral process." Yes, canvassing board members get to make judgments, but, "while discretionary in its application, the provision is not wholly standardless. Rather, the central purpose of the scheme, as evidenced by its plain language, is to remedy 'an error in the vote tabulation which could affect the outcome of the election.' . . . In this pursuit, the provision strives to strengthen rather than dilute the right way to vote by securing, as near as humanly possible, an accurate and true reflection of the will of the electorate.

"Unless and until each electoral county in the United States uses the exact same automatic tabulation (and even then, there may be system malfunctions and alike)," Middlebrooks continues, "there will be tabulating discrepancies depending on the method of tabulation. Rather than a sign of weakness of constitutional injury, some solace can be taken in the fact that no one centralized body or person can control the tabulation of an entire statewide or national election." Indeed, the more boards and individuals involved, Middlebrooks implies, the less likely anyone can steal an election.

"I conclude that the public interest is best served by denying preliminary injunctive relief in this instance. . . . Nowhere can the public dissemination of truth be more vital than in the election procedures for determining the next presidency."

"DENIED."

Middlebrooks has given Olson nothing.

★   ★   ★

Over the weekend, circuit court judge Terry Lewis was playing tennis with a pal — an active Republican, a former candidate himself — who just happened to ask Lewis if he thought any of the various election court cases were going to end up in his courtroom.

"I doubt it," Lewis said. It looked like things were going to stay in the South of Florida, butterfly ballot in Palm Beach, federal case in Middlebrooks's Miami court.

Lewis isn't thinking about any of that Monday as he listens to testimony in a case where a woman is suing her daughter for allegedly bilking her savings account. Suddenly Doug Smith — a Leon County public information officer — is in the back of the courtroom motioning for him.

Lewis beckons him to the bench.

Smith hands him a copy of a brief filed Sunday: *Canvassing Board of Volusia County v. Katherine Harris and the Elections Canvassing Commission.*

But even this the unflappable Lewis doesn't think much of. It's just an action for declaratory judgment and injunctive relief — basically a request that Lewis make Harris accept their vote tally even if it comes after the 5:00 P.M. deadline. Shoot, he'll be back on the tennis court in no time.

★   ★   ★

Shortly after noon, Judge McDermott, the Republican chair of the Volusia County canvassing board, calls a press conference.

"I think it's reasonable," he says, "to assume that we should have a definitive and official certification of all the ballots by midday tomorrow, Tuesday, OK?"

Nevertheless, McDermott announces that as an insurance policy the Volusia County canvassing board is suing Clay Roberts and Katherine Harris for the purposes of "seeking a court order for an extension for the deadline, just in case. That has been filed." The hearing will be today at 1:00 P.M. "The reason we have filed the suit is, one never knows what problems may come up," he explains. "We've had some surprises — most of them unpleasant — in connection with what we've done so far, and you're aware of those surprises. The additional three hundred twenty ballots, that was at least a ten on the Richter scale, as far as I was concerned. So, you know, Lord knows what other surprises or problems are waiting there for us."

A journalist asks, "Judge, does the recovery of the three hundred twenty lost votes justify in your mind a hand count?"

"Oh, absolutely," says the Republican. "Yes, absolutely. I was disappointed that this came to light, but, you know — and just as a matter of principle, it was the right thing to do, just for those of us here at Volusia County, but especially in view of the fact that we're dealing with the race for president of the United States and everything that entails.

"The people of the United States and — it's interesting, the polls that have been taken of ordinary citizens, the vast majority — I think it's about seventy-five percent or perhaps even more of ordinary citizens are saying, 'Look, we're as frustrated as everybody else is about not knowing the results, but it's important that all these canvassing boards and other authorities throughout the various states, chiefly Florida, of course, do it right.'"

★   ★   ★

The Gore people have decided to join with Volusia County. Hattaway's on the phone with a reporter who's asking him about it, something about a hearing at 1 P.M. He turns to Jeremy Bash, ace cub lawyer. "What's this about a hearing at one o'clock today? Something about Volusia County?"

"I think that's tomorrow," Bash says. "Tuesday."

"Well, I've got a reporter on the phone here who says it's today."

Bash goes out to the hallway, where he runs into Mitchell Berger, his Tallahassee law partner John Newton, and — straight from central casting, missing only his mint julep — aged, white-haired Democratic éminence grise and barrister Dexter Douglass.

"Is the hearing today?" Bash asks.

"No, it's tomorrow," Berger says.

"I think it's today," Bash disagrees. "Check it out."

Newton calls the court clerk. The hearing is today, in half an hour. Their brief isn't ready. Berger, Newton, and Douglass rush over. The plan is to ask the judge for a continuance.

But once they get there, Lewis says no. Debbie Kearney is there for Harris; Barry Richard is there for Bush, who has enjoined on the other side. So Douglass simply plunges in with his argument, using his folksy North Florida charm. The legal arguments aren't crisp, aren't quite fully formed. How could they be? Douglass just joined the team a matter of minutes ago.

There are two conflicting statutes here, about whether Harris is obligated to reject late vote tallies or not.

101.111 (1) reads: *"If the county returns are not received by the Department of State by 5 P.M. on the seventh day following an election, all missing counties **shall** be ignored and the results shown by the returns on file **shall** be certified."*

However, states Florida statute 102.112 (1), *"If the returns are not received by the department by the time specified, such returns **may** be ignored and the results on file at that time **may** be certified by the department."* (Emphases added.)

Now we all know what President Clinton, Parser-in-Chief, was referring to when he said the fate of the free world came down to what the definition of the word "is" is. But Harris and her attorneys have asserted that late returns *may* be allowable only in case of natural disasters. About this, Douglass goes full folk.

"Let me tell you, this is not only a hurricane, this is a bark-splitting North Florida cyclone with a hurricane tailing on the end of it. It's one that rips across the entire country. It winds its way all over the country and all over the world."

Richard, of course, disagrees. "There has been no compelling reason to order the secretary of state to do something by law she is not obligated to do," Richard says.

"How do you reconcile this statute that seems to provide a manual count if you can't get done within the time period?" Lewis asks.

"It is not our place to question the wisdom of the legislature," Richard responds.

Lewis listens to the arguments. The question for him is not so much whether the preliminary certification must take place at 5:00 P.M. tonight. It must; the statute seems clear on that. So Volusia County is screwed, temporarily, at least — they still have the contest phase to work within, if they so choose.

What is up for debate is whether Harris is required by law to ignore any returns that come in after the deadline. In other words, is Harris *required* by law to screw the canvassing boards that want to recount their ballots? Or is it something she *can* do but doesn't have to?

Harris's attorney, Kearney, concedes that the more recent statute — the "may" statute — is the applicable one. Fine, Lewis thinks. So she does have discretion. Then why is she refusing to even listen to their reasons? Why is she telling the canvassing boards that it doesn't matter what reason they cite, she's not taking any late ballots? That doesn't seem like the exercise of discretion to Lewis. Hmm.

★   ★   ★

State house senior aide Rubottom is angry.

Kearney did nothing to defend the legislature's law. He doesn't see any contradictions in the may/shall issue, it's up to Harris to accept the returns if she wants.

He calls Kearney; he calls Ginsberg; he calls Jimenez. He tells them all that the legislature is there and eager to insert itself in this conflict if necessary.

★   ★   ★

Al Gore finally appears. The nation has only seen him walking here and there, to and fro, playing a rather lame touch-football game with his family on Friday.

"There's an awful lot at stake here, and what is at stake is more important than who wins the presidency," Gore says, trying his darnedest to seem sincere, but as always falling short. "What is at stake is the integrity of our democracy, making sure that the will of the American people is expressed and accurately received.

"That is why I have believed from the start that while time is important, it is even more important that every vote is counted and counted accurately. . . . And so that's what I'm focused on, not the contest, but our democracy, to make sure that the process works the way our founders intended it to work.

"Look," he says, the human TelePrompTer trying to seem ad-libby. "I would not want to win the presidency by a few votes cast in error or misinterpreted or not counted, and I don't think Governor Bush wants that either."

Oh, yeah?

"Now, if there's any saving grace at all to the extra time that this is taking, it is this: Schoolchildren all over the United States are learning a lot about how a president is chosen in this country. [STAGE DIRECTION: CHUCKLE]

"They're learning a lot about our democracy. And families are able to make the point without fear of ever again being disputed that it matters whether or not you vote, and every vote counts. So register and vote and participate in our democracy."

Ugh.

★　★　★

Al Gore wants to know just who this Katherine Harris character is.

"What do we know about her?" he asks his communications director, Mark Fabiani.

Fabiani says that she's very partisan, a state co-chair of the Bush campaign.

"Why aren't we getting that out?" Gore asks.

No decision had been made because she obviously wields a lot of power, Fabiani says, and the legal guys are worried about picking a fight with her.

But later that afternoon, the Gore generals talk about it and decide that since it's crystal clear that she's not a friend, they might as well start trying to discredit Harris and her decisions. Soon Gore spokesman Chris Lehane is talking to reporters, calling her "Commissar Harris," a "lackey" and a "hack."

Of course, there's much more to the answer to Gore's question than just Lehane's pointed barbs. She's rich, for one, worth about $6.5 million. The granddaughter of the citrus magnate and state representative Ben Hill Griffin, Jr., Harris — born in Key West, raised in Bartow, east of Tampa — comes from a long line of Democrats. As such, she once interned for then-senator Lawton Chiles during her four years at Agnes Scott College in Decatur, Georgia.

She's been all over the map, job-wise. She's served as a marketing executive for IBM in Tampa, New York, and Dallas. In Sarasota, she worked in commercial real estate. Freshly divorced in the 1990s, Harris quit her job in real estate and served as a Vanna White–like character in a Sarasota night-club act, "Mr. Chatterbox's Sentimental Journey." In addition to giving members of the audience gift certificates to Wendy's and for dry cleaning,

Harris's primary job was to show the crowd how to perform a chicken dance.

This is the person who might decide who becomes the next leader of the free world.

Bearing in mind Harris's role in the presidential conundrum, Chiles would turn over in his grave if he knew that he played perhaps *the* major role in pushing her toward her current power. In 1991, Chiles appointed his former intern — who studied art in Spain — to the board of trustees of Sarasota's Ringling Museum of Art, known for its collection of works by Peter Paul Rubens. Harris's fellow board members eyed her warily. In 1992, however, she proved her worth by taking control of the museum's annual fund-raiser and using her marketing skills, and social contacts, to make the fund-raiser, which normally just broke even, profitable.

Not long afterward, she and her fellow board members hopped a flight to Tallahassee to lobby for restoration of museum funds that had been cut. The trip was a success, but Harris was quite dismayed with her meeting with freshman Democratic state senator Jim Boczar, who didn't seem to care about the museum. Boczar told her that as far as he was concerned, a Rubens was a sandwich.

Harris ran against him in 1994, breaking all fund-raising records for a state senate seat, raising more than half a million dollars. In November, she beat Boczar handily, 60 percent to incumbent Boczar's limp 40 percent. With her victory, a senate split down the middle 20 to 20 finally landed in GOP hands, 21 to 19. And Republican control of once-Democratic Florida began to take root. Harris was the harbinger.

For a newcomer, Harris took to the sleazy ways of Tallahassee politics pretty damn quick. A chunk of her 1994 campaign coffers cash — $20,600 — had come from Riscorp Insurance Company. Riscorp gave $400,000 to ninety-six different candidates that year, but Harris was the largest beneficiary of the company's largesse. In 1996, from her seat on the state senate's Banking and Insurance Committee, Harris offered a bill that made it more difficult for Riscorp's out-of-state competition to offer discounts for workers' compensation policies. (She also was a co-sponsor of a bill that would have required parental consent before a minor could have an abortion, a bill that Governor Chiles happily vetoed.)

Around that time, Harris not only became a big fixture in the Sarasota social scene, and a regular in the *Sarasota Herald-Tribune*'s gossip column ("ANNUAL CLAMBAKE IS A CASUAL EVENT"), she found love. Set up on a blind date, Harris was wooed by Swedish businessman Anders Ebbeson, who runs a company that makes accessories for yachts, and who took her to the opening night of the 1995 opera, where they saw Verdi's *La Forza del Destino* — The Force of Destiny. In September 1996, while cruising the Greek Isles with a dozen or so other loaded Sarasotans, they announced their engagement.

Snagging an interview with Harris at the Governor's Ball at Ringling Museum, the *Sarasota Herald-Tribune* reported the news of her engagement breathlessly.

"Will she change her last name? 'No,' said the legislator. 'I planned to, but Anders said that I had built my public life with the name Harris, and I should keep it.' Children? 'We'll see,' she said. 'Right now I love what I'm doing, what I'm able to accomplish, and there's a lot more to do.' The wedding in Paris? 'It's what Anders wants; the city is very special to him.'

"You might say that the last couple of months have been hectic for the petite legislator. Last Saturday, though, was a time for Katherine to dance with her new husband and bask in the beauty of her beloved museum."

They were married on New Year's Eve 1997 in Paris, but she was back in Tallahassee before the week was over to assume the chairmanship of the state senate Commerce Committee.

In 1998, incumbent secretary of state Sandra Mortham was set to be Jeb Bush's running mate in his second go at the governor's mansion, against recount veteran and current Lt. Gov. Buddy MacKay. Harris declared her intention to run for the office.

But Mortham fell out of favor with Jeb after she was criticized for using state funds on outings that had little to do with anything but her own self-promotion. So Mortham said she would instead run for reelection for secretary of state.

But Harris said she was staying in the race.

That same year, five Riscorp executives pleaded guilty to felony and misdemeanor charges surrounding their 1994 campaign donations, which were illegal. The company's founder — who illegally reimbursed his employees for donations to candidates — was sent up the river for five years. Mortham had received $5,825 in illegal contributions from the company. Company executives wrote checks to political candidates and received special bonuses from their boss paying them back — a clear violation of election law.

Harris's share of illegal contributions, however, was even larger, the most of any legislator, $20,292. Her campaign manager, David Lapides, was described by federal prosecutors as a "co-conspirator" or "co-schemer" in the Riscorp strategy to hide contributors' true identities; a 1994 memo from Riscorp representatives to Lapides offered instructions on how to change the addresses on Riscorp checks so they couldn't all be traced back to the company. "Katherine's office called and asked if we could give them different addresses to list for each of the checks. All the checks show the P.O. Box 1598 address and if we submit these, the newspaper will probably make the connection and track them all to Riscorp," read an internal Riscorp memo.* Harris was never linked to the malfeasance, and she returned the illegally donated funds. But she wouldn't let reporters inspect her files, unlike other politicians who took Riscorp money.

Incredibly, under the guidance of senior adviser "Mac" Stipanovich, Harris ran TV ads against Mortham for taking "illegal contributions from insurance executives." Harris beat Mortham in the September GOP primary.

Then Harris, who said she was running for secretary of state to de-politicize the office, called her children's advocate Democratic opponent "a liberal lobbyist" and beat her, 56 percent to 44 percent. That same day, Floridians voted for a constitutional amendment to eliminate the secretary of state's office in 2002.

Where Mortham had heralded an election-reform package, Harris turned her attention elsewhere. She traveled extensively, spending more than $100,000 in state money on trips to Barbados, Brazil, New York City, and elsewhere to promote trade with the Sunshine State — her travel almost three times more than Jeb's. At the Sydney Olympics, Harris spent $350,000 in taxpayer funds on a Florida Pavilion.

The amount of money she spent on reforming the state's election problems was slightly less than that.

Perhaps the most telling step in Harris's journey to power came in March, however, when she shocked her former colleagues on the board of trustees of the Ringling Museum of Art. They were talking about a plan by the GOP senate president, John McKay, to give the museum to FSU — a move that the trustees opposed.

---

* It's apparently this incident, as well as questions about how much Harris has spent on offi-cial travel, that leads Harvard Law professor Alan Dershowitz to say to CNN on November 14 that Harris is "corrupt. She's had all kind of corruption allegations about expenditures of money. She's a crook. She's a crook and an operative of the Bush campaign." Dershowitz is too smart to commit slander, but this is pretty close to it, were it not so amusing coming from an attorney who helped ensure the freedom of O. J. Simpson and Claus von Bulow.

In a conversation that she apparently didn't know was being recorded, Harris said that McKay's plan would "destroy the museum. I mean, it's bad. I don't see any upside." But, she told the trustees, she wasn't going to do anything about it. "John is immensely powerful," she told them. "And I said, if John wants to do it, it is a done deal. I have said that I can't take a personal proactive role." Other cultural establishments "are doing terribly under FSU," she acknowledged. But "I am not fighting McKay on it. . . . John McKay is powerful. . . . It's really sad to watch all of our whole work go down the drain."

After the tape of the board meeting was leaked to the press, the editorial board of the *Sarasota Herald-Tribune* slammed her. "Because she lacked the nerve to do so, she failed in her duty to all Floridians and to her office. . . . In choosing political expedience over principle, Harris may have damaged her reputation beyond repair."

Just six years! Most politicians take at least a decade to completely sell out the very cause that compelled them to run for office in the first place. But Harris is on a fast track. She wanted to run for senate this year, in fact, but Jeb had already decided that Rep. Bill McCollum would get the nomination, and he cleared the field accordingly and told Harris no.

★ ★ ★

Around this time, I get a phone call from a high-ranking Gore adviser I'll call "Strep Throat."*

Strep Throat seldom called me during the campaign, frequently not even returning my phone calls, so I am immediately suspicious. The Gore media strategy was cataclysmically poor, I thought. It's part of the same idiocy that Clinton referred to on Election Night behind closed doors — Gore was surrounded by hired guns who weren't in it because they believed in him (whoever he was that day) but rather because they were Democrats who wanted to make some money and accrue some power. This was in stark contrast to both Bush and, of course, Clinton, both of whom were surrounded by True Believers.

"What's up?" I ask.

Strep Throat wonders if I've heard the rumor that "everyone" is talking about — that Katherine Harris and Jeb Bush had, or are having, an affair.

No, I say. What's the proof?

None yet, Strep Throat says. But people are working on it. He hears that Mike Isikoff from *Newsweek* is on it. (I later ask Isikoff about this, and he says it isn't true.) Better look into it, Strep Throat says.

---

* Stolen from *MAD* magazine's December 1976 parody of *All the President's Men.*

I ask a staffer at a Democratic state senator's office about any rumors she's heard about Jeb. She gives a couple, but when asked, says she's never heard anything about Jeb and Harris.

Chris Vlasto, the ABC News producer who with Jackie Judd broke the story of Monica Lewinsky's DNA-coated Gap dress, has been given the same "tip." He asks staffers at three local hotels, inquires around town, checks out phone and e-mail records, and comes up snake eyes.

There's no evidence, Vlasto thinks. Not at all. No hint, even.

At a Tallahassee bar, Café Cabernet, I ask some local scribes about it, and though they've heard the rumor in recent days, they never heard it before this election mess.

It's vile and despicable stuff, completely untrue, and it comes from a senior adviser to Vice President Al Gore.

★   ★   ★

Theresa LePore spent Sunday organizing her office, getting ready for a hand recount, while Roberts spent her day scoffing at GOP attempts to have her removed from the canvassing board because she gave the Gore campaign money and has that bumper sticker on her Lexus SUV. But now it's back to work, and they start with a short meeting.

Local GOP attorney J. Reeve Bright is here. Some of the Republican lawyers here for Bush think Bright's something of a pain in the ass, a gadfly. But Bright knows one thing from talking to Wallace, Johnson, and Murphy yesterday: if the canvassing board requests an opinion from Clay Roberts on whether they can go forward with the hand recount, whatever Roberts says in response will be binding.

This is something that Burton still doesn't know. He continues to think it'll just be an opinion, something the board can consider and weigh and, ultimately, disregard if they feel it is inaccurate. Burton doesn't even know that the division of elections office is part of the secretary of state's office.

Bright casually says to the board that they should get this opinion before they plunge in. Carol Roberts has been advised that this would be OK as long as they seek similar guidance from Democratic attorney general Bob Butterworth.

"The request to be made in writing?" Bright asks.

"Yes, yes," Burton says. "Absolutely."

They fax requests for guidance on how to do the hand recount, one to Butterworth and one to Roberts.

Four hours later, Clay Roberts writes back: they can't do the hand recount at all. Such counts are only in the event that there has been "incorrect election parameters or software errors."

Harris writes them that: "No county canvassing board has ever disenfranchised all the voters of its county by failing to do their legal duty to certify returns by the date specified in the law."

Palm Beach County attorney Denise Dytrych is back from Middlebrooks's trial and wherever she was over the weekend. She tells the board that Clay Roberts's letter is binding.

"It is?!" Burton thinks. "I never would have asked for it if I knew it was going to be binding!" They can't count. They are now legally required to not count.

In the days to come Burton will wonder about Kerey Carpenter, who kept suggesting that he seek an advisory opinion from the division of elections but never said anything about it being binding. "Was she putting stuff in my head?" Burton will wonder. "Was she playing me?"

Carpenter, who has moved on to other legal matters, will not again set foot before the canvassing board.

★ ★ ★

As Monday's protest march reaches Narcissus Avenue, the Rev. Jesse Jackson and his team turn left.

A few blocks away, a stage has been assembled outside the West Palm Beach governmental building, at Third and Olive Streets. But a welcoming crowd does not await Jackson. Approximately two dozen Bush supporters — half of them black and all of them hostile — have reserved choice spots at Jackson's "Democracy & Fairness, Every Vote Counts, Every One Counts" rally. While Jackson & Co. are marching from the Meyer Amphitheater, near the inlet that separates Palm Beach from West Palm Beach, the pro-Bush contingent stands front and center, shouting "Jesse go home!" at the top of their lungs.

Soon they can say it right to Jackson, as he mounts the stage, around 5 P.M. And they do. And they won't stop. One of their number, holding the "I Support Sec. Harris and Florida Law" sign, is Don Black, former Alabama Ku Klux Klan grand wizard, founder of the National Association for the Advancement of White People, and a Bush voter. Black has found common cause with a half dozen African-American conservatives, the members of "Freedom Fighters International."

Whaddaya know? George W. Bush *is* a uniter, not a divider, after all!

Interestingly, the members of Freedom Fighters International — the most vociferous "Jesse Go Home" bellowers — aren't even from Palm

Beach. Rumor has it they have been bused in from Miami, though they won't say who paid for their tickets. (Finally, a busing program that conservative Republicans can support!) They all hate Gore; spokesman Michael Symonett proceeds to tell me that Gore's a murderer, since he comes from a long line of Southern Democrats.

It doesn't matter what the protest organizers do or say — whether they attempt to stop the heckling with mockery or prayer or an off-key verse of "My Country 'Tis of Thee." The Bush-backers keep yelling. They hold their signs high, blocking Jackson from the platform set up for the TV cameras.

Soon enough, Jackson leaves at the advice of police, who cite security reasons. He skedaddles back to the amphitheater, and the rally is moved there.

The Jackson demonstration is clearly a disappointment for its organizers. West Palm Beach police were told to prepare for a crowd as big as thirty thousand, but the turnout was closer to three thousand. And it is not exactly a cross section of the local electorate. For the most part, the participants seem to be among the most fervent Gore supporters. Based on their signs and banners, they come from liberal interest groups that detest Bush and all that he stands for — People for the American Way, local Gore-Lieberman activists, and the National Association for the Advancement of Colored People. The most popular sign — "Let every vote count" — is the work of the Florida Alliance of Planned Parenthood Affiliates Inc.

Jackson is staying in my hotel, so it was not tough to catch him earlier Monday afternoon. He was standing in the lobby, resplendent in a flowing black silk shirt, his well-fed belly poking out from its midst. Surrounded by cameras, his entourage, and fans seeking his autograph, Jackson is in his starry-eyed element.

"So why are you here?" I ask him. Angry Bush-backers have been slamming him for days; some Democrats have even expressed concern — albeit off the record — that his presence isn't exactly helping things.

"Disenfranchised voters have faces," Jackson answers in his famously modulated tones. "They're Jewish Holocaust survivors, they're African-Americans, they're Haitian-Americans, they're farm workers, they are students. They were turned away. They have a right to vote. And their vote must count. Because they matter. There are voices that are trying to close the door on them again. They closed the poll on them last Tuesday; they're trying to close the polls again. Democracy puts a higher virtue on fairness and accuracy than it does speed. Let's have a fair count."

"So should there be a revote?" I ask, knowing how unlikely this is.

"It could be a first vote," Jackson replies. "That's fair. Either under-counted, discounted, disenfranchised, voters need a fair vote."

What of the reports that some of the Gore chieftains weren't happy being represented by such a polarizing, controversial figure as himself?

"The right to vote is not about Gore or Bush, it's about people who are disenfranchised. I marched. Our right to vote is sacred. The issue today is not the campaign. It's essential to vote. Now, I think Gore does appreciate what we're doing. Because he knows the disenfranchised people have a right to be heard."

★   ★   ★

In the supervisor's warehouse in Fort Lauderdale, Broward County, the canvassing board — Judge Robert Lee, county commissioner Suzanne Gunzburger, and elections supervisor Jane Carroll — begin counting the sample 1 percent of the ballots.

GOP lawyer James Carroll, no relation to the elections supervisor, asks them to reconsider. But no one on the board formally brings up his sugges-tion. "The request dies from lack of a motion," Lee says.

James Carroll isn't happy, and things get heated. Lee in turn gets fired up. This is not a public hearing, he says, this is a meeting, and you are here by our good graces, not because the sunshine law applies. "If you interrupt again, I'm going to ask the deputy to remove you," the judge tells him.

They begin with a ninety-minute debate over the standards to use. The board eventually decides — on a 2-to-1 vote — to use the "two-corner" rule, meaning the chad has to be detached from the ballot in at least two corners. The county workers count all 3,892 ballots from the three Demo-cratic precincts; the canvassing board inspects any disputed ones.

The end result is a net gain of just 4 Gore votes.

Lee reads the statute that says that a full hand recount is warranted only when "the vote tabulation system fails to count properly marked" ballots. The county attorneys agree with Jane Carroll's own attorney — they shouldn't have to do a recount if there's nothing wrong with the tabulation machines and no evidence of fraud.

The Democrats vehemently disagree.

You don't get to even make an argument, Lee tells them. It's a two-pronged test as to whether the matter's even open to debate — prong no. 1 is "Is there a problem with the system?" and no. 2 is "How significant is the difference?" The 1 percent recount fails to meet either one. "Unless we conclude that there's a problem with that thing in there," he says, "we don't go to Step Two to determine if there's an effect on the outcome of the election."

The attorneys keep yapping away. Rep. Peter Deutsch and local attorney Charles Lichtman square off against county GOP chair Ed Pozzuoli, state senator Jim Scott, and Carol Licko, who resigned as Jeb Bush's general counsel in May. Yap yap yap!

After warning them three times to keep their traps shut, Lee turns to a sheriff's deputy. "Deputy? All of them — out!"

The attorneys look at Lee, stunned.

I have warned you guys, he tells them. Now you're going to be behind the window like everyone else, and you can stand over there and watch us.

"The recount has not indicated an error in the votes tabulation, which could affect the outcome of the election," Lee says aloud.

They vote.

"All in favor, aye," he says.

Gunzburger says, "Aye."

"And opposed?" Lee asks.

Carroll says, "No."

As does Lee.

"The election results stand," Lee says. No hand recount in Broward.

★　★　★

In Palm Beach Democratic HQ, discussions have been about taking Burton, LePore, and Roberts to court to force them to adopt a more liberal ballot standard.

"This standard is going to kill us," Dennis Newman says to Jack Corrigan and David Sullivan. They're not counting votes that are clearly Gore votes, he says. "We can't wait until the end of the process to challenge this, we need to get in there now and change it, get a legitimate standard going."

On Sunday evening, as Newman runs a massive training for hundreds of Democratic observers, Corrigan and Sullivan are working with Ben Kuehne on drafting the legal motions. They're going to take these guys to court.

★　★　★

In Broward, Lee and Carroll look outside at the craziness, the protesters and lawyers coagulating, the gnashing of teeth. Deutsch is holding a press conference, talking about how he was illegally forced from the meeting. A *Sun-Sentinel* reporter will later tell Lee that Democratic honcho Mitch Caesar and some others are outside talking up the notion of recruiting a well-financed opponent for Lee in his next judicial election.

"How do we get out of here?" Lee asks Carroll. The back door goes out only to the roof, where there's barbed wire. He and Carroll laugh about the image of them scaling the building to avoid the crowds.

In a way, it's just annoying, Lee thinks. He has no doubt in mind that if the current skirmish he's been drawn into were reversed, those exact same parties would be making — with the exact same vigor and vehemence — the exact opposite arguments. Democrats would be saying that the Republicans were inventing votes; Republicans would be arguing that county canvassing boards have the discretion to do whatever they see fit. It's all kind of tiresome, he thinks.

★ ★ ★

Monday night, The Flag takes a bunch of the Tallahassee operation out for dinner at The Governor's Club.

It's been a long day. Broward voted against having a hand recount, Clay Roberts issued his opinion against the legality of the very notion . . . it's clear to all that the Republicans are very well coordinated.

They sit in a nice upstairs dining room — leatherbound books, white-coated waiters, a long table. Daley and Christopher sit across from one another in the center of the table, and they're flanked by Berger, Klain, Douglass, Sandler, Christopher attorney Mark Steinberg, Berger's law partner John Newton, spokesman Hattaway, Daley aides Graham Streett and David Lane. Much of the discussion at dinner is about Bob Butterworth. About how he's done nothing for them. Daley, in particular, expresses some frustration. Butterworth is the only Democratic state official, really — the governor, house, senate, division of elections director, secretary of state, even the goddamn (purportedly Democratic) secretary of agriculture is in the Bush camp. And yet he's done nothing for their cause, he's AWOL. Silly Butterworth; unlike Harris and Jeb, he actually is trying to behave impartially.

Christopher mentions having met him, how he found him not all that impressive, rather underwhelming. As Daley goes on about Butterworth, he gets increasingly agitated. Just talking about it is pissing him off. He tells Streett to get Butterworth on the phone for him. Streett gets up, walks to the corner of the room, punches up his cell phone.

When he's got Butterworth on the line, Streett brings the phone to Daley. Daley snags it and leaves the room, whereupon he proceeds to rip Butterworth a new asshole. It's day six and Harris has already shown the world how aggressive she's going to be for Bush, and where have you been?! Daley asks. We have no friends in this state, he says. Everything we've gotten so far we've gotten on our own, while Bush has the whole thing wired. He tells Butterworth about the opinion that Roberts handed down earlier today on the illegality of hand recounts. Palm Beach asked for an opinion from you, and you didn't even give them one, he says.

The next morning, Butterworth — despite a 1993 opinion he issued that "any questions arising under the Florida Election Code should be addressed to the Division of Elections and the Department of State" — issues an opinion that differs from Harris's.

"No vote is to be declared invalid or void if there is a clear indication of the intent of the voter as determined by the county canvassing board," he writes. He was compelled to offer his opinion since Clay Roberts's take on it all "is so clearly at variance with the existing Florida statutes and case law."

It's the first and last time the Gorebies find any use for the man they'll come to think of as Butterworthless.

8

"I'm willing to go to jail."

Post-Elián, there aren't a lot of Cuban-American Republicans who have framed letters from Janet Reno on their office walls. Roberto "Bobby" Martinez — the former U.S. attorney whom Kendall Coffey replaced — may be the only one. He tries to be a voice of caution, calm, the rule of law.

Martinez is a friend of Jeb's, has been since prep school at Phillips Andover. He served as his general counsel during Jeb's transition to governor. Now he's serving as one of the lead attorneys — along with former state representative Miguel De Grandy — in front of the Miami-Dade canvassing board.

Armed with a book on election law — Martinez hasn't been involved in a recount for more than a decade, when he argued against Coffey in a state legislative race — he went into the building and checked it all out. Everything seemed in order. Judge Lawrence King, Jr., the chairman of the canvassing board, even gave Martinez a tour of the counting room. To Martinez, King seemed very proud of his staff and the process, telling him how professional it was, how careful the workers were not to touch the individual ballots, as repeated handling could degrade the cards.

In all the squabbles about recounts, Martinez knows his mission: to preserve the status quo. Martinez hasn't been told to stop any further counting, to engage in delay tactics, to stall — he doesn't have to be told.

Thus, he was delighted when the board chose to wait until today to hold its hearing on hand counting the 1 percent sample. Bush field director Ken Mehlman was especially happy. Though of the three southern Florida counties, Gore's margin of victory in Miami-Dade was slimmest — roughly 53 percent to 47 percent — Mehlman's concern is that there are a lot of undervotes — 10,750. The Bushies don't want those ballots counted by hand.

Over the weekend, Martinez and De Grandy got organized. Political consultant Al Lorenzo was hired to tell them just which precincts were what and why and whether their rates of undervote were normal. Martinez suspected that the Gorebies were going to challenge absentee ballots, so he contacted a private investigator, Hugh Cochran, a former G-man Martinez knew when he was U.S. attorney. You never know when a bit of information about something — or someone — might be useful.

Nevertheless, on Tuesday morning, Martinez remains concerned about the potential legal might of his Democratic rivals. In fact, he's more concerned than ever, because he hears that last night, David Boies flew in to Tallahassee to join the Gore team.

★　★　★

David Boies flew in last night because on Monday, Ron Klain asked former solicitor general Walter Dellinger, "Who is the best lawyer in the country that we don't have working on this case?" and Dellinger gave two names: Boies and Joel Klein, both of whom worked on the antitrust suit against Microsoft. Klein was unreachable, Boies not so.

Not that he wasn't busy. As America's hottest lawyer, Boies was in Manhattan meeting with executives from Philip Morris in the conference room of the Lexington Avenue office of Boies, Schiller & Flexner when Dellinger called. Before he could be given the message, Boies — who is known to say, "Would you rather sleep or win?" — had already zipped over to the office of another client, Manhattan developer Sheldon Solow, for whom he won an $11.5 million judgment in 1999. At Solow's office, he got Dellinger's message, which was marked "Important."

Boies called Dellinger, a friend from Yale Law School days and on various legal stuff. What's up? he asked.

As you're probably aware, there's this recount issue going on down in Florida, Dellinger said. He conference-called Klain in, and Klain gave the basic 411, asked if Boies could come down to help out for a few days.

"When do you want me there?" Boies asked.

"As fast as possible," Klain said, as they might be going to the Florida Supreme Court the next day.

Boies called his son, Jonathan, a lawyer at his firm, and had him prepare a packet of information gleaned from Lexis-Nexis and the Internet. He had a charter plane arranged to take him from Teterborough Airport, across the river in New Jersey, to Florida and proceeded to take two more meetings — with clients from Calvin Klein and from Napster — before heading to the airport, where Jonathan's research was waiting for him. He arrived in Tallahassee around midnight, cabbed it to the Governor's Inn, met Klain, walked over to Mitchell Berger's offices. The only one on the team he knew was Warren Christopher, since they'd both done some work for IBM in the 1970s, as well as the fact that they were both alumni of the University of Redlands.

Tuesday night I catch my first glimpse of Boies when I stumble in to the Governor's Inn, where The Flag is staying and where my glorious office assistant had managed to secure me a room. It's late, and he's doing a TV interview. Such is Boies. The camera loves him, and it is not an unrequited love. Boies is an intriguing figure, brilliant, nice, rumpled, pock-marked, mussed, with cheap suits and Rockport shoes and a $29.95 Casio watch oddly wrapped around the outside of his shirt.

He has represented radio talk-show host Don Imus, comedian Garry Shandling, and Yankees owner George Steinbrenner. In 1997, he left big-time law firm Cravath, Swaine & Moore to start his own firm, and in 1999, *National Law Journal* named him "Lawyer of the Year," and the reporter who wrote the story — calling him "the Michael Jordan of the courtroom" — is now following him around working on his biography. Largely this is due to his last case. Just as Ted Olson is Bill Clinton's legal nemesis, Boies is Bill Gates's.

And to hear his best friend, James Fox Miller, tell it, he always knew that Boies was headed in this direction. Miller's a past president of the Florida bar, and he's more than willing to tell me all about his buddy. As able as Boies is, Miller's hyperbole strains credibility. But he's only slightly less hypey than the rest of the media is being with news of Boies's arrival.

Boies has been Miller's best friend since four days into Northwestern Law School in 1962, he tells me. Bearing in mind that Boies has been married three times, Miller says that he "probably know[s] him better than anybody in the world." "He's the best legal mind I know," Miller tells me. "He can simplify complex legal and factual issues better than anyone I know. He can grasp the basics and the nuances of law to which he has never been exposed. He's the quickest study of any mind I have ever seen anywhere." As if his legend needed any more mythology, Boies also is dyslexic — the reason that his brain has worked so hard on overdrive to overcompensate in other areas, like his photographic memory. But no one considers his dyslexia to be anything but interesting color in his profiles. Certainly not Miller. "When Vice President Gore hired David Boies, he maximized his chances of success," Miller says.

But what of the fact that Boies isn't an expert on election law, certainly not on Florida election law? No problem, Miller says. When Boies was hired by CBS to defend the network against libel charges by Gen. William Westmoreland, Boies had never done a libel case before. But by the end of it, he was the no. 1 libel lawyer in the country, Miller replies. When Klein at the Justice Department brought Boies in to help them fell Gates and Microsoft, "he'd never even turned on a computer," Miller says.

Clearly Miller seems to hold Boies in a kind of awe usually reserved in times past for emperors. And it's been this way since that first week at Northwestern. Professors held him in such regard, Miller says, that one told him, "He is teaching the faculty, we're not teaching him." (Well, not every professor; Boies later had to transfer to Yale after he had an affair with a professor's wife, a woman who became wife no. 2.) But Boies does have his detractors. During the Microsoft case, Gates attacked him personally, saying Boies was "out to destroy Microsoft . . . and make us look bad." Robert Levy, a senior fellow in constitutional studies at the libertarian Cato Institute, says that Boies's Microsoft arguments were over the top for the benefit of the cameras. "The case played to the media. It didn't focus on substantive legal issues, but instead emphasized the ridicule of both the company and Bill Gates in particular."

When I ask his best friend about Levy's criticism, Miller says that playing to the media may have been the only way to win the Microsoft case. And Boies can hardly be faulted for pursuing a legal plan that worked, at least in the short term.

But last night I did wonder what Boies was doing gingerly, leisurely talking to David Bloom of NBC while Rome burned.*

---

* In an interview on January 15, 2001, I'll ask Boies if while he was in Florida he wasn't wasting his time when he would talk to the media instead of preparing for trial, working on the case. He'll say to me, "What do you think 'working on a case' is? It's thinking, it's answering questions, it's refining the arguments. And this was not a situation like in antitrust cases, where there are lots of obscure market-definition issues and you have to go into records and cases and research. When I got on the plane, I had in my hand the stack of statutes and cases Jonathan had pulled for me," and there weren't very many more cases he needed to learn about, he says. "This was not a situation where there was a great deal of undone legal analysis. A lawyer needs to be able to answer any questions the court is going to have; lots of lawyers have elaborate moot courts, which I don't do because I find them artificial. There weren't any questions that the Florida Supreme Court asked me that hadn't been asked to me by members of the press, sometimes several times."

★ ★ ★

On Tuesday morning, Martinez and De Grandy face off against Coffey and Democratic trial lawyer Steve Zack before the Miami-Dade canvassing board: King, Leahy, and circuit court judge Myriam Lehr. (Lehr was assigned to the board when every single commissioner recused himself or herself due to involvement one way or another with a race on the November ballot.) They're there to debate a motion from county Democratic chair Joe Geller, that Miami-Dade should conduct the "1 percent" recount of the county's ballots, as well as inspect the 10,417 undervotes.

On Election Night, Zack had been asked by Gore lawyer Chris Koch to come on board, but he'd turned him down, saying he was too busy with an HMO trial. But Zack was intrigued by the Middlebrooks case, primarily since two of his University of Florida buddies were there — both Middlebrooks and Tallahassee attorney Steve Uhlfelder, who was arguing in favor of cameras in the courtroom on behalf of ABC. So Zack had ducked in to see the trial, whereupon Coffey asked him to help him argue the recount today.

Zack's no great legal mind, but he's a skilled trial attorney, full of rhetoric and histrionics, which he often uses effectively. Zack begins by discussing the seal of the Florida Supreme Court: its motto, *Sat Cito Si Recte,* "soon enough, if done rightly"; the goddess of justice, "which is blindfolded to symbolize the impartiality of the law," and the eagle, "which has been interpreted as the power of justice ruling the world." Zack's description of the motto is cribbed, nearly verbatim, from the Florida Supreme Court's Web site. He talks about Middlebrooks. He talks about *Profiles in Courage.* He quotes Will Rogers.

"May I ask a question?" Judge Lehr interrupts. "Which three precincts?"

They are precincts 103, 203, and 234 — astronomically Democratic precincts, two largely black and Hispanic (though not Cuban) and one largely Jewish and elderly.

Martinez is called to speak. He refers to a document provided him by the Bushies, the testimony of the former director of elections for the state of Oregon, who says that the more you handle ballots, the more "their quality as evidence of the voters' original intent is degraded."

Lehr, flipping through the copy of the document that's been provided by Martinez, jumps in again. "Mr. Martinez, I apologize, what page are you on?"

Page four, paragraph six, Martinez says.

"Page four is missing," Leahy says.

"That's a major oversight," Martinez says, but continues. He argues that there has been no error in vote tabulation. He quotes Florida statute *Broward v. Hogan** and Katherine Harris. Martinez also offers a touch of rhetorical panache; not quite Zack-level, but close. "Ours is a country of laws," he muses. "It is a country that is governed by the rule of law. That is a term that this area in particular has heard quite a bit in the last year. We must respect and follow the rule of law. There are many people in this country — and in this area in particular — that come here because our system of government follows the rule of law, and they have escaped those systems of government where the governmental officials act arbitrarily."

There is more than a touch of Emma Lazarus underlining Martinez's comments. Both elected officials on the board — Judges King and Lehr — were elected with significant support from the Cuban-American community. Both retain the services of Armando Gutierrez — politico and spokesman for Elián's Miami relatives. Martinez is sending a message.

Coffey rebuts some of the arguments about ballots being degraded in the process. Zack says that *Hogan* doesn't apply until the board makes a decision. He quotes Dickens and, again, Middlebrooks. "You know, I was thinking about how prophetic the movie *2001* was," Zack rambles. "When I saw it, it was 1960-something. It's now 2001.[†] And in *2001*, a computer called Hal controlled our lives. Not individuals. Computers still in this century hopefully will not control our lives.

"You know, Bob Martinez is a very good friend of mine," he continues, as those listening strain to understand where he's going. "He came from Cuba in the sixties, and I did, too. I was born in the United States, but my grandfather is Cuban, and my mother is Cuban." (After Zack was born in the United States, his family moved to Cuba, and then he returned to the States in 1961.) "My grandfather was a refugee for the second time in his life. He had come from Russia to Cuba in the early 1900s to avoid oppression. He was obviously very, very upset having to leave Cuba, as was my mother, and I remember his words, and I asked him how he was feeling.

---

*In March 1991, Al Hogan was defeated by just 3 votes in his race for Oakland Park city council against Douglas Johnson. A computer recount increased Johnson's margin of victory to 5 votes. Hogan wanted a hand recount, since there were undervotes not read, but the Broward County canvassing board denied his request. He sued the board in circuit court and won, but in November 1992, the Fourth District Court of Appeals ruled that the canvassing board had the right to deny his request.

[†]At the time, of course, it was not 2001. It was November 14, 2000.

"He said, 'You know, it's a horrible thing to be a refugee twice in your life. I take solace in one thing, that I'm going to America. I know I will never be a refugee again, because I know that if America falls, there will be no place to go.'

"And I know that he never heard of Thomas Paine at that time before he died or at any other time. But had he, he would have stated the same thing Thomas Paine said when they founded this nation. That is, the right of voting for the representatives is the primary right by which all other rights are protected. All we are asking you today is to protect that right."

All three members of the canvassing board vote to do the 1 percent hand recount.

★   ★   ★

About eight years ago, circuit court judge Terry Lewis, appointed to the bench in '97 by Chiles, finished off a junky mystery novel and thought, "They actually paid this person? They actually spent money to publish it? I really think I could write something as good as that." Five years later, a small publishing house published his magnum opus, *Conflict of Interest,* a decent thriller about Teddy Stevens, an alcoholic Tallahassee attorney assigned to defend a young black kid for murdering a woman with whom Stevens secretly had an affair.

Katherine Harris's conflict of interest in the decision before Lewis is a little less steamy, but a lot more consequential.

Some in the Bush camp are worried about Lewis. He's a registered Democrat, and the last time he was asked to issue an injunction this weighty was in July 1999, minutes after a Jeb-backed law took effect that would require abortion providers to notify a minor's parents forty-eight hours before the procedure was performed. Lewis granted the temporary injunction almost immediately, based on state constitutional privacy issues, and in May 2000 he ruled that the law was "exactly the kind of government interference into personal, intimate decisions that the privacy clause protects against."

Bush attorney Barry Richard gives the team his take on Lewis, as he'll do for every Florida judge. He thinks Lewis is intellectually one of the most competent judges on bench anywhere, an independent judge who presides over a good courtroom. He and Lewis like each other's styles: just as Lewis appreciates the fact that Richard will acknowledge weaknesses in his case, thus earning credibility, Richard likes the fact that Lewis gets to the meat of the matter right away in his questions, zeroing in on the core issues right off the bat. He tells his colleagues not to worry.

True to his Solomonic reputation, shortly after noon Lewis issues an "order granting in part and denying in part" Volusia's motion for the temporary restraining order. "I give great deference to the interpretation by the secretary of the election laws, and I agree that the canvassing boards must file their returns by five o'clock P.M. today," he says. "I disagree, however, that the secretary is required to ignore any late filed returns absent an Act of God."

Lewis points out that the hand-recount provision in state law exists for a reason. If Harris weren't meant to accept any hand recounts, that would mean that the law were valid "only in sparsely populated counties," where such recounts can be completed by the deadline mandated for seven days after the election. "Just common sense tells you that if you have discretion, you can't decide ahead of time what the possibilities might be that a canvassing board can't get the results in," he thinks. You have to at least hear the reasons why.

"That the secretary may ignore late filed returns necessarily means that the secretary does not have to ignore such returns," Lewis rules. "It is, as the secretary acknowledges, within her discretion. To determine ahead of time that such returns will be ignored, however, unless caused by some Act of God, is not the exercise of discretion. It is the abdication of discretion.

"If the returns are received from a county at 5:05 P.M. on November 14, 2000, should the results be ignored? What about fifteen minutes? An hour? What if there was an electrical power outage? Some other malfunction of the transmitting equipment? . . . Obviously the list of scenarios is almost endless. . . . The secretary may, and should, consider all of the facts and circumstances."

That said, Lewis doesn't really get why anybody's putting up a fuss about the certification deadline. The law provides for anyone to contest the election. And since one reason for such a challenge is the "rejection of a number of legal votes sufficient to change or place in doubt the result of the election," it would seem that the canvassing boards can go ahead and count and, once completed, contest the certified results. Or Gore can. Or the guy in the street can.

So yes, the deadline stands, Lewis says. But it is "ordered and adjudged that the secretary of state is directed to withhold determination as to whether or not to ignore late filed returns . . . until due consideration of all relevant facts and circumstances consistent with the sound exercise of discretion."

Harris is no longer only using Kearney. The secretary of state's office has officially retained Joe Klock of Steel Hector & Davis, a firm with a Democratic history, where Janet Reno once practiced law. When Harris hears of Lewis's ruling, she decides to go ahead and certify tonight. But Kearney and Klock caution her otherwise. This is a legal order, they tell her. The judge is ordering you to consider reasons for returns filed late. They recommend that she at least take a breath.

★   ★   ★

In Tallahassee, in Courtroom 3-D at the Leon County Courthouse, GOP attorney George Meros is vigorously objecting. And in his objection, and perhaps as well in his subsequent bout with laryngitis, there lies a symbol of the bipartisan nonsense playing out in Florida.

Elections supervisor Ion Sancho, a forty-nine-year-old Democrat, has called a special meeting of the county canvassing board. Since Election Day, twelve absentee ballots had turned up, and Sancho wants them included in the county tally before the 5 P.M. deadline.

Since Leon County had gone for Vice President Al Gore over Gov. George W. Bush 60 percent to 40 percent, Meros, a Tallahassee attorney representing Bush, clearly thinks the twelve absentee ballots would favor Gore by a similar ratio. So he tries to have them scrapped.

You have no proof of receipt by seven o'clock on the night of the election, as the statute requires, Meros says. You have no proof that the ballots were in the safekeeping of the board, which is also what the statute requires.

But where Meros argues the rule of law, Sancho sees overzealousness. "He's treating the proceeding as if it's a criminal proceeding," Sancho thinks. Sancho had in fact investigated how the ballots ended up at the polling warehouse where the ballots are taken, and he ascertained that the ballots were legit. He explains this; Meros doesn't buy it, calling Sancho's investigation "hearsay."

Sancho explains that seven of the ballots had been filled out by county employees who had been running the polling precincts on Election Day, and therefore didn't have time to show up to their precincts and vote. The county employee who collected these seven just happened to forget to turn them in to the county's "AB," or absentee ballot, department. There were two ballots that had been sent to Sancho's office through interdepartmental mail, which — in the mail crush leading up to November 7 — no one had opened until after the election. Then there were three absentee ballots from voters who had recently changed addresses; the ballots were then hung up in the bureaucracy of the addressing office.

Meros does everything he can to block the admissibility of the ballots. Led by county judge Jim Harley, the canvassing board overrules him, pointing out that Sancho had the authority to accept them. Meros is not happy.

Then they open the ballots, right there, before Meros and the judge and about a dozen others.

Ten votes for Bush; 2 for Gore.

Meros and the other Republicans in the room start smiling.

"Are there any more objections, George?" Harley asks knowingly. Everyone laughs.

"I'm not saying another word," Meros says, thanking the canvassing board for its time and walking out of the room.

"I see it all across the state," Sancho will later say to me. "Each side is simply trying to achieve its ends, uncover votes it believes will be favorable and suppress votes it believes will be unfavorable." In the process, neither party is doing much to elevate the dignity of this process much above your average Panama City wet T-shirt contest.

★   ★   ★

Carol Roberts is fired up. "I never would have agreed" to seek an opinion from Clay Roberts "had I been told it was binding," she says, "because I believe we in Palm Beach County ought to be making that decision." She wants the team to ignore it.

Burton now wants to do the count, inspired at least in part by Wallace's annoying object-object-object stall tactics, Kerey Carpenter's suspected shiftiness and Harris's stalwart partisanship. But as turned around as he feels, the judge is not quite on Roberts's program when it comes to ignoring the law.

"As a county court judge and as a chair of this board," Burton says, "I think it is my obligation to follow the law, and the law tells me that this opinion is binding on this board, and the law tells me we have to follow it. And so based on this, it would be my motion that the manual recount be suspended."

Burton calls the vote to suspend the countywide hand recount before it even begins. LePore — now taking guidance from county attorney Denise Dytrych, not Montgomery — votes aye. Roberts votes nay. It's Burton's motion, so he's automatically with LePore.

At this point the board can't even certify the results it has because of a restraining order granted last week in the butterfly ballot case. In the afternoon, circuit court judge Jorge LaBarga — the poor dude forced to contend with the butterfly ballot revote case — dissolves the restraining order and also tells the board that it is "permitted" to conduct the full hand recount, though Harris has discretion as to whether or not she'd accept the late returns. "If she decides to accept them, fine," LaBarga says. "If she doesn't, then you need to talk to her about it."

So can the board go ahead with the count after all? The canvassing board debates the matter. Dytrych says that they shouldn't.

"What happens?" Roberts asks, at the height of her you-go-girlness. "Do we go to jail? Because I'm willing to go to jail." Democrats in the crowd cheer.

"If we start, and the supreme court tells us to stop, that's what we'll do," Burton says. He and Roberts have made up after he accused her of sandbagging him, but he's still unhappy when she goes into campaign mode.

Wallace is furious. "The entire world is watching you all and the action that you take," he says. "The chief elections officer of the state of Florida has told you that you cannot act lawfully and conduct a manual recount. What we suggest and what you suggested this morning — and nothing has changed since your hearing this morning — is that you wait for a court decision telling you it's legal or not legal to continue with the manual recount."

Roberts acts as if Wallace's microphone isn't on and calls for a vote on the recount.

All three vote aye.

"What happens if the supreme court says that the canvassing board is acting illegally by conducting this manual recount?" Wallace continues.

"Then we're going to abide by any ruling of the court, of course," Burton says. A lot of Burton's statements to Wallace include an "of course." The kid is getting really annoying, Burton thinks.

"And what would you do to preserve the sanctity of those ballots?"

"I think the same thing that's always done, Mr. Wallace."

"What is that?" Wallace asks.

"You have been in there," Burton says.

"No, this has never been done before," Wallace presses. "I don't understand what's to be done."

"All right, do we need to address anything else?" Burton asks.

"I don't have anything else," says Roberts.

Wallace is fired up. "Is the judge refusing to answer the question?"

"I think the judge answered the question," Burton says. "We have kept those ballots under security, and they'll continue to be kept in the same manner that we've done to protect the sanctity of them."

They break and agree to start the counting at 7 A.M. tomorrow, Wednesday.

Bush spokesman Eskew gripes to reporters, who await his every word. "Machine counts are accurate. Let's not forget, we've had three of them," Eskew says. "What on earth rationale is there for going to a less accurate accounting, other than to come up with a different result?"

Good question. Maybe he should ask Bush why he ever signed that 1997 Texas law.

★   ★   ★

LePore is starting to come to terms with her naïveté. She is no longer listening to Montgomery, favoring instead Republican county attorney Dytrych, whom she likes and respects and, more important, knows. And the judge. She's listening a lot more to the judge these days.

But it's not as if she thinks that the Democrats are the only ones with agendas. She's clearly resentful of Kerey Carpenter and all her lobbying. And now there's the matter of Katherine Harris and Clay Roberts. LePore is bending over backward to be as impartial as she can; she cannot believe how Harris and Roberts are behaving. "As an election official, you need to have at least the appearance of being nonpartisan and treating everything that you do in a nonpartisan manner," she thinks. She remembered when she heard that Harris was actively involved in Bush's campaign; she thought it was inappropriate then. Now it is totally out of hand. Talk about the fox guarding the hen house. Every year, the association of elections supervisors has a reception for legislators in Tallahassee. In this past one, the association was to hold a news conference announcing its statewide "Get Out the Vote" campaign with its GOTV foundation. The organizers of the campaign wanted Harris to appear, but — LePore remembers — Harris kept having it rescheduled because she was on the pro-Bush "Freezin' for a Reason" tour for the New Hampshire primary.

Elections have never been a priority for Harris, LePore thinks. Even though she's constantly a font of promises — telling the association, "We're gonna do this" and "We're gonna do that" — when it comes time to do it, she's never there. Harris didn't cough up the cash she'd pledged for the association's GOTV campaign, she barely worked with the association at all on voter registration, she's been a nonentity. Most of the time Harris didn't even attend the association's conferences, though she is — as she reminds the world now — the chief elections officer in the state.

And now, the way she's acting, so transparently pro-Bush, so unwilling to let them do a hand recount, forced by a judge to consider reasons why vote tallies might come in late . . . LePore just didn't understand it.

LePore has an opinion on Clay Roberts, too, whom she's worked with a lot: "Clay knows who his boss is," she says.

★   ★   ★

While Harris is coming at the board from the right, telling them that they can't count, Gore attorney Ben Kuehne is coming at them from the left. On behalf of the Florida Democratic Party, Kuehne files a motion before LaBarga to seek injunctive relief and make the canvassing board scrap that 1990 standard and start to loosen it up, to "review ballots based on voters' intent."

The law Kuehne cites is good ol' 102.166 (7) (b): "If a counting team is unable to determine a voter's intent in casting a ballot, that ballot shall be presented to the county canvassing board for it to determine the voter's intent."

In Fort Lauderdale, the Democrats are suing the Broward County canvassing board, too. It seems that where the canvassing boards do what they want, the Dems claim the hegemony of the canvassing board. All hail! Where they don't, they sue. Mean old board!

Meanwhile, local Democrats are spreading rumors about Lee, about the fact that Jeb appointed him, that some big circuit court judgeship is awaiting him in return for yesterday's vote. The Democratic lawyers' take on Burton is even far more angry and suspicious.

★   ★   ★

The counters in Miami-Dade take around four hours. They're interrupted to hear King read an announcement that Harris is delaying the preliminary certification until tomorrow, and will consider reasons for late tallies if faxed to her by 2 p.m. Wednesday.

Before 8 p.m., the board issues the news: Gore gained a total of six votes. Now: Should they count all 653,963 ballots?

Six votes? Martinez says. "They have not met the threshold requirement. . . . We have to follow the law here. What happened today does not rise to the level of an error."

Coffey points to the 10,750 undervotes. "Some think that there could be eight thousand disenfranchised voters who did not strike it right. Take six percent of that in the mind-boggling closeness of the election. The outcome shows that indeed there are additional votes in favor of Al Gore. We are in a situation right now where it just wouldn't be right to stop the process, the process of getting to the truth."

De Grandy has a different take, of course. "It is time to reach closure," he says.

"We need to follow the law," Martinez adds. "I can talk for hours about Dickens or *2000-and-whatever-it-was Space Odyssey*. I read fiction. That's not what you want to hear from me. I'm a lawyer, and you are a canvassing board that has to follow the law."

De Grandy knows recounts firsthand. In 1988, during his first run for public office, he beat Carlos Valdez by 9 votes in the GOP runoff for a state legislative seat.* After the absentee ballots were counted, however, De Grandy and Valdez were tied. An automatic recount had Valdez picking up a vote, De Grandy losing one, so De Grandy asked for a hand recount. The canvassing board voted 2 to 1 to conduct the count — Leahy, of course, voted against it — and while they found De Grandy's missing vote, they also found another one for Valdez. De Grandy didn't appeal.

King calls for a vote. He exercises his chairman's prerogative and asks Leahy to vote first. Leahy's been doing this for more than a generation. He's a bureaucrat's bureaucrat, a milquetoast moustachioed man of impeccable credentials and zero charisma. He believes in his machines. When he votes no, few are surprised.

Lehr's the wild card here. While King, a Democrat, has made it pretty clear that he favors a countywide hand recount, no one knows what Lehr's going to do. She's quiet. Born in Brussels, Belgium, she's married to a big GOP honcho. All eyes on her.

Lehr votes no.

King votes yes.

No hand recount in Miami-Dade. Though they do want the additional Gore votes added to the certification.

Good, Martinez thinks. He's glad. The rule of law prevailed.

---

*The one being vacated by then–state senator Ileana Ros-Lehtinen, who was running for U.S. House. More on this race in a bit.

★   ★   ★

Ticktock, ticktock.

Miami-Dade's a goose egg, Palm Beach starts tomorrow, Broward's waiting to see what the Florida Supreme Court says about the conflicting opinion . . . what about Volusia?

Volusia's done. And the new tally is good news for Gore. Gore picked up 241 votes in the hand recount, Bush 143, a net gain of 98 for the vice president.

Jack Young smiles.

★   ★   ★

In Tallahassee, Baker enters the state senate hearing room, where a bunch of us media idiots are sitting. He then rhetorically urinates in Gore's ear while announcing to the world that it's raining.

Offering "a proposal that we think is very fair," Baker says that the Bush campaign will change its position on manual recounts, accepting them as valid, as long as the counties engaging in the manual recounts finish their task by Tuesday at 5 P.M. "We are offering to accept the manual recount up to the time of the statutory deadline," Baker says.

This is of course a clear physical impossibility, as declared by the Palm Beach County canvassing board, which has said it would need six days for the operation. Additionally, whatever hand-counting the board could have accomplished Tuesday was shanked when Harris issued her opinion questioning the legality of the hand recount, thus suspending it. Nonetheless, Baker pushes this forward as a "compromise that both campaigns [could] enter into in good faith," knowing full well that the Gore team will reject it on its face. (Which happens a few minutes later, when Daley, in Washington, issues a Chicago-style deep-dish No Way.)

It is imperative, Baker argues, that the Gore team accept his offer. "More and more we see uncertainty in financial markets and we see uncertainty abroad," Baker says, insinuating that Gore may be responsible for an impending apocalypse.

Oh, sweet Moses.

Baker, his comments actually written by Zoellick, slams the Gore campaign for suing Broward County when it refused to continue with its hand recount. "The Gore campaign, which placed great weight on Florida law when it thought the provisions served its tactics, does not like *this* Florida law," he rightly says. "In sum, the Gore campaign has been unwilling to accept any finality," Baker continues, "after the vote, after the recount, after the manual recount tests in selective favorable counties, or even after the larger selective manual recounts within the time established by Florida statute. Indeed, the manual recount in Palm Beach County is at least the fourth count of these votes, because the county also undertook a third machine count."

Baker neglects to mention that the third machine count came at the request of the Republicans. Since the first one was just the regular election count, and the second was the law-mandated recount because the margin of victory was so slim, that would mean that the Democrats and the Republicans have one recount apiece done at their respective requests, the one done at the Democrats' request being manual, and uncompleted, the one done at the Republicans' request being that third machine recount.

But Baker's counting on you not knowing that.

Baker is asked how this is in any way a compromise. The Palm Beach hand recount has no chance of being concluded by close of business Tuesday, while Bush still leads by an estimated 388 votes. And — according to the Bush team — Bush will be the anticipated winner of the absentee ballots due by midnight Friday. How does this not give Bush a distinct advantage?

"How can you say that?" Baker asks, seemingly almost wounded. "There's no assurance he will win those [absentee ballot] votes. Traditionally, they have favored the Republican candidate, and we should say that; I've already said that. But there's absolutely no assurance. So if you're suggesting that we take no risk by this proposal, I would argue with that rather strongly.

"I think for them to reject it just on the grounds that it locks in a victory for us is simply not right," Baker says.

In the midst of this nonsense, Baker does make some of the legitimate, cogent arguments on his side. It is true — and somewhat disturbing — that the Democrats have yet to offer any sort of timeline for when the recount process might be over to their satisfaction. On Thursday morning on NBC's *Today* show, for instance, Lieberman was asked if his ticket would cease gumming up any finality to the Florida recount process if it got its manual recounts, and he hedged. "We have a wait-and-see attitude about that," Lieberman said, playing right into the Bush campaign's argument that the Gore team is going to keep challenging the Florida results until it finds an outcome it likes.

Baker is asked: If the Bush team objects to the "subjectivity" of the largely Democratic counties from which the Gore team wants recounts, would he therefore agree to a statewide hand recount?

"I reject that categorically, and let me explain why," Baker says. "It took fifteen hours to count four precincts in Palm Beach County. There are six thousand precincts in the state of Florida. It would take an inordinate amount of time to count six thousand precincts manually. Furthermore, we have made very clear since we've been here our problem with the fundamentally flawed process of manual counting. How it could lead to human error or even mischief — those concerns are well known.

"Many people around the country have urged both candidates to reach out to one another with a fair proposal to resolve this divisive and unfortunate process," Baker concludes. "We are doing just that."

★ ★ ★

For a woman who doesn't seem to think we have a second to spare before the winner of Florida's presidential contest is declared, Harris sure takes her time getting to her 5 P.M. press conference tonight.

Finally, at 7:35 P.M. she walks in — dress, lipstick, and pumps all precisely coordinated to the same regal maroon hue.

Harris has taken her share of hits in the last few days, receiving gator-size rhetorical chomps from Dems up and down the peninsula. That said, Harris seems calm and collected as she walks in to tell the world that all sixty-seven counties have filed their returns as of Tuesday at 5 P.M., and according to those returns, Bush leads Gore by 300 votes — 2,910,492 to 2,910,192.

Harris acknowledges Lewis's decision and leaves open the possibility that she might, in fact, accept later hand-recount totals if they come — though she offers no guarantee. "Within the past hour, the director of the Division of Elections" — Clay Roberts — "faxed a memorandum to the supervisors of elections in these three Florida counties," she continues. "In accordance with today's court ruling confirming my discretion in these matters, I am requiring a written statement of the facts and circumstances that would cause these counties to believe that a change should be made before final certification of the statewide vote."

This is bullshit, of course. She didn't even want to give this extra day, but attorneys Klock and Kearney seriously recommended that she do so. An open mind cannot be mandated by law — though the pretense of one can, I suppose.

The final certification will come Saturday, after the midnight Friday deadline for overseas absentee ballots. The deadline for the excuse letter from the three counties is 2 P.M. Wednesday, Harris says. "On advice of counsel, I will not take questions because of pending litigation," she says.

And the litigation does indeed pend. Running alongside the Democrats' legitimate arguments in favor of a full and accurate manual recount lurk the darker impulses of trial lawyers, who envision even more possible lawsuits beyond an extended deadline for hand recounts. So Tuesday I ask Klain what other lawsuits there might be. Will the Gore campaign sue Palm Beach County for its confusing butterfly ballots? Will the Gorebies claim that the ballots were illegal, thus necessitating a revote in the county? "Our options are under review there," Klain says. "Our first option is trying to get these votes counted."

I try again. What would he say to the American people who, according to polls, think there should be a full recount, by hand if necessary, but aren't prepared to go beyond that?

"I would just say to the American people that the ballots would be counted in Florida today if not for the legal and political issues to stop the count, the responsibility for which lies at the feet of the Republican Party," Klain says.

OK, fair enough, but what about beyond that? What if you get that, and Gore still doesn't win? Are you prepared to call it a day?

"Let's get the votes counted and see where we go from there," Klain says to me.

★　★　★

But which votes do they want counted?

Jack Young calls Gorebies Charlie Baker and Jill Alper in Tallahassee to talk about what to do, where his team of roughly forty should go next.

There's talk of going to Broward, to help out Sautter's team. It's pretty much a given that he won't go to Palm Beach County, where the Boston Boys — with whom Young has butted heads — are running things.

Let me take these people and send them out to other Opti-scan counties, Young says. Let's tell other canvassing boards about the Volusia experience. Judge McDermott — a Republican — has gotten a lot of good press, let's capitalize on it.

Clearly there are votes in the overvotes, Young says. People fill in the circle for Bush and then write in Cheney and the vote is discarded, unread by the machine. Lake and Duval Counties have a ton of overvotes, for instance.

But Baker and Alper are skeptical. Lake and Duval Counties are overwhelmingly Republican, they say. The plan is to count in places where Gore won.

Young reiterates the point — the one he and Sautter made in *The Recount Primer* — that if you're behind, you just increase the pool of possible votes as much as possible. (Not to mention the idea that if you actually want to count all the votes, you don't shrug off doing so in some counties because they tilt GOP.)

If you go into those counties can you assure us that Gore will pick up votes there? Young is asked by the people he calls "the politicos."

"No," he says, "I can't."

His team is sent south, to Broward and then eventually Miami-Dade.* So much for "count all the votes."

★ ★ ★

As the sun rises Wednesday morning, Palm Beach is set to do its recount, and Broward isn't.

That switches.

The Broward County canvassing-board members seek legal guidance on what they're permitted to do. They find that, since Elections Supervisor Jane Carroll was the one who received Harris's binding opinion — and not Judge Lee, the chairman of the board — they're not bound by it. So, impressed by Butterworth's opinion, Lee switches his vote.

A GOP attorney says that they gotta listen to Harris. "Then let her go get her mandamus to make us stop," Lee says, referring to the Latin word for "we command" and the legal order from a superior court. And in the meantime, they plunge away — twelve teams of counters, 609 precincts, 588,000 ballots. Two corners of the chad gotta be off in order for it to count.

From Austin, Bush spokesman Ari Fleischer, based on nothing, tells reporters that Lee's change of mind is evidence that "officials involved in the recount are succumbing to political pressure." Lee finds this ridiculous. The other night, he had heard that Democrats were saying that Jeb was promising him treats; now word on the street is that Gore had pledged to him a federal judgeship. Both sides are going crazy, Lee thinks. He's bent over backward to avoid contact with anyone.

---

* Big mistake. Lake County — where Bush beat Gore 50,010 to 36,571 — reported 3,114 overvotes. In December, the *Orlando Sun-Sentinel* will review them and clearly identify 376 Gore votes — ballots where the oval had been filled in for Gore, and either Gore or Lieberman's name had been filled in under the "write-in" section. Likewise, the newspaper finds 246 similarly botched Bush votes. This is a net gain of 131 Gore votes.

The machine rejected these ballots, but a thorough canvassing-board review likely wouldn't have.

"To publish illegal votes as legal votes would be to mislead the readers and the public," the inimitable Eskew told the *Sun-Sentinel*. "These are illegal votes, and your paper is publishing them as legal votes." He calls the media investigation "mischief."

"Scott," he said earlier in the week to his partner of five years, "until this is over, let the machine pick up all the calls." He wouldn't return any having to do with any of this. He told his secretary, Olga, to tell folks that he wasn't returning any calls until the storm had subsided.

Speaking of political pressure, the same Republican lawyer that Lee snapped at a few nights ago — Fort Lauderdale barrister James Carroll — is today sharing the love in Palm Beach, where on behalf of the GOP he's trying to get Carol Roberts disqualified from the canvassing board. He says she's been counting ballots as Gore votes that have "no hanging chads. She's been observed picking up numerous ballots from questionable ballot piles and interspersing [them] with the Gore ballot pile. She has been observed bending, twisting, poking, and purposely manipulating ballots in a manner that compromised their integrity. Ms. Roberts has been observed bending individual ballots approximately ninety degrees to determine whether the vote was valid."

One of Gore's Boston Boys, Dennis Newman, steps up.

"This motion is the most ridiculous, frivolous attempt that I've ever seen. Everyone in this room, this area, and all this media have told you of every action that every member of the board made on Saturday. There are thousands of videotapes of that. To say that one of the commissioners handled the ballots and looked at them in an unfair way is just a desperate attempt, another desperate attempt, of the Republicans to delay the fair and accurate counting of the ballots of Palm Beach County."

But it's not just Republicans like the delightful James Carroll who are playing politics; political pressure comes from the Democrats, too. Palm Beach County Democratic chair Monte Friedkin, pissed off at Burton, tells reporters that "he'll never get elected in this county. Not if I'm chairman."

"It's a political nightmare," Burton will think when he hears of Friedkin's comments. "Sure, there isn't any direct pressure, but I can read the papers, I can read quotes. Friedkin, shooting his mouth off, let him do what he wants — that's fine. But these things shouldn't be on the judge's mind." He needs to focus on the law.

As if the world isn't bass-ackward enough, Judge LaBarga rules in favor of the Dems on the standard by which the ballots are to be assessed. The 1990 standard goes against Florida law, he says. "No vote is to be declared invalid or void if there is a clear indication of the intent of the voter." The 1990 standard "restricts the canvassing board's ability to determine the intent of the voter." But it's a confusing, vague order, as befitting everything in this mess. While LaBarga rules that "the Palm Beach County Commission has the discretion to utilize whatever methodology it deems proper to determine the true intention of the voter," he also says that the board doesn't have the discretion to use the 1990 standard. "The present policy of a per se exclusion of any ballot that does not have a partially punched or hanging chad is not in compliance with the law," he rules. "The canvassing board has the discretion to consider those ballots and accept them or reject them."

Right. Well. OK. Thanks for clearing *that* up.

Harris receives the canvassing board's requests for extensions of the certification deadline. She rejects them. The Steel Hector & Davis attorneys have told her that the only excuses for late tallies are broken machines or acts of God. And though there's reason to believe that something's really wrong with the Votomatics — whether it's the fault of the machines or the voters, who can say — none of the members of the canvassing board claim that their machines were broken. Not that Harris or her legal staff gave them a heads-up that such would be an acceptable excuse.

Burton will later say about their excuse letter that he didn't think she even read it.

★　★　★

Former Clinton adviser Paul Begala is on NBC's *Today* show Wednesday morning. "She oughta recuse herself," he says of Harris. "She hasn't done so, which suggests to me she's impervious to public opinion. I mean, everybody who appears in public like she did yesterday, looking like Cruella De Vil coming to steal the puppies, is not very interested in what other people think of her."

Al Gore thinks this is hilarious. "Cruella De Vil!" he says. "Did you hear what Paul called her?"

Harris, of course, doesn't find the remark all that funny. She likes Dalmatians. And how come no one makes fun of any of the males in all of this and the way *they* look? Why aren't *they* mocked on *Saturday Night Live*? Her staffers try to comfort her — Hey! You really have to make it big to be made fun of on *SNL*! But it hurts. Still, she's addicted to it in a way. She stays up late, watching Letterman and Leno, to see what they have to say about her.

★　★　★

Bobby Martinez is pissed off.

He just got a call to head to the Miami-Dade canvassing-board hearing. Martinez thought this shit was over with, but shortly after he arrives, Miami Democratic chair Joe Geller offers the motion to reconsider yesterday's decision. Without giving the other side any notice. Without anything having changed.

After Geller springs his surprise motion on the board — after a different hearing on a recount involving a local race — King asks Martinez if he wants to say anything.

Martinez doesn't even want to concede that what Geller's doing is even remotely appropriate.

Perhaps more important, Martinez is worried about the Cuban-American community, which has been exemplary so far in its behavior during this incendiary mess, he thinks. But he knows that Miami-Dade, and its *Cubano* community, has the potential for chaos. If you want to set off a series of events to cause tensions to explode, you can do it if you set out to do it, he thinks. And this reconsideration has the potential to do that.

Geller steps up to the mike. He tells the board that Broward County canvassing-board members have decided to go ahead with the countywide hand recount, that they changed their minds, that they decided that the results after the 1 percent recount indicate maybe enough to affect the outcome of the election.

"Why did they consider a full manual recount?" Lehr asks. "What prompted them to do such a thing?"

A judge told them they could go ahead with it and ignore Harris's certification deadline, Geller says. He wants to reconvene tomorrow at 9 A.M., so the board can reconsider.

"How much time do you anticipate," King asks, "the presentation of at least —"

Geller's cell phone starts ringing.

"Please turn your phone off, sir," King says.

"I'm sorry," he says, frantically punching the appropriate button. "Sorry."

"How much time do you anticipate you'll need?"

Geller says an hour.

Leahy says that the fact that Broward changed its mind isn't enough. "I would need more than that to vote for a re-hearing," he says.

Geller reaches into his bag of justifications. Judge LaBarga ruled against Harris's deadline, too, he says. And in addition, he "issued an order striking down the Palm Beach County standards used by the canvassing board — the one-corner, two-corner rule."

"With all due respect," Lehr says, "that's only his opinion. You know? Then he can have his puppets sitting here, too. You know what I'm saying? I'm not needed, then. That's *his* opinion."

Geller scrambles, assesses the situation. Focus, Myriam, focus, Geller thinks. That's not what I'm talking about. We're not addressing standards. We'll get to standards if we actually start counting. "All I'm saying is that —"

"You know, if he wants to look at them his way, that's his prerogative," Lehr says. "You know, I have my standards. And, and you have all been behind us and watching us for the last two days, and —"

"OK," King interrupts. "So, Judge, do you or do you not wish to grant the hearing tomorrow? I know Mr. Leahy does not."

"I'm not opposed to, against granting a hearing, but maybe we should first listen to Mr. Martinez and see what he has to say," Lehr says.

I'm not prepared to argue this dumb thing, Martinez thinks.

He's very upset.

"I'm going to count to ten first," Martinez says. "I was taught as a child before responding —"

"You don't have to be mad," King snaps. "If you feel that you are emotionally involved in this case or this matter and you are counting to ten because you are irate over the issues raised by Mr. Geller, then maybe you should have someone else stand in for you. I don't like the look in your eyes, and I don't like you looking at me with the idea that you're mad."

Good, Geller thinks. Martinez is being an asshole. Rolling his eyes and sighing and being melodramatic, like Gore in the first debate.

"If you're counting to ten — and I'll let you explain what you just said on the record — but I really don't appreciate that," King goes on. "You've been given absolutely your fair share. And to be upset or to be upset about that in a manner which might upset you with respect to this panel, I'll be happy to take a few minutes, let you sit down and compose yourself, and come back to the panel. Would you like to do that?"

"No," Martinez says, chastened, but also somewhat embarrassed for King, who he thinks is making an ass out of himself. He wasn't upset at the board when he made his "counting to ten" comment! He was upset at Geller and the Democrats!

"*Thank you*," King says pointedly.

Martinez speaks briefly. "There is no provision in the Florida statutes . . . that deals with the request that Mr. Geller is making. Judge King, I hope that you would keep an open mind. I hope I can convince you, but I think frankly you have to understand that I'm focusing my attention at this time to your distinguished colleagues."

He makes his pitch.

Calmly, rationally.

King shows a bit of contrition. "I now understand, Mr. Martinez, why you stated what you did. And I apologize to you if I seemed a little distemperate with respect to the matter. . . . I'm sorry if I've gotten off on a soapbox."

In an attempt to put an additional obstacle in their way, Martinez suggests that they hold a session to determine whether or not there should be a hearing on the motion for reconsideration.

That idea goes nowhere. But, perhaps feeling guilty about his disproportionate eruption at Martinez, King suggests that they table everything until two days hence, Friday, at 3 P.M.

★ ★ ★

Speechwriter Attie comes over to NavObs Wednesday with a speech he's been working on since Saturday in which Gore calls for a statewide machine recount of all the ballots and a hand recount of those that the machine can't read. But Gore scraps this, relegates it to a sentence in his speech, a call for a statewide recount if Bush wants one. The media elite are hammering Gore for dragging this out, for the comments Lehane made about Harris, and he wants to show that he can raise the tone of it all, and that he sees a way toward completion, a reasonable plan with parameters.

But when Gore comes forward today to give the speech he'd proposed giving Saturday, it feels late, and it's delivered in typical Gore fashion — which is to say that no matter how sincere it may be, it feels oily.

"The campaign is over, but a test of our democracy is now under way," he says. "It is a test we must pass, and it is a test we will pass with flying colors. All we need is a common agreement that what is at stake here is not who wins and who loses in a contest for the presidency but how we honor our Constitution and make sure that our democracy works as our founders intended it to work."

Gore proposes "a resolution that is fair and final." The hand recounts in Broward, Dade, and Palm Beach Counties will be allowed to finish. "I am also prepared, if Governor Bush prefers, to include in this recount all the counties in the entire state of Florida. I would also be willing to abide by that result and agree not to take any legal action to challenge that result."

As Fabiani watches this, he knows that this proposal might have meant something last week, when the butterfly ballot lawsuit seemed a tad more promising. But now its litigative potential is weak, and the story's old. He shakes his head.

Gore also suggests that he and Bush meet "personally, one on one, as soon as possible . . . to improve the tone of our dialogue in America."

A few hours later, Bush goes on TV to respond. To the recount proposal — No. To the offer to meet personally to improve the tone of our dialogue in America, that would be — No.

Just as Gore seems to ooze insincerity, Bush seems nervous, twitchy, in hopelessly over his head. Neither of these guys' public appearances seems to do much to reassure anyone; in fact, they explain why this was a tie.

"As we work to conclude this election, we should be guided by three principles: this process must be fair, this process must be accurate, and this process must be final," Bush says. Fairness means no more counting. Accuracy means that hand counts can't be used. Final means Friday at midnight, when the overseas absentee ballots are due. He also offers the obligatory whack at hand recounts. "As Americans have watched on television, they have seen for themselves that manual counting, with individuals making subjective decisions about voter intent, introduces human error and politics into the vote-counting process."

Throughout the election, Gore got called on his various fibs and demagogueries, as he should have. Some of the things he said were outrageous — hinting that there was something benignly racist about Bill Bradley's health-care proposal immediately comes to mind. But Bush seems to get away with his rank hypocrisies. I have no idea why. How can he keep slamming the very notion of hand recounts when Texas has one of the most liberal hand-recount laws in the nation, thanks in no small part to him?

★ ★ ★

Then there's the complete disingenuousness of the Democrats' "count every vote" call. Which to some doesn't even make sense. Michael Carvin, down in Florida at Ginsberg's request, is confused about the Democrats' strategy.

He sees Gore speak, hears him talk about a statewide recount. As a strategy, that makes sense to Carvin. There's no way the Democrats can be under the impression that they'll be able to pursue undervotes in four Democratic-leaning counties, have those votes propel Gore to a victory, without the Bushies arguing that the *entire state's* undervotes need to be looked at. Is there?

Then he watches Christopher and Boies on TV, talking about how they are going to ask the Florida supreme court to set a standard for the whole state. This, too, makes some sense. There needs to be a statewide standard or — as the Bushies argued in the Middlebrooks brief on Monday — there might be some equal-protection arguments they could utilize against them in the U.S. Supreme Court. This is a rather sophisticated approach, Carvin thinks, but it's reasonable. They realize that if they want four counties' undervotes looked at, they'll have to accept a statewide count, which will take some time. So they're going to take the PR hit, allow Bush to be certified the winner after the absentee ballots are counted, and they're setting the stage for the contest provision, which will obviously take some time.

But then the Democrats don't file anything.

What are they doing? Carvin thinks.

The Dems' calculation isn't all that complicated, actually. They're aware of a few harsh realities: for Bush to be certified the winner will be a PR disaster; privately Democrats on the Hill are already starting to peel off. When will this end? they ask. Gore's poll numbers are starting to erode. Additionally, the legal burden in a contest is much greater. One has to argue against a certified result, the burden of proof is much tougher, and the fight takes place in courtrooms instead of before canvassing boards. So the Gorebies decide to ride the protest phase as far as it can get them, so they can enter the contest phase in the strongest possible position. Let's keep the hand recounts going, they've decided, and then we'll see what happens. The hope, of course, is that there will be enough Gore votes in Broward, Miami, and Palm Beach to dispense with Bush's 300-vote margin of victory. Then the onus becomes *Bush's*. Then *Bush* has to contest the election. Then *Bush* has to explain to the world why he's being such a crybaby.

Yep, the Gorebies figure, the better thing to do is put off the certification, get the votes counted, and take it from there.

★ ★ ★

LePore calls the Palm Beach field office of the Florida Department of Law Enforcement to let the fuzz know about an item for sale on eBay that she will not stand for. The wife of her computer guy buys antiques on eBay, and she noticed that someone calling himself Mark Bruce is selling a Votomatic, complete with butterfly ballot, for two grand.

She prints it out, and her husband gives it to LePore, who calls the cops.

Special Agent John Marinello e-mails "Bruce," who now says he wants $20,000. Marinello agrees, and at about 5 P.M., some undercover Florida Department of Law Enforcement officers go to the corner of Lantana Road and Military Trail to meet the millennial Butch and Sundance and talk turkey. They finally agree to $4,000; the cuffs come out.

"Mark Bruce" turns out to be Mark Bruce Richter, forty, a Lake Worth, Florida, schemer. It's a brilliant alias, as befitting the man who came up with the perfect crime. His partner is Steven Solomon. Under interrogation, the two reveal that the Votomatic was left behind at the Winston Trails Club House. They're booked for dealing in stolen property and unlawful possession of a voting machine — the latter of which is a felony. Solomon also gets the nice added charge of possession of a firearm in the commission of a felony, since he had a .40-caliber Smith and Wesson semiautomatic pistol in his fannypack.

It's a tough competition, but even after another month of this chaos, no one will beat Richter and Solomon for the title of Sorriest Losers in this whole grim affair.

★   ★   ★

In Palm Beach, Mark Steitz and Jeff Yarborough have been crunching numbers for Gore.

Undervotes in Palm Beach: 10,582. In Miami-Dade: 10,815. In Broward: 6,686.

If one assumes a 12 percent "revival" rate on these undervotes, that means that there are 1,269 uncounted votes in Palm Beach, 1,297 in Miami-Dade, and 802 in Broward.

Applying the proportion of the vote that Gore and Bush got in each county — 64 percent to 36 percent in Palm Beach, 53 percent to 47 percent in Miami-Dade, 69 percent to 31 percent in Broward, that means the following number of net Gore votes as yet uncounted: 730.

Other charts are assembled, with other revival rates — 10 percent, 14 percent — and other proportions of Gore votes, if one assumes that those who undervote are slightly more Democratic, as they tend to be minority or elderly or inexperienced voters. Crunching these numbers, the net Gore votes range anywhere from 615 to 1,175. The Gorebies think that the Bushies are crunching these numbers as well — which is why they're doing everything they can to stop the process.

Patrick McManus, the mayor of what was once punch-card ballotville, Lynn, Massachusetts — with eighteen recounts in twenty years, 'til the secretary of state phased cards out in '98 — has been down in Palm Beach since Monday, with a group of about a dozen others. He, of course, knows Whouley and Newman and Corrigan and the rest. McManus, a CPA and a lawyer, knows these machines, knows that as they get older, they're tougher to vote with. The rubber on the base of the machine breaks down, ending up with incompletely punched-out ballots. So McManus believes that Palm Beach County's revival rate should be much higher. They should pick up anywhere from 200 to 500 votes in Palm Beach, he thinks. If not more. If they used the *Delahunt* standard, it would be anywhere from 1,000 to 1,200.

"What would happen if we had a statewide recount?" Whouley asks.

It would depend on the standard, McManus says. And also it would depend on what ballots we're looking at. You guys are just focused on the undervotes, but there are 22,000 overvotes in Duval County, mainly from black precincts. Sometimes there are votes that can be discerned in overvotes; for example, a voter might acknowledge that he mistakenly punched the ballot for more than one candidate and attempted to rectify the problem by marking in pen whom he wanted to vote for.

If we counted all the ballots though, Gore would win, McManus concludes. Using the "intent of the voter" standard, he'd win by maybe 20,000 or 30,000. Using the stricter standard they're applying in Palm Beach, he would still win, but by maybe 2,000 or 3,000. But, he understands, the statutory deadline for calling for any more recounts has passed.

Whouley tells him to talk to Steitz.

Steitz at first worries that this is just some crackpot Whouley pawned off on him. Soon he realizes that he's not, that he knows what he's talking about. Why don't you let me put this in a spreadsheet for you? he asks McManus.

"Ah, you yuppies and your spreadsheets," he says. He tells Steitz that if it were up to him, he'd push for a statewide recount. It would be a risk, but one worth taking.

More important, McManus doesn't quite understand what's going on with the stopping of the hand recounts, with the Republican challenges to the very notion of hand recounts. Hand recounts are totally normal. He thinks it inconceivable that there's a presidential election being decided by a handful of votes, and the votes aren't being recounted. The Republicans are mocking the notion of hand counting? This makes no sense to the mayor of Recount-land.

★   ★   ★

And as if things weren't bad enough for LePore attorney Bruce Rogow, who thinks the hand recount should continue, he's got Alan Dershowitz on the phone yapping at him.

You should tell your client to start counting, Dershowitz says, you're going to cost Gore the election, you need to get her to start counting now, she shouldn't pay attention to the secretary of state.

While Dershowitz is yelling at him, Rogow's partner, Beverly Pough, starts waving to him.

"Warren Christopher!" she whispers, pointing to the phone. "Warren Christopher!"

Rogow hangs up on Dershowitz.

"Bruce, this is Warren Christopher," Rogow hears from the other line. He thinks that's odd. "Bruce"? He doesn't know him well enough to call him "Bruce." Doesn't know him at all!

"Hello, Mr. Christopher," Rogow says.

"I want to thank you for everything you're doing for us," Christopher says, apparently referring to a brief Rogow filed for the Palm Beach canvassing board, asking the Florida Supremes to resolve the conflicting advice offered by Harris and Butterworth.

This offends Rogow.

You've got it all wrong, I'm not doing anything for you, Rogow says. I'm representing some other client.

Christopher seems to sense that he ruffled Rogow's feathers, and he gets apologetic and diplomatic. But still, the message is: It would really help us if the count would begin.

It can't begin until we hear from the Supreme Court of Florida, Rogow says. Which I think will be this afternoon. The Florida justices will want to step in here.

Christopher apologizes again, asks what Rogow's views are on all of this. On the federal track, the Bushies have appealed Middlebrooks's Monday ruling to the far more conservative Eleventh Circuit Court of Appeals in Atlanta. Christopher says that his people say that they don't think the Eleventh Circuit will take it up.

Rogow doesn't know about that. There are a few justices on that twelve-judge bench whom the Gorebies better be wary of, he says. My views are that you've got to watch out for the Eleventh Circuit and the U.S. Supreme Court, because that's where the Republicans want to be, Rogow says. You need to be in the Supreme Court of Florida, and that's where I've put this now.

The call ends. Rogow considers the whole thing to have been entirely inappropriate.

★ ★ ★

Hearing that Harris has asked the Florida Supremes to consolidate all the cases, Bush legal chieftain Ginsberg calls Joe Klock to tell him that the Bushies are not happy. If the Florida Supreme Court takes the case, then

Gore will be playing on a Democratic field, Ginsberg says. The Bush team wants to play this game in Atlanta, at the Eleventh Circuit, or in D.C., with the SCOTUS (Supreme Court of the United States). But not here, in Tallahassee, with an all Democrat-appointee court.

This is where you want to feel sorry for Klock and his client. It isn't like Klock hasn't been trying to steer the secretary of state down what he thinks is a safe path. He had told Harris that there was no basis in Florida election law to allow hand recounts because of voter error. But by consolidating the cases, at least, if there is a hand recount, it can be statewide, with one uniform standard for the ballot.

Of course, that's not what Klock wants to have happen. His concern is more with all the people who voted correctly, not the ones who didn't. The way Klock sees it, the Democrats are maneuvering any way possible to get Gore more votes than Bush. The instructions were quite clear, he says:

AFTER VOTING, CHECK YOUR BALLOT CARD TO BE SURE YOUR VOTING SELECTIONS ARE CLEARLY AND CLEANLY PUNCHED AND THERE ARE NO CHIPS LEFT HANGING ON THE BACK OF THE CARD.

If the Bush folks are turning on Harris over this, then she's really going to be without friends. What Strep Throat and left-leaning pundits and Leno and Letterman are doing to her is fairly cruel, slamming her appearance and constantly ridiculing her heavy layers of makeup. Even the *Washington Post* — the paper of Woodward, Bradlee, and Bernstein — writes about her in ways that seem not only mean but even obsessive: "Her lips were overdrawn with berry-red lipstick — the creamy sort that smears all over a coffee cup and leaves smudges on a shirt collar. Her skin had been plastered and powdered to the texture of pre-war walls in need of a skim coat. And her eyes, rimmed in liner and frosted with blue shadow, bore the telltale homogeneous spikes of false eyelashes. Caterpillars seemed to rise and fall with every bat of her eyelid, with every downward glance to double check — before reading — her latest 'determination.'

"One wonders how this Republican woman, who can't even use restraint when she's wielding a mascara wand, will manage to . . . make sound decisions."

Meow.

But it's tough to muster an iota of pity for Harris. It's hard to feel bad for a woman who feels the necessity to block votes from being counted every step of the way, who's being sued by Judge McDermott, a Republican, for what he views as disenfranchisement. There are 175,000 ballots — under-votes and overvotes — that Florida vote-tabulation machines did not read. Certainly some of these folks found the Gore-Bush choice untenable and opted for no one, and surely a lot of these people fucked up their ballots with incompetent voting, and that's too bad. But it's also pretty clear that there are at least *some* votes in there, some Floridians who had a choice that wasn't recorded. Considering that Bush's presidency comes down to a 300-vote margin of victory, how can the country ever feel confident about who actually got more votes if we don't look at them? Harris wants the world to feel bad for her, wants the world to understand that she's just doing her job. But then she turns around and does exactly what Bush would want her to, gumming up the works as much as possible. Maybe Stipanovich isn't telling her what to do, as coordinated with the Bush team. But it almost doesn't matter — she's on their program with or without instructions. From almost any angle, her behavior is outrageous. Yes, the Gorebies' ploy to look for votes only in three Democratic counties is disingenuous. Gore's "offer" the night before for a statewide recount had a real used car–sales-man feel to it. Both sides are plotting, and neither is behaving as if they truly want a fair fight. It may well be that the biggest difference between Bush and Gore at this point is that Bush has a Katherine Harris, and Gore doesn't.

In any case, this one move to take the matter to the Florida Supreme Court will be the first, last, and only time that Harris does anything that isn't completely in George W. Bush's best interests. It also happens to be the last decision Harris makes without the guidance of Stipanovich.

★   ★   ★

On Friday, November 17, everybody's wondering what the Florida Supreme Court will do. The Gorebies have appealed Lewis's ruling that Harris acted within her discretion, and Palm Beach has appealed LaBarga's ruling on hand recounts, which involves both whether to count and the chad standard.

I'm an impatient man, so I call former Florida Supreme Court justice Gerald Kogan to see what he thinks.

A registered Democrat first appointed to the bench in 1987 by then-governor Bob Martinez, a Republican, Kogan says that in his personal opinion, "any recounts [that] registrars feel are necessary to get an accurate tabulation certainly should prevail." This isn't politics, he explains, it's Florida law. Of course it's Florida law as interpreted by the state Supreme Court, which is thought to lean left. The late Gov. Lawton Chiles, a Democrat, appointed six of the court's seven justices, and the seventh was appointed by then-governor (now senator) Bob Graham, also a Democrat.

Not everyone would agree with Kogan. Barry Richard has already said that the Florida Supreme Court "has no jurisdiction. If the supreme court should determine that it has jurisdiction, I think it will have to do so by recognizing a source of jurisdiction that it has never heretofore recognized. . . . The parties cannot confer jurisdiction on the supreme court by compromise or by agreement. The supreme court's jurisdiction is clearly set forth in the Florida Constitution and it is very narrow."

"I have to disagree with him on that point," Kogan says. "I would think the supreme court can have jurisdiction whenever and wherever it says it has jurisdiction."

While I'm talking to Kogan on the phone, I get an e-mail alerting me that the Florida Supreme Court has rejected Harris's requests that the hand recounts be stopped, and that the Gorebies' and Palm Beach County cases be consolidated. The court will hear arguments on Monday about hand recounts. And: without anyone even asking them to, the seven justices prevent Katherine Harris from certifying the election tonight or tomorrow or until they say when.

Kogan couldn't be less surprised.

★   ★   ★

To give you an idea of how competent Floridians are in general, you should know that after a heavy rain, there's a flood in the parking lot of Palm Beach County's Emergency Operations Center, which was opened in 1998 and activated for Hurricane Floyd.

LePore has arranged the counting for the command center, which looks like a cross between an amphitheater and a classroom, five tiers down to the front of the class, seats about 150. The count is finally — finally! — about to start Thursday night at 7:14 P.M., but the process is hobbled a tad since there's a dearth of Republican counters, only enough to form thirteen counting teams instead of the planned thirty.

Wallace wanders through the room, studying everything, focused. The aisles are packed, so Wallace clears the way for a man carrying ballot boxes.

"Don't want to be dropping ballots!" Wallace chortles.

LePore is diligent with the ballots as she hands them out to teams. One counter's pen is accidentally brandished within striking distance of a ballot. "Don't touch it with the pen!" she says excitedly.

"Remember to look on both sides," Burton says. He reminds them to follow the standard Broward County has adopted — count it as a ballot if it's punched through, hanging chad and dimples are to be examined by the canvassing board. "There's no need for a debate," Burton says. "If they say questionable, just put it in there, and we'll take care of it later."

Wallace objects. "We are precipitously adopting a standard on the very night we start counting," he complains.

Burton says to chill. The standard on "questionables" will come later, "when we're sitting together and your chin is once again placed on my shoulder."

★ ★ ★

In Broward County, GOP delay tactics are pissing off the entire canvassing board, even Republican Jane Carroll. A lawsuit from four Republican voters forces subpoenas upon all three of them.

They can't analyze disputed ballots themselves while they're in court, but Lee deputizes another judge to at least supervise the larger hand count while the three go trudging off from the Emergency Operations Center in Plantation to Judge Leonard Stafford's courtroom in downtown Fort Lauderdale, half an hour away. When they arrive, Stafford tells them they can go back.

On their drives back to Plantation, Gunzburger and Carroll receive word via cell phones that Stafford had ordered them to return to the courtroom.

Lee doesn't have a cell phone, so he gets no such notice. Which is just as well, because when Carroll and Gunzburger return to Stafford's courtroom, it turns out that he hadn't ordered them back at all. Carroll's attorney, Sam Gorman, finds out that the attorney who spread the word that Judge Stafford wanted them back is a member of the law firm run by local GOP bigwig attorney William Scherer. Scherer has certainly been on the Bush program of stalling the count before, in arguments before the board. But this is something else entirely — Gorman, livid, wants to initiate disciplinary proceedings against the Scherer attorney before the Florida Bar for misrepresenting a judicial order.

But Lee knows her and is sure that it was an honest mistake, and he talks Gorman down.

★ ★ ★

On Friday, the count continues much as it did on Day One. Only this time, there are twenty-six teams of four, Republican counters having shown up in greater numbers.

Outside, Republicans like Eskew are claiming that it's chaos in the EOC, that chad are flying in a ballot bacchanal. "Mind reading is no way to decide the presidency — and neither is a stacked political deck," he says.

But neither of the sort is going on. No one's reading minds — they're assessing ballots, just as is done in Texas. And Burton and LePore are doing everything they can to be impartial — even Roberts seems a tad cowed. Burton thinks the GOP attempt to have her recused has shaken her into more of a semi-neutral stance.

But Eskew wants the process discredited, so, as he did in South Carolina, unable to compete using the truth, he will look elsewhere for ammo.

The most unfortunate incident of all comes at around 1 A.M. Thursday morning, when a senior citizen counter drops some ballots on the floor. Sheriff's deputies and police officers move in to make sure no one touches them. *Swarm! Swarm!* An observer seated behind the counters lifts her feet so they don't touch the ballots — though one deputy will later tell Burton that at least one ballot touched her foot. An observer will later estimate that it was only about five or six ballots that fell; Tucker Eskew will tell the press that it was twenty.

The canvassing board discusses which pile the ballots belong in. "For the integrity of the process, you must recount this entire precinct," Wallace says. Burton agrees. Lock 'em up and start the precinct again in the morning, he says.

★ ★ ★

On Friday, November 17, as Broward County goes through a similar experience — the tedium of counting, the objections of Democrats to ballots not being counted as votes and of Republicans to other ballots being counted — the canvassing board in Miami-Dade County meets to decide if they want a similar fate.

Coffey points to legal rulings and decisions by other counties' canvassing boards that have gone their way. Martinez says that Al Gore, having lost the election in the polling place, is now trying to win it through aggressive litigation. "You have shown great courage in applying the rule of law, Mr. Leahy, Judge Lehr, Judge King — I know you and I disagree. Nevertheless, I respect you. I'm not going to push you. But you're being pushed now. What I ask you at this point in time is that you stick to your conviction, Mr. Leahy, Judge Lehr."

Not the right thing to say to Lehr.

"Nobody has pushed me," she says. "Mr. Coffey has made a point, and I will agree with him, that events are exploding upon us . . . I do not operate in a vacuum."

The board votes unanimously to listen to the Democratic arguments. Zack argues that the canvassing board is "not a court of law. If you are anything, you are a court of equity. You're supposed to do what's right and fair.

"You know, one of the least important things that we do is watch *Monday Night Football*," Zack goes on. "One of the most important things that we do is elect a president of the United States. . . . On *Monday Night Football*, we allow an instant replay when we're tired, when we're exhausted. We just want to turn off the TV and let the Dolphins or the Jets win, and go to sleep.

"But we say, no, we as Americans have a fundamental sense of fairness. And we say, if there is a better method, we have to use it. And you know the video camera isn't what decides what happened — it requires the decision, thank God, of a human being looking at what happened in the best possible way — slow motion, if you will. I will say slow motion is a hand count."

Coffey talks about Broward, how that county is doing right by its voters. "Can we say no because we're too busy? It's too much hassle? Of course not."

When De Grandy speaks, he mocks Zack and Coffey's appeals to the emotions of the board. "Let me tell you first what I did not hear, and then let's talk about what we know. What I did not hear was any recitation of facts or law that would justify reconsideration. . . . What I did not hear is any compelling new evidence. . . . I am going to make you one promise. I promise you that Mr. Martinez and I are not going to ask you how you feel, are not going to probe your emotions."

"We'll try not to do the same, Mr. De Grandy," King quips.

During De Grandy and Martinez's presentation, Zack interrupts. "I never believed in Della Street coming in and talking to Perry Mason, but actually we just got confirmation that the supreme court has just blocked Katherine Harris from certifying results."

"Might I ask a point of order and a point of privilege?" Martinez asks. "And that is that if Mr. Perry Mason and Della Street would just keep it quiet a little bit."

The arguments go on. But soon enough, King calls for a vote. And unlike last time, this time he votes first. "I'll vote yes in concurrence with the recount of all ballots in Dade County by hand," he says. "And this time, I'll ask Judge Lehr, if you would be so kind to make your vote."

Martinez is suspicious. Lehr seems to him to be the most vacillating member of the board, the most impressionable. Last time Leahy voted first, and she just followed him. Will she do the same here and follow King?

"I, too, am going to concur with you, Judge King," Lehr says. "I believe that the people of Dade County are entitled to have their votes counted. . . . You read the papers, and you listen to the television, and the news — a lot has been happening. And I have taken a lot of what has been happening into consideration," most recently the supreme court stay of the certification, she says.

Leahy says that the way he interprets the law, manual recounts are only for when there are errors in vote tabulation. He's a no.

The recount is on.

Martinez is stunned. They're disregarding the rule of law, he thinks. Furious, he returns to the Greenberg Traurig offices, where his team is working, and it's decided that Miguel De Grandy will deal with the canvassing board from now on, while Martinez will set his sights on what happens in the courts. "I don't want to go back there," Martinez says about the canvassing board. "There's no need for me to go back there. I want to focus my efforts on the courts. And I don't want to go back there."

It's as if he's talking about Cuba itself.

★   ★   ★

In Palm Beach, the counters grow weary. This is mind-numbingly boring work.

"I had a lot of practice for this," a sheriff's deputy says. "I was an altar boy."

"We've been going about two hours, haven't we?" one asks. "What time did we start?"

"Can we take a break in the middle of it?" one asks Denise Dytrych.

"Are you pretty close?" the county attorney asks.

"We've got another hour and a half."

"We need to protect the ballots," Dytrych says, and while the group takes a coffee break, a sheriff's deputy stands at the table and guards the ballots.

Tucker Eskew walks in and talks to a Bush observer. The observer tells him that in the past hour, he has seen five Bush ballots put into the wrong piles, sometimes the Gore pile. The observer also tells Eskew that the mistake was corrected after it was pointed out.

A little later, deputy county attorney Gordon Selfridge tells some counters to treat the ballots gingerly. "You're not supposed to be tapping it down," Selfridge says to one of the men. The man keeps tapping it down. Selfridge complains to Burton. The judge gets up and goes to the microphone. "People want to handle them like playing cards, and people are banging them and straightening them," he says. "You need to handle these very gently. Be sure the part you touch is down at the bottom, not in the middle."

At around 4:20, the canvassing board starts looking at the county's fifty-two absentee ballots received since Election Day. Before they open them up to count the vote, the board members need to determine whether the envelope carrying the ballot is legal. Does it have a postmark? Is the postmark from November 7 or sooner?

One from Japan — accept. One from Israel — reject. And on and on. Seventeen will be rejected.

Eskew points out to a reporter that the ballot boxes are lying around, and some people are propping their elbows on top.

The postmark on a military ballot is unreadable. The Democratic attorney says that it should be rejected.

"I cannot believe that our service boys fighting hard overseas, that their ballots would be disqualified, and I ask the board to reconsider their opinion," says GOP attorney Brigham McCown.

"All right, we will file a protest and arrange for a violin," says Burton.

Onward and downward.

9

"We need to write something down."

During that first weekend, in Tallahassee's Camps Bush and Gore, strategists realized that they needed to supplement their focus on hand recounts with a side-dish campaign relating to overseas absentee ballots, due Friday, November 17. Of course, there are the military ballots, which are expected to come in heavily for Bush, but there are also rumors swirling that American Jews in Israel — energized by Lieberman's presence on the ticket — have turned out in droves as well.

Fabiani points out that "no one knows" if huge packages of ballots are coming from Tel Aviv and Jerusalem, but he and others sure talk about the possibility a lot, as if those ballots will come in packed in pita or with a shmear of cream cheese. Gore garnered 80 percent of the Jewish vote a few days ago, and estimates have about four thousand Florida Jews in the land of milk and honey. Lieberman, for one, is convinced that tons of ballots are coming from the Jewish homeland. And who knows what the military voters will do; while Dole beat Clinton in 1996's Florida overseas ballots — 54 percent to 46 percent — Dole was a war hero, Clinton a draft dodger, which is not quite the dynamic here.

The Bushies had been a little spooked by an obscure news item about a Democratic lawyer trying to drum up post-election absentee ballots. It wasn't exactly a story full of facts; no one seemed to pick up on it. But it was enough for the Bushies to worry, so former secretary of state Jim Smith was instructed to go out there and lay down the strict law of the land as it pertained to overseas absentee ballots.

"The Florida law is simple, straightforward, and reason-based," Smith said. "Let me go over some of the controlling rules. First, overseas ballots must be either postmarked by November seventh, signed and dated no later than November seventh. Overseas ballots may not be completed after November seventh. With respect to this election, the time to complete an absentee ballot ended on the day of the election. Any overseas ballot completed after November seventh is invalid, invalid, and cannot be counted.

"Next, for voters mailing overseas absentee ballots, only those ballots mailed with an APO (army post office), FPO (fleet post office), or foreign postmark shall be considered valid. Ballots that are not mailed with these postmarks are invalid and cannot be counted."

Smith went on to outline seven additional laws for absentee ballots. There are a lot of requirements absentee ballots must meet, he insisted. They must be completed by the voter, have the signature and address of a witness, a witness can't verify "more than five ballots in an election unless he or she is legally authorized to administer oaths or is an absentee-ballot coordinator designated before the election," and on and on.

He then attempted to put the fear of God in anyone who might be thinking about trying to skirt these rules. "It is a felony to perpetrate, attempt, or aid in any fraud of any vote cast or attempted, such as backdating an absentee ballot," he said. He used the word "fraud" once, the word "felony" four times.

A reporter asked Smith: Why are you here?

"At the request of the Republican Party of Florida," he replied, because of "news reports that there has been some encouragement of some individuals overseas who may not have cast their ballot" but were erroneously told that "even though the November seventh date has passed, they could still do that." When pressed, however, Smith allowed that he didn't know the specifics of the story he was referring to.

Over at Democratic HQ, at the coordinated campaign center, attorney Mark Herron was working on the same project. Herron had no knowledge of Smith's press conference, though his understanding of the law was the same. But ironically, Smith had a lot to do with why Herron was sitting there in Democratic HQ.

See, Herron and his law firm — Akerman, Senterfitt & Eidson — had just parted ways. The other partners didn't want him to work for Gore and told him that if he continued to do so, they would have to split. Given that choice, Herron remembered a similar predicament back in '86, when he was with a different firm, and he was asked to run the gubernatorial campaign of former state representative Steve Pajcic. Herron listened to his law partners then and watched from the sidelines as Pajcic beat Smith — then a Democrat — in the primary. But because of the ill will between Pajcic and Smith, Smith ended up endorsing GOP nominee Bob Martinez in the general election and soon became a Republican himself. Herron was friends with both men, and he was sure that if he had been running Pajcic's campaign, none of the ugly fallout would have happened.

He swore to himself he'd never again opt out of such an opportunity. Which is what this was, he thought. So he was booted.

Over the weekend, the Gorebies had asked Herron to work on the overseas-absentee-ballot issue. What's the process? he was asked, over and over, by Nick Baldick, Ron Klain, Charlie Baker, Jack Corrigan. Herron walked them through it. Back in 1980, it was clear that Florida had an inherent defect in its election system, arising from the fact that its primary elections were so late — a September primary, then a runoff in October. How could they get the overseas ballots out when they didn't even know who was going to be on the ballot until October? The choice was either move the primaries back or give overseas folks more time. So in 1984, the state of Florida and the federal government entered into a consent decree, Herron explained, which allowed these ballots to come in up to ten days late — as long as they were postmarked by Election Day or, if they didn't have a postmark (some letters from overseas military bases aren't postmarked), signed and dated by Election Day.

In 1989, despite the consent decree, the Florida legislature ruled that only ballots with postmarks would be considered valid, and Republican Smith and Democrat Herron clearly read the conflict the same way — the 1989 law ruled supreme. Both were operating out of political interest, of course — Smith trying to guard against invalid Gore votes, presumably from Jews in Israel, Herron against invalid Bush votes, presumably from soldiers.

For once, there was something everyone agreed on. But not for long. Not after Herron, at Charlie Baker's urging, writes a memo detailing the many ways overseas ballots can be disqualified, "count every vote" be damned.

★ ★ ★

Toward the middle of the week, the Bush team's Warren Tompkins puts together a spreadsheet on the overseas absentee ballots, what had come in already, what had been counted, how many had been requested, how many were still expected in, and so on. The overseas-absentee-ballot thing was likely going to go their way, Tompkins tells people. He anticipates that the Democrats know this and are going to challenge as many of them as possible.

"You're kidding me," spokeswoman Mindy Tucker says to him. "They can't protest."

"We think they're going to," Tompkins responds.

Tucker wants to let the press know about this at once; but she's overruled. Let's wait, she's told.

★ ★ ★

Jason Unger, thirty-two, is but one of the attorneys hired by the state GOP to focus on the issue of military overseas absentee ballots. Working with other attorneys at his firm, Gray, Harris & Robinson — one of the few Republican firms in Tallahassee — he has prepared all week for deadline day, November 17.

Ed Fleming, a Republican attorney in Pensacola who represents Rep. Joe Scarborough, R-Fla., has been drafted by Unger to work on the project. In one of their conversations, Unger tells Fleming of a rumor he's heard that the Dems are going to go full-bore in challenging overseas military absentee ballots. On Thursday, Fleming asks a local county attorney if he's heard anything about the rumor. Sure, the attorney tells him. Got a memo right here about it, written by the Democrats. He faxes Fleming the memo, written by Herron, outlining the Gore strategy.

Fleming gives news of the memo to Stuart Bowen, a Bush attorney from Austin who's supervising the absentee-ballot effort in the Panhandle. On Friday morning, after making sure that Fleming obtained the memo legally, Bowen tells him to fax the memo to Tallahassee ASAP.

At 11:42 A.M., the memo arrives in Unger's office. He shows it to the senior attorneys running his shop, who have it run over to Bush HQ at the Bush Building.

"This is gold," Tucker says when it gets around to her. It's a PR jackpot — it plays into an already existing perception that the Democratic Party cares less about the military than the Republicans do. Plus there's the hypocrisy angle. "Count every vote"? Except for American soldiers?! The Bushies got ready for a full assault. From now on, they will refer only to "military ballots," not "overseas absentee ballots."

Duval County, Clay County, Escambia County, Okaloosa County — the places where there is the highest concentration of military voters — seem to be where it's the worst. The Gorebies are after ballots for not having a postmark. They're after military ballots for having a U.S. postmark, though the military will later explain that several batches of these overseas ballots were postmarked in the United States from various port cities. They're after federal write-in ballots, which are for individuals abroad who claim that they requested an absentee ballot but never received one. Along with their voting information, users of federal write-in ballots have to swear in an affidavit under the penalty of perjury that they requested an absentee ballot and didn't receive one. The Gorebies are making elections supervisors check the names of the voters against their records to see if, in fact, they did request absentee ballots.

★　★　★

Gore recount expert Chris Sautter is before the Broward County canvassing board when a team of three other Gore attorneys comes in to disqualify absentee ballots. Sautter is not happy.

Like Young, Sautter's a big believer in adopting a conciliatory tone with the canvassing board. And now here come these schmucks, sent by Tallahassee, trying to eliminate votes. Sautter's first instinct is to not even let them into the room.

Sautter has a brief discussion with them — not one of them has ever been involved in a recount before. They're carrying the Herron memo, which he has never seen before. They seem to be under the impression that their orders are to be stringent when it comes to military overseas absentee ballots but not to overseas ballots in general. To Sautter, their attitude is "We're the pros, and we're here to take over."

This is a county that Gore won with 67 percent of the vote, Sautter tells them. They don't use the Herron memo.

★　★　★

One of the Florida Bushies, state GOP finance chair Al Austin, is good friends with Norman Schwarzkopf, and he calls up ol' Stormin' Norman to see if he knows about the Herron memo. When he learns of it, the Persian Gulf War commander blows his top. But Schwarzkopf is sick with the flu, so he can't appear at any press event. Nevertheless, on the morning of Saturday, November 18, Schwarzkopf calls Tucker and dictates a statement. "These armed forces ballots should be allowed to be tallied," Schwarzkopf says. "It is a very sad day in our country when the men and women of the armed forces are serving abroad and facing danger on a daily basis, yet because of some technicality out of their control, they are denied the right to vote for the president of the United States who will be their commander in chief."

When Tucker and an aide go to the Tallahassee press camps Saturday morning armed with copies of the Herron memo, Schwarzkopf's statement, and a few other documents, reporters attack them like locusts. On TV on Saturday, and in print on Sunday, the story erupts.

Ron Klain tries to point out that the rules the Herron memo details are just the same rules that Jim Smith spelled out on Sunday, when the Republicans were fearful of sacks of absentee ballots coming S.W.A.K. from Tel Aviv. He runs over to CNN, MSNBC, Fox News Channel, distributing copies of the transcript of Smith's press conference. But not one media outlet mentions Sunday's press conference by Jim Smith or how the Bushies have shamelessly pulled a 180 on the issue, since rigorous application of the law will now clearly affect armed servicemen and -women more so than Jews abroad in Israel.* Instead, the focus is on the Gorebies' nakedly hypocritical love for election law hypertechnicalities in their mad rush to disenfranchise American soldiers. And on the fact that of the 3,733 overseas absentee ballots that have come in since Election Day, 1,527 of them have been scrapped.

★   ★   ★

In Austin, Montana governor Marc Racicot — a friend of Bush's and long-time supporter — sits in with the brain trust and hears this business. Racicot (pronounced Roscoe), once the chief prosecutor for the largest U.S. military jurisdiction in Europe back when he was in the judge advocate general's corps, volunteers to go point on this.

Armed with anecdotes that have come from the organized, information-gathering infrastructure that Enwright, Mehlman, and Eskew have assembled, on Saturday Racicot gives a televised press conference to lash out at the hand-recount process and the Democrats' absentee-ballot disqualification campaign.

Racicot is a perfect pick for this. His low-key manner combined with his prosecutor's taste for the jugular will allow him, over the next few weeks, to make the most ugly of allegations while seeming perfectly reasonable. As one of the leaders of the Libby High School basketball team in its first and only state basketball championship season, student body president Racicot set a record that still stands for the most assists in a hoops game: 32. He will give Bush a big one as well.

* In fact, the Democrats' communications shop is so harried, Mark Herron himself won't even know about the Smith press conference until I tell him about it during an interview in January 2001.

More important, he knows how to try a case, having earned a 95 percent conviction rate over an eleven-year stretch. He became Montana's twentieth governor in 1993, and he will be retiring this year, mentioned frequently as a possible member of a Bush cabinet.

"There is something, obviously, that is terribly, terribly wrong with what has been occurring," Racicot says. "We now have clear and convincing evidence — in fact, in my judgment, it's beyond that — that in Palm Beach County and Broward County, the hand counting of the ballots that is ongoing is not only fundamentally flawed; it is becoming completely untrustworthy."

The attempt to discredit the hand-recounting process by mocking the chad has not gained enough steam — especially since everything is televised and witnessed by members of both parties — so the Republicans have decided that they have to just start lying, fibbing, exaggerating, and insinuating.

They had tried. On Thursday and Friday in Palm Beach, Eskew's complaints weren't finding many takers among the reporters who were there, who saw that absent a few minor incidents of human error — all corrected — there wasn't much to gripe about. Everything was pretty orderly. So Eskew passed off his charges to Tallahassee, and a new Big Lie begins, and the campaign the otherwise respectable Racicot begins to aggressively wage here on behalf of the Bush team henceforth consists of nothing short of a goulash of truth, lies, and innuendo — most offensively against the judiciary — and served to the American people with a sprinkle of concocted moral outrage.

Right off the bat, Racicot says that the Miami-Dade canvassing board consists of "two Democrats and one Republican." That's not true. King is a Democrat; Lehr and Leahy are independent.

Racicot refers to "the taping of chads to ballots." He refers to witnesses who "have completed affidavits that indicate that a taped chad has been taped over the hole where the ballot or the notation could be made for a vote for Governor Bush." It is true that some of these ballots exist, but in every case the chad was apparently taped by voters. There is no evidence, and there are no witnesses to anyone else doing the taping.

Racicot goes on to make hay out of the mixing of piles of Gore votes and Bush votes, reading conspiracy in bureaucratic ineptitude, just as Democrats did with minority voters turned away from the polls on Election Day.

"Ballots have been used as fans," the former military prosecutor alleges. "In fact, the chairman of the Palm Beach canvassing board, Judge Burton, had to warn counters not to use the ballots as fans." This one is true; Mehlman himself saw it. Burton told them to stop fanning themselves; the fanning stopped; but not one chad was ever seen falling out as a result of the fanning. Of course, Racicot doesn't mention that inconvenient fact.

Racicot harps on: "On Thursday night at one A.M., an elderly counter dropped twenty to sixty ballots over the floor, creating a huge scene. Other observers stepped on the ballots as they were lying on the floor. Just for a minute, imagine that you have a seventy-year-old man at two A.M. in the morning trying to count thousands of small cards, many of which stick together, to see where these tiny holes are located.

"In Broward County, there's chad on the floor, on the counting tables, on the chairs," he continues. Of course this is true. When ballots with hanging chad are handled, sometimes the partially punched chad falls from the ballot. But anyone who has handled and seen these ballots knows that the chad doesn't fall out unless it was already at least partially, usually almost entirely, punched. And in all the allegations the Republicans will allege, not once will they ever produce evidence — or even one convincing story — of someone punching the chad from a ballot during the counting.

Anyone who sees the process knows that it is organized, and highly supervised, with bureaucrats and county workers slaving away, trying to do the right thing while under the watchful eyes of the media as well as political operatives from both sides. But the Bush team doesn't want America to know this. Harping on the changing standards alone isn't doing the trick, so they begin alleging fraud and corruption.

"I think when the American people learn about these things, they're going to ask themselves, 'What in the name of God is going on here?'"

One might say the same thing about Racicot's press conference. It's a pretty shameless episode in an otherwise respectable career.

But Racicot is not done, and only now does he hit on the heart of the matter. "Last night we learned how far the vice president's campaign will go to win this election," he says. "And I am very sorry to say, but the vice president's lawyers have gone to war, in my judgment, against the men and women who serve in our armed forces in an effort to win at any cost.

"Last night across Florida, they threw out between nine hundred and eleven hundred votes cast by military men and women. In Duval County, for example, forty-four votes, mostly military, were thrown out. The man who would be their commander in chief is fighting to take away the votes from the people that he would command." Even with those ballots tossed, Bush picks up 1,376 votes, Gore 750. Bush is now ahead by 926 votes.

In the Bush Building in Tallahassee, one senior member of the Bush team has a realization. "Boy, they could really use Jim Smith's words against us," the strategist says. Luckily for them, neither the Democrats nor the media do so. In fact, only one media outlet — a Web magazine — even points out the contradiction.

If two men lie, one stuttering, the other smooth and smiling, it is human nature to disbelieve the stutterer and trust the man with the confident grin. And right now, the Bush team is smiling.

★   ★   ★

Considering that behind closed doors Lieberman was the most aggressive proponent of using the law any way that the Gore team could, his seeming capitulation on the overseas-absentee-ballot issue is astounding.

But since he, not unlike Racicot, is a man who wraps harsh partisan rhetoric in a calming, reassuring package, since he is far more effective than Gore in communicating, oozing sincerity where Gore can't even dribble any, and since he is Gore's no. 2 and thus able to serve as both attack dog and cheerleader, Lieberman agrees to do all five Sunday shows — ABC's *This Week,* with Sam and Cokie, CBS's *Face the Nation,* NBC's *Meet the Press,* CNN's *Late Edition,* with Wolf Blitzer, and even Fox News Channel's *Fox News Sunday.*

On NBC, Tim Russert brandishes the Herron memo and grills Lieberman on it. Throughout the campaign, senior members of the Gore team whined that Russert, a former Democratic Senate staffer, was in the tank for Bush — Bush wanted him to moderate at least one of the debates! they point out — and today he does little to change their minds.

"Many controversies swirling in Florida," he says right off the bat. "The most recent: Democratic lawyers challenging overseas absentee ballots, some fourteen hundred and twenty were disqualified, more than either Bush or Gore won. Many of them members of the armed services, and people are very, very concerned. They point to a memo written by Mark Herron, a lawyer who assists the Gore campaign, telling Democratic lawyers, 'This is how you knock out ballots from military people overseas.' They don't have a postmark right. They're not dated properly. Technicalities, if you will.

"How can a campaign who insists on the intent of the voter, the will of the people, not disenfranchising anybody accept knocking out the votes of people of armed services?"

Lieberman says that he hasn't read the memo, that Russert's copy is the first he's actually seen of it.

"Let me just say that the vice president and I would never authorize, and would not tolerate, a campaign that was aimed specifically at invalidating absentee ballots from members of our armed services," Lieberman says. "And I've been assured that there were more absentee ballots from nonmilitary voters overseas that were ultimately disqualified. We're all about exactly what you said, having every vote counted fairly and accurately, and I think that was the end aim of what happened with the absentee ballots, and it's our aim as the hand counts go on in these three counties in Florida."

Russert reads from more Bush propaganda, a letter the Bushies secured from the deputy director of the military postal services who "says that if a sailor is on a ship, it's hard to get a postmark. Will you today, as a representative of the Gore campaign, ask every county to relook at those ballots that came from armed services people and waive any so-called irregularities or technicalities which would disqualify them?"

Lieberman crumbles like a matzoh. "We ought to do everything we can to count the votes of our military personnel overseas. . . . I would give the benefit of the doubt to ballots coming in from military personnel generally, but particularly in light of the letter and the kind of statements we've heard about that."

Elections officials are probably afraid of litigation and are therefore following the letter of the law, he says. "I'd urge them to go back and take another look. Because, again, Al Gore and I don't want to ever be part of anything that would put an extra burden on the military personnel abroad who want to vote. . . . I'd give the benefit of the doubt to ballots generally."

Among those watching *Meet the Press* Sunday morning is Herron, who is stunned to see Joe Lieberman sell him down the river. All his memo did was detail Florida law. He had written it, for Godsakes, at the direction of the Gore-Lieberman team! He'd already lost his job so he could help the effort, and here was the vice presidential nominee distancing himself from the memo when all it did was explain Florida law!

Stunned, Herron takes a walk to calm down. Baldick has a slightly different reaction. As the guy in charge of the kids who have been running around the state for Gore-Lieberman, the twenty-somethings who were yelled at before canvassing boards from Panama City to Palm Beach while protesting these ballots — so as to help get Lieberman in the White House — he's enraged at the Connecticut senator's capitulation. And how about poor Mark Herron, who was just shit-canned from his firm because he's one of the few Democratic lawyers in Florida — especially in Tallahassee! —

with the stones to work for Gore regardless of what Jeb thinks about it? "*Fuck* Joe Lieberman!" Baldick rants to anyone who will listen. If Lieberman runs for president in 2004, Baldick vows, he will do everything he can to hurt him in the two states he knows best and Lieberman will need most — Florida and New Hampshire.

★   ★   ★

Senator Bob Kerrey, Democrat of Nebraska, is watching this all unfold, and he can't believe the shit the Republicans are getting away with saying.

It's not just this matter of the absentee ballots. Kerrey is retiring from the Senate this year, heading to Manhattan to be president of the New School, but he is not going softly into that dark night. As a Navy SEAL and war hero, Kerrey left a leg in Vietnam. In 1992, when he ran against Bill Clinton for the presidency, Clinton's draft-dodging offended him to no end. In 2000, George W. Bush's draft-dodging offended him only slightly more than the cocky way Bush handled it and the free ride the media gave him.

It wasn't that Kerrey was such a Gore guy. After all, he was one of only three senators to endorse Bill Bradley in the primaries, and his later take on the glaring weaknesses of Gore's Social Security reform plans didn't do the Democratic nominee any favors. But surfing the Web in October, Kerrey was shocked to read a *Boston Globe* story detailing how Bush, then the son of a congressman, jumped ahead five hundred places in line to get in the Texas Air National Guard. He was even more stunned to learn that there was an unaccounted-for year in Bush's air guard duty, when Bush was to have reported for duty in Alabama but no one could remember him ever having been there, with no corresponding records that he ever fulfilled the obligation.

It wasn't the circumstances of his evasion of service, even though it came in the midst of an era when five hundred American GIs were dying each week, Kerrey was giving up a leg, and McCain was being held in a POW camp even though, as the son of an admiral, he'd been offered early release. No, even bearing all that in mind, it was the idea that Kerrey read the *Globe* story while Bush was talking about being guided by his conscience, by refusing to do what was politically expedient, while Bush was making the character of *Army enlistee* Al Gore an issue.

Now here it is again, Kerrey thinks, as he watches Lieberman fumbling on TV. The political surrogates who defended Gore weren't so hot, Kerrey thinks. Congressmen Hastings, Wexler, Deutsch — they were good guys and doing their best, but Gore needs someone more experienced down there to help him, someone with a national reputation. Bush was beginning to use the whole Republican Governors' Association, and they were killing Gore!

Kerrey phones up Gore.

"You need to get somebody down there, for Godsakes," Kerrey says. They were getting killed. Surrogates matter, he thinks.

Gore explains to him that the thinking in Goreland is that they want to use local politicians. That's the story they're laying out — local people, local canvassing boards, their decision.

But Carol Roberts can only do so much, Kerrey believes. It's very difficult for a local person to debate Norman Schwarzkopf on the issue of military ballots. We need the same sort of surrogates the Republicans are using. Especially in this overseas-absentee-ballot dispute, which in Kerrey's opinion is "totally bogus."

"We may have made a mistake in sending the memo out," Kerrey thinks, "but it's no mistake to say that if a ballot is illegal, it should be disqualified. It might help for me to go down there. They won't expect a one-legged Vietnam veteran Medal of Honor winner to argue that a ballot that's two weeks late *should* be disqualified. It's bullshit to say otherwise. That's one thing you learn in the military — you take responsibility for your actions, you follow orders, and even if you don't know the rules, you can be court-martialed for not following them."

But it's not just the absentee-ballot issue that's getting Kerrey fired up; he thinks the Republicans have basically launched a campaign based on The Big Lie. Tell a lie loud enough, often enough, with sufficient conviction, and sooner or later people will believe you. Take hand recounts, for instance. The Votomatic is a shitty device, one that hasn't been used in Nebraska — *Nebraska!* — since 1982, the year Kerrey was first elected governor. Everyone knows it isn't as accurate as a hand count.

In addition, Kerrey is flummoxed to hear Republicans pretend that hand recounts are anything but the norm in close elections. Everybody in politics understands that in a close election, you do a hand recount, he thinks. Racicot, a former attorney general, knows that the things he's saying aren't true, Kerrey thinks. But Racicot says them repeatedly, over and over, and because he does so, people start believing that they must be true.

And the people running the interviews don't challenge him.

Kerrey's aghast at the fact that the media allows the Republicans to even argue that the validity of hand recounts is a debatable point. Kerrey doesn't blame the Republicans, really. They're trying to prevent the hand count, that's their objective, and they're doing what they need to do. But that national journalists would actually fucking sit there and nod their heads and say, "Senator Kerrey, this is a very good point that the governor has raised," when it wasn't a good point at all! It was a joke!

And the Bush team clearly had gotten permission from their people to say anything they wanted to say. Look at House Majority Whip Tom DeLay: "The Democratic Party is prosecuting the war to reverse the results of a fair, free election by any means necessary," DeLay says. "Make no mistake, we are witnessing nothing less than a theft in progress, and the American people, the Constitution, and the rule of law are all potential victims."

They were out there saying that Gore was stealing the election, committing fraud, and what the fuck were the Democrats doing? So even though it's not quite the Gore plan, an infuriated Kerrey flies down to Florida, spends a day in Miami and a day in Palm Beach. Somebody, he thinks, has got to do *something*.

★   ★   ★

"Fucking Butterworth!" one Gorebie mutters under his breath.

The attorney general issues a letter on Monday, November 20, telling elections supervisors to allow overseas ballots from members of the military that don't have a postmark — as long as the ballots are signed and dated no later than the date of the election. "No man or woman in military service to this nation should have his or her vote rejected solely due to the absence of a postmark, particularly when military officials have publicly stated that the postmarking of military mail is not always possible under sea or field conditions," Butterworth writes. The Gorebies are not only upset with the content of the letter, they are pissed that they didn't even get a heads-up from Butterworth before it was issued.

Now the Bushies can contrast the Herron memo not only with what Lieberman said, but with Butterworth.

There go the Dems, like ships from a sinking rat.

★   ★   ★

On Tuesday, Kerrey holds a press conference.

"Having been in the military, one of the things that was driven into me when I was in the United States Navy is that failure to get the word is no excuse," Kerrey says. "Everybody that's in the military understands that. And we should not be playing politics with our military as a consequence of that standard being in place every single day for our fighting men and women. If they have a legal ballot, it should be counted. If it's not a legal ballot, it should not be counted. Men and women in the military should not expect and do not expect to be treated in some fashion that has them being a pawn in a political argument that's very tense and very passionate here in Florida.

"In the military we accept responsibility for our mistakes, we don't blame it on somebody else. And if I'm not prepared and I didn't get the word and I come to my commanding officer and say, 'Gee, I'm sorry, Captain, I didn't get the word,' my commanding officer will say, 'Lieutenant, failure to get the word is no excuse.'"

The ballots that have been tossed for technicalities are being done so because of a lack of postmark, Kerrey says. "And the day after these accusations are made, what we're discovering is signatures are not there, voter IDs are not there, addresses are not there, witnesses aren't there. . . . And we're discovering that the number of people who were thrown out this time around are no greater or no less than what happened in 1996."

★　★　★

There are three lessons Kerrey learns in Florida.

One, the Republicans are just all-out lying about the hand recounts being chaotic. He tells reporters this at one press conference, but they basically ignore him. Chaos is always a better story than calm.

Two, he thinks, the Democratic Party of Palm Beach County committed campaign malpractice by not noticing and filing a protest against the butterfly ballot before the election. An old woman approaches him to tell him how she's voted ten times in Palm Beach. She knows the rules, she tells him, she knows that the presidential candidate who's the same party as the sitting governor is listed first and the other party's candidate is listed second — so she punched the second hole, mistakenly thinking that it was for Gore. The idea that she voted for a man who denies the horror that she lived through during World War II appalls her. The woman, who has a concentration camp number tattooed on her arm, is crying; Kerrey is very moved.

Three, Kerrey sees firsthand that some of the ballots the Democrats want to be counted as votes — the dimples, specifically — simply cannot be called that. In Palm Beach County, he's shown a disputed ballot, and he thinks, "Oh my God, you can't assert that this is a vote." He says as much.

"Of course you can, you can see it right there," a Democratic lawyer asserts.

Kerrey still can't see it.

Some of the marks that the Democratic lawyers are calling "dimples" that show "intent" don't look like marks to him. But then again, that's a testament to the Democratic Party's strength and weakness, he thinks — we care about fairness. The Republicans simply don't, he thinks. Not in this battle, anyway.

He'll come to think that the Democrats' dimple lust will help the Bush people paint the entire recount as illegitimate. And he'll know, even as he flies back to Washington, D.C., that the Republicans used the overseas-ballot issue very effectively, they drove it home, and — despite his best efforts — the Gore campaign buckled and lost. It didn't matter what the truth was, it didn't matter that Racicot and Dole and Sen. Alan Simpson said what Kerrey considered to be out-and-out lies, the media was letting them get away with it, and there was nothing he could do. He tried.

In retrospect, Kerrey will come to see the dispute about overseas absentee ballots as the moment when the Bushies turned the corner and started to put this thing away.

★   ★   ★

Though no one knew it for sure at the time, there was a good reason for the Herron memo. Before the election, 23,246 overseas ballots were mailed out from the state of Florida, and more than half of them — 14,415 — had come in by Election Day. As of Monday, November 13, Florida's sixty-seven counties had received 446 military overseas ballots since November 8.

By Thursday afternoon, that number had swelled to 2,575. By Friday, it was 3,733.

Democrats like Nick Baldick were suspicious: Where did this sudden surge of overseas ballots come from, more than a week after the election? Military mail is often far more efficient than regular post office mail.

Baldick's suspicions were well founded. According to a knowledgeable Republican operative, on either November 10 or 11, after Warren Tompkins was assigned by the Bush campaign inner circle to be in charge of absentee ballots, there was a sixty- to ninety-minute conference call for political operatives scattered throughout the state. Tompkins was on the call.

Many matters were attended to. They talked about finding people to be observers. They talked about drumming up protesters. They talked about assigning operatives to different clerks' offices to wait for the overseas absentee ballots, and to report on what the Democratic operatives were up to.

According to a knowledgeable Republican operative, in the course of that conversation they discussed having political operatives abroad and near military bases encourage certain soldiers who had registered to vote — but hadn't yet done so — to fill out their ballots and send them in.

Voter registration ID made it so they could identify not only which soldiers, sailors, and airmen were Democrat and which were Republican, but which were black and which were white. They would target the right ones.

We'll get them to send them in, and we'll argue about the postmarks later, one of the operatives said, according to this source. We're gonna raise a stink and force them to count these ballots. We don't know how they're gonna come in, but we need every vote we can get.

If this idea was carried out, then the Bush political operatives involved were committing a serious crime. But barring a major law-enforcement investigation into the matter — where phone records can be subpoenaed, and operatives can be threatened with perjury charges if they fail to tell the whole truth, two powers I simply do not have — the world may never know if this plan was carried out, and if so, how it was carried out and how many votes Bush may have gained as a result. (Neither Tompkins nor Mehlman returned calls for comment.)

10

"You know what
I dreamed of today?"

In Tallahassee, the Florida State Seminoles — ranked no. 3 in the country, with a 10-and-1 record — are a religion. Same in Gainesville, where the 9-and-1 Florida Gators are ranked no. 4. So on Saturday, November 18, Gore v. Bush is pushed aside for a more important contest: Florida v. Florida State. A bunch of us — lawyers, reporters, pols — get tossed from our hotel rooms to make way for alumni and fans that had their rooms booked up to a year in advance of today's game.

Even the august Mr. Baker gets booted by the Doubletree Hotel; he moves to a rental apartment where he'll remain 'til the bitter end. Curiously, despite the fact that, when all is said and done, the Democrats will have been outplayed and overrun by the Republicans, Christopher successfully negotiates to keep his room at the Governor's Inn. Perhaps there's some deeper meaning in this. In any case, I'm not sure how well he slept — outside his window, bars were packed, bass pumping, co-eds losing themselves in pursuits Christopher probably hasn't thought about since the Carter administration.

It's cold — something like 40 degrees, in the 30s with the windchill, we're told — but that doesn't stop FSU's Doak Campbell Stadium from quickly being packed with 83,042 fans, some with faces painted, others more than a tad boozy. FSU sticker–adorned cars in the parking lot have alligator dolls hanging from the trunks.

Some of the fans' hand-painted signs, of course, allude to the other war being waged in town. A big theme revolves around comparing visor-clad

Gators coach Steve Spurrier — who led his team to a Sugar Bowl win in '96 but can't buy a victory in Tallahassee, where he has a record of 0–4–1 — to Al Gore. "Who's A Bigger Crybaby? Spurrier or Gore?" taunts one sign. "Visor Boy, your chads are dangling," reads another. Forgoing any football connection whatsoever, state GOP chair Al Cardenas and Insurance Commissioner-elect Tom Gallagher hand out "Sore-Loserman" campaign signs.

The hot ticket today is FSU president Sandy D'Alemberte's skybox, where you can find Florida Supreme Court justices Major Harding and Leander Shaw, as well as Governor Jeb Bush. Soon, none other than Katherine Harris arrives with her husband, and two bodyguards. She looks lovely, gray sweater hanging from her trim frame like a queen's robe. Harris has more than a passing interest in this game; the University of Florida football stadium, called "The Swamp," is officially named after Harris's citrus mogul grandfather, Ben Hill Griffin, a powerful Floridian worth $390 million in 1990.

Everyone in the box is sporting name tags.

"If anyone does not need a name tag, it is you," one reporter says to her.

"Really?" she asks. "I guess you're right. I went to the supermarket today. And a woman said to me, 'You shop?' I said, 'Duh, yeah.'"

"You know what I dreamed of today?" she says to another reporter. "That I would ride into this stadium, carrying the FSU flag in one hand and the certification in the other to cheers of all those around me."[1]

Joseph she ain't. She says she cannot get over her newfound celebrity. "I cannot believe this, I watch Leno, and he's making jokes about me," she says. "You know, what joke I loved the best is, 'If Katherine Harris was a sportscaster of this game, she would call the winner in the third quarter.'"

How are you holding up? she's asked.

She giggles. "What do you think?" she says. "How do I look?"

"I love this game," she adds, motioning toward the field. "We will have a winner at the end."

FSU beats Florida 30 to 7.

★   ★   ★

Strep Throat* calls me back. I haven't written anything about Harris and Jeb for a bunch of reasons, primarily because I think there is nothing to write. But I also think that it's disgusting that Strep Throat would even

---

*The only reason I don't tell you Strep Throat's name is that I made a solemn promise that I wouldn't ever do so, and I, at least, consider my credibility to be a valuable asset. Unlike Mr. Throat.

pitch the story to me, a story that, as far as I know, Strep Throat invented out of whole cloth.

Strep Throat never bestowed upon me this much attention during the campaign, which I resent. And frankly, I'm insulted that he would think I would spread such filth.*

Strep Throat tells me that he has a lead for me. The name of a guy willing to talk. He's on the faculty of the University of Miami Law School, I'm told. I don't call. A few hours later, Strep Throat calls me back and tells me that the guy is actually on the faculty of the University of Miami *Medical* School. Apparently, he was heard on talk radio saying that everyone knew about the affair.

At this point, I do call. I'm like the eleventh person to call him, the professor says. ABC, *Newsweek,* the *New York Daily News,* a ton of major media outlets have phoned before me. It's not him, the Miami guy says. There's someone else with the same name in Tallahassee or something.

This is how a senior Gore adviser is spending his time, peddling this filth. Filth that isn't even remotely true. A few weeks from now, the *New York Observer* and others will allude suggestively to "the rumor" about Jeb and Harris that the media had put a lid on. Die-hard Democrats will send e-mail after e-mail, begging us to tell the American people the truth.

★   ★   ★

True to his word, Bobby Martinez doesn't go back to the Miami-Dade canvassing board to try to get the count shanked and, more specifically, to get a judge to order the elections-board employees to stop sorting out the 10,750 undervotes.

Instead, on Saturday, Martinez tracks down circuit judge Margarita Esquiroz at a wedding in the Keys. She's the duty judge this weekend, and Martinez wants her to issue a temporary restraining order to prevent the countywide count from commencing. He argues, in particular, that sorting out the undervotes will degrade the ballots.

Really, do we have to do it today? Esquiroz asks him. I'm in the Keys.

---

*I do so now, only after the presidential dispute is all over, and because I think Strep Throat — and whoever else on Team Gore knew about it — should be ashamed. I realize that even mentioning it circulates it even further, and for that reason I had second, third, fourth thoughts about including it here. But when all is said and done, I do it because I think Democrats need to be slapped out of their delusion that their advocates acted honorably. Strep Throat was not a fringe player on the Gore campaign. Strep Throat was a senior adviser who dealt with the vice president on a regular basis.

I'm sorry, Judge, Martinez says. But they're going to sort out the under-votes tomorrow, so I really do need to do this today.

Have you told the other side yet? she asks.

Not yet, he admits. I haven't filed the brief yet. I wanted to talk to you first to see how you think we should do it.

OK, well, after you tell them, then beep me, she says.

Martinez arranges hand deliveries of the emergency motion for a temporary injunction — Esquiroz gets one in the Keys, Zack gets one at home, Coffey at Berger's law firm, and Murray Greenberg gets one, too, since the canvassing board, technically, is the one Martinez is seeking the injunction against.

They agree to hold the hearing Sunday morning by telephone.

During the hearing, Martinez tells Esquiroz that "the prudent thing is the very reasonable request that we're asking for, a very temporary pause of this matter until this afternoon, perhaps, or tomorrow morning."

Greenberg says that Leahy, a twenty-six-year expert, has already testified that he does "not believe that running ballots through the card reader will further degrade the ballots." In his experience, Leahy has already testified, any chad that falls off is one "hanging on by two corners, or one corner, [and] we have unanimously determined those to be clear votes. There may be instances where a clear hanging chad, either through manual handling or through this operation of putting them through the reader one more time, may fall off. I'm not concerned about that as a canvassing-board member. That is a clear vote. And we've already determined those to be clear votes."

Martinez pipes in. "Your Honor, when we were before the canvassing board last week, Mr. Zack . . . said, quoting from the motto on the seal of the Supreme Court of Florida, he read a quote in Latin, and he translated it for the benefit of all of us. . . . 'Soon enough, if done rightly.' . . . The right thing for you to do is to put a pause to these matters and get some guidance from the Supreme Court of Florida," which will be meeting tomorrow.

Esquiroz denies the motion.

Martinez and De Grandy will file the motion before another judge when the work week begins, but that will be denied, too.

★   ★   ★

Ed Pozzuoli is fired up.

"The Gore campaign now wants to lower the bar because it needs more votes!" the Broward County GOP chairman rants. With Palm Beach and Miami-Dade Counties utilizing looser standards, Broward decides to do so as well on Sunday, November 19. County attorney Ed Dion, a Republican, and assistant county attorney Andrew Meyers, whose wife is helping the Gore legal team, conclude that the two-corner rule is too stringent. Meyers comes armed with the Texas standard, raising the eyebrows of Republican observers who wonder if maybe his wife gave him a copy of it.

The timing, at least, is a bit suspect. With counting in 390 of the county's 609 precincts completed, Gore has picked up 105 net votes, which will not be enough. For Judge Lee, however, the more significant timing issue comes from the fact that they all just reviewed about 50 dimpled ballots from a precinct where clearly something was wrong with the voting machines.

"Any semblance of a standard of fairness in the hand-counting process in Broward County has been abandoned," says Bush spokesman Ray Sullivan.

Dion, of course, says that's nonsense. He's a Republican, for Godsakes! It's just that judges in Palm Beach and Miami-Dade Counties have ruled against a per se exclusion of any ballots. "My only job is to represent the canvassing board," Dion says. "This is an evolving situation. What we believed to be accurate legal advice on Monday is now changed."

★   ★   ★

The Palm Beach group is only a few hours into their Saturday chore when a Republican counter, a woman, angrily leaves table nine. She is enraged. "I've had it," she whispers to a reporter. "I'm not coming back. There are some real games going on here." The problem isn't the Democrats, however. It's the Republicans. The GOP observer at her table is objecting to every sixth Gore vote, a pattern that is repeating itself at other tables. These are not dimples or otherwise disputable ballots, these are clear Gore votes, punched through. The Republicans' strategy is now offending even Republicans.*

Burton realizes this, of course, and before the count began today he approached each counting team to tell them how the canvassing board was inspecting the "questionables." One precinct had 440 "questionables," he says, but at the canvassing-board table, he anticipated that Republican

---

*In a perfect example of how the shoddiness of the media benefited the Bushies, this "some real games are being played" anecdote will be reported by the Associated Press without the explanation that the Republican woman was complaining about Republican games. Then the story will be e-mailed out by Bush communications senior staffers Ari Fleischer and Dan Bartlett on November 18 at 5 p.m., with the subject line "GAMES BEING PLAYED" as an example of Democratic dirty tricks.

lawyers like Wallace and John Bolton, a newly arrived senior Bush aide, would object to "about four of them."

In fact, Bolton doesn't even wait for the ballots before he starts launching objections. He says that counters shouldn't be intimidated into not putting ballots in the questionable pile. Burton says he's just trying to "educate" the counters. Bolton disagrees.

It's the Republican strategy: gum it up. They don't like the fact that the counts are going on, so they want to ruin them. It's rather immature, not to mention vaguely anti-democratic. But it's working.

Early afternoon, a new GOP observer comes in and begins raising hell at Team Five. Everything had been going fine with Team Five until this young punk arrives. The Democratic counter — an older African-American woman — has had a routine: she picks a ballot from the stack, holds it up for everyone to look at, flips it front and back, then places it in the appropriate pile — for Bush or Gore or whomever. While she's putting it in the stack, she takes another ballot with her other hand. Young Punk has a problem with her routine, though.

"Wait until you put it in the stack before you pick up another one," he says.

"We'll be here all day," she says under her breath.

"You're doing it again," he says. "One at a time."

He raises his hand: a formal objection. Lawyers swarm.

"She's picking up two ballots at a time, calling them out like it's only one," he says, falsely.

"You know that's not the truth," she says. "You are not truthful. That's a lie."

This offends Bolton. "I don't think you have to say that at all," he says.

"Who are you?" the Democratic observer, an older white man, says to Bolton, clearly annoyed.

The cavalry — Burton, sheriff's deputies, county officials, lawyers — arrives.

"If you see something going on you don't like, you don't talk to her," Burton tells Young Punk. "You talk to your lawyer."

Burton orders Young Punk to another table. Bolton complains that this makes it look like Young Punk did something wrong. The Democratic woman agrees to change teams instead.

"Thank you very much," Burton says. "You are a lady. I think tomorrow morning we're going to have to make some changes."

Later Burton makes a plea to the observers. "I want to assure you, if you're an observer, by all means put aside a ballot if it's questionable. But if you're objecting simply to object, the board is going to have to discuss it. When we go through four hundred and fourteen objections and only six are objected to when the lawyers go through them . . ." He trails off. "I'm begging you all to be reasonable," he says.

★ ★ ★

Outside, the Elián connection is complete. We already have Gutierrez. And Coffey. And Cuban-Americans angry at the Clinton-Gore administration, and chaos in Miami, Al Gore not sure what to do or what to say, courts and lawsuits.

And now we have "the fisherman."

Donato Dalrymple got his fifteen minutes a year ago, when — out in the Atlantic on his cousin's boat — his cousin dove into the sea and rescued poor Elián. The media called him "the fisherman," even though he's a house-cleaner and that was his first time out in the boat. His cousin would later say that Dalrymple overinflated his role in the rescue. But he was there — holding Elián in his arms, hiding in the closet — on that fateful April morning when the INS stormed into the Little Havana home, forever harming Gore's chances for significant support in Miami-Dade's Cubano precincts.

So what the hell's he doing here, outside the Emergency Operations Center?

"I was a victim of this administration," Dalrymple says. "And I just came here to check it out. Before the election is actually stolen, or someone concedes, I just wanted to come and see. I'm just like any other citizen here."

You here because the media's here?

"I'm not here for the cameras," Dalrymple insists. "I just came here to support George Bush."

★ ★ ★

On Wednesday, November 8, Gore fund-raiser Peter Knight convened a bunch of the fat cats who were in Nashville for the election and secured $3 million in pledges to the Gore recount fund. On Sunday, November 14, Don Evans sent out an emergency e-mail to Bush supporters, asking each to kick in $5,000 to the Bush-Cheney recount fund.

By now, the money to the Bush and Gore recount committees has started to really pour in. Twice as much for Bush as for Gore, of course — about $7.5 million. The same people and network that made the Bush campaign the most cash-rich presidential campaign in history, to the tune of $100 million, kick in $7.4 million. To his credit, Bush has limited donations to $5,000 and is listing the names of his contributors on the Web — people like former Dallas Cowboys quarterback Roger Staubach and Kenneth Lay, chairman of Enron, a Houston-based Texas energy company that has been over the years Bush's largest benefactor. American Airlines CEO Donald Carty, Texas Rangers owner Tom Hicks, and MBNA chairman Alfred Lerner all give $5,000. With Boies fighting for Gore, Republican donors affiliated with Microsoft have twice the reason to kick in bucks; and Microsoft lobbyist Jack Abramoff; Charles Simonyi, chief programmer of Word and Excel; Bryan Woodruff, a software design engineer; and several others have all donated.

Knight's been able to bring in $3.5 million. Infoseek founder Steve Kirsch kicks in $500,000; Stephen Bing, a Hollywood writer (*Married . . . with Children*) and producer (Stallone's *Get Carter*) gives $200,000; Slim-Fast founder S. Daniel Abraham $100,000; actress Jane Fonda $100,000; the political action committee of Senate Minority Leader Tom Daschle $5,000; *Las Vegas Sun* editor/president Brian Greenspun gives $5,000. New Jersey senator-elect Jon Corzine just bought himself a senate seat with $60 million of his own money; he kicks in $25,000. New York songwriter Denise Rich, who's trying to get her slimy, sleazy, fugitive tax-evading ex-husband a pardon, donates $25,000.

★   ★   ★

By now, civil rights attorney Henry Latimer* — a former Broward circuit judge and the first black partner at the Fort Lauderdale law firm Fine Jacobson Schwartz Nash Block & England — has been designated the Gore team's go-to guy on all the complaints about voting irregularities in the minority community. He reaches out to members of the civil rights community throughout the state, tells them to let him know of anything — anything — at all. He works with the NAACP, talks to the organization's representatives in Washington, D.C., and in Florida.

He hears of things that disturb him. Black voters shut out at one precinct because the polls were closed, but two white voters are allowed to stroll in and cast their votes. Hundreds of voters, the majority of whom seem to be black or Hispanic, who should have been on the voting rolls but weren't for

---

*Not all of Latimer's work is on behalf of aggrieved African-Americans, of course. In 1984, he represented the city of Miami in a suit brought by a twenty-year-old black man shot and killed by a Hispanic city cop. In 1991, he represented Miami again when former police chief Perry Anderson, an African-American, sued the city for not paying legal fees for his private attorney when he was named in lawsuits against the police department in various police brutality cases. In the past, the city had paid for counsel to represent white police chiefs.

some reason. Other instances, where black voters were asked for two forms of picture ID. Voters complaining about cops oddly swarming about polling places. But what can be done about any of this? Latimer wonders. A lot of the stuff is just anecdotal. And you can't go to court on every complaint. The Gorebies are sensitive to the perception that they're running to court every time there's the most minute incident.

He is bothered a great deal by the fact that there was so much ballot spoilage in black precincts. Latimer doesn't hold Jeb or Harris responsible — not in the direct, conspiratorial sense, anyway. But what happened on Election Day is generally reflective of the community at large, and most people are prone to overlook the rights of minorities, Latimer thinks. It's no surprise that black precincts have worse machines, poorly trained elections clerks.

"Gee whiz," Latimer thinks, recalling his youth in Miami in the 1950s and '60s, marching for civil rights. "All these years, and I don't know if *my* vote counted."

Racism is different now than in his youth. No, they don't have Sheriff Bull Connor standing out there with bulldogs, keeping blacks from the polls by force. No, it's benign neglect these days, he thinks. Still, what can be done legally? The best thing now might be to focus on how to change this situation in the future.

*   *   *

Sunday, Bruce Rogow flies up to Tallahassee. When he arrives at the Doubletree Hotel, right there in the lobby, David Boies is being interviewed by *60 Minutes*.

"This is not where I'd be the day before a case before the Supreme Court of Florida," Rogow thinks.

Rogow's no foe of media attention, but he wonders if Boies is playing too many roles on the Gore team. He's not sure that you can keep yourself on the kind of track that you need to be on to plot the strategy when you're also being asked to be the spokesperson. When you're the lawyer, you're the lawyer, he thinks.

Boies continues with the interview.

11

"Es un circo."

Last Tuesday, the Rodgers brothers drove about seven hundred miles south to Tallahassee to protest Al Gore stealing the election.

"I'm here because I'm angry," Fred Rodgers, sixty, tells me.

It's Monday, November 20, almost two weeks since the election, and I'm up early (for me, anyway; it's 8:15 A.M.), standing outside the state supreme court, so as to ensure a seat by the time of the historic oral argument, scheduled for 2 P.M. I'm about eighth in line. They said 148 members of the public are allowed to watch the proceedings, first come, first served. Some members of the media got tickets through a lottery, but there are only so many seats.

Not everybody is here to see; some are here to be seen. Like Fred, of course.

Fred's a retired reliability engineer from Newburgh, Indiana, "a statistician," he says, "and I'm angry that they're doing a hand recount. Machines are designed to have test programs. Test diagnostics make sure the machine is performing properly. When Palm Beach County came up with over eight hundred votes added for Al Gore in the second recount, I can tell you it should not have had another recount, they should have looked for fraud."

Fred is walking up and down the street, holding a sign that says, "The Hand Recount is a Farce." On the other side it says, "Selective Recount Unfair." His sixty-five-year-old older brother, Ron, has a sign, too: "Al, if every vote counts, why not the military?" on one side, and "Al Gore: Commander-in-Thief" on the other. The one belonging to brother Jim, fifty-eight, says, "Hand Recount — a License to Steal" and "Gore/Daley/Boies 'Liars, Cheaters, and Thieves, Oh, My.'"

229

"We're just three grandpas from the heart of America," explains Fred.

This has been a big Rodgers family project. The letters on the sign have been painstakingly etched out in pencil first, and carefully colored in with black ink. The signs, in fact, are ever-changing, consisting as they do of two pieces of poster board attached with those fastener paperclip things. Every few hours, Fred Rodgers wanders off and returns with a whole new sign.

Originally this was going to be just a two-day protest. On Friday, they shuffled back into Fred's 1995 Chrysler New Yorker, the one with a hundred thousand miles on it, and drove the seven hundred or so miles back to Mount Carmel, Illinois, where Ron and Jim live, so as to see Ron's grandson play football in the state semifinals.

It was a crappy day; halfway to Atlanta, they heard that the state supreme court had put a stay on Harris's certification. Then, later that night, the Mount Carmel Aces got their butts handed to them by the Harrisburg Dogs. So on Sunday, the Rodgers brothers got back in the car and came back here. They're staying at the local Motel 6.

I get back in line. A Florida Coastal Law School student named Trevor Mask, twenty-five, number seven in line, has been saving my place; Delta Airlines flight attendant Alyson Wood, thirty, is behind me. Both are native to Tallahassee, though neither lives here anymore. Both voted for Bush and came to see a bit of history.

Down the street, "Angelina the Polka Queen" — crown on her head, clad in a red dress and sequined shoes, playing an accordion — and her partner "King Ira" — crown atop his blond wig, red sequined jacket, strumming on the old banjo — are singing against the proceedings. "George W. B. / Please put the world back in order for me," they sing. "I don't like liberals creating such confusion. / Just want all folks to respect the Constitution." They're from Gainesville, they say in between spats of mugging for various TV cameras.

"We're here to debut the queen's new song," says Ira Philpot.

"We got some great Christmas songs, too!" Angelina Woodhull chirps.

It's 9:30 A.M. now, and the line has grown to about fifty. Across the street, eight TV networks have set up tents. One of the several officers from the sheriff's office keeps approaching Alyson and whispering in her ear.

Trevor's friend from high school and Florida State, Frank Mayernick, twenty-four, a law student at FSU's College of Law, suddenly appears with doughnuts and coffee, which he and Trevor offer to everyone in the surrounding area. In front of Trevor and Frank is state senator Skip Campbell, an Orlando Democrat, with a couple of attractive female senate staffers.

With much of the line consisting of reporter types like me and professional pols like Campbell, Trevor and Frank soon become very popular among the reporters. They're real people, after all. "Are you guys the students?" a Bloomberg Business News reporter asks, pouncing. Trevor is interviewed by Bloomberg, NBC News, and *USA Today*. Frank gets Bloomberg and Orlando's ABC affiliate; he tells the *USA Today* scribe that "This is a circus," and it is noted how much better a sound bite that was than Trevor's more earnest and ponderous utterings. Soon a correspondent from Spanish-language channel Univision comes over and asks if anyone speaks Spanish.

"How do you say 'This is a circus' in Spanish?" I ask him.

"Es un circo," he says.

Frank tries it out. His accent sucks, though. The Univision correspondent turns his attention to the sweet young state senate staffers in front of us. Within minutes, Mr. Univision gets a phone number.

By noon about 175 have joined the line. Including a bunch of professional Republicans who have blatantly cut in line right behind me, RNC counsel Ginsberg, Florida state GOP chair Al Cardenas, others. In front of us, state senators Jim Scott, a Democrat, and Tom Lee, a Republican, also violate the "no cutsies" rule.

On the sidewalk right in front of the supreme court building, Baker exits an SUV like he's at the Oscars. A smattering of applause follows. Ginsberg, his hair particularly neon in the Florida sun, scampers after him.

Cardenas spots GOP power attorney Ted Olson about fifteen places behind him in line. "I got all those positive vibes right here," Cardenas says in his thick Cuban accent.

I have now officially been in line for four hours and forty-five minutes.

Finally we get in.

★   ★   ★

The supreme courtroom has a high ceiling. A large bench stands up front, the seven justices' names all writ out, but other than that, we could be in a small chapel. Frank, Trevor, Alyson, and I debate whether a certain TV correspondent is wearing a rug. You'd never know it unless you saw him from the back, where what looks like a toupé plops over the thin scraps of real hair poking out from underneath, like fringes on an Oriental carpet.

We're still debating its legitimacy when the correspondent scratches his head, and the whole deal moves like a tablecloth.

Hair still on my mind, I make a joke that Barry Richard's immense gray pompadour makes him look like he plays the sax for Billy Joel. When

Richard comes over to my row, I realize that I am sitting next to his wife, Allison. "Look how handsome you look!" she says to him. We look to the left and stare at Christopher, who appears embalmed.

Agriculture commissioner Crawford and elections head Roberts walk in and take front-row seats. Then the court marshal and another courtroom employee walk in and out of the justices' chambers, putting folders and stacks of papers before the appropriate justices' chairs. The marshal then steps down from the dais, looks down, takes a breath, and then proceeds to bellow: "PLEASE RISE! Hear ye, hear ye, hear ye, the supreme court of the great state of Florida is now in session!"

The seven robe-clad justices spill out onto the bench one by one. The chief justice settles first into his chair in the center, followed by the justice who sits to his immediate right, then the justice who sits to his immediate left, and so on, right, left, right, left — a well-choreographed presentation.

Seated, left to right, they are two old white men (Fred Lewis and Harry Lee Anstead), one old black man (Leander Shaw), the old white chief justice (Charles Wells), another old white man (Major Harding), with two stately middle-aged women — one white (Barbara Pariente) and one black (Peggy Quince) — rounding it out on the right.

Before they moved to Tallahassee upon their appointments, Anstead and Pariente were from Palm Beach (!!!) — a fact that right-wing-conspiracy theorists outside the courtroom are already citing, anticipating that not only will the largely Democrat-appointed court fulfill their liberal-activist stereotype, but somehow they'll show geographic bias.

Being a supreme court justice is a good gig. You can interrupt lawyers in mid-bullshit and tell them to fast-forward to the relevant part. You can challenge their misrepresentations and glib evasions with disdain and impatience. And instead of your impudent actions resulting in an immediate end to a press conference and a lifelong kibosh on obtaining interviews, the shysters treat you with deference, bowing and genuflecting and calling you "Your Honor."

Which is what happens here. In fact, Chief Justice Charles Wells begins the proceedings by preemptively telling the attorneys to cut to the chase. "Since we have a limited amount of time here, we would ask that we get right to the heart of the matter as you see it, because we are fully cognizant of the facts and the procedures of below that have brought you here." Wells isn't screwing around. He even tells the rest of us when our bathroom break will be.

Despite that warning, Paul Hancock, representing Butterworth, commences with a bucket of rhetoric.

"The court has previously referred to the attorney general as 'the people's attorney,'" Hancock says. "I stand here on behalf of the attorney general in that capacity. . . . The right to vote is perhaps the most cherished right in our democracy. The real parties and interests in this lawsuit are not the presidential candidates, nor the parties that support them —"

"Mr. Hancock, excuse me for interrupting," Wells says. "I would really like counsel on both sides to pay attention to a concern of mine." That concern is to figure out how to resolve this mess. "It seems from my reading that we have a continuum from November seventh to some point in December," Wells explains. "And that's when my concern is, and so I'd like to sort of get this hammered down to that framework."

Great, thinks Bush attorney Michael Carvin. They've already decided that we lost the argument about whether November 14 was the certification deadline. Usually they let you debate the matter a bit first.

"What's the date, the outside date that we're looking at and which puts Florida's votes in jeopardy?" Wells asks Hancock.

"December twelfth, Your Honor, is my understanding," Hancock says. "The electoral college meets on December eighteenth." December 12 is the "safe harbor" day on which the Florida legislature can meet and elect its electors if it so chooses, if it fears that the state's electors will be in jeopardy if they don't.

Carvin had come prepared to argue in favor of December 12 as the deadline, anticipating that Hancock and Boies would give the outside date, December 18. He's pleased that Hancock has made this point for him.

And Carvin's good luck continues, as Wells asks Boies the same question. Hancock said the deadline for all of this is December 12. "Do you agree with that?"

"I do, Your Honor," Boies says. After all, December 12 is years away. *Years.* This thing isn't going to last that long. Boies is confident that he'll successfully argue for an extension of the deadline, the hand recounts will go on, and he'll go home, just like that. Why argue with a supreme court justice over six days in December?

Carvin implores the high court not to accept a hand recount. But the court is well aware that Florida law — not to mention Texas law — finds such recounts not only legal but, at least in Texas, preferable to a machine recount. As Boies argues, "I cannot imagine how the [Florida] legislature could provide for these manual recounts and yet have those recounts be an illusory right."

"Does the secretary . . . play any role in determining whether or not there shall be a manual recount in any county?" a bulldog-faced Justice Harry Lee Anstead asks Joe Klock. Klock is reputed to be a brilliant legal strategist, a font of ideas, but in a courtroom he can be bumbling and clumsy and even a bit obnoxious. Or maybe it's just that the actions of his client are tough to defend.

"Absolutely not, sir," admits Klock.

"And so, who has the authority and responsibility for that?" Anstead asks.

"The canvassing board of the county," Klock says.

"Well, under the circumstances that we have here, then, isn't in essence the secretary of state, who has no authority to determine that, overruling a decision by the proper body that has the authority to do that?"

"To the contrary —"

"Isn't that what the net effect of this is?"

"To the contrary, Justice Anstead —"

"Well, if the secretary is saying, 'I'm not going to count the recount that started very late in the process,' and at a time in a large county where effectively the recount could not be completed before the seven days were up, isn't that the net effect?"

"Justice," Klock says, "I don't know that the recount couldn't be done in that period of time. And of course we have no trial record to know whether the recount could be done in that time."

"Don't we also end up sort of discriminating between small counties and large counties?" Anstead asks. "If we take Dade County, for instance, and Okaloosa County, clearly there is going to be a vast difference in the time that it takes in Dade County to do that manual recount compared to a small county. Would you agree?"

"Justice Anstead, yes," Klock says.

Amazing — Harris has done everything she can outside this courtroom to stop the hand recounts, but here today Klock is admitting that it was up to the canvassing boards the whole time.

Anstead presents a hypothetical anecdote that further undermines Harris's justification for discarding three counties' manual recounts. Harris, he poses, based her trashing of the recounted numbers on the statutory deadline for certifying the votes seven days after the election — a position she has clung to like Linus to his security blanket. But what if the members of the Miami canvassing board were to "go off to the islands" for a week instead of completing their vote-counting duties by the seven-day deadline? Anstead asks. Would Harris simply not accept their votes? Is the seven-day deadline absolute?

"Of course it's not absolute," Klock finally allows.

Democrats are also peppered with questions about their more dubious claims and actions. Attorney Andrew Meyers, representing Broward County — which decided on Sunday to start considering the unpenetrated "pregnant"- and "dimpled"-chad ballots along with the others — is asked by Leander Shaw whether this wasn't "unusual, changing rules in the middle of the game." Meyers says that "the important thing is that we do what's right at the end." How to read the ballots has been an "evolving area."

But the larger problem for Gore and his lawyer friends isn't dimples but resolving how the justices could allow the hand recounts without blatantly violating the Florida law that mandates last Tuesday's certification deadline. What can be done? The Democrats' attorneys are asked repeatedly for suggestions as to how they think the court could rule to keep everything within the parameters of the existing law. But they don't provide many answers. "There is some information in the record," says Boies, "but to be completely candid with the court, I believe there is going to have to be a lot of judgment applied by the court as well."

The debate returns to accuracy issues: "Is it the manual-recount process that's inherently flawed?" Pariente asks. "Isn't that the exact process that is set forth by — as has been represented to us, as the statutes reveal — in Texas law, for this exact process to take place where there's manual recounts? And that those are preferred over the machine recounts?"

"I really don't know what Texas law is," Carvin says. Of course he knows full well what Texas law is, but he doesn't think there's any sense in talking about a law from another state. From Carvin's point of view, the Florida Supreme Court is just not going to rule in their favor. As Baker puts it to him during the brief bathroom break: "Just answer the questions, and we'll get out of here."

Still, Carvin isn't ready to completely give up, and he tries a little subliminal strategy. He keeps arguing home the point that the Florida Supreme Court has to abide by a provision of the federal election code — United States Code, Title 3, Section 5 — that generally prohibits states from appointing electors according to any rules made *after* the election. The law dates back to 1887, in the wake of the disputed Hayes-Tilden election of

1876;* the U.S. Supreme Court has never ruled on it one way or another. Carvin knows that if the court abides by 3 U.S.C. 5, it will set the stage for the Bushies to complain to the Supreme Court of the United States about equal protection violations down the road if the Florida court goes ahead and orders the recount. He has a 108-year-old U.S. Supreme Court precedent at hand — *McPherson v. Blacker,* in which the SCOTUS ruled that the U.S. Constitution "leaves it to the legislature exclusively to define the method" by which each state's electors are chosen. But Carvin has no intention of telling them about this case, no intention of warning them of the argument that he, Olson, and the rest will make before the SCOTUS if the Florida Supreme Court extends the certification deadline. It's something of a trap, and Carvin is only too happy to set it.†

The justices ask Boies what he thinks of a statewide recount.

"We are not urging that upon the court," he says. "But certainly that is something that we have indicated that we would accept. And we believe the court has the power to order that or to order, as the court suggests, a window" for the hand-recount tally totals to come in.

Carvin is surprised that Boies doesn't press the case for a statewide count. Boies should say, "We think these three need to be counted, and

---

*The ugly 1876 dispute between Democrat Samuel Tilden and Republican Rutherford B. Hayes began when Florida submitted two slates of electors, one for Hayes from the GOP state canvassing board and one for Tilden from the Democratic state legislature. Congress formed an Electoral Commission, made up of five congressmen, five senators, and five U.S. Supreme Court justices. On a vote completely split on partisan lines — giving 185 electoral votes to Hayes, the popular-vote loser, and 184 to Tilden — Hayes's one-term presidency was born. To prevent this from ever happening again, on February 3, 1887, Congress passed the Electoral Count Act, which established a number of laws kicking it all back to the states, hopefully forever.

† "A clever court could have figured out a way to do this," Carvin will say to me on January 16, 2001, with a devilish grin. "But they were not particularly clever." He goes on: "The kind of cases I do — civil rights cases, affirmative action cases — I see the judges, I basically know the result, I mean a lot of times. If I'm arguing Prop. 209, and there are three Carter appointees, I basically know how they're going to come out, and vice versa if it's three Reagan appointees."

California's Prop. 209, which bans consideration of race or gender in state school admissions or in state hiring, was adopted by public initiative in 1996. Carvin argued in favor of it all the way to the SCOTUS, and the Court refused to hear arguments on the matter in November 1997, one of Carvin's many victories against affirmative action and civil rights measures. In October 1998, for instance, he worked to erase a 1993 Cincinnati city-charter law prohibiting discrimination in housing and employment based on sexual orientation.

"I've been in a lot of courts where I sort of know that I'm just here for stopover purposes. Then all you're trying to do is get through, lay down your markers, and move on."

if you want to do all of them after these three are finished, that's fine, too," Carvin thinks. After all, certainly if some counties are recounted, no definitive win can come without *all* of them recounted. Boies must figure the Florida Supreme Court's already in his pocket, Carvin reasons. But are they not looking ahead? This is the exact way to get the Supreme Court of the United States involved — which is, of course, the Bush strategy: the SCOTUS will save us! Please, throw me in this briar patch! Carvin thinks.

Boies and the Gorebies, however, are confident that SCOTUS won't rear its head. This is a state issue, they think. The current group of justices in Washington has voted again and again in favor of states over the federal government. Sure, justices like Scalia, Rehnquist, Kennedy, and O'Connor probably prefer Bush be president. And Clarence Thomas was nominated to the court by W.'s daddy, so he might feel a little personal loyalty. And while the Supreme Court's conservative pro-states' rights philosophy has frustrated the Democrats again and again, this time it works to their advantage.

"Mr. Boies, I think your time is up," Wells says.

I ask Allison, Barry Richard's wife, when she thinks the court will decide what to do.

"I keep asking my husband, 'When will the justices rule?'" she says, laughing. "He keeps saying, 'They'll rule when they rule.'"

★   ★   ★

After the arguments, Daley and Christopher say good-bye to Tallahassee. "Those guys are leaving, and they're not coming back," Klain predicts to Hattaway.

Christopher has a sick daughter, and his wife's best friend has passed away. He's needed in Los Angeles for family reasons, and though he will continue to stay in close contact with the team — especially with his colleague Mark Steinberg, who stays behind — when "Chris" leaves Tallahassee, he leaves.

Daley will return once more, but he, too, decides that his presence is better served elsewhere. He flies to D.C., shoring up support on Capitol Hill, hanging with Gore, keeping the operation running from Gore's home at NavObs, which some are now calling "the Bunker." He needs to keep the Hill in line, he needs to be where the political action is, near Gore. And frankly, with all the bashing of his dad, he's not sure that he's helping by being the public face of Gore's deal down here. Boies and Klain seem to have everything under control.

Baker, however, will remain in Tallahassee, the nucleus of the Bush atom. He has a job to finish. When Bush is crowned, then he'll leave. But not before then.

★　★　★

In Plantation and West Palm Beach, the tedium continues.

In downtown Miami, the tedium begins.

Elections Supervisor Leahy announces the plan, which is similar to that of the other two counties: more than fifty counters at twenty-five tables on the eighteenth floor of the County Building. They can be done by December 1, with Thanksgiving off, Leahy says.

The Miami-Dade canvassing board, however, has seen the havoc wreaked on the other two counts by observers objecting to unobjectionable ballots. For that reason, Leahy assumes that the 10,750 undervotes will be questionable by definition, and he begins to separate them on Sunday so the canvassing board can check them out. Additionally, Leahy, with the board's approval, gives the Miami-Dade counters very different instructions when it comes to the observers. The counters are instructed to not show each ballot to the observers. They'll put any questionable ballots in separate piles, and stack the other ballots in Gore or Bush piles. Once those Gore or Bush piles are an inch thick, the counters can hold them up as a pile for the observers to inspect. If the holes are clearly punched — and the observers can peer all the way through the aligned Gore or Bush holes — then the assumption will be that there are no problems with those ballots.

"We're going to run an orderly ship," Judge King says. "I do not expect observers to be arguing or putting into this process their personal opinion."

★　★　★

The Bushies have a real presence outside the county building. I'm somewhat familiar with New York congressman John Sweeney. A statesman he ain't. As soon as he was elected in 1998, he made a beeline for the National Republican Congressional Committee, where he quickly made a name for himself by being one of his class's most aggressive fund-raisers. Totally part of the problem. And, of course, here he is today, claiming that "Miami-Dade has become ground zero for producing a manufactured vote."

I also know Sweeney's colleague, Rep. Rob Portman, R-Ohio. He's a gentleman and a good guy. He, of course, has a slightly different tone, if the same fundamental message. "We're here this morning because we're deeply troubled by what we see unfolding in Miami-Dade County," Portman says. "At the very least, if there's going to be another recount, there needs to be clear guidelines. The eyes of the world are on Florida and Miami-Dade County, and they don't like what they see."

The Bush campaign has sent out e-mails and made phone calls and relocated its advance staffers to Florida to create the illusion of outraged voters. These professional Bush staffers have been shipped in to whip up locals into a frenzy. And Republican activists keep coming, their room, board, and travel paid for by the Bush recount fund. They're directed to Miami-Dade specifically, since Mehlman and others are concerned about the mystery of what might lie on those 10,750 undervotes. And once they've gotten to Miami-Dade, they're supposed to cause a ruckus. Which they're more than happy to do.

Thus, outside, it's getting tense.

Inside, too.

One of the lions of integrity guarding the process for Bush is GOP observer Grant Lally. Lally's a two-time losing congressional candidate who in 1998 received one of the largest penalties ever meted out by the Federal Elections Commission — $280,000 — for receiving more than $300,000 in illegal campaign contributions from his parents for his 1994 primary and general election campaigns, and then lying about it.

Lally decides to pick a fight with Ivy Korman, administrator of the elections department. He calls her "hostile" and tries to get her kicked out of the room. Both Lally and Korman are allowed to remain, but King's patience is starting to wear thin. De Grandy is objecting like crazy, which is fine; it's the observers who are talking and keeping the process from proceeding in an orderly manner.

Working with fellow Democratic observer Steve Kaufman — an L.A. attorney who does a lot of election law — Young notices something interesting about the Miami-Dade ballots. There are a whole bunch where the chad has clearly been punched out — nothing hanging, nothing dimpled — but the chad has been punched out for a nonexistent candidate. Kaufman and Young have an explanation, and using a sample ballot they demonstrate the theory to Leahy.

There is, they point out, no candidate's name next to chad no. 5. But if you put the paper ballot on top of the plastic booklet of candidates that rests on the breadbox-size Votomatic instead of in the slot under the plastic booklet, then the no. 5 is the chad next to Bush's name, which is actually in the no. 4 slot. Same for all those no. 7 votes — Young and Kaufman tell Leahy that those must be actually for Gore, whose chad is actually designated no. 6.

Once the canvassing board has been through the rest of the 10,750 undervotes, they'll come back and look at the 5's and 7's, Leahy says.

★ ★ ★

Judge Jorge LaBarga seems genuinely anguished as he walks into his Palm Beach County courtroom to rule on the butterfly ballot plaintiffs' call for a revote.

"Clearly, a great number of patriotic and deeply concerned citizens of Palm Beach County fear that they may have unwittingly cast their vote for someone other than their candidate," LaBarga rules. "While some may dismiss such concerns without a second thought" — *Hmmm. Whom do you think he's talking about?* — "this court is well aware that the right to vote is as precious as life itself to those who have been victimized by the horror of war, to those whose not-too-distant relatives were prohibited from exercising the right to vote simply because of their race or gender, and to those who have risked it all by venturing across an unforgiving sea in makeshift rafts or boats.

"However" — and you knew there was a "however" coming — "for over two centuries we have agreed to a Constitution and to live by the law."

Yes, there have been overturned elections and revotes in Florida before, LaBarga notes. The Carollo-Suarez mayor's race in '97. A Polk County commissioner's race in '96. A 1978 Liberty County school board race. A 1979 Wakulla County race for county judge. The 1972 Democratic primary race for sheriff of Columbia County. And yes, there have been races in other states — Delahunt, a '93 Pennsylvania race for state senate, a '97 state assembly race in Jersey. But "the plaintiffs in this action cite not case law authority in the history of our nation, nor can the court find any, where a revote or new election was permitted in a presidential race." The law is clear that "presidential elections must be held on the same day throughout the Unites States."

So: tough luck.

★ ★ ★

Harris's office is a virtual greenhouse, packed as it is with flowers from well-wishers all over the country. But things are not so great for her. She's received death threats, so she now has sheriff's deputies following her around. She eats most meals in her office. She doesn't sleep. She's heard the rumors about her and Jeb, and though her husband laughs them off, they still bother her.

She starts to think of herself as Queen Esther, a biblical figure known for being both brave and beautiful.

Esther was also plucked randomly into a position of power in which she made history, but it's assuredly not the most humble thought Harris has ever had. The saga of Esther took place during the 400's B.C. After being adopted by her cousin Mordechai, the beautiful Esther was chosen for the harem of King Xerxes, known as Ahashverosh in the Bible. Esther kept her Jewish ethnicity secret until Prime Minister Haman — outraged after Mordechai refused to bow down to him — tried to have all the Jews in the empire killed. It was against the law to appear before the king without being summoned; nonetheless, Esther went before King Xerxes — "If I perish, I perish," she said. She did this not once but twice, "begging him with tears," according to the Book of Esther, "to stop Haman's evil plot against the Jews." Xerxes heeds her request, the Jews survive, and the whole deal is celebrated in the Jewish holiday of Purim, the only Jewish celebration that requires intoxication. Esther is also the Persian name for Hadassah, Lieberman's wife's name.

"I reread a book about Esther last night," Harris e-mails a fan. "She has always been the specific character in the Bible that I have admired." "Esther has long served as one of my favorite role models," Harris writes to another. "Queen Esther," she e-mails a fellow Republican, "has been a wonderful role model." She makes the comparison out loud, in the office. "If I perish, I perish," she says — so much so that she starts to annoy her staff.

Of course, Esther saved Jews from being slaughtered by a Babylonian despot. As opposed to working steadfastly to apply law rigidly so as to benefit her preferred presidential candidate. But whatever.

★   ★   ★

On Monday in Plantation, Broward County, with 544 of 609 precincts done, Gore has a net gain of 117 votes.

The bigger task ahead lies in the thousands of questionable ballots that the canvassing board has to review personally. But suddenly Elections Supervisor Jane Carroll makes a surprise announcement. She's leaving. She's going on a cruise.

Lee isn't surprised. Carroll's seventy years old and not exactly the picture of health. Carroll had told him that her blood pressure was way up, that her doctor told her that if she kept going, she might have a heart attack from the stress. But this poses a real problem. Florida law states that a county commissioner should now fill Carroll's space. However, this is Broward County, the Massachusetts of Florida, and all of the county commissioners are Democrats. So the canvassing board, under these rules, will now be entirely Democratic.

This concerns Lee. We're fighting a battle here, trying to have some legitimacy, he says. Lee calls chief circuit court judge Dale Ross, explains to him the problem. We need a Republican, he says. Ross says that he'll talk to county GOP chair Pozzuoli. Eventually they settle upon circuit court judge Robert Rosenberg.

When Rosenberg reports for duty on Tuesday, Lee is immediately put off. The first two things Lee hears out of Rosenberg's mouth are that they're never gonna finish this in time and that he's not working long days.

This isn't what Lee wants to hear. They have more than 10,000 questionables to look at — 6,000-some undervotes, plus the other questionables that the Republican observers have stacked the deck with to prolong the process. This is going to be work.

Though Lee is technically the junior judge to Rosenberg, he steps up and lays down the law. Just like you replaced Mrs. Carroll, he says, you can be replaced, too. So you're either going to do it or tell me now that you're not, and we'll get someone to take your place.

Rosenberg says he'll get on the program, but he generally keeps his distance from Lee and Gunzburger. He doesn't eat with them. Instead, he dines with Georgette Sosa Douglas, the Fort Lauderdale attorney suing them in federal court. Sosa Douglas doesn't even *talk* to Lee, even though they once were friends, to the point that she spoke at the ceremony that commemorated his formally becoming a judge.

Yeah, Rosenberg's an odd duck, Lee and Gunzburger think. They notice the long, drawn-out way he examines the punch cards. Taking off his Coke-bottle glasses and bringing the ballot so close to his face that his eyes cross. Or holding up a magnifying glass to the ballot. Rubbing his eyes exhaustedly. It's quite theatrical. Lee's willing to give him the benefit of the doubt, assuming that Rosenberg's just trying to be as deliberative as possible. Gunzburger thinks he's trying to prolong the process, just like Scherer and the rest.

Gunzburger and Lee do find one silver lining in Rosenberg's appointment to the board. With Carroll, they'd been joking for some time about an "ugly picture contest." Lee's mother in Duval County would call him to tell him of unflattering photos of him in the local paper; there was one not-too-nice one of Carroll in *USA Today*. But once Rosenberg came on board, with his bulging, cross-eyed stare, which made the front page of the *New York Times*, there was no doubt who was the winner. No need for a recount on that one.

★ ★ ★

Perhaps it's only appropriate that Jeb Bush's first public appearance since this all started is in the prison town of Marianna, where he holds an "Open Office Day" on Tuesday. "It's like being an Iranian hostage," Bush tells one Floridian, Bill Slay, of the last week. "I can't even walk around outside now. It's like the seventh day of being held hostage."

When he finds out that Slay's a beekeeper, Jeb points to the reporters following him around. "These are my bees, and I'm the hive," he says.

Poor Jeb. Throughout the presidential race, W. would joke that "little brother recognizes that Thanksgiving might be a little chilly," when asked how important it was that Florida go for him. Jeb surely feels the pressure. Hence, he's been hiding from the press, pretending to have recused himself from the contest, while his chief staffers and advisers help run things behind the scenes and he lights up the phones and makes sure everything's going on track. Jeb, in fact, was the one who got Barry Richard to speak today, despite Ginsberg's and Baker's insistence on Carvin.

"I've been doing my day job here, trying to keep politics out of it," Bush tells reporters. For instance, he signs two death warrants.

What an odd position to be in! And yet, it was Jeb who was daddy's favorite, Jeb who was supposed to be the politico of the family. Big brother George was still losing daddy's money on his ill-fated oil company, still boozing to excess, still turning mom's hair white while Jeb was married, a successful Miami real-estate developer, then Florida secretary of commerce and well on his way to power in Florida. When big brother George decided — almost on a whim! — to run for Texas governor in '94, the same year Jeb ran, it pissed Jeb off at the time; he thought both of their candidacies would relegate his campaign to half of "a cute *People* magazine story." To make matters worse, big brother George won, and he lost! This despite the fact that Jeb was always the harder worker, the better student, the one who wasn't drinking and driving and smashing into trash cans. And now here he was, scrambling behind the scenes, doing what he could for his brother once again. Seemed like he was always picking up for his family's mess. There was that time in June 1999, when his wife, Columba, hid $19,000 worth of clothing and jewelry she bought on a Paris shopping spree from U.S. Customs officials. And, of course, there's today's goddamn story in the *New York Post,* which reports on his sixteen-year-old son, Jebby, being caught naked with a chick in a Jeep Cherokee parked at the Tallahassee Mall in October.

"My dad will fix it," Jebby was quoted as saying. And indeed, the *Miami Herald* and the *St. Petersburg Times* got copies of the police report, but they never wrote a word about it. The governor is given great deference in Florida. And not just by the media.

★　★　★

Burton's starting to think that maybe Clay Roberts was right, maybe these hand recounts should apply only to machine error.

He sees these little dimples that the Democrats want counted as votes. How can you legitimately call them votes? he wonders. It reminds him of when he sits in criminal court and a guy comes before him charged with his fourth DUI and says, "You know, I know I have a drinking problem, but my wife just left me and I lost my job," blah, blah, blah. It's everybody's fault but his. Burton's attitude is *gimme a break.* This "just a victim of circumstance" thing doesn't play well with him. Sooner or later you gotta say that you're responsible, that you're accountable. If it says, "punch out the chad," you gotta punch out the chad. Is that so complicated?

"Sooner or later isn't somebody going to assume responsibility and read the goddamn instructions?" an exasperated Burton wonders. "Or if they don't know what they're doing, can't they ask for help?"

★　★　★

The Supreme Court of Florida rules Tuesday night, offering a victory — at least for now — for Gore. Remarkably, the court essentially rewrites the election code, extending the deadline for counties to recount votes, or tally unread unrecorded votes that appear to be Gore's last hope. Instead of the November 12 deadline for the recounts, fanatically adhered to by Harris, counties now have until Sunday, November 26, at 5 P.M. — or Monday at 9 A.M. if Harris's office isn't open Sunday.

"Twenty-five years ago, this Court commented that the will of the people, not a hypertechnical reliance upon statutory provisions, should be our guiding principle in election cases," Chief Justice Charles Wells writes in the unanimous opinion. "We consistently have adhered to the principle that the will of the people is the paramount consideration."

The ruling isn't a total win for the Gore team, however, begging off as it does on opportunities to set a statewide standard. "We declined to rule more expansively, for to do so would result in this Court substantially rewriting" election code, the court writes. But the court does offer a strong push in the direction of permissiveness, citing the Illinois Supreme Court's *Pullen* decision,* which ruled:

The voters here did everything which the Election Code requires when they punched the appropriate chad with the stylus. These voters should not be disenfranchised where their intent may be ascertained with reasonable certainty, simply because the chad they punched did not completely dislodge from the ballot. Such a failure may be attributable to the fault of the election authorities, for failing to provide properly perforated paper, or it may be the result of the voter's disability or inadvertence. Whatever the reason, where the intention of the voter can be fairly and satisfactorily ascertained, that intention should be given effect.

And as if that weren't enough, the court goes so far as to offer specific deft slams to claims made by many in *la famille Bush,* ruling against Harris's interpretation that hand recounts can be acceptable only when there is "error in the vote tabulation," which she deemed meant error in the vote tabulation *system.* She said that such a standard "only means a counting error resulting from incorrect election parameters or an error in the vote tabulating software," the court wrote. "We disagree."

Flushed down the Florida toilet, at least for now, goes Baker's — and indeed, the entire Bush camp's — assertion that machine recounts are preferable to hand recounts, since the latter is subject to "mischief" and "subjectivity": "Although error cannot be completely eliminated in any tabulation of the ballots," the court wrote, "our society has not yet gone so

---

*The *Pullen* decision will be a side issue from here on in, with the Republicans using it to attempt to paint Boies as a liar, so it's probably worth going into here.

In the March 1990 Republican primary in Illinois, a conservative state representative, Penny Pullen, lost to pro-choice paralegal Rosemary Mulligan. After a recount, the two were tied, and a coin toss gave it to Mulligan again. Pullen appealed to the state supreme court, which in September told Cook County Circuit Court judge Francis Barth to examine 27 undervotes and assess if there were any votes that "can be reasonably ascertained."

Barth judged that 19 ballots had no clear intent. He accepted 4 with pinholes in the chad, one dimpled chad on a ballot with a pattern of misaligned punches, and three hanging chad. Of these 8 accepted questionables, 7 were for Pullen and 1 was for Mulligan. Thus, Pullen was declared the winner, 7,392 votes to 7,386.

Two years later, Mulligan ran against Pullen again. This time she beat her.

far as to place blind faith in machines. In almost all endeavors, including elections, humans routinely correct the errors of machines. For this very reason Florida law provides a human check."

Most important, however, is the court's adherence to the first line in the state constitution: "All political power is inherent in the people." Harris could ignore this only under two circumstances, the court rules: if rejecting the recount would have prevented a candidate, party, or voter from contesting an election certification, or if somehow it prevented "Florida voters from participating fully in the federal electoral process." "But to allow the Secretary to summarily disenfranchise innocent electors in an effort to punish dilatory" counties who didn't get their returns in on time "misses the constitutional mark," the court concludes.

Gore, of course, still will have to fend off other litigation from Bush and his lawyers challenging this ruling, as well as challenges to the liberal chad rules he wants and God knows what else. Plus, of course, he still has the little matter of earning more votes than Bush has. But in a state with a governor named Bush, a secretary of state who might as well be named Bush, a Republican house and senate, as well as a daunting number of Democratic voters who can't figure out how to competently vote, Gore finally catches a break in Tallahassee.

★   ★   ★

Judge Terry Lewis knows the Florida Supreme Court pretty well, and he thinks well of them, too. Justice Harding's in his Rotary Club, and Justice Wells used to play b-ball with the other judges and lawyers on occasion; Anstead still plays every now and then. Like any good appellate judge, Lewis jokes, if you give Anstead the ball, he gives it right back to you.

That said, Lewis sure is confused about this ruling, which overturned the decision he made last Thursday.

Harding said it himself during the oral arguments — where are we supposed to come up with a new date, with a new scheme? "Are we just going to reach up for some inspiration and put it down on paper?" the justice had asked. Exactly the point, Lewis thinks. Where did this November 26 date come from?

Maybe he should have made his second ruling a little bit more detailed, he wonders. There *is* a contest provision. If a candidate thinks he's got evidence of legal votes that haven't been counted, that's grounds for a contest.

Why are the Gore lawyers resisting that so much? Lewis asks himself. He doesn't have an answer.

Nor does Dexter Douglass, for that matter, who behind the scenes is also urging Klain and the others to accept the certification deadline and move ahead to the contest period. But the PR hit would be too much, he's told. Douglass says that he doesn't think in terms of a PR hit, and what would it matter if Gore wins? The nation will embrace him no matter if he wins a "protest" or a "contest," no one much cares. But he's overruled. Douglass begins to think that no one on the Gore team is really all that interested in his unsolicited opinions on anything.

★   ★   ★

The counting goes on in the counties, as if nothing happens.

In Palm Beach at 9:42 P.M., county administrator Robert Weisman takes the microphone to tell the room that the Florida Supreme Court announcement is coming, and they will put it up on the big TV screen at the front of the room.

As a perfect symbol of Palm Beach efficiency, the technicians tune to CNN but can't punch up any sound. Nobody knows what the ruling is until after the announcement has been read by court spokesman Craig Waters and the headline comes on the screen: "Supreme Court rules the recounts must be counted."

In the counting room, at least, there is no reaction.

★   ★   ★

By the time the clock strikes midnight, the world hears responses from Gore, Douglass and Boies, and Baker.

Gore's statement, made from Washington, is all about looking presidential and above the fray. "I don't know what these ballots will show," he says. "I don't know whether Governor Bush or I will prevail. But we do know that our democracy is the winner tonight."

Why does he say things like this? Has no one told him that he sounds as sincere as Eddie Haskell when he waxes lofty?

Gore also tosses out, once again, his offer to meet with Bush — knowing that Bush will never agree to do it and that every time he makes the offer and Bush rejects it, the Texas governor looks like a spoiled brat.

Back in Tallahassee, Douglass and Boies appear in the state senate hearing room that the press corps has commandeered.

"The supreme court has done what we asked it to do," Boies says.

Beyond just gloating, however, Boies tries to signal across the state that Broward and Miami-Dade counties were conducting their hand recounts appropriately — using the broadest definition of what stage of chad is

acceptable — while Palm Beach County isn't. Rattling off the page numbers and citing specific footnotes from memory, Boies notes that the court
used the Illinois Supreme Court's liberal interpretation of which chad are
kosher — a citation that he had provided to them in his brief.

"Many of you may have seen the *Chicago Tribune* article earlier today in
which it referred to the fact that under Illinois law, the indented chads, so-
called dimpled chads, are counted under Illinois law. And the *Chicago Tribune* article referred even to the exact Illinois Supreme Court case that the
Supreme Court of Florida referred to and relied on in its decision.*

"Any indication of the intent of the voter — that is what counts," Boies
explains. "We would hope that is the standard that Palm Beach County
would promptly employ. In each of those counties it's terribly important
that those votes are counted."

Asked if the Gore team would support an effort for a statewide hand
recount if Bush wanted one, Boies notes that the Bushies have repeatedly
said that they don't want one, and that the court's plan doesn't seem to
allow enough time for a statewide recount. Eventually he sidesteps the
question altogether as a hypothetical before any of us realize what he has
done.

Lastly comes Baker, at 11:56 P.M.

Despite the fact that the Republicans, and certainly Baker, had assumed
the Florida court would rule against them, Baker and his crew are livid.
They are, after all, the types who are used to getting their way. They've been
getting their way their entire lives.

His blood boiling, venom seeping from the corners of his mouth, Baker
begins by noting that Monday, Justice Major Harding asked, "Is it right to
change the rules in the middle of the game?" "The Florida Supreme Court
and some Democratic county electoral boards have now decided to do just
that," Baker says. "Florida's supreme court rewrote the legislature's statutory system, assumed the responsibilities of the executive branch, and side-
stepped the opinion of the trial court as the finder of fact. Two weeks after
the election, that court has changed the rules and invented a new system
for counting the election results."

---

*Live by the media, die by the media. Boies should know better than to trust everything he
reads in the paper; this *Chicago Tribune* article will prove to be wrong. Dimpled ballots were
not *all* considered votes in the *Pullen* case. The *Chicago Tribune* will prove to be an irritant
to the Gorebies, which we'll get to in a bit.

Then, the cue, the foreshadowing of where we go next.

"One should not now be surprised if the Florida legislature seeks to affirm the original rules," Baker says.

[Clap of thunder, flash of lightning.]

Baker clarifies, when asked, that the Bush campaign isn't going to "seek relief from the Florida legislature," just that he "would not be surprised" — *[Stage direction: Lift arms in air innocently, giving a "Who, me?" look]* — "to see the legislature take some action to get back to the original statutory provisions." He says that neither he nor Bush has been in touch with anyone from the Republican-controlled Florida legislature, though he couldn't vouch for anyone else.

What exactly could the legislature do?

Article II, Section 1 of the U.S. Constitution states that each state may select its presidential electors "in such manner as the Legislature thereof may direct." So it is not unforeseeable that the state legislature would take matters into its own hands and choose the state's 25 electors, especially if the election results remain subject to legal attack up until the deadline for selecting electors in December. What Baker doesn't have to add is that the legislature is controlled by the Republican Party. We're going to get Florida's electoral college votes, Baker's threatening, whether by stopping the recount or calling in favors.

And while he has the world's attention, having floated this unbelievable proposition, Baker slams the very concept of "the infamous dimpled chad." He notes the 1990 Palm Beach County standard. Baker says that Boies was incorrect a few minutes earlier when he said that the Illinois Supreme Court okayed pregnant or dimpled chads, which are still attached to the ballot though an indentation is visible. "The case wasn't talking about dimpled chads at all, it talked about hanging chads," Baker clarifies.

Actually, *Pullen* — which Baker calls by the wrong name from the wrong court — doesn't take a position on any specific chad one way or the other, but it does say that undervotes have to be examined to see if voter intent can be ascertained. But at this point, demanding accuracy from either side is about as silly as demanding, well, demanding someone punch their chad all the way through.

"All of this is unfair and unacceptable," Baker says. "It is not fair to change the election laws of Florida by judicial fiat after the election has been held. It is not fair to change the rules and standards governing the counting or recounting of votes after it appears that one side has concluded that is the only way to get the votes it needs. It is simply not fair, ladies and gentlemen, to change the rules either in the middle of the game, or after the game has been played."

It's a litany of whining that only a Texan could make sound intimidating. When the Connecticut-born Bush tries it tomorrow — "Make no mistake, the court rewrote the laws. It changed the rules, and it did so after the election was over" — he doesn't quite pull it off with same machismo. And how could he? After all, it's daddy's friend who's running the show down there, bailing him out, just as it's been for W. all his life.

12

"ARREST HIM! ARREST HIM!"

Tomorrow's Thanksgiving, and though some, like DNC spokeswoman Jenny Backus, will feast on wings from the Tallahassee Hooters, others — like David Boies — are on their way home for a real holiday dinner.

But before he leaves, Boies is asked if his charter plane can make one stop on its way back to Westchester County, New York: Fort Lauderdale. The Gorebies want him to convince the Broward County canvassing board to ignore Republican entreaties that their chad standards are too loose. Since Boies's daughter Caryl lives in Hollywood, Florida, and he wants her to come to his Thanksgiving feast in Armonk — joining his wife, their two kids, and two other kids from a previous marriage — he's happy to make the fly-by.

In his many daily phone conversations with Gore, Klain is always a bit amused, a bit touched, by his boss's closing line. "We're gonna win!" Gore always signs off. "That's right, sir," Klain dutifully responds. "No, I mean it," Gore says. "We're gonna win!"

But it isn't until this morning, Wednesday morning, that Klain thinks that his boss might actually be right. The counting is going on in all three counties, the Florida Supreme Court has told Harris that she has to accept the tallies, Boies is off to fend off the GOP attackers in Broward. . . . Maybe they actually *can* win, he thinks.

Not that all the Gorebies are content. In Palm Beach, for instance, the Boston Boys think Burton is disqualifying clear and legitimate votes. The Palm Beach canvassing board is still using the "two corner" rule, despite the fact that LaBarga told them not to use any specific rules. There are other controversial calls. Burton vetoes any pinhole-marked chad, though the

Florida Supreme Court Tuesday referred to the *Pullen* case in its ruling, and in *Pullen*, pinholes were considered votes. A ballot is ruled an overvote despite the fact that the voter has apparently written "mistake" over one hole having also punched the Gore hole. Burton's argument was that, according to LePore, this was a precinct where the voter could have obtained a new ballot. "Also," Burton explained, "there is no evidence who put the writing on the ballot." Burton also leads the charge against absentee ballots where voters attempted to correct any mistakenly punched holes with tape, then punched for the right candidate.

While LePore agrees with this, the Gorebies strenuously object. After all, as a Dem points out, "when the ballot is placed in the envelope, the voter has to sign. The presumption that he knows that —"

"It could have also been the guy sleeping, and his wife said, 'I don't want to vote for that guy,' and who knows?" Burton interrupts. "We don't know. That's why I'm finding an overvote, and I have been consistent."

It isn't the strongest argument, but to Burton it makes sense at a moment when so much else doesn't. Like his colleagues, Burton is exhausted and starting to numb. At the beginning, this was hectic but a tad exciting; after all, this was democracy at stake. They were in the service of their nation's highest ideals! But it is starting to feel less like a heroic public service and more like taking both a bullet for Uncle Sam and unfair and undeserved heat for trying to make sense of a bunch of ill-conceived, poorly written, and completely confounded election laws courtesy of those Einsteins in Tallahassee. The Boston Boys think that Burton's purposely working against them. They look at Burton and see a judge trying to curry favor with Jeb. They view his outbursts against Wallace and Harris as Oscar-worthy performances. Thus, the Florida Democratic Party files an emergency motion in LaBarga's Palm Beach courtroom, seeking a clarification of his November 15 order. They drag Burton's ass before LaBarga to make him testify as to what he's doing.

"The ballots we have looked at are of such wide variety of dents and dings and marks," Burton testifies. "I mean, to be honest with you, some of us leave scratching our heads: 'How did this even happen?' We have attempted to define what the clear intent of the voter is."

If the dimple is only for president, they don't count it. "If on cards where a couple or two or three and four, and we don't have any set numbers, are showing indentations or not quite full punches, then we've taken the position that that does show the intent of the voter, in that this person, obviously, had difficulty punching out." Burton admits that when it came to automatic inclusion, they did change from one-corner to two-corner, which can be seen as more restrictive. But they only did that because Broward County had that standard at the time, and they were following Broward's lead. "And I guess just recently they've gone back, so now they're going to look at dimples. So to be consistent in this election has been a very difficult task, to say the least."

Burton doesn't say what's really on his mind about Broward's change in standards: he thinks it looks bad, it looks like the Democratic fix is in.

"Some [ballots] are questionable," Burton concludes. "Some are close. Some we need to look at. Some we need to see what's going on. I mean, in all candor, determining intent from a ballot card is impossible. Would I like for Judge LaBarga to tell us, 'Canvassing board, if there is an indentation, you count it. Or if there's only one, you don't count it'? Absolutely. And we would follow whatever Your Honor says."

In his subsequent ruling, LaBarga tells Burton and his colleagues that their continued per se exclusion of votes is wrong. But he doesn't give them any specific, clearly delineated standards. He references the *Pullen* decision, quoting the Illinois Supreme Court ruling that voters who had problems with their ballots and styluses "should not be disenfranchised where their intent may be ascertained with reasonable certainty," since "such failure may be attributable to the fault of the election authorities, for failing to provide properly perforated paper, or it may be the result of the voter's disability or inadvertence." LaBarga even takes the extra step of referencing the Massachusetts Supreme Court ruling *Delahunt v. Johnston,* noting that the "court found unpersuasive that voters may have started to express a preference in a candidate, made an impression on a punch card, but pulled the stylus back because" they had second thoughts. Of course, Delahunt and Johnston were the only ones on that ballot, so undervotes for that race were far less likely.

But even with all of this, LaBarga doesn't give the board any specific, clearly delineated standards.

Not helpful.

★   ★   ★

In Broward, GOP attorney William Scherer has presented to the Broward County canvassing board a sworn statement from a local voter, William Rohloff, who claims that he almost voted for Gore and withdrew the stylus at the last minute. "If you want to count that as a vote for Gore, you disenfranchise him," Scherer says. "As you go down this journey as to how you divine voters' intent, remember William Rohloff."

But Boies calls such claims nonsense. "If you hear hooves in the background, your first assumption is not that you're being pursued by zebras," he says. Boies advises Lee, Gunzburger, and Rosenberg to ignore Rohloff. The real issue is the type of ballot.

"Throughout Florida the counties that use punch-card ballots have two or three or four or five times as many undervotes as the counties that use optical-scanning ballots," Boies says. This isn't because punch-card-county voters are less interested in the presidential race, Boies says. It's because punch-card machines are "inadequate."

"I understand why Governor Bush's advocates want to distract from the natural and logical and obvious implication of that indentation," he says, but in Texas, Illinois, California, and Massachusetts, a dimple can be considered a vote.

★ ★ ★

The Miami-Dade canvassing board meets at 8 A.M. Its members are concerned.

Since they were the last ones to begin the hand recount, news of last night's Florida Supreme Court ruling wasn't so great, giving them a deadline of Sunday at 5 P.M. — or Monday at 9 A.M. — that they never planned on meeting. And even if they had planned on it, Leahy thinks doing so would be flat-out impossible. They would have to work ninety-six hours straight, on a holiday weekend, and they've already had a rough go of it in terms of finding county volunteers. They still don't have full staffing scheduled for Sunday.

Then there's option B: counting just the 10,750 undervotes.

"If we, the canvassing board, did approximately three hundred ballots an hour — which is pushing it, but possibly doable — it would take us about thirty-six hours to do that," says Leahy. He asks the county attorney whether that's "a viable alternative."

Option C is to just stop the count right now. "But given what the board has already decided, I'm not sure that that's a practical alternative at all. We have already determined there are some votes in the undercounted ballots."

Leahy suggests that they all move up one floor, to the tabulation room on the nineteenth floor, where thirteen IBM punch-card counting machines stand like soldiers. Not all of the undervotes were separated out on Sunday — there are still about 119 precincts remaining that need to be sorted. If they go up to the nineteenth floor, they can separate the undervotes from the rest of the ballots and actually assess some of the undervotes while doing so. The room is small, so the canvassing board, Leahy's staff, and two observers from each party will be the only ones allowed in. There is a window, so the media can watch from there. A court reporter can be in there, too. A couple pool reporters, perhaps. "I think it's doable," Leahy says.

GOP attorney Bobby Birchfield — fresh from Mississippi, where he has just lost a case defending a campaign-finance loophole on behalf of big business* — says that the Bushies are willing to work with the canvassing board on crashing on the full hand recount, and they are certainly not opposed to stopping the whole thing. But option B is simply not in the statute, he says, and you guys ruled against doing it way back when the Democrats first asked you to. Additionally, Birchfield says, "the first two hundred precincts or so, our statistics indicate, voted very heavily for Mr. Gore. There are going to be other precincts in the county that voted very heavily for Governor Bush." So you can't include votes from those first precincts that were hand-counted, since that's simply unfair.

De Grandy seconds that. Black precincts have been counted one way, he says, and now you're discussing doing Hispanic precincts a different way. This will be a blatant violation of the Voting Rights Act.

And on this issue, De Grandy has more than a little credibility. During the reapportionment battles of the early 1990s — which Carvin, Ginsberg, and Olson worked on a great deal for the RNC — plans to carve up Florida's 23 U.S. House districts, and the state legislature's 40 senate and 120 house seats, were hotly contested.

After the legislature's 1992 redistricting plan was laid out, many Cuban-Americans resented what they perceived as an inequality. Then–state representative De Grandy sued the legislature on two fronts.

On the congressional front, De Grandy wanted an additional Cuban-American congressional seat and three African-American congressional seats. A panel made up of three appellate court judges found in De Grandy's favor, and as a result, the first African-Americans since Reconstruction were elected to the house — Brown, Meek, and Hastings — and Lincoln Diaz-Balart joined Ileana Ros-Lehtinen in the Cuban-American congressional caucus.

More fractious, however, was De Grandy's suit against the legislature for another Hispanic state senate seat — because this threatened to come at

---

* The U.S. Chamber of Commerce had been running ads against state supreme court candidates and not disclosing who was funding the ads, using the preposterous campaign-finance loophole that rules that such ads aren't expressly political ads if they don't use specific advocacy words, like "vote for" and "vote against." A judge ordered the ads pulled.

the expense of an African-American state senate seat. Hispanic-Americans' apportioned state house and senate seats in Miami-Dade County were of roughly equal proportion to their county voting-age population (about 45 percent of the seats for 46.6 percent of the population). African-American advocates pointed out that Hispanic seats were out of whack with the proportion of their population that had achieved citizenship (33 percent).

Cuban-American advocates countered that black state house and state senate seats were way out of line with *their* population — 29.9 percent of the county's state senate seats, 20 percent of the state house seats, and only 15.6 percent of the voting-age population.

Arguing that the statewide population of Hispanics — 12 percent — exceeded the statewide percentage of statewide legislative seats — 7 percent — De Grandy sued the legislature in federal court to get a fourth Hispanic state senate seat and two more Hispanic state house seats.

Some thought that Cuban-American claims of disenfranchisement were disingenuous. "The Cubans have ridden on the backs of Mexicans and Puerto Ricans to claim privileges which, as the only middle-class émigrés of any size that we have had in this country, they don't need," one Democratic state senator said. And after a three-judge panel ruled in favor of De Grandy on the state legislature suit, the U.S. Supreme Court in 1994 took *De Grandy v. Bolley Johnson, Speaker of the Florida House of Representatives, et al.* and ruled against him, arguing that the representation in Dade County was fair enough. Steve Zack represented the state senate in the case.

★ ★ ★

"You have counted one hundred thirty-some precincts, which are not representative," De Grandy says to the canvassing board. "And I'm not concerned with whether they are representative of the Republican Party or the Democratic Party, they are not representative of my community, which is a protected class under the Voting Rights Act."

You can't count the votes gleaned from the hand count of the 130 non-Hispanic precincts and not do so for the other precincts, he says, or "you will be violating the rights of the Hispanic community in Dade County."

But De Grandy misunderstands the plan, old-school Miami boy Murray Greenberg says. "Apparently due to lack of sleep I am not making myself understood," he says. They're not going to count whatever votes have been picked up so far in the hand recounts, they're going to start from scratch.

De Grandy now does the ol' switcheroo. You're *not* going to count those votes from those non-Hispanic precincts? Horrors! How dare you!

It's a catch-22, De Grandy knows — but it's one of their own doing. They want to count every vote, but now they're going to take back all the ones they took from the table count and discount them again? "At that point you have created irreparable error, because now you have discerned in one hundred thirty-some [precincts] that there were some votes that you could discern the intent of the voters," De Grandy says. You can't ignore them. Plus, De Grandy says, King himself said a few days ago that the board can't count only the undervotes. He can't just change his mind!

Jack Young steps in, deferring to whatever Leahy and King want to do. He'd rather have all the ballots counted; but better this than nothing.

Lawyer Birchfield says that dimples counted as votes in undervotes are not seen as such when appearing next to a punched chad — which one might then assess as an overvote, were one to be consistent — so he feels the full countywide vote is necessary.

Just like one of the many hurricanes that so frequently pound the Florida coast, they are starting to move in circles. Greenberg steps in to try to get King to hurry it all up. "I admonish you all for the last time, you heard from both parties, you heard from the supervisor, vote!"

The canvassing board votes, 3 to 0, to count the undervotes.

At 8:50 A.M., they proceed up to the nineteenth floor to start counting.

★   ★   ★

To get to the tabulation room on the nineteenth floor, you exit the elevator, enter a secured door to the elections offices, walk maybe sixty feet, and enter a small room that has a large glass window.

In this secured space between the elevators and the tabulation room stands Mayco Villafana, spokesman for Miami-Dade County, who is confused.

Why is the media so angry? he wonders.

In the past, reporters seemed more than content standing behind the glass window. And Villafana was providing, after all, audio of what was going on inside, as well as a roving video camera, the signal from which any channel could take, live, as its own if it so wished. But reporters approach Villafana and tell him that it's unacceptable that they don't have complete access to the tabulation room itself. Nicholas Kulish of the *Wall Street Journal* hand-writes a petition demanding "media representation in the counting room" . . . "in the interests of democracy." Outside the window is not good enough, Kulish writes. "To observe without hearing is not to be present essentially, so any decision to bar the media would constitute a barring of the public, who we represent. . . . We hope this can be settled without legal action." Lawyers everywhere.*

★   ★   ★

As the week has gone on, Monday, Tuesday, the protests outside the Miami-Dade county building — the Stephen P. Clark Government Center — are increasingly hostile.

After Monday's counting had concluded, Gore had gained 46 votes — though, of course, that was because the first hundred or so precincts were Democratic precincts. That didn't stop Republican officials from revving up their minions with accusations that the 46 votes were proof of fraud.

"This thing is rigged!" Republican congressman David Hobson of Ohio said. "It is a joke on our democracy." "Unfortunately Miami-Dade has become ground zero for producing a manufactured vote," adds Congressman Sweeney.

There's an RV outside the county government building, into and out of which protester organizers hustle, handing out leaflets, armed with free T-shirts — emblazened with vitriolic anti-Gore mottoes — to give to the crowds.

On Tuesday, Villafana and the building's chief of security, Ed Hollander, asked the protesters to move their RV; it was in a space for media, and reporters were complaining. But Villafana and Hollander found the Republicans combative and confrontational. An operative came up in Villafana's face, bumped him, asked him menacingly, "Is there any problem here?!"

Weird, Hollander thought. I'm here with cops and everything, and here is this guy trying to pick a fight.

They negotiated that the RV would move by the end of the day.

The protesters claim to be just outraged Americans. But Villafana and Hollander discover that the RV has been rented by Sean T. Miles, vice president of operations for the Bush-Cheney advance team.

And while the outside world might not know it, most of the demonstration is organized by Brad Blakeman, who tells reporters that he's just "a Long Island lawyer." He is from Long Island, and he is a lawyer, but he's also

---

* The petition is signed, in order, by Rachel A. La Corte, Associated Press; Ellis Berger of the *Sun-Sentinel,* Paul Lomartire and Lou Salome of the *Palm Beach Post,* Dana Canedy of the *New York Times,* Daniel McGrory of the *Times* of London, Bill Redeker of ABC News, Don Finefrock of the *Miami Herald,* Sue Anne Pressley of the *Washington Post,* Henry Goldman of Bloomberg News, Dahleen Glanton of the *Chicago Tribune,* and Jane Sutton of Reuters.

the Bush-Cheney campaign's director of advance travel logistics. Inside the RV is Republican strategist Roger Stone, last seen publicly flacking for Donald Trump's flirtation with presidential politics. And Bush communications honcho Ed Gillespie is seen on the ground Monday and Tuesday directing the crowds, steering the orchestrated ugliness. One of Bush's media advisers, swingin' Stuart Stevens, is buzzing around somewhere, as well.

Blakeman tells reporters that they are all just outraged Republicans who have come from all over the country. The truth is that while some are rank-and-file Florida Republicans, a significant number of the protesters — and not just its leaders — are Bush campaign staffers or Republican staffers from the House and Senate.

A week earlier, the following e-mail had been distributed, one of many:

Dear Friends,

I am enclosing below a request by the Bush campaign for supporters to go to Florida to assist them in monitoring the efforts there to invent votes for the inventor of the Internet. The message states that the Bush campaign will pay your expenses.

While the Florida Supreme Court ought to put an end to this chicanery, if they do not, more Republicans will be needed to keep a watchful eye on the highly selective and subjective hunt for phantom Al Gore votes that is set to begin in Miami-Dade County, where there are over a million ballots. I hope you can travel to Florida to assist the Bush campaign in this effort to preserve the integrity of this election.

Sincerely,

National Council for a Republican Congress

There were others.

Subj: Bush campaign will pay your expenses to go to Florida for recount
Date: 11/18/2000 1:40:36 PM Central Standard Time
From: Legliaison
BCC: HOUSTONRVW
FROM: Dallas County Republican Party
FROM: the Bush campaign

Can anyone help in Florida the next few days? We can't overstate the importance of this effort — so if you can go, please contact georgewbush.com. Right now, we have people down in Florida working on the recount. They have been there for eleven days under difficult circumstances, and we now need to send reinforcements. Please forward this message. The campaign will pay airfare and hotel expenses for people willing to go. Because of cost, we are doubling people up in rooms so the only caveat is that if someone wants their own room, they will need to pay for that themselves. Also, if they need to be somewhere for Thanksgiving, we will make sure that they can honor those commitments.

Thanks for all of your help. As you can imagine, this matter is URGENT so the sooner we can get the names of interested people the better. Although we need any interested person, we have a particular need for attorneys. Please contact georgewbush.com if you have any questions.

If you pay for it, they will come. And here they are.

Like Marjorie Strayer, who tells reporters she's just a Virginian on vacation in Miami. It turns out she's an aide to Rep. Heather Wilson, Republican of New Mexico.

They're obnoxious, they're hateful, they inject venom and volatility into an already edgy situation. Thank you, Governor Bush, the uniter not the divider.

When Congressman Deutsch tries to talk to a CNN interviewer, the crowd's boos prevent him from doing so. "This is the new Republican Party, sir!" Blakeman bellows on a bullhorn. "We're not going to take it anymore!" Deutsch can be so obnoxious and toxic it's almost just. But leave it to the Bushies to make you feel sorry for a guy like Deutsch. Almost.

On Wednesday, the protests take on a more legitimate feel when they are joined by maybe a hundred local Cuban-Americans, some of whom heard interviews on the local Spanish radio station, Radio Mambi, with Lincoln Diaz-Balart and Ileana Ros-Lehtinen, who slammed the canvassing board. The reporter who calls in the interviews for Radio Mambi, Evilio Cepero, plays another role at the protests, wandering around with a megaphone yelling, "Denounce the recount!" and "Stop the injustice!"

The crowd swells as recorded phone messages in Spanish, sent out by who knows who, are made, alerting local Cubanos that they're needed at the government center.

On his way back from a TV interview, Sweeney gets a phone call from two GOP observers at the Miami-Dade count — Martin Torrey, one of his aides, and Brendan Quinn, executive director of the New York GOP. They tell Sweeney that the canvassing board is moving behind closed doors! That they're just going to do a partial count!

"Shut it down!" Sweeney orders.

Quinn tells two dozen or so of the Republican operatives to storm the nineteenth floor. Emotional and angry, they immediately make their way outside the larger room in which the tabulating room is contained.

The mass of "angry voters" on the nineteenth floor swells to maybe eighty people. It includes:

- Matt Schlapp, a Bush staffer in from Austin;
- Thomas Pyle, a policy analyst for House Majority Whip Tom DeLay, Republican of Texas;
- Michael Murphy, a DeLay fund-raiser;
- Roger Morse, an aide to Rep. Van Hilleary, Republican of Tennessee;
- Duane Gibson, an aide to Chairman Don Young, Republican of Alaska;
- Doug Heye, a spokesman for Rep. Richard Pombo, Republican of California;
- Jim Wilkinson, a spokesman for the National Republican Congressional Committee;
- Rory Cooper, political staffer at the NRCC;
- Garry Malphrus, majority chief counsel and staff director for the House Judiciary Subcommittee on criminal justice;
- Chuck Royal, legislative assistant for Rep. Jim DeMint, Republican of South Carolina;
- Kevin Smith, a former GOP House staffer;
- Steven Brophy, a former aide to Sen. Fred Thompson, Republican of Tennessee; and
- Layna McConkey, a former legislative assistant to ex-Rep. Jim Ross Lightfoot, Republican of Iowa, now an employee for a GOP fund-raiser.

"Let us in!" they yell. "Let us in! Let us in!"

They bang on the doors.

They bang on the walls.

They chant.

"LET US IN! LET US IN! LET US IN!"

It feeds on itself.

Individually, these are not intimidating guys, not tough fellas you'd be afraid of in a bar. They're wimps and fatties, largely; poorly dressed Washington, D.C., geeks. Gibson, in particular, a tall bespectacled dork, is freakishly agitated, frenzied, odd. In a bar, Gibson would get the shit kicked out of him by an anorexic junior high school girl. But here he — like his socially wanting peers — clearly feels emboldened. Physically weak, here they feel mighty. And however wanting their upper-body strength may be in real life, right now they're running on adrenaline and anger.

"LET US IN! LET US IN! LET US IN!"

★   ★   ★

Inside the tabulating room, Leahy and the others can hear the protests, loud and clear.

GOP observer Neal Conolly says that the Bushies feel "that the accommodations on the eighteenth floor, where there was more room for people to observe, were more conducive and in compliance with the open-meeting law. And I would request that the board consider that.

"I don't know who the people are that are outside shouting and making noise," Conolly says. "But I think that they probably result from the fact that there's some concern of the people on the outside that what we're doing in here is limiting access to the openness of the proceeding, and I think that that perception is important."

"It is really a logistical problem at this point," Leahy explains.

Democratic observer Steve Kaufman asks how it will be possible to get other observers in and out of the room with the crowd so frenzied.

"I can't help it," Leahy says. "Hopefully the mood out front will settle down."

★   ★   ★

Congressman Diaz-Balart holds a press conference with De Grandy. They turn up the burner from simmer to boil.

"What happened was that the way they were going about it, where they were counting all votes with significant numbers of observers in a large room, opened to you, the press, and open to observers at each table, that wasn't going the way that the Gore campaign had hoped," Diaz-Balart says. "And so, now, they've decided to leave that room, to leave the sunshine of a place where you, the press, and observers can be at every table, and to go back into a room, separated from the press, where they will count only the votes where the voters of this county decided that they would not vote for president. That, I think, is an outrage, and I think that all Americans should know what is going on at this very moment in Miami-Dade County.

"If it were not so tragic, if we would not be witnessing, in effect, the stealing of a presidential election, it would be laughable," the congressman adds.

De Grandy takes the mike to pour fuel on the fire.

"We have an even greater concern, as Hispanics in this community, in terms of our voting rights being violated at this point by illegal procedures that are being implemented by this canvassing board," the lawyer says. "There were votes that were counted in the sample recount that occurred last week. Those votes were not in precincts that were Hispanic communities."

He's right that it's a mess; the canvassing board is starting the count from scratch and ignoring its last few days' worth of work. Unlike Martinez, De Grandy is only too happy to prod Miami's racial sores.

★ ★ ★

Villafana heads out to where the two dozen or so Republicans are aggressively chanting and banging on walls. He's trying to help get the media set up — a bunch of reporters are in the crowd, too — but the protesters make his job impossible. Every time Villafana opens the door to help the media set up inside, the thug-wannabes rush the doors in a very intimidating manner, he thinks. Observers can't get in, either. When the sheriff's deputies open the doors, the GOP protesters grab the door, don't allow them to close it again, and block the observers from coming in.

Villafana steps in to try to close the door.

"Don't hit me! Don't hit me!" one of the observers cries, all the while furiously kicking Villafana, out of camera view, since the lenses are focused on their faces, not the floor. Other observers push Villafana, shove him — below the waist. "Don't hit me! Don't hit me!" the protester keeps shouting. But the only person getting banged up in this case is Villafana.

Having been through Elián protests that got way ugly, Villafana and chief of security Hollander feel that this one has potential to turn into a more violent confrontation at any time. "We're going to have to keep the doors closed, and call for backup," one of the sheriff's deputies says.

Villafana and Hollander instruct the police officers to guard the doors and to allow the protesters to take control of the lobby area. The cops have other duties — guarding the ballots, maintaining the sanctity of the elections process. They don't have the time or the inclination to deal with these Republican rabble-rousers.

So the doors stay closed. And because of this decision, members of the media, and many observers, don't get to enter the area. And the system shuts down. And the hand recount can't continue

★   ★   ★

The members of the canvassing board discuss returning to the eighteenth floor to stop the insanity. The protest is loud but not nearly as ugly as it is up close, separated as they are by walls and distance and space. But they're completely aware of what's going on, completely aware that the process can't continue with things as they are — they just can't get the process flowing with the protesters being so hostile and aggressive.

"We could run this anytime," Leahy says of sorting out the remaining undervotes. "We don't have to do it today. We want to get this process started."

They agree to do so, to get to work on counting the undervotes that have already been sorted out.

Leahy is more concerned about the angry reporters than the obnoxious Republicans. He doesn't want the process, the deliberations, the counting to be perceived by the news media as not being open or public. Throughout, everything they've done has been nothing but out in the open. "It would really bother me if it were to be reported that we're in a closed-door, smoke-filled room for these deliberations," he thinks to himself.

"Let the news media know we are going to move downstairs because of the concerns about the board, that the people are not able to view the process," Leahy says to Villafana.

"You are going to give us time to work some issues out?" Villafana asks. "There is a full protest going on out in the lobby, and we cannot bring people in or out. We have people attempting to get into a fight with officers or with members of the media."

Villafana isn't sure if it's the Democrats or the Republicans outside. But whoever it is, they want a confrontation. He asks Young and Conolly if they can tell the protesters to go back downstairs.

"Agreed," Young says. "On behalf of the Democrats, agreed."

"Until the demonstration stops, nobody can do anything," Leahy says.

Bushie Joel Kaplan says, "I suspect that if the announcement was made —"

"That announcement needs to be made by someone from the party," Villafana insists. "I don't think at this point in time they are willing to listen to anyone that represents either the government or the media."

"Would the board be able to issue a couple of sentences?" Bushie Conolly asks, stalling.

"You can express that, and if you like, I will be there as well," Villafana says, "but as long — they will listen, I think, to someone from the party."

"I don't know if they would listen to us or the other side," Conolly says, "but if the board decides affirmatively, we will reconvene at X time, and we can tell them that — the board — they will respond."

"This is being driven by both parties, and I have been out there already, and it's gotten somewhat pretty dicey," Villafana says.

"We were both crushed up against the door," Conolly says.

Young pipes in, "I will say for the record that I don't believe that there's anyone that is associated with my client who is involved with this matter. And if there is, it is because they have violated an express order from the highest authority of my client. And if there is anyone representing the Democratic party involved in these activities, it is highly unauthorized, and we will deal with it, but I don't believe it is both parties."

"I would simply request that the board affirmatively state that it intends to come downstairs as soon as possible and tell us what time," Conolly says, knowingly.

The board adjourns.

But they can't go downstairs. The security personnel have decided that they want to make sure that everything's secure on the eighteenth floor. They tell the canvassing board that they'll let them know when they're ready for them to meet down there.

★   ★   ★

It's county Democratic chair Joe Geller's misfortune that in the thick of the insanity, he decides to take the elevator to the nineteenth floor to obtain a demonstration ballot to show someone how the problem of the 5's and 7's could happen.

From behind the glass window, a clerk hands Geller the demonstration ballot. It says "SAMPLE" on it.

House staffer Duane Gibson spots Geller tucking the sample ballot into his pocket.

"This guy's got a ballot!" Gibson yells. "This guy's got a ballot!"

The masses swarm around him, yelling, getting in his face, pushing him, grabbing him.

"ARREST HIM!" they cry. "ARREST HIM!"

With the help of a diminutive DNC aide, Luis Rosero, and the political director of the Miami Gore campaign, Joe Fraga, Geller manages to wrench himself into the elevator.

Rosero, who stays back to talk to the press, gets kicked, punched.

A woman pushes him into a much larger guy, seemingly trying to instigate a fight.

In the lobby of the building, a group of fifty or so Republicans are crushed around Geller, surrounding him — though thankfully a handful of cops are there to keep them off him, protecting him.

The cops escort Geller back to the nineteenth floor, so the elections officials can see what's going on, investigate the charges. Of course it turns out that all Geller had was a sample ballot. The crowd is pulling at the cops, pulling at Geller.

It's insanity! Some even get in the face of seventy-three-year-old Rep. Carrie Meek.

Democratic operatives decide to pull out of the area altogether.

★ ★ ★

Young and Kaufman return to the eighteenth floor; they're wondering what's taking the canvassing board so long to come back downstairs. In the meantime the Gorebies conduct a quick retraining on undervotes, as led by Chuck Campion and others. They get the computer system up and running. And Young tells them to prepare for a bad day and a half. We know that the next couple hundred precincts are Republican, Young says. So be forewarned; we're going to lose votes for a while, maybe for the next day and a half. We'll come back in the following few hundred, and end up netting maybe 150 votes. But we're gonna go through the hard part of this, and the politicos are gonna flip out.

Where is the canvassing board? Young wonders. They've been missing for a while. Young's concerned. You got these protesters out near the elevators raising hell, you got the clock ticking and a Sunday deadline, you got Leahy saying that they can't count all the votes, who knows what's going on here?

At 1:30 P.M., the Miami-Dade canvassing board finally reconvenes on the eighteenth floor, in the larger room. "The reason and purpose for our meeting here at this hour after we previously had decided that we felt we could reasonably meet the deadline of the Supreme Court of Florida for an expedited yet accurate count has been somewhat changed," King says, "and that's why we wanted to hear from counsel."

Murray Greenberg is upstairs in his office, passed out on the floor from exhaustion. His boss, county attorney Robert Ginsburg, steps up to address the question Leahy puts to him: "whether or not this canvassing board could request or submit a petition" to the state supreme court to ask for a deadline extension.

"I will advise you," Ginsburg says, "the supreme court opinion in its conclusion specifically negates any kind of petition for rehearing." The Sunday, November 26, deadline is "final," Ginsburg says.

"Based on that advice, we have no option but to not press forward with a full manual recount, and that was our decision this morning," Leahy says. But now, even with the task to count just the 10,750 undervotes, "I can't sit here and tell you that if we begin the process, it will be concluded," Leahy says.

King now seems to have second thoughts about just doing the undervotes, that the hand recount should be of the entire county's ballots. That combined with the fact that they may not meet the deadline makes King think that "that does not meet the test that the citizens and the residents of our county would expect of me or the rest of this board." After they moved to the tabulation room, King says, "it became evidently clear that we were in a different situation . . . than we were this morning when we made that decision."

The protesters have accomplished what they came to do. "A radically different situation," King says.

★   ★   ★

In Tallahassee, Klain has left one cubicle in Berger's office to go to another cubicle where lunch is being served. He walks by a TV and sees a meeting of the Miami-Dade canvassing board. "This must be taped," Klain thinks. After all, Kendall Coffey has been great about reporting in religiously about any kind of proceeding there. But it says "LIVE" on the screen.

"Kendall would have called me," Klain thinks.

He listens in. He starts to panic when he hears what they're saying. He grabs the phone.

"Kendall! Why aren't you at the proceeding?!" he asks.

"What proceeding?" Coffey asks. For the first time, the board never notified him.

★   ★   ★

When Judge McDermott in Volusia County sees this nonsense on TV, he shakes his head. These younger judges are too soft. Too nice. You have to be tough. That's the reason they're all having these problems. One of the reasons they succeeded in getting the count up and running and done on time in Volusia is because he wasn't afraid of hurting anyone's feelings. Not that he enjoyed being a hardass, but if you have a job to do, and you have the authority to put an end to all the nonsense, then that's what you do.

There were obnoxious protesters in Volusia, too. Both Bush people and Gore people. When McDermott heard them yelling outside, he told the deputy: "Move 'em across the street. I want them off this property now."

There's a time and a place for everything, and a canvassing-board meeting is not Woodstock, not the Million Man March. If McDermott were in charge at Miami-Dade, he thinks, he would not only have ordered the GOP protesters out of the hallway, he would have ordered them out of the building. He's surprised that Judge King didn't. Even the editorial board of the *Orlando Sentinel,* which endorsed Bush in the election, praised McDermott in an editorial entitled "Thank You, Judge," which couldn't have been nicer if McDermott had written it himself.

You can't be afraid to be a sonofabitch. It's the only way to get anything done amid all this nonsense.

★ ★ ★

De Grandy and Young are asked to speak.

Both of them are under the impression that the canvassing board has already made up its mind to end it all. De Grandy thinks that his voting rights argument from the morning has finally sunk in. All three members of the canvassing board will say that De Grandy's voting rights argument played no role whatsoever in their decision — since they were starting all over again, they never thought it was relevant. But that won't stop De Grandy from telling reporters that it was his argument that saved the day.

Young, for his part, has no idea what the hell's going on — and is suspicious about where the board was for the last hour, and just what the hell they were doing.

De Grandy refers to a count of just the undervotes as illegal, as King himself seemed to think just a few days ago. "Nowhere in the forty-some-page order of the supreme court does it direct any canvassing board to violate the law in order to complete a recount," he says. He begins to go step-by-step through the mercurial history of the canvassing board's rulings on a county-wide hand recount, on whether counting the undervotes is enough.

Judge King, De Grandy points out, "is quoted on page ninety-six and ninety-seven of the transcript stating clearly that in your opinion, sir —"

"I'm well aware of what I said, Mr. De Grandy," King breaks in. "I don't mean to interrupt, but we know clearly that the vote was taken, and that we ordered a hand recount of all of the ballots in Dade. And in —"

"Sir," De Grandy says, "either I can argue my client's position or I can't."

"We're not here for that," King says. "We're here to ask your input with respect —"

"I'm not arguing it to *you,* but to the other two members, sir," counters De Grandy.

In De Grandy's mind, he's shoving King's words back in his face — and also serving them up for Lehr and Leahy to contemplate. King's been totally testy during the process, accusing his buddy Martinez — one of the sweetest, gentlest guys on the planet, De Grandy thinks — of *looking at him* the wrong way; accusing De Grandy himself of grandstanding. That's enough, De Grandy thinks.

"No, I'm not trying to cut you off. What I'm saying is —"

The Republicans in the crowd boo.

"— I concur with you wholeheartedly, sir, that the board did what it did at those times," King finishes. "But now we're faced with a new challenge, and we're asking for your input on that."

De Grandy continues his statement as he wants. "Today there was a motion made to change the process to something which this board has determined, and which we strongly believed and had argued consistently in every hearing, to be illegal. You cannot count less than all votes. You either count them or you don't."

Young gets up to speak, though he's clearly fighting the tide. "There are ten thousand seven hundred fifty citizens out there whose vote has not been seen by man, woman, or machine," he says. "That is simply an error. It's a systematic error. It's nothing more than the way machines and the process are designed. I believe that the statute tells you to correct the error.

"The question, I think, is then one of simply ensuring that all concerned see a process that is transparent. Well, that seems to me to be something that we can do. For example, in a northern county, Volusia, Judge McDermott had one pool camera in his counting room and allowed everyone to share off that, so the media saw precisely what the board was doing.

"My experience in recounts in large states, in statewide recounts, is that where there is a will, there is a way," Young says. "And I believe that ten thousand votes can in fact be counted accurately between now and Sunday."

King takes the mike again. He is bothered by the fact that he had spoken against doing just the 10,750 undervotes and today voted for it. But the logistical concerns are primary.

"I vote no," he says. "I believe we should stop at this time. We cannot meet the deadline of the supreme court of the state of Florida. And I feel it incumbent upon this canvassing board to count each and every ballot and to not do a hand recount that would potentially — potentially, Mr. De

Grandy; not guaranteed but *potentially* — even under the proposed plan of this morning, could disenfranchise a segment of our community."

Leahy's turn. "I'm going to also vote no for two reasons," he says.

There is loud applause.

"In my opinion, there was no requirement, or it wasn't warranted, that we do a full manual recount, based on my administrative reading of the law," Leahy says. "When the board voted last week to have a full recount, I supported the decision. I've done everything I can do to carry out that decision of the majority of the board. But at this time I do not believe that there is time to carry out a complete, full manual recount that is accurate and that will count every vote, because of the limitations put on this board in terms of time."

The thing is, it would take a whole other canvassing board for them to finish. He had said they could do it only if they went through 300 ballots an hour. But upstairs they were managing only between 60 and 100 max. They just weren't going to make it.

"Judge Lehr?" King asks.

"I, too, am going to vote no," Lehr says.

★   ★   ★

The Gorebies are demoralized. Some from their number weren't sure that there were votes in Miami-Dade, but Whouley had anticipated that they would glean anywhere from 150 to 350 votes there. So they now know that there is no way Gore will be certified the winner on Sunday; if there's an election contest, now they will be the ones who have to file it.

Moreover, they are convinced that something strange is afoot.

"The idea that they could not complete a count of the undervotes in four days is just factually incorrect," Klain thinks. They file a mandamus brief before the appellate court that night, to force the canvassing board to count the undervotes, confident that the district court of appeals will rule in their favor.

They are wrong.

The court agrees that the canvassing board has no discretion to decide to stop a count before they've finished it; but the court also rules that they cannot force the board to do the impossible.

Thursday, Thanksgiving, the Gorebies try to get the Florida Supreme Court to force the board to count.

They lose that one, too.

Boies will tell me in January that the lowest moment of it all was "when Dade suspends, and we can't get it restarted, we can't get those votes counted. If we had, it would be even harder for the Supreme Court to over-turn the results of the election. If we could have gotten the votes counted in Dade, so that at the time it went to the U.S. Supreme Court there were actual canvassing-board returns that put Gore ahead, I think that would have changed things."

A lot will be said and written about the Miami-Dade canvassing board's 180-degree turn. Some of it will be lost amid the Wednesday-morning news of Dick Cheney's fourth heart attack.* Much of it will be speculation. And as David Boies will tell me on January 15, 2001, "I don't think anybody who hasn't interviewed the canvassing-board members with truth serum will know precisely why they stopped."

That doesn't mean that Democratic pols won't try.

Lieberman will come forward on Friday to give his trademark sanctimo-nious wince. "I am deeply disappointed by reports of orchestrated demon-strations on Wednesday inside a state building — a *government* building — in Miami-Dade County. . . . These demonstrations were clearly designed to intimidate and to prevent a simple count of votes going forward."

"What happened in Miami-Dade was illegal," Deutsch tells me. "Out-of-town paid political operatives came to South Florida to disrupt a federal election," he charges, alleging that such actions violate a law that prohibits crossing state lines to "intimidate" parties supervising a federal election.†

Congressman Deutsch will take those charges a step further, from rhetoric

---

*How both Bush and George Washington University Hospital deceives the public about Cheney's fourth heart attack is remarkable for no other reason than the Bushies' ability to drag a normally respected physician into their MO of prevarication. Cheney's heart attack would not have been ruled as such a year prior, before the American Heart Association changed its classifications, but still, Dr. Alan Wasserman, president of the George Washing-ton Medical Faculty Associates, assuredly knew what he was saying when right off the bat he said that neither Cheney's "*initial* EKG nor his blood work indicated that he had a heart attack." (Emphasis added.) Of course, it was Cheney's *subsequent* EKG and blood work that indicated that he had a heart attack, which Wasserman clearly knew at the time, since at that very same press conference, he referred to the fact that "a second EKG showed minor changes" — "minor changes" as in a heart attack.

Bush, too, made this same deceptive assertion about Cheney's condition when he used the very same weasel language to assert that "the initial EKG showed that he had no heart attack." And, as always, despite the blatant disdain for the American people that Bush and his lie — and Wasserman and *his* lie — would indicate, the issue was dropped soon enough, and media outrage was minimal.

† The U.S. Congress once concluded about the Civil Rights Act of 1968 that there was "no question of the constitutional power of Congress to punish private interference with voting in Federal elections, interstate travel or interstate commerce."

into the terrain of demagoguery, in a letter to the U.S. Justice Department's division of elections, calling for a federal investigation.

But all three canvassing-board members — and, indeed, spokesman Villafana, who was no fan of the protesters — will insist that they weren't intimidated. King, in particular, comes from a pretty tough family — his judge father ruled against drug kingpins, and his sister prosecutes them. Leahy will tell me, point-blank, that he was never intimidated.

What about a story in the *New York Times* that implied that he had been intimidated? "He misunderstood something I had said," Leahy will say to me. The Republican observers *had* clearly been an impediment to the process, he says, but not through intimidation. "They attempted to delay everything we did," Leahy says. Once again, trying to find the truth floating at the bottom of this Florida swamp is near impossible.

Jim Wilkinson, a spokesman for the Bush recount team who was present at the protest outside the Miami-Dade canvassing room, says to me that there was nothing orchestrated about the protest. "There were between eighty and a hundred of us" outside the room, Wilkinson says, "and it was a very emotional group of young people. But they thought the election was being held behind closed doors."

Wilkinson observes that the Democrats have their share of protesters in Miami, too. "Al Gore has union volunteers that they've bused in from out of town to down here in Miami," he says. "Jesse Jackson brings a thousand or ten thousand volunteers to Florida, and they have no problem with it. All of a sudden, we have a hundred people and we're intimidating. Republicans are using Democrat protest tactics, and they don't like it."

Jesse Jackson's a hack, but his demonstrations in Florida (which never approached the ten thousand mark), while increasingly irresponsible in rhetoric, weren't even remotely like the ugliness on the nineteenth floor. And off the record, even Bushies acknowledge that this was not their team's proudest hour. Some are worried about a PR backlash. Then there are those like Ken Mehlman who are just happy that the count ended.

In any case, there's an immediate attempt by the Republican Party, and their media allies, to pooh-pooh any acknowledgment whatsoever that the mob was hostile and tried to be intimidating and clearly played some role — if only as an obstacle, or as a last straw — in stopping the hand recount. "In my life I have never found anything more frightening than a mob of young Republicans," jokes Fox News Channel's Brit Hume on Sunday, November 26. "They have on light green corduroy pants, and they've got on little belts with little frogs on them, and little pink shirts and everything. And, I don't know about you, but those Republican preppies just scare the daylights out of me."*

On the other side of the Coin of Crap, Rep. Jerrold Nadler, D-N.Y., comes forward on November 25 to refer to the GOP protest as a "riot," charging that "a whiff of Fascism is in the air."

"A mob threatened them [the members of the canvassing board], banged on their doors, roughed up people, threatened them, and they succumbed to the mob violence and the intimidation," Nadler says at a press conference. "That is frankly un-American of the mob to do that, it's un-American of the Republican leaders to lead that, and it's un-American for the Dade County board of canvassers to succumb to that threat."

Nadler's overheated demagoguery is an insult not only to his constituents but to the memory of anyone who ever came face-to-face with actual Fascism. While it's true that Benito Mussolini once said that "Fascism is reaction," that's where the comparison ends. For Nadler to compare a bunch of obnoxious Republican protesters who probably deserved to get roughed up a little by some of Whouley's pals from Southie (a thought that crossed Whouley's mind more than once) to Fascists is nothing short of sickening. Mussolini, Generalissimo Franco, Adolph Hitler — these are men responsible for slaughter, for mass murder, for genocide.

On November 22, 2000, on the nineteenth floor of the Miami-Dade County Government Building, fifty or so Republican activists got obnoxious, and hostile, and violent, and clearly some of them should have been escorted out of the building if not arrested. On November 21, 1920, outside the Bologna, Italy, City Hall, ten newly elected Social Democratic councilmen were slaughtered in a hail of gunfire by Fascists, who soon began patroling the countryside, taking over villages and murdering labor leaders and leftists. These events couldn't be more different; Nadler should be ashamed.

Those nonpartisans who were actually there, however — as opposed to those who seldom leave the confines of the Beltway — have a slightly more nuanced take on it all.

"Was it meant to be intimidating?" asks Villafana. "I believe so. Did they intend to disrupt the process? Yes." The canvassing-board members are "in

---

* The idea that a band of agitated white Republicans is simply incapable of intimidation is intriguing, especially when one pokes the thesis beneath its surface — imagining, for example, the exact same protest, with the exact same vigor, as carried out by, say, young Democratic African-Americans, and the subsequent reaction by, say, Brit Hume.

the public spotlight, and they know how to handle it," he says, but "I think the protesters accomplished their goal. They had a victory party after the vote was stopped; they felt jubilation."

Villafana is even more offended, perhaps, by the Republican Party's lies about what was going on inside the government building. "As an American, I personally believe in hard-fought contests, but there comes a time when essentially misinformation to the public should not be part of the process," Villafana tells me. "Confusing the American people as to what a community's attempting to do should not be part of the process, and that's an issue of ethics and what you believe in."

In the end, the Democrats' attempt to argue that the Republicans intimidated the canvassing board into quitting is at least unproven. There certainly were other possible factors. Political pressures may have played a role; De Grandy's continued references to the area's Hispanic vote — as subtle as a battalion of armed INS agents storming into a Little Havana hovel before sunrise — could certainly have weighed on the minds of the elected judges on the panel.

Then, of course, there's the question of where Mayor Alex Penelas was during the whole deal.

★　★　★

Rep. Harold Ford, Jr., Democrat of Tennessee, walks into the Miami-Dade government building right as the Republican punks are storming it. There he meets up with state senator Kendrick Meek. A few hours later, after the recount is canceled, Meek invites Ford to come with him to pay a visit on Penelas.

Penelas tells them that he's as disappointed as anyone that the count isn't going to continue. He indicates that he's troubled by the board's decision and says he hopes they'll reconsider. It's not his decision, he stresses, but Penelas says that he's going to write a statement to that effect. He tells Ford and Meek that it will be completed in half an hour.

In a conversation with Gore around that same time, Penelas makes similar comments, leaving a similar impression. Though Penelas has been AWOL from the Gore campaign — he had to distance himself from the Clinton administration's Elián blunders — he'll come through on this, it seems to Gore.

Ford and Meek tell him that they'll wait in a conference room. Penelas says he'll have it done soon.

Twenty minutes or so later, Ford, Meek, and a bishop from Meek's district tell Penelas that they're going to return to the lobby.

"No problem," Penelas says. The statement will be done in a moment.

A few hours pass, and though Ford never sees the statement, he takes Penelas at his word that it is coming. "I had a meeting with Mayor Penelas today, the mayor of Miami-Dade County," Ford says via satellite on CNN's *Crossfire* that night. "And he indicated that the county was prepared to put all the resources needed to ensure that Miami-Dade — the canvassing board — be able to provide an accurate recount."

That isn't, of course, the message of the statement Penelas eventually issues, which merely states that he has "no jurisdiction over that board's decisions."

"I don't know him well enough to feel betrayed," Ford says later. "But at a minimum, I wish he'd been more candid and more truthful."

Gutierrez, who worked for Penelas years ago but no longer does so, says that Penelas's shift was just a manifestation of the thirty-eight-year-old mayor's personality. "Knowing him, he was probably trying to please everybody," Gutierrez tells me. But when other details about Penelas's activities bubble up in the *New York Times,* thanks to Florida's open-government laws, Democrats start thinking more was going on in Penelas's world of conflicting pressures than just a desire to please.

The day before the count was canceled, the *Times* story details, Penelas was in Tallahassee where he reportedly lunched at the Governor's Club with Republican state representative Mario Diaz-Balart and met with other Republican legislators. The legislature is charged with redistricting the state and adding a congressional seat, Democrats whispered; Penelas is said to want to run for Congress. Calls were traded back and forth. But it's diffi- cult to figure out what angles Penelas is playing. He phoned both the Republican cloakroom in the U.S. House in Washington, D.C., as well as several advisers to Gore. Monday night, GOP state chair Cardenas spoke with Penelas's no. 1 political adviser, Herman Echevarria.

"I don't think they were asking about the weather," Boies will later tell me.

★ ★ ★

I meet with Mayor Penelas in December. In the newspaper, his cutie face smiles as he bestows gifts upon Miami. At the Miami International Airport, his soothing voice welcomes me, personally. In the conference room this afternoon, he's ambition in a suit. Cold, prickly, hostile. A jungle cat.

What about the *New York Times* story? I ask him. Any truth to any of it?

"I don't know what the sources are," he says with steely eyes. "I usually don't respond to things that I don't know the sources to."

He says that he never told Gore that he'd ask the canvassing board to recommence counting.

So what's the deal with all the calls and meetings and conflicting stories?

"Someday I'll write my book," he says.

"I spoke to them a few times about the issue," he says about the canvassing board, just "as the mayor, to find out what was going on, because we were getting inundated with media calls about what was going on. I wanted to make sure that [Leahy] knew that we would make available to him and the canvassing board whatever resources they needed to effectuate whatever decision they made."

So if that's all, aren't you upset about the *Times* story?

"I thought it was great," he says unconvincingly. "I got my name in the first page of the *New York Times.*

"I get criticized every day here, that's part of my job," he explains. "If you take it too seriously, then you can't handle the job. When you get back in the car, turn on any one of the talk shows, and I'm getting blasted for everything that goes wrong in this town. From everywhere.

"For other parts of the country, it may be unusual to deal with all this media and all the controversy, but I've dealt with it all, y'know. I've dealt with international fugitives and five named hurricanes as mayor and, y'know, fires and a plane crash and Elián González. It's what makes this job fun."

He doesn't look like he's having much fun.

The Democrats allege that you have plans to reregister as a Republican and run for one of the new congressional districts, after redistricting, I say. Any plans to reregister as a Republican?

"I have been fielding that question for thirteen years, my friend," he replies. "And I'm still a registered Democrat. I got my voting card right here," he says, reaching for his wallet. "I'm not going to switch parties.

"I believe that more people went to vote in Florida with the intention of voting for Al Gore," he adds. "But because of a series of coincidental events, none of which I believe were intentional, Mr. Bush won the state. But I do think more people went to vote for Gore with the intention of voting for Gore but were unable to execute for one reason or another, butterfly ballots and dimpled chads and all these other things."

Well, what do you even think about the whole idea of a recount? Should the undervotes and such be counted? Should the Republicans have taken all the steps they did to stop the counting?

"I had very strong feelings about it," he says.

Ummm . . . such as?

"That's what they are: my feelings," he says. "Like I said, maybe someday I'll write my own book about this."

C'mon.

"I favor having every vote counted," Penelas finally says.

And then he gets up and, like a tiger, skulks out of the room.

★   ★   ★

There's so much unadulterated bullshit in here it almost pains me to reprint it, but here is what the Bushies put out for their surrogates in the House and Senate to regurgitate.

Subject: Updated Talking Points on "GOP" Protests
Author: georgewbush.com at Internet
Date: 11/25/2000 1:37 PM

- The protests in Miami-Dade were a fitting, proper and instant reaction to a rash attempt by the canvassing board to count ballots in secret. Imagine all those observers, in place for the purpose of monitoring the manual recount, being told there was nothing to observe because the election board, which didn't include a single Republican, decided instead to take 10,000 ballots to the 19th floor to count them in secret. That's what the Board tried to do and the reaction was spontaneous and inevitable, given the imprudent actions of the Board.
- The press also demanded access to the room where the Board intended to act in secret.
- Passions in Miami-Dade were rising because the Board also intended to count predominantly Democratic precincts, ignoring the votes cast in overwhelmingly Cuban areas. Congressman Lincoln Diaz-Balart said the morning of the protest the Board's action was in apparent violation of the Voting Rights Act.
- The Board made a series of bad decisions and the reaction to it was inevitable and well justified.
- Finally, the Board's ultimate decision not to proceed was based on the fact they couldn't finish the manual recount by the Sunday 5:00 deadline — not because of these well deserved protests.
- But how come Joe Lieberman is critical of this protest and not the protests led by Jesse Jackson on behalf of Democrats? Joe Lieberman is less interested in right and wrong and more interested in silencing his opponents. This is the latest example of Al Gore and his campaign saying one thing while doing another. The first amendment applies to both parties and to all Americans.

★ ★ ★

Mark Fabiani never wanted to stick around in D.C. for the recount; he has a wife and kids (including an eighteen-month-old) in La Jolla, California, and he had to be begged by Gore to stick around after the election. Having directly arranged with Gore a Thanksgiving break for himself, Fabiani takes off to see his family.

Daley is pissed, frustrated; he tries to reach Fabiani but has trouble doing so. Others on the ground in Tallahassee think the communications team is rather wanting. Hattaway and Backus have been doing what they can, but lots of folks think Fabiani is flaking and Lehane is slacking — though at least they do so alternatingly.*

To Daley it's all just more of the same. The campaign he inherited late was fucked-up to begin with. He tried to do what he could, but these consultants were a problem. Shrum, Eskew, Devine, Fabiani — all smart guys, all talented guys, but they leaked like the fucking *Lusitania,* they went home on weekends, they were soft. Fabiani packed up the weekend before the election, didn't come in to work that Sunday. What kind of message did that send to the kids who were pulling all-nighters, unpaid? And now, post-election, Daley's having the same problems. He tries to get everyone to work out of the same conference room at the DNC, but that lasts like all of two hours, whereupon they all scurry back to their cozy little offices. When Fabiani comes back to D.C., he's even managed to finagle a room at the Ritz, paid for by the recount committee! Christ!

In La Jolla, Fabiani is fretting about the fact that Gore is now going to be contesting this thing. From a PR standpoint, Fabiani thinks, it's devastating to have the election declared for Bush — which is what it looks like will happen come Sunday, minus the Miami-Dade ballots.

Gore and he have talked about it, and Gore, too, knows that there's a very short fuse on this thing. Gore wants Fabiani to come up with a communications plan to convey that the process is making progress, that there's an endgame that can work. So Fabiani lays out his thinking:

---

*Gorebies will be further infuriated with Fabiani and Lehane after the recount fight ends and the *Washington Post* writes a rather flattering profile of the two, despite the fact that the Gore campaign's communications weren't quite the gold standard of media strategies, especially during the recount. Though, to be fair, Bob Shrum, Carter Eskew, and Daley were of course the ultimate arbiters of everything that went out.

From: Mark Fabiani
To: Bill Daley
Date: November 23, 2000

COMMUNICATIONS PLAN:
CONTESTING THE ELECTION

Assumptions

This plan makes two basic assumptions:

- By Saturday morning, because of various adverse court decisions and local canvassing board decisions, it is clear that Gore will not have amassed sufficient votes to take the lead by the Sunday 5:00 P.M. deadline.
- Gore has definitely decided to file an election contest if he is not in the lead by the Sunday 5:00 P.M. deadline.

Fundamental Principles

- A decision to file an election contest must be explained to the country by Gore personally and in significant detail. This is not a decision that can be explained in the first instance by lawyers and spokespeople.
- Gore must announce his decision to contest as soon as possible (once the two assumptions discussed above become fact). The alternative — delaying an announcement until Monday — is untenable for these reasons:
  - If it becomes clear on Friday or Saturday that Gore is unlikely to have the recount votes to prevail, the bulk of the news coverage will shift to the issue of whether or not Gore will nonetheless contest the election. In this kind of environment, Gore's political support will quickly and inevitably erode.
  - As a result, by the time Gore is ready to make a contest announcement on Monday, he will already have come under tremendous pressure not to take such an action.
  - By making an announcement sooner rather than later, Gore at least has the chance to hold potentially wayward supporters in line.
  - In addition, an early announcement allows Gore to set the parameters of the contest and explain how it can be conducted fairly and within a strictly limited period of time.
- Everyone associated with Gore must begin immediately to speak from the same page. Already there are comments from Gore advisers in the media saying that Gore's challenge must end on Sunday evening if Gore remains

behind in the vote. In light of Miami-Dade's decision, the facts have changed dramatically, and so should the posture of everyone speaking on behalf of Gore.

The Alternative

- If Gore has decided not to contest the election, there is still great value in maintaining the viability of the contest option right up until Sunday. In this case, the dominant themes would be these:
  - An election contest would be extremely strong and stand a great chance of success. We will need surrogates to make this point again and again over the weekend.
  - Gore is weighing his options, with one overriding goal in mind: Doing what is best for the country.
  - Gore's approach throughout this entire situation has been contrasted sharply with the opposition's win-at-any-cost, the-voters-be-damned strategy.

★   ★   ★

To the Gorebies, clearly, the Miami-Dade incident is the turning point in the post-election wrangling. Their thinking: Gore would have gained around 150 votes, propelling him to victory, a stronger position in the contest provision (*Bush* would have been the one contesting), and the SCOTUS would have been harder-pressed to issue the divisive, controversial ruling that it eventually handed down.

The one problem with this theory: it's questionable that the Gore votes were there. At least in the 10,750 undervotes.

In early December, I sit down with Cuban-American political consultant Armando Gutierrez, who was doing the math, showing me that there were plenty of undervotes in the Cubano precincts as well. Eighty undervotes in Opalocka precinct 246, he calculates, where Bush beat Gore 543 to 530; 58 in Hialeah's precinct 310, where Bush won 825 to 329; 78 in precinct 311 on West 4th Avenue, where Bush won 1,067 to 431. In the precinct that he worked on Election Day — precinct 543 at Gate 14 at Orange Bowl Stadium — there were 898 Bush votes, 351 Gore votes, and 106 undervotes, which would have presumably cut the same way, roughly 3 to 1 Bush. A subsequent analysis by the *Palm Beach Post* bears this out.[1] Inspecting the 10,750 undervotes under the loose standard the Miami-Dade canvassing board had been using before it all shut down, the *Post* ruled that Bush would have actually gained 6 votes had the count been completed, 251 new Bush votes to 245 new Gore votes.

However, when the *Post* counted the 5's and 7's — the more than 2,250 Miami-Dade ballots seemingly mis-inserted in the Votomatic machines, there were 1,023 punches for the nonexistent candidate at no. 7, and only 721 punches for Mr. Nobody at no. 5.

But those ballots were being set aside, and Young was planning on trying to convince the canvassing board to count these 2,250-some votes for both candidates.

Had these been counted — and who knows, perhaps Young could have been able to convince the board to do so — Gore would have picked up 302 additional votes. Though Leahy later tells me, "I don't think the canvassing board would have changed its mind" on the 5's and 7's. "It was something for the [Democratic] party to use in a court case, in the contest." But we'll never know what would have happened, of course. At least in part because of the GOP protesters and the obstacle they put in the path of the hand count continuing, as well as who knows what else that influenced the Miami-Dade canvassing board.

13

"We're fucked!"

Internally within the Bush legal team, the initial decision to push forward with the federal case — the one that landed before Middlebrooks — was hotly debated. Did they really want to be the first to file a lawsuit? Did they really want to be asserting that the federal government should involve itself in a state's election process? Baker calmly ruled that the insurance policy was necessary, but there were those on the other side of the debate.

On the other hand, the decision to appeal the Florida Supreme Court's ruling to the U.S. Supreme Court isn't even a close call.

The brief, chiefly prepared by Olson, Carvin, and Olson's colleagues at Gibson Dunn & Crutcher, is filed Wednesday, November 22. It requests a writ of certiorari,* throwing every argument under the sun at the Florida Supreme Court ruling.

The Bush lawyers raise the 3 U.S.C. 5 issue. They also argue that since the extension was essentially a new law, it's "inconsistent with Article II, Section 1, clause 2 of the Constitution, which provides that electors shall be appointed by each State 'in such Manner as the Legislature thereof may direct.'" This decision, they claim, was also inconsistent with the 14th Amendment. Lastly, the Bushies say, "the use of arbitrary, standardless, and selective manual recounts that threaten to overturn the results of the

---

*Informally called a "cert" or a "cert petition," a petition for a writ of certiorari (from the Latin for "to be informed of") is what lawyers write when they want a higher court to reexamine any actions of a lower court. The writ itself comes when the court agrees to hear the appeal.

election for President of the United States violates the Equal Protection or Due Process Clauses, or the First Amendment."*

Something's gotta stick. Especially with a U.S. Supreme Court that consists of seven Republican appointees.

Tribe, brought back to work on the vice president's response, writes that this is a task that has been expressly delegated to the state of Florida by the U.S. Constitution's command in Article II that "[e]ach *State* shall appoint, in such Manner as the Legislature thereof may direct, a Number of Electors, equal to the whole Number of Senators and Representatives to which the State may be entitled in the Congress." (Emphasis added.) The brief "thus is a patent attempt to federalize a state law dispute over whether a manual recount is authorized and appropriate."

Equal-protection claims are nonsense, Tribe writes; "manual recount procedures, like those that are included in Florida law, are a completely ordinary mechanism for ensuring the accuracy of vote-counts in close elections." Meanwhile, Tribe writes, "different counties within states routinely use different equipment and different ballots for the conduct of their elections" — why wouldn't that fact be considered an equal protection violation?

If the SCOTUS cuts in, Tribe maintains, "it would only diminish the legitimacy of the outcome of the election."

★   ★   ★

"I have a brief statement to make," house speaker Tom Feeney tells reporters on November 22. "I would encourage you to pay close attention to it."

Feeney's itchy. He's been looking for a way to help Bush and put an end to it all since the day after the election, when Don Rubottom told him the legislature might have the power to step in. And the Florida Supreme Court just opened the door and invited him into the chaos.

---

*Article II, Section 1, clause 2 of the Constitution provides: "Each State shall appoint, in such Manner as the Legislature thereof may direct, a Number of Electors, equal to the whole Number of Senators and Representatives to which the State may be entitled in the Congress: but no Senator or Representative, or Person holding an Office of Trust or Profit under the United States, shall be appointed an Elector."

The 14th Amendment to the Constitution says that "No State shall make or enforce any law which shall abridge the privileges or immunities of citizens of the United States; nor shall any State deprive any person of life, liberty, or property, without due process of law; nor deny to any person within its jurisdiction the equal protection of the laws."

The 1st Amendment to the Constitution says that "Congress shall make no law . . . abridging the . . . right of the people to petition the Government for a redress of grievances."

"In my view, the court's ruling indicated the tremendous lack of respect that the Florida Supreme Court has for the laws of the state of Florida and the legislature," Feeney says. The court "could have given us a resolution. Instead, I fear, it has given us a potential constitutional crisis."

Deadlines exist to be followed, the state house speaker says. But the court doesn't seem to have any respect for the election scheme as designed by the legislature. This is just the latest in a long list of feuds between the two bodies — a crossfire that Al Gore has run straight into.

Feeney's charged by Rubottom's research and the work his aide's done with legal scholars. Rubottom has been in touch with UC-Davis professor Michael Glennon, who wrote a November 19 op-ed in the *Washington Post* that Rubottom liked about "a curious provision in the 1887" Electoral Count Act, which "makes it possible for the legislature of a state to resolve disputes concerning the validity of its electors. If a state fails to make a choice on Election Day — because, for example, of recounts, court challenges, or the need to count absentee ballots — the law provides that 'the electors may be appointed on a subsequent day in such a manner as the legislature of such state may direct.'" After reading that, Rubottom called Glennon, who advised them to immediately step in.

Rubottom then called around, looking for lawyers to hire. Over at the Bush Building, Jimenez and John Manning recommended a University of Utah professor named Mike McConnell. And though McConnell couldn't do it, he recommended Harvard Law professor Charles Fried, a former solicitor general in the Reagan administration and Bush–Cheney campaign adviser. Fried gladly agreed to come on board ($350 an hour, capped at $60,000), but he was savvy enough to realize that — as a former Massachusetts supreme court justice who ruled in favor of counting dimples in *Delahunt* — the state house might want a legal spokesman who didn't have to defend such a ruling. So they also brought in his Harvard Law School colleague Einer Elhauge.

Elhauge is an antitrust Harvard Law professor who wrote a November 20 op-ed in the *New York Times* supporting Bush's SCOTUS case against the Florida canvassing boards. "The Bush lawsuit is not against manual recounts," he argued, "but against an election system run by partisan county officials who lack any objective standard for whether or how to conduct manual recounts, and who have allegedly exercised their power in a discriminatory fashion."

"I have spoken to a prominent law professor today," Feeney says, referring to Fried. "I have invited him and have issued an opportunity for him to decide to give the Florida house of representatives advice about our constitutional responsibilities, our options, and prerogatives. And until I have that advice, I don't intend to take any further formal steps."

Not publicly at any rate. But Frank Jimenez spends some time Wednesday with house republican leader Mike Fasano. When asked about this, Jeb's spokeswoman, Katie Baur, tells reporters, "If the legislature were to call a special session, Frank would be the person solely responsible for advising the governor on the appropriate action."

Waitasec. I thought Jimenez had recused himself to work for the *other* Bush. Unless of course they've dropped the pretense?

*   *   *

In the actual *Pullen* case cited by the Florida Supremes, Judge Francis Barth was ordered to reexamine twenty-seven ballots with all sorts of marks on them. Barth took the Illinois Supreme Court's order to mean that dimples *could* count, but he didn't say they necessarily *would* count. A hanging chad would be a vote, sunlight through the chad would be a vote, and a dimpled chad could be a vote, based on "other considerations of the ballot itself." "I do not infer from that [the Illinois Supreme Court order] that there had to be a partial dislodgement in order for the ballot to be considered," he said.

Barth tossed out nineteen ballots for having no clear intent, he accepted four ballots with pinholes in the chad, three with hanging chad, and one other, Remand Exhibit 19. He ruled that Exhibit 19 was a vote because of a pattern of seven other dimples on the same ballot — and not one clearly punched-out chad. He referred to the *Delahunt* case twice — in which the Massachusetts Supreme Court ruled that it wasn't convincing that a voter would have come down to vote and not cast a vote for anyone.

On the other hand, Remand Exhibit 27 featured maybe twenty dimples, along with some clear punches, and Barth ruled that in that case the pinhole in the *Pullen* chad was not sufficient.

In entering the murky world of the chad rulings of Barth's courtroom a decade ago, a couple things are clear:

1. the references by both Baker and the Bush talking points to the Illinois case being only applicable to "hanging chads" are dead wrong, either a mistake or a lie; and
2. the *Chicago Tribune* account of it all, which Boies is relying upon — "An indentation in the chad can clearly indicate the voter's intent" — is too simplistic, whether the fault of the reporter or the source, Pullen attorney Michael Lavelle, or both.

On Tuesday night, Gore attorney Mitchell Berger seeks out Lavelle, after having read that day's *Chicago Tribune* story. The team is disappointed that the Florida Supreme Court didn't give them a specific statewide standard other than "intent of the voter." But since the court did cite *Pullen,* the team thinks it would be a great idea to get Lavelle to sign an affidavit testifying to the fact that dimples counted in *Pullen,* as the *Tribune story* stated.

Shortly before midnight, Berger calls former Democratic committee-man Larry Suffredin, who suggests that Berger conference-call in Illinois state senator John Cullerton, who's Lavelle's buddy, and get him to phone Lavelle.

"Sorry for waking you up," Cullerton says to Lavelle a few minutes later. He asks him if the *Tribune* story was correct today, and if so, if he minds if he gets a Gore attorney on the phone.

Sure, Lavelle says. No problem.

Berger gets on. "Is the story true?"

Yes, Lavelle says. Barth counted dimpled ballots.

"Do you have any records from the case?" Berger asks.

"No," says Lavelle, "all I have is an abbreviated file."

"Could you get the full file from the courthouse?" Berger asks.

"Well, since it's ten years old, it won't be in the courthouse, it would probably be in storage out at the warehouse," Lavelle says. "That'll take a couple of weeks."

Lavelle is asked if he would be willing to sign an affidavit attesting to the fact that dimpled ballots were counted.

"Yeah, no problem," Lavelle says. "That's what happened."

"That could be very helpful to us," Berger says, because the Florida Supreme Court's opinion today was very unclear.

Berger asks Lavelle how early he could start on it.

Well, I've gotta talk to my secretary, he says. "Certainly not before seven-thirty or eight, local time."

"Well, the earlier you can get in the better," Berger says. "I would sure appreciate it."

Wednesday morning, Lavelle gets into work early, and there's a draft affi-davit waiting for him from the hyperactive Berger. "The trial court deter-mined that seven (7) indented or dimpled ballots reflected the voter's intent to vote for Pullen and one (1) indented or dimpled ballot reflected the voter's intent to vote for Mulligan," it says. After a few changes here and there, Lavelle signs it.

That afternoon, *Tribune* reporter Dan Mihalopoulos phones up Lavelle.

He's being told by Republicans that only ballots with light shining through the chad counted. Do you have any of those records left?

Lavelle doesn't; he reduced his loads of paper long ago. He tells Mihalopoulos to check out the ballots. The warehouse where the records are kept is only a couple miles from the courthouse. If you get a hold of the PR person down there, maybe you can get a hold of the ballots, Lavelle says.

Two hours later, Mihalopoulos pages Lavelle; the courthouse employees have no idea what the hell case he's talking about, they can't find it on the computer. Lavelle gives him some more information and steers him toward the county division of the circuit court, which is a smaller division with better records.

Shortly after 5, Mihalopoulos calls Lavelle again. He found the file. While there, he also stumbled into Burt Odelson, who was Mulligan's attorney in the *Pullen* case, who was just returned by the Bushies. "Mike, I'm sorry to tell you that it looks like the only ones that counted were the ones that had light through," Mihalopoulos says.

"How many were counted with dents?" Lavelle asks.

"I can't find *any* that were counted with dents," the reporter says.

"Read me what Barth said," Lavelle asks.

Mihalopoulos reads him a few snippets from the 155-page transcript, statements by the judge from the early part of the transcript before Barth starts actually assessing the ballots.

Mihalopoulos does *not* read Lavelle the excerpt that has Barth saying, "The light standard is not the litmus test, in my view. If there is a dent, a voter's intent may be established from other considerations of the ballot itself."

Mihalopoulos does *not* read Lavelle the excerpt that has Barth looking at Remand Exhibit 19, when the judge says that "the light standard shouldn't be the only standard" while accepting the ballot because there are eight other dimples upon it and none that are cleanly punched out.

But what Mihalopoulos *does* read him, however, makes Lavelle panic. He thinks he's issued an affidavit that could be construed as misleading. He never mentioned light passing through.

Mihalopoulos goes to write his story. He's on deadline.

Cullerton calls Lavelle that night.

"I'm glad you called," Lavelle tells him. He tells him the problem, that his affidavit could be construed to be misleading. After they talk a bit about it, they get Mitchell Berger on the phone.

I think I was wrong, Lavelle says to Berger. Dimpled ballots counted, yes, Lavelle says, but according to the *Chicago Tribune* reporter, it was only dimpled ballots with pinpricks of light through the chad. So my statement was incomplete.

"We're fucked!" Berger says.

"I'm sorry about that," Lavelle says.

"We have got to get an affidavit on file!" Berger says, explaining that the Gorebies have already used the affidavit before the Broward County canvassing board and submitted it to LaBarga. "We have got to correct the record!" Berger continues. "We can't let this sit!"

Lavelle arrives early at work on Thursday, November 23. He writes a corrected affidavit, saying that he had a "mistaken recollection" that all dimpled ballots counted. He says that he was told by a *Chicago Tribune* reporter that the only ballots that counted were ballots with light shining through. At this point, Lavelle still hasn't read the transcript.

That morning's *Tribune* has a story by Mihalopoulos and D.C.-based reporter Jan Crawford Greenburg, with the sub-headline "Illinois Case Offers Shaky Precedent." *Pullen* "may not be the legal home run they [on the Gore legal team] believe will aid his quest to win Florida's 25 electoral votes and the White House, an analysis of the ruling shows," the *Tribune* story says. Barth "exclude(d) dented ballots, since he had decided he could not reasonably determine the voters' will by examining the ballots. In fact, in the Illinois case, the dented ballots were not counted at all."

In fact, this is not the case. At the very least, the reason that Barth accepted Exhibit 19 was subject to debate, and should have prevented the *Tribune* from making any definitive ruling along the lines of "in the Illinois case, the dented ballots were not counted at all." And of course, Mihalopoulos played a rather sizable role in establishing the "shaky foundation"* referred to in the story's sub-headline.

On Thursday, November 23, in Fort Lauderdale, Broward County Courtroom 6780, a GOP attorney named Michael Madigan shows up at the canvassing board with the new affidavit and the September 1990 testimony from Barth's courtroom. "You've been provided a false affidavit and

---

* At least one *Tribune* editor will attempt to distance himself from the November 21 story by calling Mihalopoulos "a suburban metro reporter," which is to a national reporter akin to calling someone a leper. Regarding the mistakes in the November 21 story, Greenburg will say, "This was a very rapidly developing story." As for the role the *Tribune* played in the post-election drama, Greenburg argues that Mihalopoulos's story was based on what Lavelle told him, and "Boies should have done his own research." On the November 23 story, Greenburg insists that Remand Exhibit 19 was ruled a vote because of the pinhole of light, which is clearly not what a careful reading of the Barth testimony indicates.

we have the court transcript, which demonstrates that dimpled ballots or indented ballots, contrary to what Mr. Boies told you, in Illinois were not accepted!" Madigan says excitedly. "It's reported in this morning's *Tribune!*"

So? Lee asks. "We have a supreme court decision of the state of Florida that trumps what the Illinois court says or what any of the other courts say," he says.

Madigan's going a little bananas. "If we do our business based on a false affidavit, and you had a gentleman that came in here and provided you with a false affidavit —"

"I need a deputy on standby to remove somebody who is out of order, please," Lee says. "I'm not going to put up with this, sir. You have not been asked to speak. I told you, we are bound by the supreme court case, I'm not basing my decision here today on anything that someone says in an affidavit." Madigan clams up.

Having failed to use the Lavelle fiasco to change anything in Broward, the Bushies now try a new attack based on the fact that the Gore legal team waits until Monday, a full four days — until *after* Harris has certified the election on Sunday — before it presents the new affidavit to Palm Beach County. And what's more, the Bushies say, Boies and Berger *never* gave the new affidavit to the folks in Broward. Berger responds to this by saying that he had been told that Lee didn't want any more affidavits, that he found the whole Lavelle business irrelevant; he was focused on the ruling of the Florida Supreme Court. And while it's true that LaBarga won't receive the new affidavit until Monday, November 27, that's because the courthouse was closed Thursday and Friday for Thanksgiving. As one senior Bush attorney will later confide to me, "That whole Lavelle thing was bullshit."

But *Pullen* will rear her head again.

★　★　★

Their work in Miami-Dade completed, the Bush protest caravan drives north on I-95 to the Broward County courthouse in downtown Fort Lauderdale.

When they're not hand-holding and canoodling, Bush advance staffers Todd Beyer and Leslie Shockley drum up the crowd. Literally — Beyer actually beats a drum. Blakeman yells on his megaphone: "You're not going to steal this election!" Meanwhile, Bush spokeswoman Lani Miller organizes protesters.

Beneath hazy gray clouds that keep the street's immense palm trees from casting a shadow, a crowd of four hundred or so Bush supporters chant, "Rotten to the Gore! Rotten to the Gore!" Other familiar faces from the campaign are scattered throughout, wearing orange baseball caps that read "W. Florida Recount Team." "You're a bunch of Dummy-crats!" one from their number shouts on a megaphone to the pathetically sparse crowd of pro-Gore protesters across the way, many of whom hold signs deriding "Bushit."

"You couldn't even get a ballot right in Palm Beach!" the pro-Bush protester continues. "What a bunch of losers! I've never seen so many losers in one place!" The Bush crowd laughs. One protester holds a sign featuring Gore's head in a noose next to the words "Gore: Hangin' by a chad." Another sign reads: "Hey, Gore, I hear Hell needs a president."

Every few minutes, the Republicans who continue to identify themselves only as "volunteers" exit the Windsor Monaco RV parked down the street and distribute T-shirts and baseball caps for free to the ravenous crowd.

"How to STEAL an Election," one popular shirt reads. "1. Count all votes. 2. Re-count all votes. 3. Re-count some votes. 4. Hand count some votes. 5. Change the rules. 6. Exclude the military."

Who's paying for those shirts? I ask a man who refuses to tell me his name.

"I'm just a volunteer," he says.

Yeah, but who's paying for the shirts?

"I dunno," he says. "I'm just a volunteer."

This "volunteer" is actually Phil Muster, a Bush political staffer. But whatever.

★　★　★

Different players in the saga have vastly different Thanksgivings.

The Bush campaign makes sure that their operatives in southeast Florida have a memorable holiday, if not one with family. About two hundred of them gather in the Fort Lauderdale Hyatt, where Bush and Cheney thank them via speakerphone and entertainer Wayne Newton recites the Lord's Prayer.

Bush spokeswoman Mindy Tucker awakens that morning and drives around Tallahassee in an attempt to clear her mind. But before long she's beckoned back to the Bush Building after the Gorebies file a brief with the Florida Supreme Court in order to force Miami-Dade to count. She goes back to work, putting out a statement, appearing on TV.

At 4 P.M., she and around twenty others have reservations at Tallahassee's Chez Pierre. On her way there, she receives a call on her cell phone; the Florida Supreme Court decided against the Gorebies.

"Good," she thinks. "Now at least I can have Thanksgiving dinner."

At Chez Pierre, Tucker's standing at the bar, waiting for a glass of chardonnay when she receives another call. Ron Klain and David Boies are holding a conference call with reporters, she's told. Gore is going ahead, preparing to contest the election. Does she have any comment?

Aargh! she thinks. Don't these people celebrate Thanksgiving? Do they not ascribe any meaning to this holiday? She phones up Ari Fleischer in Austin. "I'm livid," she says. "Tell me if I'm wrong. Ron Klain says they're going to contest this." Tucker wants to take the evening off, so she'd prefer the response to be, "We have no formal comment; it's Thanksgiving." Is that OK with Fleischer? "I think it's fine," Fleischer says. "Do it."

She sees Klain on the bar's TV, saying that Al Gore's spending the day with his family.

"Oh, my god! That's bullshit!" Tucker says out loud, to no one in particular. "Al Gore is not 'spending the day with his family' — they just did a conference call!" She starts yelling at the TV. "I cannot believe you just said that!" she says to Klain. "He is *not* spending the day with family. He was just on the phone with you!"

A few Gore attorneys are at another table, laughing at her frustration.

They send her a bottle of champagne.

She feels obliged to walk over to them, to thank them. "How did you know champagne was my favorite?" she asks.

"All beautiful women love champagne," a Gore lawyer responds.

Tucker is repulsed.

★ ★ ★

The Palm Beach County canvassing board has taken the day off. On Wednesday, a county public-information officer told the board that "we can't work tomorrow," since they were having a tough time getting counters to agree to come in on Thanksgiving.

"How are we doing?" Burton asked her.

"Well, we're picking up the pace," the director of public affairs, Denise Cote, said.

There was no discussion.

"Great, let's take the day off," Burton said. "I could use it."

Perhaps no decision to have a Thanksgiving feast has had such national implications since, well, 1621.

★ ★ ★

The Broward County canvassing board is surprised when they hear of Palm Beach's decision. But they're working through the holiday, no matter what.

When they break in the afternoon to have Thanksgiving dinner, Lee, Gunzburger, and Rosenberg have unexpected guests at their Thanksgiving dinners: sheriff's deputies.

Gunzburger, in particular, has been receiving hate mail and threatening phone calls. She's become the target of much ire on the Internet. Her son Ron, who writes for a political Web site, tells her that she's been linked romantically with Commissioner Carol Roberts.

But there's other stuff, too. She's been told that someone wrote on another site that she needed to be "taken out," and she's received forty-five thousand hateful e-mails. On one site her daughter and granddaughter's names were listed. She feels incredibly vulnerable.

One morning, while her attorney, Larry Davis, drives her to the canvassing board, she breaks down and cries. "You know, Larry, I'm doing this because I think I'm doing a public service," she says. "I want to see my grandchildren grow up. I don't want to die over this."

When Lee goes to feast at the home of his partner's sister, sheriff's deputies sit outside in their squad cars. Lee feels guilty, though, so he forces them to come inside for dessert.

On Friday, someone throws a brick through a window of the Broward County Democratic HQ with a note: "We will not tolerate any illegal government."

★   ★   ★

Baker, meanwhile, thinks that they need reinforcements. Whether or not the SCOTUS takes up their case, they need some trial lawyers on the ground in Florida. This thing's clearly going to be contested in court, by one side or the other. And Baker here makes a tactical decision that contrasts sharply with the Gorebies' team building.

The Gore team, with the possible exception of Boies,* is made up of diehard Democratic, Gore-supporting lawyers. Mitch Berger, Ben Kuehne, Steve Zack, et al. Some of them are very talented, some of them less so, but they were selected because of their allegiance to the party and the vice president.

---

* Boies is technically a Democrat. He worked with the Clinton Justice Department to prosecute Microsoft, and his legal career was given a boost early on when he worked for Sen. Ted Kennedy as chief counsel and staff director of the Senate Antitrust Subcommittee and eventually chief counsel of the Judiciary Committee. That said, Boies has given cash to former Republican congressman Tom Campbell of California, a moderate and Stanford law professor, as well as to Sen. Orrin Hatch, Republican from Utah and chair of the Senate Judiciary Committee. "I knew him from judiciary," Boies says. "I think he's a good guy; very thoughtful and very pragmatic."

Conversely, Baker starts seeking the best trial lawyers he can get. It doesn't matter to him what party they belong to, whom they voted for.

Early on in the process, for instance, Baker calls up Irv Terrell, a tall, bald, bespectacled Texan who's a childhood friend of Bush's and a colleague from Baker Botts, where Baker's a partner. But Terrell is also something of a Democrat, a man who leans left on issues like abortion and race.

Terrell can't do it, he tells Baker, he's just too busy. Plus, Terrell's reluctant to jump into another high-profile case, having participated in the *Pennzoil v. Texaco* case. "Participated" isn't even the word, really. *The American Lawyer* would refer to Terrell as Pennzoil's "hit man" in the oil company's successful 1985 $10 billion suit against Texaco for screwing them on a deal Pennzoil had made with Getty Oil. That was a case, interestingly, on which Terrell had worked with Tribe, and against Boies.* Such high-profile cases bring out the worst in people, Terrell thinks. On *Pennzoil v. Texaco,* Terrell saw one of his co-counsels, Joe Jamail, take credit away from co-counsel John Jeffords, a close friend of Terrell's who subsequently died of a brain tumor. Terrell didn't like what the media attention did to Jamail. He didn't like what it did to him, either.

Okay, then, Baker says, then who else? Baker asks Terrell for recommendations. Who else can be brought down to Tallahassee? Baker asks. Terrell recommends Daryl Bristow, another Baker Botts attorney, a Republican, though not an active party guy or anything. Another name that immediately comes to Terrell's mind is Fred Bartlit.

★ ★ ★

Bartlit — who you may recall was a young Kirkland & Ellis attorney in 1960 when the GOP hired him to investigate vote fraud in Texas — is at his daughter's wedding at the Drake Hotel in Chicago when he first gets the call, on Saturday, November 18.

It comes from Glen Summers, one of his associates from Denver; Bartlit splits his time between Illinois and Colorado. Summers says that the Bushies — he's been contacted by an old chum, Ted Cruz, who's on the ground in Tallahassee — want Bartlit to leave the wedding ASAP, to fly down to Florida, and argue for the inclusion of overseas military absentee ballots. Bartlit, sixty-eight, agrees to do it in the morning. A friend and client says that Bartlit can fly down early Sunday morning using his charter plane.

---

*In 1993, Terrell would again beat Boies while defending American Airlines in a predatory pricing antitrust suit brought by Continental Airlines and Northwest Airlines.

A West Point grad and former army ranger, Bartlit's a tough-talking guy who constantly derides what he sees as the overwhelming amount of bullshit in the world. Fed up with meetings and bureaucracy, he and a few of his buddies — namely Phil Beck, forty-nine — formed their own firm in 1993, Bartlit Beck Herman Palenchar & Scott, commonly known as Bartlit Beck.

Bartlit and Beck are a pretty big deal, known in the legal community and among corporate America, if not household names with the rest of us. They defend big corporations, and they do so successfully. They've been real innovators in the use of technology and visuals and computers in the courtroom. They don't bill by the hour — they get incentives if they win.

And win big they do. In *The National Law Journal*'s list of the hundred most influential lawyers in 1997, Bartlit was described as "personally one of the most successful corporate defense litigators ever, with a long history of big wins." These include victories for Amoco, Dun & Bradstreet, Monsanto, and United Technologies. He's been there for DuPont on patents, National Lead on claims of paint-chip injuries to kids, GM on everything under the sun. He and Beck repped Alpha Therapeutic Corporation — a company that made blood-clotting medicine through which hemophiliacs were said to have contracted HIV.

They're big guns for the bad guys, as are most successful lawyers. Bartlit and Beck are just a bit more successful than most.

Neither claim to be conservative Republicans, however. And if you ask Bartlit about his clients, he'll immediately shift the conversation to his representation of the Sierra Club in 1981 in its suit against the utilities running the Four Corners, New Mexico, coal-fired power plant that discharged sulfur dioxide into the air. He's about to take on the tobacco industry on behalf of the Canadian government. If you ask Beck, he'll mention his representation of an African-American Chicagoan in his suit against the cops who wrongfully imprisoned him.

As for their feelings on the presidency, well, both pulled the lever for Bush in November. Beck thinks that Gore's "a creep," that he has "an unhealthy obsession with wanting to be president; his whole life's been defined as to whether he'll achieve Mommy and Daddy's dream." But neither Bartlit nor Beck voted for Bush in the Illinois primary. They were among the 22 percent of Republican voters in that state who voted for Bush's nemesis, McCain, despite the fact that the Arizona senator dropped out of the race two weeks before.

Bartlit arrives in Tallahassee the morning of Sunday, November 19, and he gets to work on the overseas military absentee-ballot case. Over the course of the week, he calls Beck, tells him that it looks like there will be a contest filed, after which things are going to move very fast, around the clock, like the hostile takeover cases Bartlit and Beck have worked on before. For that, Bartlit says, the Bushies will need more than one trial lawyer.

"I think it would be the kind of thing that would be perfect for you," Bartlit says to his young partner. He has a fatherly pride for Beck, whose headstrong, occasionally idiosyncratic ways weren't as beloved at Kirkland & Ellis as they are now. "If you want to come, I'll recommend they bring you down," Bartlit says.

But by Thanksgiving Day, Beck hasn't heard a word. Before he heads off to his sister's house for dinner, he sends out the following e-mail:

From:	Beck, Philip
Sent:	Thursday, November 23, 2000 12:51 PM
To:	Bartlit, Fred; Summers, Glen
CCL	Herman, Sidney
Subject:	If you need me

Since I haven't heard from anyone, I assume we have not been put in charge of whatever contest occurs and/or that I'm not needed in Florida. If someone needs to talk to me this weekend, I will have my cell phone with me and turned on most of the time. Skip and I are proud of all of you for helping to elect our next President.*

Beck assumes that the decision has been made, but he brings his cell phone, which he seldom does.

It's a mixed crowd at his sister's — Beck's mom and sister and one of his sons voted for Gore, while he, his wife, brother-in-law, and other son were Bush-backers. Everyone's talking about the election, getting lawyer Phil's take on it all. He hasn't told them about the fact that he might even be called to come down.

Soon enough, the phone rings, and Bartlit tells him that the Gore lawyers have just announced that a contest is going to be filed. Beck doesn't

*This last line is a reference to Sidney "Skip" Herman, a staunch Democrat Bartlit Beck partner driven crazy by Bartlit's efforts.

quite know what that is, but he's on the program, he tells his family —
"they all instantly became Bush supporters," he later says — and at the
crack of dawn on Friday morning, Beck's on his way down south.

By going for the best lawyers he can find, period, and not just going after
Bush loyalists, Baker makes a very shrewd decision. Though initially, when
Bartlit is chosen to represent Bush in a suit against fourteen Florida coun-
ties for not counting certain overseas military absentee ballots, some of the
Bush loyalists — Ginsberg and Terwilliger, primarily, as well as tons of po-
litical folks — have their doubts.

★ ★ ★

Accompanied by Summers and Unger, Bartlit presents his case on Friday,
November 24, before Judge Ralph "Bubba" Smith. Beck is in the stands,
fresh off the plane in jeans.

Bartlit knows that however strong the overseas military absentee-ballot
case is politically, it has limited potential legally. There are, for example,
serious questions about venue — whether they should be dragging fifteen
counties to a Tallahassee courtroom instead of filing in fifteen different
county seats throughout the state. There are also possible procedural problems on the matter of the law; the issue has never been resolved before. No
one would say they had a great case. But, Bartlit and Baker Botts partner
Kirk Van Tine had decided, something has to be done. The Democrats
might have retreated from the Herron memo, but military votes still
weren't being included. The Bushies estimate that about 500 ballots were
rejected for technicalities that they claim they can argue against, such as
lacking a postmark. By using the confusion about whether an absentee ballot has to have a postmark — or if, lacking a postmark, since it's sent from
a ship or whatever, it's enough that it's signed and dated — the Bushies will
try to shake out every single absentee ballot they can. Some Bush pols
repeat arguments to reporters that they don't intend on making in the
courtroom: they want military ballots given every possible benefit of the
doubt. They want ballots bearing postmarks that are unreadable to count.
And, heck, not just the unreadable; they want *post*–Election Day postmarks
to count!

How much of this is rooted in the conference call on or around Veteran's
Day, November 11, is impossible to say. Who on the Bush team knows
about that conference call? Also impossible to say. But the legal maneuvers
in today's courtroom will do a great deal to further the cause to get ballots
that have been cast after Election Day — however many there are —
counted.

★   ★   ★

When Bartlit walks into the courtroom, he expects to see Gore lawyers there, to argue on his side that these ballots should be counted — the argument that, after all, Lieberman made on TV. But they're not there, which Bartlit finds a bit sleazy. Nor are they there to argue the other side of the matter, which Bartlit finds disappointing, since he has a computer file full of graphics and Lieberman quotes arguing the Bushies' side on this. Oh well, he thinks. That the Gore lawyers haven't entered the case and aren't helping out the canvassing boards will be good — it increases the likelihood that the canvassing boards will start caving.

Not that they don't have an argument.

Since the point is to get Bush votes, right off the bat Bartlit dismisses the Bushies' suit against Clay County, which then takes the 17 absentee ballots it rejected last week and accepts 14 of them. Twelve of them are for Bush.

The lawyer for Bay County asks Bartlit if the Bushies are going to dismiss their suit against his canvassing board, too, since the board members just reconsidered 12 absentee ballots, resulting in a net gain of 2 votes for Bush. But that's not good enough. "We still have differences with Bay County," Bartlit says. And Escambia, Dade, Okaloosa, Collier, Leon, Pasco Counties, etc., etc.

The list goes on. Fred Bartlit wasn't brought here to make it easy.

★   ★   ★

A comprehensive analysis of the GOP's fight for the inclusion of overseas absentee ballots shows that it's based more on the desire for Bush votes than any concern for the rights of Americans serving their country abroad. One case in point: Broward County discarded only 6 overseas absentee ballots because they lacked postmarks. Still, GOP lawyer Craig Burkhardt of Springfield, Illinois, argues vociferously that Lee and the board include them.

Lee is already suspicious of Burkhardt,* who is clumsily obvious about his partisan intentions. For example, Burkhardt wants to see where the postmark on the envelope is from before he decides whether or not to argue in favor or against an absentee ballot's inclusion.

"You can't do that," Lee would say to him.

---

*Burkhardt is a hilarious example of how so many party hacks — both Democrats and Republicans — played small roles for their parties, and did them poorly, only to return back home with a swagger, as if back from Iwo Jima with a chest full of medals. A December 5, 2000, story about Burkhardt in the Springfield, Illinois, *State Journal-Register*, entitled "Springfield Lawyer Back from Florida Recount Duties," features Burkhardt pathetically overinflating both his role and how well he did it.

During this week, when absentee ballots are being reconsidered, the Broward County canvassing board learns that 4 of the 6 absentee ballots rejected because they lacked a postmark were without such because they'd been delivered to D.C. in a diplomatic pouch. Two were from the U.S. Embassy in Bulgaria, two from the embassy in Fiji.

You have to count them! Burkhardt ordered Lee.

OK, so they did.

Four Gore votes.

Two days later, Lee opens a letter from Sullivan & Boyd, a Republican-affiliated law firm in Jacksonville. *Somehow* this firm found out about the 4 votes. And G. J. Rod Sullivan, Jr., representing GOP voters in Nassau and Duval Counties, asks "that the Board revisit its decision to accept these ballots," or else his clients might take the canvassing board to court, for a contest proceeding to disenfranchise these overseas voters.

Lee just shakes his head. Unbelievable, he thinks.

★ ★ ★

At NavObs, the vice president is fixated on the Miami-Dade mob.

He wants every link torn apart, he orders still photos to be reproduced from the news footage, and a montage video about the protest to be cut by media man Bill Knapp. Knapp's video intersperses still photos of the protesters with text stating their GOP jobs. Copies are distributed to the *Wall Street Journal* and others.

Gore spends his days buried in the minutiae of every aspect of the case. Camped out in his library — which has a TV, several comfortable couches and chairs — or, more likely, his dining room, Gore e-mails his staffers, trades briefs, talks to everyone he can. During the campaign, his sphere of advisers outside his family was pretty limited: Daley, Carter Eskew, Shrum, Devine, Lieberman. Now it's grown to dozens. He and Klain talk twice a day. He and Whouley once a day. He's taken matters into his own hands, for better or for worse.

The presence of an old reporter pal, trench coat–wearing Wendell "Sunny" Rawls — a Pulitzer Prize winner — is noted by some of the staffers. The DNC kids have taken to referring to Rawls as "The Equalizer," based on the one-hour CBS 1980s crime drama about, according to the show's promotional materials, "an ex–Company agent who applies his dangerous and often deadly skills to helping people who have nowhere else to turn."

At the DNC, The Equalizer researches the Miami-Dade thugs while also working on the link between the voting-machine manufacturer and companies in Texas. Over Thanksgiving weekend, one senior Gore adviser, after talking to the vice president, sends out this typo-ridden note to DNC researchers:

Subject: note from conversation
Message:

check out company that designed and produced the ballot in Palm beach. Based in Little rock. Two factories that subcontract. One in ARK, one in Texas.

Need to confirm that, read it the week after the election.

Research the Little rock gazette, from Nov. 8 therougth the 12th, present time. Controvsery hit the butterfly ballot. Local paper did something on it.

Find out where the subcontractors are. If one is Texas, zero in on that. Find out who runs it, contributions. Etc. same thing with Little Rock contractor.

While Gore is almost too involved, Bush is about as hands-off as a guy can get while still having a pulse. He splits his time between his ranch in Crawford and the governor's mansion, exercising, quietly preparing his transition team, letting the man he now refers to as "General Baker" run the show completely.

★   ★   ★

"What we're asking this court to do," Bartlit says, "is to hear some of the things that have taken place. And send an order down to these counties, simply saying, 'Will you please take' — not 'please' — 'Will you *take* another look at the ballots under these circumstances, given the changed events that we've seen in the last week?'"

Judge Bubba Smith seems underwhelmed with Bartlit's presentation. Bartlit doesn't know if he's just having a bit of fun with him or what; Beck thinks that Smith is also a bit clueless, he keeps talking about how he doesn't understand how and why the federal government can review Florida election laws before the laws become official. It's a technical point, and a weird thing for Smith to keep harping on, since no one else has a problem with it, but it makes Illinoisian Bartlit seem even more like a fish out of water.

"There's no state or federal law that provides for a ten-day extension for receiving overseas ballots, is there?" Smith asks.

"Yes, sir," Bartlit says. "There's a rule."

"That's not a law, that's a rule," Smith says.

But it is a law, Bartlit thinks to himself. It's a rule that's part of a consent decree, which is binding. True, it's not a law passed by the legislature, it's a judge-made law. But it's still a law. But Bartlit knows better than to argue any more on this point.

There are other issues where Bartlit's not exactly scoring points.

"So we say if it has a postmark or if it has no postmark because of the military exigencies, Your Honor, if it doesn't have a postmark, but it's signed and dated no later than the date of election, it should be counted," Bartlit says. "That's all we're saying."

"Well, you're saying quite a bit," Smith says.

Another Bartlit anecdote is a disaster. "This is hearsay, but we're receiving e-mails and phone calls from people on carriers in the Gulf saying, 'I sent my ballot in, and I heard that it's not being counted,'" Bartlit says. "So, it's not time of war, but it's not — for those fellows, and those young women — it's not time of peace either."

"Well, we certainly want every proper ballot to be counted," Smith replies. "But we can't resolve this presidential election out of your hearsay suggestions."

Summers and another Bush attorney, George Meros, decide to step in. Bartlit's getting the shit kicked out of him.

In a way, it's hardly his fault. This case was a dog to begin with. The more damning presentations, however, come from the county canvassing boards that Bartlit is taking to task; they argue that they were just following the law, and frankly they seem to know a bit more about it than Bartlit does. Says Ron Labasky, representing Leon and Pasco Counties, "We believe we all have applied the law fairly and directly, and that any ballot that was not counted didn't meet the criteria of either state law or federal law." Says Michael Chesser, representing Okaloosa County, "We think we have done exactly what the law requires us to do. I think my canvassing board went far beyond what they thought perhaps they would be required to do. I can tell the court that my canvassing board has seen no memoranda from anyone."

Chesser makes sure that everyone knows that their disagreement with Bartlit and the Bushies has nothing to do with party label. "By registration and by voting practice, Okaloosa County is highly partisan" for the GOP, he says. "It is a home to Eglin Air Force Base, which is the largest air force base in the world. . . . While it may be possible for some folks in this room to be highly partisan, it is entirely inappropriate, I would submit, either for the court — and I would never suggest that it would be — or for a canvassing board to let partisanism [sic] enter into what they do."

Some of the counties' attorneys even seem offended. "I can tell you unequivocally, with regard to what my client believed the law to be, there was no confusion whatsoever," says Collier County's Wayne Malaney. Adds David Tucker from Escambia County, "We counted those ballots; our canvassing board did count those ballots."

"The court will review what's been presented and enter a written ruling based upon that, but without any proof that any of these canvassing boards have not complied with the law, the court is very hard-pressed to grant any relief," Smith says.

Before the day is over, the Bushies will quickly withdraw the suit altogether. After all, nine of the fourteen counties contact the Bush legal team and tell them that they're going to go along with what they want them to do. The Bushies take their suit directly to the five remaining counties, away from Bubba Smith. To Hillsborough, Okaloosa, Pasco, Orange, and Polk Counties they go, in search of votes. And the trolling goes well. The suit may not have been the strongest case on the law, but it serves its political purpose.

An anti-Gore rally is held in military-heavy Pensacola. Elections supervisors are bombarded with angry, clearly coordinated phone calls and e-mails. In Duval County (Bush 152,098 votes, Gore 107,864), the canvassing board reviews the absentees and gives Bush 20 net votes. In Brevard County (Bush 115,185, Gore 97,318) — home to Cape Kennedy and Patrick Air Force Base — Bush gains 8 net votes. Late ballots are accepted in Santa Rosa (Bush 36,274, Gore 12,802) and Escambia (Bush 73,017, Gore 40,943) Counties — the latter of which gives Bush 36 net votes. The Santa Rosa County canvassing board accepts 2 ballots with postmarks of November 8, the day after the election, and 5 ballots that arrived after November 17. Clay County (Bush 41,736, Gore 14,632) accepts 2 votes that arrived by *fax*.

Eventually, Bush will pick up a net of 176 votes by Thanksgiving weekend — Unger refers to the operation as "Thanksgiving stuffing." And Bartlit will estimate that at the end of it all, the suit shakes out maybe 300 to 400 net votes for Bush.* It goes without saying that no one on the Bush team will admit to knowing anything about the conference call, where the drumming up of illegal post-election ballots was discussed.

---

*Why don't the Bushies feel more heat for their clear and unseemly trolling? I made a New Year's resolution not to continue my grumpy rants on how soft the press was on Bush. But in addition to the general idea that the media, like any profession, consists of a lot of mediocrity, it's also worth observing that the Gorebies brought this on themselves by aggressively going out and trying to disqualify absentee ballots.

★   ★   ★

More immediate good news for the Bushies on Friday, November 24: the
SCOTUS will hear arguments on December 1. Both liberal and conservative legal scholars are shocked; this seemed like the kind of case that the
SCOTUS always stayed away from. Three who are truly stunned are junior
partners of Bartlit Beck, in Tallahassee to work on the case; Shawn Fagan,
who clerked for Rehnquist, Sean Gallagher, who clerked for O'Connor, and
Glen Summers, who clerked for Scalia, all can't believe it. They didn't think
their bosses would consider this case to be in the SCOTUS's jurisdiction.

SCOTUS doesn't buy all of the Bushies' arguments — the justices are
not interested in the equal protection argument, for example. But they are
interested in the 3 U.S.C. 5 deal, and they want to hear more about the
Florida court's new deadline being "inconsistent with the Article II, Section 1,
clause 2 of the Constitution.

Plus: Tribe and Olson get a writing assignment.

> The parties are directed to brief and argue the following question:
>
> What would be the consequences of this Court's finding that the
> decision of the Supreme Court of Florida does not comply with
> 3 U.S.C. Sec. 5?
>
> The briefs of the parties, not to exceed fifty pages, are to be filed
> with the Clerk and served upon opposing counsel on or before
> 4 P.M., Tuesday, November 28, 2000.

Class dismissed until Friday, December 1.

★   ★   ★

To get to Broward County Courtroom 6780 — Judge Lee's turf — you
have to go through security, take an elevator to the third floor, walk down a
long hallway, make your way past another sheriff's deputy, and then take
yet another elevator to the sixth floor.

Republican governors like Frank Keating of Oklahoma, Bill Janklow of
South Dakota, Mark Racicot of Montana, and Christine Todd Whitman of
New Jersey have all done this and now saunter in and out of the room.
Republican representatives Steve Buyer of Indiana and Duncan Hunter of
California also show up to watch the hand recount.

Lee calls them "the pontificators." Gunzburger calls them "the spinmeis-
ters." To them, the GOP officials aren't there to observe the process, they're
there to bad-mouth it. The Republican observers who have been there the
whole time know that the process has been fair and open, Lee thinks. These

bigwigs are simply hypocrites. One time, Michigan governor John Engler walks in, sees a dimple for Bush, and agrees that it's a clear vote for his fellow Republican. Then he goes outside to the press and derides the notion of dimples.

And the Republicans keep coming. Bush staffers like Mehlman, media coordinator Megan Moran, and spokesman Ray Sullivan walk the halls and express concern to the media. "It's clear to anyone who closely observes Broward County that the majority of the canvassing board, particularly Commissioner Gunzburger, is throwing all standards aside to arbitrarily increase the number of votes for Vice President Al Gore," Sullivan says.

Democrats are there, but they are smaller in both stature and number. Representative Nadler of New York, Rep. Alcee Hastings of Florida, and Sen. Barbara Mikulski of Maryland enter the courtroom, then exit. A Gore Recount Committee aide explains that Hastings is here to appeal to black voters, Mikulski to women, and Nadler to Jews. Typical clueless Democrat balkanization.

Inside the courtroom, the board — surrounded by party observers — tries not to pay much attention to the in-and-out of reporters, the media, and the half-dozen or so members of the public.

"That's a Gore vote," says Gunzburger.

"I agree," says Lee. "OK, that's [ballot number] A024, plus one Gore."

I ask Keating why he's here.

"As all of us, we're here to encourage that the process be fair and final," he says. "It will be final, but it can never be fair when you are re-recounting exclusively Democratic counties with almost exclusively Democratic supervisors."

Keating also has harsh words for the process of assessing voter intent by studying the chad.

"They are attempting not just to divine the intent of the voter, but to invent," he says. "Listen to the language in there. They say 'intend to vote Bush,' or 'intend to vote Gore.' How do they know?

"It's one thing to intend to vote, and quite something else to vote," he says, adding that he "saw chad on the table."

Janklow, sipping a Coke and wearing a clearly underused Champion workout suit, expresses astonishment at Florida's county-by-county standards.

"How can you have one standard in Fort Lauderdale and another standard in Miami?" he asks. "And the three different [Broward] officers have three different standards," Keating points out.

This is true. Gunzburger counts every dimple. Lee counts them only if three or four other major races on the ballot also have dimples. Rosenberg counts them only if about half the ballot is dimpled. This does, of course, end up meaning that only ballots with a pattern of dimples are counted as votes. But the problems that could come with Florida's lack of a specific standard have never been so well illustrated.

Outside, the crowd is chanting.

"Na na NA NA, Na na NA NA, Hey, hey, hey, Gore lies!"

A Republican state senator from western Maryland, Alex Mooney, twenty-nine, bellows on his megaphone. "We carried almost the whole darn country except for a few cities!" Mooney yells, apparently unimpressed that Gore actually won the popular vote by more than 500,000 votes. Mooney proceeds through a list of states Bush won — "Who won Alabama?!" "BUSH!" "Who won Mississippi?!" "BUSH!" — before arriving at "And who won Florida?!"

Another "volunteer" (read: Bush campaign staffer too chickenshit, or embarrassed, to admit who he is) distributes dozens of free T-shirts that read "GOREY Mess." "I'm just a volunteer," he says when I ask him who he is and who paid for the shirts. "I just bring 'em."

The black hecklers from "Freedom Fighters International," who shouted down Rev. Jesse Jackson a week and a half ago, suddenly show. Their leader, Michael Symonett, denies that they have been paid to shout down Democrats. Symonett says that he's rich, owns his own Jaguar, and no one could pay him to be there if he tried.

Inside, a controversy erupts when the Broward County public-information officer mistakenly refers to a batch of absentee ballots that haven't been counted yet. These are actually ballots that have already been counted, lumped together since absentee ballots aren't segregated by precinct. The plan was to recount all of them at the end. But the public information officer makes it sound far more mysterious, and rumors swirl throughout the courthouse and on conservative media outlets that Broward just "found" 500 new votes from Israel.

Rosenberg makes a motion to allow GOP representatives to argue that the absentee ballots should not be reexamined. The motion dies for lack of a second. Scherer and Governor Racicot object. Lee is already annoyed with Racicot, having seen him on TV bad-mouthing Lee by name as inventing votes for Gore. "I've been on the canvassing board several years," Lee tells Racicot. "I've had so many speeches from so many of you folks that I don't care to hear any more, with all due respect."

Scherer erupts.

Lee and Gunzburger are totally confused by Scherer's behavior, have been as the week has progressed and Scherer's gotten increasingly angry. Republicans like Shari McCartney and Ed Pozzuoli have been vociferous advocates for the Republican side, but they've remained human. Scherer, on the other hand, with whom Gunzburger worked closely, has been losing it, they think. Today he outdoes himself.

"Your attempt, constant attempt to stifle us, the Republicans, from giving you our side and to give you reasoned analysis is overwhelming and is astounding, as you are trolling for votes here," Scherer fumes. "It is obvious that you know you can't get this election any other way, so what are we going to do? Recount all of these votes again?! And I understand you're going to be bringing precincts in that we didn't know anything about in a few minutes. Precincts that you didn't tell us about. Precincts that you did not discuss on this record in public that you had left out.

"You've told these lawyers to go bring you more votes, and I assume we're going to keep bringing them to you until such time as you've got a thousand votes. I think that's what you're looking for!"

Lee can barely contain his anger. It is unimaginable that Scherer will ever again appear in Lee's courtroom to argue a case.

"All right, Mr. Scherer, you're out of line," he says. "OK, and we'll go ahead and recess. I'll ask the deputies to clear the courtroom, and Mr. Scherer is not welcome back in this room. He can watch the proceedings from outside. OK, thank you. We're in recess."

As the deputy approaches him and steers him toward the door, Scherer holds his wrists out, as if he's about to be handcuffed.

"That's not necessary," she says, continuing to guide him out.

"Unless you're going to arrest me," Scherer warns, "don't touch me, ma'am."

★ ★ ★

Scherer's anger isn't show. He is genuinely outraged.

Republicans have been watching this board very carefully, and there have been comments — most notably by Gunzburger — that indicate to them that there's clear Democratic bias afoot.

In precinct 14-J, Lee announces that there's only one disputed ballot in the pack.

"No reasonable certainty on that ballot," Rosenberg says.

"I believe I can see light on three sides, and it's a clear vote for Gore," Gunzburger says.

"I agree with Judge Rosenberg," Lee says.

To many GOP observers, Gunzburger's acceptance of any dimple —
even ones she has to squint to see — says it all.

★　★　★

After the shortest Thanksgiving weekend of his life, Boies flies to Palm
Beach County, where he's presenting witnesses before the canvassing
board, who, he hopes, will help push Burton into loosening his standards.

There's retired Cal Berkeley mechanical engineering professor William
Rouverol, eighty-three, who helped design the Votomatic. "No machine
can be perfect," he says. "Dimpled or pregnant chads, if the only discernible
mark for a given race in a given column, should qualify as a vote."

There's Yale statistician Nicolas Hengartner, who testified the week
before in Miami-Dade. The Democrats needed someone to testify about
what might exist in the undervotes, and after DNC staffer Jason Fuhrman
had been rebuffed by two other academics — Johns Hopkins University
economist Christopher Carroll and Yale statistics department chairman
Andrew R. Barron — he found Hengartner.

In his clipped Québecois accent, Hengartner says that Palm Beach has a
higher rate of undervotes than elsewhere in the state, "seven times what I
would obtain with an optical method. I would try to suggest that the reason this happens is because there's a problem with first column."

Burton is cordial but doesn't sound all that interested in this last-ditch
push. "The legislature up in Tallahassee may be more interested in that," he
says to Hengartner.

LePore's reaction is altogether different, because one of the experts testifying today is her former mentor, Jackie Winchester, supervisor of elections from 1973 to 1997.

"They get more wear in that first column because it's the one we use
most in elections," Winchester says. "Because of that, we began not even to
use that first column in municipal elections. We've never seen a pattern like
this with so many not punching in the first row but punching in all the
other rows. It's just very weird to think that people came to the polls and
didn't vote for president."

Winchester had initially been supportive of LePore, defending her on
the butterfly ballot, thinking it was a mistake, but an honest mistake. But
then LePore began to make decisions that Winchester thought were wrong,
ones she saw as favoring the Bush campaign. LePore must have known that
if the canvassing board asked for the opinion from the secretary of state, it
would be binding, Winchester thought. And it was obvious that Harris was
going to say no. LePore let the voters down by doing that.

Then, after the recount began, Winchester thought that LePore and Burton had been too hard-line against counting dimples. The 1990 standard had been adopted before it was clear that there were problems with some of the equipment, Winchester thought.

Of course, Winchester knows LePore quite well, having groomed her for her present job, and she remembers the one criticism she had about LePore: "She needs to delegate some responsibility, so that she will not be overburdened," Winchester once wrote on LePore's annual job performance review. And here it was, just two days before the deadline, and LePore was *still* not delegating. She would do periodic audits of the ballots on her own, instead of letting someone else compile the stats. And every time she did this, the canvassing board would have to take a break.

Then there are Winchester's other main criticisms of her former protégé: she really isn't all that organized, and she tends to panic. Winchester remembers the written instructions she'd once put together for how to conduct a manual recount in an expeditious and efficient manner — which is not, Winchester thinks, the way LePore's done it. The undervotes and overvotes are supposed to be separated from the rest of the ballots immediately. You're not supposed to have a situation where anybody could object to everything, which the Republicans immediately saw as a way to wreak havoc on the process.

All of these things are helping to hand the election to George Bush, Winchester, a Democrat, thinks. Having made a mess of the butterfly ballot, it seemed to Winchester that LePore should have bent over backward to be fair to those voters who got screwed by counting everything.

After all, Winchester has family members who were confused by the butterfly ballot. Her eighteen-year-old granddaughter, an honors student, who cast her first presidential vote. And her daughter-in-law, an attorney.

"LePore never apologized to them," Winchester will later say. "When I think of all the elderly Jewish voters so thrilled to vote for a Jewish candidate on a national ticket, voters who seemed genuinely anguished to have learned that they may have inadvertently voted for Buchanan. She has shown callous indifference to voters. Sure, she seems nice when you talk to her, but I don't think it's nice to treat people like that. These people are suffering just as much as Theresa is."

In the coming days, after the canvassing board refuses to allow a more lenient standard, Winchester will unleash her wrath upon LePore in a series of local interviews with the media. And LePore will sit there, inside

the OEC, amazed and confused and stunned by the fact that her mentor
has turned against her with such anger.

★   ★   ★

In Tallahassee, meanwhile, Democratic lawyers are preparing to contest the
election, which is still scheduled to be certified Sunday at 5 P.M. They plan
on challenging the results from four counties, suing their canvassing
boards for four different reasons. Two of the counties are no surprise:
Miami-Dade, where the canvassing board never finished its hand recount;
and Palm Beach, where Gore attorneys still think the canvassing board has
been too stringent on its chad requirements.

But there are two others that they're thinking of including, kind of out
of nowhere.

At first blush, when junior Gore attorney Jeremy Bash tells me about
Nassau County, it sounds pretty promising. Nassau County, which is
largely Republican, has decided to report its original election returns —
rather than its recount tally — to the secretary of state Sunday, thus strip-
ping Gore of 51 votes. The law says you have to take the recount number,
Bash says, case closed.

But after I phone up one of the canvassing board members, it's clear to
me that it's not that simple. Nassau County commissioner Marianne Marshall tells me that just before 9 A.M. on Friday, November 24, she — as a
temporary member of the canvassing board — was one in a 3 to 0 vote to
use the original Election Day numbers. The vote came upon the recommendation of Supervisor of Elections Shirley King, a Democrat, who "felt
that they [the original Election Night numbers] were more accurate" than
the mandated recount numbers, according to Marshall. For whatever reason, during the Nassau recount, 218 votes weren't pulled out of the box
they were in. Forgetting to count them added a net gain of 51 votes to
Gore's total. But upon review, King realized what had happened and
decided that those 218 voters shouldn't be disenfranchised.

"If she said that that's the way she wanted to go, then I support it," Marshall says. "Shirley King has been the supervisor of elections for Nassau
County for twenty-eight years. She has always been very honest and served
with integrity, and I respect her immensely," Marshall said. Joining King
and Marshall in the vote was Judge Bob Williams, also a Democrat.

This one is clearly going nowhere.

The other county the Dems are thinking of including in their contest?
None other than Seminole County.

14

"This has to be the most important thing."

Andrew Jackson was the first American president propelled to power by a victory in the Seminole War; Bush needs to be the second.

Back then, of course, it was a defeat of the Seminole Indians, slaughtered by ol' Hickory and his troops in 1817. Jackson became a national hero, first governor of Florida, and President of the United States, elected in 1828.

This Seminole County case is similar only in its guerilla tactics. And it all revolves around a guerilla GOP warrior by the name of Michael Leach.

Leach is from Pensacola and is military through and through. His grandfather was on the U.S.S. *Independence* during World War II; his dad was in the navy during Vietnam; Leach went right into the air force after graduating high school in 1989. After his discharge, he served as a part-time deputy sheriff in Jefferson County while serving in the air force reserves.

In 1996, Leach enrolled at FSU, where, ironically, he majored in criminology with a minor in political science. When he graduated in April, he got a job with the state Republican Party as one of the eleven regional directors for the Bush-Cheney campaign, serving eight northern counties. His office in the Bush Building is resplendent with Nixon memorabilia.

In October, state political director Todd Schnick came to Leach with a problem. The absentee-ballot applications that the state GOP sent out lacked a space for voters to include their voter ID numbers; apparently the vendor who printed them up just messed up. Most counties were accepting them anyway, filling in the numbers themselves. But Sandra Goard, the elections supervisor in Seminole County, has told Schnick that she has a pile of 2,200 or so of these applications in her office that she doesn't have the time or the inclination to correct. Schnick was welcome to send someone to do the job, but the applications couldn't be removed from her office.

It was tedious work. Fifteen days, fourteen to fifteen hours a day. A couple other regional directors helped out a bit, but generally it was just Leach sitting there in Goard's office, using his laptop and VictorySuite computer program, which had the name and information of every registered voter.

Goard wasn't always this accommodating. Not to a Democrat, at any rate.

In March, Dean Ray, forty, who operates his own kitchen appliances sales-and-service shop in Sanford, Florida, submitted 831 signatures to Goard as part of the 1,862 he needed to secure his name on the ballot to run for county commissioner. Goard accepted 644 of them — while rejecting almost 200 of them for technicalities. Ray requested that she return to him the rejected ones so he could fix them; Goard refused. "They were turned into the office, and at that point they became public record," Goard explains to me.

Goard either became nicer between March and October or she has different levels of accommodation within her psyche depending on party affiliation. Leach camped out in her office for fifteen days. He made the fixes, putting the appropriate voter ID number on each absentee-ballot application — even if VictorySuite listed the voter as a Democrat, which happened in maybe fifty or sixty instances.

On November 17, Leach was checking things out in Orange County, just south of Seminole, when he got a call on his cell phone. He had been named in the lawsuit seeking to throw out all 15,000 absentee ballots in Seminole County, because, the suit alleged, the absentee-ballot applications had been improperly tampered with. By Leach.

★   ★   ★

On Saturday, November 25, while the Gore legal team considers disenfranchising 15,000 Seminole County voters — not one of whom is alleged to have done anything wrong — their political arm is holding a town meeting at the Palm Beach Airport Hilton for "disenfranchised" Palm Beach voters.

After Eleanor Holmes Norton, the Democratic delegate from Washington, D.C., compares the disenfranchisement of Palm Beachers to that of Washingtonians who pay taxes but have no representation in the House and Senate, one after another Palm Beach voter grabs the mike to tell her a tale of woe.

Democratic operatives acknowledge that there's no hope for a revote (though Berger still wants to include the butterfly ballot case in the contest trial), but they want to "put a human face" on what happened in Palm Beach County, they tell me. Only a couple of TV cameras come by, though, so how many people see — much less care about — this human face remains up for debate.

A mile or so west on Southern Boulevard, at the Emergency Operations Center, LePore and her chums on the Palm Beach canvassing board — Burton and Roberts — are tearing through the 8,000 or so disputed ballots they have left to rule on.

The county's director of public affairs, Denise Cote, walks a few reporters through the task at hand. There were anywhere from 14,000 to 15,000 disputed ballots. Over the course of the original recount, somewhere around 4,000 of these were counted. The board got through 2,000 on Friday.

Boy, that Thanksgiving break they took doesn't seem so smart right now. How on earth will they be able to get through 8,000 more by Sunday at 4:59 P.M.? I ask.

"They're committed to finishing the process," Cote says. "They're going to quicken the pace. They indicated to me that they would work through the night if need be." Anyway, she points out "it's not going to be over" on Sunday, since SCOTUS will hear arguments over a Bush petition on Friday, there will be an appeal to the ruling against a revote in Palm Beach County, "and a potpourri of lawsuits going on here."

I ask how LePore's, Roberts's, and Burton's moods are, slammed as they've been by the Republicans for even conducting the count, and by the Democrats for being too discriminating in their chad-love.

"They seem to be quite jovial," Cote says. "They work well together."

Burton rolls up a piece of trash and throws it at the trash can, hoops-style. He misses.

"You almost hit it!" Roberts says.

What of the Republicans who are quoting LePore's chad ruling from 1990, when she was deputy elections supervisor and only accepted chad that had broken off from the ballot on at least two corners?

"The policy is more extensive than that," Cote says. Rather, she says, it's up to the discretion of the canvassing board.

"Undervote," Burton says. Roberts squints and holds the ballot up to the light, then places it down on the table.

"Undervote," he says again.

A couple different times, Burton becomes amused at the ballots themselves. He holds one up for the cameras: "It's punched out, and it says 'This one,'" he says. At another point, on another ballot, the holes are unusually large. "This is somebody who wanted their vote to count. It looks like they used a shotgun," Burton says. "I mean, talk about removing a chad."

Shortly before 10 P.M. on Saturday night, there's a dispute between Burton and the GOP observers over a Gore ballot. When absentee ballots are covered with anything — lipstick, say, or maybe ketchup — they are often unable to be processed through the tabulation machine. So election workers will take a pink ballot — its "mate" — and punch the corresponding holes in it, running it through the machine and attaching it to the original ballot. But at some point a ballot and its mate have been separated, and now there's a problem. Members of the canvassing board want to count a pink Gore "mate" as a vote, expecting to find its original ballot in one of the 186 precincts they have left to go through. Wallace and John Bolton object and want the board to track down the original ballot before counting the mate as a vote.

While Burton and the Republican have at it, Roberts excuses herself and walks over to a few reporters. "We'll finish by five," she insists. "Because we understand that's how long Katherine Harris is keeping her office open."

She shouts to the table that she wants to get back to counting.

Boston Boy Newman, meanwhile, is pleasantly surprised. Hauling Burton's ass before LaBarga and presenting Friday's panel of experts seem to have had an effect on the standard he's applying. Before the panel's presentation on Friday morning, by Newman's calculations Gore was down about 10 votes, with 40 percent of the undervotes counted. But now they're picking up some. It's still not the right standard, he thinks, but it's better.

"Five," LePore says, meaning a Gore vote.

"Five," says Burton.

"Five," says LePore.

"Five," says Burton. They're tearing through the ballots now, a GOP observer sitting between the two of them watching every ballot.

"Five," LePore says.

"Over, five and six," Burton says, meaning a vote for both Gore and Buchanan, which won't count.

"Five," LePore says.

"Five," Burton says.

"Three," says LePore, meaning a Bush vote.

They finish the batch. Six 3's. Burton counts the 5's for Gore. Bolton thinks that Burton messed up the count, so they ask Roberts to count them. She gets annoyed. "Come on, guys," she snaps. "I want to get through this."

"Nobody's trying to obstruct the process," says Wallace.

"Ninety number fives" is the final count for Gore in this batch.

But that doesn't mean 90 new votes for Gore — it just means 90 Gore votes that GOP observers categorized as questionable were now officially, firmly Gore.

It might have been a net gain of 1 or 2 for Gore, or 1 or 2 for Bush, or nothing at all.

★   ★   ★

General Baker is calling in the troops. The Gorebies are going to contest this election, and General Baker's friend's son needs the best trial lawyers around.

There's mistrust of Fred Bartlit, especially by Ginsberg, Terwilliger, and the political people. Quietly they snicker at him, his bluster, the way Judge Bubba Smith slapped him, how badly the overseas military-absentee-ballot case went, even though, in reality, there was very little case there to begin with. There are mean and cruel comments — the "Ted Baxter* of the legal profession," one of the Bush lieutenants calls him.

Bartlit, for his part, doesn't care what these political lawyers think. He's no kid, and he doesn't have to genuflect before any of these guys.

There are doubts about Phil Beck, too. No one knows him, no one trusts him, no one has any idea what to think. All they know is what they saw in Bartlit and that Beck and Bartlit are a team. Ginsberg and Terwilliger want some other trial lawyers brought in. Some people they can trust. The other side has Boies! They need some more firepower!

Can't you bring some folks in from Baker Botts? General Baker is asked.

On November 25, Irv Terrell's at his beach house in Galveston with friends, when he checks his office voice mail. There are a couple messages from Kirk Van Tine, a fellow Baker Botts partner. "Look, Baker really needs to talk to you," Van Tine says when Terrell calls him back. "Call him back; you gotta come to Tallahassee."

---

*"Ted Baxter" being the blowhard idiot news anchor played by Ted Knight on *The Mary Tyler Moore Show* in the 1970s. It's a ridiculous insult; though he is somewhat blustery, Bartlit is regarded not only as one of the more successful trial attorneys in American history but as something of a visionary in that regard.

He calls him back. Baker is somber. The legal situation has become paramount, he says. They have to win at court. "You could really make a difference for us, Irv," Baker says. "I know you're busy, but this has to be the most important thing, Irv."

Terrell is torn. Baker's an icon around the office, around Houston, around Texas, and he wants to help him. And though Terrell leans left on some things, he grew up with George W., and voted for him happily — if with some concern about what his childhood friend might do to *Roe v. Wade*.

That said, Terrell is worried about some other matters. He's overworked already, for one. "How will I ever survive physically doing all this stuff?" he wonders. He's also concerned about joining another high-profile suit; he didn't like the ugly stuff he saw in his colleagues and even occasionally in himself during the *Pennzoil v. Texaco* case. If he joins up, he wants to conduct himself appropriately.

"I'll let you know tomorrow," Terrell says.

There's a long pause. Baker's silence conveys loads.

"I'm calling Daryl, too," Baker says, referring to Daryl Bristow, a fellow Baker Bottsian and one of Terrell's close friends.

Another pause.

"Irv, you *do* need to come," Baker says.

A couple hours later, Terrell calls back. "OK, I'll be there tomorrow morning," he says.

Bristow's in Hattiesburg, Mississippi, for his wife, Janet's, thirtieth high school reunion, and the Tallahassee fight is the farthest thing from his mind. Baker had called him on November 8 to join the team, and Bristow — a craggy, white-haired Texan — was excited to be part of the legal case of the century (especially considering how young the century is!). So he'd returned the call and left a message, and that was the end of that. Bristow just figured that Baker had eventually just decided against using him.

Janet knows how disappointed her husband was, so when she calls home to check the phone messages back in Houston, she's skeptical of what she hears. "I swear somebody's playing a joke on you," she tells him, "but there's a message from Jim Baker, and it sure sounds authentic!"

Bristow plays the message. "Daryl, this is Jim Baker. I'm in Tallahassee and would like to talk to you," the recording says.

Nope, that's him.

"Secretary Baker, to use an old phrase, I thought you'd never call!" Bristow says.

"What do you mean?" Baker asks. "I *did* call. I was told that you were too busy."

★　★　★

The reverence for General Baker is truly a remarkable thing to behold.

To a man, Team Bush praises him for his smarts, his cool, his legal mind, his political skills. When Bartlit and Beck came on board, they expected that Baker would be something of a figurehead. They're surprised. To Bartlit, he's "the CEO of the enterprise." To Beck, Baker's "the man," making the key decisions, directing traffic, there seven days a week. Ginsberg knows how revered Baker is as a pol, but he's stunned by his legal skills. To Ginsberg, there isn't a legal document that Baker peruses that, after reviewing, he doesn't make a suggestion to or observation of that isn't important.

On the other side of the border, Daley and Christopher have long since gone. But Ron Klain's the one who has earned a degree of awe. He sleeps maybe two hours a night. His dedication is absolute. He seldom loses his temper, and when he does, the anger is at circumstances, never at a colleague or an underling's screw-up, and it's aimed at a door or a desk, never anywhere else. Klain — far more so than any of the advisers and consultants who told Gore what to do and who to be during the campaign — is utterly devoted to the cause.

Whatever happens, to their respective teams, both Baker and Klain have earned respect in a way that the mere word could never convey. But Klain is no Jim Baker, even combined with the spiritual guidance of Whouley in Palm Beach. Whouley himself frets about this. They don't have a Jim Baker, they don't have a warrior, an Attila the Hun. They have Christopher, a diplomat, and Daley, who's back in D.C. But, Whouley wonders, when you get down to it, who do the Democrats *have,* anyway? Bob Rubin? Maybe the Democrats just don't have anyone like Baker.

★　★　★

Broward County completes its work late Saturday — 567 new net Gore votes.

Lee says that he feels "confident, confident that there were many more votes that should have been counted," that never would have been, had they not devoted the last ten days to the insanity. One ballot, for instance, on which was written: "I'm voting for George Bush." "We were able to count it, where a computer couldn't," Lee says.

A reporter asks Lee if he thinks that their political views may have played a role in how they looked at ballots. Lee tries to give an honest answer. It is not one that Republicans find reassuring. "Well, I don't know that it was overt political bias," Lee says, "but I think it's just natural that, y'know, your own personal feelings and beliefs are going from time to time to shape how you perceive something." Scherer and other Republicans do a double-take. Did he *really* just say that?!

★   ★   ★

D day, Sunday, November 26, finally arrives.

Now the world turns its weary eyes north to Palm Beach County, where it's pretty clear that the canvassing board hasn't a snowball's chance in Hell of finishing up before 5 P.M. tonight. Was it their Thanksgiving break? Was it the day before that, when the Democrats hauled Burton into LaBarga's court? Was it the Republicans' effective dragging out of the process? Katherine Harris? Jeb? God?

It's been a long day for everyone, especially the members of the canvassing board. LePore is wearing the same white sweater that she had on Saturday. Carol Roberts is dressed in the same multicolored ensemble she was sporting yesterday as well. Burton apparently brought a change of clothes, because he has switched from the aqua golf shirt he once wore into a yellow oxford with a tie. The three of them have been here recounting the last batch of approximately 14,500 "questionable" ballots for more than thirty-one hours, but the question of the moment is: Will it be enough?

★   ★   ★

Sunday morning, Terrell and Bristow hop on the corporate jet of one of the big Baker Botts clients, Reliant Energy, and land in Tallahassee by noon. They meet with Van Tine, who briefs them on all the lawsuits out there, in particular the contest.

When Baker gets off a call, Terrell and he sit down and catch up.

"Well, I'm here," Terrell says. "Just trying to get my lay of the land."

"Well, look," Baker says, "you need to talk to Ben Ginsberg."

"Fine," Terrell says. "Who's he?"

Baker explains that Ginsberg, immediately below him in the hierarchy, is ultimately in charge of the Florida litigation, while Van Tine is making the trains run on time in terms of getting all the papers filed.

Soon Terrell and Bristow meet with Ginsberg, who is clearly concerned about the contest the Gore lawyers are about to file. Ginsberg explains the concern about Bartlit — the Bubba Smith case didn't go so well, the guy doesn't take direction very well, and no one has any idea who this Beck guy is.

But Terrell's the wrong guy to bring this up with. "I recommended Fred to Baker in the beginning," he says. "There's not going to be a problem with Fred." Terrell wants to make sure that everyone gets along, that there are no egos or turf wars or any of the hideous side of man that he saw in the *Pennzoil* case. This, he believes, is one of his primary functions. "I want to make the teams work," Terrell tells Ginsberg.

Ginsberg smiles.

Bartlit and Beck have asked for a separate place to work, so they're not even in the Bush Building; they've been given some office space at Gray, Harris & Robinson. Go over there and make sure everything's going OK, Terrell is told.

Terrell and Bristow arrive at Gray, Harris & Robinson and immediately ask for Bartlit, who welcomes them warmly. Terrell tells Bartlit that he was the one who recommended him. Beck remains pretty quiet, as if he's trying to figure out who these two Texans are, what their role is going to be.

They don't know what will be in the Gore contest, Bartlit and Beck explain, but they're focusing on Miami and Palm Beach, figuring those are safe bets. They're trying to get their hands around what happened there; they haven't yet met with any experts, but they've been talking to and meeting with various GOP observers from those counties, and they've accrued some raw facts, which they're organizing and discussing.

Bartlit gives Terrell and Bristow a brief presentation on the timelines in the two counties. He seems to really know what happened in Palm Beach; his grasp on Miami-Dade seems less firm.

"Tell me about the dimples," Terrell says to Beck.

Beck launches into the theory he's been working on about dimples, about the inherent bogusness of the Gore assault, that the only way Gore could win is if they convinced canvassing boards in Democratic counties to count marks as votes.

Terrell is floored. For someone who didn't have any idea what a "contest" was when Bartlit called him on Thanksgiving to bring him down to Florida, Beck knows his shit. The all-nighters he's been pulling since he arrived on Friday are paying off.

Forget Ginsberg's warning: Terrell and Bristow like what they see. Bartlit's a hardass, but he seems to be a good guy, just like Terrell remembers him. And Beck's one sharp, fucking cookie.

So Terrell goes back to Baker and Ginsberg with nothing but enthusiasm. "This is going to be great," he says. "This is going to be a real trial! I feel good about it."

But Baker and Ginsberg remain worried. Boies took down *Microsoft,* for Godsakes.

"I can beat Boies," Terrell says. He did so before in *Pennzoil.* "I can. I can beat David. You guys need to understand that he's mortal. He's like lightning in a bottle, and it's very important to keep him in the bottle."

Okay, Baker and Ginsberg say. How are the responsibilities being divided over there? "Who's going to do what?" he's asked.

"We don't know yet," Terrell says. "But have you met Phil Beck?"

★   ★   ★

From: georgewbush.com
Sent: Sunday, November 26, 2000 1:03 PM
Subject: Sunday surrogates In Palm Beach:

Frist
Gilmore
Hunter
Asa Hutchinson
Lugar (coming to Tallahassee in afternoon)
Kingston
Pataki
Portman
Racicot (coming to Tallahassee in afternoon)

Democrats in Palm Beach
Markey, Deutsch, Sharpton, Rep. Sherrod Brown (former OH Sec. of State)

In Florida:
Senator Dole
Lynn Martin

★   ★   ★

In West Palm Beach at 1 P.M., the raison d'être of Burton's fancy shirt and tie is made clearer when he strides before the assemblage of cameras and announces that the canvassing board is faxing Harris a request for a deadline extension from 5 P.M. Sunday to 9 A.M. Monday. After all, Burton's letter states, the task of reviewing each of the ballots has "creat(ed) an extraordinary and unprecedented challenge for the canvassing board."

"We know you are interested in counting all votes as accurately as possible," Burton's letter reads, noting that he and his colleagues are "committed to reviewing each and every one of these 'questionable' ballots as quickly as humanly possible, including working through this evening.

"We do not believe this extension would prejudice the State in any way, in light of the Florida Supreme Court's opinion," Burton continues, referring to the court's judgment that the Monday-morning deadline could stand if Harris didn't want to open her office on Sunday.

After sending the letter asking for the extension, at about 4 P.M., Burton calls Clay Roberts to plead his case. "We're getting ready to send you a letter right now," Roberts tells him. "What's it say?" Burton asks. "We're not giving you an extension," Roberts says.

Burton asks for mercy. "You know, we're about two hours away from this, maybe an hour away," Burton says. "People have been busting their asses here for twenty hours a day. Please. Just two more hours."

"Hold on," Roberts says. Burton hears him talking to someone in the background. Roberts eventually gets back on the line. "We'll let you know," he says.

Five or ten minutes later, the fax comes from Harris's office: NO SALE.

According to the rejection letter, Harris claims she doesn't have the legal discretion to allow such an extension "in accordance with the explicit terms of the decision of the Florida Supreme Court." So, at 4:30 P.M., after two weeks of twenty-hour days, Burton announces that the hand recount will not be completed by the 5 P.M. deadline. The board only has 800 to 1,000 ballots left to hand-recount — out of a total of 461,988 — but he says that such a task will take another two hours or so. Since they only have half an hour left, he calls it quits.

"So the secretary of state has decided to shut us down with approximately two hours and a half left to go," Burton says, a bitter edge to his voice. "Unfortunately, at this time we have no other choice but to shut down. The supervisor of elections" — LePore — "has to hurriedly gather all the paperwork and prepare all the returns we have. We certainly don't want to get any in at 5:01."

Scarcely five minutes later, Burton comes back into the hearing room, here at the Palm Beach Emergency Operations Center, and in a symbol of the mercurial nature of this ever-evolving second-by-second story, says that they'll continue with the last few hours of work after the deadline passes.

"We are going to send a report to the secretary of state as to the returns that we have," Burton says. "And this board has decided that we are going to remain here and finish the recount. And we are going to send whatever figures we have to the secretary of state, and it will be up to her whether or not she decides to accept those."

Tucker Eskew tells them that they should just all pack it in, but Bolton and Wallace decide to stay. Wallace notes the board's hard work, objects to its self-extension of the deadline, and graciously says that his team will remain to observe for the rest of the process.

Before he recommences with the hand recount of the remaining 1,000 or so disputed Palm Beach County ballots — knowing full well that Harris may not accept late updates to the already updated vote tallies — Burton approaches the media to offer us his thoughts.

How many new votes are there? What will the new numbers that they've faxed to Harris — the totals from the first machine recount plus the new ones absent approximately fifty precincts — reveal?

"Maybe a couple hundred votes," he says.

For Gore?

He nods.

Why are they continuing the counting, despite the fact that Harris has made it crystal clear that she won't accept these new numbers?

"Why not?" he says, casually. "We all want to finish the job."

Does he blame the fact that this has taken longer than he thought it might on the GOP lawyers objecting?

"We agree, we disagree, we agree to disagree," he says. "Both sides were extremely cooperative." He says that spending Wednesday in LaBarga's courtroom was time wasted, especially considering the fact that LaBarga ultimately gave the board no guidance on which chad were kosher. "We spent all day in court, when we could've been working," he says.

A reporter asks him a leading question about Harris, trying to get him to slam her.

"Next question," he says.

Was there a moment when he realized that they weren't going to make the deadline? asks a reporter, seeking drama.

No, Burton says. "As the afternoon went on, we realized we weren't going to make it."

Why did he ask Harris for an extension?

"Given what this experience has been, I was hopeful they'd say, 'Fine,'" he says, pointing out how hard they've all worked. He says that his Democratic critics, who say that the board has been using excessively strict dimple standards, are wrong. "You simply can't count every dimple on a ballot," he says. "We didn't count every ding on a ballot card." On the other hand, he adds, "we certainly came across an awful lot of ballots that were not counted by the machine."

Any ramifications from it all, other than who will be president?

"I'm sure every state's going to revisit its election laws," he says.

And then he leaves and goes back to work.

Inside, the three keep counting, under the watchful eyes of high-profile supporters of Gov. George W. Bush, like Republicans Sen. Kay Bailey Hutchison of Texas, Governor Janklow, Gov. Jim Gilmore of Virginia — the latter of whom is being escorted around by Phil Muster, who just a day or so ago was telling me he was just a "volunteer" handing out T-shirts at the protest outside the Broward County courthouse.

Muster doesn't seem to care that he might be recognized, which again raises the question: why do the Bushies refuse to tell the truth about their role here? They're certainly legally allowed to hand out free T-shirts, or to protest peacefully.

Deutsch walks in and sits across the aisle from Hutchison, Janklow, and Gilmore. No pleasantries are exchanged. No friendly acknowledging glances. Rep. Ed Markey also wanders in. Then he wanders out. Soon Rep. Corinne Brown, D-Fla., joins Deutsch.

"Hey hey! Ho ho! Al Gore has got to go!" chant the pro-Bush protesters outside the Emergency Operations Center.

"Thou shalt not steal," reads one sign. "Who let the chads out? Who? Who? Gore Did!" reads another.

A smattering of pro-Gore protesters is here as well. "Bush hates all minorities," reads a sign from their number.

Subtle.

"One-ninety-three-C," Burton says inside.

"Who's got one-ninety-three-C?" Roberts asks.

As I walk from my car to the Emergency Operations Center, I pass a woman who has camped out on the sidewalk, waving a Bush-Cheney sign for the motorists who pass by. I ask her how she's doing.

"Good," she says. "Who are you with?"

"Salon.com," I reply.

"Oh," she says. "You're one of *those*."

★   ★   ★

The Bushies know that their man will be certified the winner of Florida in a couple hours. Now they have to decide whether or not they'll continue to press ahead with their case in the U.S. Supreme Court. They got their certification, Bush is the official winner, why keep fighting? Why take the risk that the SCOTUS will do something wild and unpredictable? Bush's own case is buying Gore time, giving him cover to contest the election results. Why not just pack up and go home? It's a real dilemma.

The arguments on both sides are outlined for Bush in a thirty-minute conference call with Austin. Zoellick and Bush domestic-policy adviser Josh Bolten are worried — what if they lose? Then the Florida legislature will be completely demoralized. But others — Olson, Carvin — are more optimistic. We're right on the law, they say. We're going to win it. The toughest thing is to get the U.S. Supreme Court to accept the case to begin with, so we're over that hurdle. Plus, it's good to have the SCOTUS out there, hovering around. It will keep the Florida Supreme Court on its toes.

Bush considers it the toughest choice he has to make.

"We're going to stick with the appeal, because it's the right thing to do," Bush finally says.

★　★　★

When Harris, Clay Roberts, and Agricultural Commissioner Bob Crawford walk into the cabinet room at the state capitol and step up to officially declare victory for the man all three of them endorsed, the news is watched with angry eyes in Palm Beach County.

"I think it's over," says Crawford. "It should be over."

Then he botches the famous Yogi Berra quote "It's not over 'til it's over" (Yogi said "ain't") but makes a cogent point. "Both sides have enough legal talent to keep this tied up through Christmas," he says. "But the one thing the lawyers can't do for us is to bring this country together."

Of course, one wonders if Crawford would be saying that if he were declaring Gore the winner. One wonders what decision Harris would have made about late returns from Palm Beach County if *Bush* had needed them to win.

No, one doesn't, actually. One knows.

Harris "hereby" declares that "our American democracy has triumphed once again," and gives the certified vote results for Florida: Bush beats Gore by 537 votes — 2,912,790 to 2,912,253.

In Washington, Lieberman is there to immediately rain on the parade, lest anyone think that there's a chance that his side finds this decision final. "How can we teach our children that every vote counts if we are not willing to make a good-faith effort to count every vote?" Lieberman asks. Good question. One he might put to his own lawyers and pols down in Florida who are decidedly not putting forth any serious effort "to count every vote." "Vice President Gore and I have no choice but to contest these actions."

At 9:30 P.M. EST, bookended by American flags, a *somewhat* presidential-looking Bush appears before the cameras and waxes bipartisan. So much of the Bush strategy, dating back to before the primary season, has been about inevitability, about declaring himself the winner. And tonight — despite reports that he's been sulking about his 500,000-person popular-vote loss — Bush is on top of his game. He wants to work with Democrats and Republicans alike, he says, on education, tax reduction, Medicare reform, a prescription-drug benefit for seniors. "I will work to unite our great land," he says. "Now that the votes are counted, it's time for the votes to count." He says that Cheney will set up the transition team in Washington, and former transportation secretary Andy Card will be his chief of staff.

Bush says that he's heard Gore's lawyers are talking about contesting the election. "I respectfully ask him to reconsider," Bush says. "Now that we are certified, we enter a different phase." Protesting votes before the certification is one thing, Bush argues, but "filing a contest to the outcome of the election — that is not the best course for America."

Ginsberg does a conference call with reporters. "It's impossible to overstate the importance of having the certificate," Ginsberg says. "Governor Bush and Secretary Cheney have been declared the winners of this contest," and now the burden is on the Gore team to overturn that — not an easy task.

★   ★   ★

In Berger's Tallahassee office, Klain and Boies are doing the math. They have a conference call with Gore scheduled for Monday morning, 9 A.M., and they need to decide what will be in the contest lawsuit.

Boies is downing Diet Cokes, and Klain is popping M&M's, as they tear through the figures.

How can they make up the 537-vote gap?

When I call Bash to find out what's up, I get a strange comment.

"We won!" he tells me, based on the Gore team's new math.

First off are the 192 votes that Palm Beach County handed in about two hours past the Florida Supreme Court–mandated deadline, though it did get them in before Harris's announcement. Why not count them? the Gore team asks. Shouldn't Harris have used her discretion to count votes?

But when I ask Ginsberg about them, he responds that it's the simple question of a deadline missed. The Palm Beach canvassing board knew what the deadline was and followed through with typical Democrat incompetence. So tough shnoogies.

Then, the Gore folks say, there are the net 157 Gore votes from the partial hand recount of Miami-Dade County that was never completed. Those are 157 votes that the world already knows belong to Gore.

C'mon, says Ginsberg. "The law makes it clear that partial-recount results can't be included in election certification, for any number of reasons. If you were going to accept partial returns, you could just recount the most Democratic precincts in a county, then call off the recount and say, 'OK, we win.' It's just not done," Ginsberg says.

The final tally should also include 51 Gore votes from Nassau County, the Gore team says. "The law says we have to have it," Klain says.

But in Nassau County, Ginsberg counters, "the Election Night votes were counted and reconciled. In the recount, the votes for both candidates were lower. So rather than disenfranchise voters, the board decided to go back to their Election Night statistics."

With those three figures — 192 + 157 + 51 — that's 400 votes right there, the Gore attorney goes on. That means just 137 more to win! And, the Gorebies say, there are more!

But this is nonsense; the Gorebies are talking crazy talk. Do they really think that the Bushies can't counter with votes to chip away of their own? It's precisely this shortsighted, desperate approach to the vote count that has completely lost me. Bush has now won the certified election. The only vote total that could replace tonight's in legitimacy is one that comes with a statewide recount of *all* the undervotes and overvotes, by *all* the canvassing boards in *all* the counties. The Gorebies original plan — to enter the contest phase with as many new votes on the board as possible — is now lost amid a pathetic scramble — here a vote, there a vote, everywhere, a vote vote. The clock is TICK TICK TICKing in their ears, and they can't think of anything but how to get Gore votes on the board. But that means this isn't about "counting the votes" — it's about counting all the Gore votes.

Like the dimples. According to Democratic observers of the Palm Beach hand-recount process — the one that didn't count — there's a net gain of 846 dimple-chadded ballots that belong to Gore. If the 846 dimpled Gore votes counted, Gore would lead Bush by 709 votes, Bash says.

Then there's the rest of the Miami-Dade hand count that the Gore team thinks should have proceeded. After all, the net gain of 157 Gore votes came after only 20 percent of the 400,000 or so ballots were recounted. Since Gore won Miami-Dade 53 percent to 47 percent, that 6 percent edge could provide enough votes for Gore to eke out a win. But to include this 20 percent — largely Democratic precincts — without the other 80 percent is completely unfair. Not to mention, as De Grandy pointed out, a possible voting rights violation.

"The ten thousand ballots that they claim were the subject of an undercount, they were counted," Ginsberg says. "First on Election Night, then in a machine recount, so those ballots have been counted at least twice already."

Okay, that's not quite true either. The Bushies have now taken to referring to undervotes as "no votes," as if there's nothing there at all. By that logic, the ballots *were* counted; it was just that the Floridians in question didn't want to vote for any of the presidential candidates. And further, a hand count or any other sort of recount is a waste of time, because there's nothing to find.

As of Sunday evening, the Gore legal team is leaning against suing Seminole County. "Our legal papers will be about just trying to get the votes counted," Bash says to me. "We don't want to deal with mischief — although clearly this was mischief — but we want to keep the argument clean: Just count the votes." They're still thinking of challenging some of the more dubious military absentee ballots that were allowed by counties that were, at the time, being sued by the Bush campaign. They call these ballots "backwash," before eventually deciding on a nicer name, which the Bushies are using, too: "Thanksgiving stuffing."

By now, I can't really truck either side. Klain and Boies conclude that they'd support a statewide recount, but their energy and their rhetoric is devoted elsewhere — to plucking up Democratic votes wherever they can find them. After all, Gore offered a statewide recount on national television — twice — and Bush refused both times, they say. We've been reminded again and again that Florida law lacks a mechanism for a candidate to legally compel a statewide recount, so the only way to get one is to go to all sixty-seven canvassing boards individually, and ask them, individually, to agree. And the only way to make that happen is if both parties agree — otherwise, there would be sixty-seven separate lawsuits to file.

So what seems to be left for Gore? Sketchy vote plucking that makes the Gorebies seem like desperados, scrambling for a vote here, a vote there, with no strategy focused on counting all 175,000 of the state's undervotes and overvotes.

Is there a Gore vote in that garbage dump at the edge of town? Quick!
Berger! Get over there!

That said, at least the Gorebies support a statewide recount, at least they
acknowledge that there *are* unread votes that need to be examined. The
Bushies stand in the way of votes being counted, an extremely offensive
notion on its face. They demean, they deride, they insinuate, they lie.
They've fought tooth and nail to maintain the status quo, to keep us in
limbo. "Limbo" is a good word for it, if only because it happens also to be
the name of a party game, the object of which is to see how low you can go.

As the country sinks deeper into the quicksand of torts, one man, at
least, emerges outside the Palm Beach Emergency Operations Center to
offer a solution. To reporters and real people alike, an entrepreneur hands
out T-shirts. They say: "Just Keep Bill."

★   ★   ★

From: Bush communications team

Talking Points for Monday, November 27, 2000

- Rather than give the American people the finality that they deserve, Al
  Gore has chosen to take the extraordinary step of contesting the presidential election in Florida, the first in the history of our nation. Gore
  should reconsider, do the right thing and respect the outcome of this
  election.
- Gore says he is contesting this election because every vote should be
  counted. But every vote has been counted, and recounted. And some
  votes have been selectively counted three and four times. As Governor
  Bush said last night, the votes have been counted, now it is time for
  the votes to count.
- Al Gore is not interested in counting every vote, he's simply interested
  in selectively recounting the votes he thinks will help him overturn
  the results of this election.
- Gore wrongly claims that 10,000 ballots weren't counted in Miami-
  Dade County. These ballots were counted and recounted, as required
  under Florida law. The voters who cast those ballots did not cast votes
  for President, so now Gore is seeking permission to have those
  selected ballots "interpreted."
- Thousands of these "undervote" ballots exist in other counties in
  Florida and in other jurisdictions around the nation. Yet Gore is not

interested in those ballots, he's only interested in "interpreting" the selective ballots that he thinks can overturn this election.

- If Gore truly believes that every vote must be counted, then he shouldn't be actively pursuing cases to have legitimate votes thrown out. In Nassau County, Gore is trying to get 218 valid ballots thrown out. In Seminole County, Democrats* have filed a lawsuit to have thousands of valid absentee ballots thrown out. . . .
- Opening more ballots up for more interpretation by Democratic canvassing boards would simply open up this process to more human error and mischief. . . .
- Every campaign must have a conclusion. After the votes in Florida were counted, Governor Bush was declared the winner. After they were recounted, Governor Bush was declared the winner. And after some Democratic counties performed manual recounts, Governor Bush was again declared the winner.
- Elections should be decided in voting booths, not in courtrooms. It is time for the lawyers to go home. The people of Florida have voted, and deserve to have some finality.

Thing is, there are Gore lieutenants who — if not agreeing in full to the more-than-a-little disingenuous and hypocritical Bush talking points — concur with at least one cutting observation: Whatever happened to "count every vote"?!

Tonight, Gore lieutenants are disappointed that the contest isn't statewide, as they'd been led to believe it would be. Some of the middle-tier politicos who had told ground soldiers like Jack Young to focus on the four Democratic counties did so with the understanding that sooner or later all 175,000 ballots as yet unrecorded would be checked by hand. The decision came down from above, however, by those whom the lieutenants would refer to during the campaign as "The Matrix," in reference to the superb 1999 sci-fi thriller about an evil artificial-intelligence computer power that controls the world autocratically. And in this case, The Matrix — Klain, Whouley, Shrum, Eskew, Daley, Christopher, Lieberman, and Gore — is disillusioning some of its deputies who actually thought there was meaning behind the empty rhetoric.

* Note use of word "Democrats," not "Gore," in reference to Seminole.

15

"Like getting nibbled to death by a duck."

Al Gore thought that this would be over by now.

"The Friday after Thanksgiving at midnight we all turn into pumpkins," Gore said to a friend on the night of Wednesday, November 15 — after he'd made his first, half-hearted offer to abide by a state recount if Bush wanted one.

But that was centuries ago, it now seems, and throughout Thanksgiving weekend it became clear to all involved that Gore was going to go through with the contest. The morning of Monday, November 27, the last and final pre-contest conference call finally comes.

Gore, Lieberman, Daley, and others are in D.C., Christopher is in L.A, the legal team of Boies Klain is in Tallahassee.

What to contest? A few things are no-brainers: the Miami-Dade under-votes, the Palm Beach late returns, and 846 dimpled net Gore votes, according to the Boston Boys, that the Palm Beach canvassing board deemed to not be votes. There are the 51 net Gore votes from Nassau County that Boies is hyperbolically betting his law license on.

Berger's still all over the butterfly ballot. Donnie Fowler and Whouley's shop in Palm Beach have ten thousand affidavits on hand. There's no question that voters were confused. And if they can't get a revote, there are alternative solutions, Berger says. Allocating some of Buchanan's votes for Gore, for instance. The law can create a remedy. And being that the Gorebies think of themselves as within 100 votes, any remedy could be significant.

But Gore, Klain, and Boies swat the butterfly ballot case. Bob Bauer's firmly convinced that the case has no merit; Coffey's wishy-washy on it. And ultimately, they decide, there's no time to try it.

Klain is more intrigued by the possibility of including the Seminole County case, and a similar lawsuit in Martin County, in the contest. Not because he thinks they're winners — actually, of all the lawyers, Klain is one of the most skeptical of the legal merits of *both* cases. No, Klain wants to include Seminole and Martin for strategic reasons. He explains: Republicans have the luxury of being able to make one set of arguments in the Seminole and Martin cases — the intent of the voter is ultimate, you can't throw out ballots because of hypertechnical adherence to the law — while they're simultaneously making the opposite argument on the Miami-Dade and Palm Beach ballots. Klain wants to set up a situation where the Gore team would say — publicly and to a court — "Look, there are two ways to resolve this dispute. We can either say 'count all the votes,' in which case we'll lose Seminole and Martin but we should get our votes counted in these two southeastern counties. *Or* we should have really technical and rigid Florida compliance rules, in which case maybe we don't get our votes counted in the southeastern counties but the ballots should be tossed from Seminole and Martin." The Republicans have been going on and on about different standards. Well, two can play that game, Klain argues.

Boies isn't sure what he thinks about this. Since Klain first mentioned it, he's been exploring whether or not he could make an understandable argument on the matter. But in the past few days, he's been trying this spiel out on people, and he's become convinced that nobody understands it as anything other than a bartering chip, which doesn't play very well.

And Christopher doesn't think including Seminole and Martin is a good call. "For the sake of your own political viability, we have to set a very high standard here," he says to Gore. "We can't have any tactical moves, there can't be any long shots. We have to have the highest standards when it comes to the merits of the cases."

Gore finally rules.

"Chris, I agree with your comments — with one exception," he says. "I don't care about my political viability. Joe's political viability will take care of itself. But my political viability should be the least consideration here. I have much greater competing obligations. I have an obligation to the Democratic Party. And I have an obligation to the fifty million Americans who voted for me and Joe. And I have the highest obligation to the country and to the Constitution.

"I cannot imagine that there will ever be a revote in Palm Beach," Gore says. "And I can't imagine disenfranchising the people in Seminole and Martin Counties."

A number of the lawyers are quite taken aback. This isn't the Al Gore they've known — the cold, calculating, Faustian, self-centered s.o.b. who's been running for president since 1993. They know it sounds hokey, they know that when they tell friends — especially journalist friends — about it, it sounds like horseshit. But, they think, Al Gore's become a different guy as this whole thing has progressed. There's something markedly different in the way Gore has been treating people, they think, in the way he thanks them, in the way he seems, well, nice.

And yes, it's true, he didn't particularly seem all that nice before.

Klain has sure noticed it, talking to him two or three times a day, the most he's talked to Gore since he was his chief of staff. And Klain is frankly a little stunned to find Gore incredibly gracious, even sweet. He was grateful for everyone's hard work, and he expressed it constantly. He would ask Klain all the time — is there anyone on the team whom he should call and thank? He would call their spouses. He called one lawyer's mom who was on her deathbed. It was not a side of Gore people had seen in a long time. If ever.

It kind of mystifies Klain, who'd been shut out of GoreLand so coldly just over a year ago. But he's happy to see it, and even more delighted to play a leading role in the crusade.

Whouley has noticed it, too. Gore has gotten into what Whouley calls a "please-and-thank-you" routine. He would call the field people, thank them, tell them he appreciated the sacrifice they were making. As Corrigan remarks to Whouley, "adversity does that to people."

Speaking of adversity, on Monday, November 27, the Gorebies' fears about the effect of Bush being certified come true. On that day, post-certification polls show that 60 percent of the American people are saying that this mess should end now and Gore should just concede. This includes a quarter of Gore's own supporters.

Behind closed doors, Gore might be rediscovering himself, might be — *might* be — learning that there are principles more important than just winning. But out in the real world, his act is wearing way thin.

So the Gorebies decide that they need a full-frontal PR assault.

At around noon on Monday, leading congressional Democrats Sen. Tom Daschle of South Dakota, the Senate minority leader, and Rep. Dick

Gephardt of Missouri, the House minority leader, make a great public show of their support for Gore. You gotta wonder just how sincere any of it is. Gore and Gephardt were once the bitterest of enemies; it isn't overstating things to say that they hated each other. At one debate during the contentious 1988 presidential primaries, Gephardt compared then-senator Al Gore to Al Haig. Gore responded that in making that remark, Dick Gephardt sounded like Dick Nixon. And it's safe to say they haven't gone on any fishing trips together ever since.

But Monday afternoon in the Florida state senate hearing room, Gephardt casts that baggage aside. With Daschle, he holds a press conference — and then a totally staged conference call, with Gore and Lieberman in Washington, D.C. — just hours after Gore's legal team formally files its contest papers. In the face of this controversial and unprecedented legal action — and amid rumors that certain Democratic members of the House and Senate are growing weary of Gore's relentlessness —everyone holds hands and puts on a happy face.

Behind closed doors, however, Gore lieutenants are under the impression that Gephardt and Daschle are not totally with the program. They're here today, they'll defend Gore on the Sunday shows, but the message the Gorebies have discerned is that the VP shouldn't push it when it comes to their involvement.

This is a problem. Gore doesn't have the level and quality and number of surrogates that Bush does. Kerrey was great, but Butterworth and Sen. Bob Graham have basically been AWOL. When it comes to statesmen, the Democrats have a fairly weak bench. And it's not as if the rising stars of the party — Sen. John Edwards of North Carolina or Sen. Evan Bayh of Indiana, for instance — are hopping up and down to make the case for Gore.

Whouley, too, is disappointed with his party. The girls and guys on the ground in Florida have been fuckin' fantastic, he thinks. But they still don't have a guy like Baker to run the show, they don't have a warrior. He's trying to serve as a sort of spiritual political leader of the operation — Baldick's always referring to the ground troops drinking Whouley's Kool-Aid — but he's a bit demoralized. Though he loves Gore these days, maybe like never before. He's just become an even guy, and nice. Really nice. One day he had Gore call a couple of his Boston Boys — Sullivan and Corrigan. No small thing to call Corrigan, since he'd been Dukakis's field director when Gore ran against him in '88. But Gore was fuckin' great. He thanked the guys. Then he said to them, "Hey, when this is over, you can have whatever country you want." The guys loved it. But it's not enough. They need to be tough. They shouldn'ta backed off the absentee-ballot stuff, Whouley thinks. They need to be tough. They need to be brutal — just like the Bush guys are being.

Oh, well.

He's happy to see Gephardt and Daschle down here, though.

"We support the contest filed by the Gore campaign this morning, asking that these votes be duly counted and certified," Gephardt proclaims from behind the lectern in the Florida senate hearing room. "This is the right thing to do for the people of Florida, for the people of America and our democracy," Gephardt says. "Al Gore and Joe Lieberman won the popular vote by over three hundred thousand votes* in the country. And they have a lead — they are three votes shy of a majority — in the electoral college. We believe that a full, fair, and accurate count will show that they won in Florida as well."

Then the press is shepherded — like pigs into a slaughterhouse, one reporter gripes — to a small room, where Gore and Lieberman just happen to be having the casual conference call with Gephardt and Daschle.

Just a few guys rappin', you know, no big deal.

"We were just given a new tally this morning that says that if we counted all the votes that have already been counted in some of the recount, we'd actually be ahead by nine votes, so we're encouraged by that," Daschle tells Gore. "I think there's overwhelming support for your effort and a realization that if we completed the count, there is little doubt that you'd be ahead. So we wanted to come down and be as emphatic as we can that we support you and your effort, and we support this full and fair recount."

The 9-vote figure that Daschle cites is actually outdated. It comes from subtracting a few clumps of votes (51 from Nassau; a new number they're asserting came from the late Palm Beach County tally, 215 net Gore votes; 157 from the uncompleted Miami-Dade undervote exploration; plus 123 "Thanksgiving stuffing" votes) from the certified 537-vote difference.

---

*Gore's popular-vote margin of victory will eventually end up exceeding Bush by more than 537,000 votes. Of course, this is irrelevant to a presidential victory. Except to those with, er, evolving takes on the electoral vote.

Like, say, NBC's Jonathan Alter, who said before the election — when the conventional wisdom had Bush winning the popular vote and Gore the electoral vote: "As many Americans know, the person with the most votes doesn't necessarily win. The election is decided by the electoral college."

By November 8, Alter was proclaiming, "If it turns out that Al Gore wins the popular vote nationally, there will be intense pressure in this country to have him become the president. Most people think the guy with the most votes wins."

But by now the "Thanksgiving stuffing" has been excluded. "We made the decision this morning not to do the overseas ballots," Bash tells me, saying the team wanted "a clean, crisp contest action that just dealt with counting errors." They are, however, hoping for a reexamination of 3,000-some Palm Beach ballots that the Boston Boys think Burton ruled against unfairly, and for a look at all of the 10,750 Miami-Dade undervotes.

So that 9-vote nonsense is, like, so two hours ago. But someone forgot to tell Daschle.

"Al and Joe," Gephardt says casually on the conference call, "let me just add, that [as] Joe knows, we've been having many conference calls with the House Democrats. And they have been entirely supportive and continue to be entirely supportive of going ahead with this contest for the purpose of finding out how everybody voted in this election. Our members feel very strongly that this needs to be done."

Daschle chimes back in with one of the lamest endorsements I've ever heard.

"Our colleagues were impressed with your offer to count all of the counties and to live with the results of that effort," the soft-spoken minority leader says to Gore. "And to have that concept endorsed by the [Florida] Supreme Court also, I think, impressed a lot of our colleagues. As I've talked to a number of people, I think the fact that you've repeated it now a couple of times is also, I think, an encouraging sign that you're willing to live with the results, and so are we. . . . We just want to applaud your efforts and thank you for carrying on as you have so far."

From Washington, the vice president's voice buzzes in. "Thank you both for your friendship and for your participation in this," Gore intones in his typical attempt at sincerity. (If you think Gore's bad on TV, you should hear him on speakerphone.) "You and I believe very strongly that every vote has to be counted," Gore says. "We hear statements on the other side quite frequently to the effect that we had a count and a recount and another recount — but that's really beside the point.

"What we're talking about is many thousands of votes that have never been counted at all," Gore says, apparently referring to both the late Palm Beach County numbers, and the 9,000 or so ballots in Miami-Dade County that were rejected by the machines and haven't been hand-counted. "The integrity of our democracy depends upon the consent of the governed, freely expressed, in an election where every vote is counted.

"I appreciate all the hard work that you guys are doing," Gore adds. "And Joe is right here with me."

Then Lieberman briefly peeps up. "Very briefly, thank you, both of you are leaders," he says. "You have been steadfast and direct in the most encouraging way. Thank you for taking the time to go to Florida."

As if the world needs another display of Democratic Kumbaya, minutes later, at 2:20 P.M., the Gore team arranges a conference call for reporters to talk to the two congressional leaders. At this point, Daschle has clearly been told that the 9-vote margin was no longer operable, because he's dropped it. "We think that there may be a hundred votes that separate the two candidates," Daschle now says. He notes that all the uncounted ballots and such will be available for review under the Freedom of Information Act, and surely someone will review them. "There *will* be an accurate count," he noted, calling it "tragic" that the world might learn of this accurate number three or four months hence. "That's in large part our message today," he says.

Now *this* is an interesting argument, maybe the first one I've heard from the Gorebies for quite some time. Oddly, this tack — perhaps Gore's most compelling argument for continuing the recount — originally comes from conservative activist Larry Klayman. On November 22, Klayman, head of the conservative organization Judicial Watch, secured the right under Florida's sunshine law to inspect the Palm Beach County ballots. Klayman has been using his ballot access to allege malfeasance by what he deems are Gore-supporting ballot counters. "If Klayman can do that," Klain realizes, "then of course the media will." And sooner or later, the reasoning goes, it will be known who actually garnered more votes in Florida on November 7, officially or unofficially. The *New York Times* will have its tally, Klain reasons, as will the *Wall Street Journal,* Fox News Channel, NBC, CBS, CNN, ad infinitum. So with this as a given, Klain's question is: Should the ballots be counted by judges now, before America officially has a forty-third president? Or should it be the *New York Times* and ABC News a few weeks after Gov. George W. Bush is sworn in?

And, assuming that Gore is shown to be the actual winner — which the Bush team clearly worries about, otherwise it wouldn't be doing everything it can to stop the recounting — one has to wonder what kind of mandate will that leave Bush? Under this scenario, he could be revealed to be not only the popular vote loser by more than 500,000 votes, but not even the legitimate winner of Florida, except by a host of superior legal and political maneuvering.

Of course, Gore might not actually have all that many votes among the 10,750 undervotes of Miami-Dade. And there are 175,000 undervotes and overvotes statewide, which might end up indicating an even larger Bush margin of victory than his current 537-vote landslide. No one knows. But amid all of these unknowns, one thing is pretty clear: Americans will eventually know who actually won Florida. It's just a matter of timing.

Klain will tell Tribe about this argument, and it will make its way into Thursday's SCOTUS brief. But still, the Gorbies never make a move to have all 175,000 unread ballots examined.

★　★　★

Gephardt is asked: What about poll numbers that show that Americans want this thing to be over?

Gephardt says that their feelings are "based on the supposition that what the secretary of state said was accurate. When people find out . . . that this thing is really a fifty- or hundred-vote difference," they'll change their minds.

But Gephardt and Daschle soon take leave of Tallahassee. And then two Bush allies make appearances — two men who at no other time in this nation's history would seem more powerful than either the United States Congress' House or Senate minority leader. But they sure are BMOCs about Tallahassee today.

The first is state senate president John McKay — a Republican from Bradenton, just north of Sarasota — presenting a "friend of the court" brief to help Bush's case before the SCOTUS. "Today the Florida legislature has filed an amicus brief asking the U.S. Supreme Court to stay part of the [Florida] Supreme Court ruling," McKay says. "We firmly and unequivocally believe that the Florida Supreme Court overstepped its proper boundaries in an arbitrary manner, because this matter is purely a legislative responsibility."

McKay's known about town as pragmatic, sensitive to the winds of public opinion, savvy enough to bounce from scandal back to power in the blink of an eye. During a messy divorce in 1997, McKay's ex accused him not only of battering her but of having an affair with a phone company lobbyist who was behind a bill McKay, then chairman of the senate Budget Committee, was shepherding through the senate. He resigned from the Ways and Means Committee, but bounced back soon enough, rising quickly once again to helm the whole joint as president of the senate.

At 3 P.M. or so, across the capitol rotunda, Florida house speaker Tom Feeney announces plans for a special committee that will meet Tuesday morning to examine the legislature's role in selecting the state's electors. "The Joint Legislative Oversight Committee on Electoral Certification, Accuracy and Fairness" was formed by Feeney and McKay to "address voting irregularities," which one might assume would include voter irregularities that Democratic voters experienced as well as complaints voiced by Republicans.

But one would be wrong.

Feeney's a firebrand, mild in demeanor but extreme in thought. As Jeb's running mate in '94, the Christian Coalition Legislator of the Year was made a campaign liability by Florida Democrats. Every hard-right move he ever made was trotted out: a call for the state to secede if the national debt were to exceed $6 trillion; support for a move to teach students that American culture is superior; the drafting of a bill requiring hospitals to send the state age and race records of any woman who obtains an abortion. Chiles called Feeney "spooky," "sort of the David Duke of Florida politics."

Tom Feeney remembers how he was treated.

Appearing jointly with Feeney, state house Democratic leader Lois Frankel expresses concern about the committee, the brief McKay filed earlier, and the cost of the three attorneys Feeney has retained. These attorneys are: Elhauge and Fried for the state house, and Roger Magnuson, who will advise the senate. Magnuson has written extensively against gay rights, and is dean of Oak Brook College of Law in Fresno, California, an unaccredited school that declares in its mission statement that its purpose is to "establish the Biblical foundations of truth, righteousness, justice, mercy, equity, integrity, and the fear of God in legal education and in the professional arenas of law and government policy."

Personally, Frankel likes Feeney, gets along with him just fine, but she is amazed by the brazenness of what she sees as an obvious Bush power play. Feeney and McKay, she thinks, are clearly coordinating with the Bushies so as to set up a safety net just in case Gore wins the contest provision and ultimately any recount. And she's right; McKay has talked with Jeb about calling a special joint committee of the legislature to do so. This week, Jeb will call the formation of the committee an "act of courage."

While Ginsberg was originally cagey when Rubottom called him to coordinate, there has since been tremendous communication between the two camps. Rubottom has been talking to Terwilliger; Jimenez has been coordinating with Ginsberg, Jeb, and a whole bunch of folks in the state house; state GOP chair Cardenas and Jeb have been calling the legislature's GOP leaders, checking in, seeing what's going on and how they can help.

Before the legislature even drafts a bill, Rubottom walks over to the Bush Building with Jeb's counsel, Charles Canady, to talk it over with Terwilliger and others on the Bush team. No one wants this to be the way that Bush gets the White House — through a partisan maneuver and a bill signed by Jeb — but they're sure not going to rule it out.

But all the while, the Bushies are doing everything they can to make it seem like they're not having anything to do with the legislature's decision. On December 7, Bush spokesman Dan Bartlett will lie, "The Florida legislature made this decision on its own. It's a separately elected body. We have not participated in their making their decision."

The state house minority leader sees this all going on, hears Bartlett's lie, and can't believe it. It's no secret that the Republicans in Tallahassee are cutthroat — leaning on businesses and corporations to stop donating money to Democrats, even leaning on one to cancel a reception for new Democratic legislators. But Frankel sees two reasons for Feeney and McKay's moves. Yes, they're setting up another safety net for Bush, but she also thinks that the moves of Feeney and McKay are intended to add to the "circus atmosphere" of it all, creating a chaotic situation, so that the country will eventually say "enough is enough."

Still, Frankel thinks, whaddaya gonna do? The Democrats are powerless. When she suggests names of specific Democrats to sit on the special joint committee, Feeney ignores her. Instead, he picks soft-spoken state senator Ken Gottlieb and two Democrats with constituencies that make assertiveness on this issue tough: the mild state representative Annie Betancourt, who represents a Cuban-American area of Miami, and conservative Dwight Stansel, who represents northern Florida areas that were totally Bush country.

Frankel realizes something sophisticated is happening. These guys aren't just deciding on their own, "OK, now we're going to take care of the Bush campaign." And despite Jeb's low profile, he isn't just sitting at home in front of his fireplace twiddling his thumbs. This thing's just a game, she thinks, and everyone knows it.

★ ★ ★

The contest papers are filed at 12:14 P.M., Monday, and a computer selects a judge to preside over the contest: circuit court judge N. Sanders Sauls.

"This is the worst judge we could have drawn," Dexter Douglass tells his fellow members of the Gore legal team. "This is a *looong* draw." He's a slow judge, Douglass says, and he'll be an obstacle in their goal to have an expedited trial so they can be done with before December 12, the "safe harbor" day six days before the electors are to meet. Feeney and McKay have made it clear that the Florida legislature will step in and appoint Bush the electors he needs if this thing hasn't resolved itself by then.

More important, Douglass tells the team, "Sauls is a dyed-in-the-wool Southern Democrat who's for Bush." Douglass, seventy-one, doesn't know this for a fact, of course. But he's known Sauls, fifty-nine, since Sauls was a boy. And he knew Sauls's mom, chair of the Jefferson County

Democratic Party and a tax collector; he even knew Sauls's father, a clerk of the circuit court.

Douglass sees Sauls as one of a breed of North Florida Democrats that clings to the ways of the past. "I could have been very much like Sauls," Douglass will later say, emphasizing that his direct contact with African-Americans throughout his life is what made him ultimately stick with the Democratic Party — despite what he deemed in the '60s and '70s to be some radical moves. To be sure, his concern for African-Americans started out paternalistically, but Douglass — a Korean War veteran, losing congressional candidate in '62, close friend and former general counsel to Chiles, and cattle farmer — has evolved. He doesn't think Sauls has.

We're not going to win with Sauls, Douglass says.

And just to complicate things further, Douglass says, Sauls really got into a public pissing match with the Florida Supreme Court. In November 1998, he explains, Sauls fired the longtime liaison between the Second Circuit and the Leon County government. The administrator had publicly questioned a hiring decision Sauls had made that ignored a search committee's recommendation for a family law administrator; Sauls had instead hired a friend's daughter. But the larger issue was whether Sauls — as chief circuit court judge — was running the Second Circuit in an autocratic and divisive manner, as both court employees and other judges complained. Sauls was hauled before the justices, who chewed him out. The next morning he resigned as chief judge.

The tensions involve more than that one incident, however. Sauls isn't respected by the Florida Supreme Court, Douglass says. His rulings have been overturned more than pancakes on the griddle. Appellate courts are constantly reversing his decisions, often finding that he too strictly enforces technical administrative matters.

Berger and one of his Tallahassee partners, John Newton, have another concern about Sauls. Newton has a history of publicly and financially supporting candidates who have run against Sauls. As a result, at one Florida Bar event, Sauls refused to shake Newton's hand. Newton has heard from any number of people that Sauls doesn't like him, that somehow he even holds him responsible for his problems when he was essentially fired by the Florida Supremes as chief judge. Newton, truth be told, thought it all a bit odd, and immature. But since Newton was Gore's attorney of record in Tallahassee, his signature the one at the bottom of the briefs, this was something that Klain and Gore needed to at least know about.

The Gorebies now debate whether or not they should move to have

Sauls recused. The friction with Newton alone could be grounds for Sauls to recuse himself under Florida's rather expansive recusal laws. Zack, back in Tallahassee to work on the evidence for the trial, is in favor of the recusal motion. But Boies doesn't think it's such a hot idea. If we're going to win this case, in order to maintain the legitimacy of that win, we don't want to have anybody with a view or argument that we're engaged in judge-shopping, he says. Appellate courts and courts generally do not favor recusal motions, he reminds the team. And, Boies thinks, in a way we might be better off appealing an adverse judgment from Sauls because of the bad blood between him and the Florida Supreme Court.

Ultimately, Gore and Klain decide not to ask for Sauls to recuse himself. They do make a more subtle attempt to remove the case from his courtroom, however, making a motion to consolidate the case with the *Volusia v. Katherine Harris* matter. Were Sauls to grant that motion, the case would return to Judge Lewis's courtroom. But Sauls rejects the motion.

★   ★   ★

As another step in the Gorebies' media plan, Gore himself goes before the cameras to personally explain to the world why he's taking the unprecedented step of contesting the election.

Public appearances by Gore are always fiercely debated within the Gore camp. Donna Brazile thinks that Gore isn't doing enough, she thinks he should be out almost campaigning again. Pollster Stan Greenberg, on the other hand, thinks that Gore's completely ineffective as a spokesperson — the less seen of him, the better. Fabiani's attitude is: Look, this is our candidate. And he needs to explain what he's doing.

Gore steps up to the podium, and immediately the flashbulbs start going off. The Bushies don't allow photographers to take pictures during their man's speeches — it ends up creating a distracting strobe effect. Usually the Gorebies don't either, but there's a screw-up, and the photographers start shooting CLICKCLICKCLICK, totally ruining the mood.

"A vote is not just a piece of paper," Gore says. "A vote is a human voice, a statement of human principle. And we must not let those voices be silenced. . . . Ignoring votes means ignoring democracy itself. And if we ignore the votes of thousands in Florida in this election, how can you or any American have confidence that your vote will not be ignored in a future election?"

CLICKCLICKCLICKCLICKCLICKCLICKCLICKCLICKCLICK

"That is all we have asked since Election Day, a complete count of all the votes cast in Florida, not recount after recount, as some have charged, but a single, full, and accurate count. We haven't had that yet."

That is, of course, not true, and it is nothing short of amazing that Gore would make this claim. Gore has now twice suggested a statewide recount — but half-heartedly, and a statewide recount is not the goal of either his legal or his political teams down there.

CLICKCLICKCLICKCLICKCLICKCLICKCLICKCLICKCLICK

"Great efforts have been made to prevent the counting of these votes," Gore says, accurately. "Lawsuit after lawsuit has been filed to delay the count and to stop the counting for many precious days between Election Day and the deadline for having the count finished." In Miami-Dade, Gore charges, "election officials brought the count to a premature end in the face of organized intimidation."

This is artfully phrased, since it doesn't actually state that the intimidation caused the count to end, but Gore's insinuation borders on demagoguery.

CLICKCLICKCLICKCLICKCLICKCLICKCLICKCLICKCLICK

"There are some who would have us bring this election to the fastest conclusion possible," Gore says. "I have a different view. I believe our Constitution matters more than convenience. So, as provided under Florida law, I have decided to contest this inaccurate and incomplete count in order to ensure the greatest possible credibility for the outcome."

CLICKCLICKCLICKCLICKCLICKCLICKCLICKCLICKCLICK

Gore's poll numbers continue their free fall.

★   ★   ★

On Tuesday, November 28, Baker parades what one CNN correspondent refers to as "the Boies Killers" before the TV cameras, and Phil Beck's about to faint.

It's not because he's nervous. It's because he quit drinking coffee about a year ago, so he could sleep better. This morning, however, after pulling a near all-nighter studying the case, his ass is dragging. As he was about to be introduced to the press corps with great aplomb, he thought he should violate his system's caffeine embargo. GLUG GLUG, two giant cups of coffee.

He almost instantly regrets it. He's completely lightheaded. He thinks he's going to pass out. Baker's talking to the packed room of reporters, who have no idea who Beck is. Beck's standing there before them alongside Terrell and Bristow and Barry Richard, who also have no idea who he is. And all Beck can think about is how he's about to faint in front of the world and be sent home in a box.

"This is an extraordinary procedure, and we are entering new, uncertain, and controversial territory," Baker says. "Therefore, I would like to introduce the senior members of the litigation team, who will be defending the vote of Floridians in favor of Governor Bush and Secretary Cheney."

The white-maned Richard steps up. "We believe that the election contest is without legal substance," he says. "We have divided up the issues among the lawyers, and each one here with us today is prepared to comment on a specific issue."

Terrell's first up. "I'd like to talk to you about one of Mr. Gore's pet theories in the case, and that is the myth that there are ten thousand votes that are not counted in Miami-Dade County," he says. "In fact, those are non-votes. And indeed, it is not unusual for people not to vote fully in every election on a ballot. In fact, those ten thousand non-votes are about 1.6 percent of the votes cast in that county."

Then comes Bartlit. "I'm going to talk about myth number two," he says. "That's the myth that Miami-Dade would have conducted the manual recount unless a — if it wasn't for a Republican mob that intimidated the canvassing board. A Gore lawyer, Ron Klain, said that a mob stormed the counting facility to stop the count. That's the myth.

"Here are the facts," Bartlit says. One, the protest was over the fact that the move to the nineteenth floor "was a violation of the Florida sunshine law."

Second, Bartlit says, laying it on a bit thick, the protest was benign, "peaceful" even. "There were babies in the crowd. There were little kids there. There was, in some ways, a holiday atmosphere."

Beck steps up, mentions the butterfly ballot case, which is heading toward the Florida Supreme Court. It "is not fair to wait until the votes have been counted and then, if you don't like the outcome, to say that . . . there was something wrong with the form of the ballot," Beck says. He does not faint.

Lastly, Bristow pops up to talk about Nassau County, throwing the "count every vote" rhetoric back in the Gorebies' faces. "These two hundred eighteen votes were real votes by real people who did what they needed to do to express their will," Bristow says. "No one, at no time, declared these votes illegal. . . . The board unanimously voted — including two Democrats, and that included the supervisor — that this should be done to express the will of two hundred eighteen people who had really cast their votes."

Later that day Bartlit and Beck watch a TV news broadcast about their press conference that will marry Bartlit's "holiday atmosphere" audio with videotape from the ugly, aggressive Miami-Dade protest.

"'Holiday atmosphere,'" Beck will quip. "Yeah, it was Bastille Day."

☆   ☆   ☆

Desperation has an aroma.

It repels singles in bars, clients from Willy Loman–esque salesmen, employers from the laid-off. And this week, in the Florida state capital, that smell is starting to fill the air, and it's coming straight from the campaign of those who oppose Bush's claim to the presidency. It's coming from Al Gore.

The stench can be detected on Capitol Hill in Washington. There, some Democratic congressional leaders who are vociferous in their public support for Gore reveal — off the record and behind closed doors — that they think the man should pack it in.

Even among those who support Gore and are calling for patience, "there's a sense of despair," confides one senior Democratic Senate staffer. "Every day the scenario becomes less and less probable."

Even some of the earnest Democrats slaving away for Gore on the ground in Florida don't hold out much hope that this is going to end well for the vice president. The legal hurdles are too daunting. In order for Gore to end this in the White House, each one of the following dominoes must fall precisely right in the next twelve days:

1. Circuit judge Sanders Sauls — or, alternatively, the Florida Supreme Court — must allow the following net votes for Gore: the 215 late Palm Beach County votes; the 157 votes that came from Miami-Dade County's partial manual recount; and Nassau County's 51.
2. Sauls or the Florida Supreme Court must rule against the Palm Beach County canvassing board's decision to exclude the 3,000-odd "dimpled chad" ballots, and against the Miami-Dade canvassing board's decision not to evaluate the 10,750 undervotes. Almost no one believes that the Florida Supreme Court, which has already ruled that acceptance of "dimpled chad" ballots is at the discretion of local canvassing boards, will direct Palm Beach to change their standards.
3. These ballots must contain enough votes for Gore — combined with the 215, 157, and 51 votes gleaned in the sequence outlined above — for him to overcome Bush's certified 537-vote margin of victory.
4. SCOTUS must not rule that the Florida Supreme Court overstepped its bounds in extending the deadline for ballots to be received by the secretary of state's office.
5. The GOP-controlled Florida legislature must decide not to assign its own electors if the above hasn't been decided by December 12, as seems likely.

Other long-long-long shot alternatives: The Florida Supreme Court could rule that Palm Beach County's butterfly ballot was an illegal ballot and demand a revote. Ain't gonna happen. Or a judge could toss out Seminole County's 15,000 absentee ballots or Martin County's 10,000. Also, ain't gonna happen.

On Tuesday, the desperation comes from Gore via the Rev. Jesse Jackson.

Accompanied by members of the Congressional Black Caucus — Democratic representative Charles Rangel of New York, Rep. Eddie Bernice Johnson of Texas, and Rep. John Conyers of Michigan — Jackson calls for Attorney General Janet Reno to investigate his charge of a clear conspiracy to suppress black turnout. "It is far too widespread for it to be accidental," pronounces Jackson, providing no affidavits, no names, not any backup information at all for his claims, even after being asked. "That Bush, Cheney, Trent Lott, Strom Thurmond, Jesse Helms, Orrin Hatch, Tom DeLay, Bob Barr, plus the Supreme Court of Clarence Thomas, Scalia, and Trent Lott [sic]" are on the opposing side, Jackson says, is no surprise. "We can afford to lose an election, but not our franchise," he declares. Bush "can't look at voters who were stopped by police and asked for their driver's license and their ID badges in a hostile way [and say], 'Your pain, my gain, I'm your leader.'"

After the press conference — which steps on a previously scheduled conference by the Gore recount team in which further voting "victims" were trotted out — Jackson et al. hold a sparsely attended afternoon rally outside the state supreme court.

"Who can vote a butterfly ballot anyway?!" asks Conyers, apparently unaware that more than 93 percent of the voters of Palm Beach County figured out how to use the ballot correctly. Of the Justice Department, Conyers, the ranking member of the House Judiciary Committee, said, "They're asking us to send them the evidence. Well, you come down here and find the evidence! Then we'll have a fair vote." Rabbi Jacobs of Los Angeles adds that one woman who felt that her ballot wasn't counted correctly "said that it reminded her of standing in line at the concentration camp, waiting for a piece of bread."

Perhaps the Democratic zeitgeist is best summed up by the raspy-voiced Rangel. Asked about the approaching December 12 deadline, Rangel says, "Those of us who fought so hard for Al Gore to become the president of the United States, we still want to believe that there is plenty of time for the judges and the courts" to complete the process. "What could we do in the Congress? As a member, I think the first thing I would do is apply for my pistol." Yowza! Hard to imagine a conservative congressman getting away with such a comment.

Almost every single Republican governor has been in Florida arguing Bush's case. Wednesday morning the Dems send four of their own before the media (one of whom — Pedro Rosello of Puerto Rico — isn't even from a state). They wander into the state senate hearing room to tell the media that they, too, support Gore's latest legal gambit.

"We're here in support of Vice President Gore's very principled position that all the votes legally cast in the Florida presidential race should be counted," says Gov. Paul Patton of Kentucky, president of the Democratic Governors' Association. Using the Gore recount team's latest in a series of coulda-woulda-shoulda vote calculations, Patton says that if the votes from Palm Beach and Miami-Dade Counties had been counted, it would have left Bush with a "one-hundred-fifteen-vote margin." With such a slim margin, Patton argues, who knows what would happen when and if the court counted the 10,750 Miami-Dade ballots that haven't registered a presidential choice.

Both Iowa (which went for Gore) and New Hampshire (which voted for Bush) reportedly registered more than 10,000 undervotes in this election, and their two governors, Tom Vilsack of Iowa and Jeanne Shaheen of New Hampshire, are half of the Democratic gubernatorial force here on Wednesday. Both of those masses of ballots could have swung either state the other way. So I ask Vilsack and Shaheen: Are you as concerned about those ten-thousand-ballot chunks as you are about the mass from Miami?

"I can speak only, obviously, to the Iowa situation," Vilsack says. "There is no accurate count of any undervote for the state of Iowa. The figure that you're quoting, I believe, is a guesstimate on the part of the Iowa state Republican Party. . . . I'm not certain, and I've not seen any specific definitive proof that indeed undervoting took place."

There were, in fact, almost 13,000 undervotes in Iowa, a state that Gore won by 4,144 votes. And while Florida's undervotes amount to 2.86 percent of the total votes counted, Illinois, Idaho, and Wyoming had even higher percentages.

"The state Republican Party was invited if they felt that there was an inadequate vote count, or inadequate attention paid to the voters in the state of Iowa, to have a recount," Vilsack continues. "We were prepared to have a recount. They chose not to have a recount. I think that's a fundamental difference here.

"We do know, in the state of Florida, and in Miami-Dade, there are ten thousand seven hundred identified ballots that are apparently on their way to this very city that have not been counted," he continues. "I think of the people that cast those votes. We don't know who they are. But there's the possibility that a Congressional Medal of Honor winner could have cast one of those votes. Or a mother with two children who took the day off from work just because she felt strongly about this election could have cast that vote. . . . Their vote does, in fact, matter."

Yeesh. This is what it's come down to. Hypothetical Congressional Medal of Honor winners.

Shaheen then steps up.

"I am in fact concerned that every vote in New Hampshire be counted," she says. "We have a process to recount votes. . . . We've had twenty-six recounts as a result of this election in the state, and we've just finished those up this week. That's my concern about what's happening here in Florida. There has been a process to recount, and that's been delayed, it's been obstructed, through partisan political maneuvering."

Patton returns to the mike. "We're here to support the principle that every vote counts," he says.

Every vote in Broward, Miami-Dade, Palm Beach, and Volusia Counties, that is. Not necessarily those in the other sixty-three counties in the state. And the fact that this is their position allows the Bushies to slam it — again and again and again. As Cheney tells Larry King on CNN, "every single vote in Florida has been counted. Every single vote in Florida has been recounted. Now, there are some that were not marked for president, and therefore didn't register on the machines, but that's not at all unusual in Florida. They've focused in on the ten thousand votes in Miami-Dade County that supposedly are unmarked. But there are some thirty-four counties in Florida that have a larger percentage of unmarked ballots for president than those in Dade County. . . .

"What he wants to do now is go back in, in one heavily Democratic area — two counties — and direct these election supervisors, most of whom are Democrats, who have already made their own independent decisions to redo the whole process in a manner that will favor him. And that's clearly inappropriate."

Cheney's comments that the 10,000 undervotes are just simply not votes isn't true, and he must know that. But the fact that the Gorebies still haven't formally called for a statewide recount of the 175,000 unread ballots is now not only indicative of the disingenuousness in their call to "count all the votes," it is a major political miscalculation.

★ ★ ★

Sauls allows a few random citizens to intervene in the case on a limited basis. There's Larry Klayman, of course, but there are also random Bush-backing Floridians and their hack attorneys — the GOP equivalent of the myriad butterfly ballot citizens, shysters, and suits. Which is maybe why no one pays much attention to any of them. Which may be too bad, in at least one case.

On Wednesday, November 29, Tallahassee attorneys R. Frank Myers and Lawrence Gonzalez — on behalf of Stephen and Teresa Cruce, Terry Kelly, and Jeanette Seymour — make a motion that if the court orders any recount, they order a full statewide recount of all the undervotes and over-votes. "In a statewide election with national implications," they write, "it is self-apparent that 'the will of the people' means the will *of all the people of the Great State of Florida,* not just those who happen to live in a particular county." Myers and Gonzalez set forth a few ground rules, notably that the court sets "the objective and uniform standards to be applied state-wide," as well as a deadline. But the brief just joins a stack of others like it in an endless room of papers no one reads.

★   ★   ★

From: Mark Fabiani

<h3 align="center">PROPOSED GORE SCHEDULE</h3>

Daily Model

Daily Goals

- Gore personal appearance for television to communicate his message of the day
- Move news about disenfranchised voters in FL
- Offensive move against opposition (beginning with voter intimida-tion off of today's *Washington Post* story and tomorrow's pending *New York Times* stories)
- Demonstrate Democratic solidarity

Daily Events

- One Gore statement for television, articulating the message of the day
- At least one major Gore sit-down television interview
- One event focusing on disenfranchised voters in FL
- One event focusing on offensive message against opposition (voter intimidation)
- One event demonstrating Democratic solidarity

Proposed Gore Schedule

Tuesday
- Gore lunch with Larry Summers
- Gore statement in front of his house. Message: Gore has instructed his legal team to file a schedule with the court that would allow his challenge to be decided in advance of the December 12th deadline
- Gore interview with Today Show
  - Pretaped today for airing Wednesday morning
  - Claire Shipman
  - Walking around NAVOBS with Mrs. Gore
  - Ten minutes

Wednesday
- Gore meeting with Roy Neel*
- Gore statement in front of his house, or in front of the White House, articulating the message of the day.
- Gore network interviews, taped Wednesday for airing Wednesday night, with all three network anchors and CNN.

Thursday
- Ted Koppel/Nightline day in the life, taped Thursday for airing Thursday night
- Gore availability, if necessary
- Gore White House meetings

Friday
- Gore public statement on the message of the day
- Barbara Walters interview, taped Friday for airing on Friday night's 20/20 broadcast
- Supreme Court argument

Weekend
- Instead of the Nightline/Walters combination, Gore could do 60 Minutes with Leslie Stahl on Sunday

★   ★   ★

Fabiani thinks that there are just two targets for presidential communications: the front page of the *New York Times,* and NBC's *Today* show. Both

*Heading up Gore's transition efforts in D.C.

dictate to every other reporter what is "important." If *Today* producer Jeff Zucker gives you time on his show, Fabiani thinks, then every other TV producer throughout the land notices. Thus, the taped interview with Claire Shipman.

"Did you win this election?" she asks.

"I — I certainly believe that I did," he says. "I — I — I understand that there is considerable doubt about that, and that's why this . . ."

"Do you think you should be president-elect right now?" she asks. "Do you?"

"Well — well, look, no, because I — I — the votes haven't been counted. I think that a clear majority of the people who went to the polling places and tried to — to vote, did vote for — for Joe Lieberman and me. That happened in the country as a whole. I think it happened in Florida. But, the votes have not all been counted yet."

Shipman points out that there are 1.2 million undervotes across the country. Gore dodges the question. When asked how he's dealing with it all, he says, "I sleep like a baby. I've been getting seven, eight hours of sleep a night. And I'm — I am not tortured over what-ifs at all. And, in fact, I — I believe we're going to win this election."

In Tallahassee, Dorrance Smith, a freelance TV producer in town to help the Republicans coordinate media — he was President Bush's assistant for media affairs from 1991 to 1993 — watches Gore being interviewed by Shipman. Not a bad media hit, he thinks. But what greater indication is there that Monday night's speech — CLICKCLICKCLICK — was a disaster than the fact that here's Gore again, still pushing the issue, still trying to seal the deal?

In the Bush Building, producers start calling Smith. Gore has put out the word that he's willing to sit for an interview with almost anyone — ABC, CBS, CNN, NBC. Who does Smith have to offer, they ask. Can we get Bush?

Smith talks it over with Bush's Austin triangle — Karen Hughes, Karl Rove, and Don Evans. They agree: Gore can go door-to-door trying to sell his case, but that doesn't mean they have to follow suit. Christopher has disappeared, Daley's in D.C., Boies is buried in legal work when he's not doing TV. They decide to let Cheney go out there, bop Gore on the head a few times, but they're not going to try to compete with Gore on his media plan.

Watching Gore's interviews bears this out.

"I've never used the phrase 'steal the election,'" he tells CNN's John King. "I think that's an intemperate phrase."

"Mr. Vice President, if the U.S. Supreme Court rules against you on Friday, will you then give it up?" CBS's Dan Rather asks.

"Mr. Vice President, there are another one hundred and sixty thousand of those ballots in the state of Florida, and you're not asking for them to be recounted," says NBC's Tom Brokaw.

This is going great, Smith thinks. They're kicking the shit out of him. The clincher is Peter Jennings on ABC. "You have not, sir, been completely clear or consistent about a date certain on which you will no longer continue the legal challenge," Jennings says. "Do you believe that date is December the twelfth?"

"I think this is going to be over with by the middle of December," Gore replies.

"The twelfth of December is indeed the middle of December," says Jennings, perhaps a bit irritated.

Jeez Louise, Smith thinks. Gore's like Captain Queeg on the deck of the *Caine*. When your principal becomes your surrogate, you've lost.

He brings a tape of the Jennings interview to Baker.

"I want you to watch this," says Smith. "It helps our case. It shows you how desperate they really are."

Baker soon stops by Smith's desk.

"Yeah, that was tough," he agrees.

That night, Wendy Walker Whitworth, senior executive producer for CNN's *Larry King Live,* calls Smith.

"Who do you have for us tomorrow?" Whitworth asks the Republican.

"We have Gore!" Smith laughs.

★ ★ ★

"This case has to move on a fast track. I think all parties have to agree to that," Sauls says, as he takes up *Albert Gore Jr. v. Katherine Harris et al.*

But for the Gorebies, it's nowhere near fast enough.

The Gore legal team starts filing motions, pulling out stack after stack of papers like one of those term-paper factories that advertises in the back of *Rolling Stone.* They want the trial put on the fastfastfast-track. They want the ballots brought up and counted. Yesterday.

On Monday, the Gorebies present Sauls with a proposed schedule that Zack has devised that can have it all done in time for him to issue his order on December 9 at the latest. This they file, despite the fact that Sauls has already fashioned a schedule of his own.

Joe Klock — still purportedly Harris's attorney, though he might as well get a red phone to Austin — points out that the "Expedited Trial Calendar" doesn't give Harris enough time to respond under "minimal due process" requirements. Moreover, Klock rightly points out in his brief, the Gorebies' deadline problems "are entirely of the plaintiffs own making" — (well, theirs, and Harris's zombielike obedience to whatever is best for Bush) — "having demanded a greatly expanded protest period at the expense of the evidentiary contest period."

'Tis true. The clock's TICKTICKTICKing in the contest is precisely because the Gorebies deemed it so important — primarily for PR reasons — that they fend off the certification date until they squeezed all the votes they could out of the southeastern tip of the state.

On Tuesday Team Gore files to have the 10,750 Miami-Dade undervotes and the Palm Beach 3,300 disputed ballots brought up to Tallahassee and counted immediately. They propose that the ballots be inspected and counted by the clerk of the circuit court, or by the clerks from those two counties, or by "Special Masters" named by Sauls. But the Boies Klain team wants "the count of the contested ballots (to) begin immediately by whichever of these procedures the court elects."

Phil Beck and Barry Richard, of course, object to any of these ideas, arguing that no one's proven that anything needs to be looked at at all, much less counted.

Sauls is exasperated. "Have you attempted to confer, and have there been any matters at all, has anybody even been able to agree on the time of day?" he asks Tuesday evening.

"Yes, sir!" Douglass says. "We agree that it's twenty minutes 'til six."

We know we're filing a lot of papers, Boies says. But we need to get the ballots examined ASAP. "And to get that process started . . . we have been pestering the court with as many papers as we have submitted."

"A little bit like getting nibbled to death by a duck," Sauls says.

Douglass points out that the Bushies are trying to stall, and every time Sauls rules with them, he's standing in the way of the process resolving itself. But Sauls says that "at this junction I have just about stripped the defendants down to the bares of due process." He doesn't know how much more he can expedite this.

Murray Greenberg's on the speakerphone, and Sauls asks him about transporting the ballots up. How long will it take?

"Is it supposed to come up regular mail, UPS, FedEx, security?" Greenberg asks. "We need to know that, please." Sauls says that whatever Leahy thinks is best is fine.

Richard still wonders why the ballots need to be brought up. Is Boies claiming that there was an abuse of discretion by the Miami-Dade and Palm Beach canvassing boards?

Boies says no. "Our argument is that those ballots were voted for Vice President Gore and Joe Lieberman. We think the court needs to look at those ballots — directly or indirectly — and conclude whether we're right or wrong. It has nothing to do with canvassing-board discretion." Miami-Dade didn't count, so there was no discretion exercised, Boies says. And with respect to Palm Beach, "it's a question of what are these votes."

In the end, Sauls decides to split the difference. He's going to order the undervotes shipped up, but he's going to keep the schedule the same. "I think that this is the best that I can fashion to at least be unfair to both sides — equally," Sauls says.

Beck rises. He says that voting machines need to be brought up with ballots.

"Well, there's my friend Mr. Greenberg to the rescue perhaps," Sauls says about the accommodating assistant county attorney. "Let's find out."

The courtroom explodes in laughter.

"Go ahead, Mr. Greenberg," Sauls says.

Comes Greenberg's nasally charm via speakerphone: "Your Honor, we will send up with our ballots, along with all the instructions and a sample ballot," he says.

"You know, I really like that guy," Sauls says.

★   ★   ★

In Miami-Dade County, Leahy supervises the separation of undervotes. But a stocky GOP observer, Marc Lampkin, is in his face all day, complaining. Having served as Bush's deputy campaign manager during the GOP New Hampshire primary, a state Bush ended up losing to McCain by 19 points, Lampkin is finally proving his worth here in Florida.

Lampkin never yells; his tone is even and measured. But he is relentless. He will not stop whining about this, about that. There isn't anything Leahy can do to satisfy him.

Eventually Leahy comes to a conclusion: this guy is here with the express order to irritate me. To get me to delay things. And he is very good at it.

★   ★   ★

On Wednesday in the Bush Building, Beck is not feeling the love.

Richard's going to be handling opening and closing arguments, Terrell's handling the Miami-Dade deal, Bartlit's on Broward and Nassau, Bristow's been dispatched to Orlando to help the Republicans fend off the Seminole war.

Beck's in charge of destroying the Gorebies on dimples. But every time the team meets with Ginsberg and Terwilliger to discuss strategy, and Beck tries to turn the conversation to what might happen should Sauls — or, more likely, the Florida Supreme Court — actually order ballots to be recounted, Beck starts talking about what standards he feels the Bushies should push for, and the Bush lieutenants blanch.

We don't ever want to get to the point where there's a hand recount of anything, Ginsberg and Terwilliger say. We don't want to concede the point!

Beck knows this. Yes, he says. *Of course.* But if there ends up being a count, we need to have standards we can argue. Hanging chads, sunshine, dimples — they need to be prepared to argue in favor of what Beck thinks are honest standards, like the ones Burton used in Palm Beach.

But the reaction Beck gets doesn't fill him with confidence. *Like the ones Burton used in Palm Beach! Where Gore picked up votes in that bogus recount?* It's my job to be a defeatist, Beck responds. That's my job — to prepare for anything that can happen.

There's another argument Beck is preparing that is met with a degree of reluctance: the idea that undervotes come not from anachronistic voting devices but from the clear fact that there were a lot of people out there who found both Gore and Bush unpalatable. It's not that anyone tells Beck not to make the argument that plenty of Americans found both Bush and Gore rather wanting. Indeed, in a way the Bushies' "no vote" claim is in sync with this line of thinking. But when Beck articulates the idea that millions of Americans gagged at the prospect of either one of these jokers at the helm, the Bush lieutenants wince. When Beck explains it to guys who've lived the last several months trying to persuade America to vote for Bush, their automatic reaction is to cringe.

It had been agreed on Tuesday that when Boies tried to get Sauls to bring the Miami-Dade and Palm Beach undervotes up, the Bush lawyers would argue that all the ballots should be brought up. They want to plop the whole 1.8 million — all 653,000 Miami-Dade ballots, and all 462,000 Palm Beach ballots — in front of Sauls. Make him see the absurdity of it all, gum it up. And, of course, the statute never refers to undervotes, it refers to all the ballots. But Richard, taking the lead, never really made that position clear. Still, they got so much that it seems debatable whether to ask for any more.

On Wednesday, reports from GOP observers in Miami-Dade — mostly Lampkin — indicate, if you're inclined to believe them, that there's some question as to how the ballots were being handled as the undervotes were being sorted out. Beck is preparing to argue that there were questions as to whether the integrity of the ballots was being preserved.

As he's leaving the Bush Building, heading to Sauls's courtroom, a guy Beck thinks is Bush's senior legal adviser approaches him.

"Tell the judge that he's gotta bring *all* the ballots up," the guy says.

"I can't tell him that," Beck says. "That was yesterday's argument, and that ship has sailed. He's already decided that only the undervotes are coming."

The guy looks at Beck, as serious as a funeral.

"Tell him that he's gotta bring *all* the ballots up," the guy repeats. "It's important. Tell him he's gotta bring *all* the ballots up."

Beck nods. OK.

Terrell and Beck get into the elevator.

"This is just great," Beck says. "I got the client giving me these impossible instructions. We're going to look like jerks; the judge is going to think we're idiots. But, you know, he's the Bush legal adviser, so I gotta do it."

First thing before Sauls, Beck raises the point: if you're going to bring them up, you need to bring them all up.

Sauls asks Greenberg via speakerphone: is this possible?

"We will do that if Your Honor so rules," the ever-agreeable Greenberg says. But it wouldn't be until late Thursday night before we could get all of them packaged up and driven up to Tallahassee.

The voice from Palm Beach County says the same.

"Is it going to be a convoy?" Sauls asks. "How many semis?"

Beck says that the Bushies are worried about the ballots. Our observers saw some things they didn't like, he says. You gotta bring them *all* up, Beck insists.

Greenberg objects to Beck's characterization of what's going on, but Beck doesn't respond to this. He just keeps stating that something is rotten in the county of Miami-Dade, and that all the ballots need to come up to Tallie.

And he wants to have a representative in the convoy.

"You got a spare tire on the back of any of those that somebody could ride for each side?" Sauls asks Greenberg.

"I have a lot of ideas, Your Honor, but I won't enunciate them," Greenberg says.

Boies steps up and says that there's no reason why the undervotes can't come up at once. They don't need to wait for the rest of them to be shipped up.

Wrong, says Beck, vociferously. "I'm concerned about the integrity of the evidence here," he says. "And we've had a lot of sorting that I don't think should have taken place. . . . I think we ought to get all the ballots up in a unified way, ensuring the integrity of the evidence."

"I'm going to leave it to them," Sauls says. "What do you all want to do down there?" he asks Greenberg. "Do you want to send up two times or do you want to do it once? It's your call."

"One time, from Miami," Greenberg says.

"One time it is," Sauls rules. Court dismissed 'til tomorrow.

★   ★   ★

On the way out of the circuit courthouse, and back in the Bush Building, Beck is a hero. Everyone's congratulating him for the stroke of genius. Beck thinks that the lawyers are looking at him with a newfound respect. Like, "Oooh, this guy takes the initiative!"

Amid the minor celebration, Beck confides in Summers.

"The reason I did this was because Bush's legal adviser over here told me to," Beck says. "I don't even know the guy's name."

"That's not Bush's legal adviser," Summers says. "That's just some precinct captain who wandered in."

What? Beck asks. You mean this is just some hanger-on who button-holed me and was just giving me a piece of mind?!

The two crack up.

★   ★   ★

Wednesday, Theresa LePore finally sends Katherine Harris the official Palm Beach results. She had to audit the final count, double-checking numbers on the spreadsheets.

It's not 192 net Gore votes, as the Gorebies were asserting Sunday night, nor is it 215 net Gore votes, as they're asserting in their legal briefs. It's 174 net Gore votes.

LePore keeps hearing the Democrats using this "215" number. She asks Newman where they got it. Newman tells her that that was *their* count. LePore's amazed. That's simply not the number.

★   ★   ★

Over at the legislature, the fait accompli is well on its way.

When it starts up on Tuesday afternoon, the committee has changed its name to The Select Joint Committee on the Manner of the Appointment of Presidential Electors. And as the old name is tossed, so is any pretense that this is about anything other than setting up a safety net in case somehow Gore ends up with the state's 25 electors.

McKay says that he and his colleagues "firmly and unequivocally believe the state supreme court overstepped its proper boundaries in an arbitrary manner." And the Select Joint Committee on the Manner of the Appointment of Presidential Electors' "unbiased" experts say the same thing. Argues

Elhauge, "There is no doubt of the right of the legislature to use that power at any time." "It is your constitutional duty" to appoint Florida's electors if none are yet chosen by December 12, says John Yoo, a constitutional law professor at Cal Berkeley and a former clerk for Supreme Court justice Clarence Thomas. "I don't think it would be appropriate to avoid that duty by waiting until the last minute. . . . You don't have the discretion *not* to pick the electors." The legislature has to appoint electors, says anti-gay author Roger Magnuson. Your power to do so is "plenary and full and absolute."

What a coincidence! That's just what McKay and Feeney were thinking! And Jeb, too!

"If there is uncertainty, the legislature has clear delegated authority from the U.S. Constitution to seek the electors. I admire them for at least on a contingency basis accepting that responsibility and duty," W.'s younger brother states.

Democrats are just plain pissed.

"Are we meeting to set the stage for a special session to guarantee the presidency to George W. Bush?" asks Democratic state representative Ken Gottlieb. "We should not serve as an insurance policy for a Bush presidency. We should serve to ensure every vote is counted and the real winner, whoever he may be, receives Florida's votes to be the next president."

"Why are we here?" adds senate minority leader Tom Rossin, from West Palm Beach. "Florida *has* its legal electors."

Rossin doesn't appreciate the amicus brief Feeney filed on Bush's behalf before the SCOTUS. "This brief hardly represents the Florida legislature," he says. "There was not one meeting held, not one vote cast.

"Do you think the Supreme Court knows this brief only represents the views of one party?"

But a better question might be: do you think it cares?

16

"We're going to massacre them."

The SCOTUS is *the* place to be Friday morning. An A-list affair with lines down the block to get in.

One pew alone features, from left to right: Daley, Christopher, former GOP Senate majority leader Howard Baker of Tennessee; Sen. Fred Thompson, R-Tenn.; Barbara Olson; and Sen. Ted Kennedy. Karenna Gore Schiff is in the house, as is the Republican governor of Michigan, John Engler, and Judge Burton. Al Cardenas is here, with losing Senate candidate Rep. Bill McCollum, R-Fla., by his side. As are Gore veep short-lister Sen. John Edwards, D-N.C., and former Clinton Justice Department Microsoft nemesis Joel Klein.

In a show of solidarity, the chairman and ranking Democrat of the Senate Judiciary Committee, Senators Orrin Hatch, R-Utah and Patrick Leahy, D-Vt., walk over to the hearing together. But Hatch and Leahy's brief bipartisan stroll ends at the U.S. Supreme Court building, and that's where any figurative common ground ends as well.

"The Honorable, the Chief Justice, and the Associate Justices of the Supreme Court of the United States!" bellows the marshal. "Oyez! Oyez! Oyez! All persons having business before the Honorable, the Supreme Court of the United States, are admonished to draw near and give their attention, for the Court is now sitting! God save the United States and this Honorable Court!"

Sitting in the center, high atop the mahogany mountain, in this historic room, with its maroon-and-golden curtains and sculpted marble portraits of, among others, Moses, Solomon, Confucius, Hammurabi, and Charlemagne, Chief Justice William Rehnquist gets right to business. "We'll hear arguments this morning in no. 00836, *George W. Bush v. the Palm Beach County Canvassing Board,*" he says. "Mr. Olson?"

Daley's concerned. Seven of these justices were appointed by Republicans — Rehnquist by Nixon; Stevens by Ford; O'Connor, Scalia, and Kennedy by Reagan; Souter and Thomas by Bush Sr. And though Souter and Stevens have since turned out to be quite a bit more liberal than anticipated, Daley sees the deck as stacked against them. To Daley this has never been a legal battle, it's been political from Day One, a political dogfight cloaked in law. That's just the nature of election law cases, he thinks. And if you were to agree with Daley's thesis, you couldn't find worse judges than Rehnquist and Scalia.

Rehnquist, seventy-six, was Nixon's assistant attorney general before he was named to the bench in 1972. Then, and when Reagan nominated him to be chief justice in '86, the Senate confirmation hearings were full of allegations that Rehnquist had long been hostile to the rights of minorities. As a private attorney in Phoenix in the '60s, Rehnquist opposed a plan to end school segregation and a public accommodations ordinance. There were even allegations — which Rehnquist denied — that while heading up a GOP ballot-security program, the future chief justice "personally challenged the eligibility of minority voters," according to a disputed Democratic Senate report. An intellect, and a pleasant-seeming man, Rehnquist has steered his Court on a decidedly conservative path.

And then there's Antonin Scalia, who in manner almost makes Rehnquist look like liberal Ruth Bader Ginsburg. Brilliant and confrontational, Scalia is a true-blue Believer in the conservative cause — for which he is both beloved and despised. In 1974, as an assistant attorney general, Scalia had been given the task of deciding whether newly resigned President Nixon had to hand over his infamous tapes and documents. Scalia ruled that Nixon didn't have to do so; he was unanimously overruled by the Supreme Court. In '86, Scalia — then a U.S. Court of Appeals judge for the District of Columbia — was confirmed unanimously, sneaking past the Democrats in the Senate amid a bitter battle over Rehnquist's promotion to chief justice. On the stump, Bush has cited both Clarence Thomas and "Antonio" Scalia as the kinds of Supreme Court justices he admires.

Democratic attorneys keep telling Daley that Rehnquist's Court is known for exercising judicial restraint, for bending over backward to let states decide their own laws. *Whatever,* Daley thinks. Here we are, right?

Ted Olson steps up and immediately addresses what many feel is the weakest claim in the Bush argument — that the issue here involves a federal law and necessitates the Court's attention.

"The election code that the Florida legislature developed [for elections] conformed to Title 3, Section 5 of the United States Code," Olson says. "That provision invites states to devise rules in advance of an election to govern the counting of votes and the settling of election controversies." The Florida high court made new rules after the election, Olson argues. He's well prepared, having worked long nights with his Gibson, Dunn & Crutcher partners plus Carvin, Terwilliger, and others — including a stable of former Supreme Court clerks who bring with them a certain understanding of what arguments appeal to their former bosses, like Manning, who once clerked for Scalia, and Ted Cruz, who worked for Rehnquist.

But Olson is scarcely two minutes into his opening statement when Justice Sandra Day O'Connor, seated immediately to Rehnquist's left, jumps in.

"Well, Mr. Olson, isn't Section 5 sort of a safe-harbor provision for states?" she asks, meaning isn't it just in case of emergency, if and when the electors aren't selected by December 12. "I would have thought it was a section designed in the case some election contest ends up before the Congress, a factor that the Congress can look at in resolving such a dispute." After all, as Justice Anthony Kennedy, immediately to O'Connor's left, says, "We're looking for a federal issue."

Justices Stevens, Scalia, and Stephen Breyer, a Clinton appointee, also get down in there, mixing it up, probing and poking and examining Olson's position. Scalia asks Olson if he would hold Florida to such a tough standard if this were a debate about speed limits and highway funding. Stevens points out that Olson's whole argument is "based on the premise that the Florida court overturned something that the statute had done. Is it not arguable, at least, that all they did was fill gaps that had not been addressed before?"

Kennedy cites the *McPherson v. Blacker* case from the Bushies' briefs. It's up to the state legislature to design the scheme by which electors are selected. "The state legislature *could* vest it in the judiciary if it wanted, as I read the *McPherson* case," Kennedy says. "And here they've done something less."

Right, Olson later says, when Souter brings the same issue up. The Florida Supreme Court was "doing what this court said in the *McPherson v. Blacker* case that it cannot do, is allow itself to insert itself or the Florida constitution above what is required by Article II, Section 1 of the Constitution," that it's up to the state legislature to decide how it's to be done.

Justice Ginsburg, also a Clinton appointee, seems perhaps the least convinced that she and her colleagues should overrule their Florida counterparts. In "even the very cases that you cite, as I checked them," she notes,
the high court ruled "that we owe the highest respect to the state court
when it says what the state law is."

Ginsburg argues that if there are two possible readings of the Florida
court's ruling — "one that would impute to that court injudicial behavior,
lack of integrity, indeed dishonesty, and the other that would read the
opinion to say we think this court is attempting to construe the state law,
but it may have been wrong, we might have interpreted it differently, but
we are not the arbiters, they are" — then why should the highest court in
the land assume the worst?

In deference to her concern, Olson amends his earlier statement. "I don't
mean to suggest, and I hope my words didn't, that there was a lack of
integrity or any dishonesty by the Florida Supreme Court," he says. "What
we're saying [is] that it was acting far outside the scope of its authority."

But both sides get beat up in Supreme Court cases; it's the nature of the
beast, since to make it so far up the judicial ladder, both parties have to
have compelling arguments. So, after a few brief remarks from Joe Klock
and Paul Hancock (representing Bob Butterworth), Gore's main man,
Harvard law professor Lawrence Tribe, undergoes the same ordeal.

Tribe starts by slamming Olson's argument as merely a sound bite.

"Although it is part of the popular culture to talk about how unfair it is
to change the rules of the game, I think that misses the point when the
game is over, and when it's over in a kind of photo finish that leaves people
unsure who won," he says. "And then the question is: How do you develop
great, sort of, greater certainty? And a rather common technique is a
recount, sometimes a manual recount, sometimes taking more time. . . .
It's nothing extraordinary."

Kennedy raises an eyebrow. "You're saying, no important policy in 3
U.S.C., Section 5?" he asks. "In fact, we change the rules after?"

Tribe backs down a bit: "Certainly, not, Justice Kennedy." But, he adds, "if
you look at the language, I think it's really much too casual to say . . . that
all of the laws must stay fixed." Moreover, he says, "that's really not a question for this Court, but rather for the Congress."

Tribe reads the law in question, arguing that it provides for the courts to
step in if need be, so no big deal, no harm, no foul. But O'Connor doesn't
take to this. Florida law states that certification should have taken place on
November 14, she notes, and the state supreme court changed that.

"'Here is the certification date,'" she says, as if quoting the legislature. "How could it have been clearer? . . . Perhaps the Florida court has to be aware of the consequences to the state of changing the rules."

Tribe says that the "provisions are in conflict" in the Florida law, so the Florida court took the state's emphasis on the right to vote and used it "as a tiebreaker." But Justice Scalia doesn't like that. "Mr. Tribe, I don't agree with that," he says. "I don't think that the Florida Supreme Court used the Florida constitution as a tool of interpretation of this statute. . . . I read the Florida court's opinion as quite clearly saying, having determined what the legislative intent was, we find that our state constitution trumps that legislative intent. I don't think there's any other way to read it. And that is a real problem, it seems to me, under Article II" — the provision of the Constitution that gives state legislatures the authority to decide how they select their electors.

Scalia keeps needling Tribe, making it more than clear that he doesn't approve of the Florida court's ruling. "I just find it implausible that they [in the Florida legislature] really invited the Florida Supreme Court to interpose the Florida constitution between what they enacted by statute and the ultimate result of the election," Scalia says.

O'Connor and Kennedy, too, seem rather skeptical and disapproving. Under questioning, Tribe at times steps back a little from his own arguments. He even appears to strain occasionally for new ones, at one point actually telling the justices that "disenfranchising people isn't very nice."

Finally, Rehnquist calls it a day.

"The case is submitted," he proclaims as the gavel goes BANG! Justice Clarence Thomas is, as usual, the only one who didn't speak.

★ ★ ★

Also on Friday, those crazy, wacky liberals on the Florida Supreme Court rule on the butterfly ballot appeal that Henry Handler, Andre Fladell, et al. have filed.

They rule against them with prejudice.

"They claim that the ballot is patently defective on its face in that the form and design of the ballot violated the statutory requirements of Florida election law," the court writes. "The appellants contend that the ballot was confusing and, as a result, they fear that they may have cast their vote for a candidate other than the one they intended." Even if one were to accept the "allegations," the court writes, the butterfly ballot isn't anywhere near "substantial noncompliance with the statutory requirements mandating the voiding of the election."

"NO MOTION FOR REHEARING WILL BE ALLOWED," the justices unanimously rule.

★ ★ ★

Bush wants attention to be paid to his Thursday meeting with Colin Powell, his likely secretary of state. It's all part of the "Inevitability Image." A seven-vehicle caravan arrives at Bush's Crawford ranch shortly before noon; the Cheneys and Powells exit a blue Chevy Suburban and enter the side door of the Bush ranch's temporary house; construction of the main house being, like so many things these days, behind schedule. Ten minutes later the alpha males, with wives following them dutifully, approach the media. Bush is at his DKE president best, winking and mugging to the scribes.

"We're really thrilled that Colin and Alma took time out of their lives to come down," Bush says. "We're going to spend the afternoon talking about our transition, and in particular we're going to talk about national-security matters and foreign-policy matters, and no better person to talk about that with than Colin Powell. He has a great deal of experience. Dick and I trust his judgment, so I look forward to a really good afternoon.... Colin, thanks for coming."

"Thank *you*, governor," Powell says. "I look forward to our conversations this afternoon on matters of international affairs and foreign policy and also transition issues. So thanks for having me, and congratulations on your success in the election." When asked if he's officially been anointed secretary of state, Powell says, "I have not yet been asked, and if that question should be posed to me, I think I should answer it directly to the governor at that time before answering anyone else."

Asked if he's concerned about the legislature's stepping in, and whether that might be seen as a power play, Bush says, "As far as the legal hassling and wrangling and posturing in Florida, I would suggest you talk to our team in Florida, led by Jim Baker."

Asks another reporter, "With Gore all over the airwaves, are you having this press availability to respond to criticism that you've appeared out of touch, out of mind, out of touch the last few days?"

Bush laughs. "That's a pretty good one. Thank you all for coming."

★ ★ ★

All day Thursday and Friday, airtime is taken from Powell and given to the ballot-filled trucks from Miami-Dade and Palm Beach as they make their way to Tallahassee.

From West Palm, the ballots come in a yellow Ryder truck driven by Tony Enos, the actual designer of that fucking butterfly ballot. He probably owes the citizens a little more hard labor than just an extended road trip, but this is the task he's been given. From Miami, the ballots come in two white vans that leave Leahy's watch at 6 A.M. Friday. Behind them, in a silver Pontiac, rides a Gore observer named Chad. Chad Clanton.

The five-hundred-odd-mile, eight-hour trip proceeds up the Florida Turnpike north, past Disney World to I-75 North, to I-10 West to Tallahassee. The truck and vans are followed by news choppers, so CNN and MSNBC and all the rest can periodically give images of the caravans. Clever and original newscasters and reporters all note the similarity with the coverage of O. J. Simpson's Ford Bronco ride. An AP reporter even tracks him down to see what he thinks. "Boring," says the Heisman trophy–winner and acquitted double murderer, now a Florida resident. "In my case, it may have been a little more intriguing, because people didn't know what was going to happen. Here, they know the ballots are going to get to Tallahassee."

★ ★ ★

The Gorebies' point man on minority voters' irregularity complaints, Henry Latimer, learns that in Duval County, 27,000 undervotes and overvotes were tossed — disproportionately from black precincts in downtown Jacksonville. In some black precincts, 1 in 3 ballots was discarded, about four times more than in white precincts.

Latimer learns this after certification, and he's pissed. Now it's too late to do anything about it. He'll work with the Congressional Black Caucus and the NAACP in urging the Justice Department to look into the problems, to hold hearings, to try to get to the bottom of what happened, so that it never happens again.

But what did happen? What was the reason for the 27,000 trashed ballots? Latimer wonders. Was it the confusing "caterpillar ballot"? Was it all the new black voters? Did someone intentionally double-punch the ballots?

In a way, it almost serves the Gorebies right. Duval Democrats had been trying to get members of the Gore team to listen to them for weeks. There were votes in the overvotes, they insisted. African-American voters who had been confused by the caterpillar ballot had written Gore's name in. There was clear intent there. But few were then taking the notion of overvotes seriously. Well — some were. Young and Sautter. And African-American Democrats in Duval. But no one was listening.

★ ★ ★

"If anyone's wondering," one member of the Gore legal team jokes, "Steve Zack's available for *Nightline* tonight."

Quite a few on the Gore legal team don't understand why Boies spends so much time with Steve Zack, who seems to some to be something of a self-aggrandizing bullshit artist. Maybe this was just jealousy. Everyone wanted to be close to Boies, but it was Zack who would have dinner every night at the Silver Slipper, billed as "a place for Florida's movers and shakers," with the Microsoft killer, and some didn't quite get why Boies liked him.

There has been much debate within the Gore legal team as to how to proceed. Berger thinks that the only evidence needed is the un-recounted ballots from Miami-Dade, and the 3,300 disputed ones from Palm Beach. Coffey, meanwhile, wants a litany of experts to show that there was something wrong with the machines, as well as to establish that the Miami-Dade GOP protesters intimidated the canvassing board. Another consideration — not to mention evidence, in the Gorebies' mind, of the Bush delay-and-draw-out strategy — is the fact the Bushies have compiled a list of almost one hundred witnesses. If this is a race against time, maybe less evidence would be better.

In the end, Boies and Klain decide to introduce a ton of evidence but not a lot of testimony. Zack will prepare two witnesses to establish two matters: that there were uncounted votes that need to be inspected, and that there was something wrong with those Votomatics that caused the problem to begin with. This will show that there were legal votes that hadn't been counted, the counting of which could likely change the outcome of the election.

While Zack and his elections expert examine the machines in Miami-Dade, the assistant director for the supervisor of elections, John Clouser, tells them that some of the Votomatics haven't been cleaned in eight years.

Other questions are raised, too. Why do some people have problems punching holes? And why does it just happen on column one, on the left? The left side is used most often, which, some theorize, increases the rigidity of the rubber. Could that be it?

Zack's no expert on any of this. The first time he heard the word "chad" was when he was sitting in Middlebrooks's courtroom, Monday, November 13. But he has a theory. Most people are right-handed. So when they put the machines down on the voting table, they must bring them in from the right side, and inside the Votomatic the chads migrate to the left side as that corner is put down first.

Yes, that must be it, Zack thinks.

★   ★   ★

Bartlit, meanwhile, is preparing what he feels is an excellent case on Broward, compiling odd quotes from Gunzburger and Lee, preparing to call in Judge Rosenberg himself to hammer the canvassing board on its liberal standards. Gunzburger and Lee argue that they agreed around 80 percent of the time, but Bartlit is under the impression that Rosenberg will slam them on the stand.

Another bomb Bartlit plans to drop involves Michael Lavelle, despite the fact that Lee has said that the Lavelle affidavit did not affect the board's decision one way or the other.

Moreover, Lavelle has since reviewed the September 1990 transcript and has concluded that Judge Barth did, in fact, allow two dimples to count as votes. His original recollection *was* correct, he thinks. And Mihalopoulos's phone call to him, in which he read partial excerpts from the transcript, was misleading, if unintentionally so.

The *Tribune,* of course, is reporting the opposite. "Mistake in Citing Illinois Case Gives Bush Ammo," Jan Crawford Greenburg writes on Friday, December 1. Her story still doesn't mention the role that Mihalopoulos played either in bringing Lavelle to Berger and Boies's attention to begin with or in convincing him that his original memory was wrong. Plus she's still making assertions like "the judge in fact ultimately excluded those [dimpled] ballots," which Lavelle, at least, believes not to be true. Far be it from the *Chicago Tribune* to point out its own sloppy reporting has fed into the mess it now is writing about.

Deposed by the Bush lawyers in Illinois on December 1, Lavelle reads from the September 1990 hearing transcript, reciting Barth's comments that "the light standard is not the litmus test, in my view. If there is a dent, a voter's intent may be established from other considerations of the ballot itself." He also testifies that neither Berger nor Boies ever pressured him "to include information in that affidavit that was not true and correct as [he] understood it to be," thus countering an ethics complaint against Berger and Boies filed by the conservative National Legal and Policy Center in McLean, Virginia.

Boies is aware that Lavelle's videotaped deposition is better for his team than the Bushies would have it. Both he and Berger are under the impression that there is little more going on here than an attempt to paint them as liars, when in actuality, the biggest liars about the *Pullen* case have been Baker and the Bushies for arguing that the case had to do with hanging chad only. The big mistake was assuming that the *Tribune* stories were accurate; but since then, it's pretty clear that in the *Pullen* case dimples were in fact considered, and were even counted on at least one occasion. Late one night, Sean Gallagher faxes Berger notice that the Bushies intend to show Sauls the videotape of Lavelle's deposition.

"Tell Bartlit that not only are we going to cross-designate" the videotape, Boies tells Berger, "but if he wants to drop any parts that he thinks are bad for us, we want them in." They *want* Lavelle to become part of the record, they *want* the Bushies to run the video.

The Bushies decide not to.

★   ★   ★

Friday evening, Zack deposes a tall cowboy named John Ahmann. Ahmann, one of the refiners of the punch-card ballot back in the 1960s, is a Bush witness flown in from California to try to shoot holes in Zack's chad buildup theory. Sometime during the deposition, Ahmann mentions that he holds a patent for a new kind of stylus.

"You know what? I bet he's got other patents," Zack thinks. He calls Jennifer Altman, a partner at the Miami office of his forty-lawyer firm, Zack Kosnitsky, and asks her to find out everything she can.

Altman spends the weekend, she later says, "looking for anything on this guy. I spent a lot of time on the phone, on the computer, finding whatever research I could."

★   ★   ★

Before statistician Hengartner testified before the Palm Beach canvassing board last Friday, he was up all night preparing the affidavit he was going to present to the board. In it, he hoped to outline his predictions of how many votes should turn up while they waded through the undervotes. One of the comparison races Hengartner used involved the 1998 Palm Beach ballot, and the fact that there were more undervotes in the senate race than there were in that year's governor's race. His guide in Palm Beach was Neal Higgins, twenty-five, a second-year Harvard Law student, who, Hengartner believed, told him that the governor's race was in the second column — thus lending credence to the theory that there were more problems in the first column.

But after he's flown to Tallahassee, Hengartner still hasn't seen the 1998 Palm Beach ballot, he still doesn't have the hard data. So he asks one of the Gorebies, Mike Farber, to take the reference to those 1998 races out of his proffer* before Sauls. This does not escape the notice of one of Beck's favorite witnesses, Laurentius Marais, a statistician from South Africa whom corporate America — Big Tobacco, lead-based paint manufacturers, etc. — relies on quite a bit to shoot down the theories of plaintiffs. Theories

---

*A written statement a witness presents to the record in a trial as to what he or she is going to say.

like, say, Philip Morris misrepresented the health effects of smoking. Or that kids who chew on lead-based paint have slower intellectual development.

Marais calls Palm Beach, obtains a sample copy of the 1998 ballot that Hengartner referred to in his Palm Beach affidavit, about which he has removed all mention in his proffer. "I think we may have a piece of information that will be quite useful in your cross-examination of Professor Hengartner," he says to Beck.

He explains.

"Holy shit," says Beck.

★ ★ ★

That night, Bartlit Beck junior partners Shawn Fagan and Sean Gallagher are about to go depose Hengartner and Brace, respectively.

Beck tells them about all the good stuff he has on Hengartner and Brace, the ways he's planning on taking them down. So he tells Fagan, a Harvard Law grad who clerked for Rehnquist, and Gallagher, a Michigan Law grad who clerked for O'Connor, to take a dive. Beck doesn't want them to tip off the Gorebies' witnesses as to what they have, so they can adjust their testimony.

"You are under strict instructions not to ask any smart questions," Beck says with a smile. "I want you guys to take the worst depositions ever taken. If you ask anything about the 1998 Palm Beach ballot, you're fired," he says to Fagan. And to Gallagher, he says, "I don't want you to ask anything about the rubber on the left-hand side of the Votomatic. We got great stuff, and I don't want to scare them off."

Fagan and Gallagher go off, spending most of their depositions asking the Gore witnesses what courses they taught in college, what books they used as course materials, where they went to school, inanities such as that.

Afterward, they huddle with Beck, talk about the few things they were able to learn, and brag about which deposition was dumber. Before they all retreat to their hotels for an hour or two of sleep before the trial, Terwilliger and Ginsberg grab Beck. Whaddaya think? they ask.

"I suppose I should be lowering expectations," Beck says. "But the truth is, we're going to massacre them."

17

"You were relying on the Gore legal team to give you the straight facts, weren't you?"

In Courtroom 3-D, circuit court judge Sanders Sauls doesn't look like he's enjoying this any more than the rest of the nation is. He's scowling, even frowning a bit. Sauls had said that he wanted this to be a twelve-hour hearing, winnowing down the number of Bush witnesses from ninety to twenty.

Doesn't he know that nothing happens quickly in Florida? Heck, that's why people *live* in Florida. This is the state where a quartet of senior citizens can paralyze a four-way intersection for an hour while they wait for the other Cadillac to move first.

"Let's get all the fluff off," Sauls said on Friday. Following his lead, Boies and Richard begin Saturday with a bipartisan motion-and-second to try to keep their opening remarks concise.

And we're off. Though we've all learned by now that this thing could end up anywhere — being decided by the U.S. Supreme Court, the Florida legislature, the U.S. House and Senate, or the fat Baldwin brother — Gore's legal team has pinned a lot on this case. If not on Sauls, then at least on the case they're about to present here.

Boies steps up and declares that "the issue before this court is 'Is there, or are there, legal votes that have been rejected?'" It doesn't matter why Harris didn't accept Palm Beach County's post-deadline numbers, Boies argues. What matters is that the county tabulated votes that Sauls now should include for Gore, votes that could certainly affect Bush's margin of victory,

Boies notes, "which, as everybody in the country and probably the world knows, is five hundred thirty-seven."

He ends after about fifteen minutes, telling Sauls that he's "not going to spend time arguing 'the right to vote,' or any of that."

Now it's Richard's turn, and he comes out swinging, saying that Boies's arguments are "unreasonable and contrary to Florida law." "If we accept Mr. Boies's premise, there is no reason for a tabulation on Election Night," Richard says. Just ship all the ballots to Tallahassee after the election and have all the judges count them. Rather, "the conduct of the canvassing boards comes to this court with a presumption of correctness."

And besides, Richard continues, Boies has to prove "whether or not the Miami-Dade, Palm Beach, or Nassau canvassing board has abused its discretion, not only that it acted wrongly but also acted in a fashion that no reasonable person would have done." Boies, Richard points out, has soft-pedaled this premise since first introducing it on Tuesday to a somewhat skeptical reaction from Sauls.

Other attorneys in the room get a moment to speak. Fresh off his U.S. Supreme Court appearance, Klock has a quick give-and-take with Palm Beach County canvassing-board lawyer Andrew McMahon. Michael Mullin, representing the Nassau County board, says that he will easily and handily dispense with the Gore complaint against his board.

Throughout the day, a cluster of protesters remains gathered outside the courtroom. Gore supporters are singing "This Land Is Your Land," as one from their number strums an electric guitar. The Bush backers hold signs jeering Gore as a sore loser; one from their crowd is dressed as Darth Vader. A man in sackcloth with a fifteen-foot crucifix argues that only Jesus can bring this nation together.

Inside, Zack calls the team's first witness, Kimball Brace, dressed like the prototypical D.C. bureaucrat, shaggy beard like Grizzly Adams.

The Gorebies haven't devoted an inordinate amount of time to tracking down the very best witnesses. After Hengartner had testified before the Miami-Dade and Palm Beach canvassing boards, DNC staffer Jason Fuhrman had e-mailed Klain and a couple others, asking them if they wanted to keep using the Yale statistician. The DNC had since talked to other statisticians who were both more experienced and higher profile. But the Gorebies were happy with Hengartner; Boies thought he had done a fine job in Palm Beach, and after all, Hengartner was a known quantity.

But what about his idea that there was something wrong with the voting machines? That somehow, for some reason, it became tougher to punch holes in ballots in the first row? Rouverol, at eighty-three, was a little long in the tooth. So Zack looked through newspaper articles and saw that the expert quoted most was Kimball Brace, president of Election Data Systems, a consulting firm in the D.C. area.

"Can you help us?" he asked Brace, after explaining what he was looking for.

"Yes," Brace responded. And now here he is.

Brace says that for the last twenty years, his company has compiled information on "what kind of voting system is used in every single county in the country." Zack brings Brace's own Votomatic out, Exhibit 52, and Brace proceeds to show how it's supposed to be used: ballot slid into Votomatic, stylus through the hole of the machine and the ballot underneath, chad punched out. "Unfortunately," Brace says, "it doesn't always work that way."

Beck objects. Brace, Beck says, is "a professional demographer" without the expertise to talk about the Votomatic. Beck steps up for a voir dire* examination, says that "in fact what you've been doing for the last twenty-five years is things like advising the Democratic Party in redistricting fights." Brace's degree, Beck reveals, is in political science, not mechanical engineering.

The point won, the task of questioning returns to Zack. Brace says that after looking at the Palm Beach voting devices earlier in the week, he concluded "that there was more extensive wear of that template on the left-hand side than on the right-hand side, which would be understandable and normal in the course of business, in terms of the use of the voting equipment. The left-hand side of these machines gets more use, because when an election administrator sets up the ballot, he generally starts from the left-hand side and moves to the right-hand side as the ballot is filled out."

Brace says that dimples can be formed when ballots are put on top of the Votomatic instead of slid inside them.

"I want to inquire, if I may," Sauls asks. Do the voter instructions say to make a dimple?

"Well, they're not instructed to create dimples," Brace says, "they *do* create dimples."

---

*From the Old French for "to speak the truth," voir dire is usually the term used during jury selection when lawyers try to figure out a prospective juror's possible biases. But opposing counsel can also voir dire a witness, especially on the matter of the witness's expertise, to see whether an expert witness has an interest in the case, which he or she, of course, is not supposed to have.

There are other ways, too, dimples can be formed, Brace says. If "the machines are not cleaned out on a regular basis and there's chad buildup and, therefore, the voter may not be able to push down as firmly." Or if the stylus goes in the hole at an angle, instead of straight in. Or if the rubber strips on the device aren't "properly maintained," and they "become old, brittle, hard, and keep a voter —"

"Your Honor," Beck jumps in, a 180-pound sneer, "may I voir dire on this expertise?" Sauls holds him off; cross-examination is coming. Brace ends by saying that hand recounts are necessary.

Now Beck is ready to roll. He asks Brace to use the machine and vote without making a dimple.

He does.

"Did it work?" Beck says.

"Yeah," Brace replies. "I voted for number five." Gore.

"You don't have to say who you voted for, " Sauls says to laughter.

"And if somebody actually puts the card in the machine like they're instructed to, and attempts to vote, rather than attempts to make a dimple, it's not all that hard to knock out the little chad, is it, sir?" Beck asks.

"Well, it depends on the template in there," Brace says. He shows how it can be difficult to punch it in sometimes. "Well, I mean, I'm hitting right here . . . I'm pushing down, and finally, it went in."

"*Long last,* you're able to vote," Beck says. This is like slapping a punching bag.

"Do you know the difference between synthetic rubber and natural rubber?"

No.

"Do you know whether natural rubber over time tends to get harder or softer as it ages?"

No.

And on and on. He's cooking now, sounding and carrying himself in a way that's eerily reminiscent of Kevin Spacey at his Oscar-winning, arrogant best.

Brace is not cooperative. "Would you answer my question?" Beck impatiently asks him.

"I thought I did," Brace replies.

"No," Beck says. "Answer yes or no. Then if you need to explain . . ."

"OK. That would certainly be the main thing that I . . ."

"You're supposed to answer yes or no," Beck says.

"Yes," says Brace.

"Yes?"

"Yes," Brace says again.

"*Thank you,*" Beck says, his voice dripping with a candy-covered combination of exasperation and disdain.

Beck soon turns to chad buildup.

"The theory is that there's a bunch of people voting for president of the United States, and all these little chads fall down, and they kind of stack up on one another, and then they stop somebody from pushing the stylus through the hole, right?"

"Not necessarily," Brace says. It stacks up on the left side, he says.

"Do you know how many people, on average, use one of these voting machines in the presidential election?"

"I don't," Brace says. "It would be a good number to know."

How many chads would have to be in a Votomatic to cause chad buildup? Beck asks.

"I don't know."

Beck then wonders how chad can build up on the left side in a Votomatic when the devices are taken to and fro, hither and yon, in between elections. Brace has no answer to that.

Zack has two of the actual Votomatics from Palm Beach County. He's hoping one of them will be full of chad. When no one's looking, he opens the latch of one of them, looks underneath, and sees that it's empty. He pushes the device back into place. He opens the second one — it's full of chad. He smiles. It's his birthday today, and this is his present, he thinks.

He takes this second Votomatic over to Brace. "Have you ever seen somebody, after they get through voting, go ahead and shake it up so that they get all the chads moved around?" he asks, shaking the Votomatic, hoping to discredit Beck's theory about the chad getting shaken. "Have you ever seen anybody do that?"

"No, I have not," Brace says.

Zack brings the device to Brace.

"There's a lot of chad falling out," Brace says.

Zack asks him "to remove this cover, and, Judge, I want to show that this cover, this machine is full to the brim with chads. . . . May I dump this, Your Honor, on a piece of paper?"

"You need my knife?" the hammy Sauls asks, quickly brandishing a blade. Brace accepts it.

I ask a courtroom cop if a lot of judges carry knives. "I dunno, I never searched one," the cop says. "A couple carry sidearms." But then again, the cop says as he takes out his own knife, "We all carry knives in the South."

Brace opens the machine and chad confetti spills all over Sauls.

"I'm putting chad all over Your Honor's counter," he apologizes. Gore attorneys smile, seeming to think that the fact that masses of chad built up in this third-party-selected machine proves their point.

Beck asks Brace to read the Votomatic's instructions, under "Important Notice to Voter." Brace does: "Look at the back of the ballot card, then be sure all holes are cleanly punched, and then pull off any partially punched chips . . . that might be hanging."

"They don't even talk about the *possibility* that somebody could come in here and end up just dimpling the thing rather than punching through, do they?" Beck asks.

"Dimples are a newer phenomenon in American electoral history," Brace says. Not a good answer.

Brace steps down, and it sure feels like Beck just ate Brace alive.

★   ★   ★

Beck returns to his table. He likes cross-examining [read: destroying] experts more than anything else, ever since he was a kid in the 1950s watching *Perry Mason* on TV. (I wonder if the producers of *Perry Mason* know how many baby-boomer lawyers they inflicted on the world. Terry Lewis, Steve Zack, Phil Beck all cite the show as one of the many reasons they entered the law.) He's been waiting his whole career to get someone to confess on the stand to being the real murderer, he jokes. But this is pretty good, too.

Richard hands him a note: "One of the finest cross-examinations I've ever seen." Terrell, too: "That was brilliant."

In the court administrator's office — where the Bush legal team has set up shop for breaks — the responses are the same. Beck is getting slapped on the back, high fives.

"You should dial it back a little," Bartlit says. "You were having a great time up there, and you did a nice job, but you were close to going over the top. You should dial it back a little for the next guy, rather than be quite as theatrical and flamboyant."

"I don't think I can," the cocky Beck replies. But he promises to try.

Bartlit loves Beck, thinks he's fantastic, talented, has loved watching him blossom at the firm they created together. And he knows that lawyers love wiseass remarks and clever sarcasm, which Beck is great at. But in past cases, Bartlit Beck has conducted tests of Beck's arguments on potential jurors, using focus groups of judges and lawyers and just plain folks. And every time Beck unleashes one of his cutting remarks, the approval meter ratings go up with the lawyers and down with the jurors. The judges tend to be mixed.

Just dial it back a little, Bartlit says again.

★　★　★

Hengartner is next up, Douglass announces.

Douglass has largely been relegated to the position of Team Gore MC. He doesn't volunteer much in terms of suggestions or ideas; he doesn't think Boies Klain and the others want him to.

Gore attorney Jeff Robinson — the only African-American attorney I've seen on either side — begins questioning Hengartner, a gangly Canadian who, Robinson quickly establishes, isn't a Democrat, or someone being paid for his testimony, or even an American citizen. At Yale, he teaches applied statistics, probability, and the theory of statistics. He's here today because "it's an exciting problem, it's important," and "it provides visibility for both Yale University and also for myself."

Hengartner discusses charts that show that there were far more under-votes in Palm Beach County than anywhere else in Florida — an aberration the Gore team wants Hengartner to say can only be because of the county's faulty punch-card machines. Only 0.3 percent of the votes cast in optical-scanning machines have "no recorded votes for president," Hengartner says. By contrast, 1.5 percent of punch-card ballots were under-votes. And that figure was 2.2 percent in Palm Beach County.

Robinson then tries to get Hengartner to provide evidence that some-how Palm Beach County's hand recount wasn't done correctly. During their hand recounts, the canvassing boards in Broward and Miami-Dade Counties recovered votes in 26 percent and 22 percent of their counties' undervotes, respectively, Hengartner says. But in Palm Beach, the recovery rate was much lower, 8 percent.

Beck comes at Hengartner hard, too, seeking first to paint his knowledge of the undervote figure as incomplete, and then going after his credibility. Hengartner, Beck establishes, doesn't know about undervotes for other offices. Why didn't he ask Harris for the data?

He did, he says, but "she was less than helpful." Surprise, surprise.

To test your hypothesis, though, you'd have to look at other offices, right? Beck asks.

"It would be interesting," Hengartner says. "But I want to remind you, again, not all the races in each county will be competitive. . . .There would be popular judges, and hated judges —"

"That's why you would look at all the counties," Beck says, "rather than picking one county where there is the dirty rotten judge, and one county where there is a real popular judge —"

"Can we move this to another subject?" Sauls asks, always a jokester. But Beck has made a point.

Beck produces the Hengartner affidavit from Palm Beach County — to Hengartner's surprise and, it would seem, confusion.

Gore's attorneys start objecting frantically. They seem to know what's coming. Beck points to Hengartner's analysis of the undervotes in the 1998 Florida senate race versus those in the governor's race. Using a projector, Beck shines the offending graph onto the wall, as Robinson and Boies whisper to one another frantically.

"A closer inspection of the Palm Beach County ballot reveals that the senatorial race was recorded in the first column, and the gubernatorial race in the second," it says. The document goes on to say that "it seems unusual and indicates that the punch-card reader does not record all the votes cast in the first column."

"You bought into their hypothesis about the left-hand column," Beck presses.

"I am trying to put one and one together," Hengartner says in his stilted English.

"You haven't inspected the ballot," Beck asks, even though Hengartner's statement said that "a closer inspection" of the ballot helped prove the Gore team's thesis.

"Have you?"

"I have not seen the ballot," Hengartner admits.

Well, guess who has?

Beck says that he subpoenaed the elections board and has a copy of the ballot from November 3, 1996. With Sauls's permission, he approaches Hengartner on the stand and shows it to him.

Both the Senate *and* the governor's race are listed in column 1.

Bum-bum-*BUMM!*

Robinson stands; he wants to see the ballot.

"It's the only one we have," Beck says mockingly. "If you want to come up here and stand with us, I sure invite you to."

"You said in your statement that what was in column one was in column two," Beck charges. "That just wasn't true, was it, sir? You never even looked at the ballot."

"It contained a mistake," Hengartner says.

"When you signed that sworn document, you were relying on the Gore legal team to give you the straight facts, weren't you?"

"Well, I relied on the facts that I received, yes," Hengartner says meekly.

"That's all I have, Judge," Beck says, as he glides back to his seat.

Bartlit is so proud of Beck his eyes well with tears.

It's a pretty devastating moment, and Hengartner leaves the courtroom visibly rattled.

I've seen it a million times in D.C.: Democrats can be so fucking sloppy.

★   ★   ★

During a break, Terrell approaches Dexter Douglass. He likes Douglass and knows that Baker — who was friends and hunting buddies with Chiles — likes and respects him, too.

"You ever get to Texas?" Terrell asks him.

"Not much, Irv," Douglass says. He's very guarded.

"Don't you know about the *Pennzoil-Texaco* case, and which side I was on?" Terrell asks, smiling.

The lightbulb goes off over Douglass's head. "You were on the plaintiff's side, weren't you?" Douglass says. "So you're not *all* bad, are you?"

"No, I'm not all bad," Terrell says.

Douglass notes that Terrell has stayed pretty low-key with the media. "I haven't seen you grabbing the microphone," he says.

"That's true," Terrell acknowledges. "I have seen people grab the mike, and it didn't serve them very well." He tells him a little about the *Pennzoil* case, how Jamail burned his friend, how he himself thought his shit didn't stink for a spell there. Things have been OK on this case, though. Some of the Bush lawyers grouse when Barry Richard books himself on *Larry King Live* — he and King are old friends from Miami. And of course, there's the tension with Bartlit, much of which goes on behind Bartlit's back. But things are relatively serene.

The conversation soon turns to Douglass's Herefords, and cattle, and Boies.

"You really got yourself a horse there," Terrell says, motioning to the lead Gore lawyer.

"That's true," says Douglass. "But my horse gets tired."

★   ★   ★

The Republicans get to call their witnesses now, and they start with Burton. At the front of the room, Sauls is rocking back and forth in his leather chair, his lips pursed like he's about to whistle.

Having been slammed by both sides in Palm Beach, Burton is embraced by the Republicans in Tallahassee. And why not? With his chad standard, Gore picked up only 174 votes, and under his leadership, the count wasn't completed in time. Palm Beach could have blown everything for Bush. But with Burton, it's pretty much blown over.

Bartlit walks Burton through the evolving process by which they assessed ballots in West Palm: LePore, Carol Roberts, Dennis Newman, Ben Kuehne, LaBarga, Jackie Winchester, the 1990 standard, one-corner rule, two-corner rule, hanging chad, dimples, patterns of dimples, and on and on.

"Basically three Democrats?" Bartlit says of the canvassing board.

"Three people trying to do the best job they can, yes sir," Burton replies.

Boies, interestingly, doesn't attempt to undermine the Palm Beach standard as too rigid in his cross-examination. Instead, he decides to try showing that Palm Beach found votes — legitimate, actual, real-life votes — in its hand recount, thus hoping that Sauls will include them even though they were a little late and also force the same standard on the 9,000 yet-to-be-hand-recounted ballots of Miami-Dade.

Sauls wants to know more about the 1 percent recount, if there was any established rule as to when the results from it would necessitate a full county recount.

"I felt not," Burton says, "because, quite honestly, I think statistically to say that would mean nineteen hundred votes, that was incorrect. . . . I wanted to go about this in a more reasoned approach and analysis, and I wasn't given that opportunity. And I guess since that day, I guess I've been the one accused of trying to block this recount, which is not the case."

"Absolutely not," Sauls says. "I'll have to salute you as a great American, as a matter of fact."

A great American? Boies thinks. OK, well, clearly Dexter's right, Sauls is not inclined to rule for us.

Even Burton thinks Sauls's comment is "weird." Commenting on what a witness was saying, giving his editorial take on it? "OK, whatever," Burton thinks.

He steps down. Outside the courtroom, Barry Richard approaches him. "I really want to get together when this is all over," Richard says to him. "One Democrat to another."

★ ★ ★

Beck brings a rubber expert before the court, Richard Grossman, technical director for the the Hammond Group's Halstead Division, which manufactures "heat stabilizers and other additives for rubber and plastic composition." But Zack points out that Grossman told him in yesterday's deposition that he has never seen a Votomatic. He gets Sauls to go along with the thesis that Grossman can talk only about the composition of rubber — not the operation of the Votomatic — and when Beck even *thinks* about anything other than that, Zack objects over and over. To Sauls's clear annoyance.

"This is *an expert*, Mr. Zack," Sauls says. "Overruled."

But Zack gets some points in on cross-examination — for what they're worth, since Sauls seems to be showing his cards. Zack gets Grossman to acknowledge that he knows nothing about the maintenance of the rubber in the Votomatics. Soon it becomes pretty clear that Grossman doesn't really have much to offer.

The clock strikes 6:20 P.M. Sensing no end in sight, Sauls, weary, impulsively hammers it all to a close until Sunday morning, bright and early.

The Gore attorneys are mixed on how the day went. Klain and Douglass think that the witnesses were inexperienced and pretty horrible. Boies thinks that it doesn't really matter that much, the important evidence is the ballots, and they just need to get to the Florida Supreme Court. Zack has a more positive spin on it, of course. Brace was adequate, he thinks — better than Beck's rubber guy!

Of course, the onus is on what Beck has taken to derisively referring to as "the Gore legal team" to put on stellar witnesses. The Bush team has no obligation to prove a thing. They're just here to waste time and lay groundwork for an appeal, which would waste more time. And they're doing a swell job.

Outside, the attorneys host dueling press conferences. Gore aides point to a *Miami Herald* analysis of the 175,000 discarded ballots from all over the state, somehow ending up with Gore winning Florida by 23,000 votes. The *Herald* analysis is ridiculous, assuming, as it does, that everybody voted successfully, assuming that everybody voted for president, that no one abstained.

The Bush team tries to explain contesting procedures it filed earlier in the morning, challenging the election results in Volusia, Broward, and Seminole Counties. They say they did so because in order for Sauls to rule in Gore's favor, the outcome of the election needs to be in question; by throwing these counties on the table, it will become clear that anything and everything can be disputed when you get down to it. It's as if by making an even bigger mess, they'll make the prospects of cleanup well nigh impossible.

Meanwhile, the lovely little town of Tallahassee is hosting a parade and winter celebration. Citizens have a fun run, cheered on by spectators, while rides and treats and festive lights wow the town's kids. As the town joins together to light the ceremonial Christmas tree, locals seem happily apathetic about the political and legal manipulations taking place only yards away.

☆ ☆ ☆

Immersing yourself in one state's politics is like attending a Royal Family reunion: the incestuous relationships you come across are just staggering.

You have Miami-Dade assistant county attorney Murray Greenberg, who attended junior high school with Barry Richard, who lost his primary race for attorney general to Jim Smith, whose law partner is Brian Ballard, whose sister is Palm Beach County commissioner McCarty, whose nemesis is Carol Roberts . . . and on and on . . .

Holland & Knight attorney Steve Uhlfelder of Tallahassee embodies this web. Within a few days of the Election Night anticlimax, Uhlfelder — who served as counsel for the '96 Clinton-Gore state campaign and was a member of Democrats for Bush this year — was called to work for Gore, for Bush, and for ABC News. He chose the last. Uhlfelder is close with Jeb, whom a few years ago he introduced to his good friend Barry Richard. He's a law partner of Richard's wife, Allison Tant, ran the judicial retention campaign of both justices Lewis and Anstead; as a student at the University of Florida, he, Steve Zack, and Donald Middlebrooks met "Walkin'" Lawton Chiles at the Gainesville city limits; his dad was close friends with Carol Roberts and her husband when president of the Palm Beach synagogue Temple Israel. When he was at Steel Hector & Davis, he hired Donna Blanton, one of Katherine Harris's attorneys; his wife, Miffie, and Jeb's wife, Columba, take yoga together; he was counsel to Democratic governor Reubin Askew in '78 and is GOP senate president John McKay's business attorney now. And on and on.

On Saturday night, December 2, the Uhlfelders and the Richards go out to eat at the Governor's Club. Soon, of course, the straight-laced Richard announces that he has to call it a night. "I'm really tired; I need to go home to prepare for tomorrow," the attorney says.

It's a nice night; the town's Jingle Bell Run is in full operation. And, in keeping with the nature of state politics, after they bid Barry and Allison adieu, whom should they stumble upon but David Boies, holding an empty wine bottle in one hand on his way back to the Governor's Inn.

"Hey, Steve," Boies says, having met him through his commentary work for ABC News. "What's going on?"

Boies says that he's returning from a great dinner at the Silver Slipper with Zack. As a connoisseur of wines, he enjoyed the bottle he's holding and didn't want to forget the vintage.

"Let's have some more!" Uhlfelder says. At the Governor's Inn, they do.

Uhlfelder tells Boies that his team seems pretty disorganized; he'd spoken to Gore attorney Deeno Kitchen earlier, and Kitchen said that he didn't quite know who was in charge. They talk about Microsoft, about civil rights; Boies, on his third or fourth screwdriver, says that he doesn't quite get why the Bushies are putting up such a stink about counting the Miami-Dade undervotes — he's not even sure that Gore would gain votes there, when all is said and done.

Uhlfelder studies Boies. He likes him. Thinks he's one of the most honest and open people he's ever met. But he also wonders if Boies is the kind of guy who has to be all things to all people. He's boozing it up with him tonight, he's been interviewed on TV every morning. And then, of course, there's that court case.

★　★　★

Sunday morning, back in Miami, Zack's colleague Altman is still looking into John Ahmann's stylus patent when she finally finds the U.S. Patent and Trademark Office's Web site.

Bingo.

The Bush team's star witness — there to reassure Judge N. Sanders Sauls that everything was totally cool with the punch-card ballot devices — holds two patents for instruments designed to vastly improve said devices. And in order to secure the patents, Ahmann slammed the original voting machines he was in the courtroom to laud. Ahmann's deposition before the patent office reads like Zack had written it himself.

Altman, a registered Republican who voted for Gore, is pleased with her discovery. But she's even more worried about how she can deliver this information to Zack, who's already in the Tallahassee courtroom. Zack's cell phone is off. Its mailbox is full.

Altman frantically calls Berger's law firm on Monroe Street in Tallahassee. She faxes the information to them and begs them to rush it over. Jessica Briddle, a Gore recount-committee staffer, grabs the material and sprints down Monroe Street to the courthouse. Near the elevators, she gives it to Jeremy Bash, who gives it to Gore attorney Andrew Shapiro.

In the courtroom, while Ahmann is being sworn in, someone — Zack's still not sure who — puts the file on his lap with the typed note Altman had sent: "Steve, urgent, read now."

Zack does.

Beck, meanwhile, is doing direct examination of the bolo tie–clad Ahmann, who says that "it punches real easy. . . . I seriously doubt that the voter would be unable to push through on a normal voting device."

As for the theory that chad buildup under Gore's name prevented people from voting for him, Ahmann says, "I do not believe it's possible. . . . I know no way that could happen."

What about if, as Zack yesterday pointed out can happen, the device hadn't been cleaned out in a decade?

"I would first say, no," Ahmann says, "but then that would also depend on whether you had an election every week, or if you only had an average of two or three elections a year. . . . In order to fully fill it up, you could go fifty years."

In Miami, Altman isn't even sure if Zack has gotten her fax. She's watching the trial on MSNBC, but it has switched to a commercial break or different programming or something. So she switches to C-SPAN. Zack's on his feet now, cross-examining Ahmann.

"Would it be relevant to you to know that the machines purchased by Palm Beach County had an inferior plastic, a harder plastic?" Zack asks.

"It's not unusual that when a manufacturer puts out a product that the initiation of that product might not be perfect," Ahmann says. "When IBM first came out with its Votomatic, it had to be reworked, and that's when I got involved."

Zack smiles. "I really appreciate your mentioning that," he says, trotting out Ahmann's October 27, 1982, patent application.

Klock objects on behalf of Katherine Harris. Of course; shouldn't the lawyer for the chief elections officer of the state try to hide problems with the Votomatic from the court? I guess this one thinks so.

"Overruled," Sauls says.

Zack starts to read his patent application back to Ahmann.

"Could I have a copy of whatever documents are being read from?" Beck asks.

Now it's Zack who can cockily say, "I only have one copy."

Zack continues quoting the application.

"The material typically used for punch board and punch card voting can and does contribute to potentially unreadable votes because of hanging chad or mispunched cards.

"If chips are permitted to accumulate between the resilient strips, this can interfere with the punching operations and, occasionally, it has been observed that a partially punched chip has been left hanging onto a card, after the punch was withdrawn, because the card supporting the surface of the punch board had become so clogged with chips as to prevent a clean punching operation. Incompletely punched cards can cause serious errors to occur to the data processing operation utilizing such cards."

Zack next questions Ahmann about his stylus patent, which Ahmann says was designed to "align better" than the styluses used in Miami-Dade County.

"We wanted to reduce template wear, which will keep the stylus on the chad, so that they have clean punches rather than gouges, or pinholes, or hacking chad," Ahmann says.

In his final question, Zack asks him about the need for manual recounts after elections "when you have hanging chads . . . lots of them because machines aren't tearing them off correctly."

To which Ahmann replies, "You need either reinspection or a manual recount if you have that situation, yes, you do."

Precisely the opposite of what the Bush team wants him to say.

"Any redirect?" Sauls asks Beck.

Ahmann is now a witness who might say anything, Beck thinks. Sure, what Ahmann said will have limited, if any, impact on Sauls, but Beck knows this is a big PR loss. Time to pull out.

"No, Your Honor," Beck says.

In Miami, Altman is loving it. "The person had gone up on the stand and said X, when in fact, in a sworn deposition before the U.S. patent office, he had said Y," she'll later say. "Lawyers dream about impeaching someone that way."

Though GOP attorneys are quickly dispatched to the TV cameras to compare the old punch card–ballot devices with other fully functional though not quite cutting-edge machinery — windshield wipers without the "blink" mechanism, for example, or black-and-white televisions — members of the Gore legal team are clearly delighted with Ahmann's testimony. And TV pundits start saying that maybe things have finally shifted Gore's way.

After Ahmann's testimony, a beaming Zack leaves the courtroom during a break and gushes to the media. "We feel that's it," he says. "It goes to the fact that there was a problem with the machines. And it proves that in a close vote, you gotta hand-recount the vote."

In the court administrator's office, Ginsberg approaches Beck.

"Did you know about the patent?" he asks.

"I knew about the patent, but I hadn't seen this document," Beck says. "I don't think it's going to be a significant deal, though."

Beck explains: Whether John Ahmann thinks hand recounts are a good idea in a close election makes for good television, he says. But it will mean absolutely nothing to Sauls, who's trying to decide whether these county canvassing boards abused their discretion — discontinuing the hand recount in Miami-Dade or applying a more rigorous standard in Palm Beach. Yes, it's going to be played as a big deal in the press, and everybody's going to be saying that John Ahmann flipped us on this key point. I know it's going to be played as a *Perry Mason* moment — especially because Boies and Zack are good at manipulating the press — but I also know it's not going to impress Sauls at all.

Ginsberg nods his head. "Yeah, you're probably right," he says.

★   ★   ★

The day goes on. Beck calls to the stand William John Rohloff, the Broward County cop Scherer found who claims that on Election Day he placed the stylus over Gore's chad and withdrew it because he just *couldn't* bring himself to vote for Gore. Rohloff now fears that he left a dimple that the Broward County canvassing board may have erroneously deemed a Gore vote. It's probably safe to say that voters like Rohloff are about as common as a day Katherine Harris avoids eyeliner, but the point is that the Republicans have found him, and here he is.

Laurentius Marais has a teddibly erudite-sounding South African accent and a distant, callous bearing; when he steps up to testify, the temperature in the room drops 10 degrees. Douglass passes a note to Miami-Dade County attorney Murray Greenberg that Marais "would fit right in with the Third Reich."

That's a bit harsh, but Marais does seem like a precision-oriented SOB, handily sneering at many Gore claims as bad science and incomplete research, repeatedly dissing Saturday's testimony by Hengartner, implying that it was "slipshod and slapdash." He also says that "it would be a factor to consider" that there were so many undervotes in Palm Beach because — as Beck hypothesizes — some voters were confused and "may have just thrown their hands up in the air and said, 'I can't figure this out; I'm not going to vote for any of these guys.'"

"From a statistical point of view," Beck concludes, "is there any valid basis for drawing the conclusion that people were in the Votomatic voting booths trying to vote for Al Gore, but they simply weren't able to push the stylus through the chad?"

"Absolutely none," Marais says. *Brrr!*

On cross-examination, Boies tries to slam Marais as the statistician equivalent of a hit man. He paints Marais as someone who makes a living out of killing the testimony of other statisticians at the behest of evil interests, claiming that whatever he's hired to dismiss "does not meet your standards as to a thorough scientific analysis. . . . For example, you testified that certain statistical analyses that linked lead paint with injuries in children didn't meet your standard for statistical scientific analysis, correct?"

At this, Beck jumps up and objects.

Boies "is trying to tar him," Beck charges, asking Marais to discuss "a case Mr. Boies thinks would be unpopular with the public, and that doesn't have any relevance here." Beck asks Judge Sauls to direct Boies to stop dragging in other cases, to "admonish" Boies to take issue with Marais's methods and his methods only. "Otherwise, all he's doing is grandstanding," Beck says.

"Your Honor," Boies says, "I'm not grandstanding."

But Sauls sustains the objection. Marais's whoring for the lead paint industry is not relevant here.

Beck objects again when Boies describes something Marais has said in a way Beck thinks is misleading. Boies allows that maybe he's confused about the matter, but before Marais can clarify, Sauls jumps in and lays out all the arguments Marais had made.

I wish I'd said it that well, Marais jokes.

Sauls's comments impress the hell out of Beck, and reassure him that the judge gets it. "If anybody thinks this guy is anything other than a sharp guy really paying attention, they're wrong," Beck thinks. "He's paying more attention than anybody else in the courtroom to what's being said on the stand."

★   ★   ★

Irv Terrell calls GOP Miami pol Tom Spencer to the stand. Spencer was an observer in Miami-Dade throughout the canvassing board's fickle month, and he basically reads excerpts from hearing transcripts, establishes that Democratic judge King pushed for the recounts while independent Leahy didn't want to do them at all. Spencer seems like a straight shooter, a friend of Leahy's, and Terrell picked him to help tell the Miami-Dade story precisely because of that. Spencer says that there were lots of problems during the hand recount, that on November 19, "an entire tray of ballots from precinct two hundred fourteen . . . fell and splashed all over the floor and was picked up, and then put back in the tray in order."

And then comes Tom Spargo.

Terrell had the Miami-Dade "intimidation" part of the case, and he privately considered it to be probably the Bushies' ugliest moment. He spent the week talking to Miami-Dade GOP witnesses and, frankly, found a lot of them wanting. He especially needed someone to testify that hundreds of chad were spit out when the third machine sort was conducted to sort out the undervotes. Show some evidence that the process was off the rails, and maybe the near riot would be a bit more excusable. Tom Spargo was the only witness he had who could testify to this.

Terrell has asked each of his three witnesses the question lawyers always ask: Is there anything — *anything* — in your background, *anything at all,* whether or not it's true, whether or not it's been misinterpreted, anything that I should know about that the other side can use against you? Because you're about to go on national TV, and if there is anything, it will stain you forever. All three said no. Nothing there.

Terrell has his suspicions about Spargo, but what can you do, he said he was clean. So he calls him to the stand, and Spargo testifies about the chad.

When it's time for Kendall Coffey's cross-examination of Spargo, he doesn't waste any time brandishing the blade.

"Good afternoon, Mr. Spargo, I'm Kendall Coffey, one of the attorneys for the vice president and senator. As I understand it, part of the thrust of your testimony this afternoon is to, in effect, discredit, if you can, the reliability and integrity of some of the processes that were used by Supervisor Leahy and the staff, correct?"

"I only testified, I believe, to what I observed but I, all right —"

"Isn't it *true*," Coffey asks, "that the last time you were on the witness stand on matters of reliability and integrity in an election scenario, you took the Fifth Amendment nineteen times?"

Terrell's on his feet even before Coffey's sentence is completed. "This is what you call your basic bushwhack," Terrell says. "He knows it's not proper. He's coming in to embarrass him, and I suggest he tender whatever evidence he's got. I think it's irrelevant."

"Your Honor, I have background information which I think goes to the reliability of the witness," Coffey responds.

Sauls calls the attorneys back to his chambers to talk about this.

★   ★   ★

Spargo's a New York GOP hack, counsel to lame politicos with short shelf lives, like Lt. Gov. Betsy Ross and Republican-turned-Democrat-turned-unemployed congressman Michael Forbes, back in Forbes's first incarnation. In the Empire State, Spargo's known for trafficking in the ridiculous, like a 1990 lawsuit against then-governor Mario Cuomo for claiming his family's Queens home as his voting residence, though the governor, of course, primarily resided at the governor's mansion in Albany. Or his 1998 suit on behalf of defeated attorney general Dennis Vacco against newly elected Democratic attorney general Eliot Spitzer, in which Spargo alleged, but never remotely proved, that fifty thousand illegal aliens voted on Election Day. He'd been counsel to the state GOP until he resigned in 1990 under investigation of an ethics commission. This involved the role, if any, that he played in a 1985 campaign-financing scandal that funneled cash from the developers of a Poughkeepsie mall to local officials. After Spargo failed to submit to questions about the alleged political payoffs, a state supreme court justice issued a warrant for Spargo's arrest. This was lifted when Spargo agreed to testify before a State Commission on Government Integrity investigation, though his testimony was hardly forthright, as he did, indeed, invoke the 5th Amendment nineteen times.

In a trial held on a normal schedule, it's likely that neither Hengartner nor Ahmann, nor Brace, nor — especially — Spargo would have been called to testify. But this is fast-track, baby.

Sauls, Coffey, Terrell, Richard, and Klock spill into the hallway behind Courtroom 3-D.

Terrell is furious. He notices the conspicuous absence of Boies and Douglass.

"We believe that this witness is subject to impeachment," Coffey says, outlining Spargo's sketchiness, most notably the times he pleaded the 5th Amendment.

"Might I ask counsel a question?" Terrell fumes. "When did this occur?"

I think it was ten or eleven years ago, Coffey says.

"Was he convicted of a crime?" Klock asks.

"It's showing a propensity to refuse to provide candid testimony in matters involving elections," Coffey says.

"As counsel for Governor Bush," Terrell says, "at least in the state of Texas — Mr. Richard and Your Honor will speak for the state of Florida — that's not admissible." Since he was never convicted of anything, certainly not of a felony, and this all happened more than ten years ago, none of it is admissible in a court of law.

"It's the same in Florida," Barry Richard says.

"It's improper," Klock says. "I'm surprised."

Sauls sustains the objection. "Anything further as to that," he says to Coffey, "and we're going to have a hearing on contempt tomorrow morning." Sauls marches back to the bench.

"And if there's anything else like that," Terrell warns him, "*I'll* move for contempt on you."

Coffey shrugs. "You've gotta do what you've gotta do."

"Listen to me, counsel," Terrell whispers. "You will be damaging yourself if you continue. What you heard out there and in here is mild compared to what I'm going to say about you if you keep going like that."

They reenter the courtroom. Terrell approaches Spargo and whispers to him. "He will not be asking you any more questions like that," he says. "You're doing great, you're doing well as a witness. Keep hanging in there."

Then: "Tom, there's something I must know, and you must tell me: is there anything else?"

"Irv, I'm so sorry I didn't tell you before," Spargo whispers, repentant.

"I know," Terrell says. "But I must know, you must tell me."

"No, that's it," Spargo says. "I'm so sorry."

But Coffey's not done yet. He has a photograph of Spargo actually demonstrating — clapping and chanting — at Miami-Dade on Wednesday, November 22. He asks him about various hypocrisies of GOP tactics in Miami-Dade — that Martinez tried to get a court order to stop the separation of undervotes from the rest of the pack, for instance, and only days later, Republicans protested when the canvassing board went to the nineteenth floor to separate the undervotes that hadn't yet been separated.

Richard leans over to Terrell, who's still enraged, and tells him about the stripper Coffey bit back in '96. Terrell is horrified. He looks at Coffey like he's an animal. Terrell becomes worried that he's so mad, he'll say something about Coffey's incisors to the court, or to the press. But he doesn't.

Soon enough, Coffey's done with Spargo. Terrell, of course, does not take the opportunity to ask him any more questions.

When his rage subsides, Terrell will wonder why Coffey raised the issue in such a clumsy way. He could have pointed out that Spargo is the only one who supposedly saw the thousands of chad spilling out, pointed out that the court is being asked to take Spargo's word for it. He could have talked to him about his word, about how a man's word relies upon his ethics, principles, and beliefs, asked him if he'd ever been accused of being unethical. Then Spargo would either have had to admit it or lie about it, and Terrell would have had to object, putting an end to it with the world — and Sauls — perhaps believing the worst.

Not only was Coffey's tactic unethical, Terrell thinks, it was bad lawyering.

★ ★ ★

During a break, the Bushies regroup a bit. Beck approaches Terrell.

"You know, not everything goes perfectly," Beck jokes. "Sometimes your guy endorses hand recounts," he says.

Terrell smiles. "Sometimes he pleads the Fifth Amendment."

Bartlit feels that he has a bang-up case on Broward to present, but Ginsberg and Terwilliger want to end it. They don't need to push for much more of a case, they don't need to put on many more witnesses.

Bartlit disagrees. He's gonna roast Gunzburger. And Lee, to a lesser extent. He has damning quotes of Gunzburger talking about voting her conscience instead of a standard, and he has Rosenberg ready to assail her. Plus, Bartlit says, if they lose in the Florida Supreme Court, they should be prepared to put the Broward ballots back in play. But even Beck thinks that they should quit while they're ahead. The Gore case is weak. The Bushies are winning. Who knows how many Ahmanns and Spargos are lurking in their witness lists?

★　★　★

The last quarter or so of the trial is full of quiet and minor developments. Marc Lampkin gives his testimony, alleging that when Leahy and his team began sorting out the undervotes on Wednesday, the ballots were damaged.* And, as one member of the Bush legal team later tells me, Lampkin, an African-American, is also there to show the country that the GOP isn't entirely made up of white Presbyterians.

Twenty-year Nassau County supervisor of elections Shirley King comes next; none of the Gorebies want to cross-examine a sweet little old lady, so Dexter Douglass gets the job. He already knows the Nassau case is hopeless — he told Boies as much after reviewing the facts. "They're not going to throw those ballots out," he said. "I hope you didn't really bet your law license on this one."

Soon the Gorebies try to introduce the ballots as evidence. Terrell objects. The ballots have been through all sorts of "reshuffling," he says. And the Gorebies never even proved "through any witness the authenticity of those ballots, they didn't call Supervisor Leahy, they didn't call anybody from Miami-Dade to actually put those ballots before Your Honor in an appropriate way."

Sauls agrees that the reshuffling argument is understandable if the Gore team wants to argue for the ballots' "utilization" — that is, to count them,

---

*What goes unmentioned is that Leahy thought Lampkin's whole purpose that day was to "get in his face and irritate him sufficiently to delay the process."

to handle them, to show that there are votes in them thar boxes. But to admit them into evidence isn't that big a deal. A few of the "real people" intervenors get up and speak; Hengartner returns to try to clear his name, but rebuttal testimony isn't supposed to be about "rehabilitat(ing) your witness that has been impeached," Klock objects.

Soon — *YAWN*, it's like 10 P.M. — it's time for closing arguments. Douglass thanks Sauls for the expeditious way he ran the case — finishing up even before Zack's schedule would have had them done — and Boies stands up, one last chance to work his magic before the skeptical judge.

He's a fascinating guy, occasionally mesmerizing in the legal arena, just as a gifted thespian, or talented tennis player, can be. But his case has not felt, at least to me in the stands, all that strong. Hengartner and Brace were duds; disgraced in one instance, discredited in the other. Sauls has seemed underwhelmed by the Boies magic that has worked so well on us in the media and on judges like Thomas Penfield Jackson in the Microsoft case. And whether or not Boies Klain is shooting for the Florida Supreme Court as an endgame, the Sauls case is important both for PR purposes as well as to establish a record that the SCOTUS and its frisky conservative justices — like, say, Scalia — might want to poke around in.

It just doesn't feel like they've made their case. Not even a bit. And the fact that they never tried to get all 175,000 undervotes and overvotes counted has caused a complete erosion of support for the "count every vote" charge among reporters, many of whom would like to know who actually won the presidency, as crazy as that sounds.

Instead, Boies talks about Nassau County, hoping to make the convincing case that Douglass never managed. "The statutory direction is that when you have a discrepancy, you pick the mandatory machine recount" number, not the count from Election Night. The Nassau canvassing board could have recounted the ballots again; it didn't. It just relied on what *Harris* of all people told them to do.

"The court heard Judge Burton, called by the defendants, testify that they had been able to identify the clear intent of the voters," Boies says. "There is no evidence in the record that suggests that those two hundred fifteen votes are not legal votes that need to be included." The fact that they were two hours late is no reason to keep them out of the final vote tally, he says. Of course, they weren't two hours late, they were actually three days late. And there weren't 215 net Gore votes from Palm Beach, there were 174.

"He says, 'Well, maybe there are some votes there, maybe there are some people who intended to vote. But it's too late, and that's that,'" Boies says of Richard, characterizing this euphemistically as a "bad things happen" argument. "With respect, Your Honor, Florida statute and Florida case law do not permit the court to say, 'Well, we're simply going to ignore the will of the voter.'"

As for Miami-Dade, Boies continues, whether you believe the bumbling Nicolas Hengartner or the creepy Laurentius Marais, the canvassing board there "was able to discern the clear intent of the voter in between one-fourth and one-fifth of all the ballots that the machine could not read. . . . So what needs to be done with these nine thousand ballots? We think the answer is obvious. They need to be counted. They need to be reviewed."

What about counting *all* the ballots statewide? "I challenge them to cite the case that says that," Boies says, "because the statute doesn't say that." The contest statute asks us to prove that there are legal votes that haven't been counted, Boies says. "And we've done that."

Richard's turn. Two weeks ago, he says, the Florida Supreme Court ruled, in *Palm Beach v. Harris,* that "the decision whether to conduct a manual recount is vested in the sound discretion of the board." Well, the Miami-Dade, Palm Beach, and Nassau County canvassing boards exercised their discretion responsibly. And no one has proven otherwise. "I kept waiting for a witness to come in here and testify that there was a problem somewhere in this state, and that the problem was of sufficient magnitude to overturn the county anywhere," Richard says. That witness never showed up.

Boies is misreading the statute he cites for Nassau County, Richard says. The statute "is not about the difference between the first machine count and the second machine count, it's talking about the distinction between the machine count and the returns that were submitted" to the canvassing board. "A voter can't come into court and say, 'I forgot to go to the polls on Election Day,' and say, 'You need to give me another chance.' And the voter can't say, 'I went to the wrong precinct and voted the wrong place; let me vote again,'" Richard pleads. "Why is it any different when a voter walks into the booth and either fails to read the instructions properly or, if he can't read them or she can't read them, fails to ask the personnel who are available for such person to help, and votes wrong? . . . The voter has some obligation to do it right."

The burden of proof is on Gore's team, Richard says. "We are light-years from any carrying of that burden. There is no proof of any problems. There is nothing but two witnesses with speculation. There is no evidence."

He puts it to Sauls: Is Florida "prepared to tell the American people that it will disqualify its electors and possibly hinge the election of the presidency on the only two witnesses presented by the plaintiffs?"

Under pressure to speed things up, the Gore team limited their case to two witnesses. Just as the Gorebies' original decision to limit the hand recount to four counties, rather than all sixty-seven, was rooted in the pressure they felt to have the matter resolved quickly, the Bushies successfully spin the results of their opponents' hypersensitivity to PR and the ticking clock as evidence of an inherent disingenuousness.

★ ★ ★

In the midst of some of the riff-raff closing arguments — Klock's, and some of the voters' attorneys — there's an off-the-record discussion about Shirley King, elections supervisor of Nassau County. Sauls says, "I salute Miss King as a great American." That makes two great Americans in one trial. Not bad.

Terwilliger steps up and makes a motion to dismiss. "The relief they have asked for is a partial recount of votes. And here they disagree in their papers without contention that a manual recount has to be *all* the votes, or that any recount has to be of *all* the votes." Boies said that the Bushies needed to cite a case in order to push for a statewide recount. "We don't need a case," Terwilliger says. "The statute says it all. It is self-evident, and logic dictates that it be all the ballots that would be subject to a recount."

In fact, the Bushies are now convinced that the Gore legal team will never go for a statewide recount. They believe that the Gorebies think that they would lose a statewide recount — especially one with clearly defined standards — and so, even though the Bushies don't want one, they shrewdly seize it as a PR and legal maneuver.

As for their argument that the Miami-Dade canvassing board erred by not continuing their hand recount, though its members were convinced that they could never make the November 26 deadline, this is ridiculous, Terwilliger says. "Surely the irony is lost on no one, no less Your Honor, that the board is now being sued" for not abiding by a situation that the Gorebies, using the Florida Supreme Court, created, "for failure to meet a deadline that the Gore-Lieberman campaign asked for."

At 11:18 P.M., the case is closed. "I will give you a decision in the morning," Sauls says.

★ ★ ★

"I think Barry Richard's a fine lawyer," Boies says to a scrum of us. "I think he made the best case he could with the material he had to work with." After recouping in a conference room in the circuit court judges' chambers, Boies is handed a beer, which he guzzles in the elevator down to the parking garage.

It seems to escape at least a few of those following this whole mess that it has now become a war between thieves. Perhaps it always was. Bush doesn't want any recounting of ballots, and you don't need to be a politics junkie to know what that means. If you're confident you scored the touchdown, you're not going to worry too much about the instant replay. But Gore, bar a few offers he knew would be rejected, hasn't exactly wanted a replay, either. He's only wanted to review a select chunk of Florida where statistically he should clean up. Yes, an argument could be made that limiting the recount to those few counties made lots of sense; it would be logistically much more feasible than a statewide recount, and it certainly was playing by the rules to choose the counties where they wanted a second look. Bush could have chosen some Republican counties if he'd wanted to, but of course he didn't want any recounting anywhere.

Was there any way Gore could have avoided getting to where he is right now, his top lawyer heading for his car, his case in tatters? Possibly not. Maybe in California or New York or Illinois. Maybe in Massachusetts or New Mexico or Oregon. But this is Jeb Bush's backyard. This is Katherine Harris's home. They pull the strings, they hold the cards, and they're the ones folks like Sauls and Burton and Penelas are going to have to answer to once David Boies and Ron Klain have gone back home. But even if this is the Jeberglades, there was never — not once — a good-faith effort by the Gorebies to go statewide and find out who really won if the 175,000 unread ballots were examined. There were Republican officials — not a lot of them, but enough, like Nebraska senator Chuck Hagel — who had said that a statewide recount seemed the only reasonable solution; Gore could have taken cover by standing with him. But he didn't, because his lawyers and his pols told him he didn't have to, and that he might not win that way. So in enemy territory, Gore ceded the small amount of high ground he had. Between that and the fact that the Bush team has out-lawyered, out-intimidated, and out-maneuvered the Gore folks at just about every turn, it is hard not to be left with an inescapable conclusion. Al Gore may well have won more votes than George Bush here in the Sunshine State. But assuming the SCOTUS keeps to form, this is over.

Boies should probably think about a second beer. At least.

18

Subject: gore clean up

We in the media may not have been paying much attention to the Seminole County case up until now, but the Gore and Bush teams sure have been. And even before the case is tried, all sorts of odd machinations go down.

After Thanksgiving weekend, Seminole County circuit court judge Debra Nelson is preparing to hear the suit, when her campaign manager reveals that Nelson's campaign, too, had forgotten to put voter ID numbers on absentee-ballot applications, and thus it, too, had fixed about five thousand applications. The Republicans move that the case be shipped to Tallahassee to be consolidated with the Sauls case. They get one out of two: it moves to the capital but to the courtroom of circuit court judge Nikki Ann Clark.

"I think this might be the sleeper case over here," an intrigued Judge Terry Lewis says to Clark. "Everybody's looking at the Sauls case over there, but we've got thousands of votes over here, and if they get thrown out, the election will go the other way."

Some of the Bush legal team chieftains are intrigued as well. Clark's an African-American woman, an appointee of Governor Chiles. Sounds to them like a Gore voter. They want her recused.

But Barry Richard disagrees. She's very intelligent, very independent, she's a good judge, he tells them. She'll rule on the case on the merits, he says. Others on the Bush team aren't so sure. Ginsberg, Terwilliger, and Baker learn that Clark was one of eight judges who'd been nominated in September to fill a vacancy on the Court of Appeals for the First District — and one of six whom Jeb Bush *hadn't* selected. They decide to ask her to recuse herself. Her failure to get a promotion is entirely a secondary consideration.* But it gives the Bush team a barely legitimate-seeming excuse to ask for her disqualification.

Barry Richard disagrees. This "promotion" thing is a ruse; the recusal motion is because she's black, a woman, a Chiles appointee — and the reaction of his colleagues offends Richard. That she wasn't promoted to the appellate court is nowhere near grounds for recusal, he says. And it could look bad, too. But the Bushies don't care about the merits or how people will interpret their actions; all that matters is that there are 15,000 absentee ballots that Judge Clark could possibly throw out, and they have to stop her.†

Though he's signed almost every Leon County court motion that comes out of the Bush Building, Richard refuses to sign the recusal motion against Clark. A Tallahassee lawyer named Segundo Fernandez does so instead.

On Wednesday, November 29, the Bush lawyers file the motion. After Clark denies it, the Bush lawyers on Thursday appeal the decision to the district court of appeals — using language that even Baker Botts attorney Daryl Bristow finds a bit harsh. The DCA also rejects the motion. And though there have been concerns expressed that both the motion and the appeal might garner them bad press, neither action merits much media coverage at all. Once again the Republicans are given a pass. So much for the "liberal media."

Clark has been in highly charged situations before — assistant state attorney in Miami, assistant public defender in West Palm, appellate defenders' office in Detroit, staff attorney with Legal Services of North Florida, aide to Chiles, assistant attorney general of Florida under Butterworth, director of legislation for the Florida Department of Environmental Regulation under Carol Browner. And that, in many ways, was the whole point. She wanted to be where the action was. Growing up in Detroit in the '60s, she could see that the legal arena was the place to be if you wanted to make a difference. In her mid-teens, she'd cut class to watch civil rights lawyers like Elliot Hall making their cases. She didn't know what those lawyers were even saying, but she knew that they were right, and that they were making a difference.

---

*In an interview in January 2001, I asked Richard why the motion for recusal had been made. "A number of people in the Bush campaign assumed that she would not be a good judge for us," he said. "She's black, a woman, a Democratic appointee — all traits of a likely Gore supporter. Also, days before, she'd been passed over for a promotion. So they wanted to get a different judge. . . . My feeling was that she was independent and intelligent and would make the right decision based on the law. I didn't think we had any basis for asking for a recusal, her not getting that promotion was not a legal ground. So I wasn't going to sign it."

†Interestingly, Clark's sister, Kristin Clark Taylor, was director of media relations for then-president George H. W. Bush.

Yes, she is exceptional: the first African-American to be named to the bench in the sixth circuit on any level and the only black female circuit court judge. But so what? And for that matter, how can anyone think that her social conscience means that she'll just hand the election over to Gore regardless of the law? Or that her failure to get kicked up to the district court of appeals will foment such resentment against anyone named Bush that she won't be able to preside? Most of the DCA judges have tried two, three, four times before they finally got promoted.

But if the media gives the Bush strategy a free ride, it doesn't always ignore Clark. Radio host Lowell Ponte calls Clark Gore's "Great Black Hope," "an arrogant African-American Democrat judge in Florida [who] may decide whether to throw out thousands of ballots cast mostly by whites, thereby tilting the statewide outcome and keeping her political party in the White House." Ponte blasts her for "lack of judicial ethics by refusing to step aside in a case where she appears to have ideological as well as selfish and personal [motives]."

At the same time, Clark is also aware that some African-Americans who don't perceive the system as being fair are looking to her courtroom as a place where at least this case might get a fair hearing. Jesse Jackson himself sat to watch a pre-trial hearing, though Clark didn't pay him much attention. Still, it is not inconsiderable pressure.

"This could be a real sticky one," Lewis, her colleague down the hall, says to himself, looking at some of the filings. "You clearly can't condone this kind of stuff," he thinks. "Clearly, you got stuff here that looks like at least they did something they weren't supposed to do. Yet you've clearly got people who voted, and nobody says that the people who voted weren't voters or that they did anything wrong."

He gets his chance to explore the same issues on Friday, December 1, when the saga of Martin County comes to his courtroom.

★ ★ ★

In 1925, when Floridians just north of Palm Beach sought to have their area officially incorporated as a county, they had a clever idea: they proposed that the new county be named after the governor at the time, John Martin. The residents of Martin County have a long history of playing the angles with the folks in charge.

Democratic electrician Ron Taylor had been outraged to hear that Martin County supervisor of elections Peggy Robbins let the treasurer of the Martin County Republican Party, Tom Hauck, remove several hundred Republican absentee-ballot applications from her office, do whatever the hell Hauck wanted to do to them, and then bring them back. Hauck had also been permitted by Robbins to camp in the elections office to fix any incomplete or mistaken applications. All in all, Robbins's cooperation with the GOP brought 673 Republican votes back into the world. To Taylor, Robbins made even Seminole elections supervisor Sandra Goard look good.

A full 9,773 absentee ballots were cast in the county, and Bush received 6,294 of them to Gore's 3,479. Taylor wants all 9,773 ballots tossed, which would result in a net gain of 2,815 votes for Gore, and the presidency of the United States.

It's decided that Lewis and Clark will stagger their trials so that lawyers like Richard can run from courtroom to courtroom on Wednesday, December 6.

★   ★   ★

When Daryl Bristow was taken off the Sauls case and put on Seminole, General Baker didn't sugarcoat it.

"Daryl," Baker said, "I've got something I'm asking you to do where you've got no upside." He told him about the case. "We oughta win," Baker said, "but if we lose, it's premier. And we gotta have someone with white hair to take the heat. Depositions start in Orlando tomorrow."

To Bristow, that seems like a year ago, though not even two weeks have passed. By now he's met with the Seminole County canvassing board's attorney, Terry Young, and with both the elections supervisor, Sandra Goard, and Michael Leach, the Republican operative who had camped out in her office for those fifteen days. Almost immediately Bristow realizes that he doesn't want either one of them up on the stand. Goard is scared stiff; also, clearly, she played a little fast and loose with the law, and she showed her GOP hand a bit. Leach is a nice young man, Bristow thinks, but it would be easy for the Democrats to paint him as a partisan thug. Bristow decides that if he can, he'd rather enter an agreement with Democratic attorney Gerald Richman stipulating as to the facts, rather than parading Goard and Leach before the country. To his astonishment, Richman — who wants things to proceed as quickly as possible so as to meet the December 12 deadline — goes along with it.

Richman agrees because he's so convinced that the facts in the case are so indicative of a clear, egregious, corrupt abuse of power by Sandy Goard that he doesn't even feel the need to cross-examine her or Leach in court. Perhaps he's not seeing things clearly; he's juiced up on eleven-year-old resentments. And he's been itching to put it to the Bushies from Minute One. The day after the election, Richman had been working with Berger's firm on filing a butterfly ballot suit. Richman was personally fired up about it all — he himself says that he almost voted for Buchanan because of that damn butterfly ballot. He hates Bush. And he thinks the Republicans play dirty. Correction: he *knows* the Republicans play dirty — firsthand.

When the late great Rep. Claude Pepper died in May 1989 at the age of eighty-eight, Richman ran against then–state senator Ileana Ros-Lehtinen for his seat in an ugly, ugly race that political mudslinger Lee Atwater helped run out of the Bush White House.

After Atwater said that electing a Cuban-American to the seat was his top priority, Richman replied, "This isn't an Anglo seat. It isn't a Jewish seat. It isn't a Cuban-American seat. It's an American seat. It belongs to all the people."

Atwater and Ros-Lehtinen took the second-to-last sentence in that graph — "This is an American seat" — and ran with it, making it seem as though Richman had been insinuating that Cuban-Americans aren't Americans. "Tell Mr. Richman that we too are Americans," read one Ros-Lehtinen brochure.

The day of the election, Radio Mambi and another Spanish-language station equated a vote for Richman with one for Fidel Castro. Richman lost with 47 percent of the vote. Ros-Lehtinen became the first Cuban-American elected to Congress.

Since that race, Richman had been convinced that there wasn't anything Republicans wouldn't do to win. So he was only too happy to collect butterfly ballot affidavits on behalf of the Gore campaign. And when he received a phone call from Gore lawyer Joe Sandler on November 20 — saying that "we have a major Democratic Party contributor who needs a good lawyer, we can't get involved in it but your name has been suggested" — Richman was only too happy to help.

The next morning he flew to Sanford, Florida, to meet with Harry Jacobs and a bunch of lawyers drafted by Jack Corrigan and other Gorebies trying to help Jacobs's cause, even though Gore himself continues to have nothing to do with his lawsuit and knows nothing of his underlings' actions.

Richman thinks Goard and Leach violated the law, of course. But there is never any question about the fact that he and Jacobs are motivated primarily by a desire to disqualify Bush votes so Gore will win the presidency.

The Gorebies are gun-shy, wimpy, Richman thinks, while the Bushies are hungrier, more willing to do anything they can to win. The Gore team's worried about the inconsistency of trying to get votes counted here, and votes *dis*counted there. They'd been burned on the overseas military absentee ballots and don't want to get directly involved with Seminole.

Richman and Jacobs didn't think that way; they didn't care. Like good Seminole warriors, they recognize that this is a guerilla war. And they want to win.

★　★　★

On Saturday, December 2, Young deposes Jacobs. He establishes a few interesting facts: Jacobs had given $50,000 to the DNC, had financed a TV ad against Cheney's professed ignorance of, and seeming indifference to, human rights abuses in Myanmar, with whom his oil-related business, Halliburton, knowingly got into bed. He also admits having spoken with both Berger and Sandler. The Bushies immediately leak this information to the media, so as to prove collusion with Gore.

They should be so lucky, Richman and Jacobs probably think. They're actually pissed off that the Gorebies aren't helping their cause *enough*. Berger wants to help them, of course, but he's rebuffed at every turn. In fact, Richman's being helped by the Gorebies, though surreptitiously, with various Gorebies drumming up attorneys to volunteer to fly down to Florida to help out. Labor lawyers like Jack Dempsey, general counsel of the American Federation of State, County and Municipal Employees, and New York attorneys Eric Seiler, Katherine Pringle, Jonathan Abady, and John Cuti soon arrive in Tallahassee and help Richman any way they can. Paralegals provided by AFSCME root through absentee-ballot requests. But overall, the Gore team isn't helping much at all.

In fact, Richman might have had to pack it in already if not for a surprise sugar daddy. Infoseek founder Steve Kirsch had called him one Sunday, after being stranded when his US Air flight had been cancelled. "I want to help you," Kirsch said. He'd sold Infoseek to Disney for $2.5 billion in stock options. So when he said, "What do you need?" he meant it. Richman soon had a chartered plane to Tallahassee; $150,000 in legal costs came soon after.

Still, Richman is mad. They have no direct support from Gore financially, and Lieberman himself has even publicly distanced himself from the case. What if Judge Clark were to hear that even Gore didn't support their actions?

★　★　★

But Kirsch's involvement does not end here. He hires a PR agent to the tune of $50,000 to pitch the Seminole and Martin stories to the media — many of whom seem to utilize the same tiresome clichés: "Gore's 'Hail Mary' pass," for instance. On Sunday, November 26, Kirsch also phones up and retains an attorney, William H. Davis of the Tallahassee law firm Wadsworth & Davis, whom he regales with theories of statistical extrapolation and proportional allotment of Palm Beach County overvotes. At first, the programmer's riffs on votes as data and such strike Davis as a tad eccentric. But soon Kirsch's theories seem quite brilliant — if something of a legal stretch.

Florida was a statistical tie, Kirsch says. So why not give Bush 12½ electoral votes and Gore 12½? He devises many methods on what might serve as a reasonable remedy for the butterfly ballot case — giving ½ a vote to Gore and ½ to Buchanan for each Gore-Buchanan overvote. Or random allocation of these overvotes to all the candidates. Or proportional allocation. The one result all of Kirsch's various number crunchings have in common: each one of these plans would hand Gore the presidency.

On Monday, November 27, Davis speaks with Dexter Douglass and David Boies about Kirsch's various remedies. They're gracious but not really interested. They've decided against pursuing anything in the butterfly ballot realm, they say. Kirsch's remedies end up working their way into various footnotes and supporting documents in the Seminole, Martin, and butterfly ballot lawsuits. But nothing really ever comes of the hard work and wacky ideas of the California billionaire who founded Infoseek.

★   ★   ★

Before Judge Sauls can give his judgment on Monday, December 4, the SCOTUS steps in. The SCOTUS justices had spent the weekend unsuccessfully trying to find a way that they could rule unanimously. Breyer, Ginsburg, Kennedy, and Stevens saw the Florida Supreme Court as having tried to iron out contradictions in the state law; O'Connor, Scalia, Souter, Thomas, and Rehnquist felt the court essentially rewrote the law that had set certification for November 14. Moreover, they were not satisfied that their Florida colleagues had done so using sound legal reasoning.

Justice Ginsburg had been the one with the brainstorm; during oral arguments on Friday, she had said, "I suppose there would be a possibility for this Court to remand for clarification." And so sayeth the SCOTUS on Monday morning: "After reviewing the opinion of the Florida Supreme Court, we find that there is considerable uncertainty as to the precise grounds for the decision. This is sufficient reason for us to decline at this time to review the federal questions asserted to be present.... The judgment of the Supreme Court of Florida is therefore vacated,* and the case is remanded for further proceedings not inconsistent with this opinion."

---

*Set aside, possibly to be completely nullified.

This is not the victory they could have been given, Carvin explains to one of his colleagues in Tallahassee, but it's good enough. It smacks down the Florida court's decision, essentially saying that the SCOTUS is mystified, unanimously, as to how they came up with that November 26 deadline. So mystified that they've sent the whole thing back with a demand for a better explanation.

The Bushies obviously feel this bodes well for them in the different case in front of Sauls. With Sauls in his chambers mulling over the most important judicial decision of his life, it will surely help their case for him to know that all nine SCOTUS justices think that the Florida Supreme Court was wiggety-whacked when they came up with that November 26 date.

Still, predictions of what's going to happen next run the gamut. The strutting Beck is confident, as he always is in every case, that they'll win on every count. Bartlit wonders if Sauls might rule for them while also ordering some counting to take place in anticipation that he'll get reversed by the Florida Supreme Court. Ginsberg, as always, is the worrywart, refusing to take anything for granted, giving into his never-ending, world-is-too-much-with-him angst until the facts prove his pessimism wrong.

The Gorebies tend to side with Beck on this one. Anticipating a resounding bitch-slap, they write up their notice of appeal, typed nice and neat, and stick it in Jeremy Bash's briefcase.

At 4:40 P.M., Sauls calls us back into Courtroom 3-D. Beck was right: Sauls gives the Gorebies *nothing*, not a thing, not a scratch or a lick or a whit of what they wanted. A big fat Southern-fried No.

"The court must find for a fact that a legal basis for recount must exist before ordering such a recount," Sauls drawls in his North Florida accent, glasses perched on the edge of his nose. "It's not enough to show a reasonable possibility" that the outcome of the election would have been changed because of illegal votes counted or legal votes not counted, Sauls says. "Rah-ther, you have shown a reasonable *probability*. In this case, there is no credible statistical evidence" that such a case was proved. The Gore legal team, Sauls says, didn't "establish any illegality, dishonesty, gross negligence, improper influence, coercion, or fraud in the balloting and counting process."

One by one, Sauls goes down the Gore claims and crosses them off the list of arguments he was willing to buy. They didn't show that votes from a partial hand recount should be counted. They didn't show that the Miami-Dade, Palm Beach, or Nassau county canvassing boards abused their discretion.

He declares the matter over, notes that the hundreds of thousands of ballots that had been shipped to Tallahassee via Ryder Truck would remain in court custody pending an appeal, and leaves the room.

Christopher's associate from Los Angeles, Mark Steinberg, motions over to Bash, sends him on his way. The appeal will be filed before any of the Gore lawyers even leave the room. Boies, Douglass, Zack, Berger, Steinberg, et al., politely congratulate the victors who so ably represented Bush: Richard, Beck, Terrell, Bartlit, Ginsberg, et al.

"David, nobody else could have even made this close," Terrell says to Boies.

Boies walks out of the chambers with a big grin plastered on his face, very Gore-like in a way.

When are you going to appeal?

"Right now," he says.

Douglass is asked the same question.

"It's probably being done as we speak," he says.

Terrell approaches Terry Madigan, one of the attorneys who represented actual Florida voters — Bush backers, all — who were allowed to act as intervenors.

"We appreciated it," Terrell says, presumably of Madigan's efforts.

"Thank you for saying that," Madigan says.

"Well, we mean it," Terrell says.

Cameras and boom mikes surrounding them like piranhas, the Gore team turns left, to a holding room near the circuit court judges' chambers, while the Bush team turns right, to the court administrator's office.

In the Bush room, there's a huddle among the twelve lawyers, a round of bear hugs and back-slapping. In Goreland, things are less jubilant. Boies asks if they should go down to the rotunda on the first floor and talk to the press. Hattaway tells him, "We can hold here" since "the Republicans beat us to the podium."

"No, let's go down and see what the other side has to say," Boies says.

Klock is at the podium when they arrive. He's describing Sauls as "a very thoughtful judge" who pays "a lot of attention to the law."

Turns out the rest of the Bush team is still celebrating, so Boies, Douglass, and Zack approach the podium, though only Boies speaks. Before he can even finish, the Bush lawyers show up and huddle at the side of the media throng before politely retreating to near the information desk several yards away. Boies faults Sauls for not even looking at the ballots in dispute. "You can't resolve that contest without actually looking at the ballots," he says. He says he's never heard of such a case, when a judge in an election contest didn't even look at the ballots in question. He adds that the fact that they were examined by canvassing boards is irrelevant to this particular legal phase. "The contest statute does not provide for any discretion by the canvassing boards," he says. Then, momentously, Boies says: "They won. We lost. This is going to be resolved by the Florida Supreme Court. I think whoever wins at the Florida Supreme Court, we'll accept that."

Next come the Republicans. Richard says that Sauls's ruling much resembles his closing argument from Sunday night. "Judge Sauls hit every point," he says. "He even got one I didn't think of."

Which one was that?

"I'm not going to tell you which one!" he smiles.

Upstairs, behind Courtroom 3-D, Sauls thanks his staff. He takes a personal call, removes his robe, takes the elevator downstairs to the parking garage, and skedaddles on home.

★ ★ ★

At one of the many TV tents across the street from the Florida Supreme Court, Mark Silva, the legendary political writer for the *Miami Herald,* kindly informs me that some of the Bush attorneys are celebrating at Andrew's Capital Bar & Grill.

I thank him and phone up ABC's Chris Vlasto, who's at the Doubletree. It's good to have a wingman at times like these, and Vlasto has now become a pal. I tell him what Silva told me, and that I'll call him back if the scoop proves correct. Which it does. Within minutes, Vlasto and I are downing drinks in the midst of Irv Terrell, Fred Bartlit and his wife, Jenna, and Phil Beck. Plus their many, many junior attorney admirers. Bartlit's singing the praises of his graphics people; Beck's downing beers in a circle of worship. Terrell chats with Jenna.

They're not too impressed with the Democrats' case, the lawyers in this bar tell us while they rack up a $2,000 aggregate bar tab — which includes three bottles of fine champagne.

"As an attorney, I was embarrassed about their case," one says.

When I tell another that the Bushies put on a great case, he says, "No, we didn't. We put on a mediocre case. But they put on no case."

Bartlit tells me that he feels bad for Boies. "I told him, David, no one in corporate America is ever going to hire you again," Bartlit says, honestly concerned for an adversary he respects.

There's time for idle chitchat, too. Vlasto and I tell Beck how eerily similar in manner he is to Kevin Spacey. He says we're not the first to tell him that. Bartlit is flying off to Delaware tomorrow morning bright and early to represent Micron; for a sixty-eight-year-old, the dude has some major stamina. Terrell seems kind of eager to tell us that he's pro-choice and supportive of civil rights. They all seem like pretty decent guys.

I tell them all that if it weren't for Vlasto, none of us would be standing here. They don't understand. With Jackie Judd, Vlasto broke the story of Monica's semen-stained dress, I say. Were it not for that, Clinton would still be denying the affair, and Gore would easily have gotten 1,000 or so Florida votes in the process. Drinks all around.

★   ★   ★

On Tuesday Terrell tells Baker that for all intents and purposes he thinks that it's over.

"For what it's worth," he says, "we've got them pinned between a trial-court victory in front of a Democratic judge, which the nation has watched, and that Supreme Court remand."

But soon the Florida Supreme Court announces that it will hear arguments on Thursday for Gore's appeal. So it ain't over yet.

★   ★   ★

With everything on hold, in Austin and Washington, D.C., it seems like the time to let the alpha males out, to show that they're still around, to convey whatever messages they feel are in their self-interest. For Lieberman and Cheney, that message is that there is support for their causes on Capitol Hill. For Bush, that message is one of peace and understanding and a display of sympathy of questionable sincerity, if excellent execution, for Al Gore. For Gore, that message is desperation.

"Good morning," Bush says. "Had a good briefing this morning. I appreciate the administration's willingness to send a member of the intelligence community over to give me a security briefing." Does he think Gore should concede? "Well, that's a decision the vice president has to make," Bush says. "It's a difficult decision, of course. And I can understand what he may be going through. It's been a very interesting period of time for both of us. It's been one month from today that the people actually showed up and started to vote, and here we stand — and here I stand, still, you know, without a clear verdict."

Standing with House Speaker Dennis Hastert of Illinois, and Oklahoma representative J. C. Watts, Cheney has a different take on that. "Obviously," he says, "I think those two court decisions" — Sauls and SCOTUS — "were affirmations of the fact that, with respect to the vote in Florida, the votes have been counted and recounted and now certified. And Governor

Bush and I feel that it validated the decisions that had been made previously, and indicate, once again, that we did prevail in the election in Florida." There's an election possibly being stolen — by one side or the other or possibly both — and this is a rare chance to put a major player on the spot. But again the press doesn't bother. Instead, Cheney's asked whether he pronounces his name CHAY-nee or CHEE-nee. "It really doesn't matter," he says.

A few yards away is Lieberman. "Dick Gephardt made a point the other day that I think is so important to keep coming back to," he says, "that next year, someone — some university or a group of students — will under a Freedom of Information action in Florida go in and gather these ballots and count them. And it will not be good for our country, it will not be good for whoever is president then, if the result of that count would justify the seating in office of someone other than the one who was there."

At NavObs, Gore comes out to the reporters. "I don't really have an opening statement," he says. "If you want to ask any questions, feel free."

Gore's asked how efforts to toss the 25,000 absentee ballots in Seminole and Martin County jibe with his call to "count every vote."

Gore immediately starts babbling untruths about the cases. He says that in Seminole "there were more than enough votes to make the difference that were apparently thrown into —" He catches himself. "The *applications* for ballots were thrown into the trash can by the supervisor of elections there, apparently. Even though they were missing the same number that the Republican Party workers were allowed to come in and fix the other applications with."

He backs off a bit. "So I don't want to speculate on what remedy might be — I'm not a party to that case or the Martin County case" — But he can't help himself. "More than enough votes were potentially taken away from Democrats, because they were not given the same access that Republicans were," he says. "Remember, according to what's come out in that case —"

He catches himself. "Again, I'm not a party to it, but I've read about it," he says.

"Apparently the Democratic Party chair was denied the opportunity to even look at the list of applications," Gore says. "Whereas the Republican Party workers were allowed to roam around unsupervised, inside the office and bring their computers in, and fix all of the valid applications for one side, even as the Democrats were denied an opportunity to come in, denied a chance to even look at the applications, and those applications were thrown out. Now, that doesn't seem fair to me."

No, it doesn't seem fair. Of course, it also doesn't seem *true*.

An e-mail is soon sent within the DNC.

Subject: gore clean up
We need to get his seminole remarks, and the "democratic ballot applications that lacked the id number were thrown in the trash," stuff checked and put in to talking points for everyone.
He made a little news and we need to document what he said and get it out to everyone. . . . . .
asap — i have four reporters really pushing me on this.

For all the various untruths, pufferies, evasions, exaggerations, and downright lies that Gore has said in his life — and been slammed repeatedly for, sometimes fairly, sometimes not so, during this election — his crazy riff on Seminole seems to go generally uncriticized in the media. It may be that reporters are busy, it may be that no one's really sure of what the facts are in the Seminole case. And it may be pity.

In fact, a lot of reporters are imbued with odd feelings about Gore these days. Especially since Gore — who during his campaign once went sixty-two days without holding a press conference — is now reaching out to so many of them. He regularly phones up network TV anchors and producers, explaining where he's coming from, pitching them stories. At one point he strikes at least one of these network superstars as having gone a bit off the deep end.

One piece Gore pitches comes from an obscure news story written in 1989 about the Mack-MacKay Senate race, which has a speculative *X-Files*-esque conspiracy riff on the idea that Votomatic software could be programmed to not count, say, every tenth vote. There was and is no evidence to this theory, other than the fact that *it could have happened!* And in the face of the Gore legal team's argument that there are design flaws inherent in punch-card ballots, it doesn't even make much sense. But Gore becomes fascinated — some might say unhealthily so — by the story, which one of his old journalist buddies has found and brought to his attention. Gore calls a buddy at ABC, becomes convinced that *20/20* is going to investigate the matter. Some of his advisers suggest that such a story is just not going to happen so late in the game, but Gore is convinced that something's there and that ABC will investigate.

On Web site Voter.com, legendary Watergate newsman Carl Bernstein gets 1988 Florida senate candidate Buddy MacKay to riff, *Parallax View–*

like, as to what might happen if some bad guy had the source codes. "What could have happened in 1988," MacKay tells Bernstein, "and we couldn't get to it at the time, was that the machines could have been programmed so that in my big precincts, every tenth vote got counted wrong."

But outside of Bernstein's highly theoretical story, media investigations into the rather suspect charges don't go very far. ABC News's Cokie Roberts calls ABC News Florida legal consultant Steve Uhlfelder — who was one of MacKay's co-counsels in that 1988 race — to see if there's any truth to the matter. Uhlfelder tells her that it's crazy talk; no one ever talked about a conspiratorial nefarious computer programmer back then. Punch-card ballot machines are anachronistic junk, that's all. The primary reason for the vast number of undervotes was that the Mack-MacKay race was at the bottom of the first page of many counties' ballots, under the presidential contest, so people didn't notice it. They had suspected that the software might not be working right, but testing the software reassured them that it was functioning properly, at least in the counties where they tested it. But it was never about a purposefully inserted computer glitch, this "software discrimination" thing. Uhlfelder's surprised that MacKay's saying otherwise.

Some reporters who hear about this conspiracy theory begin to wonder about Gore. Is he completely losing it?

★   ★   ★

Martin and Lewis commence at 7 A.M. Wednesday. Ninety minutes later they break, and the Bush lawyers run down a flight to make the same arguments before Judge Clark. Half an hour after Clark finishes up, Lewis will resume and preside all through the night, until the Martin County case is done. Two hard facts collide in both these cases: one, clearly both Goard and Robbins were extending preferential treatment to the GOP, and engaging in some shady dealings as it pertained to Florida law, specifically the 1998 absentee-ballot application statute. The second: there's nothing really to be done about it since no one is alleging that anyone other than actual voters cast their ballots.

Clark gets to this right off the bat. There are two issues, she says. "The first is whether the addition . . . or completion of voter registration ID numbers is sufficient to invalidate the absentee ballots. And then the second issue I see is whether or not the Democratic Party and Republican Party were treated differently . . . to the extent that the validity or integrity of the election process was compromised."

Richman says that the first question is rooted in the matter of Goard's "intentional wrongdoing." Goard, he points out, "testified under oath that she did not know the name of the Republican operative, when the testimony will clearly show that she did." To the Democratic team, that's sure evidence she was trying to cover something up.

But in his opening argument, Bristow points out that state Democratic chair, Bob Poe, knew what Leach was doing while it was going on, *before* Election Day. "He knew that he could go into that office, and he did not. He knew that if there was any kind of violation of law, he could have gone ahead, and he could have filed suit, and he could have done something about it beforehand."

Helping Bristow as an intervening attorney representing absentee voters in both the Seminole and Martin County cases is — despite his rather soft, inclusive rhetoric in this case — one of the more active members of Florida's Christian Right. Matthew Staver, president and general counsel of the Christian activist Liberty Counsel, hosts a conservative radio talk show and represents all sorts of conservative causes in courts, defending prayer in Duval County public schools, filing a brief against gay and lesbian civil unions in Vermont, and representing the Rev. Ed Martin, an anti–abortion rights protester accused of harassing women entering the Ocala Women's Center. But Staver is careful not to mention any of this now, and not a single member of the media realizes who he really is.

Staver says that many of his clients voted absentee "because they are disabled. . . . We should not let this hypertechnicality disenfranchise these voters." Staver trots out Helga Powell, born in Nuremberg and raised as a member of the Hitler Youth. The Bush-backing former Nazi doesn't want to be disenfranchised, knowing "firsthand the price that citizens of a country pay when they have no right to vote for representatives and have no voice in the governance of their country." When it was the concentration camp survivors in Palm Beach who were confused, the Republicans sure didn't seem as sympathetic as they do now toward this poor alumna of the Hitler youth.

The fun starts when the Democrats and Republicans start stealing one another's rhetoric from the Sauls case. Seminole County's attorney, Terry Young, cribs from Gore when he says that a ballot "is not just a piece of paper. It is a voice. It's a right to be heard, it's a right to participate. And a voice at all costs should not be silenced." The Democrats, conversely, are suddenly strict adherents to the letter of the law. Richman calls Steven Hall to the stand. Hall, a painter and construction worker who served as the campaign manager for a Democratic candidate for state representative, met with Goard on August 18, and in a "tense" and unwelcoming meeting,

Goard told him that if absentee-ballot request forms didn't have all the necessary information, "they would be discarded." Richman reads the deposition of a Republican voter and Korean War veteran, Ronald Livingston, who in September 1998 wanted an absentee ballot and was given no help by Goard, no help at all. He was told he'd need to put his request in writing, with his voter ID number, but Goard's office wouldn't tell him what his number was. Two years later, when Livingston found out that she had bent over backward to help the state GOP, he called her to complain. "Hey, if you don't like it, file a protest," she replied. Richman establishes fairly conclusively that Goard's story kept changing — first she said Leach had been in her office for one or two days, then ten or eleven, then Leach said it was closer to fifteen, and one of Goard's subordinates said it might have been three full weeks. Richman also hammers home the question of whether or not Goard was open about knowing Leach, or either of the field operatives who assisted him, or the GOP official who first arranged their little expedition. Even Leach says in his deposition that "clearly" she knew them.

Richman even establishes some sound arguments pertaining to the law. As in the Carollo-Suarez mayor's race, absentee ballots are in Florida case law considered a privilege, not a right, and they have been tossed before. And clearly the elections office was compromised in some way; these offices are not meant to be temporary work spaces for partisan operatives. Did Leach tamper with any other absentee ballots? There's no proof that he did. But he sure could have, and in that, the process was arguably sullied.

But there's a big "but": Richman has found no smoking gun that shows that Democratic voters suffered because of Goard's actions — the Democratic Party's absentee-ballot request form, after all, in almost all cases had the space for the voter ID number properly filled in. And an elections employee testifies that of the 263 applicants that didn't receive an absentee ballot, 176 of these were Republicans and 16 were Democrats.

Richman calls to the stand a statistician, Cal Berkeley economics professor James DeLong, who offers a suggestion, based on proportions, of how many votes they can throw out so as to be fair, while not tossing all 15,000. But as with Hengartner, DeLong's inexperience serves Bush well. Richman sees him fall apart on cross-examination, expressing opinions outside his area of expertise. He sees from Clark's body language that she's not accepting his testimony. Or forget body language: her *language* is enough for Richman to know he's in trouble. In his rebuttal closing argument, Richman says that this "is a case that has to send a message and establish a very important precedent. . . . What else would come next if the court does not enforce the law?"

"My job is not to send a message," Clark snaps back. "My job is to rule on the case that is before me. My job is to apply the existing case law and statutory law to the facts as I find them from the evidence."

★   ★   ★

Court is in recess. Thirty minutes to Martin County.

Except: Where the hell is Judge Lewis?

Having not gotten much exercise since this all began, while the ball was in Clark's court, Lewis went to shoot a little hoop. He brought his cell phone, but it didn't ring. Court administrators are going bananas. Where the hell is he? At 7:20, Lewis's wife runs into the gym. "Clark got through early!" she says. "They're looking for you! They can't find you!"

"Oh, my goodness," Lewis says. After a quick shower, he "hauls buggy" back to court.

★   ★   ★

Incidentally, just in case anyone was wondering what the Florida legislature intends to do, on Wednesday, McKay and Feeney sign a proclamation that Florida's 25 electors are going to go to Bush.

"The action taken today is done so with considerable reluctance on my part," says McKay, whose affair with that lobbyist he left his wife for was probably consummated with considerable reluctance as well. "My primary objective is simple: to ensure that the voters of Florida are not disenfranchised. . . . If the election disputes are resolved by December 12, there may be a possibility that the legislature will not have to act," he explains.

Feeney is asked about the extent to which he and McKay have been setting up the safety net in cahoots with the Bushies.

"I haven't had any contact with any members of the Bush team probably since" — and here he pauses a second to think about it — "in a good twenty-four hours," he reassures the world.

Democrats "have raised concern," another reporter asks, "not just about both of you supporting George W. Bush, but about the fact that you are electors, about the fact that Mr. Feeney ran with Jeb Bush in his unsuccessful bid for governor. How do you convince the American people, whose votes are all at stake, that this is not partisan but a constitutional concern?"

"I think what they need to do is watch us," says McKay. "The proof's in the pudding."

And what does house minority leader Lois Frankel think about all this?

"I think it would be naive to believe that the speaker of the Florida house and the senate president are really calling the shots here," she says. "I think that they waited as long as they could in hopes that the courts may have decided in Mr. Bush's favor or that Al Gore would have conceded. And that hasn't happened, and I think what we see is just them following through on something that they had predetermined.

"The only thing missing from the proclamation today was the postmark from Austin, Texas," she says.

★   ★   ★

Bush spokesman Dan Bartlett's lie about the Bushies' coordination with the legislature has just been rebutted by no less than Feeney himself. So *finally*, on December 8, thirty days after communications began between Feeney and the Bush team — on the one-month anniversary of Rubottom's communiqué with Jeb counsel Canady — Tucker Eskew acknowledges that Bush lawyers "provided legal interpretations when asked by legislators.

"No one could be surprised by that," Eskew adds. Indeed. Thanks for that.

★   ★   ★

The Martin County case has a few different shades of gray. As opposed to Leach, the Republican operative in this case is evasive, responding, "I don't recall" or "I don't know" more than thirty-five times in his deposition. Additionally, the man Hauck reported to, Martin County's GOP committeeman, Charlie Kane, is a former CIA security chief. But in the end, other than the fact that Hauck was permitted to actually remove the ballots from the elections office, the issues are the same, and the parties assume the same rhetorical exchange.

Robert Harper, representing the Democrats, again preaches the Gospel of Hypertechnicalities, urging that the 9,000 or so ballots be tossed, since absentee voting "is not a right, but a privilege." Attorney Edward Stafman tells Lewis that previous case law could have Lewis "throwing out all of the absentee ballots" as a result of the Republicans' shenanigans, but if not, he could at least go for some sort of proportionate slice — like removing 673 of the 9,000-some ballots. Which — *hey! Whaddaya know?!* — would also deliver the presidency to Gore.

Bristow counters that this is all nonsense. No vote should be tossed as a result of what was merely a "hypertechnical computer glitch fix," he says.

The Martin County case treads until 12:30 A.M. Thursday, then picks up again seven and a half hours later before trudging to a close.

"By noon tomorrow I will have something," Lewis says, "and I want to consult with Judge Clark, who has a similar case — similar issues. . . . But I hope at least by lunch tomorrow I'll have something for you."

And then Lewis and Clark go off into the wilderness to decide just what they're supposed to do.

★   ★   ★

A bunch of the Bush lawyers and staffers convene for a nice dinner in one of the two upstairs dining rooms at Chez Pierre. Unfortunately, an FSU fraternity mixer is raging in the other one.

Don Evans and Missouri senator John Ashcroft are special guests of the small group. They're here to buck up the troops, thank everyone. It's almost over, they say. The end is near. But every minute or so, the door to their room opens and Evans's and Ashcroft's words to the troops are drowned out by the sounds of Rick James's "Superfreak": "That girl is pretty wild now / (The girl's a super freak)."

★   ★   ★

One last dinner for the Democrats at the Governor's Club Wednesday night. Klain isn't here; he pulled an all-nighter the night before, but Boies is, in his white turtleneck, one of the only variations in what seems to be a never-ending supply of the exact same nondescript dark suit.

"Win, lose, or draw, we've accomplished some important things," Boies tells the team. "People all across the country know in their hearts that Al Gore won Florida. The facts are on our side, the law is on our side, and now it's up to the court to do the right thing."

19

"A little matter down the road."

It's Last Call at the Last Chance Bar & Grill.

"Hear ye, hear ye, hear ye!" bellows the marshal. "The supreme court of the great state of Florida is now in session! All who have cause to plea, draw near, give attention, and you shall be heard!" And indeed, David Boies once again draws near and gives attention, explaining Al Gore's cause to plea.

But before he can do so, Chief Justice Charlie Wells has a bone to pick. Last time they all were here, no one said a lick about the U.S. Supreme Court case *McPherson v. Blacker*. But then they went off to the SCOTUS, and *McPherson v. Blacker* was all the rage.

Boies insists *McPherson v. Blacker* shouldn't mean anything to Wells, because in Florida, "the legislature has provided this court with the authority to interpret these laws." What's more, Boies says, it's true that the legislature has the "power to determine the manner of the selection. I don't think they've got the plenary power to determine the time of choosing." That power was left up to the U.S. Congress, which picked November 7, so clearly it's the election *method*, not the schedule, that the legislature has discretion over. (As has been the case throughout this mess, when federal law works, that's the way the Gorebies or Bushies will argue. If state law can be read in their favor, they'll go state. When it comes to consistently choosing one or the other, both sides have dimpled chad.)

Despite Boies's assurances, Wells is clearly fired up, almost like he's mad at what Boies talked him into doing last time. "What you're asking this court to do is to have the courts of this state get involved in any instance in which someone comes in and merely alleges that there needs to be a count. . . . Someone would say they lost by one hundred thirty thousand votes in Dade County, and we'd have to have the court count those votes."

Boies, of course, sees it differently. "This is not a situation in which somebody has simply come in and said, 'We've lost. We'd like to have a recount under the contest statute.' This is a situation in which we have identified specific votes, many of which were agreed by the district court were votes in which you could clearly discern the voter's intent." He lays them out, including the nonexistent 215 Palm Beach County votes, citing John Ahmann, who "testified that you had to have a manual recount in a close election" if you use punch-card ballots.

So why not hand-recount all punch-card ballot counties instead of just those three? Quince asks.

Boies's answer is no more satisfactory to Quince than it is to many of us. "That's where ballots were contested," he says.

"Did anyone ever pick up one of the ballots and hold it up and show it to the judge and say, 'This is an example of a ballot which was rejected but [on] which a vote is reflected?'" Harding asks. Boies says no. Boies says, "although we did tender them in evidence and we did ask him [Sauls] repeatedly to look at the ballots as part of the evidence."

This is one of the central thorns the Bushies have snared the Gore lawyers' britches on. From the get-go, the Gorebies had asked Sauls to look at the ballots, to examine them, so he could see that there were uncounted votes. (Not that Boies thought he needed to do so — to him, the mere fact that so many votes had been found in the 20 percent of the 10,750 Miami-Dade undervotes that had been counted indicated that there were votes in the other 9,000.) But every time the Gore legal team tried to get Sauls to take a gander, the Bushies made the argument that Richard makes today, when asked by Justice Anstead if Sauls examined the evidence: "I think there was no basis in law for the trial court to do that until after the plaintiff had carried its burden of proving that there was some necessity to do so." That is, until the Gore lawyers proved the undervotes contained votes, Sauls had no need to examine the ballots. But until Sauls examined the ballots, it was impossible to prove they contained votes.

Richard (who is the main man today; Carvin's up in Washington, D.C., working with Olson and the other constitutional lawyers, preparing the brief for when the Florida Supreme Court responds to the SCOTUS homework assignment from Monday) immediately agrees with Justice Wells's take on *McPherson*. "This court does not have the ability in this particular case, involving presidential electors, to disregard the statutory scheme and fashion a remedy based upon extraordinary equitable powers of the court set forth in the constitution," Richard says. "The legislature . . . has given us five, and only five, grounds for an election contest, and one of them is not that there is a close election in which Votomatic machines are used."

When the Third District Court of Appeals rejected the Gore team's Wednesday, November 22, writ of mandamus to force the Miami-Dade canvassing board to continue its hand recount, the DCA judges did so because they felt unable to compel someone to accomplish the impossible. But the Third DCA also made mention that while the canvassing board had the discretion to order a hand recount or not, it did not have the discretion to stop in the middle of the process. When Miami Bushie Bobby Martinez read that section, he winced. He thought it gratuitous, thought it might come back to bite the Bushies in the ass. And here it comes.

The DCA found "that they did have a mandatory obligation to continue the count," Anstead says of the Miami-Dade canvassing board. "How can we overturn that ruling?"

"This court also said you must have votes by November 26," Richard replies, throwing the court's own fabricated deadline back in its face. "And the canvassing board, having made the decision it was impossible, had two choices. One was to not continue the count. And the second was to send up a partial count, which, according to the evidence before the board, would not only have cut off a substantial number of precincts that might have been significantly different from the result, but also would have disenfranchised a particular minority within Dade County.

"They have not met their burden of proof," Richard insists. "The only thing they did was put two witnesses on the stand to say that they were speculating that Votomatic machines are inherently unreliable. And so, in essence, what Mr. Boies is saying to this court is any time there's a Votomatic machine in a close election and somebody says count all the ballots, you must do so."

A supreme court case is like an amusement park game in which you have to knock down the bare majority of cans. They need four here. And Justice Leander Shaw, Jr. — Florida's first African-American chief justice (the chief justice position rotates) — doesn't look like a can that Boies can knock down. Shaw speaks only three times, but every time, it's to talk about Sauls, and the fact that he found "that there was no credible statistical evidence and no other competent, substantial evidence to establish by a preponderance of a reasonable probability that the results of a statewide election in the state of Florida would have been different."

Boies tries to argue that Sauls made three errors of law, but even Al Gore, watching on TV hundreds of miles away, can see that Shaw's a lost cause.

As is Wells. On rebuttal, Wells makes his displeasure even clearer. How could Miami-Dade have been counting only its undervotes? That's not what the law says. "Shall recount manually, recount all the ballots," Wells says, quoting the statute. "That would definitely be a change in the law." You can tell he's bitter about all the cries that his court is made up of crazy liberal activists. Wells was once talked about as a possible senator, governor. Now *this* is his legacy.

Boies says that it's possible to interpret the law a different way, manually recount all the ballots that have been requested to be recounted. "And they stopped only because they didn't have time," Boies adds, forgoing the allegations of Miami-Dade "intimidation."

Pariente asks, "In terms of the remedy . . . what is the time — we're here today, December seventh — what is the time parameter for being able to complete a count of those undervotes?" And how much time does it take to count undervotes?

"The record shows that the canvassing boards were doing about three hundred an hour," Boies says. "That was obviously slower than it would be if it were being done by one judicial officer. We believe these ballots can be counted in the time available. Obviously, time is getting very short. We have been trying to get these ballots counted, as this court knows, for many weeks now."

Anstead has one last question for the Gore team, about "the problem that continues to reoccur in the case of not having recounts in other counties where the same voting mechanisms were used and where there may have been undervotes, but that the proportion of votes, for instance, may have favored your opponent." Not only that, but there are five days until December 12 — the date that, during the first Florida Supreme Court arguments, assistant attorney general Hancock had asserted, and Boies had readily agreed, is the deadline. "How can we resolve an issue like that at this late date?"

Boies says, "There's never been a rule that says you have to recount all the ballots in an election contest."

"Thank you, Mr. Boies," Justice Wells says. "I think your time is up."

★   ★   ★

How'd it go? How'd it go?

Very few in the Florida legal community seem to think the Florida Supreme Court is going to rule for Gore. Daley doesn't think so, either. Gore is more optimistic, though he's ruled out the votes of Shaw and Wells. Boies and Terrell go to dine at Andrew's Capital Bar and Grill — one suspects Boies didn't order the "Jeb-burger" — and they agree on one thing: the court will be split 4 to 3. They just disagree on which side will get the swing vote. Richard thinks he's going to win, maybe even 5 to 2.

In Austin, Bush is continuing as he's instructed. The self-coronation goes on. In addition to picking his cabinet, Bush has a lot of homework to do. This has been a frustrating thing for some of his advisers; Bob Zoellick and Condoleezza Rice have lost their patience with Bush in the past: he's unwilling to read a memo longer than a page. "General Powell and I discussed the Middle East," Bush says on Wednesday. "Condi [Rice] and I are in constant discussion about the Middle East. And what concerns me is peace."

Yowza. On Friday, Bush opens the governor's mansion to the press again. In a small room called the conservatory, Bush sits at a small table with Karen Hughes, Karl Rove, and Andy Card. X-mas decorations about; one has Santa twirling a lasso.

"We've just been in a conference call with our folks in Washington and continuing making progress on the White House setup and just had a long discussion with Secretary Cheney and [gubernatorial chief of staff] Clay Johnson about potential cabinet officers," Bush says. "I also had a good visit with Jimmy Baker today. Our folks in Florida anticipate a decision, and they feel like our lawyers made a good, strong case. . . . We are hopeful that we'll finally see some finality when it comes to this election. . . . We're prepared to, if need be, take our case back to the Supreme Court. But I hope that doesn't have to happen."

Have you finalized White House staff?

"I haven't decided on a couple of them," he jokes, casting sidelong glances at Rove and Hughes. "I don't know whether or not they can pass the background checks, if *yaknowwhatImean*." Big yuks all around.

★   ★   ★

Lewis and Clark spend Thursday conferring, talking about their interpretations of the law, how they're going to rule.

This is exactly what Gerald Richman was worried about when he heard Lewis say that he was going to consult with Clark. Lewis is more conservative than Clark, he thinks. Is he going to sway her views? Of course, in many ways, this is in the same neighborhood as the attitude of the Bushies who assumed she was going to march lockstep with whatever Rev. Jackson wanted her to do.

Clark, in fact, is decidedly not doing so, she is ruling on the law. Both Lewis and Clark are leaning heavily on the 1976 Florida Supreme Court precedent *Boardman v. Esteva*,* one of Boies's favorite cites when he was arguing for an extension of the certification deadline. Boardman argues that when voters are in substantial compliance with the law, their votes should be heard — with that value paramount, that "courts are to overturn" elections "only for compelling reasons when there are clear, substantial departures from essential requirements of law." Which does not seem to be the case here.

"The proof offered at trial failed to show that she [Goard] treated other political parties differently than she treated the Republican Party," Clark writes. "That the supervisor's judgment may be seriously questioned and that her actions invited public and legal scrutiny do not rise to the level of a showing of fraud, gross negligence, or intentional wrongdoing. . . . Faulty judgment is not illegal, unless the legislature declares it so."

Lewis comes to essentially the same conclusions. Elections Supervisor Robbins clearly allowed violations of election office protocol, but the same laws in question provide no remedy for such violations. And more important, Lewis writes of Martin County, "there is no evidence of fraud or other irregularities in the actual casting of the ballots, or the counting of the ballots."

Early afternoon on Friday, Leon County Court administrator Terre Cass reads the summary of both Clark's and Lewis's decisions. "Based upon the evidence presented and in accord with the controlling legal precedent of the Florida Supreme Court, the trial courts in both the Seminole County case and the Martin County case have determined that despite irregularities in the request for absentee ballots, neither the sanctity of the ballots

---

* In the October 3, 1972, election for a seat on Florida's Second District Court of Appeals, Edward Boardman beat Henry Esteva by 249 votes — a margin of victory rooted entirely in the 3,389 absentee ballots. Esteva, who received 404 more machine votes than his opponent, brought suit in the circuit court, alleging 1,450 irregularities in the absentee-ballot process. A trial judge found only 88 actual problems — 13 with no voter signature, for instance. He ruled for Boardman. The District Court of Appeals overturned this, ruling for Esteva. Then the Florida Supreme Court overturned the DCA, ruling once, and finally, for Boardman — a victory for the principle that courts should bend over backward to count votes, even in the face of clear screw-ups by elections bureaucrats or the voters themselves. In this instance, such a principle works for Bush, and against Gore.

nor the integrity of the elections has been compromised and that the election results —"

The Bush-backing crowd cheers. HURRAY!

"Hold on," Cass says. " '— and that the election results reflect a full and fair expression of the will of the voters. Accordingly, all relief requested by the plaintiffs has been denied and judgment entered for the defendants.' Thank you."

A Bush press conference breaks out. "We are, of course, gratified with the two strong rulings from the two judges here on the Leon County circuit court affirming the right to vote," Ginsberg says. Quite wary of Clark before, Ginsberg now seems as though he's about to break into a chorus of "Ebony and Ivory."

A reporter asks Bristow what he thinks about a comment Richman made, arguing that the state attorney should pursue criminal charges against Goard.

"This is a very fine woman," Bristow says, "and I think it is absolutely pure one hundred percent bogus."

Do you regret trying to get Clark recused?

"Well, we — that was a motion to bring to her attention an issue, so that she could consider it," Bristow says. "We never wanted history to look back and have any second guess about this proceeding. She had it, she considered it; she decided that she did not have an issue that would influence her. And as everybody on our team and every team knows, she handled this case in a masterful way."

Is this a final blow to the Gore campaign, in your opinion?

"We have one more case still pending," Richard says, motioning toward the Florida Supreme Court. "A little matter down the road."

★   ★   ★

Florida Supreme Court spokesman Craig Waters finally has this all down to a science. Being fairly Web-savvy, he was already ahead of the game when it came to preparation to put court materials on-line in the blink of an eye — he even set up a secondary backup server for when the first Web site gets too much traffic, which it does. On November 13, http://www. flcourts.org scored two thousand hits; by now they're getting 3.5 million hits a day. His one mistake was to have included his cell phone number on the site, resulting in all sorts of yahoos buzzing him in the middle of the night, urging him to tell the Florida Supreme Court justices how to vote.

"The court today has issued its opinion in the case of *Albert Gore, Jr., versus Katherine Harris, George W. Bush, and others*," Waters says. "By a vote of four to three, the majority of the court has reversed the decision of the trial court in part. It has further ordered that the circuit court of the Second Judicial Circuit here in Tallahassee shall immediately begin a manual recount of the approximately nine thousand Miami-Dade ballots that registered the undervotes.

"In addition, the circuit court shall enter orders insuring the inclusion of the additional two hundred fifteen legal votes for Vice President Gore in Palm Beach County, and the one hundred sixty-eight additional legal votes for Miami-Dade.

"In addition, the circuit court shall order a manual recount of all undervotes in any Florida county where such a recount has not yet occurred. Because time is of the essence, the recount shall commence immediately. In tabulating what constitutes a legal vote, the standard to be used is the one provided by the legislature. A vote shall be counted where there is a clear indication of the intent of the voter.

"Chief Justice Charles T. Wells and Justice Major B. Harding have written dissenting opinions. Justice Leander J. Shaw, Jr., has joined in the dissenting opinion of Justice Harding. Thank you."

The patient has a heartbeat. Al Gore's execution has been stayed.*

"It's even better than I expected," Boies says when he hears the ruling.

From reading the documents it is clear that Justice Wells didn't just write a dissenting opinion. He wrote hate mail, a blistering condemnation of his colleagues' ruling, one that Baker reads from liberally soon after. The majority's decision "cannot withstand the scrutiny which will certainly immediately follow under the U.S. Constitution." Wells stated that the decision has "no foundation in the law in Florida as it existed on November 7, 2000.

"Prolonging the judicial process in this counting process propels this country and this state into an unprecedented and unnecessary constitutional crisis," he continues, a crisis that will inflict "substantial damage to our country, to our state, and to this court as an institution."

Baker immediately announces that his legal team is on the case. In Atlanta, at the Eleventh Circuit Court of Appeals, the Bush legal team petitions for an emergency hearing. In Washington, D.C., the team will deliver an emergency petition to U.S. Supreme Court justice Anthony Kennedy, under whose purview the eleventh circuit lies, to stay the Florida court's

*I myself got this one totally, embarrassingly wrong, having written a piece for Salon.com called "Stick a fork in him, Gore's done," which outlined the myriad reasons the Florida Supreme Court was going to reject Gore's appeal.

ruling until the eleventh circuit rules. The court's "reasoning and result places the court once again at odds with the sound judgment" of lower courts, the Florida legislature, and local canvassing boards, Baker said. He said the court's decision "could ultimately disenfranchise Florida's votes in the electoral college."

"This is what happens when, for the first time in modern history, a candidate resorts to lawsuits to try to overturn the outcome of an election for president," says Baker. "It is very sad — for Florida, for the nation, and for our democracy."

Christopher listens to this. *Oh, please,* he thinks, finding Baker's remarks over the top.

However much Baker may now love to quote Wells, he was but a dissenter; his four colleagues on the bench wrote the decision that matters. And they think Gore is fundamentally right: there are votes that have yet to be counted.

"The Legislature has expressly recognized the will of the people of Florida as the guiding principle for the selection of all elected officials . . . whether they be county commissioners or presidential electors," said the four. "The clear message . . . is that every citizen's vote be counted whenever possible." They seem most concerned about Sauls's refusal to let Boies show him even one ballot. It presented Gore with "the ultimate Catch-22," they wrote, "acceptance of the only evidence that will resolve the issue but a refusal to examine such evidence."

They even sent out a footnote to their three colleagues, saying that "the dissents would have us throw up our hands and say that because of looming deadlines and practical difficulties, we should give up any attempt to have the election of presidential electors rest upon the vote of Florida citizens as mandated by the Legislature. . . . We can only do the best we can to carry out our sworn responsibilities to the justice system and its role in the process."

Daley immediately heralds the court ruling as "an important victory for what has been Al Gore and Joe Lieberman's basic principle since Election Day, and that is a full and a fair count of all the votes."

It's a "victory for fairness and accountability and for our democracy itself," Daley says, adding that the court "wisely" ordered that the hand recount take place "in every Florida county where undervotes have yet to be counted. Then Florida and America will know with certainty who really won the presidency." Well, if that's so wise, it would have been nice if Boies hadn't been arguing against it. But whatever.

★   ★   ★

Carvin's cursing at his computer. The first time the Florida Supreme Court ruled, the clerks were nice enough to give them a fifteen-minute heads-up, so they could log on before the rest of the world did, and download and print the ruling. This time they got no such call. And the server is busy. Busy. Busy. For forty-five minutes Carvin can't get on the site.

Finally he gets through. Downloads it, prints it out. He starts looking for the part that responds to the SCOTUS remand from earlier in the week. Carvin's been working on that part of the brief, anticipating their argument, and he wants to see how close he came to guessing how they would justify their action.

But there's nothing there.

Nothing about the remand. No response at all. They just ignored the Supreme Court of the United States. Who does that?! he wonders. When a cop pulls you over for going sixty and you get off with just a warning, you don't pull out and start doing eighty-five!

"We won," he says to himself. No way the U.S. Supreme Court doesn't get involved now. George W. Bush has just sealed the presidency.

★   ★   ★

There are some who aren't so shocked by Chief Justice Wells's stinging dissent: those who know him.

"That's a typical Charlie Wells dissent," says former chief justice Kogan with a chuckle, when I ring him up. "This is not something that is new. Read some of his decisions in capital cases, and you'll find that's what he does. He'll be just as strident, and he'll take the whole court to task when they don't agree with him."

What of Wells's warning of a constitutional crisis?

"That's going overboard, way overboard," Kogan says. "This republic has endured for over two hundred twenty-five years. I dare say it's going to last much longer than that. People have a way of healing very quickly."

But what of the "substantial damage" he says the court will suffer because of its rather bold ruling?

"Oh, that's just Wells," Kogan says. "He says that a lot of times when he writes his dissents. It's just the way in which he does things. I don't think they risked their credibility at all."

★   ★   ★

On November 8, Bush led Gore by 1,734 votes. The state-ordered machine recount brought this down to 357. On Wednesday, November 15, Harris's partial certification put his lead at 300. Then absentee ballots brought the margin back up to 930. After Broward County's hand recount, the tally was then certified with Bush up by 537.

But the Florida Supreme Court has just ordered 157 votes from Miami-Dade and 215 from Palm Beach counted.

Bush's lead has dropped to 154 votes.

One-hundred-and-fifty-four fucking votes! Yikes!

Even if you factor in the real number of votes Gore won in Palm Beach, that's still a Bush lead of only 193. Who knows what will be found in the 60,000 or so undervotes out there? Duval County went for Bush 57 percent to 41 percent — but Democrats insist that many of the county's 4,967 undervotes come from black precincts. A lot of the undervote counties are Bush counties: Collier County with 2,082; Hillsborough with 5,531; Indian River County has 1,058; Lee County 2,017; Marion County 2,445; Katherine Harris's home county, Sarasota, has 1,809. But there are Gore counties in there, too. Pinellas County, which Gore won by 15,000 or so votes, has 4,226; Pasco County 1,776; Orange County with 966; Osceola with 642 . . .

Anything could happen. Anyone could win.

For the second and last time, Ron Klain actually thinks that Gore might really end up the forty-third president.

In Washington, D.C., the chieftains of the Gore team go out to celebrate at the Palm Restaurant.

Their underlings, and Bush's, spend the night arranging for chartered planes full of hundreds of observers to zoom in at once, to supervise.

★   ★   ★

Richman and Jacobs are appealing Seminole to the Florida Supreme Court. "Jesus Christ," Daley says. A message is left with Richman to call Daley. He wants to put an end to this nonsense. But Richman refuses to call him back. He calls Berger — a friend — instead.

"Tell them: the vice president wants to count votes," Daley says to Berger. "He does not want to be *not* counting votes."

This is the most difficult task of Berger's whole experience. In his heart, he wanted Seminole to be part of the contest. He thinks that the law was seriously violated. And Berger knows how hard Richman and Jacobs and Richman's partner — and Berger's close friend — Alan Greer have worked on the case, essentially without their help. It's actually a painful experience for him. He thinks of himself as the Tom Hanks character in *Saving Private Ryan*, a captain doing what he's told, sent off on a mission he doesn't agree with. He meets with them and shares Gore's thoughts.

"We can't drop the case," Richman tells him. "The only way we would even consider it is if Gore personally asks us to do."

Richman still feels good, that if he looks the Florida Supreme Court justices in the eyes, they'll do the right thing. Chief Justice Wells is an old law school classmate of his. They simply will not be able to deny giving us relief, Richman says. The disparate treatment is so clear in the record.

★ ★ ★

The Florida Supreme Court order for the undervote recount is shipped back to Sauls, but he isn't going to have anything to do with it. No, siree. Those liberal fools want to make up another law, fine, but he sure isn't going to play a part in it. Not when he doesn't think it's constitutional.

So Terry Lewis gets called back into the game and commences a hearing at 8 P.M.

Beck, who has been preparing to argue standards almost since he started on the case, scurries with his briefcase full of chad-related notes back to circuit court. He says that he's "concerned that this is a proceeding that's fraught with peril constitutionally and otherwise."

Douglass, conversely, wants everything to start as soon as possible. There are going to be counties that aren't going to do a thing 'til they get a court order from Lewis telling them to do so. "That's all that we have to offer, really, is to get this going."

Klock objects, of course. He objects to Lewis supervising the counting of the Miami-Dade ballots when they're to be counted by a three-person canvassing board, he objects to the overvotes not being counted, he objects to the fact that all the votes aren't being counted. He's right about the overvotes, of course. But no one's listening.

"This is how we believe you ought to proceed, Your Honor," Beck says. "These votes or these ballots need to be evaluated using a consistent standard, because if instead you let several people start evaluating ballots using a purely subjective standard that varies from person to person, you've guaranteed yourself several legal problems."

"Let me stop you for a second," Lewis says again. "Didn't the supreme court indicate exactly what standards apply?"

Not really, says Beck. "The supreme court said, look at the voter's intent. And what we had was a two-day trial, and much of the evidence went to how one would ascertain voter intent from indentations and dimples on a ballot. And so we have a wealth of evidence on that, Your Honor, and unfortunately Judge Sauls has recused himself. And so we're frankly going to need to educate you." We're going to put together a presentation tonight and maybe show it to you tomorrow, Beck says. Keep slowing it down.

Lewis now comes face-to-face with one of the complaints Olson, Carvin, et al. filed in their complaint to Middlebrooks way back when. "What's the legal standard in Florida for determining" the intent of the voter? he asks. After Beck refers to the 1990 Palm Beach County standard, Lewis asks, "was that a statewide standard?"

No, Beck says. He catches himself on one of the Bush campaign's own right-hook, left-hook combinations. He says there is no legal statewide standard, then says that coming up with a new one would be changing the rules in the middle of the game.

"You're confusing me," Lewis says. "I thought you said there was no standard, so how can I change it?" Regardless, "the standard is what the supreme court says it is, because that's what I'm bound by."

"What I think you ought to do, Judge, with the other counties . . . is tell these counties that job number one is to segregate the undervotes in a way where they keep records, accurate records, this time around, of how many votes are being recorded for Bush and how many are being recorded for Gore and how many are being recorded as undervotes."

The Gorebies think Beck is stalling. "We think the court meant immediately when it said immediately," Boies says. "Hours make a difference here."

Beck doesn't see it that way. He tells Lewis that he's being "cooperative." They don't want the counting to occur, but if it does, they want it to be sound. They want it to be able to pass constitutional muster. Their field guys — Mehlman, Enwright — insist that with their idea of a real standard, Bush will win, even statewide.

But Beck also wants this standard reapplied to Gore votes he thinks are sketchy. The Broward County surge, for example, should be reexamined. He also suggests that when Lewis supervises counting the Miami-Dade undervotes tomorrow, he should start all over again since the 20 percent that were counted were done so with a loose standard, and at the very least a different standard from the one Lewis will probably use. Otherwise, "a lot of Hispanic voters who tended to vote Republican in this last election are going to have their votes evaluated under a standard that's different than was used for the Democrats. That creates big problems under the Voting Rights Act for a protected group like Hispanic-Americans."

But Lewis is not going to take Beck's advice. He wants the Miami-Dade ballots to be counted starting at 8 A.M. tomorrow at the local library; he puts out word to Leon County judges that he'd appreciate their help. The other sixty-three counties have until 2 P.M. Sunday to finish and by noon Saturday to fax him information on what their plans are. He gives out his fax number on international TV; big mistake. Faxes start humming in from all over. Cartoons. Angry letters. Jokes about chad and Palm Beach County voters.

Beck continues to talk about standards. About hanging chad. About patterns. About how just dimples cannot be considered votes. On and on. He agrees that if all the votes on the ballot are just dimples, that should count as a vote, but he asks Lewis to check out any questionables.

Lewis, of course, has seen that the Florida Supreme Court has begged off the opportunity — not once, but twice — to set standards. He's certainly not going to infer that they want *him* to come up with something. But Beck's not even talking to Lewis anymore. He figures that canvassing-board members have their TVs on and are watching, and worrying, and wondering what the hell they're supposed to do tomorrow, what standards they're supposed to apply. He's hoping that they'll take his advice. After all, he's the only one offering any. And even if they're not watching, well, he's confident that a U.S. Supreme Court justice or two might be watching the Phil Beck show right about now.

20

"Boy, that was some Election Night, huh?"

It's 6:22 A.M. Saturday morning, and I'm on my way back to Tallahassee. My cab driver is from St. Lucia, and he doesn't understand just what the hell's going on with the elections here.

"It is much simpler there," he says of voting in St. Lucia. "It is one man, one vote. We count all the votes by hand."

St. Lucia stands in stark contrast with St. Lucie County, Florida, this morning. In St. Lucie County (Bush 34,705, Gore 41,559), there are 537 undervotes that have yet to be inspected. According to my cabbie, at least, that never would have happened in St. Lucia.

There are three Democrats on my plane into town — two from Boston, one from D.C. — all of whom have been asked by the Gore recount team to fly down to the Panhandle and help supervise the statewide hand recount of the undervotes. After the connecting flight from Atlanta lands in Talli, about a dozen Democrats converge near the Avis rental car counter, where they are given car keys and instructions on where to drive. As with teams of Republicans, they're being farmed out to supervise the recount efforts across the state, from Pensacola to Naples.

★　★　★

Peter Greenberger, twenty-seven, worked under Baldick for Gore in New Hampshire during the primaries and then helmed the western Pennsylvania effort for Gore-Lieberman, but he'd spent the recount period in D.C., waiting to be sent to Iowa or Wisconsin in case those states had recounts. They didn't, so Greenberger watched it all on TV. Until Friday afternoon,

425

that is, when three different DNCers called him, attempting to draft him into three different assignments in three different Florida counties.

Saturday morning at 6 A.M., Greenberger shows up at the Signature Airlines terminal at D.C.'s Reagan National Airport. It's a sea of Republicans. Two hundred, maybe 250. All with orange "W." caps, better dressed than the few Democrats, sporting far more pearls. Greenberger huddles in the corner with the other six Democrats. It's easy to pick them out — two of them are black, one's Native American, you got Greeny, a Jew, and two others.

When their seven-seater charter plane lands in Tallahassee, they're met by a staffer who throws them rental-car keys and a map. Greeny takes the I-10 to Madison County, on the Georgia line, drives into the town of Madison, and instinctively looks for the clock tower. When he finds it, he learns that the canvassing board has already finished up its review of the 31 undervotes — plus 4 for Gore, plus 2 for Bush. So he calls in to Tallahassee, and is sent to the town of Mayo in Lafayette County. He drives there, looks for the clock tower. When he finds it, he learns that Lafayette didn't have any undervotes, so there's nothing to do here, either. There are *over*votes in Lafayette, but the Florida Supreme Court didn't order anyone to inspect those, so again, nothing to do here for Greeny. He calls in again. This time he's sent to Suwanee County. All that Greeny knows of Suwanee County is Bugs Bunny singing that "Way Down Upon de S'wanee River" song. He's about to learn a whole lot more.

When Greeny walks into the county seat building, in Live Oak, and announces that he's with the Democratic Party, he's greeted with silence. The canvassing board and four Republican observers are about a third through the Opti-scan undervotes. Greeny's told that Bush has picked up 4, Gore 1. Greeny asks to see the five newly discovered votes. Two of the Bush votes are fine, good, exactly why these things need to be looked at. But what the . . . ?

One of the new Bush votes has solid checks by the name of every Democrat in every race except for president, and no vote for either Gore or Bush. There's a slight pencil mark near Bush's name, but certainly nothing like the definitive checks for this voter's picks elsewhere on the ballot. Greeny objects to this. I mean, the voter went for all Democrats! All Democrats plus Bush?! That's crazy to think that, Greeny says.

"Well, you're looking at someone who did that," Greeny is told by Judge William Slaughter, the chairman of the canvassing board. In fact, all three members of the Suwanee County canvassing board are Democrats. Old-school Southern Democrats, to be sure. But Democrats nonetheless.

The other questionable Bush vote has check marks by the names of two or three presidential candidates — but, in Greeny's view, just a slightly bigger check mark next to Bush's name.

"This is an overvote," Greeny says. "I want to protest these two."

"You can't protest them, we're not in the 'protest' phase anymore," Slaughter says. "This is the contest phase."

"Well, then I want to contest them," Greeny replies. But he's told he can't do that, either.

Greeny is hit with two emotions. One is suspicion: What would this board have counted if he hadn't shown up? The other is sympathy. So this is what it must have felt like for Republicans when they were before what they perceived to be hostile canvassing boards, he thinks. Shit happens in situations like these, and if no one representing the candidate you didn't support is there — if the GOP or Democratic observer is clueless, or lost, or stuck in traffic, or late — why wouldn't someone fudge a bit on two or three ballots? And if that happens in sixty-seven counties, with Bush having a winning margin of only 154 votes, well, there's your election right there.

★   ★   ★

While it was the Republicans who had to play catch-up in those first few days after the election, the GOP now has the state wired. The Florida Supreme Court issued their ruling at around 4 P.M. on Thursday, and within five hours, at least 120 Republicans were on the ground in Tallahassee.

That night, on the first floor of the Bush Building, Enwright, Mehlman, Mark Wallace, and a few others spent ninety minutes training them on what to do, what to expect. The room was overflowing. Suitcases outside the room were lined up, a scene that reminded Enwright of the first day of summer camp. By 1:30 in the morning, everyone was ready to go. Minivans shipped the observers around; by 7 A.M. Saturday morning, they have observers in each of the sixty-three counties where hand recounts are scheduled.

Drafted by Enwright the night before, Tallahassee GOP consultant David Johnson is at the Bush Building by 6:30 A.M. He's sent to Gadsden County, but the canvassing board there isn't quite ready to get started yet, so he returns to Tallahassee, where he picks up another local pol, Steve Madden. Johnson's in the Republican uniform: blazer, white shirt, tie, khakis. Madden, a burly giant of a man, overslept, so he's cutting quite a different figure with his unshaven face, black sweater, jeans, and hiking boots. Johnson and Madden's destination: Liberty County.

As Johnson and Madden shoot west on Highway 20, they figure they're gonna arrive in the county seat, Bristol, right on time. It's 10:15 A.M., and Liberty County's set to start counting at 10 — but Liberty's in the central time zone, they figure, so they should be pulling up right when the undervotes come out. As they approach the town, Madden phones the courthouse in Bristol to get directions.

"You can't miss it, we're having our winter festival today, and it's all taking place in front of the courthouse," Madden's told. "But we started a few minutes ago."

"You did?" Madden says. "But I thought you weren't going to start until 10."

"That's right," he's told.

And then it hits both Madden and Johnson: Bristol isn't in the central time zone, it isn't west of the Apalachicola River — it's in the eastern time zone, just like Tallahassee. Kind of weird that they didn't realize that, they think. Maybe they were overcompensating for the networks screwing up on Election Night and forgetting that *any* of the state was in central time.

Anyway, they get there. Five Gore operatives are there, and they sneer at Johnson, instantly making the guy in the tie and khakis as a Republican. Hilariously, however, the Gorebies approach Madden, introduce themselves to him, apparently assuming that such a big ol' slob could only be a Democrat.

When it's all over, inspecting Liberty County's 29 undervotes will end up netting Gore a grand total of 1 new vote.

★　★　★

Jackson County, on the Panhandle and the Alabama border, doesn't have a lot of citizens like Joshua Green, who flew in from New York, N.Y., to supervise the goings-on for Gore. The Jackson County courthouse this morning is not a hospitable place, Green thinks. Especially after he starts to wonder about the weird white stickers on hundreds of the county's Optiscan ballots.

"What's this?" Green asks the supervisor of elections, Sylvia Stephens, and her deputy, Vicki Farris.

Stephens explains. As Jackson County has been doing for years, before elections workers put the county's 17,000 or so ballots through the machine for the final Election Night count, they separated the 1,400 or so ballots that the machine didn't read — undervotes and overvotes. Where the elections officer could determine the intent of the voter — say, some-one filled in both the Bush oval and also the write-in oval next to which he or she wrote "Bush" — the officer covered the superfluous oval with a white sticker so the machine could read the ballot.

Farris tells Green that they did this to 300 or so ballots. Green looks around; the only ballots he sees fixed like this are Bush votes.

This is a county that Bush won 9,138 to 6,868.

★   ★   ★

"The Library is CLOSED TODAY please see the branches," reads the sign on the front door of the LeRoy Collins Leon County Public Library, at 200 W. Park Avenue. Inside, instead of a blood drive or an exhibit of elemen-tary school art, four tables are set up and the recounting of the 9,000 or so remaining undervotes from Miami-Dade County has been under way since 9:55 A.M.

Each table hosts two judges, two deputy clerks, and two observers — a Democrat and a Republican. David Leahy is in the house, as is county attorney Murray Greenberg.

A typical counting period, at table three, begins with a deputy clerk walking to a side room and picking up a white envelope full of ballots, then taking it back to the table.

"Precinct two-sixty-seven, eighteen votes," the deputy clerk says, reading what's written on the outside of the envelope.

The other clerk opens the envelope and counts the ballots, verifying the number.

Judge Charles Francis takes a ballot. "No vote," he says.

Judge Janet Ferris assesses the ballot as well. "No vote," she agrees.

There are five shoe boxes on each table. This ballot is placed in the box set aside for the "no" votes, as others are for Gore, Bush, "other," and ballots on which the judges disagree. Lewis said Friday night that he would assess these disputed ballots himself. If any of the observers have any objections, they are told to record them and make their protests known at a later time. The observers seem to be scribbling furiously.

Subdued and serious, the four tables are working briskly, assessing about 1,000 ballots an hour. At this rate, they could conceivably be done before the SCOTUS even rules on the Bush team's request for an injunction to stop the count. Each table takes a brief lunch break — sandwiches and chips.

"Precinct two-sixty-seven, eighteen votes," ends up being 18 no votes. Table three soon goes through the 25 votes of precinct 372. Inspection of this envelope results in one additional Bush vote, 24 no votes.

One out of every 10 or so ballots bears closer inspection. Most seem to be no-brainers.

At 11:58 A.M., some chitchat from deputy clerks and deputy sheriffs in the back room seems to annoy Ferris and Francis. The judges glare; immediate silence follows.

At table four, the result is a bit different. Judge Tim Harley and chief circuit court judge George Reynolds hit a run of Gore votes. Reynolds occasionally uses a magnifying glass. There seem to be no moments of the judges holding the ballot up to the light, perhaps divining the chad.

At 12:10 P.M., Pataki walks in. He mingles in the back of the room.

Outside the library, Sen. Barbara Boxer, D-Calif., speaks to TV cameras about the importance of "counting every vote," while Bush protesters try to shout her down. "Go back to the left coast!" one yells.

"Al Gore! Three-time loser! Al Gore! Three-time loser!" the small crowd bellows. "Disbar the Supreme Court!" chants Bill Engledow, thirty, from Warren Robins, Georgia, who has a megaphone.

"I'm just a voter who's outraged," Engledow says to me when I ask him what's up.

The Gore supporters are less exuberant and fewer in number. Every time the small Gore huddle tries to get a chant going, it gets smashed by the megaphone and aggression of the fifty or so Bush supporters.

★ ★ ★

"For all the loose talk about crisis or confrontation, let's be clear about why the votes haven't already been counted," Minority Leader Gephardt says, standing with Daley at the Capitol.

"The Bush campaign has done everything it can to stop a full and fair count," Gephardt says. "They and their allies have filed lawsuit after lawsuit to stop the counting of votes. Two weeks ago, Republican Whip Tom DeLay dispatched staffers to Florida, not to observe the count but to disrupt it." Other Bushies have been attacking "the integrity of the courts," Gephardt decries, unlike Gore and Lieberman, who "have lost several cases during this process, and not once have they criticized the judicial branch."

Effuses Daley in a rare moment of optimism, "We are very close to knowing who actually won Florida and who, therefore, won the presidency."

★ ★ ★

Inside the Leon County library, deputy clerk Miriam Jugger approaches Judges Harley and Reynolds at table four. "We are one-third of the way through," she says. "Please expect to be here until nine or ten."

At table three, deputy clerk Denise Bertelsen motions toward the TV camera. "I should turn my head so my family could see me," she says.

Judges are sharing mints, apparently mindful of the close quarters. When table two returns from lunch, Judge John Crusoe asks, "Anyone have onions?"

★   ★   ★

The SCOTUS brief is signed by Olson, Carvin, Terwilliger, Richard, and Ginsberg. It requests an immediate halt to the recount until various questions are resolved, so as to prevent Bush and Cheney "from suffering irreparable injury as a direct result of the erroneous decision" made by the Florida Supreme Court.

"The period between November 7 and today has, unfortunately, been characterized by chaotic and standardless manual recounts requested by Democratic presidential candidate Vice President Gore in four heavily Democratic counties and by an outburst of litigation flowing from that process," they complain. "Because of the Florida Supreme Court's judicial amendments to the legislative structure for choosing Florida's electors, absent a decision by this Court, the election results from Florida will remain under a cloud of uncertainty.

"The consequence could be a constitutional crisis."

There have been errors in the vote counting, the Bushies say, a bit hyperbolically. "During the manual-recount process, ballots were poked, prodded, rumpled, creased, twisted, dropped, stained, tabbed, and otherwise mishandled. Not surprisingly, this rough treatment caused massive damage to the ballots." The whole thing has been chaos, they say, and it's Al Gore's own fault. The "standards for evaluating ballots were changed repeatedly during the recounts. . . . In Palm Beach County, a court ordered the canvassing board to consider 'dimpled' chads, even though the board's pre-existing 1990 policy precluded treating mere indentations as valid votes. . . . On November twentieth, the Florida Democratic Party asked the Florida Supreme Court to fashion even more expansive new standards. . . . Vice President Gore repeated that request to the Florida Supreme Court on November thirtieth."

They cite 3 U.S.C. 5 (changing the rules in the middle of the game). They cite due process. They cite Article II (that electors need to be chosen "in such Manner as the Legislature thereof may direct"). They cite the Voting Rights Act.

And they cite equal protection. Indeed, though the SCOTUS has never shown a willingness to buy into the equal protection argument as it pertains to this case, the Bushies hit this one home hard. "By permitting further inconsistent and standardless recounts to be conducted during the contest proceeding, the court's order guarantees disparate treatment for similarly situated ballots both in other counties and within the counties subject to the order. The equal protection violations are compounded by the fact that the court adopted a standard of 'selective deference' to the decisions of the county canvassing boards that . . . only benefits the Gore Respondents.

"Florida Supreme Court's decision imperils Governor Bush's proper receipt of Florida's twenty-five electoral votes. The Florida Supreme Court's decision raises a reasonable possibility that the November 26 certification of Governor Bush as the winner of Florida's electoral votes will be called into doubt — or purport to be withdrawn — at a time when the December 12 deadline for naming Florida's electors could preclude Applicants' ability to seek meaningful review by this Court."

And, as if the SCOTUS needs reminding, Olson, Carvin, et al. remind the Court that, "remarkably," the Florida Supreme Court "did not respond to the questions posed by this Court's December 4 opinion vacating the Florida Supreme Court's decision in Harris."

★   ★   ★

In the Leon County library, Leahy is stunned. He doesn't quite get what this hand recount of his ballots is all about.

Because of Marc Lampkin's annoying stall tactics, not all of the undervotes were separated from the county's ballots. They finished up 614 precincts, but there were still about 50 precincts they had left. Leahy tells the judges that there's still some work to be done, that there are still precincts that needed undervotes to be segregated. He tells them about the process by which it can work, that it will take half a day at most — which can be done concurrently with their counting of the undervotes that were segregated.

But the judges completely ignore him.

★   ★   ★

The Gorebies are running a spreadsheet.

Madison County finishes by 12:15; net gain of 2 Gore votes.

Escambia County finishes around 1:30; net gain of 3 Gore votes.

Sixteen minutes later comes news from Osceola — net gain of 4 Gore votes.

Fourteen minutes after that, at 2 P.M., Liberty County. Two for Gore, 1 for Bush.

At 2:18, they hear that Manatee County found 26 votes in their 111 Opti-scan undervotes, resulting in a net gain of 2 Gore votes.

It's nerve-racking. But they're getting there.

2:45. Highlands County. Punch cards. Three for Gore, 1 for Bush.

★   ★   ★

Beck was up all night, working with Sean Gallagher on various objections he had to file in Lewis's courtroom by 8 A.M. "The Florida Supreme Court put this court in a frankly impossible situation," the brief states. "The court's order also robs George W. Bush and Dick Cheney of even the rudiments of due process."

After Beck and Terrell — who wrote a brief on the spoliation of the Miami-Dade ballots — filed their papers at 7:55, the two hit the talk-show circuit, designated to talk about how the recounts are unfair. After entering Bushworld to much suspicion, Beck is now a full-fledged GOP superstar. The fact that he voted for McCain in the primaries — even after McCain had dropped out — is not often mentioned.

"We're going to have one county where judges look at the ballots," Beck tells CNN. "We're going to have other counties where other employees of other branches of the government are drafted into service. So, we've got inconsistent treatment right off the bat. Number two, no matter how well-meaning the judges may be, they're not given any guidance. They're not given any standards to evaluate the ballots."

Not all is lost, however. The GOP pols in the field report back to Mehlman and Enwright, and Beck hears that the percentage of undervotes being considered votes is very low, maybe 5 percent.

"They're applying real standards," Beck thinks.

There are other reports that Beck hears — counties practicing what he considers acts of civil disobedience. The Bay County canvassing board, he hears, faxes Lewis a letter stating that they might refuse to comply with his order, insisting that they did it right the first time. More than thirty of the sixty-four counties don't send Lewis the letter he requested, explaining their plans.

Out of gas, Beck heads back to the Radisson to pass out.

★   ★   ★

In D.C., Daley gets word that the Miami-Dade undervote count isn't going so hot. The standard the judges are using is pretty tough.

No surprise. Daley always knew that if regular judges looked at the ballots — people who had never looked at a ballot in their life, as opposed to elections judges, who look at ballots, who have seen this shit — they'd be skeptical, they'd say, "What *is* this?"

The judges are really moving through those things, Daley's told. And they're not counting many for Gore at all. This thing is much closer than some of the political people think. This thing is still going to come down to just a few votes, one way or the other.

★ ★ ★

Klain's on the phone with Gore, briefing him on how the recount's going, when an assistant sticks her head in and tells him that Andy Pincus, a Gore attorney in D.C. working on some of the U.S. Supreme Court briefs, is on the phone.

"I can't talk to him," Klain says, turning to Jeremy Bash. "Jer? Can you?" Bash picks up the phone.

"Hey, Andy," Jeremy says.

"I need to talk to Ron," Pincus says, sounding like he was just kicked in the stomach. *"It's an emergency."*

"He's on the phone with Gore," Bash says. "He's gonna have to call you back."

"Jeremy," Pincus says. *"The Supreme Court just granted a stay."*

"Ron!" Bash shouts. "The Supreme Court just granted a stay! Andy's on line six!"

"Hold on, sir," Klain says, putting Gore on hold.

★ ★ ★

Daley was right, it *does* come down to just a few votes.

Five, to be precise: Rehnquist, Scalia, Thomas, O'Connor, and Kennedy.

They vote to grant the stay on the Florida Supreme Court ruling. The case is set for oral argument on Monday, December 11, 2000, at 11 A.M.

And just in case Al Gore feels even the slightest bit confident, Scalia writes a totally unnecessary love note to Bush. "It suffices to say that the issuance of the stay suggests that a majority of the court, while not deciding the issues presented, believe that the petitioner has a substantial probability of success."

Counting votes that the Bushies consider to be "of questionable legality does in my view threaten irreparable harm to petitioner, and to the country, by casting a cloud upon what he [Bush] claims to be the legitimacy of his election. Count first, and rule upon legality afterwards, is not a recipe for producing election results that have the public acceptance democratic stability requires."

Scalia's note is written in reaction to Justice Stevens, who puts forward an atypical dissent. "To stop the counting of legal votes, the majority today departs from three venerable rules of judicial restraint that have guided the court throughout its history." The SCOTUS has always deferred to the state supreme courts when it comes to that state's own laws. "On federal constitutional questions that were not fairly presented to the court whose judgment is being reviewed, we have prudently declined to express an opinion," Stevens writes, a reference to the fact that the Bushies kept their main U.S. constitutional questions — like *McPherson* — out of the Florida Supreme Court so that they could bring them up before the SCOTUS. "The majority has acted unwisely."

Moreover, Stevens says, any questions about the legitimacy of the next president will come precisely from the majority's action. "Preventing the recount from being completed will inevitably cast a cloud on the legitimacy of the election," Stevens writes.

★ ★ ★

One of the myriad faxes Lewis receives is an order from the U.S. Supreme Court sent to him personally by someone calling himself "William Rehnquist," telling him to stop the counting. It's on official-looking stationery and letterhead, and Lewis would have bought it completely if it hadn't named him personally, as opposed to the more traditional reference to the Leon County Circuit Court.

This time, though, it's different. He hears of the stay from CNN first. And though he doesn't doubt the cable news network, he wants something official before he orders the recounts halted. And he gets it. This time it doesn't mention him personally. This time it's real.

Lewis has a mixed reaction. A lot of people had been working hard to make the recounts work. He was heartened by the response of his Leon County judicial colleagues, most of whom willingly were giving up their weekend to make the Miami-Dade recount work.

On the other hand, maybe the thing's finally over.

★ ★ ★

Boies and Zack are at Andrew's, finishing up lunch. On one of the TVs, news flashes across the screen: *11th Circuit Denies Stay.*

"Of course they denied it," Boies says. "How can you ever have 'irreparable harm' from counting legal votes?"

"I guess you can order dessert," Zack says.

But within minutes, another TV, on another channel, has another headline. *U.S. Supreme Court Grants Stay.*

"I guess we'd better go back," Boies says.

★ ★ ★

"Please stop the machines, Mark," says Ion Sancho, Leon County's supervisor of elections.

Then: "We should start packing up the ballots. We've got to stop the recount. I don't think it's going to start again."

In Hillsborough County, Elections Supervisor Pam Iorio hasn't yet opened the first box of undervotes — there are 5,553 total — before she hears word that the SCOTUS has stepped in.

"Just another day in Election 2000," Iorio says with a sigh.

The crowd of GOP observers starts chanting: "Bush! Bush! Bush! Bush! Bush!"

In Pinellas County, the canvassing board is two hours and 224 ballots into reviewing its 4,226 undervotes. Gore's up 2, Bush 1.

Computer expert Noel Poyntz flew from Miami to Jacksonville, Duval County, Saturday morning to install software to separate the 4,967 undervotes from the 291,000 ballots. Poyntz had just finished, when the canvassing-board chairman, chief administrative judge Brent Shore, gets paged by his wife.

He calls her back; she holds the phone up to CNN. Shore tells the rest what's going on and leaves the room to hit the Internet to find out more.

★ ★ ★

At around 2:45 P.M., word of the U.S. Supreme Court decision spreads inside and outside the Leon County Library like those glow-in-the-dark germs in the movie *Outbreak.*

"SOOOOOOOOORRREE loser," the Bush protesters chant. "SOOOOOOOOORRREE loser."

The Gore forces weakly cry back: "This is America! Every vote counts!"

At 2:59, Leon County court administrator Terre Cass pokes her head out to tell us what's up. "All I can tell you is that we are in recess right now until we can figure out what has happened," she says. "The teams finished up the precincts they were currently working on." The judges have yet to receive official word from the SCOTUS, she says.

Inside, Reynolds is given the official word from Lewis. He tells everyone to stop counting. Maybe fifteen minutes later, Cass steps to the podium.

Reporters scramble around her.

"OK, are we ready?" she asks.

We nod.

"We've just received a call from Judge Terry Lewis," Cass says. SCOTUS has ordered a stay on the Florida Supreme Court's Friday decision.

The Bush protesters erupt with boisterous cheers. "It's time for Gore to go! It's time for Gore to go!" they cry.

"This is good," Tom Rush, a Leon County Republican official, says softly to a woman next to him, motioning at the excited, somewhat angry, Bush mass. "It's my job to harness this and keep it going."

A Republican observer is running around, telling reporters that Bush was up a net 42 votes in the library when Lewis called them and put an end to it all.

Judges start leaving the building, escorted by sheriff's deputies. Reporters and cameramen chase them. One camera nearly falls, catching on a POLICE LINE DO NOT CROSS yellow tape that has separated Gore protesters from Bush protesters. Someone else pulls up the tape to make his way through, and it catches a young African-American man, John Campbell of Lakeland, Florida, under the neck, nearly strangling him for a second.

Deputy clerks spill out into the parking lot, holding shoe boxes. Inside are supplies, we're told, not ballots — the ballots are being returned under armed guard to the Leon County circuit courthouse.

"We tried," says a deputy clerk as she gets into her friend's powder blue GMC Sonoma. "We had a good system going. I'm a little disappointed. We came to do a job, and we didn't really get to do it."

Outside the library, protesters and reporters and sheriff's deputies mill about. What do we do now? Where do we go? What's going to happen next?

County clerk David Lang comes out of the building.

"We're all in a state of suspended animation, just like you are," Lang says to a mass of reporters. "When the British surrendered at Old Yorktown, they marched to the tune of 'The World Turned Upside Down.' I'm going to go try to find a copy of that."

★　★　★

At 3:11, Gore sends Lehane an e-mail on his portable Blackberry.

"Please make sure that no one trashes the Supreme Court," it says.

★　★　★

Beck is sleeping when Bartlit calls him from his Colorado office.

"Did you hear what happened?"

"No," Beck says, still asleep.

"The U.S. Supreme Court stayed the recount!"

Beck's first reaction: he has to go back to court. He's convinced that some counties are going to refuse to stop counting. At the Bush Building, his fears are confirmed. He runs over to the circuit courthouse, finds someone in the administrative office, and explains to the clerk that some counties are continuing, despite the SCOTUS order.

The clerk calls all four of them. Members of the Okaloosa County canvassing board report their plans: they're going to continue the counting but seal the results. If you do that, you won't only be held in contempt of the U.S. Supreme Court, but also Judge Lewis will hold you in contempt, they're told.

Another county wants to continue sorting, but they promise not to count. Better not, says the clerk. Within an hour, all four counties have been persuaded to stop.

★   ★   ★

In Austin, *Time* reporter John Dickerson sits shotgun in Bush's immense gray Chevy Suburban. Managing editor Walter Isaacson sits in the back with Bush aide Gordon Johndroe, and Isaacson's wife, Kathy, sits in the way back, as Bush drives them around his 1,600-acre ranch in preparation for their "Person of the Year" issue.

Bush sure seems chill. As they tour the land, Bush jokes about a bull whom they stumble upon mid-mating. "Puttin' on a show," he jokes. In the kitchen at lunch, he chastises Spot. "What is it you tracked in here?" he asks him. Back outside, at a stream, Isaacson cups his hands to the water and asks, "Can you drink this?"

"Sure," Bush says, as Isaacson lifts the water to his mouth. "Except for the cow shit."

Dickerson is trying to figure out if Bush is really this serene, or if it's an act. They've been here since 10 A.M. — five hours now — and still no sign of artifice. It seems legit. Especially when they enter an enclosed wood.

"It does just all fall away," Bush says to the group. "I could give a damn about the Supreme Court. Well, of course I do care, but you forget."[1]

He doesn't need to care. And Isaacson — who has an appointment with Gore for next week, too, just in case *he* ends up meriting the "Person of the Year" honor — need not fly into D.C.

A call from Don Evans will make that appointment eminently cancelable.

"That's great news. Terrific," Bush says to Evans on his cell phone. "That is good news," he says. He goes to call Baker, but only after he's driven Dickerson and the Isaacsons to their car.

★   ★   ★

"I have just spoken to Governor Bush," Baker tells us in the state senate hearing room, "and of course we are pleased by the United States Supreme Court decision this afternoon to stay the mandate of the Florida Supreme Court and to grant our petition."

Is it over?

"Of course not," Baker says, rather unconvincingly. "They haven't ruled on the merits. This is a stay."

What's it been like for Bush these past twenty-four or forty-eight hours?

"It has not been just these past twenty-four or forty-eight hours," Baker says. "It's been ever since we began this process, this odyssey, on November the eighth. It changes from day to day. It's one day — one day you're up, one day you're down."

★   ★   ★

As Ron Klain walks into the hearing room, he's on the phone with DNC spokeswoman Jenny Backus, and she's giving him a number: 58.

"Okay, thanks," he says, hanging up the phone, as he and Boies step up to the microphones. Klain has heard about the Bushies' spreading it around that the counts weren't going so well for Gore, and he wants to nip that in the bud. They don't want Sunday newspapers and Sunday talking-head shows regurgitating this notion that no matter what the Supreme Court rules, Gore's a dead man regardless.

Klain announces that his team was "quite pleased with the progress being made at the counts under way here in a number of counties. Our latest information shows that thirteen counties had completely or partially completed their recounts, and in those counties, Vice President Gore and Senator Lieberman had gained a net of fifty-eight votes."

What's more, Klain says, "five of those counties were heavily Republican counties. So we believe that the progress made in the count thus far indicated that we were clearly on a path for Vice President Gore and Senator Lieberman to make up the difference and to pull ahead, had the count been fully completed."

Boies is asked if the Gore legal team plans on using the 58 votes in its SCOTUS arguments on Monday.

"Well, I don't think the fifty-eight votes has anything to do with what the Supreme Court decides, or at least directly," Boies says. "I think the fifty-eight votes indicate that if this count continues to go forward, it looks like right now, although nobody can be absolutely certain, that Vice President Gore and Senator Lieberman would win the popular vote in Florida, just as they won the popular vote outside of Florida."

What about the December 12 deadline? Arguments are set for Monday, December 11. Is there going to be enough time?

"I think the timing issue is probably the single most disappointing thing about what the Supreme Court has done," Boies says. He, of course, agreed to the December 12 deadline way back during that first Florida Supreme Court argument.

Boies now says, "I think there's no doubt that December eighteenth is the final deadline. We've all been trying to get it done by December twelfth. I think that in the last week, everybody has recognized that at least, under certain scenarios, it would not be done by December twelfth. For example, the legislature said that if it acted, it probably wasn't going to act until December thirteenth, and that the December twelfth deadline was not any magical end date."

Speculation, and common sense, designate that Kennedy and O'Connor are the justices to watch, the moderate conservatives whose shifts hand victories to one side or the other. On a single Wednesday last June, O'Connor leaned left — with Breyer, Ginsburg, Souter, and Stevens — in overturning a Nebraska law banning late-term abortions, and then went with Rehnquist, Kennedy, Scalia, and Thomas on allowing the Boy Scouts to ban gays.

Boies is asked what arguments he hopes will take hold with either of the two swingers. He lays out a few arguments, saying, "I'm not sure which one's the best, and I probably won't be arguing it. And that person will have to decide what the best argument is."

★ ★ ★

The Bushies are livid. First of all, they think that "58" number is utter bullshit. It may have been real a few hours ago, before the Miami-Dade recount at the Leon County Library hit the Latino precincts, but when the SCOTUS stopped the count, the Bushies' numbers had their man in the lead.

Moreover, they had told their observers to keep the numbers quiet; they had argued before Lewis that the numbers needed to stay secret until the very end, and Lewis's ruling indeed stated that "no partial recounts shall be reported, either formally or informally."

Some of the younger lawyers — ones Beck would later describe as "hotheads" — want to bring Klain and Boies before Lewis on contempt-of-court charges. Older, more seasoned lawyers agree to an emergency motion that will shut Boies and Klain up, though nothing as harsh as a formal contempt motion. Besides, they have an idea of Lewis's MO by now, and the even-keeled author isn't going to hold anyone in contempt for one ambiguous line he wrote in his motion late at night. It wasn't even part of the oral complaint Lewis issued. Let's not get crazy here, they say.

So at 5:03 P.M., Jason Unger files an emergency motion, complaining that Boies and Klain "are in violation of this Court's Order . . . in that they are reporting, formally or informally, partial counts." They "must cease and desist immediately," says the complaint.

Klain's still pissed off — and a little anxious. He understood the gag order to have applied to canvassing boards, not parties in the legal dispute. It seems nonsensical. The counts were in public, AP was reporting the results every hour. And he considers the motion to be close enough to a contempt charge to be insulting.

Truth is, Lewis did mean it to apply to everyone. He was trying to avoid a circus-like atmosphere, with press conferences every three minutes. He's not going to take any action against Klain; the order was pretty vague, whatever. Still, as a matter of policy and protocol, he reminds the Gore team that it would be better for them not to report the partial totals anymore. Not that it matters.

★   ★   ★

Democrats will forever wonder what would have happened had the SCO-TUS not stepped in and stopped the count. There are two reasons why they shouldn't. One: the Florida Supreme Court's order to count the undervotes, without counting the overvotes, was wholly without logic. If the intent of the voter can be discerned in the approximately 65,000 undervotes, then there is no reason why the 110,000 overvotes shouldn't have been given the same opportunity. The Florida Supreme Court order, therefore, was based on a faulty comprehension of what any real attempt to truly get to the bottom of the matter would entail. As the experiences in Gadsden, Jackson, and Volusia Counties proved, there were clearly discernible votes in the overvotes.

Second, the "58" number that Jenny Backus told Klain to use at the press conference shortly after 4 P.M. was complete bullshit. According to the spreadsheets put together by the Democrats' numbers guy, Achim Bergmann, at no time during the day was Gore up 58 votes. Before Klain and Boies went out to speak to the press, the numbers Bergmann had in his computer had Gore up 31 votes (+3 in Escambia, +2 in Highlands, +1 in Liberty, +2 in Madison, +2 in Manatee, +10 in Okechobee, +18 in Orange, +4 in Osceola, −1 in Collier, −3 in Desoto, −3 in Pasco, −1 in Pinellas, and −3 in Suwanee). This may be a net gain, but it is not 58 votes, leading one to the conclusion that the "58 votes" number was invented out of whole cloth.

Moreover, the numbers that came in to Bergmann subsequent to the Boies-Klain press conference showed Gore losing votes, so that Bush was actually ahead by 15. (Gore registered −44 in Miami-Dade, −1 in Flagler, −5 in Okaloosa, −8 in Santa Rosa, +7 in Franklin, +2 in St. Lucie, +1 in Taylor, +2 in Wakulta.) As throughout the whole fracas, those Gore backers looking for reassurance in their hopes for the Gore strategy would be advised to steer clear of the hard numbers and concrete facts.

★   ★   ★

Boies wants to argue the case before the SCOTUS. He doesn't want Tribe to do it, he wants to do it. And he's not alone.

It's a real debate, because Tribe is one of the most esteemed Supreme Court attorneys alive, while Boies has argued before the SCOTUS only once before. He lost the decision, 9 to 0. And he was arguing against Tribe.

Klain and Daley think that Gore should stick with Tribe. This is his terrain. But Boies has his backers, too: Christopher and Gore's brother-in-law Frank Hunger. And, ultimately, Al Gore. Gore makes this decision based on the fact that the case will probably revolve a great deal around Florida law, which Boies now knows cold. Also, Gore feels that Boies deserves it — he poured his heart and soul into the case, has been on the ground in Tallahassee since that second week. Rightfully, personally, emotionally this is Boies's case, Gore feels. Not that it's not a close call. As Klain puts it, it's like choosing between Magic Johnson and Larry Bird. Christopher sits Tribe down and tells him that he'll be on the bench Monday.

★   ★   ★

Unless they're permanent Supreme Court reporters, journalists are assigned fairly crappy seats at high-profile oral arguments. Not that we won't take them; hey, we're happy to be there. But we're thrown together in rows of cheap chairs wedged behind immense gray columns. If you're lucky, you can see two justices at a time. It's my luck that I see the two whom everyone's watching: Kennedy and O'Connor.

While all the other legal cases in the Florida fracas have had names like *Volusia County canvassing board v. Katherine Harris et al.* and *George W. Bush and Richard Cheney v. Palm Beach County canvassing board et al.*, today's showdown finally has the right name: *Bush v. Gore.* Throughout the ninety-minute hearing — thirty-five minutes for Olson, ten minutes for Klock, forty-five minutes for Boies — O'Connor and Kennedy hold their heads in their hands. Perhaps they're just trying really hard to concentrate. But it looks as though the burdens of their pending decisions are literally weighing them down.

They offer conflicting clues. Democrats take heart in the fact that Olson's only 125 words into his opening argument when Kennedy grabs the Achilles' heel of his case. "Where's the federal issue here?" is the first question of the day.

Kennedy and O'Connor both seem skeptical of — or at least reluctant to embrace — Olson's proposition that this is just *obviously* a federal issue. But both also seem concerned that the county-by-county judgments of ballot standards might violate the equal protection clause of the Constitution.

"Can you begin by telling us our federal jurisdiction?" Kennedy asks.

O'Connor soon chirps up. "I have the same problem Justice Kennedy does, apparently," she tells Olson. Article II of the Constitution, which sets out the rules for assigning electors, "certainly creates a presumption that the scheme the legislature has set out will be followed, even by judicial review in election matters. I would have thought that that would be sufficient," O'Connor says, rather than to make a federal case out of it.

Olson replies that "there is a breakout with respect to various aspects of Florida statute and Florida election law. There's a specific grant of authority to the circuit courts. There's no reference to an appellate jurisdiction."

"It may not be the most powerful argument we bring to the Supreme Court," Olson allows.

"I think that's right," Kennedy says, to laughter from the crowd.

At the previous SCOTUS hearing, it seemed a majority of the justices were concerned the Florida court had rewritten the law, while at the same time a majority also seemed skeptical that this was a "federal issue" that warranted a federal court's meddling. Its subsequent unanimous ruling, which asked the Florida court to better justify its action based on Florida law, seemed a reasonable middle ground, one that kept them — for the time being — from entering the political fray. There are no such options here. The ticktocks from Tallahassee are deafening, and the very fact that the Court put a stop to the manual recount of Florida's approximately 65,000 "undervotes" seems to indicate the SCOTUS's serious disapproval of its Sunshine State counterparts.

Olson refers to Friday's ruling by the Florida court as "a major, major revision" of Florida law.

Stevens takes issue with that, asking why Olson's arguments "rely very heavily on the dissenting opinion in the Florida Supreme Court" by Florida chief justice Wells. Who cares what Wells wrote in his one-man dissent? Stevens asks. "Which opinion do we normally look to for issues of state law?" he asks.

More important, Olson is asked by Breyer, if the Court were to allow the recounts to continue, "What in your opinion would be a fair standard, on the assumption that it starts up missing the twelfth deadline but before the eighteenth?"

Olson doesn't really have an answer for this, except to say that he would hope that the standard would be uniform. "At minimum, Justice Breyer, the penetration of the ballot card would be required," he says. When asked, he seems perfectly willing to let Harris set a standard. This apparent hypocrisy — Olson giving a rah-rah to the idea of Harris setting a post-election standard while objecting to the Florida court's post-election rulings, saying the court changed the rules after the game — gets Ginsburg's back up.

"You have said the intent of the voter simply won't do. It's too vague, it's too subjective," she says. "But at least those words, 'intent of the voter,' come from the legislature. Wouldn't anything added to that be — wouldn't you be objecting much more fiercely than you are now if something were added to the words that the all-powerful legislature put in the statute?"

Florida statute, after all, allows for "the circuit judge" to "fashion any order he or she deems necessary to prevent or correct any wrong, and to provide any relief appropriate under the circumstances," she says. "I couldn't imagine a greater conferral of authority by the legislature to the circuit judge."

Olson is also taken to task by the left wing of the Court after he asserts that "undervotes" are actually not votes, since the machine didn't read them as such.

"As to the undervotes in which there is arguably some expression of intent on the ballot that the machine didn't pick up, the majority of the Florida Supreme Court says you're wrong," Souter says. "They interpreted the statute otherwise. Are you saying here that their interpretation was so far unreasonable in defining legal vote as not to be a judicial act entitled in effect, to the presumption of reasonable interpretation under Article II?"

"Yes, that is our contention," Olson replies.

"Very well, Mr. Olson," Rehnquist says.

Klock approaches the mike to give us a few moments of levity. The somewhat-unpolished lawyer twice refers to justices by the wrong names. He calls Stevens "Justice Brennan," a reference to the legendary jurist who died in 1997. He'd done this in his practice moot courts, too. Klock, an active University of Miami Law School alum, used to see Brennan periodically when the justice would come down to Miami during the winters. Brennan would set up dinners, meetings, and Klock got to know him a bit. And for some reason, Stevens reminds him of Brennan.

Then, in the middle of answering a question by Souter — but thinking about something Breyer had just said — Klock commits a second faux pas, calling Souter "Justice Breyer." It gets to the point that when Scalia comes forward with a question for Klock, he feels the need to introduce himself. "Mr. Klock? I'm Scalia," he says mischievously, to much laughter from the VIP crowd — which includes Dole and Jackson; Republican senators John Warner of Virginia, Arlen Specter of Pennsylvania, Orrin Hatch of Utah, and Judd Gregg of New Hampshire; Democratic senators John Kerry of Massachusetts, Patrick Leahy of Vermont, Harry Reid of Nevada, and Chris Dodd of Connecticut; Daley; and Evans, among others.

After Klock's entertaining name-fumbling, Boies steps up. In only his second Supreme Court outing, Boies gets only twenty-six words in before Kennedy interrupts and asks about the jurisdictional issue. He then rips Boies for defending what much of the Court clearly sees as the Florida court's post-election formulation of law.

"I'm not sure why if the legislature does it, it's a new law, and when the Supreme Court does it, it isn't," Kennedy says pointedly.

Boies insists that that's not the case, and reminds the Court that "the standard" as to whether or not Florida Supreme Court justices overstepped their bounds should be "the standard this Court has generally applied in giving deference to state supreme court decisions." Potential swing vote O'Connor seems doubtful of this. "But is it, in light of Article II?" she asks. "I'm not so sure."

"You are responding as though there were no special burden to show some deference to legislative choices in this one context," O'Connor, former GOP majority leader of the Arizona state senate, says to Boies. "Not when courts review laws generally, for general elections, but in the context of selection of presidential electors, isn't there a big red flag up there, 'Watch Out'?" Whether or not the Florida court acted properly is "a concern that we have," O'Connor says.

Not that the state court has even bothered to respond to the Supreme Court's previous concerns, which caused it to vacate the Florida court's extension. "I did not find, really, a response by the Florida Supreme Court to this Court's remand in the case a week ago," O'Connor says, sounding rather schoolmarmy. "It just seemed to kind of bypass it and assume that all those changes in deadlines were just fine, and they'd go ahead and adhere to them. And I found that troublesome."

The Bush team slams Florida's election law for essentially being ruled by chaos. But, one could counter, was it Gore's fault that Jeb Bush, Harris, and the GOP-controlled state legislature had allowed that law to remain without clarification? Fairness, of course, is seldom at issue when it comes to debating law.

"That's very general," Kennedy says of the Florida standard of ascertaining "intent of the voter." "Even a dog knows the difference in being stumbled over and being kicked," he says. "You would say that, from the standpoint of the equal protection clause, each — could each county give their own interpretation to what 'intent' means, so long as they are in good faith and with some reasonable basis finding intent? Could that vary from county to county?"

"I think it can vary from individual to individual," Boies acknowledges.

Souter seems even more concerned about Florida's shifting county-by-county standards. "There is no genuinely subjective indication beyond what can be viewed as either a dimple or a hanging chad," he says. It "varies, we're told, from county to county. Why shouldn't there be one objective rule for all counties? And if there isn't, why isn't it an equal protection violation?"

Assuredly making Gorebies everywhere shake in their Doc Martens, Souter says that this issue is "bothering Justice Kennedy, Justice Breyer, me, and others."

After all, as Scalia offers, "It was clear that Broward and Palm Beach Counties had applied different criteria to dimpled ballots. One of them was counting all dimpled ballots; the other one plainly was not. . . . That's just not rational."

Providing a speck in an electron in an atom that's part of a glimmer of hope, Souter says that if the Court responds to this issue, then "we would have a responsibility to tell the Florida courts what to do about it." He asks Boies, "What would you tell them to do about it?"

For once, the brainiac motormouth is speechless.

"Well, I think that's a very hard question," he finally says.

"You'd tell them to count every vote," Souter jokes.

"I think I would say that if you're looking for a standard — and I say that not because of the particular aspects of this election — the Texas standard, if you wanted to specify something that was specific, it gives you a pretty good standard," Boies says.

But Kennedy soon rains on this, returning to the argument that the certification deadline was extended by the Florida court only by creating "a new law, a new scheme, a new system for recounting at this late date."

"I'm very troubled by that," potential swing-vote Kennedy says.

Boies tries to change the subject. "I think at this stage you have to leave [that] aside — because at the contest stage, what you're doing is you're contesting specific ballots, whether or not they were included in the certification; it's absolutely clear under Florida law that that's what the contest is about. So at the contest stage, the only question is, can you complete the contest of the contested ballots in the time available?

"Everything that's in the record is that we could have, and indeed we still may be able to, if that count can go forward," Boies says.

But Rehnquist seems skeptical. "Including appeals to the Supreme Court of Florida and the other petition to this court? If this all goes forward, there's going to be an appeal to the Supreme Court of Florida and likely another petition to this court. Surely that couldn't have been done by December twelfth. . . . Or could it?"

Boies says that it can be done, that briefs and arguments and a decision have been done so far in this fiasco "within twenty-four hours," and, with a handful of exceptions, most of the counties can finish up within a day or so. "As I understand it, some of them have taken advantage of the time —"

Rehnquist starts to ask a question. But Boies, the smartest kid in the class, isn't done speaking.

"Wouldn't the —" Rehnquist says.

"— to get the procedures ready to count —" Boies continues.

But there's no question who wins the argument over whose turn it is to speak.

"Just a minute, Mr. Boies," the chief justice intones authoritatively, and Boies shuts his mouth.

Souter tries again to get Boies to admit that there's something troubling about every county having its own ballot-reading standard. Boies tries a new argument — that since Floridians vote differently county by county, optical ballots here, punch cards there, what he's asking for isn't such a big deal.

"There are five times as many undervotes in punch card–ballot counties than in optical-ballot counties," he says, so "some difference in how votes are being treated county by county" already exists. "That difference is much greater than the difference in how many votes are recovered in Palm Beach, or Broward, or Volusia, or Miami-Dade. So that the differences of interpretation of the general standard are resulting in far fewer differences among counties than simply the differences in the machines that they have."

Soon enough, time's up. "The case is submitted," Rehnquist says. Leaving the courtroom, Sen. Tim Hutchinson, R-Ark., yawns. In the auditorium, senators Dodd, Specter, and Tom Harkin, D-Iowa, huddle, trying to figure out what's going to happen. But even those esteemed senators are just as clueless as the rest of us.

★ ★ ★

Tribe is troubled. And confused. There was far too much discussion about the equal protection argument, he thinks. The justices had never before shown any inclination to buy into that argument. In fact, twice before, the SCOTUS rebuffed the Bush team's efforts to get the equal protection argument before them. What changed? In Tribe's mind, nothing. Nothing in the law or in the record, at any rate. But now, a day before the December 12 "safe harbor" deadline, suddenly the Supreme Court is intrigued by equal protection?!

Tribe is also a bit bothered by the Florida Supreme Court, and how it didn't respond to their Supreme superiors' questions. There were some pretty obvious questions that the Florida court hadn't yet answered satisfactorily: Where did the November 26 date come from? for instance. Or, how much did they lean on the state constitution, as opposed to state law, when they made their first ruling?

Then there was Boies. Tribe, of course, wanted to argue before the U.S. Supreme Court and disagreed with the decision to go with Boies, who had been there only once before, in a case where Tribe had handed him his hat on a 9 to 0 ruling. He understands the decision, thinks the world of Boies, but also knows that arguing successfully before the U.S. Supreme Court takes more than an agile mind and a familiarity with Florida law. It's a very specialized tribunal, one in which experience and familiarity help.

Tribe is very fearful of the equal protection argument, though he thinks it completely ridiculous. He wishes Boies had argued more forcefully against it, emphasizing more how the methods of voting are vastly unequal county by county, how, for whatever reason, voters in Miami-Dade and Palm Beach are less likely to have their votes count than those in Sarasota or Sanibel. He wishes Boies had mentioned that dimples are randomly distributed, and not just a mark that tends to show up more on Democratic ballots.

Boies himself seems to acknowledge a smidgen of this — if only briefly — after the argument. "There were questions that I wasn't prepared entirely for," he allows in a press conference.

★ ★ ★

On Monday, December 11, the five justices who stayed the recount seem ready to rule for Bush. The Florida Supreme Court created a new law, based on God knows what, and that's a clear violation of both 3 U.S.C. 5 —

the "changing the rules in the middle of the game" deal — as well as Article II, that electors need to be chosen "in such Manner as the Legislature thereof may direct." The justices order out for Chinese food for their clerks, so they can hand down a decision that night. But then the Florida Supreme Court finally turns in its homework assignment from the week before, and in so doing throws a wrench into the works.

When Florida Supreme Court spokesman Craig Waters walks outside to the steps of the court in Tallahassee, not one — *not one!* — reporter is there to hear what he has to say. But O'Connor and Kennedy sure hear. The Florida court explains the method by which it arrived at its first decision, how it wasn't rooted in the state constitution but rather state law, as written by the state legislature.[2]

Suddenly O'Connor and Kennedy are no longer with Rehnquist, Scalia, and Thomas on 3 U.S.C. 5 or Article II. Nothing's going to be decided tonight.

★　★　★

It's Tuesday, December 12. Gore believes that the SCOTUS is either going to rule for him or is going to decide not really to involve itself. Daley thinks he's living in a dreamland — "Fuhget it!" he says to Gore. "Five Republican judges. We're going right in the tank" — but Gore is confident that they'll be counting the ballots again, soon.

He's not alone. Both the Bushies and the Gorebies have kept their observers scattered throughout the state of Florida, in preparation.

★　★　★

From: georgewbush.com
Sent: Tuesday, December 12, 2000, 10:16 AM
To: Jack Oliver
Subject: Surrogates for recounts

Talked to Joe and Mindy and Mehlman this morning. This is what we want to do for press purposes. Mehlman is going to talk to Joe about what they need for observation of counting purposes – that will have to be a much bigger operation than anything we can handle out of our mini–press office. The following needs to be ready if the Court calls for a recount. If a larger surrogate operation is put into place, we can fold these folks into that pro-gram as well.

We need to be prepared to cover the following major media markets in FL:

1. Miami
2. Palm Beach
3. Tampa/St. Pete
4. Orlando
5. Jacksonville
6. Tallahassee
7. Pensacola

Because Congress is in session, Governors and non federal surrogates should be the easiest to get.

Suggestions: in NO order of preference — All are retired or federal office-holders

Gov. Racicot
Gov. Pataki
Gov. Thompson
Gov. Engler
Gov. Whitman
Gov. Gilmore
Gov. Keating
Gov. Ridge
Sen. Alan Simpson
Ken Blackwell
Gov. Taft
Gov. Cellucci
Sen. Ashcroft
Howard Baker
Lynn Martin
Bob Dole
Elizabeth Dole
Lamar Smith
Susan Molinari

★ ★ ★

Gore calls speechwriter Eli Attie. He's working on an op-ed for the *New York Times* about why it's important that the fight be carried on, and he wants some help.

"How soon can you get here?" he asks him. Attie says he can be there in five minutes, but when he goes to catch a cab, he realizes he's out of money.

He goes to a money machine, but it's broken. So he walks over. Since he's now late, he decides to walk in the front gate instead of the back.

Big mistake. Reporters have been calling Attie, a dozen a day, to see if he's working on a concession speech. Attie hasn't been, really, though every now and then he sketches out an idea, unbeknownst to Gore. Now that he's here, walking through the front gate, however, reporters are convinced that he's here to work on the concession speech. Attie runs in, fending off ABC's John Yang, among others. He hasn't even arrived at Gore's house before Gore senior aide Monica Dixon calls him on his cell. "What are you doing at Gore's house?!" she asks him. "I just got calls from five reporters asking me why you're there!"

When Attie walks in, Gore greets him with a shake of his head. "You should've used the back gate," Gore says.

★   ★   ★

Meanwhile, everyone in the world is wondering what the justices are up to. Speculation about political biases fills the air. Does it matter that Scalia's son works for Olson's law firm? Or that Thomas's wife is collecting résumés for the new Bush administration? Or that Thomas himself owes his job to Bush's pop? Or that O'Connor and Rehnquist clearly want to retire, and clearly want to do so when a Republican is in the White House? Or that Ron Klain himself led the team that selected Ginsburg? Or that she and Breyer were appointed by the Clinton-Gore administration? Maybe; who knows? It's naive to pretend that the justices aren't as human as the rest of us, that their politics don't play any role whatsoever in their decisions, just as the Florida Supreme Court justices' biases surely reared their heads on one or more occasions.

Rehnquist, Scalia, and Thomas are fired up against the Florida Supreme Court. They want to vacate this decision, too. They feel that the Florida Supreme Court stepped on the legislature's job. O'Connor and Kennedy no longer see it that way. But they, like Souter and Breyer, do have equal protection concerns about the standardless, county-by-county way the ballots are being analyzed. Of course, this potential problem was pointed out in the Bush legal team's first argument, not to mention in its brief before Middlebrooks, so they're coming to terms with this issue a little late.

Ginsburg and Stevens don't think that the SCOTUS should have ever even taken this case to begin with. The Court almost never steps in to tell a state supreme court how to interpret their own law.

Souter and Breyer don't want the Court to issue a ruling that can be seen as divisive, political. They suggest to Kennedy and O'Connor that they all try to fashion a solution to the equal protection problem, establish a standard, send the thing back to Florida, and have them do it right. But Kennedy and O'Connor aren't biting. They don't think that there's really any way to come up with standards. They don't trust the Florida Supreme Court to supervise a recount that will pass muster. What's more, time runs out at midnight tonight, the date that the Florida Supreme Court set — with Boies's consent — as a deadline for any count to have been completed.

Soon Breyer and Souter leave the Supreme Court altogether. TV news networks show them buzzing out of the underground SCOTUS parking lot.

Stevens thinks the whole equal protection argument is nonsense. The ballots of voters in counties that use punch-card systems are more likely to be disqualified than those in counties using Opti-scan systems, he says.

Nonetheless, Rehnquist, Thomas, and Scalia — despite never having shown much interest in the issue — join with Kennedy and O'Connor on the equal protection argument. They will reverse the Florida Supreme Court's decision and send it on back to Tallahassee. They — and their clerks — begin writing. Rehnquist, Thomas, and Scalia then write another opinion, overturning the Florida court on 3 U.S.C. 5 grounds.

What the majority produces on equal protection will not be known as one of the better written, or more carefully reasoned, arguments to come out of the Supreme Court. The precedents they use to back up their equal protection argument are questionable at best. Sure, the argument can be made that county-by-county standards are unfair. But what of the clear votes — 174 solidly identified in Palm Beach, who knows how many else unexamined — that have yet to be counted, especially those in counties where there is a higher rate of ballot spoilage due to punch-card ballots? Why is there any less of an equal protection argument when one compares the overvotes of Lake County with the previously worthless overvotes of Volusia County, since discovered in the hand recount and included in the final vote tally? What about the Jackson County overvotes fixed on Election Night? How come there's no equal protection problem comparing those with the 110,000 or so overvotes remaining in Florida? Thus, given a choice between two potential equal protection violations, why not try to chart a course to find a solution? Or, if one supposes that there isn't enough time to chart a solution, why not defer to the plan the state supreme court already has in place? These questions will never be answered satisfactorily.

Stevens and Ginsburg are furious. Stevens writes an angry — uncharacteristically furious — dissent. The federal questions in this case "are not substantial," he writes. "The Florida Supreme Court's exercise of appellate jurisdiction was wholly consistent with, and indeed contemplated by, the grant of authority in Article II." The canvassing boards' "intent of the voter" interpretations are no "less sufficient," nor did they "lead to results any less uniform than, for example, the 'beyond a reasonable doubt' standard employed every day by ordinary citizens in courtrooms across this country."

Moreover, Stevens writes, the majority's thought process doesn't even make sense. This recount isn't being conducted correctly, so we're just going to put an *end* to it?! "Under their own reasoning, the appropriate course of action would be to remand to allow more specific procedures for implementing the legislature's uniform general standard to be established," Stevens writes. "In the interest of finality, however, the majority effectively orders the disenfranchisement of an unknown number of voters whose ballots reveal their intent—and are therefore legal votes under state law—but were for some reason rejected by ballot-counting machines."

And then Stevens writes the paragraph that he will be known — both beloved and derided — for in perpetuity:

> What must underlie petitioners' entire federal assault on the Florida election procedures is an unstated lack of confidence in the impartiality and capacity of the state judges who would make the critical decisions if the vote count were to proceed. Otherwise, their position is wholly without merit. The endorsement of that position by the majority of this Court can only lend credence to the most cynical appraisal of the work of judges throughout the land. It is confidence in the men and women who administer the judicial system that is the true backbone of the rule of law. Time will one day heal the wound to that confidence that will be inflicted by today's decision. One thing, however, is certain. Although we may never know with complete certainty the identity of the winner of this year's Presidential election, the identity of the loser is perfectly clear. It is the Nation's confidence in the judge as an impartial guardian of the rule of law.

At least Stevens signs his blistering letter "I respectfully dissent." Ginsburg's doesn't even come with the "respectfully" (though, to be fair, this isn't unprecedented for her). She points out that the SCOTUS has directed a state supreme court on how to interpret its state's own laws only three times that she can think of — in 1813, 1958, and 1964 — the latter two times being when southern states resisted civil rights laws.

Just last year, she says, a prisoner in Pennsylvania claimed that the state had been mistaken in its interpretation of state law, and we sent it back to the Pennsylvania Supreme Court for help. "The Chief Justice's willingness to reverse the Florida Supreme Court's interpretation of Florida law in this case is at least in tension with our reluctance in [that case] even to interpret Pennsylvania law before seeking instruction from the Pennsylvania Supreme Court." We're always telling federal courts to exercise a "cautious approach" to matters of state law. Why aren't *we* being so cautious?

What's more, Ginsburg continues, how can the majority argue that tonight's deadline is the problem, when it's the Court itself that stayed the recount on December 9? There are at least three other dates that the Court could assume to be the deadline: December 18, when the electors are set to meet, December 27, when Congress is to request certified returns from the secretary of state if there still aren't any electors for that state; even January 6, when Congress is to determine the validity of the electoral votes.

Stevens, Ginsburg, Breyer, and Souter, however, are but four on a bench of nine. And without a fifth, they're pretty much guaranteed that any future colleagues, appointed by now-all-but-finally-declared-President-elect Bush, will keep them in the minority for at least another four years.

★   ★   ★

Legal correspondents are on TV even before they've had a moment to read a page of the majority's complex ruling, penned by Kennedy. Live, skimming pages, they stumble on telling passages.

"The question before us, however, is whether the recount procedures the Florida Supreme Court has adopted are consistent with its obligation to avoid arbitrary and disparate treatment of the members of its electorate," reads one passage. "The problem inheres in the absence of specific standards to ensure its equal application."

In Washington, one of Tribe's protégés, Tom Goldstein, is faxing the decision to Tallahassee, where Bash runs each page, one by one, from the fax machine to Ron Klain, who has two phones going — Boies on one, Gore on the other. Klain reads the pages aloud. They're trying to figure out what this muddled mess means.

"This is a crazy opinion," Klain says. "There must be something missing." He tells Bash to make sure all the pages are there.

There is no standard, the majority writes. And "[t]he want of those rules here has led to unequal evaluation of ballots in various respects. . . . As seems to have been acknowledged at oral argument, the standards for accepting or rejecting contested ballots might vary not only from county to county but indeed within a single county from one recount team to another."

In the Bush Building, the Bush lieutenants — Ginsberg, Terwilliger, Van Tine — are all in General Baker's office. In an effort to psychically force the Supremes to issue a ruling, earlier in the day, Don Evans and Ginsberg had even taken a walk to get their shoes shined, hoping that by being out of the office and away from the TVs, the Court would have no choice but to rule at that very moment. It didn't work, but here it is. They're trying to figure it out. The decision's complicated, and each channel they turn to has a different take on what it all means. Evans is on the cell phone with Bush. "Find Olson," Bush tells him. "Find out if we won."

They get him. Olson says yes, they won,

"Congratulations, Mr. President-elect," Baker says to Bush.

The majority opinion goes into the record as established at the Sauls trial. King, Lehr, and Leahy all using different standards. Palm Beach County changing its standards twice — the 1990 standard, then the Sunshine Rule, then the 1990 standard again — during the 1 percent recount on Saturday, November 11. "Then the board abandoned any pretense of a per se rule, only to have a court order that the county consider dimpled chads legal." Miami-Dade's undervotes were counted differently midstream. Broward's standards differed from Palm Beach's, the former using "a more forgiving standard than Palm Beach County, and uncovered almost three times as many new votes, a result markedly disproportionate to the difference in population between the counties." Recounts in Broward, Miami-Dade, and Palm Beach were not just of undervotes, but of all the ballots — but the Florida Supreme Court ordered a statewide recount of just all the undervotes. And what of the 110,000 overvotes?

"This is not a process with sufficient guarantees of equal treatment."

The SCOTUS majority make the motions about how, in a perfect world, they could correct this problem instead of just giving the presidency to Bush. In order to do it and not violate equal protection or due process, standards would have to be established statewide — complete with arguments, procedures for implementation, judicial review.

"That sounds like a devastating paragraph for Vice President Al Gore," NBC anchor Tom Brokaw suggests to correspondent Dan Abrams. "They're saying time has run out. We can't come up with a standard, nor could we review it in time to resolve all of this. Would that be a correct reading, Dan?"

"Tom, I can't answer that question quite yet," Abrams says.

The majority opinion goes on, outlining what they'd have to do to get a legit hand recount going. The voting machines would have to develop programs to screen out the undervotes. And the overvotes. Harris would have to evaluate the accuracy of the software. And it is here, in this graph, that the answer seems to lie. Because Florida statute "requires that any controversy or contest that is designed to lead to a conclusive selection of electors be completed by December 12. That date is upon us."

> Because it is evident that any recount seeking to meet the December 12 date will be unconstitutional for the reasons we have discussed, we reverse the judgment of the Supreme Court of Florida ordering a recount to proceed.

Klain pauses after he reads this. "Sir," he says to Gore, " I think this means you're hosed."

He turns to the rest of the lawyers in the room. "I need everyone to leave the office. Now."

★   ★   ★

Brokaw interviews DNC chair Ed Rendell. "Do you think that it's time for Vice President Al Gore to concede, Mr. Rendell?"

"Oh, I think he will concede, Tom," Rendell says.

Inside the DNC, Democrats are booing their chairman.

Inside NavObs, Gore is angry and incredulous. How could Rendell, *the DNC chairman*, have just said that?! Relations between the Gore campaign and the former Philly mayor have always been tense — the feeling's been that Rendell's too much of a loose cannon, not loyal; he wasn't much help during the primaries. As if Gore needed more reason to dislike him, here he is calling for Gore to concede on national television!

Brokaw tries to get Tribe to say the same thing, but twice he demurs until he's read the opinion. Finally he gets his hands on a copy, and he joins Rendell.

"I'm sure that Vice President Gore has the kind of reverence for the Supreme Court as an institution that he will not really undertake to be less than complete and gracious in his acceptance of this result," Tribe says.

Not that Tribe's happy about the decision. "As I teach it to my students over the years, I'm going to be rather critical of what the Court did, both in terms of some of the legal reasoning and in terms of the institutional performance, having so precipitously stopped the recount dead in its tracks, now to say in effect, 'We're shocked, we're shocked that it can't be completed by midnight on December twelfth,'" Tribe says to Brokaw. "It does come across as not entirely convincing. And to be divided seven to two is somewhat misleading, because it's five-four on some of the critical issues. To be divided closely on the one instance in American history where the Supreme Court chooses the president rather than the other way around is not likely to sit well over time either with the American people or with historians. But I think the Court's place in our lives is such that we should all rally around, even if we disagree with the result."

Klain yells at Bash, "Tell Larry Tribe not to say Gore should concede!" Bash calls Tribe, delivers Klain's message.

"CNN still has up on the screen 'Tribe says Gore should concede'!" Klain yells. Bash calls the CNN assignment desk, delivers Klain's message.

Klain calls in Douglas Hattaway and Jenny Backus. Take a deep breath, he tells them. Relax. We're not sure what's going to happen yet.

★   ★   ★

President Clinton is sleeping at the Belfast Hilton Ireland when all this comes down. His aides decide not to wake him. This has been such a nice trip for the president. The negotiated peace in Ireland is one of his greatest foreign-policy accomplishments. He'd spend the earlier part of the day in the Republic of Ireland–Northern Ireland border town of Dundalk, where sixty thousand greeted him so enthusiastically, so effusively, in a way Americans just haven't since the whole Lewinsky thing.

"Why wake him up in the middle of the night just to tell him bad news?" asks White House deputy chief of staff Steve Richetti.

The next morning, at 8:15 or so, a bunch of senior White House staffers are meeting in the lounge area of the senior staff room, running through the day. There's Richetti, and national security adviser Sandy Berger, White House counsel Bruce Lindsey, and press secretary Jake Siewert. They're preparing for the day, preparing to debrief the president. He'll have a meeting later with individuals who, four years ago, wouldn't have even sat in the same room with one another — namely Sinn Fein's Gerry Adams and Ulster Unionist leader David Trimble.

Doug Band, the president's aide, calls Richetti. "The president needs to see you right away," he says. Clinton just heard about the Supreme Court's decision.

Oh boy.

Richetti, Berger, Lindsey, and Siewert make their way up to Clinton's suite. There are already three or four copies of the decision there by the time they arrive. Clinton's leafing through one of them. He's in a full state of outrage.

"It's an incredibly political decision," the president fumes. He points out that the majority decision was issued per curiam, issued on behalf of the Court instead of signed by any justices in particular — kind of an odd thing to do, being that there were four such strong dissents. "No one wanted to sign the thing!" Clinton says.

He starts tearing through the Stevens dissent, reading parts aloud. "That's right!" he says after he finishes a sentence he agrees with. "That's right."

"Um, you're going to have to take questions on this later today," Richetti says.

"I don't think you should say any of that in public," Berger cautions, stating the obvious. But Clinton takes the bait.

"I am *not* going to be *silent!*" the president responds, fuming. "I will *not* validate this opinion in *any way, shape, or form!* I don't wanna be sitting around ten years from now, saying I signed off on *the most political* decision the Supreme Court has *ever made!*" He starts tearing through a list of other notorious Supreme Court decisions he feels this one will earn a place next to — *Dred Scott,* which in 1857 ruled slaves property not citizens, *Plessy v. Ferguson,* which in 1896 codified legally enforceable segregation.

"I am *not* going to be on the wrong side of history on this!" Clinton fumes.

The president is reminded that Gore has yet to give a statement on the matter. He probably shouldn't say anything until Gore does, at least. Clinton agrees; he asks them to check with Daley first, find out what Gore's going to say. And with that, Clinton is put back in his box. For the time being.

Phew!

★   ★   ★

Gore and Daley have one last talk Tuesday night before a decision is made.

"I think it looks pretty bad," Gore says. "There seems to be unanimity" among the lawyers' opinions.

Not Samurai Klain, of course, who wants to keep fighting until the last breath he draws, but among all the others. Boies, in particular, thinks that this is the end of the road, if for no other reason than that he doesn't buy the Supreme Court's equal protection argument at all. Every county in Florida does have the same standard, he thinks — the "intent of the voter" standard. It may be a very general standard, but it's Florida law. They had asked the Florida Supreme Court not once but twice to give them a more precise explanation, a more detailed statewide standard, and both times the court balked. The SCOTUS itself could have suggested something back after the December 1 hearing — it's not as if the Bushies weren't complaining about this very issue as long ago as in their very first briefs before Middlebrooks, submitted on November 11.

Moreover, Boies thinks — and says, often — if a single general standard is unconstitutional, then elections in many, many states for many, many years have been a violation of the equal protection law. And the difference between counties in terms of the application of that standard is much less significant than the differences in counties based on different voting machines. The difference between how counties might apply the intent standard is a lot less than the difference between juries in the North and the South in terms of putting somebody to death — or even in terms of the difference in the application of the death penalty in Broward County versus Leon County! So if there's an "equal protection" problem on this, then it's a problem that pervades much of what local government and courts do.

All of which is to say, Boies concludes: the SCOTUS was going to find a way to put an end to this one way or another, and this was the way they chose, and that's all she wrote.

The next morning, Daley returns to NavObs. Gore's working on his speech.

★ ★ ★

Klain and his team — O'Melveny & Myers Los Angeles partner Mark Steinberg, Ohio State University professor Richard Cordray, Mark Messenbaugh, Dan Feldman, Bash — work all through the night, preparing a brief to the Florida Supreme Court. It explains how a statewide recount can be done in keeping with equal protection. It establishes a statewide standard based on *Delahunt*'s slutty standards — with any "discernible indentation or mark, at or near the ballot position for the candidate." It asks the Florida Supreme Court to clarify to the SCOTUS that December 12 — which just passed — was not the deadline, despite what Boies told them at that first state supreme court argument. It's a brief that will never be filed.* At around 8 A.M., Klain gives the team the news: the vice president has decided to suspend all efforts. Klain delivers an emotional thank-you. "I'm privileged to have worked with a group like you," Klain says. "It's time for us to stop."

At 11 or so, Gore himself calls. He's put on speakerphone. "Boy, that was

---

The New Republic, in its December 25 issue, will refer to this as the "secret brief," to be revealed "when the identity of Deep Throat is revealed." See the appendix for a full copy of the "secret brief." And then call *The New Republic* and ask them who Deep Throat is.

some Election Night, huh?" Gore jokes. He thanks them all. "I can't tell you how much that meant to me and the country. Tipper and I are grateful. You people are unbelievable, just unbelievable. Your performance was absolutely astonishing."

It's an emotional moment for Klain in many ways, pushed that much closer to tears because he hasn't had a good night's sleep in more than a month. Finally he had been put in charge of a Gore campaign. He didn't win. But he had done everything he could, and, he feels, there are few serious tactical errors — if any — that could have been anticipated and could have definitively changed the outcome. And, after all, Gore hadn't officially won Florida even once, and it came this far. And while the battle had gone on, not only did Klain prove himself to Gore, but the Al Gore whom Klain had admired — and liked, even — had reemerged.

Gore breaks up the moment with another joke. He's having a party at NavObs Wednesday night, everyone's invited. They shouldn't have any problem finding the place, Gore says. "You'll know it when you see a group of people shouting, 'Get out of Cheney's house!'"

But even as the Gore attorneys pack away their legal-size manila folders, and Fabiani reaches for his bourbon, other Democrats are in denial. Richman and Jacobs are looking into a way to appeal the Seminole County lawsuit at the U.S. Supreme Court. Then there are the three Florida house Democrats who call for Gore to continue to pursue whatever legal avenues remain available in his quest for the presidency. And in the protests of representatives Alcee Hastings, Peter Deutsch, and Carrie Meek, it's made crystal clear that many Americans will forever harbor lingering doubts about Bush's legitimacy as president.

"The vice president should not concede and should actually use that opening the Supreme Court has given him," Deutsch says in a conference call with reporters Wednesday. "There's still time to count the votes." Despite legal experts' claims to the contrary, Deutsch insists, the Supreme Court ruling, in remanding the case back to the Florida Supreme Court, leaves an opportunity for the recount to be reordered on constitutional grounds. The actual final deadline "is January 6, when Congress accepts the electors," Deutsch says. They slam the SCOTUS for what they consider to be a partisan ruling precluding, according to Meek, "my African-American constituency" from having a "chance of having their votes counted." The Court's decision "reminds me of some terrible, horrible mistakes of the past," she says.

Hastings says that the ruling turned American politics upside down.

"Rather than be a place where presidents choose judges, these were judges choosing a president." Deutsch says that his ten-year-old son summed up the perception problem of the Court Wednesday morning when he said, "It's not fair." "It looks like a political decision," Deutsch says, calling the ruling "maybe [the Supreme Court's] darkest hour ever." While Hastings, Meek, and Deutsch allow that they will live with a President Bush, Hastings calls the decision a "stain on democracy. . . . The people are going to be left saying, 'I'm not certain this guy won this election.'" Factor in the various disputes surrounding the Florida election, Hastings says, including the butterfly ballot, the failure of various hand recounts to be completed, the fact that some ballots were "on an eleventh-grade reading level" and on and on. After all that, "you tell me that you know that George Bush won this election, I will tuck myself under the legitimacy that you have just falsified. The legitimacy of any president where the votes are left uncounted is automatically a consideration."

Yes, they'll work with him. "He'll 'be' the president," Hastings says. "And if the Middle East explodes tomorrow, we will rally around him as we would Al Gore." Still, the wounds from this election may be slow to heal, Meek says, particularly among black voters, who are especially wary of the legitimacy of Bush's presidency. "Our voters are suspect [sic] of the judicial system," Meek says. "They feel there's something rotten in Denmark. There have been too many circumstances that belied honesty and integrity in this process. They don't believe that Gore has been treated fairly. They feel that their votes have not been counted."

"I don't think this thing is over," Deutsch says. "Just think about every Bruce Willis movie you've ever seen."

"I prefer *Friday the 13th* and Freddy Krueger from the *Nightmare on Elm Street* films," jokes Hastings.

But even Bruce Willis movies roll the credits at some point. What about the members of the Gore team who are saying that it's all over?

Deutsch refers to them as "the people in Al Gore's office who want to go back to being lobbyists" and "don't want to offend a Bush administration," because they're "afraid of losing their clients." Deutsch says that he knows Gore fairly well and that "I know in his heart I don't think he wants to stop."

★ ★ ★

Carter Eskew pitches in, makes some suggestions about Gore's speech. As do Attie, Daley, Bob Shrum, Tipper, Karenna, Kristin, the Gore family in general. Even historian Richard Goodwin throws in an idea or two. But Al

Gore's speech is largely his own. He's working hard, finding the right tone, working on delivery, making sure that it's the speech of his life. There's some debate about whether or not he should use the word "concession." He decides he'd better.

His speech is human, heartfelt, self-deprecating, completely and absolutely deferential to President-elect George W. Bush. Gore steps to a podium in the Old Executive Office Building. He seems to take a moment to mentally prepare himself; a barely perceptible shift from a wince in horror to a sigh of relief.

"Just moments ago, I spoke with George W. Bush and congratulated him on becoming the forty-third president of the United States," Gore says. "I promised him that I wouldn't call him back this time," he jokes. Gore spells out his concession so clearly that no pundit could read any doubt into it, or slam him for anything but unconditional surrender, "offer[ing] my concession . . . and accept[ing] my responsibility, which I will discharge unconditionally, to honor the new president-elect and do everything possible to help him bring Americans together."

Without trying to justify his hard-fought legal battle to have the Florida undervotes counted, Gore acknowledges that he "strongly disagree[s] with the [Supreme] Court's decision." But he also says: "I accept the finality of this outcome, which will be ratified next Monday in the electoral college."

Showing a glimmer of the pugilistic "Fightin' Al" who felled Bill Bradley and so turned off the media, Gore says that "some have asked whether I have any regrets. And I do have one regret: that I didn't get the chance to stay and fight for the American people over the next four years, especially for those who need burdens lifted and barriers removed, especially for those who feel their voices have not been heard. I heard you, and I will not forget. I've seen America in this campaign, and I like what I see. It's worth fighting for, and that's a fight I'll never stop."

He quotes Sen. Stephen Douglas telling Abraham Lincoln, "'Partisan feeling must yield to patriotism.'" He says that "what remains of partisan rancor must now be put aside, and may God bless his stewardship of this country." He thanks the Liebermans for not only bringing "passion and high purpose to our partnership" but for "open[ing] new doors, not just for our campaign but for our country." (In case anybody forgot: Lieberman's a Jew!)

The camera cuts to Tipper, sandwiched between Lieberman and wife, with a tearful daughter Karenna and husband, Drew Schiff, behind them, as well as a mop of blond hair from an unidentified Gore daughter.

Karenna must have lost it when Gore quoted his father (quoting poet Edwin Markham), saying, "As for the battle that ends tonight, I do believe, as my father once said, that no matter how hard the loss, defeat might serve as well as victory to shape the soul and let the glory out.

"I personally will be at his disposal,* and I call on all Americans — I particularly urge all who stood with us — to unite behind our next president," Gore says.

"And now, my friends, in a phrase I once addressed to others" — namely President George H. W. Bush and Vice President Dan Quayle in 1992 — "it's time for me to go," Gore says.

Boy! the pundits exclaim. If only he had spoken like that during the campaign! And this is how it always is, which is something for civilian Al Gore to remember. Because when the pundits praise Gore over the next few days for his grace and class, they are merely doing what the media always do with presidential losers.

"A Concession Speech with Grace and Class," headlined the *Washington Post* . . . on November 5, 1980, for President Jimmy Carter.

"Bush, Gracious in Defeat, Promises Smooth Transition," wrote the Associated Press . . . on November 4, 1992, about President George H. W. Bush.

"Dignified Ending to Dole's Gutsy, Arduous Campaign," headlined the *St. Louis Post-Dispatch* on November 6, 1996, about Sen. Bob Dole.

And so, what's next for Gore?

"I know I speak for all of you and for all the American people when I say that he will be our president, and we'll work with him. This nation faces major challenges ahead, and we must work together. And I extended my best wishes to him and to Mrs. Bush and to the members of the Bush family."

That's not Gore speaking. It was Massachusetts governor Michael Dukakis in 1988.

And he was interrupted by the Democratic crowd.

They cheered: "'92! '92! '92! '92! '92! '92!"

★   ★   ★

At the Governor's Club, Ginsberg has taken a few dozen of the Florida state GOP staffers out to dinner, "all the folks we displaced," as he later puts it.

---

*Again, this is as much a Washington tradition as traffic on the Beltway. "Dole May Get to Advise Clinton Foreign Policy," *Washington Post* headline, post-election 1996.

Before the champagne toasts to Bush and their efforts, they all watch Gore's speech silently. Ginsberg will later call it "graceful."

Down the street, at Po' Boys, Gore's speech gets a different reaction from Speaker Feeney.

"What a loser," Feeney says, according to a *Sun-Sentinel* reporter who Feeney doesn't know is there. He calls it "an evil speech."

★   ★   ★

Just as Gore didn't seem slick or fake or insincere or arrogant or condescending — even humbly referencing his need to "mend some fences" in Tennessee, both "literally and figuratively" — Bush, in his acceptance speech, successfully steers clear of his oratory foibles.

He doesn't smirk, doesn't mispronounce any words with more than two syllables, doesn't seem — as he too often does — a few California rolls short of a sushi platter. His tongue darts in and out of his mouth a tad too often (dry mouth?), but Bush seems sturdy, strong, and a good winner.

In stark contrast with his campaign staffers who drummed up Florida crowds with anti-Gore vitriol, Bush even suggests that he understands, even empathizes with, Gore's attitude of the last few weeks. "Gore and I put our hearts and hopes into our campaigns," Bush says. "We both gave it our all. We shared similar emotions. So I understand how difficult this moment must be. . . . He has a distinguished record of service to our country as a congressman, a senator, and as a vice president."

(Bush doesn't work into his speech Gore's service in Vietnam during the war. Gore, helpfully, did.)

Bush asks for prayers for him and his family, prayers for Gore and his family, for "this great nation," as well as "for leaders from both parties." With the Creator in mind, Bush puts a karmic spin on the last thirty-six days, saying, "I believe that things happen for a reason, and I hope the long wait of the last five weeks will heighten a desire to move beyond the bitterness and partisanship of the recent past."

Bush emphasizes his desire to work with Democrats, ticking off reforms that everyone can agree on in the broadest, most superficial terms imaginable: education, Social Security reform, Medicare, tax relief, foreign policy "true to our values," and a strong and superior military. Bush does seem better suited to co-leading a bipartisan consensus on Medicare and Social Security reform than Gore, but the bloody, ugly divisiveness of the last six weeks may prove far more powerful than the glossy sheen Bush tried to coat his incoming presidency with.

Speaking of divisiveness, having lost the black vote by a larger percentage than any Republican presidential candidate since Gerald Ford in 1976, Bush even marginally reaches out to the black community — heralding "our shared American values that are larger than race or party," and adding that "the president of the United States is the president of every single American, of every race and every background."

Comparing this tight race to the hard-fought 1800 race that delivered the presidency to perhaps America's most brilliant president, Thomas Jefferson, the man who is probably not even in the top fiftieth percentile says he would "be guided by President Jefferson's sense of purpose: to stand for principle, to be reasonable in manner, and, above all, to do great good for the cause of freedom and harmony." Perhaps hoping to increase the sales of his campaign "autobiography," *A Charge to Keep* (written by spokeswoman Karen Hughes), Bush says that "the presidency is more than an honor, more than an office, it is a charge to keep and I will give it my all."

★   ★   ★

It's a great speech, given to thunderous applause from the Democrat-controlled Texas house of representatives, highlighting Bush's boasts of having reached across the aisle to work with Democrats. Or so it appears. After being introduced by Democrat speaker of the house Pete Laney, Bush refers to the chamber as "a place where Democrats have the majority, Republicans and Democrats have worked together to do what is right for the people we represent. We had spirited disagreements, and in the end, we found constructive consensus. It is an experience I will always carry with me, and an example I will always follow. The spirit of cooperation I have seen in this hall is what is needed in Washington, D.C."

It turns out that dozens of Democrats actually weren't invited. "We weren't asked to come," says state representative Garnet Coleman, vice chairman of the Texas house's Public Health Committee and a member of the Appropriations Committee. Calling the Bush team's failure to invite Democrats "phony" and "hypocritical," Democratic state representative Kevin Bailey, D-Houston, says that "it was kind of surprising that we weren't invited."

"It shows you how good they are at presenting impressions," adds Coleman.

★   ★   ★

Gore spokesman Douglas Hattaway is at Café Cabernet with some friends and colleagues. He's approached by Michael Leach, of Seminole County fame.

"Hey!" Leach says after introducing himself. "Great speech! Except when he attacked the Supreme Court."

"What part was *that?!*" asks Hattaway.

"You know," says Leach, "when he said he disagreed with them."

"You know what?" says Hattaway. "I need a fucking drink."

Postscript

The Plot to Steal the Presidency

Walk into the Grand Atrium of the Ronald Reagan Building on Friday night, January 19, 2001, and you'll be treated to some interesting scenes.

There's Fred Bartlit over there, hugging Ken Starr.

There's Phil Beck, warmly introducing Dr. Laurentius Marais to fellow guests. "My star witness!" he says.

Ginsberg, Carvin, Terwilliger, Van Tine. Olson's over there — they say he might be solicitor general!

It's the Baker Botts reception for former president and Barbara Bush. A black-tie affair, packed to the gills. Tomorrow, George W. Bush will be sworn in as president of the United States.

"George W.'s first job was in the mail room of Baker Botts," Baker says to the crowd.

Soon it's Bush Sr.'s turn to speak. "I want to thank Jim, who went over there and did that superb job." He also thanks the "many lawyers from Baker Botts and across the country who went down there at their own expense and did a fantastic job of getting out the truth and protecting, I'd say, the rights of all of the voters in Florida." The lawyers, Bush says, "went over there and, in my opinion, Barbara's opinion, did the Lord's work."

He has praise, in particular, for Baker. "I mean, Christopher never had a chance up against this guy — I'm telling ya!" Bush says. "He was in over his head when Baker took him on."

"Without reminiscing too much about the event, those terrible thirty-seven days," Bush says, with Jeb's son George P. Bush by his side, "I think one of the things troubled me the most were the gratuitous attacks on this boy's father. The attacks on Jeb Bush, the governor, the most honorable, honest man in the world. It really burned me up, and Barbara, too.

"I don't know why I'm getting off on that tangent in this night, but this seemed like a friendly crowd to tell that to."

There are balls and parties all over town. Ginsberg and his law/lobbying firm, Patton Boggs, host one for the Bush legal team. Greenberg Traurig's D.C. office hosts Barry Richard. At the Florida Ball, in the National Building Museum, in a black, ruffled, strapless, floor-length silk gown, wearing a large diamond choker and a wrap is Katherine Harris. She may be appointed to a position in the Bush administration yet — one that doesn't require Senate confirmation. Or she may run for Congress; there's reportedly a GOP House seat opening up in the Sarasota area.

"I want you to know how very much I missed you and how very pleased I am to be back in circulation," she says to a mass of Floridians.

There's John Ellis, of Fox News Channel, over there, talking about the Bush "dynasty." "For all the press jabber about dynastic pretensions, I've never heard anyone in the family talk about it," he tells a fawning reporter from the *New York Times,* whose subsequent story doesn't even mention Ellis's role in his cousin's presidency. "It's viewed as an amazing thing, not a dynastic thing. I don't think it's a coincidence. I think George W. and George Herbert Walker Bush both worked very hard to get where they are today. But it's extraordinary that it happened. If you wrote it in a book, nobody would believe it."

★   ★   ★

Bush's Florida team has been rewarded. Olson was nominated to be solicitor general; Allbaugh is head of the Federal Emergency Management Agency; Josh Bolten is White House deputy chief of staff. As I write this, they're talking about putting Baker at the helm of the World Bank. Zoellick was named U.S. trade representative. Ken Mehlman is White House political director. Brad Blakeman is deputy assistant for appointments and scheduling. John Bolton was nominated undersecretary of state for arms control and international security affairs. Ari Fleischer was named White House press secretary. Dan Bartlett is a senior communications staffer. Mindy Tucker was named spokeswoman for the Justice Department. It took new White House spokesman Tucker Eskew only a matter of seconds before he was caught in a lie so egregious he was slammed by both the *National Review* and the *Wall Street Journal.** But, as has been the case, after the puff of smoke cleared, Eskew kept going.

*Tucker told reporters that Bush's nominee for labor secretary, Linda Chavez, didn't know that a woman who had stayed at her home was an illegal alien. Chavez herself told reporters that not only was that not true but that she had told that to Eskew.

As of this writing, of course, many Gorebies are still trying to figure out what to do with their lives. Bill Daley has an office in the same complex where Monica Lewinsky once lived and that Bob Dole still calls home — the Watergate. David Boies returned to his lucrative law practice. Warren Christopher and Ron Klain are back at the L.A. and D.C. offices of O'Melveny & Myers; Klain just hired Jeremy Bash. Whouley's back at Dewey Square, shuttling between Boston, where Newman and other Boston Boys are, and D.C. Young, Sautter, Alper, et al. are back in D.C.; Fabiani finally got back to La Jolla; Hattaway's in Boston.

Most of the lawyers from both sides are back in business — Bartlit in Denver, Beck in Chicago, Terrell and Bristow in Houston, Ginsberg, Van Tine, Carvin, Terwilliger, Olson, et al. back in D.C. The Florida lawyers from both sides seem well, if not better than ever — Richard, Martinez, De Grandy, Wallace, Scherer, Zack, Berger, and Kuehne are all fine, the Bushies maybe a bit more so than their Gore-backing counterparts. According to sources, Coffey no longer works for the same law firm, because one of his former law partners, a Cuban-American, has political ambitions and did not want to be associated with a man who was associated with Al Gore.

Indeed, Hurricane Chad may have left Florida, but there is damage in its wake. Judge Lee has reregistered from the Democratic Party to "no party"; Judge Burton and Theresa LePore were considering doing the same as of January 2001. David Boies and Mitch Berger were cleared by the Florida Bar Association of any ethical wrongdoing in the Lavelle matter. Republicans were gearing up to unseat the four Florida Supreme Court justices — Quince, Anstead, Pariente, and Lewis — who voted to begin a hand recount of the state's undervotes.

Jeb Bush launched a commission to look into how voting can be improved in his state. Harris and Clay Roberts were hauled up and embarrassed before a U.S. Commission on Civil Rights hearing in Tallahassee that looked into the state's elections problems. "I heard, today especially, from supervisors who were desperate, desperate for your help," said Commissioner Victoria Wilson. "And the word that comes to mind is that you abandoned them. They were abandoned by your department." Throughout the hearing, Harris, the chief elections officer of the state, had to turn to Roberts to find out the answers to questions.

Additionally, television networks have been revisiting their rules on calling winners based on VNS data. A typical result: an investigation of CNN, commissioned by CNN, concluded that "CNN's election night coverage was a debacle." A study of VNS commissioned by VNS was less harsh, ruling that the Election Night mistakes were "the product of a number of system errors that tended to work in concert at various points in the evening," and recommending "stricter quality control and quality standards." No shit. Networks will indubitably be more circumspect about calling a state in the future. But to be realistic, about the only thing we're probably guaranteed will never happen again is you won't hear Dan Rather say, as he did on Election Night, "When *we* call a state, you can take it to the bank."

Speaking of taking it to the bank, the whole deal looks like it will cost Florida more than $3 million. Not to mention a whole lot of respect. Joe Klock and his Steel Hector & Davis team handed Katherine Harris — and Florida taxpayers — a bill for $682,266. The attorneys insisted that they cut costs wherever possible; Klock slept at a friend's house while in Tallahassee, for instance. For 3,724 hours of work, the taxpayers got a bargain, the law firm said. Including the $10,000 to send the lawyers to Washington, D.C., in a Lear Jet to argue before the U.S. Supreme Court. Other expenses Floridians will end up footing the bill for: around $300,000 for the constitutional scholars hired by Rubottom, Feeney, and McKay. Sixty grand for extra security measures in Miami-Dade. Palm Beach County paid Bruce Rogow $100,000 to represent LePore. A quarter mil went to defend Seminole County's Sandra Goard. The private attorney for Agriculture commissioner Bob Crawford charged taxpayers $46,477; weeks after the election debacle concluded, Crawford resigned to take a cushy job with the Citrus Department. About the only expense that seems worth it is the $2,500 Volusia County spent to feed its vote counters.

★　★　★

As America returns to its blissful slumber, perhaps the most severe divisions created are those within the U.S. Supreme Court, where reportedly the actions of the majority — and the failure of O'Connor and Kennedy to work with Souter and Breyer on trying to fashion a solution to the problem — have left clerks and justices demoralized.

Beyond the closed doors of the U.S. Supreme Court building, it is disturbing how few conservative legal scholars have proved to be intellectually honest enough to read the majority's December 14 ruling as nothing other than a slapdash piece of work at complete odds with conservative legal thinking. One of the few to do so was John DiIulio, Jr., who wrote, in a December 25 *Weekly Standard* piece entitled "Equal Protection Run Amok," that to "any conservative who truly respects federalism, the majority's opinion is hard to respect." DiIulio continues:

The arguments that ended the battle and "gave" Bush the presidency are constitutionally disingenuous at best. They will come back to haunt conservatives and confuse, if they do not cripple, the principled conservative case for limited government, legislative supremacy, and universal civic deference to legitimate, duly constituted state and local public authority.

"In most cases," acknowledge Rehnquist, Scalia, and Thomas, "comity and respect for federalism compel us to defer to the decisions of state courts on issues of state law." There are, however, "a few exceptional cases," and "this is one." Why?

Why, suddenly, do inter-county and intra-county differences in election procedures, which are quite common in every state, rise in the Florida case to the level of "equal protection" problems solvable only by uniform standards (by implication, uniform national standards) and strict scrutiny from federal courts?

How can the conservative jurists on the Court find prima facie fault with what the Bush legal team disparaged as "crazy quilt" local laws and procedures? Why, in any case, weigh the alleged problem in Florida without taking cognizance of how election procedures vary from polling station to polling station and from county to county in, say, Pennsylvania? And why, in reversing a state's highest court for not following the U.S. Constitution, and for infringing upon the state legislature's authority, does the nation's highest court substitute its own resolution of the ultimate "political question" for the Constitution's explicit, black-letter reliance on state legislatures and, if need be, the U.S. Congress? . . .

I would like to believe there was a time when conservatives would have instinctively recoiled at the way we have all now fallen into thinking of and battling for the presidency as if it, rather than the Congress, were constitutionally the first branch of our national government. There was a time when conservatives understood that the localisms of little platoons and county governments were good and to be preserved and protected by law and custom unless proven bad by experience. . . . There was even, I suppose, a time when conservatives would rather have lost a close, hotly contested presidential election, even against a person and a party from whom many feared the worst, than advance judicial imperialism, diminish respect for federalism, or pander to mass misunderstanding and mistrust of duly elected legislative leaders.

If there ever was such a time, it has now passed, and conservatives ought to do what they can to bring the country back to this future.

Regrettably, *Bush v. Gore* does no such thing. Desirable result aside, it is bad constitutional law.

As I write this, media organizations are conducting their statewide recounts of the election. On January 27, 2001, Dennis Newman sent out an e-mail to the dozens of members of the Gore recount team — Charlie Baker, Jack Corrigan, Michael Whouley, Nick Baldick, Donnie Fowler, Mitch Berger, Ron Klain, Dexter Douglass, Ben Kuehne, et al.

"As we all know," Newman wrote, "Burton, Harris, Scalia, Jeb, et al stole the election from us. The attached article from today's *Palm Beach Post* is further proof. Basically it says that if Burton had counted the ballots objectively we would have picked up an additional 672 votes. This is in addition to the 174 votes (should be 215 but that's a whole other dispute) that the Board had given us in the recount, but Harris refused to count.

"In addition, other media counts since the election have shown that we picked up an additional 130 votes in Lake County and 120 additional votes in Hillsborough County. This gives us an additional 672+174+130+120= 1096 votes. Please circulate this information as widely as you can. Anything to get National media attention to this would obviously be helpful."

The *Palm Beach Post* story, however, showed nothing of the sort. It showed that "[i]f Democrats had gotten their way and dimpled ballots in Palm Beach County had been counted as votes, Al Gore would have picked up 682 votes, which is more than President George W. Bush's 537-vote statewide margin of victory, according to *The Palm Beach Post*'s examination of disputed ballots."

But not even in Broward County were *all* dimples — regardless of whether or not there was a pattern — considered votes. And this is the inherent fallacy of the media-funded recount. A truly accurate tally would reflect ballot counts that adhere to the way each county's canvassing board would have ruled. Since a majority of the sixty-seven counties never stopped to reconsider undervotes or overvotes, there is no precedent as to how they would have ruled. So it doesn't really matter what the counters hired by the *Washington Post* or any other paper judges to be a vote. All we can get is a set of hypotheticals.

Nevertheless, it's silly to pretend that reasonable people shouldn't wonder who, indeed, garnered the most votes in Florida — especially considering that Al Gore gleaned more than half a million votes more than Bush in the popular-vote contest. The world entered the swamps of Florida on Wednesday, November 8, with 175,000 unread ballots throwing the Ellis-anointed Bush coronation into serious doubt. We left it on December 13, with those same ballots unread, the vast majority of them still uncounted.

Certainly George W. Bush and his minions did everything they could to stand in the way of anyone — witness Tucker Eskew's discrediting of the media attempts to examine the ballots — trying to get to the bottom of whom tax-paying, God-fearing, Americans voted for.* Baker said "NO RECOUNTS" early on, as was his right, and the lawyers and pols followed through, almost entirely within the legal system. GOP lawyers on the ground — Wallace, Scherer, Martinez, De Grandy — stalled, whined, obstructed. Politicians and spinners — Fleischer, Eskew, Racicot — exaggerated, misled, lied. Lawyers in the courts set traps, like Carvin, and disingenuously represented the facts as they wanted them to be seen by the court, like Olson. The trial lawyers hired by Baker — Bartlit, Beck, Terrell, Richard — went after victory in court regardless of The Truth or, in some cases, even their own personal politics. Political operatives — Mehlman, Blakeman, the emboldened Miami-Dade wusses — injected venom into the air, making an already tense situation even uglier. Bush and Cheney sat back and reaped the benefits of the ugliness their organization was putting out there.

In other words, the American system worked exactly as it's supposed to.

Was the Gore team any better behaved? With two exceptions, no. Generally, the Democrats were just as disingenuous, just as power-thirsty, and just as hypocritical. They co-opted Theresa LePore and lied about the official number of votes that came in from Palm Beach County after the extended deadline. They, too, cajoled, misrepresented, misled, lied. Daley bullied Butterworth; Wexler lied about LePore; Gore told the American people just plain falsehoods about Seminole County; Strep Throat spread malicious gossip about Harris; Burton and Penelas were slammed for selling out voters for their own personal gain, with little evidence to back up the claims.

But in two respects, the Gore team was better behaved. First, the Democrats were more restrained on the ground, and with a few exceptions — Nadler, Jackson, Dershowitz — more responsible in their rhetoric. Of course, maybe they had to be calmer. After all, they were the ones asking for hand recounts, getting deadlines extended, contesting the election. Gore was never officially ahead in the Florida vote count; they *had* to be more temperate.

---

*Incredibly, in its series about the Florida madness, the *Washington Post* allowed this line from Bush to stand unchallenged: "We survived the recounts. I didn't mind a recount."

And, let's not forget, Gore *did* call, however lamely, for a statewide hand recount, the only thing that could have truly and honestly brought us to at least the neighborhood of an answer as to whom a majority of the citizens of Florida really chose on November 7. But, on the other hand, despite Gore's lofty rhetoric, at no point did his political operatives or lawyers make an attempt to have all the votes counted. Not during the protest, not during the contest, not on the ground when various counters called and asked if they wanted the votes in, say, Lake County, checked out.

Throwing a huge question mark into any depravation assessment, of course, is the Republican overseas-absentee-ballot conference call. All the other shenanigans that took place in this mess — delaying tactics, vote trolling, standards adjusting — did so within the confines of the law. Except for this. If this order was carried out, it was illegal. If ballots cast after the election came in, and were counted, that was cheating.

I seriously doubt, however, that there will be any investigation into the matter. People want this thing to be over with. And remember who's in charge of the country now. There is, in my mind, a much greater likelihood of Bush team dirty-tricksters and spinners launching a campaign to discredit this author and this book than there is of any sort of law-enforcement investigation into the overseas-absentee-ballot matter. Despite the fact that this book also points out examples of nasty behavior of Democrats, and lies by Gorebies ranging from the Veep himself to Reverend Jackson to Congressman Wexler, since the Republicans are in the White House, the charges against them might seem harsher. After all, at this point, who really cares if Harry Jacobs lied on *Hardball?* But this, too, is part of the problem.

★ ★ ★

The race was hardly over before the second-guessing began, and journalists and pols began asking what, if anything, could have been done differently.

To be sure, Daley, Boies, et al., had an uphill fight from the first minute. The Republicans had four things going for them. First, Bush had been declared the winner that night by the media, i.e., the TV networks. This was in no small part thanks to John Ellis, *unbelievably* put in charge of calling the election results for Fox News Channel. Second, and perhaps most important, Bush actually *did win* the vote tally that night, by 1,500 or so votes, and the machine recount, by 300 votes, and the system is set up to make it rare that an election is overturned. Third, Bush's brother was the governor, and he had the state wired, top to bottom. And fourth, the Bush team did a better job during the recount.

Team Gore took a horribly chaotic situation — created by shortsighted state legislators with rather limited legislative gifts — and made it worse. It was all too easy for five justices of the U.S. Supreme Court to step in, find a troublesome constitutional issue swirling around in the stew, and slam the lid down, putting an end to the madness. It was the Democrats who asked canvassing boards to change their standards, who took them to *court* to change their standards, not because they were concerned that voters were being disenfranchised, though that was the rhetoric in which they cloaked their cause. They did it because they felt that was the only way they could get enough votes so Gore could win.

Of course, the Gorebies were also hobbled by what David Leahy calls "the horrible law." "All the politicians were complaining, '*This* judge,' '*This* court,'" Burton said to me in January 2001. "But *they* wrote the laws! The laws are horrible! 'Intent of the voter'?!"

True enough; there was no mechanism for a statewide recount. But would it have been impossible? Judge Lewis likes to fantasize about how he would have solved the problem, had he been assigned the election contest. He would have gotten both Bush and Gore themselves in his courtroom, laid out the problem, and worked with them from the bench to resolve it. Maybe he would have even let Bush choose the standard.

This was fantasy, of course. And the case ended up before Sauls. But what kind of a case did the Gore legal team present? Not a strong one, not a particularly convincing one. And yet, Boies points out that Sauls's judgment was ultimately overturned, and had it not been for the SCOTUS stepping in, the undervotes, at least, would have been counted.

Indeed, Team Gore did have this one ally. Even if they didn't have Butterworth — who clearly took his position as an impartial arbiter of state law far more seriously than the disturbingly ambitious Harris ever did — the Gore team had the Florida Supreme Court. The seven justices in the first ruling, and then the four justices in the second, were willing to take a bold stand to ensure that votes were counted. But with the guidance of Boies, the justices manufactured an ill-conceived way to get to the bottom of it all; first clearly rewriting Florida election code, then ordering only the undervotes counted.

In some ways, it's not the justices' fault. Harris and the secretary of state's office (Kerey Carpenter, for instance) abused their positions. They may have ruled that way so as to retaliate against the clearly partisan actions of individuals like Commissioner Carol Roberts, but they did so nonetheless.

The Florida Supreme Court was trying to figure out a way to smooth out the wrinkles in contradictory statutes and provide aid to counties shanked by Harris's partisan maneuvers. But they did so in a way that awoke the slumbering giant of the U.S. Supreme Court — as nudged by Olson, Carvin, Terwilliger, etc. — who clearly outwitted the Florida justices. Thus the Florida Supreme Court tried to help the "Count Every Vote" cause, but they did so in ways that ended up hurting the state's chances of ever finding out who really got the most legal votes.

It didn't have to be this way. There was, after all, the *contest* phase of the election, which could have put the entire statewide deal in front of one judge. Gore and his legal team wanted to avoid this for PR reasons — not exactly a lofty excuse. And when they did finally contest it all, it wasn't the statewide results they wanted examined — it was 51 votes here, 157 votes there, 215 votes that never were. "Count every vote," indeed. How easy for randy SCOTUS justices to deride. Hell, the Gore team had given them a layup.

Sadly, none of this should have come as a shock to the Democrats. Sitting right there in their files, in the postscript of *The Recount Primer*, was a lesson no one learned.

The Ultimate Recount
(Indiana's 8th Congressional District — 1984)

There is no better case to demonstrate how and how not to conduct a recount than the 1984 battle between incumbent Democrat Frank McCloskey and his Republican challenger Richard McIntyre for Indiana's 8th Congressional District seat.

The 8th Congressional District of Indiana has become known as the "Bloody 8th" because of the closeness of its election outcomes and the intensity of its political campaigns. . . . Election night results . . . showed a handful of votes separating McCloskey and McIntyre. Over a period of six months, three complete vote tallies were conducted: an election night canvass, a state recount and a federal recount. Eventually, McCloskey was seated based on a margin of four votes out of a quarter of a million cast. . . .

The 8th District recount illustrates most of the key points addressed in this primer.

First, the importance of quickly gathering data. McCloskey's team immediately identified areas of information to be gathered, created a format to insure consistency, and had workers in the field within two days after the election, gathering information. . . . Thus, strategic decisions concerning the conduct of a state recount, such as the probable effect of the lack of district-wide rules, were made on the basis of reliable information.

On the other hand, once the state recount started, McIntyre's campaign blindly charged ahead seeking new votes, indiscriminately disqualifying McCloskey ballots and pursuing immediately advantageous positions without regard to their impact upon the contest districtwide. Thus, McIntyre's aggressive, but misguided, strategy played to the advantage of McCloskey.

The immediate effect was to provide McIntyre with a Pyrrhic victory of over 500 votes in the state recount. But this margin was reached by rulings so seemingly inconsistent as to appear part of an improper use of the nominally Republican dominated election system to benefit the McIntyre cause. Particularly susceptible to being made offensive was the disqualification of thousands of ballots for technical reasons in predominantly black precincts in Evansville, Indiana. Ironically, these disqualifications were not needed by the McIntyre interests, a fact apparently not known to his team at the time. McCloskey supporters were able to characterize the state recount as a sham and obtain a federal recount overseen by the House of Representatives.

Sound familiar?

★　★　★

Some Democrats have no interest in a serious analysis of what happened in Florida, however. Like Terry McAuliffe. Clinton money-man and, as of February 3, 2001, chairman of the Democratic National Committee.

"Folks, let us never forget it," McAuliffe says at his inaugural address as DNC chair. "Al Gore won that election. . . . If Katherine Harris, Jeb Bush, Jim Baker, and the Supreme Court hadn't tampered with the results, Al Gore would be president, George Bush would be back in Austin, and John Ashcroft would be home reading *Southern Partisan* magazine.

"George Bush says he's for election reform. Reform *this*," bellows McAuliffe. "I say park the state police cars, take down the roadblocks, stop asking people of color for multiple forms of ID, print readable ballots, open the polling places, count all the votes, and start practicing democracy in America."

McAuliffe later claims that his speech was just intended to fire up the Democratic base, but such rhetoric is just as overheated, spurious, and fact-deficient as the various speeches made by Republicans — like, say, Racicot — during the recount. Which may be, regrettably, the lesson Democrats learned from this: Lie all you want, it doesn't matter. The media won't call you on it, and if they do, who cares? Surely this is not a healthy development.

But what *of* the charges of wholesale intimidation of African-Americans? I have no doubt that there were shady instances where blacks didn't get to vote, but even Henry Latimer, the civil rights attorney made point man on this issue by the Gorebies, doesn't allege any grand conspiracy. That surely won't prevent Democrats like Jesse Jackson and other demagogues from making claims devoid of fact, or evidence, of continuing to exploit Florida for political gain.

Truth is, though the NAACP and other civil rights organizations continue to rail against the disenfranchisement of black voters, the most glaring instances of black Floridians' votes not being counted — in Duval County — is due to a toxic combination of two things: (1) ballot spoilage from new voters and uneducated ones, and (2) inattentiveness to the issue of ballot spoilage, rooted in the indifference of elections officials. It might score McAuliffe political points to paint a picture of Election Day in Florida that conjures images of Bull Conner and civil rights struggles of generations ago, but the reality is far more complex.

When I asked David Leahy about the voting machines that failed that Election Day morning test at Dunbar and Evans Elementary schools (mentioned in chapter 1), he said that he wasn't concerned, since the machines had worked fine in the warehouse. This seemed a rather flippant comment to make about the precincts with the highest percentage of unread ballots in the county. But while African-American activists in Miami-Dade are fired up and trying to get the caucasian Leahy replaced, they should remember one thing: a lot of the elections workers — like Evans Elementary precinct clerk Donna Rogers — are African-American. And Rogers, when I interviewed her, not only didn't accept any responsibility for what happened in her precinct, she refused to even believe that it happened. Undervotes, overvotes, and hanging chad have been around for a long time. Where were Congressmen Deutsch and Wexler — or Commissioner Suzanne Gunzburger, for that matter — when Broward County supervisor of elections Jane Carroll, a Republican, was trying to secure funds to buy Opti-scan machines for the county? How could Iowa governor Tom Vilsack rail against undervotes in Florida when his own state had its share as well?

That said, when elections supervisors complained to Katherine Harris and Clay Roberts about poorly functioning machines, or about the horribly inaccurate ChoicePoint felons list, many were greeted with what they felt to be complete and utter disregard. Did the fact that these problems hurt black, Hispanic, and underclass voters disproportionately play a factor in their indifference? I don't know. But it's probably safe to say that if these problems had been causing a stir among Sarasota Republicans — or if election reform had been a pet cause of state senate president John McKay — then Harris would have been a bit more attuned to it, committed to working on it. Who knows? Maybe she would have even allocated some of the funds she spent jetting off to Australia to set up the Florida pavilion at the Olympic Games.

But while we're looking for people to blame, let's not forget how Harris and Roberts got to their positions of power. Clay Roberts was appointed by Jeb Bush who, along with Harris, was elected by the good citizens of Florida on November 3, 1998. Many of the same good citizens whose votes didn't count because they didn't bother to check the instructions on the ballot box and who now are looking for a scapegoat.

★ ★ ★

Which is the point: We, as Americans, are to blame for what happened in Florida. Whomever you think the subtitle of the book applies to, we are the ones who let him try to steal a presidency. We are the ones who haven't cared about hanging chad in the past, who didn't inform new voters of how to make sure their votes are read by the machine, who elected legislators who passed vague and conflicting laws, who nominated Gore and Bush to begin with. Gore, whose advocates bullied various Florida elections officials, who was willing to stake a presidential victory on dimpled ballots that not even Bob Kerrey considered votes in three Democratic counties. Gore, who said "count all the votes," but made no true move to have that done. Gore, who couldn't even win his home state, who had to struggle to win an election against a candidate as weak as Bush at a time of unprecedented peace and prosperity. Gore, the self-proclaimed champion of environmental and consumer causes, whose lusty capitulation on such issues propelled the candidacy of Green Party candidate Ralph Nader — who garnered roughly 97,000 votes in Florida alone. Gore, who was, at the very bottom of it all, a rather unappealing candidate who seemed to have not only no sense of vision but no sense of himself.

And then, of course, you have the winner, George W. Bush, who let General Baker run it all for him, who thought what happened in Miami-Dade was funny, who let Hughes, Fleischer, Eskew, Rove, Bartlett, Racicot, Baker, go out and say things on his behalf that just simply were not true, things that bashed judges and justices who were — however imperfectly — trying to make sense in an insane world.

The man in charge of the overseas absentee ballots for Bush was Warren Tompkins, who we all know was also in charge of the ugliest primary contest in modern history — the battle for South Carolina, fought against Sen. John McCain. How was it that Bush was allowed to walk out of South Carolina without the media or the Gore campaign reminding him of the disgraceful, disgusting, loathsome way he and his campaign secured a victory? How is it that our president is on a first-name basis with a man like Warren Tompkins to begin with? Or does the mere fact that Bush has been preceded by characters like Clinton and Nixon make that question asked and answered?

We have set up a world where great men do not get nominated for the presidency — only ruthless, power-mad pols with hollow centers, surrounded by political mercenaries. We have set up a world where the candidate with the more effective liars and more cutthroat scoundrels wins. Perhaps our displeasure with the products of this machinery is the reason we got into this mess in the first place.

Dirty politics and hollow rhetoric are not new to America, but in recent decades, as money and television and mass marketing have saturated the political process, the office of the presidency has been terribly tarnished. Nixon and Clinton certainly did their damage, but they weren't the only ones. We're a coarser society, an angrier place, made all the more so by the billions of dollars to be made in exploiting the worst in us. In 2000 we had two men running for the highest office in the land, and many of us thought neither of them truly up to the task. So perhaps there really wasn't a presidency left to steal. You can look at dimpled ballots, questionable judicial decrees, lazy reporters, family ties, and too much money. You can scour the Florida swamps in search of submerged Votomatics. You can file Freedom of Information Act requests to track down mash notes between people who were supposed to be neutral and folks who were rabid partisans. You can look at Florida — or Iowa, or New Mexico, or just about any state — and wonder how its residents feel, knowing so many votes are routinely misread and discarded. You can look at sleazy political operatives and cutthroat lawyers and politicized judges. But if you really want to know who's responsible for what went down in the Sunshine State, you might want to take a look in the mirror.

Notes

Chapter 1

1. Tamala Edwards, "O Brother, Where Art Thou?," Salon.com, Dec. 19, 2000.
2. Maxine Jones, "The African-American Experience in Twentieth-Century Florida," essay in *The New History of Florida,* Michael Gannon, ed. (Gainesville: University Press of Florida, 1996).
3. Glenda Alice Rabby, *The Pain and the Promise: The Struggle for Civil Rights in Tallahassee, Florida* (Athens: University of Georgia Press, 1999).
4. Gregory Palast, "Florida's 'Disappeared Voters': Disfranchised by the GOP," *The Nation,* February 5, 2001.
5. John Mintz and Dan Keating, "Minority Undercount Rate Higher," *Washington Post,* Dec. 3, 2000.
6. Paul Brinkley-Rogers, "County Had Highest Rate of Invalid Ballots," *Miami Herald,* Dec. 3, 2000.
7. Mintz and Keating.
8. Frances Robles and Geoff Dougherty, "Ballot Errors Rate High in Some Black Precincts," *Miami Herald,* Nov. 15, 2000.
9. William Cooper, Jr., and Alexandra Clifton, "Glades Blacks' Ballots Tossed More Than Average," *Palm Beach Post,* Nov. 18, 2000.

Chapter 2

1. John Ellis, Inside.com, Dec. 2000.
2. Jane Mayer, *The New Yorker,* Nov. 20, 2000.
3. Evan Thomas and Michael Isikoff, "The Truth Behind the Pillars," *Newsweek,* Dec. 25, 2000.
4. Alicia C. Shepard, "How They Blew It," *American Journalism Review,* Jan. 2001.
5. Seth Mnookin, "It Happened One Night," *Brill's Content,* Dec. 12, 2000.
6. T. Trent Gegax, *Newsweek,* Nov. 20, 2000.
7. Gegax.

Chapter 4

1. Glen Simmons et al., *Gladesmen, Gator Hunters, Moonshiners, and Skiffers* (Gainesville: University Press of Florida, 1998).

Chapter 5

1. Adam Cohen and Elizabeth Taylor, *American Pharaoh: Mayor Richard J. Daley, His Battle for Chicago and the Nation* (New York: Little, Brown, 2000).
2. Edmund Kalina, *Courthouse over White House: Chicago and the Presidential Election of 1960* (Orlando: University of Central Florida Press, 1988).

Chapter 10

1. The Harris quotes from the Florida-FSU game come from the ABC News producers Chris Vlasto and Eric Avram, great Americans both.

Chapter 12

1. Clay Lambert and Bill Douthat, "Miami-Dade Ballot Recount," *Palm Beach Post,* Jan. 14, 2000.

Chapter 20

1. John Dickerson, "Home on the Range: The Bush Ranch Is the Way He Likes to See Himself — Rugged and Thoroughly Texan," *Time,* Dec. 25, 2000.
2. Much of this is common sense to anyone who delves into the opinions, but I'm indebted to the best Supreme Court reporter in the country, Joan Biskupic of *USA Today,* for her Jan. 22, 2001, story, "Election Still Splits Court."

APPENDIX

The Unfiled Gore Brief of December 13, 2000

IN THE SUPREME COURT
OF THE STATE OF FLORIDA

CASE NO. SC00-2431
On Appeal from the Second Judicial Circuit
CASE NO. 1D00-4745

ALBERT GORE, Jr., Nominee of the Democratic Party of the
United States for President of the United States, and
JOSEPH I. LIEBERMAN, Nominee of the Democratic
Party of the United States for Vice President of the United States,

Appellants,

vs.

KATHERINE HARRIS, as SECRETARY OF STATE
STATE OF FLORIDA, and SECRETARY OF AGRICULTURE
BOB CRAWFORD, SECRETARY OF STATE KATHERINE HARRIS
and L. CLAYTON ROBERTS, DIRECTOR, DIVISION OF ELECTIONS,
individually and as members of and as THE FLORIDA ELECTIONS
CANVASSING COMMISSION,

and

THE MIAMI-DADE COUNTY CANVASSING BOARD, LAWRENCE D.
KING, MYRIAM LEHR and DAVID C. LEAHY,

as members of and as THE MIAMI-DADE COUNTY CANVASSING BOARD, and DAVID C. LEAHY, individually and as Supervisor of Elections,

and

THE NASSAU COUNTY CANVASSING BOARD, ROBERT E. WILLIAMS, SHIRLEY N. KING, AND DAVID HOWARD (or, in the alternative, MARIANNE P. MARSHALL), as members of and as the NASSAU COUNTY CANVASSING BOARD, and SHIRLEY N. KING, individually and as Supervisor of Elections,

and

THE PALM BEACH COUNTY CANVASSING BOARD, THERESA LEPORE, CHARLES E. BURTON AND CAROL ROBERTS, as members of and as the PALM BEACH COUNTY CANVASSING BOARD, and THERESA LEPORE, individually and as Supervisor of Elections,

and

GEORGE W. BUSH, Nominee of the Republican Party of the United States for President of the United States and RICHARD CHENEY, Nominee of the Republican Party of the United States for Vice President of the United States,

Appellees,

CASE NO.

ALBERT GORE, Jr., Nominee of the Democratic Party of the United States for President of the United States, and JOSEPH I. LIEBERMAN, Nominee of the Democratic Party of the United States for Vice President of the United States,

Petitioners,

vs.

KATHERINE HARRIS, as SECRETARY OF STATE STATE OF FLORIDA, and SECRETARY OF AGRICULTURE BOB CRAWFORD, SECRETARY OF STATE KATHERINE HARRIS

and L. CLAYTON ROBERTS, DIRECTOR, DIVISION OF ELECTIONS,
individually and as members of and as THE FLORIDA ELECTIONS
CANVASSING COMMISSION,

Respondents.

BRIEF OF RESPONDENTS ALBERT GORE ET AL.
ON REMAND FROM THE UNITED STATES SUPREME COURT

W. Dexter Douglass
Florida Bar No.0020263
Douglass Law Firm
211 East Call Street
Tallahassee, Florida 32302
Telephone: 850/224-6191
Facsimile: 850/224-3644

Ron Klain
c/o Gore/Lieberman Recount
430 S. Capitol St.
Washington, DC 20003
Telephone: 202/863-8000
Facsimile: 202/863-8603

Andrew Pincus
c/o Gore/Lieberman Recount
430 S. Capitol St.
Washington, DC 20003
Telephone: 202/863-8000
Facsimile: 202/863-8603

Kendall Coffey
Florida Bar No. 259861
2665 S. Bayshore Drive, Suite 200
Miami, FL 33133
Telephone: 305/285-0800
Facsimile: 305/285-0257

David Boies
Boies, Schiller & Flexner LLP
80 Business Park Drive, Suite 110
Armonk, New York 10504
Telephone: 914/273-9800
Facsimile: 914/273-9810

Jeffrey Robinson
Baach Robinson & Lewis
One Thomas Circle, Suite 200
Washington, DC 20003
Telephone: 202/833-7205
Facsimile: 202/466-5738

Mark R. Steinberg
2272 Live Oak Drive West
Los Angeles, CA 90068
Telephone: 323/466-4009

Benedict E. Kuehne
Florida Bar No. 233293
Sale & Kuehne, P.A.
100 S.E. 2d Street, Suite 3550
Miami, FL 33131-2154
Telephone: 305/789-5989
Facsimile: 305/789-5987

John J. Corrigan, Jr.   Dennis Newman
896 Beacon St.   580 Pearl St.
Boston, MA 02215   Reading, MA 01867
Telephone: 617/247-3800   Telephone: 781/944-0345
Facsimile: 617/867-9224   Facsimile: 617-742-6880

COUNSEL FOR ALBERT GORE, JR., AND JOSEPH I. LIEBERMAN

INTRODUCTION

This case is before this Court on remand from the U.S. Supreme Court, which has returned the case for further proceedings "not inconsistent with this opinion." *Bush v. Gore,* No. 00-949, Slip op. 13 (U.S. Dec. 12, 2000). An appropriate response to the U.S. Supreme Court's decision is a clarification of key points of statutory construction under Florida state law. The U.S. Supreme Court suggested that *this Court* has held that in a Presidential election, Florida law places primacy on trying to meet the so-called "safe harbor" provision in 3 U.S.C. s5 (which is **never even mentioned** in the Florida statutes) rather than on ensuring the fundamental democratic principle that the will of the people not be frustrated in accurately ascertaining the outcome of a popular election. *Id.* at 12. Yet this Court has never so held, and Florida's elections laws cannot remotely bear such a construction. This Court should respond to the U.S. Supreme Court's remand with a statement of Florida law that clarifies this point.

The U.S. Supreme Court has identified limited equal protection problems with the recount of undervotes this Court had ordered to complete a full and fair tally of the votes cast in this election. It has indicated, in particular, that a recount could be conducted consistent with the Fourteenth Amendment if two conditions were met: (1) adoption of "adequate statewide standards for determining what is a legal vote"; (2) "practicable procedures to implement them [and] orderly judicial review of any disputed matters that might arise." *Id.* at 11. The Court's opinion also suggests some need to address the question of so-called "overvote" ballots. As discussed below, these conditions could be met by an immediate order of this Court, and a full and accurate tally of the votes could be achieved, just as this Court directed as a matter of state law five days ago.

At bottom, the issue here is whether this Court — on a fundamental issue of state law which it holds the definitive authority to construe — believes that a mere "legislative wish to take advantage of the 'safe harbor'" afforded by federal law, *Bush v. Palm Beach County Canvassing Bd.*, No. 00-836, Slip op. 6 (Dec. 4, 2000), trumps the intent of the Legislature, which runs deeply and constantly through Florida's elections law: *i.e.*, that "the right of Florida's citizens to vote and to have elections determined by the will of Florida's voters [are] important policy concerns of the Florida Legislature in acting Florida's elections code." *Palm Beach County Canvassing Bd. v. Harris*, Nos. SC00-2346, *et al.*, Slip op. 31 (Fla. Dec. 11, 2000). The proposition is particularly unpersuasive now that the Legislature has provided powerful new evidence in its current special session that it is more concerned about making a selection of electors than in meeting the supposed December 12th "safe harbor" deadline.

If instead, as we believe, this Court's recent provision for a "manual recount" of undervotes to determine accurately the rightful winner of this election should not be "eviscerated and rendered meaningless" by a time limit that is not mandatory, but should "accommodate the manual recount," *id.* at 22, then the Florida Supreme Court has the lawful authority, on remand, to correct this misunderstanding about Florida law, and to order a resumption of the manual recounts, to be completed within 48 hours. Coupled with the few basic steps discussed below, this Court could exercise such authority properly under the U.S. Supreme Court's remand, and in so doing, would vindicate democracy and the rule of law in Florida before the Electoral College convenes on December 18, 2000.

I. THE CLEAR AND CONSISTENT INTENT OF FLORIDA LAW IS THAT ELECTIONS MUST FAITHFULLY REFLECT THE POPULAR WILL.

Three days ago, this Court stressed the importance "to remind ourselves that the Florida Legislature has expressly vested in the voters of Florida the authority to elect the presidential electors who will ultimately participate in choosing a president." *Palm Beach County, supra,* Slip op. 31 (citing 103.011, Fla. Stat. (2000)). In that case, the Court held that an arguably mandatory deadline "must be construed in a flexible manner to accommodate the manual recount" needed to ensure an accurate count of the votes cast in this very election. *Id.* at 22. In large part, the Court reached this conclusion because of the "important policy concerns of the Florida Legislature in enacting Florida's election code" to preserve and protect "the right of Florida's citizens to vote and to have elections determined by the will of Florida's voters." *Id.* at 31.

Nor, as this Court noted, was this the first time that an apparent deadline in the Florida election laws was extended to accommodate competing policy concerns. In particular, the overseas ballots must be counted if they are received any time up to ten days after the election pursuant to an administrative rule that balanced competing concerns of related federal and state laws. *Id.* at 25.

Moreover, this Court has repeatedly stressed that the fundamental purpose of Florida's election laws is to determine and effectuate the will of the people. *See, e.g., Harris,* Slip op. 31 (Fla. Dec. 11, 2000) ("Courts must not lose sight of the fundamental purpose of election laws: The laws are intended to facilitate and safeguard the right of each voter to express his or her will in the context of our representative democracy"); *Chappell v. Martinez,* 536 So. 2d 1007, 1008 (Fla. 1988) (the people effecting their will through "balloting, not the hypertechnical compliance with statutes, is the object of holding elections"); *Boardman v. Esteva,* 323 So. 2d 259, 267 (Fla. 1975) ("It is the policy of the law to prevent as far as possible the disenfranchisement of electors who have cast their ballots in good faith") (quotation omitted), *cert. denied,* 425 U.S. 967 (1976).

Thus, where putative deadlines or matters of administrative convenience would cause legal votes cast not to be counted or otherwise frustrate the will of the people, they must give way to this paramount concern. *See, e.g., Harris II,* Slip op. 22. The same overriding concern with enfranchising as many citizens as possible is reflected in Florida's universal standard for determining the legal validity of ballots that are cast in elections. *See e.g., Darby v. State,* 75 So. 411, 412 (Fla. 1917) (ballot marked to plainly indicate voter's intent should be counted "unless some positive provision of law would be thereby violated"); *State ex rel. Carpenter v. Barber,* 198 So. 49 (Fla. 1940) (vote should be counted "if the will and intention of the voter can be determined"); *Nuccio v. Williams,* 120 So. 310 (Fla. 1929). Hence, in a case of allegedly mismarked ballots, this Court held that the Florida courts "should not frustrate the will of the voters." *Beckstrom v. Volusia County Canvassing Bd.,* 707 So. 2d 720, 726 (Fla. 1998).

Weighing against this bedrock policy of Florida law is not the need to comply with any firm, mandatory deadline, but consideration of a voluntary choice of whether to strive to meet a provision of federal law that *both parties have agreed* offers only encouragement and some penumbral protection for the electoral votes that Florida submits to Congress. As the U.S. Supreme Court noted: "The parties before us agree that whatever else may be the effect of [3 U.S.C. §5], it creates a 'safe harbor' for a State insofar as congressional consideration of its electoral votes is concerned." *Bush I,* Slip op. 6. The parties were unable to find any more meaning or substance in this provision, which has been characterized as "all carrot and no stick." Indeed, this year 21 states did not even bother to submit their paperwork to the National Archives by the prescribed date. *See District, 29 States Submit Electors,* AP Online (Dec. 12, 2000). One reason for this unconcern may be that a successful challenge to a state's electors requires the concurrent of both chambers in Congress, which is virtually impossible if different parties control the two chambers when Congress meets to count the electoral votes, as is true this year.

What is important, however, is that a mere "safe harbor" provision designed to offer encouragement to the states cannot sensibly be transformed into a deadly vortex that sucks into its maw the rights of voters, the rights of candidates, and all of the legal and democratic procedures established under Florida state law. Noting that all provisions of the Florida election statutes must be read *in pari materia,* this Court held that a "comprehensive reading" of the laws "required that there be time for an elections contest pursuant to section 102.168." *Harris II,* Slip op. 30 n.22. As a matter of statutory construction, therefore, this Court fashioned a remedial system carefully designed to safeguard the mandatory judicial contest provided by the Florida Legislature. And this Court recently reiterated the principle "that the primary consideration in an election contest is whether the will of the people has been effected." *Perez v. Marti,* 2000 Fla. App. LEXIS 11542, at *5 (Fla. 3d DCA Nov. 3, 2000). Once again, there is nothing to commend a reading of Florida law that would cast overboard the contest proceeding, and with it any hope of an accurate rendition of the people's will, merely for an ephemeral date that need not even be followed, has no practical effect in this instance, and in fact is widely ignored. *See Submit Electors,* AP Online, *supra,* at 2 ("the law does not require penalties if that deadline passes," but "lists of electors should be sent to the archives 'as soon as practicable' on or after Dec. 12").

The U.S. Supreme Court's opinion rests on a confused reading of Florida law that this Court should clarify. While, as the U.S. Supreme Court held, there is doubtlessly a "legislative wish to take advantage of the [Title 3's] 'safe harbor'" *Harris.,* Slip op. 6, that "safe harbor" cannot be transformed from a shield for this State into a sword dangling above *this Court.* Moreover, the assertion that "the Florida Supreme Court has said that the Florida Legislature intended to obtain the safe-harbor benefits of 3 U.S.C. §5," *Id.,* Slip op. 12., comes from a passage in *Harris II* that does not even support the statement. Under Florida law, judicial contests, along with the rights of voters and candidates they are designed to safeguard, cannot be terminated to achieve compliance with an administrative deadline that approximately half the states honor only in the breach.

On remand, this Court may want to consider the U.S. Supreme Court's opinion as effectively certifying the following question to the Florida Supreme Court: "Does Florida law hold that the state *may* select electors by December 12, 2000, or does Florida law hold that the state *shall* select electors by that date?

The answer here, as it was in *Harris II,* must be informed by the importance in Florida law of preserving and protecting the will of the voters. And that answer must be that Florida law makes compliance with the safe harbor date preferable, but not compulsory. As Justice Breyer noted, though the proceedings to date rendered it impossible to qualify for the "safe harbor," it would be possible to complete all manual recounts necessary to conclude the contest proceeding by December 18, 2000, the date the Electoral College convenes. The Court did not disagree, but expressed the view that it was bound by the Florida Supreme Court's supposed construction of Florida law to end all such proceedings on December 12. *Bush II,* Slip op. 12.[1]

II. THE U.S. SUPREME COURT HAS HELD THAT TWO CONDITIONS MUST BE MET FOR ANY RECOUNT: ADEQUATE STANDARDS, AND PRACTICABLE PROCEDURES WITH JUDICIAL OVERSIGHT.

The U.S. Supreme Court held that recounts previously ordered by this Court require more clarity before they can proceed. In particular, the Court held that the recounts required adoption of "adequate statewide standards for determining what is a legal vote," as well as "practicable procedures to implement them [and] orderly judicial review of any disputed matters that might arise." *Bush II,* Slip op. 11. Both conditions can be readily met and the recounts promptly concluded.

A.   Adequate Standards for Determining Votes

The proper standard for counting the remaining votes must be consistent with and determined by the Florida Legislature's direction that "[n]o vote shall be declared invalid or void if there is a clear indication of the intent of the voter." Fla. Stat. §101.5614(5). It is a fairly straightforward task to provide more specificity to this general standard pursuant to the broad authority vested in the courts under Florida law governing contests. See §102.168(8), Fla. Stat. (2000).[2] The touchstone, of course, as in any case where the U.S. Supreme Court has remanded to the state courts to cure an equal protection violation, is to impose a remedy that is best calculated to carry out the intent of the legislature. *Wengler v. Druggists Mut. Ins. Co.,* 446 U.S. 142, 152-53 (1980).[3]

In determining the appropriate standard to govern the manual count, the U.S. Supreme Court has decided that in dealing with inanimate objects like ballots, "[t]he search for intent can be confined by specific rules designed to ensure uniform treatment." *Bush II,* Slip op. 7. Thus, the necessary clarification does not result in abandoning or moving away from the general "intent of the voter" standard, which could raise its own constitutional problems, but merely making this standard more specific and objective.

In identifying the appropriate standard for determining voter intent under section 101.5614(5), this Court is guided by its own recent opinions construing the statutes, which do not permit restrictions that would substantially limit the number of ballots counted and thereby contradict the Legislature's intent. Again, this Court has just emphasized "the right of Florida's citizens to vote and to have elections determined by the will of Florida's voters as important policy concerns of the Florida Legislature in enacting Florida's election code. *Harris II,* Slip op. at 31. The recount provision specifically "strives to strengthen rather than dilute the right to vote by securing, as nearly as humanly possible, an accurate and true reflection of the will of the electorate." *Id.* at 17 n.4 (quotation omitted). We believe that there are two possible approaches for setting such standards.

1. Meaningful Guidance Can be Found in Texas Law

This Court can derive guidance from other state statutes regarding the appropriate uniform standard for determining "intent of the voter" on punchcard ballots.

For example, the Texas Election Code provides such specific guidance while remaining consistent with Florida law's "intent of the voter" standard. Under Texas Election Code 127-130(d), a vote is to be counted if:

(1) at least two corners of the chad are detached:
(2) light is visible through the hole;
(3) an indentation on the chad from the stylus or other object is present and indicates a clearly ascertainable intent of the voter to vote; [or]

(4) the chad reflects by other means a clearly ascertainable intent of the
voter to vote.

Under the Texas standard, an "indentation of the chad" on the ballot, *see
id.*, indicates the *intent* to cast a vote; the failure to puncture the ballot indicates only a *physical* failure by the voter or the stylus to express that intent
by dislodging the chad. These substandards would serve to clarify Florida
law and accommodate the Legislature's direction that the "intent of the
voter" must be determined with the U.S. Supreme Court's interpretation of
the Equal Protection Clause in this case. This approach would be consistent with Florida law, but would provide the added specificity that the U.S.
Supreme Court held to be a prerequisite for going forward.

2. Alternatively, This Court Should Clarify That Any Indentation on the Ballot to Indicate Voter Intent Satisfies Florida Law

Alternatively, plaintiffs thus urge this Court to adopt a uniform standard
recognizing indentations on punchcard ballots as clear expressions of
voter intent. This approach is supported by the Massachusetts Supreme
Court's interpretation of a similar statutory standard. As the Court held,
the trial judge concluded that a vote should be recorded for a candidate if
the chad was not removed but *an impression was made on or near it.* We
agree with that conclusion." *Delahunt v. Johnston,* 671 N.E.2d 1241, 1243
(Mass. 1996) (emphasis added). The Court continued:

> It is, of course, true that a voter who failed to push a stylus through
> the ballot and thereby create a hole in it could have done a better job
> of expressing his or her intent. Such a voter should not automatically
> be disqualified, however, like a litigant or one seeking favors from the
> government, because he or she failed to comply strictly with
> announced procedures. The voters are the owners of the government,
> and our rule that we seek to discern the voter's intention and to give it
> effect reflects the proper relation between government and those to
> whom it is responsible. *Id.*

The Massachusetts Court also rejected as "unpersuasive" the argument that
such indentations did not reflect an intent of the voter, *viz.*, that "voters
started to express a preference in the congressional contest, made an
impression on a punch card, but pulled the stylus back because they really

did not want to express a choice in that contest." *Id.* As the Court recognized in language particularly apt to the present circumstances, such a scenario was implausible: "The large number of ballots with discernible impressions makes such an inference unwarranted, especially in a hotly contested election." *Id.*

In response to the U.S. Supreme Court's remand order, this Court must now clarify application of the long-settled Florida principle that the intent of the voter must be ascertained and is the paramount consideration in tallying votes. *See* '101.5614(5), Fla. Stat. (2000) ("No vote shall be declared invalid or void if there is a clear indication of the intent of the voter"). *This Court should direct the counting of all ballots which contain a discernible indentation or other mark, at or near the ballot position for the candidate, unless other evidence on the face of the ballot clearly indicates a voter's intention not to vote for that candidate.*

Indeed, this standard is compelled by both Florida statutory and case law. The manual recount statute itself provides that counting teams are to manually examine punchcard ballots "to determine a voter's intent" and, if they are unable to do so, "the ballot shall be presented to the county canvassing board for it to determine the voter's intent." '102.166(7)(b), Fla. Stat. (2000). As this Court recently stated, these statutes require "that so long as the voter's intent may be discerned from the ballot, the vote constitutes a 'legal vote' that should be counted. As the State has moved toward electronic voting, nothing in this evolution has diminished the longstanding case law and statutory law that the intent of the voter is of paramount concern and should always be given effect *if* the intent can be determined." *Gore v. Harris,* No. SC00-2431, at 24-25 (Fla. Dec. 8, 2000) (citations omitted), *rev'd on other grounds, Bush II.*

These principles were originally set forth in the era of paper ballots. In *Darby v. State,* 75 So. 411 (Fla. 1917), this Court was required to ascertain whether an "x" marked on the wrong side of the ballot question rendered the vote improper. It determined that this mark reflected the intent of the voter and, accordingly, counted the vote. "Where a ballot is so marked as to plainly indicate the voter's choice and intent in placing his marks thereon, it should be counted as marked unless some positive provision of law would be thereby violated." *Id.* at 412.

It seems apparent that the standard for discerning the intent of the voter in Florida consistent with Florida's statutes and cases must be a standard consistent with *Darby.* Just as in *Darby,* when an "x" marked the spot and it was clear from the "x" that the voter was casting his or her vote a certain way, so it must be that when a voter punches the chad with a stylus and it is clear from the ballot that the chad was intentionally punched, the vote must be counted. *See id.*

Similarly, for optical scanner machines, when it is clear that the pencil was used to color in or otherwise mark the oval or arrow assigned to the indicated candidate, that mark should be counted as a vote. This is not a new standard in Florida. It has been Florida law since its inception. When a vote can be counted, the will of the voter will be recognized. Simply because machines usually aid in tabulation does not mean that when those machines *detract* from tabulating legal votes this Court should void legal votes contrary to common sense. This standard is uniformly consistent — whenever a legal vote can be discerned, it should always be counted. *See also Pullen v. Mulligan,* 561 N.E.2d 585, 611 (Ill. 1990) ("to invalidate a ballot which clearly reflects the voter's intent, simply because a machine cannot read it, would subordinate substance to form and promote the means at the expense of the end").

B.   Practicable Procedures and Orderly Judicial Review

In describing the recount process imposed by this Court in its order of December 8, 2000, and implemented through Judge Lewis' order of December 9, 2000, the U.S. Supreme Court noted that the recount was not designed to be conducted in a manner "well calculated to sustain the confidence that all citizens must have in the outcome of elections." Slip Op. 11.

"Orderly judicial review" means procedures by which disputes can be identified, brought to the attention of the court or one of its judicial officers for resolution, and appealed should disagreement remain after that resolution. *Cf. Press v. Pasadena Independent School District,* 326 F. Supp. 550, 553 (S.D. TX. 1971) (Texas created scheme of *orderly judicial review* of Texas Railroad Commission decisions by appeal to a state district court and subsequent review by a court of appeals and the Texas Supreme Court). To assure that a process of orderly judicial review is available with respect to any recount procedures ordered by this Court, this Court (and by direction the Leon County Circuit Court) should impose procedures that include essentially the following requirements:

1. Each counting team shall consist of two persons who shall not be from the same political party. Each counting team member shall read the attached instructions on counting the ballots and shall sign at the

bottom of the sheet to reflect that they have read and understand the instructions.

2. Governor Bush and Vice President Gore may each designate a person for each team to observe the process. That person may not make a verbal objection or challenge to any particular ballot determination nor in any way disrupt or interfere with the counting process.

3. To insure that all objections are handled in a uniform manner, any objections an observer may have to the process or to the disposition of a particular ballot shall be made in writing and shall be immediately filed (together with the disputed ballot, if applicable) with the local canvassing board. Any objections to the disposition of a ballot shall remain with the ballot until all disputes concerning that ballot have been finally resolved.

4. If the members of the two-person counting teams disagree as to whether a ballot clearly evidences the intent of the voter or for whom the ballot should be counted under the rules announced above, they shall present that ballot for review to the local canvassing board.

5. If a dispute remains after the local canvassing board has reviewed the ballot, the ballot shall be delivered to that board's Circuit Court for automatic review. The Circuit Court shall then determine whether, under the interpretive rules stated above, the ballot reflects the clear intent of the voter to vote for a single candidate. Unless there is an appeal, the Circuit Court's determination will be reported to the local canvassing board, which will then record the ballot in accordance with the ruling.

These procedures for implementing the standards specified above, and to resolve disputes over those standards, are adequate to meet the Equal Protection concerns raised by the U.S. Supreme Court in its opinion.

III. THIS COURT NEED NOT ORDER COUNTING OF OVER-VOTES; IF SUCH A COUNT IS ORDERED, AN APPROPRIATE PROCEDURE FOR COUNTING THESE VOTES CAN BE EASILY ESTABLISHED.

In its decision, the U.S. Supreme Court expressed certain concerns over a recount that excludes overvotes. *Bush II*, Slip Op. 9, 12. However, it did not order that any recount include those votes. Moreover, even if this Court determines to conduct a recount on remand that includes overvotes, such a recount can be completed without much difficulty.

A.   Overvotes Do Not Need to Be Included in a Recount

While the U.S. Supreme Court did raise issues concerning the exclusion of overvotes from a recount, it did *not* mandate that such ballots be included on remand. *See, e.g., Bush II,* Slip Op. 12 ("*If* a recount of the overvotes were also required . . ."). Thus, this Court is under no obligation to order such a count on remand.

There are ample reasons not to include such ballots in a recount. First, as Justice Breyer pointed out, "[the defendants] presented no evidence, to this Court or any Florida court, that a manual recount of overvotes would identify additional legal votes." *Bush II,* Slip Op. 1 (Breyer, J., dissenting). Neither at trial, nor on appeal, did the defendants present any evidence concerning the nature of the ballots found to be overvotes. Nor have the defendants, at any stage in the proceeding, sought a count of overvotes — as was their right in a contest proceeding. §102.168, Fla. Stat.

The U.S. Supreme Court noted two distinct types of overvotes:

- First, voters whose ballots reflect two marks, but whose intent can nonetheless be discerned (such as a voter who punched and wrote-in for the same candidate or mistakenly marked in the area designated for another candidate but then also for the candidate of choice);
- Second, ballots counted by machines as legitimate votes, that were indeed illegal overvotes.

Bush II, Slip Op. 9. Neither category merits inclusion in a statewide recount.

First, while there may be some ballots that fall into the first category, defendants did not produce at trial, nor does the record contain, any evidence that they are particularly numerous in nature — or that they tend to favor one candidate over the other. To the extent that evidence exists in other judicial proceedings concerning this same election, it suggests that a large number of overvote ballots may have reflected an intent to vote for Vice President Gore, not Governor Bush. *See, e.g., Fladell v. Palm Beach County Canvassing Board,* No. SC00-2373 (December 1, 2000). Thus, there is no reason to believe that exclusion of overvotes from the recount disadvantages defendants.

Moreover, common sense suggests that the number of overvote ballots with discernable evidence of voter intent will be few and far between. Unlike "undervotes," where any evidence of voter intent on the ballot will indicate a legal vote, "overvotes," by definition, reflect evidence of multiple intents. Only in the rarest instances could these ballots be read as reflecting a single intent.

With regard to the second problem — a voter who marks two votes on his ballot, only to have a single vote read by the machine (and thereby, has his illegal ballot counted as a legal vote) — what the U.S. Supreme Court fails to recognize is that if inclusion of these votes presents constitutional issues, the same issues are presented by the earlier certified vote tallies. That is, such ballots are included — not just in any certification to emerge from this proceeding — but from the two certifications that the Court suggests were somehow more legitimate. Yet those earlier certifications included all ballots that the machine read, *whether or not they were true overvotes.*

In the end, there is no reason to include so-called overvotes in any statewide recount. Defendants have not presented evidence to suggest such a remedy is needed; they have never asked for it; nor has it been shown that the absence of it harms either party — or even leaves out any appreciable number of legal votes for either party.

B.   If This Court Orders Counting of All Ballots That Have Not Been Counted by Vote-Counting Machinery, There Is a Practicable Manner for Completing It Fairly Quickly.

If this Court concludes that a count of the so-called overvotes is required or desirable, it can be completed practicably and efficiently.

This process can be accomplished in the time remaining before December 18. It does not require that every ballot in the State of Florida be manually recounted. A full manual recount of all ballots is unnecessary because there is no dispute that a vote for presidential candidate tallied by a vote counting machine is a lawful vote. The only question is whether a ballot that has been *rejected* by a vote-counting machine, whether for failure to register *any* vote for president or for having registered *two or more* votes for president, in fact contains a lawful vote. It is only this second group of ballots — those that have failed to register one and only one vote for president — that must be manually inspected to determine whether each contains a lawful vote.

The process for segregating machine-countable from non-machine countable ballots is well-developed. The Supreme Court's opinion, in an attempt to make remedial action here appear impossible, expressed concern that:

> The Secretary of State has advised that the recount of only a portion
> of the ballots requires that the vote tabulation equipment be used to
> screen out undervotes, a function for which the machines were not
> designed. If a recount of overvotes were also required, perhaps even a
> second screening would be necessary. Use of the equipment for this
> purpose, and any new software developed for it, would have to be
> evaluated for accuracy by the Secretary of State, as required by Fla.
> Stat. §101.015 (2000).

Slip Op. 11-12. However, this vastly overstates the logistical difficulty. In fact, most if not all vote-counting machines in Florida, whether they use a punchcard or opti-scan type ballot,[4] are already equipped to segregate uncounted ballots (those that contain either undervotes or overvotes for president) from ballots on which a machine can detect one and only one vote for president. The software that makes this segregation possible is already included in most vote-counting machines and has already been evaluated by the Secretary of State, as required by Florida. Stat. §101.015 (2000).[5] Indeed, plaintiffs believe that segregation of undervote ballots was already completed or in progress in every county where such segregation was necessary in response to the order of this Court and the Circuit Court when the Supreme Court issued its Stay Order on December 9. The same technology can segregate overvotes as well as undervotes by simply changing the designation on the vote segregation and tabulation system. It does not require new software as implied in the Supreme Court's opinion. For those counties whose machines do not have that capacity now, the necessary software is readily available, free of charge.

Segregating non-machine countable ballots from machine countable ballots is a routine process that can easily be accomplished by the county canvassing boards. Here is how the process could work: First, all ballots would be run through the counting machines. The counting machines would tabulate votes on those ballots that register one and only one vote for president. The machines are designed to stop when they encounter a ballot on which there is no vote for president, or on which there is more than one vote for president. *See* Miami-Dade Tr. at 4 (Nov. 18, 2000). Those ballots would be rejected by the machine and segregated into a separate pile. They would then be manually inspected and legal votes determined thereon tabulated. The results of this tabulation of rejected ballots would then be added to the results of the tabulation of machine-readable ballots to create a single tally of votes for president in each county.

This process has already been used successfully by several counties following the November 7 election. *See The New York Times,* Nov. 16, 2000 (in some counties such as Gadsden, "election officials counted by hand only the ballots that counting machines had rejected, usually a small percentage of the total"); *The New York Times,* Nov. 12, 2000 (stating that election officials in Seminole County — Democrats and Republicans — agreed to hand count ballots that had not been counted by electronic voting machines); NBC News Transcripts, *Meet the Press,* Nov. 12, 2000 (James Baker, Republican advisor to George W. Bush, noting same).

Although the number of ballots is large — approximately six million were cast in the State of Florida — the recount we propose can be timely completed. The machine segregation and count will take only a short time. The manual inspection of an estimated 177,000 undervote and overvote ballots will be spread across the State. Most counties will have little trouble finishing their count in under a day. Plaintiffs estimate that 43 of Florida's 67 counties will have to inspect less than a thousand ballots. An additional fourteen counties will have to inspect less than 4,000 ballots. And, as this election season has amply demonstrated, Florida's counties have the resources and dedication to complete their ballot count quickly and efficiently when called upon.

The process that plaintiffs are proposing — machine counting every ballot that can be read by the machine, and manually counting those ballots that are rejected by the machine — is intuitively obvious. It satisfies the equal protection concerns voiced by the Supreme Court by ensuring that every ballot is adequately inspected to give effect to the intent of the voter, if any, expressed thereon. The mechanisms to accomplish this process are already in place in the counties. And the process can be completed in a matter of days, if not hours. In view of the grave importance of ensuring that every vote is counted in this historic election, plaintiffs respectfully submit that this Court has no real alternative but to order this remedy.

The Supreme Court decision maintains that there are equal protection problems with this Court's recount order not only because of its failure to include overvotes in the manual recount, but also because of the absence of a uniform, specific standard to guide the recounts.

Counting "overvotes" as well as "undervotes," and using a clear and uniform standard to do so, will remedy both these concerns. The standard to be used is the same one proposed for undervotes — all ballots should be counted which contain a discernible mark, at or near the ballot position for the candidate, unless other evidence on the face of the ballot clearly indicates a voter's intention not to vote for that candidate.

This standard is well established in both Florida statutory and case law. *See* §101.5614(5), Fla. Stat. (2000) ("No vote shall be declared invalid or void if there is a clear indication of the intent of the voter"). *Darby v. State* first held more than 80 years ago that, "Where a ballot is so marked as to plainly indicate the voter's choice and intent in placing his marks thereon, it should be counted as marked unless some positive provision of law would be thereby violated." *Id.* at 412. There is nothing different about the basic task and approach today. *See, e.g., Pullen,* 561 N.E.2d at 611 ("The legislature authorized the use of electronic tabulating equipment to expedite the tabulating process . . . not to create a technical obstruction which defeats the rights of qualified voters").

Because the counting machines, particularly those used in counting optical scan ballots, would read such ballots as overvotes without recognizing the voter's clear intent as expressed on the ballot, these voters will be disenfranchised unless a manual recount of the undervotes is undertaken. A manual recount of overvotes, employing a clear and uniform standard as described previously, would finally allow these voters' plain words and other markings to be read, and their votes to be finally counted.[6]

In *Beckstrom v. Volusia County Canvassing Bd.,* 707 So. 2d 720 (Fla. 1998), ballots which were defectively marked and thus unreadable by the scanner had to be hand-counted to determine the intent of the voter. Manual recounts may be particularly necessary in reviewing overvotes on optical scan ballots, where it is frequently clear that the voter colored in or otherwise marked the oval or arrow assigned to the indicated candidate, but that mark was not counted as a vote for that candidate because other marks also registered on the machine. Just as in *Darby,* when an "x" marked the wrong spot but it was clear from that "x" that the voter was casting the vote a certain way even though the ballot was not marked in the manner specified by the voting instructions, so it must be that when there are markings on an overvote ballot that make it clear from the ballot who the voter's intended candidate was, that vote must be counted. *See Darby* 75 So. At 412.[7]

This is not a new standard in Florida. It has been Florida law since its inception. When a vote can be counted, the will of the voter is recognized. Simply because machines aid in tabulation, when those machines fail to tabulate legal votes, this Court should not let such failures void legal votes and thereby disenfranchise Florida voters.[8]

CONCLUSION

For the reasons stated, on remand from the U.S. Supreme Court, this Court should address the three conditions necessary to conduct the statewide recount of contested votes that this Court had already found was necessary to complete the pending judicial contest and determine the rightful winner of Florida's electoral votes. As discussed herein, this Court should: (1) adopt adequate statewide standards for determining legally valid votes; (2) impose practicable procedures to implement them; and (3) provide for orderly judicial review of any disputed matters that might arise. These conditions can be met by an immediate order of this Court, and a full and accurate tally of the votes could be finally achieved, just as this Court directed as a matter of state law five days ago.

Respectfully submitted,

W. Dexter Douglass
Florida Bar No.0020263
Douglass Law Firm
211 East Call Street
Tallahassee, Florida 32302
Telephone: 850/224-6191
Facsimile: 850/224-3644

Ron Klain
c/o Gore/Lieberman Recount
430 S. Capitol St.
Washington, DC 20003
Telephone: 202/863-8000
Facsimile: 202/863-8603

David Boies
Boies, Schiller & Flexner LLP
80 Business Park Drive, Suite 110
Armonk, New York 10504
Telephone: 914/273-9800
Facsimile: 914/273-9810

Jeffrey Robinson
Baach Robinson & Lewis
One Thomas Circle, Suite 200
Washington, DC 20003
Telephone: 202/833-7205
Facsimile: 202/466-5738

Andrew Pincus
c/o Gore/Lieberman Recount
430 S. Capitol St.
Washington, DC 20003
Telephone: 202/863-8000
Facsimile: 202/863-8603

Kendall Coffey
Florida Bar No. 259861
2665 S. Bayshore Drive, Suite 200
Miami, FL 33133
Telephone: 305/285-0800
Facsimile: 305/285-0257

John J. Corrigan, Jr.
896 Beacon St.
Boston, MA 02215
Telephone: 617/247-3800
Facsimile: 617/867-9224

Mark R. Steinberg
2272 Live Oak Drive West
Los Angeles, CA 90068
Telephone: 323/466-4009

Benedict E. Kuehne
Florida Bar No. 233293
Sale & Kuehne, P.A.
100 S.E. 2d Street, Suite 3550
Miami, FL 33131-2154
Telephone: 305/789-5989
Facsimile: 305/789-5987

Dennis Newman
580 Pearl St.
Reading, MA 01867
Telephone: 781/944-0345
Facsimile: 617-742-6880

COUNSEL FOR ALBERT GORE, JR., AND JOSEPH I. LIEBERMAN

Notes

1. In any event, Justice Breyer correctly pointed out that whether it would be possible to finish or not was "a matter for the state courts to determine," *Id.* at 3 (Breyer, J., dissenting). Even more, this is a prediction of fact, not a point of law, on which the record was inconclusive.
2. This Court can therefore impose an interim plan to remedy the equal protection problems noted by the U.S. Supreme Court. The Legislature would be free at a later date to choose the same or a different remedy to govern future elections.
3. When quick action is needed to remedy an equal protection problem that threatens an active election cycle, courts may propose an interim solution to remedy the problem pending legislative action. *See, e.g., Burns v. Richardson,* 384 U.S. 73, 85–86 (1966); *Reynolds v. Sims,* 377 U.S. 533 (1963).
4. 65 out of 67 counties in Florida use either opti-scan ballots or punchcard ballot systems. In addition, Martin County uses both punchcard ballots and a mechanical voting system and Union County uses manually-tabulated paper ballots. See election.dos.state.fl.us/votemeth/cvs.shtml.

5. During proceedings of the Miami-Dade County Canvassing Board Hand Recount, Supervisor of Elections David Leahy stated that the unvoted ballots had been separated out by the card readers the previous day. See Miami-Dade Transcript (Nov. 20, 2000), at 7. *See also* Miami-Dade Tr. at 4 (Nov. 18, 2000) (Judge King stating that his "first recommendation is to use the software and the program that was developed for us to identify the undercounted ballots in the presidential race . . . and that we would run the ballots through the readers"). Again, the software program is designed to stop where there is not a punch for a presidential candidate and those ballots would be segregated but kept with the precinct.

6. Examples of overvote ballots in the record include a damaged ballot on which the voter wrote in the phrase "Al Gore for President" but was not counted (Tr. Palm Beach County Bd. 11/18/00, at 94–97), and ballots where the voter mistakenly voted for one presidential candidate, taped over the wrongly punched chad and then voted for Al Gore, but was not counted (Tr. Palm Beach County Canvassing Board, 11/19/00, at 66, 75–76, 82, and 84–85). The clear intent of the voter standard outlined herein would address these overvote ballots and allow them to be counted for the appropriate candidate.

7. This standard is well represented in Florida law through the years. *See State ex rel. Carpenter v. Barber,* 198 So. 49 (Fla. 1940) ("The intention of the voter should be ascertained from a study of the ballot and the vote counted, if the will and intention of the voter can be determined, even though the cross mark "x" appears before or after the name of said candidate") (*citing Wiggins v. Drane,* 144 So. 62; *Nuccio v. Williams,* 120 So. 310; *State ex rel. Knott v. Haskell,* 72 So. 651).

8. As this Court noted in its quotation from the Illinois Supreme Court case of *Pullen v. Mulligan,* "The legislature authorized the use of electronic tabulating equipment to expedite the tabulating process and to eliminate the possibility of human error in the counting process, not to create a technical obstruction which defeats the rights of qualified voters. This court should not, under the appearance of enforcing the election laws, defeat the very object which those laws are intended to achieve. To invalidate a ballot which clearly reflects the voter's intent, simply because a machine cannot read it, would subordinate substance to form and promote the means at the expense of the end." *Harris v. Palm Beach County Canvassing Bd.,* Slip op. at 34–35 (*quoting Pullen v. Mulligan,* 561 N.E.2d 585, 611 (Ill. 1990)).

Index